AN
INTRODUCTION
TO
SOCIOLOGY

Edited by

WILLIAM MELOFF & DAVID PIERCE

Nelson Canada

I(T)P ™
International Thomson Publishing
The trademark ITP is used under licence

Published in 1994 by
Nelson Canada,
A Division of Thomson Canada Limited
1120 Birchmount Road
Scarborough, Ontario M1K 5G4

Canadian Cataloguing in Publication Data

Main entry under title:
Introduction to sociology

Includes bibliographical references and index.
ISBN 0-17-604184-2

1. Sociology.   I. Meloff, William, 1940–
II. Pierce, W. David.

HM51.I67 1994   301   C94–930266–X

Acquisitions Editor Charlotte Forbes
Editorial Manager Nicole Gnutzman
Developmental Editor Heather Martin
Art Director Bruce Bond
Designer Sharon Chow
Cover Illustration PELLAN, Alfred   Canadian   1906–1988
            Femme d'une Pomme, 1943
            Art Gallery of Ontario, Toronto
            Gift of Mr. and Mrs. Charles S. Band, 1956

Printed and bound in Canada

1 2 3 4   **WC**   97 96 95 94

Contents

Preface

The concept was simple: develop a textbook for the introductory sociology market, with the proceeds to go to a charitable society devoted to furthering the work of sociologists at the University of Alberta. The implementation, needless to say, was not as simple. It required convincing some thirty potential authors to put their own creative work on hold to write one or more textbook chapters for which they would receive no direct remuneration and the prospects for scholarly recognition were well down the road, at best. Nonetheless agreement was obtained and the work commenced. It should be noted here that the original idea came not from a sociologist but from a psychologist — Frank Epling, who communicated the idea to his friend and colleague David Pierce. Pierce enthusiastically took the idea to the chair of the Department of Sociology at the University of Alberta, Robert Silverman, and the two of them began the project.

The initial committee consisted of Robert Silverman, David Pierce, William Meloff, and Harvey Krahn. Once the plans were fleshed out, the Department of Sociology faculty met to determine interest and potential commitment. The response was extremely positive, and work began in earnest. Existing textbooks were reviewed and introductory sociology instructors were consulted to determine which topics should be covered, and in what order. Finally, the chapter assignments were organized and the authors went to work.

Once the first draft of each of the chapters was in, it was decided to establish a relatively small (forty students) section of the introductory sociology course for the 1992 winter term using the book both as a text and as the base for lectures. Students were invited to register for this section and were advised that they would be using the rough draft of a new text and that, in addition to the normal course requirements, they would be asked to critically review the text. They were assured that all criticism would be gracefully accepted, no matter how negative or outspoken, and that their course grade would reflect only the amount of work they put into the course, not how they felt about the text. William Meloff agreed to teach the course, with the assistance of two graduate students — Barbara Heather and Reevan Dolgoy — who were given the responsibilities of working with students on an individual basis as required, as well as making up a testbank for each of the chapters, and providing their own critical chapter-by-chapter reviews. When the course was over, students, graduate assistants, and instructor had achieved an exemplary level of rapport through the vehicle of mutually analyzing and criticizing the material in the text, along with learning it. The materials available to us when the course ended included the original manuscripts returned by each student, annotated with detailed notes in the margins, and a two-page critique of each chapter that required the students to respond to a number of specific questions. The task of collating these responses, computing summary scores, and organizing the chapter materials for each of the authors fell to Jennifer McMullen. To the students in that section of Sociology 100 go the sincere thanks of each of the authors for their assistance and dedication. It is not often that an author will have the benefit of this type of critical review when a textbook is still in the development stage.

The thanks of the authors are extended as well to a number of others who had a hand in the production of the text: Tracey Dvorkin, Guy Germain, Sheila Luck, Charlene Marshall, David Odynak, Hannah Scott, Robert Silverman, Erica van Roosmalen, and Barbara Demers.

The typesetting of this book was done by Laura Hargrave, on whose head were also piled the multiple tasks of wheedling chapters and revisions from the authors, formatting the text, making sense out of the tables, and ensuring that the end result was a logical and systematic text. The editors and authors assume full responsibility for any errors or omissions. Any accolades should be directed first and foremost to Laura Hargrave.

Finally, our thanks to the thousands of students in introductory sociology courses at the University of Alberta over the past twenty-five years. Those of us faced with the task of walking into a room of anywhere from 40 to 500 students and attempting to impart knowledge understand that these students have taught at the same time that they have learned.

Introduction

William A. Meloff, W. David Pierce

Now dawns the age of Nothing. Once, not so long ago, people thought little of Nothing. They pretended Nothing ever happened when, in fact, Nothing was happening all around them. Back then, Meaning was everything, and people sought only larger truth. Those who dared to ponder the Meaning of Nothing could not expect to be taken seriously.

Bill Zehme, "Jerry & George & Kramer & Elaine,"
Rolling Stone, 660/661, July 8–22, 1993, p. 40.

One of television's most popular shows, *Seinfeld*, bases its claim to fame on the fact that the show's episodes deal with "nothing" — small snippets of life that focus on mundane topics. The show does not focus on serial killers or on the violently aggressive behaviour of someone whose natural parts have been replaced with titanium and silicon. It does not focus on the evil business and sexual doings of a wealthy Texas family or on the excitement and rigours of space travel. Nobody carries a gun, or a scalpel, or a law book. The show deals with "nothing" . . . or does it? Perhaps what the show really does is focus on the "somethings" to which each of us can relate: those moments in life when things happen that — even though in retrospect they may be considered trivial — have an important impact on our lives for the moment, quite possibly with long-term implications for our behaviour well into the future.

Sociology, perhaps, is the *Seinfeld* of the science world. It has been criticized for studying "nothing." Virtually everyone who has taught in the area has been told by a student that the topics were "trivial" or "common sense." With all due respect to those who feel that way, sociology is really the scientific study of "something" rather than "nothing." That "something" involves those things that touch our lives most frequently, and with the most important consequences: human society and social behaviour. If the study of sociology is viewed as common sense, it is because each of us lives in a social environment and thus has become an "expert" on the human condition — or at least our own. As this book will demonstrate, however, the systematic tracking of human society by sociologists has resulted in information about our social world that in many cases directly contradicts what common sense would tell us, or gives us insights into relationships among social phenomena that we never knew existed.

From the time that human beings were capable of reflective thought, there is evidence that they speculated on human nature. In all cultures, folklore has involved the telling of stories — passed on orally and, ultimately, in written form — reflecting the nature of the society in which they originated. Stories of good and evil, morality and immorality exist in every culture and society. The early philosophers speculated at great length on "the human condition." For some, humans were essentially good; for others they were essentially evil. In mythology, folklore, and religious writings, beliefs about the how and why of human behaviour have been a major preoccupation.

It was not until the end of the 19th century that the myths and speculations about human society and human behaviour were put into a more objective context. The development of sociology as a systematic study of human society and social behaviour required as a precondition the acceptance of the scientific method — a way of examining the phenomena around us in a manner that replaces belief and emotion with logical and replicable methodologies.

The techniques of science, of course, have been around much longer than the science of sociology. Auguste Comte suggested that the study of human behaviour was delayed because human beings were reluctant to study those things that affected them most directly. According to Comte, mathematics was the first science since it was the least threatening to society's established belief systems. Eventually the other sciences developed, but it was not until the 19th century, with Darwin's work on evolution, that we began to examine scientifically those aspects of our world that could challenge beliefs held for thousands of years. To this day, the debate over creation versus Darwinian evolution persists in some quarters. At the same time, sociologists have begun to view the assumptions of the scientific method more critically, understanding that it is itself a value system which, if not used carefully, can introduce its own biases into the accumulation of knowledge. Further, significant sociological research is now being carried out using nontraditional techniques that are more amenable to the topics being investigated.

Sociology has emerged not only as one of the newest sciences, but also as one of the most broadly based. As this introductory text demonstrates, the concerns of sociologists range from the most basic two-person (dyadic) interaction to the broad-based areas of work, minority group relations, and fads and fashions. The chapters in this book present both the theoretical and empirical cornerstones on which the science of sociology is built, along with an overview of the substantive areas within the discipline. The book is divided into two parts. Part 1 (Chapters 1–7) lays the basic groundwork for the science of sociology, while Part 2 (Chapters 8–16) examines specific areas that interest many contemporary sociologists.

We begin in Chapter 1 by tracing the historical development of sociological theory, outlining the "classical masters," and concluding with the current state of theoretical writings.

Chapter 2 presents the scientific methodology employed to ensure findings are bias-free and capable of replication by others. A major criticism of sociology has been that it is just common sense wrapped in science. The chapter on research methods shows why sociology is much more than common sense and illustrates the methodologies that allow us to present our knowledge of sociological phenomena with confidence.

Chapter 3 deals with culture and society, and examines the large-scale social organizations into which each of us is born. How we behave, how we relate to others, even how we speak are essentially products of our culture and of the society in which we live. Beginning with the distinctiveness of human social existence, the chapter explores elements of culture, with specific Canadian references, and outlines the composition and forms of societies. Finally, the theoretical perspectives on cultural and social change are explored and analyzed for their importance to virtually every area of sociological inquiry.

Chapter 4 — social psychology — presents the basic elements of human behaviour, acknowledging that each person is born into a social environment that has a profound effect on his or her development. At this level, there is a natural bridge to one of the other major sciences of human behaviour — psychology. Many of the concerns and interests of sociologists working in social psychology are shared by psychologists working in the same area. Inevitably, however, there is a difference in perspective, because sociology is essentially the study of human social organization, whereas psychology is based on the study of individuals.

In every society, there are statuses and roles that are either ascribed to or achieved by every individual within it. An ascribed role or status is one over which a person has no control. It exists because of society's definitions of specific genetic traits. For instance, we had no choice in being born "male" or "female," and are subject to various cultural expectations as a result. An achieved status, on the other hand, is one we prepare for and consciously decide to attain. Every society, no matter how democratic or open, has its "haves" and "have-nots," and while every status is relative, the fact that inequalities exist has profound effects on the individuals who live within it. Chapter 5 discusses social stratification, with particular emphasis on stratification in Canada, with its unique blend of cultures, races, and religions.

The sociology of work is examined in Chapter 6. Industrialization and the development of a capitalist economic system brought profound changes to the nature of society. Virtually every adult is expected to get a job and the "rules" of the workplace will affect not only the total lifestyle of the individual, but the total makeup of society as well. In a rapidly changing technological environment, the implications that the nature of our work holds for each of us are serious and complex. These and other issues are carefully examined, with particular emphasis on Canada's situation.

Chapter 7 deals with the influence that politics — the distribution of power — has on the development and structure of a society. Canadian society has been profoundly influenced by its two founding cultures, on the one hand, and by its proximity to the United States, on the other. Today we are struggling with the national aspirations of Quebec, the expressed needs of the aboriginal peoples of Canada, the implications of free trade, and a plethora of other issues whose ultimate resolution may very well require a redistribution of power, and hence a significant change in our society.

Taken as a whole, these seven areas have an impact, in lesser or greater degree, on the work of every sociologist, irrespective of that sociologist's specific area of interest. That is because they define the framework within which each member of a society lives.

Chapter 8 deals with crime and deviance, offering important insights into the research that tries to explain why some individuals operate outside the established norms and expectations of their society. All societies do not necessarily share the same definitions of deviance; what is deviant in one may be expected or valued in another. This chapter describes the varieties of deviance and crime, and explains the procedures and problems in measuring these phenomena. Sociological theories that try to explain crime are presented along with some factors that are correlated with criminal behaviour. Finally, some examples of noncriminal deviance are presented.

Chapter 9 on race and ethnicity explores factors that have led to some of the most destructive actions in human history and which, even in the most enlightened society, have the potential for turning neighbour against neighbour. The "realities" of race and ethnicity seem, like so many social phenomena, cultural rather than intrinsic. The ways in which society defines these categories have profound consequences for the social conditions under which each of us learns and lives.

Chapter 10 recognizes that inequalities within a society are not limited to matters of race and ethnicity. We are just beginning to explore the differential treatment of males and females in our society — a treatment based not on innate physiological differences but rather on culturally established differentials that serve to empower one group while discriminating against the other. The sociology of gender is a relatively new but extremely important area for our assessment of human societies, and reflects issues that are being hotly debated today. While the evidence of gender inequity is indisputable, sociologists are increasingly being asked to clarify the issues in an objective manner so that methods of dealing with the problems can be devised and implemented.

Chapter 11 examines the process of aging and its impact on the social structure. As the "baby boomer" generation moves through the life cycle, the proportion of older people in our society will increase. That fact, coupled with the myriad medical advances that extend our life spans, presents new challenges for our society with its traditional focus on youth. This chapter systematically explores aging as an organizing principle and social construct, reviews the theories of aging, presents the current statistical picture of the Canadian population's age structure, and explores social policies related to aging.

Traditionally, we have viewed the family as the most important social unit in the development of the individual within society. Where we could once speak of the "traditional" family unit, however, we now have to deal with a wider range of family types than could ever have been imagined a couple of generations ago. Chapter 12 examines the current issues in the area of the family, including the theoretical orientations, changing demographic trends, variations in family and marriage forms across cultures and time, and the complexity of forms that are found in Canadian society today.

Across time, it appears that a universal tendency has been to try to explain and give meaning to human existence. Chapter 13 (the sociology of religion) looks at the variety of belief systems directed toward the supernatural that have developed, the organization of those belief systems, and their effect on both the individual and the society in which he or she lives. The challenge for sociologists is to provide a framework for the systematic study of religion without allowing value judgments on the "goodness" or "badness" of particular religious beliefs to intrude on its objectivity. The impact of religion on personal life has undergone significant change in our society, although some form of religious belief is still relevant to most Canadians. The variety of religious practices and the variations in the depth of belief present yet another challenge in describing the current nature of our society and in predicting its future.

It may not be immediately obvious, but issues relating to the medical profession, health and health care, and death and dying all contain a significant sociological component. Chapter 14 explores these topics, outlining the role of sociological research and understanding in this context. The fact, for example, that Canada has universal health care while the United States does not is not a function of the medical technologies employed within these two countries, but rather a social result of their different public philosophies. At some stage in our lives, each of us will require medical attention. At some point, each of us will have to deal with the issues of death and dying, both our own and of those close to us. Again, the procedures for doing so and the way in which those procedures will affect each of us as individuals and society as a whole tend to be sociological rather than technological. As this chapter will show, sociology has a major role to play in helping us to understand and deal effectively with the issues.

Demography, the study of the growth, stability, and decline of populations, is covered in Chapter 15. The disparate sizes of the populations of China and Canada suggest that the population of any society plays a major role in determining the nature of that society. Using a different comparison, Canada's population is approximately equal to the population of California, contained within an area larger than the United States. What are the ramifications of this fact for maintaining the unity of our country? What effect does the tremendous and continuous growth in California have on the quality of life in that area? Where natural population growth can not ensure an adequate population for a society, what are the implications for immigration policy? Is the earth in serious danger of becoming overpopulated in the near future, and if so, what efforts need to be taken to reduce or eliminate that problem? As this chapter will show, the work of demographers in determining the answers to these and other questions of population growth and composition are crucial to the planning that must take place in every society.

Finally, Chapter 16 — on collective behaviour — deals with the shared behaviours of people who may never have met, and may not even be in physical proximity. Societies have changed significantly through the combined actions of large numbers of people polarized around a single issue. Whether we are dealing with the latest fad or the development of a social movement aimed at bringing about significant change in some aspect of society, the science of collective behaviour offers some important insights into the phenomena surrounding a major characteristic of every modern society — social change.

This text represents the cooperative work of many faculty members, graduates, and graduate students of the Department of Sociology at the University of Alberta. It is a large department, with a broad base of interests and orientations. This text represents that diversity, presenting a cross-section of current approaches and methodologies in the field of sociology.

It has been suggested that Canadians' view of ourselves is always modified by our proximity to the United States. Much of the way we see the world is shaped and modified by our exposure to the media sources emanating from the United States. While the mass media have done much to bring about the "global village" predicted by Marshall McLuhan (1962), there are many aspects of our society that are a direct product of our unique identity as Canadians. Wherever relevant, this text examines the issues from a Canadian perspective in the hope that through the science of sociology a better understanding of our society and culture will be attained.

History of Sociological Theory

Raymond A. Morrow

INTRODUCTION

An initiation into classical and contemporary sociological theory is a bewildering experience. Part of the shock stems from the fact that neither common sense, nor the mass media, nor even most high-school curricula really convey the complexities and uncertainties of our efforts to understand social reality. But there is also a more optimistic side to all of this: there are conceptual resources for making sense of much that has been — and will be — happening in the world.

After working through the various topics of an introductory text we find that the centrality of theory begins to make concrete sense and becomes a new form of *common sense*. Theory is practical if you wish to reconstruct your understanding of society and history in ways that involve **sociological imagination**. But it is also disturbing to realize (and ask why) only a very few — mostly the relatively privileged like yourselves — have even a chance to understand these questions, let alone the range of proposed responses. Sociology can help explain why, and perhaps what is to be done — if you have the patience to give it a chance.

The task of this chapter is to survey the *history* of **sociological theory**. Sociological theory is concerned with the development of sociology's most general conceptual frameworks for interpreting society. First we will consider the debates surrounding whether or not — or in what sense — sociology can be *scientific*. Then we will turn to the origins of classical theory in the early 19th century as a response to the emergence of a capitalist, industrial society, culminating in the classical masters of sociological theory from the mid-19th century until World War I. The institutionalization of sociology as a discipline is traced to the rise of the democratic welfare state in the first half of the 20th century. As we shall see, in Canada this institutionalization took place somewhat belatedly after World War II, with a quite separate tradition in French Quebec. In the concluding section we will review the leading contemporary theories of society.

The concepts used by sociological theories are often difficult because their terms are not familiar to us or differ from common sense. To make matters worse, most of the theoretical concepts in sociology are not even defined in standard dictionaries. Consequently, you will find that using more specialized dictionaries and encyclopedias for the study of sociological theory is necessary and helpful (e.g., Abercrombie et al., 1988; Jary and Jary, 1991; Borgatta and Borgatta, 1992).

IS SOCIOLOGY A SCIENCE?

Whether sociology is a science presupposes an answer to the question, "what is science?" Philosophers of science have long wrestled with this problem in order to answer questions like "how do we tell the difference between a pseudoscience such as astrology and a real one such as astronomy?" Such questions are the concern of the branch of philosophy called **epistemology**. The traditional **empiricist** philosophy of science emphasized a single, universal "scientific method": a body of observational methods that can validate a theory based on general laws by ensuring that it corresponds to the facts. Empiricists (also called, in their most extreme form, **positivists**) held that the most successful sciences such as physics followed this model and that the social sciences should emulate the natural sciences. Over the past two decades, however, **postempiricist** philosophers and historians of science have criticized empiricist and positivist epistemologies for being too inflexible even for the natural sciences. For example, many crucial findings in physics are not directly observed. Also, various competing theories may all be backed up by facts, so choosing between theories depends on many other factors as well. Finally, examining different natural sciences suggests that general laws are only one of many possible explanations of the causes of a given phenomenon. The use of a model (or theory) to describe or explain the basic structure underlying a phenomenon is held to be the most important basis of explanations in many areas of inquiry.

Today there are three main approaches to sociology as a science that compete for the attention of social researchers: **positivist social science, interpretive social science,** and **critical social science** (Neuman, 1991).

• POSITIVIST SOCIAL SCIENCE

Positivists stress logic and scientific methods. Positivists think the ideal of the social sciences is to measure variables, establish correlations between them, and then discover general laws that explain their causes. The primary objective of sociology should be to analyze the social structures (elements) that determine human behaviour. Empirical research should thus focus on facts. Meanings, according to most positivists, can also be studied objectively (e.g., as attitudes defined by questionnaire scales) just like any other phenomena. However, this position has often been identified with the claim that sociology should be **"value-free"** in order to avoid bias and keep politics out of research. By learning about social laws as revealed through analysis of social facts, positivists hope to enable societies to control unwanted social outcomes in much the same manner that engineers seek to control nature. But the question of how to use this knowledge is often completely separated from research itself. This approach to theory has dominated modern sociology, though it has been seriously challenged over the past two decades.

In contrast, **antipositivists** reject the assumption that there is some kind of unified scientific method revealed by formal logic. Like the postempiricists, they believe that the idea of one scientific method is too inflexible. They argue that sociology requires distinctive methods and concepts to study meanings and so should not follow the natural sciences directly. Further, they contend that questions of value are an integral part of research.

• INTERPRETIVE SOCIAL SCIENCE

Interpretive theories and methodologies stress understanding the meanings of social relations. From this perspective sociology is a social, not a natural science. The methodological focus is on participant observation and interpreting the symbols of a culture or group. "Participant observation" is what takes place when a researcher joins others who are engaged in a naturally occurring event. The primary objective is to understand how people make sense of the world they inhabit, rather than analyze the causes of behaviour. Erving Goffman's study of the way people present themselves to others is a well-known example of interpretive social science. Interpretive theorists are not usually interested in controlling social life because they are more concerned with understanding their subjects of study than changing or judging them. Interpretive social research thus tends to favour **value relativism**. Though interpretive researchers acknowledge that they bring their own values into research, they try to avoid judging the people they study. Value relativism is commonly used in cultural anthropology, which is dominated by interpretive theory.

• CRITICAL SOCIAL SCIENCE

Critical social researchers argue that meanings are partly determined by their social contexts. As a consequence, people often misunderstand their own motivations or how society works. To this extent they agree with positivist researchers that it is important to understand causal factors in social life and how they shape perceptions of reality. Critical researchers, however, focus on the important factors of power, domination, and exploitation in social life. They agree that social research can be scientific, though in a manner distinct from natural science, because they hold that the study of meanings is also crucial — a belief they share with interpretive researchers.

History of Sociological Theory

Critical researchers, however, argue that meanings should also be studied as **ideologies,** value judgments that often reflect power relations and political beliefs such as conservatism, liberalism, and socialism.

For critical researchers, ideologies are both enabling and distorting: they help people act to maintain or change their way of life, but they may also distort understanding of what is really going on. Nor can sociologists fully escape this process. Therefore, critical social research seeks to be both self-aware about its own value assumptions and aware of those of other social actors. Those involved in the study of poverty, for example, should use their knowledge to criticize existing policies and social conditions.

Feminist theory shows the distinctive features of the critical approach. It suggests that positivist social science has excluded methods that would take the unique experience of women seriously as the basis for a type of social knowledge. Further, it argues that both analysis of objective power relations and interpretive knowledge should be used to criticize existing institutions that reproduce the inequalities suffered by women.

ORIGINS OF CLASSICAL THEORY

Sociological theory arose in response to the industrial revolution in the late 18th and early 19th centuries (Zeitlin, 1987; Coser, 1977). The earliest forms of sociological thinking were closely bound up with political ideas. As a consequence, there was a tendency to view changes in society more or less directly from the perspective of one of the three main social classes in early capitalism. At first these interpretations expressed social values rather than social scientific theories. In other words, early sociological formulations were more concerned with what *ought* to be than with establishing facts by systematic observation. Nevertheless, they posed the issues they examined in a way that was distinctive enough to open the way for the "classical masters."

Although these early 19th-century ideas have familiar names, their meanings have changed. The original meanings referred to a form of society that has long since disappeared. The most optimistic idea is associated with classical **liberalism** — the political philosophy of new capitalist entrepreneurs (i.e., the "bourgeoisie") and closely associated liberal professions. Liberal thinkers identified capitalism with industrial progress, and tended to downplay its negative effects on the working class. Classical liberals adopted the position of **laissez faire** — the idea that governments should let market forces run freely with limited regulation. Only toward the end of the 19th century did liberals reverse their position and argue, as even now, that significant state intervention was necessary to make capitalism operate more humanely and fairly. Today, the classic liberal position is called **neoconservatism**.

In the beginning of the industrial revolution, the dominant economic group — the landed gentry and aristocracy allied with the clergy — was ambivalent toward capitalism; the resulting **conservatism** was a view that the traditional feudal order must be defended against change. Hence conservatives defended the right of governments to intervene to preserve the old order. The formation of another new social class — the working class — brought forth the most radical critique of the new industrial system: **socialism**. Early socialists advocated strong government intervention in the economy, even to the point of abolishing capitalism.

• THE ENLIGHTENMENT AND THE DISCOVERY OF SOCIETY

The discovery of the New World (after 1492), the worldwide expansion of markets, and rapid urbanization had profound effects. The 15th-century Renaissance envisioned a **humanism** that encouraged individuality and the importance of nonreligious aspects of life. The 16th century brought the Protestant Reformation led by Martin Luther, which successfully challenged the Catholic Church's monopoly on cultural life, and thus opened the way to new forms of thinking and cultural expression. This new intellectual freedom culminated in the 17th century with the rise of modern science as represented by Newton's theory of gravitation. Then, in the 18th-century Enlightenment, the principles of reason (i.e., scientific thinking) were applied to philosophy and politics, resulting in the French and American revolutions that called for the end of monarchy and its replacement by natural rights and democracy. Finally, the 19th century brought the full emergence of capitalism, along with the expansion of its two new social classes — the working class and the bourgeoisie. The origins of sociology can be traced to the early 19th-century, post-Enlightenment intellectuals who attempted to make sense of this new order from the perspective of these two new social classes.

With a handful of exceptions, 18th-century Enlightenment thinkers could not explain the origins of the changes brought about by the industrial revolution except in terms of how the church had previously suppressed free thinking. The reason for their inability to explain social and historical change is that they did not have an understanding of **society** as a theoretical concept (Frisby and Sayer, 1986). Only with the rise of sociology — and the discovery of society as a topic of inquiry, a completely new mode of thinking — did an adequate understanding of these historical processes become possible. The founder of sociology was the French aristocrat Montesquieu (1689–1755) who sought to link the characteristics of diverse legal and political systems with various geographic, economic, and social determinants. Until Montesquieu, no one had clearly grasped how historical change was caused by the social factors constituting a society.

• Liberalism as Sociology

The origin of the term *sociology* and its development as a systematic mode of analysis are usually traced to the work of Auguste Comte (1798–1857) in France, who first used the term *sociologie* in print in 1838. Many of his ideas stemmed from his work as a secretary for Saint-Simon (1760–1825), who had the first coherent vision of an emerging industrial society in which experts and business would take over from incompetent aristocrats. In his "Law of Three Stages," Comte justified sociology as a new kind of science, arguing that all knowledge evolved in phases: the theological, the metaphysical, and the scientific. Comte argued that only in his own work had sociology emerged as a "positive" science of society in two senses: that it was constructive (uniting order and progress), unlike the negativism of the French Revolution; and that it produced certain (positive) knowledge. The key to his understanding of society was the **organic analogy,** which compares society to an organism with integrated structures and functions.

In Britain, the most famous 19th-century sociologist was Herbert Spencer (1820–1895). Spencer's theory of society was influenced by Comte and combined Darwinian evolutionism (which he interpreted crudely as the "survival of the fittest") with a biological theory of progress through differentiation. According to this theory, societies advance by developing more complex and specialized parts that recombine into new forms with the evolution of the division of labour. Spencer drew the hasty conclusion that his theory legitimized the British Empire as the pinnacle of social evolution. Later users of Spencer's theory often used racial arguments about the supposed superiority of white races to try to justify European colonialism.

The liberalism that united these different views of society stemmed from the principle Comte called "progress with order." These views championed the role of the new, leading economic class of capitalism (i.e., the bourgeoisie), and saw the state as having only a minor responsibility for regulating the excesses. This sociological perspective was complemented by the new economic theory of Adam Smith (a central figure in the Scottish Enlightenment and the founder of modern economics), who argued that the "invisible hand" of the market required laissez-faire policies to operate efficiently and fairly.

• Conservatism as Sociology

Classical conservatism romanticized and idealized the traditional communities of the feudal system. Conservative sociologies developed in response to the challenges of liberalism and socialism. To classical conservatives, the ideal society was one in which the aristocracy ruled peasants under the watchful eye of the church, and industrial cities had yet to appear. The basic principle of classical conservatism was that individuals are by nature weak and violent, and thus strong forms of government authorized by a powerful elite are necessary. This form of sociology stressed the dangers of rapid change — especially revolutionary change — for social order. The most famous precursor of this position was that of Thomas Hobbes (1588–1679), who argued that citizens should voluntarily surrender their individual rights to a monarch in order to ensure social order.

By opposing the capitalist and the French revolutions, conservative theorists were sensitized to analytical questions omitted by liberal and socialist writers. The most famous British conservative was the political philosopher Edmund Burke (1729–1797), who criticized the French revolutionaries on the grounds that they did not understand that meaningful change could not be created by force and pure reason. The failures of the French Revolution and the eventual counter-revolution led by Napoleon confirmed aspects of this argument. For sociologists the most important 19th-century conservative was Alexis de Tocqueville (1805–1859), who developed a more progressive analysis based on the importance of a balance of power in a society to avoid the dangers of revolution.

• Utopianism as Sociology

The socialist writers were also concerned with the restoration of community and the negative effects of capitalism, but looked more to the future than the past, and spoke from the view of the working class, not the aristocracy. Utopian thinkers envisioned an ideal society and were strong on criticizing the present and envisioning new forms of social life that were nowhere to be found in the present; but they were weak on analyzing society empirically and on finding ways to change it.

Writing mostly in the 1830s and 1840s, **utopian** socialists criticized the savage consequences of laissez-faire capitalism — child labour, the brutal effects of factory work, unemployment, the destruction of communities — and tried to envision an alternative system of production and politics that could combine new technologies with more humane and egalitarian social relations. "Back to the land" communes derive their inspiration from this tradition. The argument was that economic as well as political (democratic) revolution was required. First, utopian socialists pointed out that most people could not vote because they did not have property (a requirement for voting then), and, second, that effective use of democratic rights required economic rights as well. Robert Owen (1771–1858) in Britain — one of the founders of the labour movement — attempted to show in his own factory that through education and improved working conditions workers could become effective members of a democratic society and thus should have the right to vote.

THE CLASSICAL MASTERS

The debates of modern sociology refer most often to three key figures: Marx, Weber, and Durkheim. They outlined the basic methodological, theoretical, and value issues that continue to guide sociological debate today (Collins and Makowski, 1989; Coser, 1977; Zeitlin, 1987; Parkin, 1982; Thompson, 1982; Giddens, 1971).

• MARX

The history of sociology is often referred to as a debate with "Marx's ghost," because his theory of society was the first to provide a way to understand and change the ills of capitalism. Although he captured many features of capitalistic society, Marx studied capitalism only during the early phase of its development. His pessimistic diagnosis was based in part on his analysis of a form of capitalism in which only a small minority had voting rights, trade unions were illegal, and workers had virtually no legal protection. He felt that the state could never become truly democratic because if it did the working class would take over and abolish capitalism. As a consequence, the capitalist ruling class would always prevent full democracy, thus contributing to eventual social and economic breakdown and revolution.

Marx claimed that theory should not only describe the world, but also contribute to its practical transformation by making people aware of real possibilities for change: capitalism *should be* transformed into a classless social order so that all citizens could realize their full human possibilities.

The core of Marx's approach was a set of general concepts that formed the basis of a science of history called **historical materialism**. This approach stressed the primacy of economic power and class in determining social relations. Marx's most elementary assumption was that social being shapes consciousness. Social being involved the economic foundation of life, or what he called the **mode of production**. Every mode or type of production was defined by the way its dominant elite extracted an economic surplus from its subordinate class (or classes). All historical modes of production have also been systems of *exploitation* because these subordinate groups did not receive a just share of wealth and income. Different types of labour exploitation meant that human history was a history of class struggles conducted between various classes. Exploitation caused human beings to be cut off in different ways from their potentialities by systems of class domination. In the case of capitalism this takes the form of **alienated labour**.

A mode of production is defined by the *forces of production* (essentially technology) and *relations of production* (the organization of labour exploitation). The rise of capitalism as a mode of production was thus characterized by the application of new technologies (especially the steam engine) to new relations of production — i.e., wage-labour as part of free labour markets. These social relations of production in turn defined the specific form of class antagonism between the owners of capital and simple labourers. The key sociological proposition that followed from this conception of society became known as the **base–superstructure metaphor**. According to this analogy, the economic system (the "base") determined the other aspects of society (the "superstructure") such as governments, law, education, and other aspects of culture.

The antagonism between labour and capital could not be resolved within capitalism itself, and a transition to a new mode of production was therefore inevitable. Part of the argument was that capitalism was inherently characterized by boom and bust cycles that would gradually inten-

Box 1.1

KARL MARX

Karl Marx (1818–1883) was born in Germany, but later fled to Paris and finally London because of political persecution. In London he met his lifelong collaborator, Friedrich Engels (1820–1895), who introduced him to the writings of English political economists such as Adam Smith. Marx's sociological approach was based on three streams of thought. First, he used English political economy to analyze capitalism. For Marx, the boom and bust cycle of capitalism and its exploitation of workers could only be overcome by a new type of economic system. Second, he argued that social life was based on dialectical change involving conflict and opposition that inevitably led to new ideas and historical epochs. Third, he drew upon the vision of a future society based on French utopian socialism, but argued that such possibilities were built into the working out of the contradictions of capitalism itself.

sify the alienation of labour and create the objective conditions for revolution. Because the state was directly controlled by the capitalist class in Marx's time, he did not foresee the possibility of a fundamental reform of capitalism through working-class participation in the political process.

As a political activist, Marx not only wanted to interpret society, but he also wanted to change it. Revolution was the specific means that he thought necessary to abolish exploitation and alienation. Still, even though he participated at various points in his life in working-class political associations, he was not an important political leader. Indeed, in that role he earned only brief mention in specialized European working-class political histories. This experience was important, however, in shaping his understanding of how revolutionary change might take place. He was convinced that the gradual formation of working-class parties would force a confrontation between labour and capital. Capitalists would eventually try to use force to prevent the working class from taking over the government, but the working class would rise up and resist. At this point the workers would set up a new form of democracy after a brief, transitional "dictatorship of the **proletariat**" — i.e., the working class.

• WEBER

Weber's position is often called **historicist** because it stresses that theory is a human construction somewhat arbitrarily imposed on a continuously changing reality. Weber did not believe that sociological theory could be reduced to natural laws, even if it could provide useful accounts of causal relations in specific cases. Although there could be no *general law* of revolutions, in other words, it would be possible to develop a theoretical analysis of a specific revolution (say, the French Revolution) or a particular type of revolution (say, peasant revolutions).

For Weber, the rise of capitalism should be understood not only for its economic causes, but also in terms of the new systems of meaning that guided social conduct. The resulting **interpretive sociology** emphasizes the crucial role of **Verstehen** ("to understand" in German). It is the process of interpreting meanings, or Verstehen, that Weber says differentiates the natural from the social sciences.

Weber thought that social institutions should be analyzed and compared as **ideal types**. So, for example, the ideal type of a bureaucracy is a model of the general features that all bureaucracies tend to share (a hierarchical structure, clearly defined positions, etc.). Only in this way is it possible to look beyond unique cases in order to see general causal processes at work. Whereas a traditional historian might develop a theory of the French Revolution, a Weberian sociologist would construct an ideal type of revolution and develop propositions about that type.

Finally, Weber argued that sociology should be **value-free**: sociologists should not mix up observational statements with value judgments. The fact that one has values opposed to a particular political party, for example, should not be allowed to distort the empirical analysis of its operation and role in society. Many critics have inaccurately concluded that Weber wished to exclude political issues and values altogether from sociology. Weber held that sociologists might address value questions as long as they separated this task from their role as social scientists and did not suggest that their value claims had a scientific foundation.

Box 1.2

Max Weber

Although Max Weber (1865–1920) is regarded as Marx's most important critic, Weber also learned a good deal from him. For this reason each represents a type of conflict theory. A key aspect of Weber's writing is based upon an analysis of the new stage of capitalist development arising in response to the revolutionary Marxism that ultimately led to the creation of the Soviet Union. As a nationalist liberal in Germany, Weber accepted the need for more working-class political participation, but strongly opposed revolutionary socialism because it represented a new form of bureaucratization.

Weber criticized Marx for his tendency to claim that social life is *nothing but* a response to economic factors. Though Marx usually was not guilty of such reductionism, very many of his followers have been. This critique of Marx is most apparent in Weber's **Protestant ethic thesis**. Weber argued that understanding the rise of capitalism required not only an analysis of economic factors, but also of "ideal" ones — the role of ideas (cultural processes) in social change. Hence, he tried to show that, in the early years of capitalism, Protestants were more inclined to business ownership than Catholics because of their greater ability to postpone gratification, given a more immediate need for tangible signs of future salvation. This point is based on his methodological assumption that explanations should take into account the *meanings* of actions, as well as social and economic causes.

The central theme of Weber's analysis of social class is that class relations cannot be understood exclusively in terms of the mode of production. For Weber the symbolic aspect of class, as expressed in *status* or prestige, was also important. The power of a social class could not be derived directly from its economic position. Social class involved collective forms of consciousness as evidenced by political parties (the state was not directly under the control of the dominant class, but was rather the site of struggle among classes).

For Weber, relations of **domination** in some form — the existence of rulers and the ruled — are an inevitable part of social life. Weber distinguished among three types of legitimation or rule by **authority**. *Traditional authority* induced obedience based on custom; *rational-legal authority* was based on the belief in the rationality of law backed up by reference to the testimony of experts; and *charismatic authority* was exercised when leaders provided a new moral vision of social order.

The most novel and prophetic side of Weber's work is his theory of bureaucracy or complex organization. The key to bureaucratic organization is the impersonal rule of experts oriented toward the most efficient means for the realization of organizational objectives. The modern factory, military organizations, and state agencies are the most important representatives of this form of organization.

Weber used the term **rationalization** to refer to the process whereby increasing numbers of tasks in society become subject to rational calculation rather than guidance by tradition. The result was a *disenchantment* of social life that followed from the decline of magic and the rise of science in its place. In this context, religion could no longer bring together different parts of society. Rationalization undermined not only religion, but also individuality, by locking people into the "iron cage" of organizational life.

Working within the tradition of German sociology, Weber became preoccupied with the consequences of the shift from **Gemeinschaft** (or intimate community) to **Gesellschaft** (abstract, bureaucratic society). Feudal society had been characterized by intimate social relations of community. In contrast, capitalism had eroded community relations when feudal peasants moved to the cities and large, impersonal organizations of business and the state were created. Under conditions of Gesellschaft, or abstract societal relations, people lived alone in an increasingly **mass society** — one in which traditional class differences were eroded by public education and the new media.

Weber's theory of bureaucracy and rationalization bears some resemblance to Marx's narrower theory of alienation. Bureaucracy in effect provided a new form of order, but one very different from that of traditional "communities." Crucial to the bureaucratic organization was its impersonality. Bureaucracies were thus continually expanding as part of a more general and inevitable process of rationalization. For this reason, Weber thought socialism a futile alternative because it would only create even more bureaucracy, even if it did produce greater social justice and equality.

Weber was very pessimistic about the human consequences of rationalization. Part of the problem was that he did not believe it possible to choose rationally between basic value positions.

He saw value questions as ultimately a "war between gods" — a matter of irrational faith — without any possible rational solution. The consequence was a value relativism that came with the disenchantment of the world brought about by the decline of religion and the rise of science.

Unlike Marx and Durkheim, Weber did not develop a fully coherent approach to values. On the one hand, he was much engaged in politics, but his positions were specific to the liberal German politics of his generation and not of great interest for social theory today. On the other hand, where he did engage in value inquiries of broader scope, his ambivalent and mostly pessimistic conclusions were not of the type to inspire any kind of political movement or vision of social change.

• DURKHEIM

Durkheim viewed sociology as a science and suggested that sociologists could treat **social facts** (e.g., birthrates) as "things" analogous to the data of the natural sciences. He argued that the knowledge produced by this science could be "applied" like any other.

Durkheim developed a statistical analysis of dependent and independent variables in order to account for different rates of suicide. Less known, however, is Durkheim's later work on the sociology of religion where the analysis he develops of the structures of religious thought is much closer to a kind of interpretive sociology of the kind proposed by Weber. Durkheim should be considered the founder of sociology modelled on the natural sciences.

In his first major book, Durkheim introduced his theory of modern society. His thesis is that societies evolve like organic systems through a process of social differentiation and specialization in which new, more complex structures (divisions of labour) replace simpler ones. Primitive and feudal communities were characterized by a **mechanical solidarity** where individuals were very similar because there existed a limited division of labour, and their actions were coordinated by a cultural consensus. Modern societies, on the other hand, are characterized by an **organic solidarity** in which there is greater social diversity and individuality. This new system of coordination provides the basis of a superior form of social integration. Durkheim's theory provided a response to the negative interpretations on the left and right that saw capitalism only from the perspective of its harmful aspects. In contrast to this general theory, Durkheim's more specialized work on suicide in part served to confirm some of his more general arguments about **anomie,** or lack of rules, increasing social disorganization, and the need for reforms that would facilitate social integration.

Durkheim's study of primitive religion emphasized the formation of cultural consensus. The result was a definition of religion that suggested that society could not exist without the symbolic cement provided by religious beliefs. Central to this definition is the distinction between the **sacred** and **profane** character of things in everyday life. Certain objects — such as items used in religious rituals — have a continuous sacred significance. Others can be at different times both sacred and profane: whereas a soldier's sword is profane during his life, it might take on a sacred

Box 1.3

EMILE DURKHEIM

Emile Durkheim (1858–1917) was strongly influenced by the liberal sociology of Saint-Simon and Comte. His theory was based on the organic view of society as a system of interrelated parts that progressively evolved through increasing differentiation into more complex, higher forms. Durkheim was the first classical sociologist to have a university position in sociology and exert a broad political influence. His liberal-reformist conception of sociology preceded the rise of the **welfare state.** A welfare state is distinct from laissez-faire rule in that the government actively regulates the economy. Also, the government introduces safety nets (such as mass education, and unemployment and medical insurance) to protect citizens from negative effects of economic instability or their individual lack of foresight.

Table 1.1

CLASSICAL MASTERS OF SOCIOLOGICAL THEORY

	Marx	Weber	Durkheim
Metatheory	*Historical materialism*	*Historicism*	*Positivism*
Analytical Theory	• Class conflict interests	• Ideal and material	• Evolution from mechanical to organic solidarity
	• Contradiction in modes of production	• Bureaucratization and rationalization	• Anomie
	• Alienation		
Normative Theory	• Critique of exploitation	• Critique of mixing facts and values	• Diagnosis of social pathologies
	• Call for revolutionary change	• Ambivalence about the future	• Call for reformist change

symbolic function when buried with him upon death. Without such integrative symbols, levels of anomie (i.e., normlessness) rise and societies become unstable.

RISE OF THE WELFARE STATE

Whereas the debates of classical theory revolved around the implications of the rise of capitalism, modern theory has been preoccupied by the **welfare state**. The rise of the welfare state required the revision of older concepts of capitalism and the creation of new ones; sociology as a *historical* discipline must keep reconstructing its concepts in order to keep up with changes in reality. The origins of the welfare state can be detected in the 19th century in such things as legislation against child labour, the beginnings of mass education, and some welfare schemes in Bismarck's Germany. Mostly, welfare capitalism is an outcome of the impact of the Great Depression of the 1930s and World War II. The outcome was the transition from a laissez-faire capitalism where the state has limited functions to an organized form in which the state plays a central regulatory role. The implications of this transformation of the role of the state constitute one of the central themes of 20th-century social theory.

This shift was anticipated in the work of Durkheim and in Weber's theory of the state and bureaucracy. (Though some of Marx's concepts could be adapted for this purpose, his work remained more directly applicable to the Third World.) But before contemporary theory emerged in the post-1945 period, the direction in which the crisis tendencies of early capitalism were leading had to be clarified.

The epochs or stages of social development become visible only once they are past. During periods of transition it is often very difficult to know what kind of new social formation is in progress. Such was the case in the turbulent years from 1914 through 1945 — the period marked by World War I, the Russian Revolution, the Great Depression, and then World War II. During this period of transition it was unclear what kind of society might follow the demise of unstable forms of laissez-faire capitalism. The three main contenders offered rather different solutions to the problems of the instability of unregulated market systems: *Soviet communism* (based on *Marxism–Leninism*) suggested the creation of a "dictatorship of the proletariat" organized by a party vanguard; *fascism* offered order through a powerful leader, nationalism, and imperial expansion; and **social liberal** and **social democratic** parties offered the possibility of a democratic welfare state. The military defeat of fascism, the discrediting of communism with Stalinism, and the stability provided by the formation of a European economic and political community opened the way for the welfare state after 1945.

• THE WELFARE STATE DEBATE

Many ex-Marxists joined the social democratic and social liberal camp after World War II, arguing that Marxism was a "god that failed" along with fascism. The new stability and growth provided by the emerging welfare states created a climate that was bringing about an "end of ideology" in the earlier extremist sense. In welfare states all of the major social groups competed within a basic consensus on values and political processes. Value consensus allowed groups to negotiate their conflicts and differences without recourse to violence or threats to the system. From this perspective, for example, the differences between the Progressive Conservative, Liberal, and New Democratic parties in Canada are minimal compared to their shared assumptions about the constructive role of the state in a democracy. The pluralist or multiparty welfare state was conceived as the best type of political-economic system one could rationally hope for.

Such a political theory was closely associated with the **functionalist** or organic conception of social order. Functionalist views did capture important aspects of change where liberal democratic regimes were successful. On the other hand, the functionalist approach did not take into account the residual conflicts and antagonisms in this new form of society, let alone emergent sources of tension and conflict. Nor did functionalist views deal with the problem that in many areas of the world (e.g., Latin America) democratic institutions and the state were weak and directly served the interests of the dominant classes.

Others, though vehemently rejecting Soviet Marxism, argued in diverse ways that the emerging welfare state was still incapable of dealing with all of the negative effects of capitalist growth (Kettler et al., 1984; Eldridge, 1983; Craib, 1992b). Within this tradition of conflict theory, a more hopeful assessment was given by Karl Mannheim (1893–1947) — writing in Germany and England in the 1930s — who attempted to bring together ideas from Marx and Weber about the possibilities for democratic social planning. Under the influence of Mannheim's approach, C. Wright Mills (1916–1962), the founder of radical conflict theory in North America, concluded in the 1950s that the actual character of the new form of capitalism found in the United States did not fully justify Mannheim's optimistic diagnosis. Above all, the emergence of power elites undermined many of the democratic pretensions and planning capacities of a liberal democracy. Further, the emergence of new forms of white-collar work suggested a new type of class structure that could not be easily interpreted through traditional class analysis.

The most pessimistic diagnosis of the new welfare state was the **Frankfurt School** tradition of **critical theory**. Its most famous representative — Herbert Marcuse (1898–1979) — spoke of a new type of "one-dimensional" society in which real political competition was no longer possible because political parties did not really represent significantly different options. From the pessimistic perspective of critical theory, the control of consciousness by the mass media, coupled with a popular blind faith in science and technology, prevented criticism of society from developing or having any effect.

• ORIGIN OF SOCIAL PSYCHOLOGY

Though the classical sociological theories included a social psychological analysis (e.g., alienation in Marx, anomie in Durkheim, subjective understanding in Weber), **social psychology** did not emerge as a distinctive theoretical tradition until this transitional period. Social psychologists have been concerned with three types of inquiry: the study of social interaction, the effects of structural features of society on individuals, and the experimental analysis of behaviour and cognition in controlled situations (Franklin, 1982). Sociologists have been primarily concerned with the first two, and psychologists, the latter.

The origin of **symbolic interactionism** is linked to the tradition of American pragmatism, especially the work of George Herbert Mead (1863–1931). According to pragmatism, the key to understanding social life was to study how consciousness is formed in social contexts. The founder of symbolic interactionism, George Herbert Mead, argued that the self was essentially a social construct emerging from social interaction. From this perspective, so-called "deviant" subcultures could be studied through participant observation and not be seen as fundamentally different from "normal" social relations.

Behavioural and cognitive social psychology were both experimental and based on surveys. Experimental research focused primarily on group processes and social learning. Survey research has been widely used in all of the subfields of sociology to understand change in attitudes.

ORIGIN OF CANADIAN SOCIOLOGY

The origin of Canadian sociology was connected to increasing state responsibilities for providing social welfare and dealing with social problems. From the outset, however, Canadian sociology has had two distinctive sociological traditions, despite mutual influences (Hiller, 1982; Kroker, 1984; Brym and Fox, 1989; Whyte, 1992).

The earliest sociologists in English Canada were allied with the Christian social gospel movement. Their main concern was with the plight of the poor and disadvantaged. A key task of early research was to describe and measure the extent of various kinds of social problems. Though these earlier efforts have left virtually no theoretical traces, sociological theory continues to be influenced by the second phase, peaking in the 1940s and 1950s.

One major contribution to this second phase was the economic history and historical sociology associated with Harold Innis, at the University of Toronto, who stressed the role of communications technology (including railroads) in social change. Until the late 1960s, however, there were very few sociology positions available in either universities or governments. Most students had to go to Britain or the United States for advanced degrees, and sociology remained very marginal in the university system.

The third phase of the development of English Canadian sociology can be traced to the late 1960s. With the rapid expansion of universities and the emergence of many doctoral programs in sociology, Canada belatedly became a major centre of sociological training and research.

In Quebec, on the other hand, the institutionalization of sociology was closely associated with reformist impulses within the Catholic Church in the 1930s. The influence of French social theory was strong from the outset, as was a close relationship between sociology and the nationalist aspirations of francophone Quebec.

In its second phase, Quebec sociology contributed to the modernization of the province's politics and culture. French-speaking sociologists helped eliminate clerical control of universities in 1960. Sociologists were particularly concerned with analyzing the sources of francophone Quebec's relative "backwardness," locating them in the power of the Catholic Church, the economic and political dominance of English Canada, and the perceived inferiority associated with having French as one's native language in North America.

In its third phase, Quebec sociology has had close relations with both Marxist theory and the independence movement. On the one hand, many of the leading theorists were convinced that francophone culture could only thrive and survive in the context of sovereignty-association. On the other hand, critical sociologists such as Marcel Rioux questioned whether independence was worth the trouble if it did not include fundamental changes that would improve the position of disadvantaged groups (Rioux, 1978; Morrow, 1986).

CONTEMPORARY THEORIES OF SOCIETY

Contemporary theories of society still work within the shadow of these earlier debates about the welfare state. Specific theories are divided among symbolic interactionist, functionalist, and conflict theories of society (see Chapter 4 on symbolic interactionism) (Wallace and Wolf, 1986; Ritzer, 1992; Craib, 1992b; Collins, 1988).

• FUNCTIONALIST THEORY

The term *functionalism* has several meanings (Turner and Maryanski, 1979; Hamilton, 1983; Crothers, 1987). A functionalist method is used by any theory stating that some part of society exists because of its contribution to the smooth functioning of society as a whole. Thus, many of Marx's concepts are functionalist in this sense — e.g., the notion that the ideological superstructure functions to provide the cultural order necessary for capitalism. But more commonly, functionalism has an analytical meaning as a type of social theory based on the organic model (following liberal social theory from Comte through Durkheim).

The two most influential sociological versions of functionalism can be found in the work of Robert K. Merton (1910–) and Talcott Parsons (1902–1979) in the United States. The development of modern functionalism was polarized between their two strategies of inquiry. Merton advocated a more cautious strategy of developing **middle-range** theories (about deviance, roles, bureaucracies, etc.), which would eventually provide the foundation for a synthesis. Merton's approach is sometimes termed *conflict functionalism* because his empirical orientation gave attention to *dysfunctions* (the negative consequences of structures) as well as positive functions. Further, he emphasized that consequences may be different for particular subgroups than for society as a whole. The police may have a positive function for preserving public order for society as a whole, but may be very dysfunctional for a social group (e.g., blacks in Toronto or Los Angeles) trying to resist what they perceive to be discriminatory policing practices.

Merton's key contribution to functionalism was based on a distinction between functional methods and *structural functionalism* as a general theory promoted by Parsons and others. For Merton, the functional method assumes that a society is made up of a set of structural parts that may or may not have some function for the whole. The distinctive character of sociological theory was its ability to search for *latent functions* as opposed to the *manifest functions* of institutions. Whereas manifest functions were available to the consciousness of participants and could be related to their overt intentions, latent functions could be analyzed only through sociological concepts and the study of the *unintended consequences* of social actions.

For example, poverty persists despite great overall gains in the standard of living. Poverty is puzzling because it is difficult to come up with any clear explanation of the manifest functions of poverty, either for society or subgroups. But a closer look suggests that there may be significant *latent* positive functions of poverty. For society as a whole the fear of poverty may encourage the work ethic as a norm. For specific subgroups — those in social services and related professions — the existence of poverty may provide good jobs.

Merton also focused on the dysfunctions of social structures. Poverty has some manifest negative effects: for society there is the cumulative cost of underutilized human resources; for the poor people there is the cumulative cost of material deprivation and psychological crisis. Again, a closer look reveals some less obvious, latent dysfunctions: poverty contributes to higher rates of family dysfunction and deviance — to the detriment of society and those labelled as part of the poverty problem. Ethnic and other stereotypes about the poor as personal failures are reinforced.

In contrast to Merton's conception of middle-range theory, Talcott Parsons's theory was the most influential in the English-speaking world from the 1940s through the 1960s. This approach focused almost completely on the positive functions of social institutions, at the expense of social conflict and dysfunction.

Parsons's work can be divided into three phases. During the early period in the 1930s he sought to synthesize the implications of classical theory in the form of a theory of action fairly close to that of Weber, but also based on insights drawn from Durkheim. But he quickly abandoned this position in the second phase in the 1940s, when he shifted attention to Durkheim's examination of society as an integrated system. Parsons became interested in **systems theories** that had been developed in natural sciences, especially biology. As he saw it, these new biological systems theories required updating the biological analogy in the form used by Durkheim. Of particular importance here was the study of feedback mechanisms characteristic of *cybernetic* (or self-regulating) systems.

According to Parsons, any conceivable form of society can be analyzed in terms of what is sometimes called an **AGIL schema**: adaptation (economic processes), goal-attainment (political processes), integration (communities), and latency or latent pattern maintenance (cultural consensus). Of particular concern for Parsons was the transition from feudalism to modern societies. He argued, based on an organic model similar to Durkheim's, that this involved a process of modernization characterized by a shift from low levels of social differentiation (i.e., a limited division of labour) to high levels of complexity. These shifts could be observed in each of the four functional contexts described by the AGIL schema.

For example, in traditional societies adaptive (economic) functions were carried out within the kinship unit; in complex industrial societies, though, these processes become differentiated in specialized economic institutions. The political functions of goal-attainment were realized by part-time leaders in tribal societies, but delegated to full-time leaders in specialized legislative institutions in modern ones. Whereas the functions of social integration were originally organized around tribal law and Gemeinschaft-type communities, in modern societies they are carried out by legal systems. Cultural integration also shifted from observance of homogenous religious customs to pluralistic secular practices based on specialized educational, media, religious, and other institutions.

In the third phase in the 1960s, Parsons tried to resolve the difficulty his systems theory had in dealing with social change. He returned to a biological model in order to uncover the role of "evolutionary universals" in society. Applying this extremely complex model led Parsons to an optimistic analysis of the progressive evolution of societies toward higher and higher levels of integration. Thus, he saw emerging in contemporary society a kind of knowledge society that could maximize technology and expertise for human needs. As critics have often noted, Parsons's theory has the effect of implying that the United States represents the ideal toward which all other societies are evolving.

• CONFLICT THEORIES

Conflict theories emphasize conflict among groups, but also concern themselves with processes of integration (much as functionalist theories discuss aspects of conflict). What really differentiates conflict theory from functionalism is the concept of *domination*, a term that is used in a special way by Marx and Weber to include both the symbolic and coercive aspects of power. The term should *not* be associated with the common-sense notion of domination as simple oppression or coercion. Rather, conflict theory argues that the basis of every social order is a system of domination — characterized by groups of rulers and ruled — backed up by legitimate authority based on political symbols. People voluntarily accept rule by authority that may conflict with their own interests. For example, in primitive societies slaves tended to believe the official ideology that it was their nature to be slaves. As a consequence, the key to social order in a slave

Box 1.4

Neo-Weberian Conflict Theory

As the term *neo-Weberian* implies, such research extends Weber's basic concepts. Ralf Dahrendorf in Germany was a pioneer in the 1960s who combined Weber and aspects of Marx into a general theory of class and power. Against Marx, Dahrendorf argued that economic class is only one of many structural bases of power and legitimation in societies.

The most influential and productive neo-Weberian conflict theorist today is the American sociologist Randall Collins (Collins, 1992). A central theme of his research is that educational credentials have become a new basis of class stratification, leading to an excessively expanded educational system as individuals compete for higher and higher qualifications to get jobs. An important extension and generalization of this approach is a kind of **social closure theory** pioneered by Frank Parkin in Britain, which analyzes the processes social groups use to try to maximize the advantages of their social positions. From this relativistic perspective, there is no essential difference between capitalists, workers, or ethnic groups organizing to define their interests. Most of such research remains faithful to Weber in refusing to develop the normative implications or envision a practical resolution of the problems identified.

society was not merely exercise of force by the rulers, but also the slaves' beliefs that they deserved their fate. According to this theory, contemporary societies also combine coercive and symbolic controls in ways that block understanding of the system and how it affects the life chances of individuals and groups.

• POLITICAL ECONOMY

As a theoretical approach, political economy borrows much from Marx in that it explores the effects of economic and class structures on social order (Morrow, 1992). Research guided by political-economic theory was sparse in North America until the late 1960s. Until that point the understanding of Marx's work as it applied to social science was very limited. In Europe, however, Western Marxism (as opposed to Soviet Marxism) developed largely underground in the 1920s and 1930s and was integrated into sociological debates after World War II. This movement was aided by the discovery of Marx's early writings, which demonstrated the relevance of his approach to sociological theory. Of course, Marx's concepts had to be adapted to the new conditions of the 20th century, especially the rise of the welfare state, the emergence of the new middle classes, and the shrinking of the traditional working class. Nevertheless, the revival of Marxism had a profound effect upon sociological theory in the 1970s, in the wake of the disillusionment with functionalism.

Recent work has tried to show the continuing importance of class and economic factors in reinforcing racism, sexism, and an exploitative and antagonistic system of work relations. Political economy has had a particularly strong impact in Canadian sociology as a strategy for understanding changes in the production process, the international division of labour, and public policy. A central theme has been the manner in which political-economic constraints severely limit and distort the goals of a welfare state in addressing problems of growth and inequality. Reform is viewed as superficial and ineffective, serving indirectly to maintain the position of the dominant classes.

Political economy is often concerned about the power relations between different societies. According to the concept of **dependency,** originally based on the experience of Latin America, weaker societies (often referred to colloquially as "banana republics") fail to develop in a balanced and sustained way because of the external dominance of the major economic and political powers. Problems faced by the Third World countries derive from their economic and political dependence on advanced societies. Further, there is a Canadian dependency theory according to which early colonial relations with Britain and later dependence upon American capital have distorted the development of the Canadian economy.

According to Immanuel Wallerstein's **world systems theory,** no individual society can be understood outside of its relation to the worldwide market system. For example, any business regulatory decisions made by Canadian governments are in relation to the transnational organization of capital and the possibility that investment will be shifted elsewhere if business does not like Canadian trade rules.

• CRITICAL THEORY

Critical theory refers to a tradition of social philosophy originating in Germany in the 1920s called the *Frankfurt School.* Today *critical theory* is used to designate a broad set of writings influenced by the Frankfurt tradition and adapted to historical changes within specific nations (Morrow, 1985; Craib, 1992a; Billings, 1992). Though originally the Frankfurt tradition was close to neo-Marxism, contemporary variants have broken in crucial ways with the Marxist tradition and are sometimes called *post-Marxist.*

Critical theory today is distinctive in at least three key respects. First, critical theory emphasizes the problem of the relationship between agency and structure — i.e., how people's actions may be constrained by class and economic structures but are not fully determined by them. Second, one of its standard bearers, Jürgen Habermas (Pusey, 1987), has focused on the cultural and social psychological bases of social domination. The foundation of his approach is that **communicative action** ultimately has priority over work and labour in social life. A central theme is how the controlled expansion of technology and the subordination of human need to economic rationality has disoriented the basis of everyday life.

Finally, critical theory has been an important source of *ecological* criticism because it has questioned the blind faith in science and technology. In part these insights stem from a novel reading of Weber's theory of rationalization. Critical theory has also been concerned with how new social movements — such as those relating to women, the environment, natives, etc. — have created a new agenda for fundamental political change.

• Cultural Studies and Postmodernism

The development of critical theory is also linked with **cultural studies** (Morrow, 1991). Popular culture is part of everyday life, as opposed to specialized cultural activities such as going to museums or operas (Gruneau, 1988; G. Turner, 1990). A central issue is whether the rise of the mass media and new information technologies has transformed — or is in the process of transforming — the nature of contemporary society. Will children growing up as part of a global information network with rock videos and Nintendo games see and experience reality differently? If so, what will be the consequences for social change?

Postmodernist theory challenges the traditional assumptions that science and technology would automatically bring freedom, reason, and happiness to all. Critics argue that the rise of industrial society has not clearly brought progress. World wars and civil strife have made the 20th century the most violent in history. Environmental disaster is not far away. As well, there are multiple signs of psychological discontent: the rise of religious fundamentalism and the proliferation of cults; increases in violent crime, suicide, and substance abuse; and conflicts between genders and within families. C. Wright Mills identified the dilemma back in the 1950s:

> Now we confront new kinds of social structure which, in terms of "modern" ideals, resist analysis in the liberal and socialist terms we have inherited.
>
> The ideological mark of The Fourth Epoch — that which sets it off from The Modern Age — is that the ideas of freedom and of reason have become moot; that increased rationality may not be assumed to make for increased freedom (1968: 167).

Two forms of postmodernist social theory can be distinguished. *Critical postmodernism* extends arguments already developed in political economy and critical theory. Michel Foucault (1926–1984) has argued for the importance in modern societies of the diffuse forms of *disciplinary* power or social control embedded in experts and institutions of social control in prisons, educational systems, and so on (Smart, 1985). Such power is held to control not merely externally through coercion, but is deeply internalized into our bodies, hence out of reach of our conscious awareness. *Relativistic postmodernism,* on the other hand, argues that any effort to construct a grand theory of society or history is based on false dreams of sociology as a universal science. Instead, such sceptical postmodernist social theories argue that social scientists should focus on analyzing issues of limited scope and stress the inescapable differences among people, rather than prescribing some kind of arbitrary standard (usually that of the dominant groups) as "normal." As a consequence, critics have charged that relativistic postmodernism undermines the very project of social science.

• FEMINIST THEORY

The emergence of **feminist theory** over the past decades represents the most important new development in social theory (Sydie, 1987; Wallace, 1989; Ritzer, 1992). But it is also important to note that there are feminist *theories* — i.e., a diverse body of work. Feminist theories have been allied with many different ideological positions (e.g., liberal, socialist, Marxist, postmodernist, etc.) and all the varieties of conflict theory. There is nevertheless an underlying unity to feminist theory based on a shared empirical focus (the social consequences of gender, for women in particular) and a critique of "sexism": the assumption that throughout history women have been intentionally deprived of economic and social opportunities, and of equality within intimate relationships. Partly in response to these debates, the area of *men's studies* has emerged both to complement feminist theory and to develop theoretical issues that allow men to pose new questions about their own experience and needs (Brod, 1987).

In the human sciences, therefore, the concept of feminist theory has come to designate an *interdisciplinary* set of concerns that challenges traditional social science. Gender bias is found throughout the history of sociological thought. As a consequence, feminist scholars argue that sociology and other disciplines need to be revised to address women's issues. A central objective of feminist inquiry has been to link theory and practice.

Some *radical feminists* reject the empiricist conception of scientific method. They argue that research should focus on the experience of women as uniquely understood by women (Smith, 1990). In contrast, *empirical feminists* stress that the credibility of feminist research depends in part upon using the standard objective methods and quantitative research to establish a reliable body of knowledge about the effects of gender (Eichler, 1988b). Finally, critical *postmodernist feminists* attempt to link the feminist critique of science to other forms of questioning naive faith in science and progress. In the process they have warned against the dangers of exaggerating the differences between men and women and point to the importance of fundamental differences among women themselves (Nicholson, 1990).

Most feminist approaches require new strategies of inquiry to ask questions never asked before because of gender bias. Such questioning has forced the rethinking of basic issues in most other areas of sociological theory (Wallace, 1989). Of particular importance has been the rethinking of the relationship between gender and class. For example, the sociology of work has focused mostly on *paid work*. From this perspective, the tasks women do at home — domestic labour — were not even considered work. Most recently, so-called *Third Wave* feminist theory has questioned the dominance of middle-class and white women in setting the agenda for research and practice. Feminist theory has, in short, challenged every specialty area of sociology. It is at the centre of many important internal debates.

Feminists strive to overcome gender-based forms of domination identified by theory and research. The specific strategies for accomplishing change vary from enforcing existing equal rights legislation to restructuring basic institutions. Still, the cause of women is often linked with that of all other groups that experience similar disadvantages. More specifically, it is often argued that, given their relegation throughout history to roles demanding cooperative and nurturing skills, women have been more highly sensitized to new possibilities for making social relations less violent and destructively competitive.

SOCIOLOGICAL IMAGINATION AND THE CRISIS OF SOCIOLOGY

Recent developments have challenged the sharp distinction between ideology and social science. In various ways critical, feminist, and postmodernist theories have made evident the close and inevitable interplay between values and facts. Some sociologists continue to view social research as scientific investigation. Others argue that only by linking ideological questions to empirical research can sociology recover its mission as envisioned in classical theory. The origins of this kind of debate can be traced back to the 1950s in the radical conflict sociology of C. Wright Mills in the United States with his call for **sociological imagination**. Mills argued that the scientific aspirations of sociology cannot be mechanically realized by copying natural science through quantification with little regard for historical reality. The goal of sociology should be rather to translate what appear to be *private problems* (e.g., unemployment, poverty, alienation) into *public issues* by showing their origins in social conflicts and inequalities. For Mills, that required not only information and reason but also the quality of mind he identified as the sociological imagination, which "enables us to grasp history and biography and the relations between the two within society" (1967: 6).

SUMMARY

Sociological theories are concerned with three distinct types of questions: debates regarding the methods of sociology and its status as a social science; analytical claims about the empirical structures of society; and value interpretations that bear on the relationship between sociological research and advocacy of social change. Broadly speaking, three distinct answers to these questions can be characterized as paradigms of research:

- *Positivist social science* attempts to imitate the logic and methods of the natural sciences in order to find general laws of social life; these laws can then be applied to control unwanted effects.
- *Interpretive social science* attempts to understand the meanings of social interaction and show how people construct social reality in social contexts; such understanding is not concerned with controlling people, but rather with understanding and respecting different ways of life.
- *Critical social science* analyzes the interplay between the conscious actions of agents and the deeper structures that constrain them in order to demystify existing ideologies and empower groups to transform their situation.

The rest of this chapter has been devoted to the historical development of sociological thought:

- the origins of classical theory in the 18th and early 19th centuries (Enlightenment precursors, early classical theory);
- the three late 19th-century classical masters (Marx, Weber, Durkheim) whose approaches were described as historical materialism, historicism, and positivism;
- the mid-century transition associated with the rise of the welfare state, the emergence of social psychology as a subfield, and the rise of sociology in other societies such as Canada and Quebec;

- contemporary functionalist theories of society, as divided between middle-range theory (Merton) and general theory (Parsons);
- contemporary general conflict theories: neo-Weberian theory, political economy, and critical theory;
- the emergence of cultural studies as a focus of inquiry, along with related debates about postmodern culture and postmodernist social theory;
- the recent emergence of feminist theory that has provided the most important new challenges for methods, empirical analysis, and questions about values.

KEY CONCEPTS

AGIL schema

Alienated labour

Anomie

Antipositivism

Authority

Base—superstructure metaphor

Capitalism

Communicative action theory

Conflict theory

Conservatism

Critical social science

Critical theory

Cultural studies

Dependency theory

Domination

Empiricism

Epistemology

Feminist theory

Frankfurt School

Functionalist theory

Gemeinschaft

Gesellschaft

Historical materialism

Historicism

Humanism

Ideal types

Ideologies

Interpretive social science

Interpretive sociology

Laissez faire
Liberalism
Mass society
Mechanical solidarity
Middle-range theory
Mode of production
Neoconservatism
Neo-Weberian theory
Organic analogy
Organic solidarity
Positivism
Positivist social science
Postempiricism
Postmodern culture
Postmodernist social theory
Profane
Proletariat
Protestant ethic thesis
Rationalization
Sacred
Social closure theory
Social democracy
Social facts
Socialism
Social liberalism
Social psychology
Society
Sociological imagination
Sociological theory
Symbolic interactionism
Systems theories
Theory
Utopian socialism
Value-free
Value relativism
Verstehen
Welfare state
World systems theory

REVIEW QUESTIONS

1. Compare positivist, interpretive, and critical approaches to social science.
2. Discuss the origins of sociology as a response to the rise of industrial society, giving particular attention to its relation to the ideologies of classical liberalism, conservatism, and socialism.
3. Compare the approach to sociology of Marx, Weber, and Durkheim with respect to the conception of sociology as a science, empirical analysis of capitalist society, and value assumptions.
4. Discuss some of the distinctive features of sociological theory in Canada.
5. Compare the functionalist approaches of Parsons and Merton with the general approach of conflict theories.
6. Compare any two of the following forms of conflict theory with respect to their implications for social theory: neo-Weberian theory, political economy, critical theory, postmodernist theory, feminist theory.

Research Methods

John Gartrell, David Brown, and Judith Golec

INTRODUCTION

Sociological methods describe how sociologists do sociology: how they go about finding out about the social world around them. Research methods have a very active, practical, and exciting flavour to them. One of sociology's strengths lies in its diversity of method. The major objective of this chapter is to communicate the range of this diversity without getting lost in endless variety. We present one research strategy associated with each of the three major traditions: positive, interpretive, and critical social science. In so doing, the intent is not to teach you how to actually do research. Rather, we try to help you become a more informed reader of sociology, one who can read critically and recognize the often unstated assumptions and methodological choices embedded in the published accounts of specific studies.

As you know from the preceding chapter, the dominant conception of social science is logical positivism. This doctrine has a deep and continuing influence on how sociologists conduct their research. In fact, the methods used to generate the information in the topical chapters that follow are generally positivist — usually quantitative — and only occasionally historical, comparative, interpretive, or critical. This chapter begins with an overview of logical positivism. This is followed by a discussion of survey research, the sociological research strategy we most often associate with positivism. Interpretive research is illustrated through a classic field study; then some of the features of critical research are discussed using a recent Canadian feminist critique. In the final section, we review some of the ethical rules governing social research.

THE METHOD OF LOGICAL POSITIVISM

Although statements justifying positivism appear early in sociological thought — for example, in the 19th-century writings of Auguste Comte — it is the 1920s formulation called **logical positivism** that has had such a profound and enduring influence on sociological methods. In this view, sociology is no different from the natural sciences, most particularly physics. Logical positivism is what most people understand as the "scientific method" effectively personified by the character "Spock" of *Star Trek* fame.

In logical positivism knowledge of the real world must be **empirical** (positive) or, in other words, based upon observational methods. We may observe directly through the use of the senses or indirectly through the use of measuring instruments. *Formal logic,* including inductive and deductive reasoning, forms a bridge between research methods based on observation and theories based on general laws. The scientific process, therefore, uses empirical observation, formal logic, and lawlike theory to produce and verify social knowledge (Derksen and Gartrell, 1992; Kaplan, 1964).

Theory is extremely important in the practice of social research. Theory provides a basis for beginning research; it sets up the areas of inquiry and the questions to be addressed. Theory also provides a framework through which we make sense of the observations. Theory is thus the goal of research. The progress of scientific knowledge is circular, and cumulates as separate tests of different investigations of a theory: theories are developed and tested and new data give rise to new theories, which are in turn tested (Figure 2.1).

When our focus is **deductive** we are "testing" theory. We have developed expectations (called hypotheses) about the social world that we are testing against observations collected in some systematic manner. Here the strategy of the researcher is first to derive specific hypotheses from a general theoretical perspective, and then to see if those hypotheses about events or relationships in the social world hold true. It is this strategy that enables us to determine whether the theory corresponds to the facts and in turn to decide whether or not the evidence supports the theory.

When our focus is **inductive** we primarily work from observations of the social world toward theory. The aim is to come up with patterns rather than try to confirm or refute a particular theory.

Figure 2.1

THE RESEARCH CYCLE

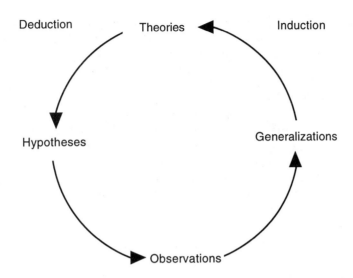

Source: Adapted from Wallace (1971).

Sometimes it is necessary to follow this course because there is no theory in a given area or because a particular theory has not shown itself to be useful in making sense of particular observations. On the basis of concrete observation, we make guesses about which other groups and situations these findings might reasonably be thought to apply to. Generalization is the first step toward the development of a more broadly applicable theoretical framework.

Theories consist of "lawlike" statements (propositions) that specify relationships between properties (concepts) of the units sociologists study (individuals, social collectivities). Universal laws are generalizations about the social world that hold true across time and place, and in many different circumstances. Positivism presumes that in spite of historical and cultural variety there is something enduring and regular about social life that can be captured in generalizations and abstract laws. An additional assumption of this view is that social regularities, like those in the natural world, display a cause–effect pattern.

The explanatory style that is most consistent with logical positivism is **nomothetic**. This style does not try to achieve an exhaustive description of all the events and circumstances that surround a particular social arrangement or action. On the contrary, the goal of the nomothetic model of explanation is to uncover the general pattern of cause and effect and to provide the greatest amount of explanation with the least number of concepts. A social phenomenon is "explained" when it is shown to be a particular instance of, or covered by, a universal law.

Theories must be "testable," which implies that they must include "how to" measurement information to translate abstract concepts into empirical observables (as variables) and to specify relationships between the concepts as statistical measures of association, such as correlations. Indeed, this emphasis on empirical theory — theory that can be empirically examined — is the basis for the preoccupation of American positivism with statistical techniques and research instrumentation. Statistical analysis requires **quantification,** the representation of observed properties of individuals and social collectives with numbers.

Another important goal for scientific investigation is to produce **objective** knowledge, free from subjective bias and the values of the researcher. Admittedly, the researcher's personal values influence the selection of the research topic, but once the topic for study is chosen the researcher's

Research Methods

values and prejudgments are not supposed to influence the production of knowledge. The search for objective truth rests on an assumed separation between the knowing subject (researcher) and the objective to-be-known world. Extensions of this idea are reflected not only in the value-free idealization already noted but also in the priority given to data obtained through the senses, in the importance accorded to standardized instruments of measurement, and in the prescribed detachment of the researcher from the subjects under study.

Survey Research

There are several research strategies, including experimental and survey methods, favoured by sociologists working in the positivist tradition. In sociology, research topics having a social psychological focus are those most amenable to experimental manipulation; for this reason, applications of experimental research are discussed in Chapter 4, which discusses social psychology. In this chapter the focus is on survey research. An example of this method — a study of social inequality within rural villages in India — is presented in Box 2.1.

Box 2.1

Survey Research

A Study of Inequality within Rural Villages in India

Not so long ago one of the authors was working toward a Ph.D. He had previously travelled around the world, studied in India for a year, and afterward added an M.A. in Indian studies to his B.A. in sociology. But that is another story. It does partially explain, however, why he was interested in studying the influence of community development programs on village stratification systems in rural India. Studies had already been done on this topic with widely varying results, but the results were difficult to compare because the methods employed were never quite the same. What was needed was a systematic study designed to see if relatively well developed villages had different stratification systems (greater inequality?) than villages that were less well developed. After a year of applying for research grants (and getting support from all five agencies to whom he had applied), the young sociologist and his family headed for Hyderabad, where he had lived as a student five years before.

In order to collect a wide range of information about each community, the research design included plans to interview four knowledgeable informants about each village: the village community development worker, the headman-mayor, the record keeper, and someone from the regional development office (often an agricultural extension officer). From general knowledge and on the basis of their records, they could detail the development inputs that the village had received and many characteristics of the village as a whole (village size, occupational distribution, number of different castes and modern organizations, percentage of electrified households, etc.). However, they couldn't be expected to know some things: the value of privately owned resources (land, livestock, etc.) or how much agricultural production each village turned out. Officials didn't keep track of how education, income, status, or consumption were distributed across village households, or how many cultivators knew about, had tried, and still used agricultural innovations. Such information would have to come directly from villagers.

Since not every villager could be interviewed, estimates for each village could be obtained only from a survey of a representative sample of households — one sampling for each village studied. Thus, several problems arose in picking communities to study and people to interview — "sampling" problems — beyond the very real problems of time and money.

The first sampling problem was to establish how many villages would be studied and how to pick them. Historically and geographically, the state of Andhra Pradesh had been divided into regions: the dry inland plateau and the better irrigated coastal region. To maximize differences in development levels, separate samples of villages would be drawn from these two regions. Three districts were selected from each of these regions (one rich, one medium, and one poor), and 14 villages were randomly selected from each of these districts.

The 1961 census of India had produced lists of villages and published limited information about them (population size, occupational distributions, and so on). The listed villages were numbered separately within irrigated and nonirrigated regions (sampling strata), and the 14 villages were selected from each district by using a table of random numbers — a book of numbers with no pattern to their order. The number of the 14 villages chosen from each strata was proportionate to the size of that strata. Thus every village had the same chance of being selected, and the resultant proportionate random sample could therefore be said to "represent" the hundreds of villages in that district. Six districts with 14 villages each gave 84 villages, representing, it was hoped, a wide variety of economic and social conditions.

The second problem was how to pick a sample of households to represent each village. Within each village a stratified random quota sample of households was selected (again from a list of households the census had prepared). It was stratified into three groups — cultivators, agricultural labourers, and others — on the basis of identifications made by villagers as the households were selected. The quota for each of these three divisions was established from the proportion of that occupational group in the last census. The total number of households to be selected was based on a minimum of 15 for the smallest villages (40–50 households) to a maximum of 60 households for the largest village (over 800 households). This disproportionate sampling was based on the knowledge that what mattered to the accuracy of estimates of community characteristics was the absolute size of the sample. Relatively more households were therefore needed for accurate estimates for the smaller villages.

To gather comparable information on each village, the same questions had to be put to each set of four knowledgeable informants, and another set of different questions had to be addressed to each sample of household heads. Four standard interviews were therefore designed (for the four different knowledgeable informants), with a fifth interview devised for the household heads. All the interviews had to be translated into Telugu (and then back-translated to check for accuracy), and all the interviews had to be pretested (in villages not included in the sample) to try to make sure that they were the right questions, and to make sure that people could understand and answer them. Three pretests were necessary before all the difficulties were ironed out.

An advertisement for research assistant interviewers had brought several hundred qualified replies. Six assistants, all with social science graduate degrees and experience working and living in rural villages in Andhra Pradesh, were hired. To reach the sample villages, the assistants and the Ph.D. student had to deal with all sorts of unanticipated logistical problems: arranging for accommodations, dealing with vehicle breakdowns, coping with floods (one interview team was completely stranded for a couple of days), and searching for villages (one village had actually moved in anticipation of the building of a large dam). Field work was definitely an adventure!

After about seven months, the data collection was complete. Over 2000 interviews with villagers had been completed and 84 sets of knowledgeable informants had been questioned. Manual coding of interviews was completed and checked, and then completely redone, and the punching of the 20 000 IBM cards began. A computer was found at the South Central Railway to write a magnetic tape (in the middle of the night, since the computer was tied up with the census), and the tape was carefully passed through innumerable airport security checks (not through X-ray machines) on its way back to North America where thousands of errors had to be edited over a period of about eight months before the data could be analyzed.

Village-level estimates were generated by running descriptive statistics programs on the 84 surveys (sequentially). Then a data set was constructed by merging the 84 sets of survey estimates with the information from knowledgeable informants to produce a truly prodigious amount of statistical information and thousands of pages of computer output.

Source: Gartrell (1977); Gartrell and Gartrell (1981).

• WHAT IS SURVEY RESEARCH?

In a typical survey, the researcher selects a sample of respondents from a study population and administers a standardized questionnaire to them. By answering researchers' questions, respondents report on their own opinions and behaviour and describe their circumstances.

• THEORY AND SURVEY RESEARCH

In our Indian community development example, a general "law" derived from Marxist theory covered the relationship between development and stratification. It held that under capitalism, with its private ownership of the means of production, the greater the surplus produced, the greater the inequality in its distribution. In the eighty-four Indian villages, this law was used to explain the observation that large differences in wealth (gross crop income and land owned) existed in some villages and more moderate differences in wealth prevailed in others. *Large differences* in wealth and income (high inequality) were observed in villages with a *high level* of wealth and income (high surplus). *More moderate differences* in wealth and income (lower inequality) were observed in "less-developed" villages with *lower levels* of wealth and income (less surplus). In other words, there was a strong *positive correlation* between indicators of community development and indicators of the degree of stratification within the community. Under the initial condition of agrarian capitalism, where land and its produce were privately owned, if the level of development (wealth or surplus) was high for a village, then we also tended to observe high inequality in the distribution of surplus and wealth.

A distinction is made between abstract **concepts** and empirical observables. Abstract concepts classify or categorize reality in such a way that properties of the things we study, such as individuals or social collectives, are defined **nominally** (literally, "named") in terms of other concepts (ones we understand). Empirical observables, on the other hand, are defined by **operational definitions** — instructions as to how to observe phenomena and rules of measurement for the assignment of symbols (usually numbers) to quantify the property observed as a **variable**. In the Indian village example, "community development" was conceptually defined as the level of technical, economic, and social welfare resources. One way in which the level of technological development was operationally defined was to observe the percentage of households that village records showed to have electrical connections (number of households with electrical connections divided by the total number of households times 100). Other operational definitions referred to reports by knowledgeable informants as to the number of tractors or other modern machines, and the percentage of land in the village records shown to be irrigated.

If there is a relationship between two variables, they go together in some way — that is, they are **correlated** so that changes in one accompany changes in the other. If the relationship is such that increases in one variable are accompanied by increases in the other, the relationship is said to be *positive;* if, however, increases in one are accompanied by decreases in the other, the relationship is described as *negative* or *inverse*. The paired relationships between variables are the building blocks of causal explanations. In a **causal** statement, the direction of the relationship is specified such that one of the variables is **dependent** and the other is **independent**. The independent variable is assumed to cause changes in the dependent variable.

The survey researcher attempts to discern causation by first noting correlations between variables. And here we need to point out that statistical descriptions operate on the level of probability. A statistical correlation means that one variable tends to vary with another. While this pattern or relationship may not be found in every case observed, it is still considered a social regularity and one that is potentially causal. Within survey or statistical research there are three criteria that must be fulfilled before claiming cause. First, there must be an observed empirical relationship or correlation between two variables. Second, the causal or independent variable must precede the dependent variable in time. And third, the observed relationship cannot be explained by any other cause (variable). In other words, the empirical relationship must not be **spurious**. Implicit in these three criteria is the recognition that two variables may be highly correlated without either one determining the other. In other words, all cause implies correlation, but not all correlation implies cause.

It is important in survey research, as in all forms of quantitative inquiry, to state in advance the expected relationships between the dependent and independent variables. By stating the **hypothesis** (the statement of the expected relationship) in advance, the researcher is able to test the adequacy of the theoretical ideas against empirical observations.

• THE STANDARDIZED QUESTIONNAIRE

Operationalizing the variables and the hypothesized relationships is the procedure that permits the researcher to define precisely the procedures, or operations, for translating variables into empirical observations and for measuring or assigning numbers to them. In survey research, these procedures are normally contained in a standardized questionnaire, which consists of a series of questions used to gather information from respondents. In the India study, you will recall, the researcher constructed five different questionnaires for different types of respondents: four to be adminstered to the four different kinds of informants and one for the 2040 male heads of households.

The questions composing the questionnaire may be of two types. **Closed-ended questions** have a fixed range of possible responses. Either the respondent or the researcher marks certain categories of reply to the questions asked — e.g., "Yes/No/Don't know" or "Strongly agree/Agree/ Disagree/Strongly disagree." Since there are only a small number of categories to which numbers can be assigned, closed-ended questions have the advantage of producing comparable data that are easily coded and tabulated into machine-readable form. Sometimes, **open-ended questions** are included to permit the respondents to express their views in their own words. Such questions may produce more in-depth information on a given item, but the overall objective of survey research makes closed-ended questions the format of choice.

The wording of questionnaire items and the method of administration are given serious attention in survey research. The India study highlights the important role that cultural knowledge and language play in the construction of questions. It took three pretests for the researcher to be satisfied that the wording of the questions communicated the appropriate meaning for the population being studied. Questionnaires may be administered by a trained interviewer in a face-to-face meeting, or the researcher may choose to have trained interviewers ask questions over the telephone. Questionnaires may also be self-administered, with the respondents filling them out at home (and returning them by mail) or at a central location to which they have been invited.

• SAMPLING

In theory, the researcher could administer a questionnaire to every individual in the population (a census). But rarely do sociologists have the money, time, or resources to study every individual in large populations. Therefore, survey researchers have needed to develop techniques allowing them to select a small sample that can serve as the basis for making generalizations about the larger population from which it was drawn. In order to permit such inferences, the sample must be drawn by methods intended to make it *representative* — that is, to have it possess the same distribution of characteristics as the population from which it is drawn.

The "gold standard" of these techniques (the one to which others are compared) is the form of **random sampling** known as *simple random sampling*. The selection process gives every member of the study population the same chance of being selected. Every member of the population to be studied is listed and numbered (the list is called a **sampling frame**), and then a sample is drawn using a table of random numbers or a computer program. This process operates just like a lottery, and chance determines who is picked. The larger the sample, the more likely it is to accurately represent the population. However, there is always some chance that the sample will not be like the population from which it is drawn, even if the best methods are followed. This chance is referred to as **random sampling error**.

Simple random sampling is not always practical or cost efficient. For example, sometimes the cost of travelling to reach respondents spread over a large geographical area is prohibitive. Often, therefore, we attempt to improve on random sampling by using a **stratified random sample**. Instead of drawing cases from the general population, the population is first divided into relatively homogenous subgroupings (strata based on a characteristic of the population that the researcher is using as a major independent variable), and then individual cases are selected within the strata using random procedures. In the Indian community study stratification was used twice. Villages were sampled from high and low irrigation areas and the households within villages were sampled within occupationally defined strata. In both cases, the number of units selected from each strata was proportionate to the relative size of the strata in the population. These are examples of *proportionate* stratified sampling.

Under some conditions, researchers might also deliberately oversample a particular stratum and this is referred to as *disproportionate* stratified sampling. For example, if researchers are interested in how perceived health differs over the life course (by age), they might design their sampling methods so that respondents of different age strata are represented in *equal* numbers (note that researchers have to have prior knowledge of the population in order to stratify). Such a sampling design might be used if the subgroup in question were particularly important to the study (perhaps, in a health survey, because older people were more likely to get sick) and if that subgroup constituted a relatively small proportion of the total population. National samples in Canada, if they want to also represent each province, must overrepresent smaller provinces such as Prince Edward Island because the accuracy of survey results for a sample depends on the sample's size, not on the sampling fraction (sample size divided by population size). In this sense, it is relatively more difficult and expensive to study small or rare groups.

Cluster sampling divides the population into geographic areas and then draws a probability sample within each area. The cluster is similar to a stratum except that instead of using a population characteristic to divide the population, the researcher takes advantage of the naturally occurring geographic groupings (clusters). In the India study, the sampling design for selecting the villages took advantage of the natural divisions (irrigated and dry) in the state of Andhra Pradesh to disproportionately sample from different regions so as to increase the diversity of community development.

Many modifications to simple random sampling are possible. In all cases, sampling designs try to proceed from the principle that they should maximize variation (differences) within the sample in the independent variables (the causes) so as to maximize the chance of observing corresponding differences in the dependent variables (the effects).

Under the broad term *survey research* there are many variations in sampling techniques, including several nonprobability sampling methods. This presentation attempts not to provide an exhaustive treatment but rather to suggest the complexity of the decisions involved in sampling design.

• ISSUES RELATED TO RESEARCH DESIGN

Sociologists give a great deal of consideration to the design of their research prior to beginning a project. Although this design is often modified slightly during the course of the research, a plan or strategy for approaching the research problem is required. As we have emphasized, the design of the research cannot be separated from its theoretical interests. In fact, the researcher selects the design and methods according to how well they allow for the documentation or collection of data that will enable us to discern the social world in causal or structural terms.

As the theoretical interests of the researcher vary, so will the design of the research itself. In all cases, however, the design is considered adequate to the degree that it enables the researcher to fulfil theoretical objectives while balancing a number of important objectives.

The idea of systematic comparison is a constant in all social inquiry. Research is valued to the extent that its design enables us to compare our unit of analysis across different circumstances and across time. Comparisons not only serve the function of testing theory, as in the formal experimental models; they also enable us to develop theory by observing groups or individuals in groups in varying conditions and over time. As a result we are able to formulate empirical generalizations. These enable us to make claims about the social and historical configurations under which certain social processes operate.

With respect to the temporal dimension, research designs can be classified into two basic types: **cross-sectional** and **longitudinal**. With a cross-sectional design, we examine a social situation at a single, fixed point in time, as in the study of social inequality in India. However, even cross-sectional surveys may include retrospective questions about the past. In general such questions are limited by memory. We can expect people to report accurately on relatively unimportant things in their lives only if they date from the recent past; generally we limit questions about attitudes and feelings to the near present. Larger events such as marriage and divorce, birth and death, employment and education can often be reliably recalled over a lifetime. This introduces a time dimension into some studies, such as when we study the effects of education upon occupational and income attainment.

The General Social Survey (GSS) conducted by Statistics Canada each year on a different focal topic uses an essentially cross-sectional design, but it has an interesting way of dealing with time. The GSS is based on 10 000 telephone interviews (approximately thirty minutes in length) with a national probability sample of Canadian adults. The focal topics are rotated through a five-year cycle (health, time use, victimization, education and work, family and friends), and the data are made available to university researchers across Canada. Repetition of the focal topics on this five-year cycle provides for comparisons that form part of a longitudinal design. In addition, since many of the independent variables such as age, income, education, ethnicity, and so on are measured in every survey, year-to-year longitudinal comparisons can be made for those variables.

One type of longitudinal design used with survey research is called a **panel** design. In a panel study, the same subjects are interviewed over a period of time. Professors Harvey Krahn and Graham Lowe (1991) of the University of Alberta have been conducting a panel study of the transition from education to jobs (and back) in a cohort of Edmonton students (with comparison samples from Sudbury and Toronto). The study began with a sample of 3564 high-school and university students (split about 60:40) in 1985, just before they graduated. They were recontacted (using a short, mailed questionnaire) in 1986, 1987, and 1989. After four years, 1605 responded. The study found that the transition from school to work was much more prolonged than expected. Half or more of the students worked while they were in school, and the two roles continued to be mixed long after graduation. Higher education was necessary to get good jobs; many of those with high-school diplomas were trapped in low-paying jobs without much chance of advancement. Those who experienced unemployment lowered their occupational aspirations, but at least in the short term, unemployment did not appear to damage self-esteem or mental health.

While it is obviously more expensive and difficult to interview people more than once, panel designs provide additional information on the ordering of cause and effect in social phenomena. In some cases, such as with the Longitudinal Study of Income run by the University of Michigan, panels may be followed over a number of years to study the long-term effects of changes in people's lives. Unfortunately, there are no large, well-known, reasonably funded examples of long-term panel studies in Canada.

Surveys can reveal the "comparative dimension of circumstance" — how different social phenomena vary under different conditions. In the 1990 All Alberta Survey, Linda Derksen and

John Gartrell (1993) asked more than 1200 respondents how concerned they were about the environment, using a typical seven-point scale to indicate responses ("Very concerned" to "Not concerned"). They also asked respondents whether or not they recycled each of a list of items (newspapers, bottles, cans, etc.). Derksen and Gartrell found that while most people said they were concerned about the environment, the level of their concern was not correlated to the number of different items they recycled. Recycling was much more prevalent in Edmonton households living in single-family dwellings (the only households in the province that then had access to a curbside blue-box program). In addition, there were some "spillover" effects in Edmonton (higher recycling even without access to the program), and there was a higher rate of recycling in urban areas generally than in rural areas of the province. The only circumstances in which individual attitudes made a difference in the amount recycled was for households in Edmonton who had access to the curbside recycling program. Those households recycled more if they said they were more concerned. Social structure (the blue-box program) had a large effect on behaviour, although attitudes had an effect only where social structure facilitated it. It would seem that money would be better spent on instituting programs than on educational campaigns designed to influence attitudes.

In both research design and consideration of results it is important to avoid two pitfalls: the fallacy of reductionism and the ecological fallacy. We commit the **fallacy of reductionism** when we try to explain a complex social phenomenon, such as everything that happens in a family, in terms of one set of explanatory factors — say, economic factors. Reductionism leads us away from the real complexity of social phenomena, even though analytically we may separate the various kinds of explanations considered.

We commit the **ecological fallacy** when we ascribe characteristics to specific individuals in our sample on the basis of the summary descriptions we apply to the sample as a whole. Although based on trends across a large number of individuals, our summaries may not reflect the pattern found for any specific individual within the sample. For example, in an Introductory Sociology class, we might find that the average age of students is 25. However, that does not mean that every student or any particular student in the class is indeed 25 years of age. This reflects the difference between observations of specific individuals and the summary of the **aggregate**.

We can now turn to the criteria for evaluating the design and outcome of survey research. The first of these, and perhaps the most important, is validity. **Validity** can be understood, in its most basic terms, as the extent to which the claims we make through our descriptions fit the phenomena that we have studied. So, in the case of survey research, validity can be understood as the correspondence between our theoretical concepts and the way we measure them (*measurement validity*). For example, you might ask whether the social class indicator that a researcher has selected for a survey is a valid indicator of the concept "social class." Is the level of education reported on a questionnaire a valid measure of social class?

The second and related criterion for evaluating the design and outcome of sociological research is that of reliability. **Reliability** refers to the extent to which our selected indicators work in a consistent manner, especially when they are used repeatedly. Are the indicators accurate, whatever they measure? Would the measurement methods used produce the same answers if the survey were done again? This problem underlines the need to pretest our questions on survey instruments thoroughly before executing the design. Thus, in survey research we are concerned with composing questions, as indicators of our concepts, that are not only valid but also reliable. Indeed, reliability is a necessary (but not sufficient) condition for validity.

The third criterion for evaluating survey research refers to the degree to which the findings can be *generalized*. In a fairly narrow sense, **generalizability** is a function of sampling. Results obtained for a representative sample can be inferred only to the population from which the sample was drawn. In a broader sense, generalizability may be said to rely on the universality of the abstract concepts with which we work and the range of variability in the phenomena we study.

The question of **replicability** refers to the research design as a whole. Can the design be made explicit enough that further researchers could enter into the same social situation and repeat the study? In practice, much social research is never replicated. Perhaps political factors and funding preferences are among the most significant reasons for this. Research proposals aimed at discovering new knowledge are more highly valued than research aimed at confirming already existing knowledge. Related to this last criterion is the important principle in research that the method designed and used be reported in as full a manner as possible. It is on the basis of this kind of accounting that research activity is opened to criticism.

AN INTERPRETIVE ALTERNATIVE: FIELD RESEARCH

In North America, the influence of interpretive sociology on research practice was first evident in the field studies done during the 1920s and 1930s by a group of researchers at the University of Chicago. Their views on methodology were influenced by Weber's writings on *Verstehen*, anthropological field studies of different cultures, and journalistic styles of investigation. The distinctiveness of social reality, according to the interpretive critique, requires a distinctive methodology rather than one imitating the methods of natural science. This strategy should emphasize subjective meaning rather than objective factors, observations gathered in natural rather than artificial settings, and qualitative rather than quantitative procedures. Among the several versions of interpretive or qualitative methodology are field studies (such as those done by the early Chicago School), case studies, and life histories, as well as contemporary studies of everyday life.

In this chapter we draw on William Foote Whyte's *Street Corner Society* (*SCS*) to illustrate the features of the field study as one variant of interpretive research. *Street Corner Society* is a study of the social life of second-generation Italian immigrants who lived in Cornerville, a slum neighbourhood located in a large U.S. city (called Eastern City) during the late 1930s. The methodological reflections first appended to the second edition of *SCS* (1955, 1981) have become a landmark statement, which general (Burgess, 1984; Hammersley and Atkinson, 1983) and specialized textbooks on field research (Emerson, 1983; Miles and Huberman, 1984) continue to extend, refine, and debate. Recently (Adler et al., 1992), the *SCS* text was incorporated into current discussions on the construction of narrative knowledge.

• WHAT IS FIELD RESEARCH?

Field research is sometimes called *ethnography* (a term anthropologists prefer), **participant observation** (with reference to the technique of collecting data), or *qualitative methods* (indicating the non-numerical quality of most field data). Field research is the study of a social phenomenon through first-hand observation by becoming immersed, for an extended period of time, in the ongoing social activities of the people being studied.

Field researchers "immerse" themselves in the setting. They study from within, as Whyte points out, in order to discover from locals "the nature of the society in which they live" (1981: xvi). Relying only on an outside perspective, we are told in the introduction to *SCS*, results in distortion such as the then current but misguided view of Cornerville as a dangerous and disorganized place. Understood from the inside, Cornerville "reveals itself" as a "highly organized and integrated social system" (1981: xvi). But getting an insider's perspective requires more than simply watching others. The researcher must also participate directly and personally in routine activities and learn to assign meanings in locally approved ways. This kind of immersion, aimed at understanding without judging, is called participant observation. It is common, as in the case of Whyte, "to begin as a nonparticipating observer" and to find later, when the previously unknown has become familiar, that one is in danger of "becoming almost a nonobserving participant" (1981: 321).

• FIELD RELATIONS, MEMBER ROLES, AND QUALITATIVE DATA

To be "of" the natural setting and not merely "in" it, means that the field researcher must include in the research design plans for gaining entry, establishing close personal relations, learning the ropes, and maintaining lasting relationships. These may seem like ordinary activities, but the success of participant observation depends as much on developing social competence within the setting as on applying technical skills.

The literature on field relations speaks of gatekeepers, sponsors, key informants, and co-researchers — a list of some of the most important relationships bearing on the success of a field project. In *SCS*, the description of the rackets, which provides a context for understanding corner life, remains partial because **gatekeepers** (persons in an organization who have authority to control access) were able to prevent undesirable outsiders, like Whyte, from fully penetrating the organizational front. He was more successful at the community level. After several months and a few false starts, he met a social worker who volunteered to help find an "in" on the corner. As Whyte's **sponsor** (someone with the credibility to make introductions), she put him in touch with Doc, who subsequently became one of Whyte's most important **key informants**. As leader of the Norton Street Gang, well respected on the corner, Doc was able to introduce Whyte to members of his own gang as well as to others in Cornerville; to neutralize the suspicions that his presence raised; to vouch for his trustworthiness; and to help teach him the ways of corner life. Over time, Whyte ceased to treat Doc "as a passive informant" and began instead to relate to him as a **co-researcher,** discussing with him the "puzzling problems" in his data. In fact, Whyte tells us, "Some of the interpretations I have made are his more than mine, although it is now impossible to disentangle them" (1981: 301).

The **member roles** — i.e., the social roles a researcher occupies in the setting — depend to a large degree on the field relationships that are formed and developed over the course of the study. Whyte tried to occupy peripheral roles (e.g., recording secretary) that would place him close to the action but not so close as to influence or interfere with its natural unfolding.

The researcher is the instrument in field research both for generating and for recording data. Within the limits of existing field relations and established member roles, the researcher transforms field experience into detailed **fieldnotes**. Some notes may be extremely detailed. An event that in reality lasts for only five minutes may yield ten or more pages of single-spaced typed description. Part of the rigour and discipline of field work lies in producing fieldnotes that are comprehensive and detailed enough to lead to fruitful analysis.

Researchers treat their own experiences and personal feelings, and the accounts people give to explain their own behaviour, as data to be recorded in their fieldnotes. Subjective data are important both in themselves and for interpreting social reality. Such data provide important clues for discovering the shared but taken-for-granted meanings that are normally difficult to articulate. These data are often supplemented with formal interviews and a variety of other documentary materials (diaries, photographs, memos, maps, and other artifacts) that help describe what is going on in the setting. Fieldnotes may contain some numerical data, but most field data are **qualitative**.

• DESIGN AND SAMPLING

The researcher's direct involvement in the setting means that the design in field research is much less structured than in survey research. A field researcher does not normally begin with a standardized set of instruments and a clear hypothesis to test. Instead, the field researcher typically begins, like Whyte, with "a vague idea" (1981: 283) and an openness to exploration. *Flexibility* is considered an advantage in field studies because it allows the researcher to shift direction, follow unanticipated leads, and seize opportunities as they present themselves.

The shape of the design in field research has been described as a funnel that becomes progressively narrowed. Initially, the research is *de-focused*. The scope of the research topic is broad and the researcher is open to all kinds of information, including information that at first glance does not appear relevant. The early research experience seems like "fumbling and searching" (Whyte, 1984: 274). Fumbling and searching for what? For a sense of the overall picture and for the "relevant" questions to ask of this particular setting. A clearer sense of the picture evolves as the researcher is socialized into the setting, examines the initial data, and begins to make provisional inferences. As a pattern emerges, the researcher begins to *focus* the scope of the investigation and pay particular attention to specific ideas, questions, and themes. By the time the researcher considers leaving the field, the inquiry is highly specific, aimed at filling gaps in the data or testing ideas that arise in the final stages of analysis.

Focusing calls for a sampling strategy. In field research the process of sampling within the setting is purposeful rather than random. This is called **theoretical sampling,** because it is guided by the researcher's developing picture or theoretical conception of what is going on. Field researchers may sample times, locations, interactions, activities, individuals, groups, contexts, and so forth. Accordingly, Whyte's rationale for determining who and what to observe was not based on principles of random selection but on theoretical criteria derived from his evolving conception of how Cornerville was organized.

Validity, in this context, refers to whether our interpretations of the situation correspond to those held by insiders, whether the researcher's interpretation meets the test of **meaning adequacy.** This is not at all a straightforward issue. The researcher and the members of the community being studied may well have quite different perspectives. The question is not so much whether there is one correct perspective, for we know that multiple perspectives are possible and are to be expected. The issue for the qualitative researcher is in having a thorough enough grounding that the various perspectives are represented and can be understood even if not reconciled.

• THE ROLE OF THEORY AND QUALITATIVE DATA ANALYSIS

In the introduction to *SCS,* Whyte tells the reader that the "general pattern [in this context, read "theory"] is important, but it can be constructed only through observing the individuals whose actions make up that pattern" (1981: xix). Whyte's commitment to building theory from data rather than conducting research to verify existing theory is typical of the *inductive* approach that characterizes field research. Building **substantive theory** — i.e., theory constructed from and used to explain the phenomena studied — is a major goal of field research.

Proceeding from the particular to the general rather than from the general to the particular is thought to be necessary if the biasing effects of *misconceptions* are to be avoided. Some researchers interpret this to mean that all preconceptions, even theoretical ones, are to be avoided, preferring instead to "let the data speak for themselves." Whyte, however, avoids this extreme position by noting that even the act of recognizing an event as "an instance of a phenomenon" presupposes a theory. This theory, logically prior to substantive theory, is called **orienting theory** —"orienting" in the sense that "it indicates what phenomena deserve particular attention and what other phenomenon can be disregarded or be accorded less attention" (1984: 275). Interaction theory provided Whyte with a simple set of orienting concepts that led him to study, first, the actions and interactions of members of a group, and then, interactions between groups, and finally, the larger context of Cornerville in which these interactions take place.

Instead of formulating laws, field researchers normally organize their generalizations into a **framework of concepts.** These generalizations are close to — some say grounded in — the data, and represent only a low level of abstraction. The primary objective of the framework is *holistic,* and the framework therefore consists of the concepts and their interconnections within the specific social context. In this kind of theoretical presentation an action or event has been "explained" when the researcher has shown how it fits into the larger framework of which it is a part.

There is a close interplay between theory building, data collection, and analysis of qualitative data. The analysis of qualitative data is concerned with *concept formation*. It begins with the act of perceiving a pattern, and is followed by a process of testing, reformulating, and retesting through comparative analysis.

Perceiving a pattern consists of more than simply applying the formal rules of logic to empirical observations. Research ideas, Whyte tells us, "grow up in part out of our immersion in the data and out of the whole process of living," much of which proceeds "on the unconscious level" (1981: 280). Whether the pattern appears as the result of a chance occurrence or through the careful weighing of evidence, once the researcher thinks a pattern has been found, he or she begins to systematically review the fieldnotes, looking for evidence that the pattern "represents the life we are observing" or alternatively that it is "simply a product of our imagination" (1981: 280). Part of the rigour of field research comes from carefully and methodically rereading fieldnotes, comparing instances of the pattern, making links between fragments of a supposed pattern, posing questions based on an alternative interpretation, gathering new data, searching for contradictory data, reformulating ideas, and repeating the cycle many times. In this respect, the relation between theory, data collection, and data analysis is said to be *cyclical* rather than linear.

The final report of field research is not organized around mathematical equations or lawlike propositional statements. Rather, in the final report, often called an ethnography, the researcher usually presents the qualitative data in a narrated form that aims to admit the reader into the subjective world of "particular people and . . . the particular things that they do" (Whyte, 1981: xix). Accordingly, *SCS* presents an **ideographic** description of Cornerville told through, first, the story of Doc's life and through him, the story of the Nortons; then Chick's life and through him, the story of the Italian Community Club; and so on. We are led in the discursive and contextualizing style of the narrative from particular stories to general claims. Diagrammatic representations of the conceptual schema (1981: 13, 49, 95, 185, 189) and generalizations are woven through the text. We learn that in general, part of what distinguishes corner boys from college boys is a different moral code. Further, we learn that in general, the values embodied in the corner boy code (free spending and loyalty to friends) serve to garner prestige on the corner but in the long run will trap corner boys in Cornerville and in a life of relative economic disadvantage. In contrast, the middle-class values of thrift and self-interest embodied in college boy morality tarnish one's reputation on the corner but in the long run lead to occupational mobility and relative economic advantage.

• CURRENT DIRECTIONS

It is a short leap from general statements to the identification of variables and hypothesized relationships. Some researchers consider the task of identifying variables and their relationships a legitimate goal of field research. In recent years, sociologists have looked favourably on an approach referred to as **triangulation,** wherein different research designs are combined within a single project. Thus, for example, we might do a survey of individual members of a community alongside an ethnographic study of the social relations and culture that connect the members within the community. Triangulation is valuable in that it can underline the importance of acknowledging the complexity of social phenomena and the limitations of any single research approach.

Other sociologists have begun to look critically at the product of field research, examining the ethnographic text *as text*. Under the influence of a postmodern sensibility, **textual analysis** rejects as naive the argument that research texts are factual representations mirroring the world of experience. Instead, it views texts as social constructions open to the influence of their biographical, social, and historical contexts. Within this perspective, texts may be examined in relation to the context in which they are produced as well as to the rhetorical devices researchers use to create for the reader the appearance of an objective description. It is in this respect that the special issue of the *Journal of Contemporary Ethnography* (Adler et al., 1992) offers a range of new insights on the original text of *SCS* and on the general issues of interpretation in field research.

A THIRD OPTION: FEMINIST CRITIQUE

The critical alternative is the most recent and the least likely to be included in textbooks on social research (Newman, 1991 is an exception). Perhaps it is even somewhat premature to present **critical research** as an "option," since it lacks a coherent programmatic statement or agreed upon standards for conducting critical research, although feminist scholars have written substantially on methodological issues (Cook and Fonow, 1990; Reinharz, 1992). Nonetheless, critical researchers have challenged the traditional claims for objectivity and value-neutrality in research; therefore, some attention, however brief, is warranted.

Variants of critical research may be identified by their theoretical interest — in particular, how it applies to the study of power relations. Two major variants are class analysis, focusing on class structures, and feminist analysis, focusing on gender relations. This discussion makes reference to a recent feminist critique (not a label the author uses, however) by Leslie Bella, entitled *The Christmas Imperative* (1992).

The Christmas Imperative is a study of women's experience of Christmas. Christmas is likely to evoke pleasant images of leisure, family, and friends; of feasting, festivity, and gifts. But is Christmas fun and leisure for everyone? Not for Bella or the women she interviewed in this study. For the people who usually "produce" Christmas, the experience is one of ambivalence — possibly more of work and anguish than of leisure. Yet women still feel compelled every year to try to reproduce the perfect Christmas for imperfect families. How is this compulsion (the "imperative") to be understood? What are its origins and impact, and how might its transformation be promoted? These are the research questions addressed in *The Christmas Imperative*.

• WHAT IS CRITICAL RESEARCH?

Critical research employs empirical evidence and critical thinking to go beyond the surface appearance of reality to uncover hidden ideological structures and power relations. Its purpose is to help people construct a better world for themselves. Critical theory espouses a blend of empirical and normative elements in sociological research. The empirical work of critical inquiry is rather *eclectic*. Bella's study, for example, relies on various sources of data, including (among others) interviews, diaries, survey results, historical documents, literary texts, and department store advertisements.

"Objective" data by themselves are treated with suspicion in critical research because the surface appearance of social reality — that which is by definition immediately available to the senses and common sense — is itself superficial and may be misleading. The deeper and normally unseen power structures and cleavages that lie behind surface appearances are the real object of critical inquiry. Uncovering the veil of surface appearance and revealing the deeper structures requires a self-reflexive or *critical* attitude. To think critically one needs a good theory. Bella begins the study with a critical analysis of the concept "leisure," revealing the gender bias that it contains: men (and children) enjoy the warmth and magic of Christmas with few obligations for producing it; women labour to create the festive "holiday" for others with little opportunity to enjoy it. Guided by an alternative concept — Christmas is women's work — Bella proceeds to explore historical and contemporary data showing the origins, development, and consequences of Christmas as *women's work*.

The explicit adoption of a **value-laden** stance suggests a further challenge to both positivist and interpretive social research. Like other feminist researchers working in the critical tradition, Bella's work is not *about* women but *for* women. She is clear that the aim of her research is not simply to explain or understand women's experiences, but rather to transform them in ways that entail less work and more pleasure for women.

In Bella's study the implications of the value-laden stance are limited to the notion that knowledge is itself empowering. Some critical researchers, however, have advocated a closer relation between research and action.

ETHICS IN SOCIAL RESEARCH

All sociological research, regardless of the methodology employed, poses ethical dilemmas. Accordingly, most professional associations, universities, and funding agencies have developed written statements or codes of ethics like the one adopted and updated by the Canadian Sociology and Anthropology Association (1993). Such codes are intended as guidelines to protect the rights of human subjects without impeding the search for knowledge.

The overriding principle is that human subjects should not be harmed by their participation in research. Several rules exist to achieve this end: (1) participation in a project should be voluntary; (2) consent should be given prior to taking part; (3) consent should be informed—i.e., given after full consideration of the risks associated with the research project; and (4) subjects should be free to decide to withdraw from the project at a later time without penalty. Although codes of ethics differ in their precise wording, there is general agreement that this set of rules should be adhered to; if it is waived, this should be done only with compelling justification.

This raises a question: is deception in social research justifiable? The answer to this question is not as clear-cut as one may wish. The example presented in Box 2.2 will help illustrate this point.

Box 2.2

DECEPTION IN SOCIAL RESEARCH

Deception was used in *Tearoom Trade* (1975, 1970). In this study Laud Humphreys assumed the role of lookout to observe men engaging in impersonal sex in "tearooms" (i.e., restrooms) located in public parks. The men Humphreys observed did not know that he was conducting research. But this is not the full story of the deception. Humphreys also secretly wrote down the licence plate numbers of the cars of the men he observed in the tearoom. Later, with the cooperation of the local police — but without their knowledge of his real purpose — he was able to match the licence plate numbers with names and home addresses. At yet a later date, he managed to have his sample of tearoom visitors combined with another sample, a random sample drawn for a health survey that was being conducted in the same city by other sociologists. To conceal the identities of the men in his sample from the survey researchers, Humphreys went to the homes of the tearoom visitors and administered the health questionnaire himself. He disguised himself on these visits by changing both his physical appearance and the car he drove. Finally, prior to administering the questionnaire, he explained the purpose of the survey and the sampling methods used, but he misled the men about his full intentions by omitting any reference to the earlier study or to the "special" circumstances that led to their inclusion in the health survey.

Tearoom Trade is a landmark study. Part of the reason for this is that the deception used in the study became the centre of one of the most controversial debates in sociology (leading, incidentally, to the creation of ethical codes within funding and educational institutions), and part of the reason is that the findings of the study helped shatter conventional ideas about male homosexuals. Humphreys was able to show that most of the tearoom visitors had all the trappings of a straight lifestyle: wives, families, respectable jobs, good incomes, social reputation, and suburban homes. In most respects, then, the men who engaged in the tearoom trade were indistinguishable from "conventional" men. These findings were clearly at odds with the general views of most ordinary citizens and many public officials. Debunking false conceptions is one of the worthwhile contributions of social research, and we might agree that the study was beneficial because of the knowledge it produced. But is the knowledge gained valuable enough to warrant deception?

Should Humphreys have disguised himself as a lookout? Given the fact that he was observing a deviant activity subject to police surveillance, he probably could not have done the study without deception. But should he have done it at all? Is this a topic worthy of sociological investigation? Some sociologists think not. Should Humphreys have omitted telling the police about his real interest in tracing the licence plate numbers? Yet if he had told the police, would he not have exposed the men to police action? Should he have disguised his appearance when he went into the homes of the tearoom visitors? If he hadn't, would he perhaps have unintentionally revealed the men's secrets to their wives and families? In these circumstances, did deception actually operate to protect the participants from harm? Or did Humphreys "go too far"?

Social researchers have an obligation to make their findings public. Indeed, making knowledge public is one of the main contributions that social research can make to foster open discussion and informed debate in society. But in reporting their findings, researchers are expected to consider the harm that might result from revealing the identity of research subjects or from linking specific findings to particular individuals. In survey research, it is often possible to develop procedures that render all data anonymous so that even the researcher is unable to connect respondents' identities to specific data. In field research, subjects' identities are often disguised under pseudonyms. Confidentiality poses less of a problem when the researcher is using historical documents that are in the public domain.

Since information gathered by researchers does not enjoy the same legal protection as client information obtained by lawyers, it can be subpoenaed by the courts. Promising confidentiality is not the same as ensuring confidentiality. Extremely sensitive topics require creative procedures if the promise of confidentiality is to be given material weight. A recent U.S. study (Ruch et al., 1991) of sexual assault victims provides a good example. The researchers sought and obtained a certificate of confidentiality from the U.S. attorney general. These certificates protect an accused in the case of self-disclosure bearing on a criminal offence. In similar fashion, the certificate protected research participants from having research information used later in any trial proceedings.

Most ethical codes require researchers to submit a proposal for approval by an ethics review committee before undertaking research. In this way, a committee of peers determines, to the extent possible, that the ethical issues of the study have received full and serious consideration and that the safety of human subjects will not knowingly be compromised.

As the tearoom trade study (Box 2.2) suggests, conducting ethical research is not a simple matter of following the right rules and avoiding a fixed list of wrong practices. Real-life situations are often ambiguous, and outcomes are not easily predicted. In practice, ethical research depends on the integrity of the individual researcher. It is less a matter of following hard-and-fast rules and more a matter of exercising judgment, assessing incomplete information, weighing risks against benefits, and reconciling competing interests.

SUMMARY

- Research in sociology is conducted by diverse methods. The identification of three traditions of social science — positive, interpretive, and critical — suggests but does not exhaust the richness, for even within these broad divisions there is substantial variety among research strategies.

- Logical positivism has a profound and continuing influence on the way sociologists conduct their research. Of the several principles associated with this position, the assumption that social reality can be investigated using the same methods as the natural sciences has been fundamental.
- Survey research, one of the research strategies associated with the positivist conception of science, emphasizes the role of formal logic in theory development, a hypothesis-testing model of research, measurement procedures, and quantitative analysis.
- Field research, one form of interpretive social science, attempts to gain an insider's perspective on social reality. This research strategy favours participant observation, a flexible design, qualitative analysis, and narrative presentation.
- Feminist critique, one of the research styles influenced by critical social science, offers an approach that combines empirical and normative elements in research practice.
- Most professional associations, universities, and funding agencies have developed ethical codes to guide social research. However, conducting ethical research involves more than simply following the right rules and avoiding wrong practices.

KEY CONCEPTS

Aggregate

Causal relationship

Closed-ended questions

Co-researcher

Correlation

Critical research

Cross-sectional research design

Deductive

Dependent variable

Ecological fallacy

Empirical

Fallacy of reductionism

Fieldnotes

Framework of concepts

Gatekeeper

Generalizeability

Hypothesis

Ideographic

Independent variable

Inductive

Key informant

Logical positivism

Longitudinal research design

Meaning adequacy

Measurement
Member role
Narrative
Nominal definition
Nomothetic
Objective
Open-ended questions
Operational definition
Orienting theory
Panel
Participant observation
Qualitative data
Quantification
Random sampling
Random sampling error
Reliability
Replicability
Sample
Sampling frame
Sponsor
Spuriousness
Stratified random sample
Substantive theory
Survey
Textual analysis
Theoretical sampling
Triangulation
Validity
Value-laden
Variable

REVIEW QUESTIONS

1. Identify and discuss the major tenets of logical positivism.
2. Explain how survey research embodies the tenets of logical positivism.
3. Explain how interpretive and critical methods depart from logical positivism.
4. Compare survey research, field studies, and feminist critique with respect to the role of values and theory in the research process.

5. How do survey research and field studies differ in their methods of data collection, approaches to sampling and conceptions of validity?

6. Choose a research topic and consider how you would approach the same topic from the three perspectives.

7. Continuing the challenge posed in question 6, discuss the ethical issues you would anticipate given the nature of the research programs.

Culture, Society, & Change

Sharon McIrvin Abu-Laban and Baha Abu-Laban

Culture, Society, and Change

INTRODUCTION

This chapter focuses on three important concepts in sociology: culture, society, and social change. First, we examine culture and the role it plays in relation to human behaviour. **Culture** refers to the sum total of the heritage of a people: their language, customs, beliefs, knowledge, learned behaviours, and understandings. We explore two major sociological perspectives. One has a long tradition; the second is a more recent approach that has inspired a rapidly growing research tradition of its own. This discussion includes an examination of issues such as cross-cultural diversity and diversity among cultures, and includes a critical assessment of culture and its role in social inequality, the perpetuation of elite advantage, and the maintenance of superordinate and subordinate relations.

Next, we discuss the concept of society. The concepts of culture and society go hand in hand because culture is reflected in human association and it is also created by humans in association with one another. Society at a more general level often meshes with the boundaries of nation-states. But this is not always the case. **Society** is better described as a complex, all-encompassing level of human relationships within a defined territory and with fairly distinctive culture and institutions. This section looks at diverse societal types, ranging from hunting and gathering societies to modern industrial societies and on to discussions of postmodern and post-industrial societies.

Third, we address the issue of social change. **Social change** refers to any observable difference or modification in social organization and/or patterns of behaviour over time. In the social world things do not remain the same; they are not static. The processes of social change and stability have long fascinated sociologists. In a world of change, transitions (whether personal, technological, or political) are close to the lives of all of us. Questions are raised here concerning the different components and sources of change and the degree to which social and cultural change can be predicted and explained.

Together, culture, society, and social change encompass major concepts in sociology, ones critical to understanding and explaining our social world. But before discussing these, we need to address the basic building material — the biological base. Early philosophers argued that the infant is born as *tabula rasa,* a "blank slate" upon which society can write the determining character. This contention sidesteps the fact that the neonate enters the world with biological attributes, important potentials, and basic limitations. This reality cannot be ignored. All humans, whether in Auckland, Ottawa, Cairo, or Beijing, begin from a species-specific biological base. But humans are immensely adaptable. The social organization of biological capacities, *human agency* (the ability to act independently of social constraints), as well as the social factors that work to take away our agency contribute to the resulting diversity among and within societies and cultures.

DISTINCTIVE HUMAN SOCIAL EXISTENCE

The uniqueness of the human species is often demonstrated by comparison with animals; humans are distinctive in a number of ways. While the instinctual component is sizable among nonhumans, humans are not born with inclinations to build nests, stake out territory, or engage in seasonal migration. The courting behaviour of any one pair of amorous robins is quite predictable to an ornithologist. In contrast, the courting behaviour of any one pair of humans from one of the many different cultures on earth can encompass a range of complexities: from matchmaker introductions to chance encounters in singles' bars; from crooning ballads under the balcony of a beloved to giving one's sweetheart a prized pig; from dancing cheek-to-cheek to the Big Band Sound to line dancing to "Cadillac Ranch." We learn to be human, to love, to give meaning, to respond to others, and sometimes to deceive, exploit, and control. The bundle of characteristics that comprise each individual reflect her and his cultural and social background as well as individual experiences. We learn to be human, but we receive varied lessons. The lessons we do receive are shaped by culture, history, biological inheritance, and personal choice.

Some distinctive attributes of humans have particular consequences for social life. The social life of people is distinctive. It is (1) adaptable; (2) group based and organized; and (3) reliant on symbols.

• ADAPTABILITY

The unique intelligence of the human animal contributes to versatility and flexibility in human social life. The human animal has a large, complex brain, hence the capacity for language and for the creation of scientific formulae, political cartoons, and religious canons. The degree of human intelligence means that people are highly adaptable across a wide range of physical settings. Thus humans can live in Inuvik, at the equator, and in space stations circling the earth. It also means that humans can share past experiences with each other, plan futures, and try to chart a better world.

Humans are distinguished from other animals by their consistently upright posture, by their bipedal (two-footed) walk, and by characteristics as seemingly "simple" as an opposable thumb and forefinger, common to only a few higher-order primates. In fact, this is a critical anatomical structure that allows tools to be grasped, adapted, and used. Our hands open up an immense range of technological possibilities. It is ironic that humans are distinctive in their ability to joke and laugh while at the same time they are distinctive in the extent to which they kill their own kind (no other animal is so destructive). In contrast to other animals, humans have the capacity for year-round mating. It is argued that this characteristic contributes to stability and bonding between men and women. Intimate relations might be very different if Canadians had seasonal rather than year-round mating patterns.

• GROUP BASIS AND ORGANIZATION

Human existence is group based. As well, the long period of human infant and child dependency has profound social implications. This dependency is unique in the animal kingdom. Whether cannibals or kings, we are all born helpless and remain weak, vulnerable, dependent, and unable to fend for ourselves. The human infant needs to be cared for by adults who themselves were cared for and **socialized** (trained) by other humans. This living chain of cooperative effort is essential to the biological survival of the human species.

What would happen to Homo sapiens without a human group? For the child, it could prove disastrous. Although there have been accounts of such children (including the legend of Romulus and Remus, the mythical founders of Rome, supposedly raised by wolves), these tales remain in the category of folklore or urban legend. The existence of so-called **feral children** (children abandoned by adults, living in a state of nature and/or raised by nonhumans) has never been reliably established. We do know, however, from reports of abused children raised in near-isolation from human contact, that these children suffer immense loss of human potential, deficits in language and other measurable attributes of intelligence, and ignorance of socially accepted behaviour. The fledgling human faces a variety of complex learning demands. We acquire our distinctive human attributes interacting with human groups, whether they number two or two thousand. Groups are the focus of sociological study.

Culture, Society, and Change

Box 3.1

CULTURAL TRANSMISSION

The hit Rogers and Hammerstein musical *South Pacific* was a long-running stage play, as well as a successful film. Its theme centres on the romantic love between a Caucasian American sailor and a Polynesian islander. This song reflects on the bigotry and opposition generated against the relationship.

You've got to be taught to hate and fear,
You've got to be taught from year to year.
It's got to be drummed in your dear little ear,
You've got to be carefully taught.

You've got to be taught to be afraid,
Of people whose eyes are oddly made,
Of people whose skin is a different shade.
You've got to be carefully taught.

You've got to be taught before it's too late,
Before you are six or seven or eight,
To hate all the people your relatives hate.
You've got to be carefully taught.
You've got to be carefully taught.

• RELIANCE ON SYMBOLS

As humans we give meanings to our cultural productions (whether our houses, religious artifacts, or wedding rings) far beyond their physical status. A **symbol** is an object that takes on another meaning. Symbolism infuses the social world with layers of meaning with important social consequences. A classic example is a piece of fabric that symbolizes a country. Americans have raised countless controversies over their "Stars and Stripes" or "Old Glory." In the United States criminal charges have resulted from acts defined as disrespectful to the flag, such as burning it in a demonstration or using it to patch clothing. All flags from all countries can be seen simply as pieces of cloth, but this neutral view is uncommon.

Canadians, too, have been embroiled in intense disagreement regarding the national flag. For much of our history we didn't have a specifically Canadian flag. There were three attempts — in 1925, in 1946, and again in the 1960s — to replace the "Red Ensign" with a distinctive national flag. Each attempt produced controversial and highly emotional debates. In 1965, after a six-month debate in the House of Commons, the familiar red-and-white flag with a red maple leaf became official. Today our flag stands as a common, generally uncontested, national symbol. But it is a symbol that would have been unrecognizable to residents of 19th-century Canada.

To say that human beings are reliant on symbols is to acknowledge the powerful importance of language, one of the greatest of human social inventions. Human society is language based. Words and their meanings are socially created and agreed upon. It is through language, the spoken and the written word, that individuals can transmit personal history, and knowledge can accumulate. Language is the chief mechanism for cultural transmission, social learning, and abstract thinking. Human languages are systems of learned symbols. They form the foundation of culture and society.

HISTORY OF RESEARCH ON CULTURE

The early work on culture, the majority of which was done by anthropologists and sociologists, examined human diversity cross-culturally and provided a rationale for greater tolerance and understanding regarding human differences. In the 19th century more Western (mainly European) elites were able to travel to colonized parts of the world. These travellers (including adventurers and missionaries) described, interpreted, and tried to "explain" the differences they encountered. Some writers emphasized visible or imputed racial differences among people. Evolutionary theory inspired by the work of Charles Darwin and fuelled by **scientism** (holding unrealistic expectations about the ability to apply methods of natural science to the social sciences) was applied to society in Social Darwinism. **Social Darwinism** is a term for theories that apply Darwinian principles of natural selection to human societies to justify the status quo. In contrast, studies in culture offered a social explanation for differences rather than one grounded in physiological/racial traits. They emphasized that people *learn* to be human and that learning creates understandable differences between and among people. Out of this evolved the concept of **cultural relativity** — i.e., that cultural differences are better understood not by imposing alien judgments or values from another culture, but instead by assessing a culture on its own terms, in its own context. Implicit in the notion of cultural relativity is a broader image of humanity. Any single Canadian experiences only a corner of life. Humanness, however, takes many forms. Whether male or female, easterner or westerner, lender or debtor, to understand the social world one needs to look beyond the blinders of personal experience. The challenge is to find ways to approach this goal.

• CULTURAL DIVERSITY AND ETHNOCENTRISM

We may best become aware of our culture when we contrast it with another. It is at the point of contact with other cultures that people become aware of their own. Cultural diversity is revealed in comparisons between cultures and, as well, by examining the variety within a "single" culture.

When we are exposed to other cultures, there is a temptation to judge them against what is familiar. **Ethnocentrism** refers to the practice of viewing other cultures through the framework of one's own. It is usually judgmental and includes the belief that one's own culture is morally or culturally superior.

THE MOUNTIES: A CHANGING CANADIAN SYMBOL

Box 3.2

The mounted police force, as a Canadian symbol, has long intrigued British and American observers. Vivid images of the force can be found in Hollywood films and romantic novels. The expression "Mounties always get their man" is a North American cliché. Since established by Parliament in 1873, the force has evolved from a police force for the North-West Territories, the North-West Mounted Police (NWMP), to the Royal North-West Mounted Police (RNWMP) in 1904, and to the Royal Canadian Mounted Police (RCMP) in 1920.

Originally, it was seen as a temporary creation, but as early as the 1880s constables with scarlet coats were appearing on Canadian immigration pamphlets and in tourist ads. Over time, along with the name of the force, the Mounties' dress requirements have changed. Now the scarlet coat and navy blue trousers are used only on formal occasions. They are no longer the everyday working uniform. When women were first allowed to become constables in 1974, this too introduced shifts in the dress code. More recently, some controversy erupted regarding the "symbolic propriety" of constables of the Sikh faith wearing turbans, as required by their religious precepts. Among other things, the dispute reflected an ahistoric understanding of the RCMP. As societies change, their distinctive symbols and traditions may also undergo change. Like other social creations, the RCMP, a visible, venerable Canadian symbol, has changed over time.

• CULTURAL RELATIVISM

Traditionally, researchers have tried to take a less biased approach to understanding the cultures around them. The positivist tradition (see Chapter 1) argues that the observer should stand apart and adopt scientific "detachment" in assessing other cultures. A term that is important to the early study of culture is **cultural relativism** — a perspective for understanding cultural differences by not imposing alien judgments or values from another culture. This approach holds that a culture may be better understood on its own terms and in its own context than when judged against another culture whose values are held up as absolute. This goal has become an ideal in research on different cultures.

• CULTURAL UNIVERSALS

How similar are different cultures? A **cultural universal** is a feature held in common by all societies. George Murdock (1965), a major contributor to this area of study, argued that there were more than sixty cultural universals, including taboos, sports, dancing, gift giving, funeral ceremonies, and controls over sexuality. While the forms may differ depending on the culture, Murdock thought that these features are found in all cultures. Our shared biological inheritance and the exigencies of social life create commonalities in the human condition. For example, all peoples experience the dependency of infants and the reality of death and grief. A number of early researchers argue that these common experiences create common issues that result in broadly similar attempts at resolution: these are cultural universals.

TWO VIEWS OF CULTURE

Two major contrasting perspectives on culture developed, each with a differing research tradition. The traditional perspective views culture as a shared heritage arising from common norms and values. The more recent, "expanded" view tends to emphasize culture as a symbolic product linked to issues of stratification and power.

• THE TRADITIONAL VIEW: CULTURE AS SHARED HERITAGE AND NORMS

The traditional view sees culture as an underlying base for social interaction. In this perspective culture is the sum total of the heritage of a people: their language, customs, beliefs, knowledge, learned behaviours, understandings, and societal products — all of which can be shared and passed on to future generations. It includes both *material* (artifacts) and *nonmaterial* (social conventions) products that define and shape the characteristics of members of a society. Culture is not innate. It is socially created and taught through the process of socialization that occurs in families, schools, peer groups, the mass media, and other social institutions. From this it follows that culture consists of the artifacts of social life in a particular time and place; at the same time, it is a blueprint for social life. However, it is a shifting blueprint. Culture is an unfolding design for living.

Since in this view culture consists of our human conventions and inventions, it includes things like the constitution, religious ceremonies, Father's Day, textbooks, environmentally sound shopping bags, and that Lamborghini in the showroom window. Behaviour in a culture is usually predictable not because one knows the usual behaviour of any one particular individual but because a particular group's behaviours have become "culturally standardized" (Stephens, 1963: 83).

Culture, we have seen, is contingent on time and place. The norms (rules or expectations), attitudes, possessions, and behaviours of Canadians today are different from those of the last century. Codes of sexual conduct provide an interesting contrast. Nineteenth-century Victorian standards of morality prompted some people to cover the legs of their pianos because they feared "legs" might trigger "impure" thoughts. By the early 20th century, when Dr. Scholl, the foot-care specialist, first began marketing his products, there were cries of public outrage because Scholl's advertisements exhibited the human foot in the nude, except for arch supports or bunion plasters. These behaviours, the cultural products of socially created codes of moral conduct appropriate to the 1890s, seem far removed from the behaviour of most contemporary Canadians.

In the traditional perspective, culture is organized and made possible by behavioural rules. These rules differ from one culture to another; therefore, human societies differ. To varying degrees, we are subject to **social control,** which is how a group modifies and influences the behaviour of its members. Social control can be formal or informal. The church that excommunicates a priest is exercising social control. So is the patrol officer who tickets an overparked car. **Sanctions** are the specific behaviours that either punish nonconformity or reward conformity. Thus we speak of positive sanctions and negative sanctions. Parents use positive sanctions when they praise and encourage a child who complies with family rules (norms). Our day-to-day lives are lived within a context of social expectations. These may be powerful, indeed.

• Normative Continuum

In the traditional view cultures are held together by distinctive systems of norms and values. **Norms** are agreed-upon societal rules and expectations specifying appropriate and inappropriate ways to behave in a particular society. Normative expectations tell what to do, how to do it, where to do it, and why it is to be done. Expectations are not constant for every member of a society; they vary by age, gender, and position in society. For example, when on a warm spring day in 1992 a Guelph, Ontario, woman decided to cool herself on a walk home by removing the clothing from her upper body, she was charged by the police. If she had been a male, the absence of clothing would not have resulted in police intervention.

With an understanding of cultural norms, we can better predict others' behaviour. Norms vary in intensity, importance, and the degree • to which they are enforced. Any society's normative

---

Box 3.3

SOCIAL CONTROL

Social control is exerted in subtle ways. A banquet in a bathroom is a violation of Canadian folkways. In fact, it verges on being a taboo. Thus, it had interesting implications for Greyhound Bus Lines employees.

Eating dinner in a bus depot washroom may not be to everybody's liking, but it certainly got a message across to Greyhound employees. John Munro took over as vice-president of Greyhound Bus Lines 18 months ago, with the assignment to improve customer service. The first thing he discovered was that many depots were in desperate need of janitors, Munro said Wednesday in a speech to the Kelowna Chamber of Commerce. He called the regional managers together, told them customers "want to travel in a friendly, safe, clean environment." Two months later, when that didn't work, Munro called them back together and told them "every month I'm going to meet with regional managers and have dinner — in Greyhound washrooms — and not tell you where." Depot managers started cleaning up their washrooms and sending photos of their own in-house washroom dinners to Munro.

Source: *The Edmonton Journal,* September 21, 1990, p. A2.

expectations can be visualized on a continuum reflecting degrees of societal importance from folkways to mores to laws.

Folkways

Most expectations are termed **folkways:** day-to-day social conventions reflecting a given culture. They represent expectations that may or may not be met. If they are not met, other members of society may mildly disapprove. Christmas trees are not put up on Mother's Day. Grass, not onions, adorns the lawns of suburbia. Soup is not lapped up from a saucer. It is inappropriate to while away the time before a class lecture by singing military drills and marching up and down the aisle. Those who break the conventions of folkways receive a raised eyebrow, a look askance, or negative comments. Local gossip networks may bristle with commentary about the individual's behavioural peculiarities but the wrongdoer is unlikely to face the criminal justice system.

Folkways are not strictly enforced, and when violated generate relatively mild disapproval — from critical comment to gossip or avoidance. It is apparent that such expectations change over time, and are sometimes imposed selectively.

Some folkways last longer than others. **Customs** are a society's enduring folkways. The tradition of giving gifts during the December holiday season is a well-established custom in Canadian society. Other folkways, in contrast, are transitory. In an age of mass-media influence, fads such as mood rings, pet rocks, and Teenage Mutant Ninja Turtle T-shirts can quickly come and go.

Mores

Further along on the continuum of normative social control, **mores** are norms that are considered extremely important and morally right for the welfare of the group. They represent a society's important ethical rules treating basic issues defined as critical for group survival or group integrity, such as admonishments against stealing, rape, or murder. These are the obligatory expectations of society that more clearly focus on right and wrong. Mores are major norms; their violation may cause horror, shock, or outrage, and may lead to punishment.

Laws

Laws are rules enforced by delegated authorities. They provide for formal behavioural control through force or the threat of force. Laws rooted in mores, such as those against killing, tend to be the most effective. Laws with more ambiguous status may be followed grudgingly — e.g., traffic laws or income tax laws. When laws are at odds with folkways or mores, which is sometimes the case, they may be differentially enforced or even skirted. For example, it was illegal to give birth control advice in Canada until 1967. People could be prosecuted if they used "artificial" means to limit or space their children. Yet Canadians found pharmaceutical and mechanical ways to limit their family size. Still another example of the behavioural consequences of lack of fit between laws and mores can be found by looking at the prohibition era in Canada. Prohibition reached its zenith in the early 1920s when the sale and drinking of alcoholic beverages were forbidden by law. However, alcohol was available by prescription. The lure of this legal mechanism for acquiring a drink was such that, during the Christmas holiday season, pharmacists faced virtual epidemics of "sick" customers, lining up with prescriptions in hand, waiting for their holiday cheer.

Laws as social creations are subject to change. Until 1918, it was illegal for Canadian women to vote in federal elections. When Canadian women won suffrage (the right to vote) it was two years before their American counterparts, just across the border, could also vote. Our laws are artifacts of our symbolic culture and as such are alterable social products.

Values

Implicitly or explicitly, cultural norms, in particular mores and laws, express societal values. **Values** are the core ethical ideals and central beliefs characterizing a culture. While norms are situation specific, values reflect broad basic beliefs that encompass multiple norms. The initial research interest in values assumed that societies cohere through consensus on shared values. This assumption has since been challenged by the recognition that societies can be deeply divided, yet continue to cohere.

Values are not as easy to identify as norms since they are more encompassing and less visible in day-to-day life. But we can infer values by examining common, important norms. The basic values of society influence the content of its norms.

For example, Clare Brant, a practising psychiatrist, attempts to single out some of the traditional values that continue, in varying degrees, to differentiate aboriginal communities in Canada from the majority culture. He suggests that the "ethic of noninterference" is probably one of the oldest and most ingrained values for aboriginal people. Brant estimates that it is some twenty-five to thirty thousand years old. It continues today in varied form.

Clare Brant argues that aboriginal people, in contrast to the majority culture, tend to see interference in *any form* as rude. How does this work in daily life? In the larger society, if someone announces at a party that she will be buying a new car next week, she is likely to receive suggestions on make, dealer, engine specifications, and so forth. For people who follow the ethic of noninterference, things are quite different. Unsolicited advice is forbidden. For example, if a car owner gives a ride to a group of aboriginal people, no passenger would think of "backseat driving." Even if the driver faces a problem (e.g., a mudslide or flat tire), to give the driver suggestions or advice would violate the ethic of noninterference. In Brant's words: "We are very loath to confront people. We are very loath to give advice to anyone if the person is not specifically asking for advice. To interfere or even comment on their behaviour is considered rude" (Ross, 1992: 13).

For years researchers have attempted to understand the core values of different societies, seeing this as critical to interpreting and understanding culture and normative behaviours. (For a recent comparison between Canadian and American values, see Baer et al., 1990.)

In the approach that sees culture as shared heritage and norms, diversity tends to be problematized. **Subcultures,** relatively integrated cultural systems that differ from the dominant culture, are recognized components of complex societies. The earliest research on subcultures focused on ethnocultural groups and deviant youths. For example, researchers looked at socialization into competing values as an explanation for criminal activities.

West Edmonton Mall, touted as the world's largest shopping centre, has a number of subcultures. WEM, the local nickname for the massive mall, is the city's most popular tourist attraction. Some 60 000 people spend time at the site each day. The mall has more than shoppers and salespeople. There is an underground subculture of some 200 youths, some with very troubled lives and some homeless, who try to live in the maze of halls and tunnels. The so-called mall rats divide into smaller groups by staking out turf, wearing distinctive clothing and hair styles, and holding common normative expectations (e.g., "Don't report friends to mall security") (Arnold, 1992: 1, 2). In other words, the teenage habitués form a subculture. The glittering, marbled, mirrored mall has another subculture concealed in its executive offices. Top management offices are hidden behind huge one-way mirrors overlooking the shoppers. The mall and its inhabitants are observed by unseen administrators.

In the traditional perspective of culture, subcultural diversity is likely to be seen as resulting from the absence of "consensus" or as a product of such factors as inadequate (faulty) socialization or group isolation (e.g., immigrant groups who "have yet" to assimilate into the dominant cul-

COMMUNITY NORMS AND ALCOHOL FOR ALCOHOLICS

The province of Alberta controls the sale and distribution of alcoholic beverages and, until recent moves toward privatization, purchases could only be made through government liquor stores. In Edmonton, these stores opened at 10:30 a.m. Alcoholics who are poverty stricken don't have the money to stockpile supplies, so they often make their purchases daily. Since there was the possibility that inner-city problem drinkers, unable to buy an early-morning drink, might instead resort to dangerous alcohol-based hair sprays and disinfectants, the rules were changed for one group of Edmontonians. One liquor store in the inner city was allowed to open at 8 a.m. Meanwhile, alcoholics in suburbia waited for their liquor stores to open at 10:30 a.m. How might one explain this norm flexibility?

ture). For some researchers this approach seemed too narrow and too static. In addition, debates over cultural universals have raised questions concerning the importance of *meaning* in human social life. For example, to group all rituals surrounding the death of a member of society under the concept "funeral ceremonies" is to overlook important variations that hold differing meanings for the participants.

• THE EXPANDED VIEW: CULTURE AS CONTESTED SOCIAL PRODUCT AND EXPRESSIVE SYMBOL

An expanded approach recasts the study of culture into an *interpretive* perspective aligned with the new interdisciplinary trend in cultural studies (see Chapter 1). This approach moves away from a belief in a single, extant, reality "out there" waiting to be discovered, just as it moves away from scientism. In this expanded view of culture, power is a significant factor in the distribution, use, and evaluation of cultural products. Dominant groups, it points out, have access to important cultural symbols and they work to perpetuate their power.

• Culture as a Contested Arena

Culture becomes a contested arena in this perspective. Language is a cultural product, an artifact. In turn-of-the-century Canadian society some forms of multilingualism were regarded harshly, as markers of "foreignness." Schoolchildren who spoke (for example) one of the aboriginal languages, Ukrainian, or German on the playground could face punishment. The powerful (dominant) majority controlled access to its ranks and defined the "better" language. Today, many Canadian schools offer courses in "second languages" and, to an extent, the retention of ancestral languages other than English or French is encouraged, reflecting some of the changes in an increasingly diverse society. In a multilingual society, then, languages may be hierarchically evaluated. But hierarchies are rarely constant. They fluctuate, as this example shows.

At a still earlier period, Latin and Greek were exclusive languages, the languages of class elites. Greek and Latin represented "gentleman's scholarship." Women rarely had the opportunity to study them. In this way, powerful elites enjoyed yet another male prerogative and language became a symbol of conspicuous display. Anyone who pursued study in these languages had to have discretionary time and funding. Hence, access to them was determined by class and gender. (At other times these languages have been enshrined within the protected confines of the church, again ensuring their exclusivity.) Classical literary studies and our attempts to understand antiquity rely on recovered texts produced and perpetuated by men of advantage. Bias, therefore — including class and gender bias — may be present in texts that have long been admired. Clearly, language, a critical human creation, is a cultural marker and a way to demonstrate status and power.

Universities are larger examples of a similar process of culture and control: they are hierarchically ordered. One university is assessed more favourably than another. Fields of specialization, the obstacles that must be surmounted to obtain a degree, quotas, grades, gatekeeping (restricting access) — all these facets of educational culture are situated in a context of power. None of these are absolute; they carry variable meanings and are subject to change. Power groups prevail; those in power play a part in defining what is "appropriate" knowledge or "appropriate" interpretation, and they control access. Consider how this may extend to any number of different identity groups in society: the portrayals of warfare by opposing sides, the interpretations of "correct" science or medicine, visions of a better future, and so on.

In this view, culture is a product of struggle between social groups defined by economic (or class), racial, ethnic, gender, or age divisions. Pierre Bourdieu (1984) suggests that those who amass cultural capital can use it to further their advantage. This broadened view of culture has opened a wealth of research possibilities. Highly valued cultural products are more accessible to the powerful. This can be seen in the variety of barriers that dominant groups use to control access to cultural institutions, but it can also be seen in daily life. Video technology can be differentially accessible. Research evidence suggests that among couples, males are more likely to monopolize the remote control of the television set (Gray, 1986, as reported in Brown, 1990). Control over the remote empowers one person to make program selections and channel changes. This control over cultural technology allows the person "in charge" to define and legitimate the "worth" of particular programs. Gray's study found that men in charge of the remote control were more likely to watch sports programs and to be dismissive of daily serialized fiction programs. Their women partners who were fond of "the soaps" felt constrained in their own viewing and shared their program interests in confidence with other women, with an undertone of shame.

• Divisions within a Culture

At the popular level, *culture* may refer to a certain standard of taste and refinement. For sociologists, it is this and more. Attending the ballet or street dancing; eating with sterling silver cutlery or plastic forks; studying sociology or the art of dog grooming — all of these are cultural activities

Box 3.5

CULTURE AND THE TREATMENT OF ANIMALS

Humans' attitudes and behaviours toward animals are socially constructed and vary according to time and place. For example, in both Old Testament and Muslim tradition dogs are condemned as unclean. Yet over half of contemporary North American families have pets, largely cats and dogs, but also fish, birds, guinea pigs, and snakes, among others. Animals become the heroes or the victims of cultural preferences. Each year, Canadians devote massive sums of money to pet-related expenses: special food, health care, and accessories (including winter boots and toothbrushes). Companion animals may serve as confidants, dinner dates, recreation partners, and protectors. The relationship between some people and their animal of choice may last longer than their marriages or other human intimacies.

While animal meat is a staple in the average Canadian diet, not all animals are at equivalent risk. Those that do not grace our dinner plates can evoke great sympathy. In January 1992, the city council of Malibu, California, formally met and voted to declare dolphins "citizens" of Malibu. Other animals have been accorded less illustrious distinctions. For centuries, the people of Spain have honoured one of their departed saints in an annual ritual that involves hurling goats off the tops of church towers. Each year, a sizable number of goats are sacrificed. Now that Spain is part of the European Union, protests have arisen that this practice isn't "European." Of course, what is and is not "European," or "Canadian," or "American" is not only socially defined but subject to change. So, too, is our treatment of animals.

to the sociologist. In the culture-as-contested-social-product view, the fans of the television soap opera and the fans of Luciano Pavarotti are equally of interest: both represent portions of the larger society. But the socially constructed evaluation of cultural activities is of considerable significance. Sociologists, like others, make distinctions between different forms of culture.

High Culture

High culture consists of the cultural practices and products considered more profound, serious, intellectual, and demanding, and accessible only to a few. High culture is, by its very label, evaluative and hierarchical. High culture is available to some members of a society (the privileged elites) but not to all. It is defined by power and its status is maintained by its inaccessibility. In our society, high culture is characterized by such phenomena as opera, classical music, the ballet, and fine wine.

The products of high culture, such as the informed appreciation of classical music or abstract art, require specialized knowledge and skills. These skills can be expensive to acquire, perform, produce, and/or instruct. They demand funds and discretionary time, which are not evenly distributed among the population.

Popular Culture

The expanded perspective on the sociology of culture has focused on contemporary cultural forms and institutions, and their influence across society. The new interdisciplinary work in cultural studies focuses heavily on popular culture as a contemporary social form (See Grossberg et al., 1992). **Popular culture** refers to cultural practices that appeal to the mass population, or non-elites. Mass communication has the effect of promoting commonalities and encouraging consumption of similar things. Thus, bestseller lists and top ten tunes not only document commodities but encourage emulation.

Newspaper tabloids sold at supermarket checkout counters in Canada and the United States are prospering in an age when people read less and concentrate for shorter time periods. The largest tabloid newspaper, *The National Enquirer*, which documents the personal lives of the famous and defamed, sells a reputed eight million copies weekly — more than the two largest hard-news magazines, *Time* and *Newsweek*. Tabloids are eminently accessible, a characteristic that on its own contributes to the fact that they are not part of high culture.

In the perspective of the new cultural studies, the everyday products of the late 20th century are ripe with meaning. Commercials are an often-studied cultural product. Research on beer ads is instructive. These ads are aimed almost exclusively at a mainstream, mostly male audience. Their stated purpose is to motivate people to purchase beer. Lance Strate argues that such ads can also be seen as gender guidebooks, providing "a manual on masculinity" (Strate, 1992: 78). In Strate's view these ads carry messages regarding challenge, risk, and mastery — over nature, over technology, over other people in good-natured "combat," and over oneself. Beer drinking itself can be seen as a test of mastery (display of bravado and manliness) in that it requires performance under pressure.

• Oppositional Groups

Although both perspectives on culture share an interest in cultural diversity, the second model is more likely to see diversity as linked to power and social location (e.g., class, gender, ethnicity). Cultures also contain **oppositional cultures** — subcultures that show clear antagonism to the hegemonic majority culture. Thus the "hippies" of the 1960s were seen as an oppositional culture or **counterculture** resistant to a dominant culture, challenging U.S. involvement in the Vietnam War, and conventions regarding sexual expression.

The newer perspective on culture has moved beyond the study of dominant cultural values and subcultural values to a recognition that in modern life people may be involved in more than one subculture and that these may have varying degrees of importance or meaning in their lives. It is the presence of oppositional groups, particularly, that contributes to cultural change.

• The Attribution of Meaning

Cultural products are specific to a culture, time, and place. The expanded perspective sees culture not only as a human product but as infused with human meanings. Culture is a symbolic product. This is illustrated in Sarah Matthews's (1979) sensitive study of older women concerned over the distribution of their personal possessions after death. The question of which beneficiary should receive which item is not an issue of distribution, but one of meanings and attributed meanings. What is the meaning of an act, a behaviour, *in context*? What meaning will the recipient give to inheriting a particular piece of jewellery or handicraft, for example? Some of the older women studied distributed their possessions before death to ensure the best placement for valued objects. For many, inheritance strategies promised a form of ongoing influence, even after death. In this case, a brooch or embroidered towel, as an object, is actively engaged by its user and is inscribed with a distinctive meaning unique to her life and to the way she hopes she will be remembered. Both the aging woman and her inheritors actively assign meaning to these cultural products. Research that is sensitive to meanings recognizes that such multiple "realities" and perspectives on the social world arise out of human diversity.

Culture and society are sometimes treated as alternative ways of describing the same thing, almost like different camera angles on the same subject. But culture is embedded in society.

SOCIETY

In day-to-day conversation, the term *society* often refers to an association of people with common interests and goals. Hence we speak of the Society for the Prevention of Cruelty to Animals or the Royal Society of Canada. In these cases, the word *society* is used in a narrow sense inadequate for sociology. Sociologists use the concept of **society** to describe a complex, all-encompassing level of human relationships within a defined territory and with fairly distinctive culture and institutions. The term refers to human groups with strong internal connections, permanence, and self-perpetuation.

Society functions in time and space. Some societies — e.g., Babylon, ancient Egypt, or ancient Greece — are no longer in existence; according to Fry (1985), some 3000 exist today. Although it is common to equate societies with the boundaries of nation-states (as in the example of Canadian society or British society), society and territorial boundaries on the map do not always coincide. For example, the territorial base for some Bedouin tribes in the Arabian Peninsula crosses national boundaries between Saudi Arabia, Kuwait, and Iraq. Also, one can legitimately refer to more than one existing society within a national boundary. Thus, the designations French-Canadian society and Inuit society — all within Canadian society — are sociologically correct.

Society provides a background against which interaction occurs at all levels of social organization. In modern societies, small groups, voluntary associations, social classes, communities, institutions, and the like all function not in isolation but in relation to the larger society. These units are major parts of society and, as such, are highly interdependent. In this sense society is said to have a determined social structure that involves **patterned** (i.e., recurrent) relationships and reflects a high degree of permanence and continuity over time. Hence, society outlives any one of its individual members.

The study of society, however, can not be reduced merely to a study of its parts. Kingsley Davis (1949: 26) provides an interesting analogy: "It is like a house which, though composed of bricks, nails, mortar, and pieces of lumber, cannot be understood purely in terms of these materials; it has a form and function as a complete house." Davis's cautionary remark is important to keep in mind, but it should not be interpreted to mean that it would be fruitless to study the parts that make up society.

• THE SOCIAL STRUCTURE

Each society is uniquely organized with a framework of its own. The term **social structure** refers to "the enduring, orderly and patterned relationships between elements of a society" (Abercrombie et al., 1984: 198). The metaphor of structure is used to describe the recurring, predictable, and organized patterns among the component parts of human social behaviour. Five components are important in understanding social structure: (1) social roles; (2) statuses; (3) groups; (4) social stratification; and (5) institutions.

• Social Role

A **social role** refers to a specific pattern of behaviour expected of people in a particular position. Roles are typically associated with certain rights, duties, and obligations that form part of the cultural fabric. Whether a person behaves according to expectations is a different matter. For this reason, sociologists often distinguish between the terms *role* and *role behaviour*. The latter term refers to the actual behaviour of the incumbent of a position, which may or may not meet expectations.

In the broader context, one individual may assume multiple roles. For example, a university professor may, in addition to being a teacher, alternately perform such roles as wife, mother, daughter, aunt, cousin, sister, friend, committee member, chair of a department, volunteer worker, counsellor, researcher, and sports fan. Most people in modern society juggle a variety of roles.

At the organizational level, one can observe a larger number of roles that are designed to complement each other. For instance, within a university the roles of a professor and a student are obvious. However, these roles are complemented by many others in order to ensure the effective functioning of the organization. Figure 3.1 shows varied roles within the university that involve not only specialization but also a great deal of coordination.

When the expectations for a given social position are incompatible, as in the case of the position of supervisor — a position that may carry different expectations from workers and from management — the incumbent may experience **role conflict**. Role conflict in this case is probably inevitable as a result of the adversarial nature of labour–management relations in Canada and elsewhere. In other situations role conflict may occur where the individual occupies two different positions that register incompatible expectations — as when a teenager is caught in a tug-of-war between the expectations of peers on the one hand and parents on the other.

• Status

The concept of **status** is very much related to that of role. In this sense, status

> refers to the level of *prestige* that is accorded a group member by virtue of the particular role he plays. Status (prestige) is thus seen as a *consequence* of social ranking; an individual enjoys a high level of status or suffers a low one because the role allocated . . . is ranked high or low in the group's hierarchy of roles (DeFleur et al., 1971: 46; italics in the original).

Figure 3.1

SELECTED POSITIONS IN A NETWORK TYPICALLY FOUND IN A LARGE CANADIAN UNIVERSITY

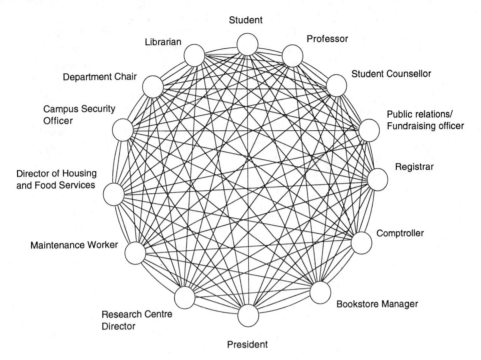

Note: Some of the recorded relationships are mediated, and some are linked directly.

How status is attained in society interests sociologists. One principle of allocation is merit: an individual's qualifications determine whether he or she will be allocated a given status. This is commonly called **achieved status**. There are, of course, different levels of skill or education in a population; according to the principle of merit, skill level is matched with status. We know as well that there is a second principle of status allocation: ascription. **Ascribed status** has little to do with achievement and more to do with such characteristics as age, sex, ethnicity, and social inheritance. In the latter case, the status of an individual is very much influenced by parental status and resources.

According to some sociologists, chance also plays a role in status allocation. Lowell J. Carr (1948: 47) even thinks that chance constitutes a third principle of status allocation. While chance may indeed play a role (as in becoming a millionaire by winning the lottery or in being in the right place at the right time for an unexpected opportunity), it is premature to elevate it to the level of a principle. However, intriguing questions are raised when considering the extent to which achievement, ascription, and even chance can play a role in status attainment in Canadian society.

• Groups

Human experience centres on the group. A **group** is two or more individuals engaged in meaningful communication and interaction for the purpose of achieving a common goal. The latter criterion distinguishes a group from street or casual encounters where, for example, one person asks another for directions. This definition includes such things as family, gang, tribe, committee, caucus, and dinner party. But it excludes social categories such as blue-eyed men, people whose annual income falls between $30 000 and $40 000, teenagers, and other collections of individuals who have only shared socially significant characteristics in common.

Several years ago Theodore Mills (1967: 2) noticed the pervasiveness of groups in human existence. Mills estimated that every person on the planet belonged to an average of five to six groups. In 1991, there were 5.4 billion people in the world. Even allowing for overlapping groups, Mills's estimate suggests that the total number of small groups in existence could number many millions. Human groups, then, are pervasive and they are influential.

Groups differ in size, function, degree of formality, and degree of permanence. Variation in these attributes results in significant differences in how group members communicate and interact with each other. These differences are reflected in how the group as a whole looks upon its own members as well as upon outsiders.

Degrees of Intimacy and Formality

Groups can also be distinguished based on the degree of intimacy and formality among participants. **Primary groups** are small, intimate, face-to-face and lasting forms of association. The characterization of primary groups by the early sociologist Charles H. Cooley remains classic:

> By primary groups I mean those characterized by intimate face-to-face association and cooperation. They are primary in several senses, but chiefly in that they are fundamental in forming the social nature and ideals of the individual. The result of intimate association, psychologically, is a certain fusion of individualities in a common whole, so that one's very self, for many purposes at least, is the common life and purposes of the group. Perhaps the simplest way of describing this wholeness is by saying that it is a "we"; it involves the sort of sympathy and mutual identification for which "we" is the natural expression. One lives in the feeling of the whole . . .
>
> A primary group is not only an agency through which we satisfy our social and emotional needs, it is also an agency of informal social control in the sense that the members' behaviors tend to be influenced by group expectations (1909: 23–24).

In contrast to primary groups, **secondary groups** are impersonal, function-specific, and short-lived forms of association. Many of our contacts in contemporary society are through such secondary groups. Such is the case, for example, when we pay bills, register for a course, volunteer at the blood bank, talk with the long-distance operator, schedule an appointment, receive a parcel, make a speech, or attend a concert. On the other hand, the impulse to establish primary relationships is strong. So important are primary groups that they are formed and re-formed throughout an individual's life. Large groups often separate into smaller primary groups. For example, a university, which can be seen as a secondary group, contains countless primary groups. Similarly, other formal organizations, such as large workplaces, contain informal structures with primary relationships.

Secondary groups lack the emotional bond characteristic of primary relationships. Typically, secondary groups are based on a social contract in which expectations for the relationship are very specific. This contract may be unstated, but it is part of a larger system of mutual expectations. When a shopper goes to a department store, the relationship he establishes with the salesperson is impersonal, specific, and transitory. When a returning Canadian traveller declares her purchases to a customs officer, the interaction is function-specific. As soon as the task is accomplished, the relationship ends.

The controls applied to secondary relationships are formal rather than informal. They are often based on written codes of conduct and specific expectations. If one of the two parties to a secondary relationship does not comply with the norms governing the particular situation, formal sanctions may be introduced to resolve the dispute.

The Impact of Group Size

The early sociologist Georg Simmel argued that size is an important consideration in the study of groups because it exerts considerable influence on the nature and quality of interaction within the group.

For example, the **dyad,** a group of two individuals, has special characteristics that terminate even if only one more person is added to the group. Simmel noted that the dyad is the smallest group in which a secret is no longer the property of one person, and at the same time it is the largest group in which the secret can be preserved relatively securely. Perhaps because of this, secret (or underground) societies are often organized in such a way that only two members see each other at any one time. Finally, there is an "all or none" quality about a dyad. If one member withdraws, the group ceases to exist. However, once there is a membership of three, the group can persist even if one member drops out.

The **triad** is a group of three individuals. This is a group with still another distinctive structure. It differs from the dyad in that it permits the formation of alliances and coalitions. For example, in a family or in a friendship clique of three people, two of the participants may "gang up" against the third. Insight regarding coalition formation in a triad may be reflected in the advice counsellors often give to parents to "stand united" in dealing with their child. (The concern here is a coalition may form between the child and one parent against the other parent.) Triads are uniquely susceptible to these coalition alliances. Hence, the relations between two people in a dyad may be either strengthened or disturbed by the addition of a third. The triad does not have the same degree of intensity and vulnerability that is found in the dyad. Where there are disagreements in a dyad, delay in resolving them is a threat to the continued survival of the group. In a triad it is easier to reach an agreement.

Beyond the triad, four-person and five-person groups have their own points of interest. A four-person group is the smallest unit in which coalitions can be of equal size, while the smallest group in which two coalitions of unequal size can occur is the five-person group.

The influence of size on group dynamics can be seen in a variety of settings. In decision-making groups the opportunity to participate in the process declines with size. For this reason, researchers in the area of formal organization suggest that groups of seven or nine persons are more ideally suited for distributed (somewhat equal) participation than groups of fifteen or twenty. Closer to home, the impact of group numbers is illustrated in university classrooms, where fifteen to twenty students allow for seminar-like participation and discussion, whereas larger classes, in varying degrees, inhibit active student involvement.

• Institutions

An **institution** is an enduring complex of norms and values developed to regulate behaviour around certain basic social needs. Table 3.1 lists ten institutional areas: familial, educational, religious, medical, economic, political, scientific, military, legal, and sport. In each instance examples of social needs, norms, values, institutional statuses/roles, and groups are provided. These institutional areas are interlinked and affect each other.

In pre-industrial or simpler societies, institutional functions such as the educational, medical, economic, and recreational are fused with the family institution. The needs of the sick, the young, or the aged may be met at home, along with the performance of recreational and economic activities. At the same time, other institutional areas such as the legal, military, and scientific may appear in an elementary form outside the home in the collective action of the larger group. The important point is that societies vary in terms of how sharply social institutions are differentiated (i.e., how separate and distinct they are). The highest degree of institutional differentiation, or **institutionalization,** occurs in modern industrial societies.

Table 3.1 MAJOR SOCIAL INSTITUTIONS

Institution	Some Social Needs	Some Values	Some Norms	Some Statuses/Roles	Some Groups
Family	Regulate sexual behaviour; provide care for children	Marital fidelity	Have only one spouse	Husband Grandmother	Relatives
Educational system	Transmit cultural knowledge to the young	Intellectual curiosity	Attend school	Teacher; student	Student clique; university seminar
Religion	Share/reaffirm community values and solidarity	Belief in God	Attend worship services	Priest; rabbi	Congregation; synod
Medical system	Care for the sick	Good health	Save life if possible	Physician; patient	Hospital staff; ward of patients
Economic system	Produce, distribute goods and services	Free enterprise	Maximize profits	Accountant; vendor	Corporate board; labour union
Political system	Distribute power; maintain order	Freedom	Vote by secret ballot	Senator; lobbyist	Parliament; political party
Science	Investigate social and natural world	Unbiased search for truth	Conduct research	Physicist; anthropologist	Research team; scientific society
Military	Attack or defend against enemies of the state	Discipline	Follow orders	General; soldier	Platoon; army division
Legal system	Maintain social control	Fair trial	Inform suspects of their rights	Judge; lawyer	Jury; cell mates
Sport	Provide for recreation and exercise	Winning	Play by the rules	Umpire; coach	Hockey team; fan club

Source: Adapted from Robertson (1987: 94).

Institutions exhibit a high degree of integration of norms and values. In other words, the norms of behaviour governing an institutional area are not just an aggregate but rather an inter-connected set whose elements cohere and reinforce each other. For example, in the educational institution the prescription that children should attend school is integrated with norms governing the behaviour of teachers and other students whose purpose is not to discourage attendance. Thus, where roles are complementary, mutual expectations are ordinarily not in conflict. However, in periods of rapid social change, many institutional norms may be questioned, resulting in problems of integrating norms.

Societal institutions are closely interrelated. This means that a change in one institutional area may, and often does, have a positive or negative impact on other areas. Should the Canadian government introduce universal day-care legislation, for example, this would have ramifications not only in the political system, but also in the family, educational, legal, and economic systems.

Institutions function through different forms of social organization including, for example, different types of groups, voluntary associations, and administrative arrangements. Of particular interest in the study of institutions is **bureaucracy,** which is a goal-oriented form of administration organized as a secondary, formal group. According to Max Weber's (1946) classic description of bureaucracy, this organizational form is distinctively characterized by

1. the distribution of tasks among different positions as official duties;
2. the arrangement of offices into a hierarchical authority structure;
3. the development of rules and regulations, rationality, and efficiency;
4. personnel recruitment on the basis of merit and promotion on the basis of merit or seniority;

5. impersonality both among employees and with clients; and
6. development of professional careers.

This is an idealized characterization of bureaucracy that lacks empirical accuracy. Research into bureaucracy in the past fifty years has underlined problems of inefficiency, rigidity, and blind adherence to rules, which are all counterproductive.

Bureaucracy constitutes an important aspect of the social structure in most modern societies. A large proportion of Canadians work in a variety of bureaucratic organizations; bureaucracy is the standard form of administration in practically all institutional areas listed in Table 3.1. Finally, bureaucracy has had an inestimable impact on our behaviour and mode of thinking. To understand contemporary Western societies it is essential to understand how bureaucracy works.

• Social Stratification

An important aspect of "the enduring, orderly, and patterned relationships between elements of a society" is social stratification, or the hierarchical arrangement of people based on selected criteria. **Social stratification** is a system of institutionalized inequality. For the sociologist, the study of social stratification (or the social class system, as it is sometimes called) involves two questions:

1. How are scarce and valued resources distributed in society?
2. What relations exist between social strata or classes?

The first question refers to the distribution of such resources as economic power, political power, and prestige. The second question involves "relationships or exchanges among individuals and groups from the point of view of their reciprocity or symmetry." Relational inequalities refer to asymmetries in exchanges between units such that, for example, one person gives more of something to another than he or she receives in exchange, or one social class benefits at another's expense (Hunter, 1986: 4).

Social inequality can be seen as a direct product of status and role differentiation in society and of the degree to which society is based on a subsistence economy or on an economy of surplus. All the different institutions, groups, and organizations that exist in society interact and, as well, intersect with roles and statuses to produce a particular system of power and privilege. Obviously, in the stratification systems of modern industrial societies, some individuals and groups are more advantaged than others and some individuals and groups gain their advantage at the expense of others. As a consequence of this, the structure of the stratification system is unique to each society, even if it exhibits similarities to stratification systems elsewhere. This is a critical — perhaps *the* critical — reason for the differences in social structures around the world.

• SOCIETAL TYPES

The average Canadian takes many things for granted and lives a life of relative abundance. In Canada and, generally, in countries of the Western world, there is less uncertainty about securing the basic amenities of life including food, clothing, and shelter than in other parts of the world. This is a matter of considerable interest to the sociologist and calls for an explanation. For the sociologist, differences in advantage or disadvantage among peoples of the world cannot be satisfactorily explained either by divine providence or by claims to biologically instilled aptitude. Nor can differences in societal advantage be explained merely by reference to natural resources. While geography, climate, and other environmental factors are related to well-being, these factors play only a small role in social and economic development (Heilbroner, 1963). Obviously, the availability of natural resources may make economic development easier in some countries and more difficult in others. But there are poor countries with abundant natural resources and affluent countries that are poor in natural resources. These inconsistencies have forced sociologists to recognize the decisive role that social, cultural, and economic factors play in societal well-being.

During the mid-19th century, sociological interest in societal types was very high. It was a period of rapid industrialization and urbanization; a time when the old feudal system was being replaced with new class structures; a time of questioning individual rights and obligations; and at the same time, a period of Western colonial expansion. Europeans were exposed to dramatic changes at home, and privileged European travellers were returning home from their journeys with fascinating stories of people in faraway lands. The differences between people were often explained through some form of evolutionary theory and the idea of progressive development of human groups through stages of civilization.

In 1887 the German sociologist Ferdinand Tönnies developed a major distinction between societies. Tönnies proposed two societal types, which he labelled **Gemeinschaft** (translated as "community" or "a climate of supportive relationships") and **Gesellschaft** (translated as "association characterized by individualism and self-interest"). Each societal form promoted distinctive types of relationships. Gemeinschaft was best represented by the family. Gesellschaft, on the other hand, reflected weakened social ties. Tönnies saw societies moving historically from Gemeinschaft to Gesellschaft, a process he viewed as a negative transition.

Shortly after Tönnies's formulation, Emile Durkheim in 1893 proposed a binary conception of society as well. Durkheim, in his landmark book *The Division of Labor in Society*, argued that society is moving from **mechanical solidarity** to **organic solidarity**. Less complex societies with little division of labour are united by the fact that the members of the society are similar and have common practices and beliefs. Thus they demonstrate mechanical solidarity. However, in more complex societies, with elaborated structures and highly specialized roles (particularly occupational), the form of interdependence or linking can be described as organic solidarity. The members of society differ but they need one another. Thus, Durkheim, in contrast to Tönnies, tended to see societal modernization as beneficial. Durkheim believed that in modern societies with organic solidarity, even though the extended family unit weakens, the marital unit becomes stronger. Even if support needs cannot be met by the spouse or extended family, they will be met by occupational groups. (See discussion in Chapter 1.)

The important beginnings made by Tönnies and Durkheim focused on dualistic views of society. More recent typologies group societies on the basis of such features as contrasting political-economic and organizational complexity, as well as on the basis of contrasting levels of cultural possessions and technological efficiency.

Lenski (1966) suggests five types covering a wide variety of societies.

1. **Hunting and gathering societies:** These are simple, small societies that may be nomadic or semi-nomadic, but in either case they live at the subsistence level and have little or no economic surplus. Technology is elementary, involving simple tools and weapons. Social inequality is minimal in this type of society.

2. **Simple horticultural societies:** This type of society is economically a little more advantaged than the hunting and gathering type. Because gardening is the dominant economic activity, simple horticultural societies are characterized by permanent or semi-permanent settlement patterns. Here we begin to see the growth of cities, but metal tools and weapons are at an elementary level of development. Social inequality in wealth and power is much greater than in hunting and gathering societies, and there is increased division of labour in the economic, political, and religious spheres.

3. **Advanced horticultural societies:** The most distinctive features of advanced horticultural societies include metal tools, hoes, and weapons; further advancement into more permanent settlement patterns and population growth; the growth of the state and state power; and increased occupational inequality.

4. **Agrarian societies:** The development of this type of society coincided with the invention of the plough and metal tools. Surplus food is associated more with agrarian societies than any of the preceding types. Different classes such as the merchant class, retainer class, priestly class, and peasant class, begin to take shape. Cities grow larger in size, as do the state and government. Bureaucracy takes firmer root in agrarian societies.

5. **Industrial societies:** The most distinctive features of industrial societies involve efficiency and the use of varied sources of energy. In their more advanced stages, industrial societies have shifted emphasis from manufacturing to service industry. Occupational differentiation is at its most advanced stage and extreme social inequalities remain, but perhaps to a lesser degree than in advanced agrarian societies (Lenski, 1966). Social stratification is complex and government social policy is designed to ease the burden on the poor.

Today we are witnessing a shift in modern industrial societies toward a knowledge-based society resulting from the tremendous advances in automation, telecommunications, and computer technology. The implications of this shift from early industrialization to an emphasis on information and the production of new knowledge are not yet clear.

• SOCIAL CHANGE

A Greek philosopher once remarked that one cannot step into a river twice. At the second step, he or she is not the same person, nor is it the same river. This is an illustration of the ubiquity of change. The sociological perspective acknowledges the pervasiveness of change but, in addition, insists that change must be observable and also measurable.

At the conceptual level, it is useful to distinguish between social and cultural change. **Social change** refers to any observable difference or modification in social organization and/or patterns of behaviour over time. What this definition underscores is the fact that change is a process. We may study it over short or long spans of time, depending on the unit under consideration and the research agenda. Moreover, the definition emphasizes the need to observe and hence to measure social change. The unit of analysis may be society as a whole or a segment such as a region, a community, an institution, a primary group, or a secondary group.

The importance of studying the culture when addressing issues of social change and transition is reflected in Judith Tucker's (1985) sociohistorical research on peasant and lower-class urban Egyptian women from 1800 to 1914. This was a period characterized by rapid socioeconomic change as Egypt adapted to European intrusion and British colonialism. Tucker argues that women in the early 1800s had a degree of power and control, even though the setting was patriarchal. Precolonial *indigenous* institutions contributed to this. She argues that women were relatively empowered by their personal access to Muslim religious courts that spelled out their rights and by a cultural ideology that supported women in the public sphere, as producers or traders. Tucker's evidence suggests, in fact, that Egyptian Muslim women *had more power before Europeanization and colonization than after.* Such research counters the argument that equates the East with static traditionalism, challenges the practice of neglecting indigenous structures, and points to the importance of studying culture to understand the dynamics of change.

To study change, the sociologist may examine, for example, one or more of the following aspects of change: its direction, rate, source(s), and controllability. The unit of analysis is variable and the focus may be social or cultural change, or both.

• Direction of Change

Is the direction of change evaluated in a positive or negative way, and by whom? Language legislation in Quebec in the past few years has moved in the direction of linguistic assimilation of ethnic groups and an emphasis on French-only commercial and other signs. Norms and patterns of behaviour have been influenced by this legislation. Reactions to this change within and outside Quebec have ranged from extremely positive to extremely negative. In southern Alberta the Oldman River Dam (completed in 1992) is evaluated positively by many farmers and extremely negatively by native communities who fear the loss of their way of life and damage to the environment.

• Rate of Change

The rate or pace of change can also vary. Revolutions tend to bring about radical changes over short periods of time. In the area of gender equality in Canada, the rate of change is viewed by some to be slow. It should be emphasized that the terms *fast* and *slow* are based on evaluative judgments: what is fast for some people may be slow for others. In any case, the study of change requires that assessments be made about the speed with which it occurs.

• Source(s) of Change

It is possible to identify influences on social change. Population is one important influence as evidenced by the baby-boom period following World War II. The sudden increase in birthrates had both immediate and long-term effects on the expansion of services provided by educational, economic, political, health, and other institutions. The baby-boom generation has now assumed a larger burden of taxes to pay for the multitude of social programs. Population change resulting from immigration and from the increase in the proportion of the aged has also had far-reaching impact on Canada's social structure and culture.

Another source of change is technology. The birth-control pill, for example, has had an impact on sexual mores, population control, and women's participation in the labour force. The computer provides a current example of the impact of technology on social and cultural change. The computer has revolutionized relations in the workplace, allowed more and more people to work at home, and created a new form of economy — the so-called knowledge-based economy.

Sociologists often consider the physical environment as a source of change. In his classic book *The Developing Canadian Community,* Clark shows the historically important role of the frontier in shaping not only economic development, but also changes in forms of social organization in Canada.

> The establishment of the fishing industry in the Gulf of St. Lawrence led to the traffic in furs with the Indians and to the settlement of the Annapolis and St. Lawrence valleys. To fish and fur was later added the important staple of timber, opening up for agricultural exploitation the interior of New Brunswick and the new Province of Upper Canada. Expansion of the fur trade to the West brought about the sudden rush for gold in British Columbia, and eventually in the Yukon, and the settlement of the wheat lands of the prairies, and these developments hastened the growth of

industrial capitalism in the East. The pushing out of the frontiers of manufacturing, and the exploitation of the mining and pulp and paper resources of the North mark the final phases of the frontier expansion of economic life in Canada (1962: 3–4).

Finally, innovation is another source of change that merits examination. Societies vary in the degree to which they reward inventions and discoveries, and even the same society may reward innovation differently at different periods of time. In contemporary Western societies, including Canada, governments, industry, and other institutions have invested heavily in research and development (R and D) and science and technology (S and T) in the hope of gaining an edge over competitors. Presumably, the payoffs from encouraging and facilitating innovation will far outweigh the investment.

The sources of change may be *endogenous* (i.e., coming from within the society) or *exogenous* (i.e., coming from the outside). In some cases they are a mixture of the two. Endogenous factors encompass the above-noted sources of change — population, technology, physical resources, and innovation; exogenous factors refer to diffusion, the process by which cultural elements spread from one society to another. There are not many societies in the world today that live in complete isolation. A variety of material and nonmaterial cultural traits have diffused from East (Asia) to West (Europe and North America), as well as from West to East. The advanced state of our transportation and communication technology today has made diffusion a truly global process.

• Change and Human Control

Human beings expend a great deal of effort trying to control events in their daily lives. On a broader scale, institutions and societies attempt to control social and cultural change in various ways. In the economic sphere the pace of technological change is controlled by negotiations between labour and management. Legislation is another way of controlling change, either by regulating its pace or preventing it from taking place altogether. Related to this is the fact that governments attempt to control change by planning and coordinating activities of many groups through boards, commissions, and task forces.

Hutterites in western Canada (members of a Christian sect that lives communally) provide an interesting example of a community that attempts to control the process of change. The behaviour of all colony residents is under constant surveillance; violations of group norms are not tolerated. In addition, the Hutterite elders go through a very deliberate process of critically examining cultural elements from the larger Canadian society (e.g., dress codes, new farm equipment, labour-saving devices) before deciding on the acceptability of any change. Once a major decision is made, it tends to be implemented simultaneously in all the colonies in Alberta, Saskatchewan, and Manitoba.

European and North American societies are still undergoing further transformation and industrial development. Meanwhile, many societies in the world are trying to catch up. These are the developing or Third World countries. These countries have made intense efforts to improve their own conditions through programs of social and economic development. Their experiences have been mixed. The difficulty faced by many of these countries may be attributed, at least in part, to the fact that their development plans have not been comprehensive enough to take account of the interconnectedness of social institutions and norms of behaviour. Moreover, for the most part Third World countries are dependent on the West and at the same time, the world economic system is structured primarily to serve the interests of the Western industrialized countries and not the interests of developing ones (Frank, 1969). Despite these difficulties, development continues to be a priority in countries of the Third World.

THE INTERSECTION OF CULTURE, SOCIETY, AND CHANGE

Human behaviour in general is not random or haphazard, not hit-or-miss, not purposeless, unsystematic, or rigidly static. It is, rather, goal oriented, patterned, and potentially predictable. While human behaviour is influenced by genetic makeup and physiological needs, it is influenced even more by cultural and social factors. Norms, values and ideals, and institutions define how people in a given culture should behave, but with allowance for some degree of freedom of choice. Conceptions of right and wrong, acceptable and unacceptable, and tolerable and intolerable behaviour are all culturally defined. Deviation from the norm tends to invite negative sanctions.

It is remarkable that human beings are capable of adapting to environmental extremes, from equatorial to arctic climates. Thus, it is natural to expect variations in how societies are organized and how human beings satisfy their needs. But human societies have commonalities, too, certainly in form but also in substance. In all societies members are assigned roles and statuses to keep the societal enterprise going, to ensure survival. In this respect, people are aided by their own socially created institutions, which regulate human behaviour around certain needs. Human existence the world over is group based. And human social life in any given society is or tends to be integrated through the collective efforts of the group.

Neither culture nor society is a rigidly static entity. A key premise of sociology is that change is an inherent feature of culture and of social organization. The process of change is potentially subject to human control, but not completely. In point of fact, there is an ever-present tension between the forces of tradition and the forces of change — regardless of whether the sources of change are endogenous or exogenous. Attitudes toward the direction and rate of change can vary widely within the same society.

DINING IN CHANGING TIMES

Box 3.6

A typical day begins with Randa Ryan rushing out of her Austin, Texas, home to coach the 6 a.m. swimming practice. She grabs a cup of yogurt on the way out the door. Husband Steve, also a University of Texas athletic department administrator, and her two sons, Seth, 14, and Rhett, 10, start breakfast. Most days, the guys make do with frozen waffles and pancakes popped in the microwave or the hard-boiled eggs and whole-wheat bread Mom keeps in the refrigerator.

The family arrives home from work and school at different times. Randa Ryan says they "hardly ever sit down to an evening meal." When they do eat, "it's staggered and in shifts" — often a Lean Cuisine from the freezer, warmed-up lasagna made on Sunday, a casserole made by the boys or soup left on the stove for whomever, whenever.

The days of the traditional family meal are numbered. "Families are putting less emphasis on sitting together and sharing a meal," says Marlene Johnson, consumer information director for The Pillsbury Company, which recently completed a 15-year study of our eating habits. "If trends continue, the family meal could be extinct by the year 2000."

. . . The whole idea of the dinner hour seems to be on the wane . . . For generations, families have used the evening meal for conversation, catching up on the day's events, even inculcating the young with such social graces as using a knife, fork and spoon (and no slouching).

But what are 50 percent of adults doing at dinnertime? Eating with Tom Brokaw and Vanna White, according to a Roper Report's study this year, which found TV viewership during meals up from 33 percent in 1977. Bombarded with food choices, busy schedules and convenience products unheard of 15 years ago, many families are dining "restaurant-style, with everyone eating different meals at different times."

Source: Abridged from "The Family Dinner: Becoming Extinct." In *Diversity in Families*, 2nd ed., edited by Maxine Baca Zinn and D. Stanley Eitzen. New York: Harper and Row, 1990, pp. 8–9. Excerpted from Laurence Sombke, "How Our Meals Have Changed," *USA Weekend*, November 11–13, 1988, pp. 4–5.

It is easy, sometimes even tempting, to overstate the role that culture and social structure play in controlling human behaviour. Although we are all influenced by the culture and society in which we live, nevertheless it is well to remember that norms, values, and organizations are social creations and not completely imposed on us from above (e.g., by divine or societal authority). Human beings are active agents and as such, they can act on and modify the norms and institutions that they created in the first place. Culture and society are abstract concepts — the creation of the human mind — and they should not be reified or turned into concrete suprahuman entities presumed to impose upon us a will beyond our own. In more ways than one, human beings influence their destiny.

SUMMARY

- Human social existence has several distinctive characteristics. It is highly adaptable, group based, and organized to an extent not found in animals. It is reliant on symbols and the elaborated use of language.
- Culture refers to the physical and social creations of humankind.
- Two perspectives have evolved on the study of culture: (1) a traditional view that emphasizes culture as shared heritage and norms and (2) an expanded view that stresses culture as contested social product and expressive symbol.
- The traditional culture-as-shared-heritage-and-norms perspective emphasizes normative control in creating and maintaining cultural unity. It tends to assume a coherence in the larger culture and emphasizes research objectivity, frequently promoting a scientific model for studying culture. Often, researchers in this mode have searched for cultural universals.
- The more recent, expanded perspective on culture sees it as a symbolic and social product. This view emphasizes the creations of culture, their meanings, and their effects. The user of culture is assumed to be an active participant who assigns meaning and interprets events. Hence, culture is a symbolic product.
- Although both models of culture are interested in cultural diversity, the first model is more likely to see diversity as a product of factors such as inadequate socialization or group isolation. The second model is more likely to see diversity as expectable, linked to power and social location (e.g., class, gender, ethnicity) and contributing to social change.
- Culture as a component of social stratification is reflected in the work done on elite and mass culture. Those in power define elite culture and limit access. Such mechanisms reinforce and maintain power and privilege.
- The products of mass consumer society also work to enforce the social locations in society; thus, gender, race, and class divisions may be produced and reproduced through language, education, and the media.
- Subcultures predominate in modern societies. People may be members of several subcultures in a way that may not threaten the dominant culture. When these subcultures are oppositional (countercultural), the possibilities for social change increase.
- *Society* refers to the totality of human relationships within a defined territory and with distinctive culture and institutions. The term *society* may be applied to a particular people (e.g., the Zulu of South Africa) or to a complex nation-state such as France. Society and culture are two sides of the same coin.
- The term *social structure* refers to the organizational framework within which human beings interact. The main elements of social structure include roles and statuses assigned to individual members, groups (which vary in size, function, and other characteristics), institutions, and the stratification system (which reflects social, economic, and political inequalities). Characteristically, all these elements function within a distinctive cultural environment.

- Societies may be contrasted in terms of their unique social and structural features. Comparative analysis is often facilitated by the development of societal types. An early societal typology identifies Gemeinschaft and Gesellschaft types of society. A more recent and elaborate societal typology has been developed on the basis of economic and political factors as well as levels of cultural possessions and technological development. In this scheme, five societal types have been identified: hunting and gathering societies, simple horticultural societies, advanced horticultural societies, agrarian societies, and industrial societies.
- The successor to industrial society is the knowledge-based society, which is still in the making. This emerging societal type encompasses the latest transformations in human group life.
- Closely associated with the study of culture and society is the study of cultural and social change. The latter field of inquiry directs attention to aspects of change including the direction, rate, and sources of change, as well as the degree to which human beings can direct and control change in culture and social organization.

KEY CONCEPTS

Achieved status
Ascribed status
Bureaucracy
Counterculture
Cultural relativism
Cultural universal
Culture
Custom
Dyad
Ethnocentrism
Feral children
Folkways
Gemeinschaft
Gesellschaft
Group
High culture
Institution
Institutionalization
Law
Mechanical solidarity
Mores
Norm
Oppositional culture
Organic solidarity
Patterned behaviour

Popular culture

Primary group

Role conflict

Sanctions

Scientism

Secondary group

Social change

Social control

Social Darwinism

Social role

Social stratification

Social structure

Socialization

Society

Status

Subculture

Symbol

Triad

Values

REVIEW QUESTIONS

1. What are the main characteristics of human social life? Discuss.
2. How useful is the concept of culture from a sociological point of view?
3. Two perspectives on the study of culture have evolved: culture as shared heritage and norms and culture as contested social product and expressive symbol. Compare and contrast these two perspectives.
4. How would you explain the difference between subculture and counterculture?
5. Distinguish between folkways, mores, and laws.
6. Point out the possible interconnections between culture and society.
7. What are the main elements underlying the concept of social structure? Briefly discuss any two of these elements and indicate their significance for the study of society.
8. How would you explain the difference between primary and secondary groups? Of what significance is the distinction between these two types of groups?
9. Outline the main issues involved in the study of social and cultural change. To what extent can human beings control or direct social and cultural change?

Social Psychology & Socialization

W. David Pierce, William A. Meloff, and W. Andrew Harrell

Social Psychology and Socialization

INTRODUCTION

Although many sociologists study groups, communities, and institutions, there are other researchers who are interested in the interplay between the individual and society. Social psychology is a *bridging discipline* between the study of the individual (psychology) and the study of society (sociology). At a basic level, social psychologists assume that people's actions, thoughts, and feelings are primarily the outcomes of interaction with others. To illustrate, *status* refers to a person's position in society. These positions are rewarded differently depending on cultural practices, and evaluated as better or worse by members of a society. (For example, in our society doctors are highly valued but street cleaners are not.) Based on these differences, people learn to value the performances of higher-status persons more than those of lower-status persons. In addition, people come to expect better performance from superiors and worse from subordinates.

These beliefs about competence — known as **performance expectations** — in turn determine our susceptibility to social influence in new situations. People often yield to the opinions of higher-status persons even if status has little relevance to the task at hand — so that, for example, the views of an engineer may sway a jury's decision. At the same time, they do not listen to the opinions of others with lower status, even if these people have the most effective solution to a problem; this may be the case when opinions of workers are disregarded by management. Studying the effect of status on social influence is one example of how social psychologists analyze individual actions in a social context (Berger et al., 1972; Webster and Driskell, 1978).

• THE SUBJECT MATTER OF SOCIAL PSYCHOLOGY

The subject matter of social psychology is social behaviour, the mutual and reciprocal relationship between the behaviour of one person and the behaviour of another (or others). The study of social behaviour concerns how the actions of an individual are regulated by the behaviour (and characteristics) of others and, in turn, how the behaviour of others is affected by what an individual does. Social psychologists also try to show how aspects of the social structure necessitate certain kinds of human interaction.

A university is an institution that structures the social interaction of faculty and students. One kind of interaction is a lecture — involving the behaviour of the professor and the class. Although the informal norms of university require that students pay attention to the lecture, there is great variability in behaviour. The attention of students may depend on the lecture style. The way a professor delivers a lecture (tone of voice, intonation, etc.) is one of the factors that contributes to listening and observing by the students. In turn, class attention may cause the professor to continue a line of reasoning, while inattention may lead to a change of topic or example. A social psychological account of this episode would point to the general conditions (or variables) that regulate the behaviour of a speaker and the factors that contribute to the reactions of an audience (context, facilitating and inhibiting factors, outcomes, etc.).

Social psychology deals with issues that are intrinsically interesting to most people. In everyday life, we often wonder how people form social relationships, why we change our opinions, what makes people (and nations) aggressive and violent, and how we come to see others (and ourselves) as having distinct emotions, attitudes, and thoughts. We often discuss the actions of our friends, relatives, and acquaintances. For example, Fred and Sally seem to have a stable, happy relationship, but one day they have a fight and Sally leaves. Was it something about Fred (or Sally) that led to the fight? Perhaps there were economic circumstances that contributed to the conflict. Why didn't Sally stay — was their marital relationship weak, unstable, or violent? Was it a question of adultery or child abuse, inequality of roles, strain, or personal achievement? Clearly, the topic of social behaviour and its causes is something we all care about.

SOCIAL PSYCHOLOGY: A SCIENTIFIC DISCIPLINE

Box 4.1

Social psychology is a field that systematically studies human social behaviour. But is social psychology a scientific discipline like physics, genetics, or biology? One answer comes from Kenneth Gergen (1973), who believes that social psychological statements hold only for a given historical period. Because of this and other limitations, social psychology cannot be a scientific field.

Gergen's views have not been adopted by most social psychologists, who agree with Barry Schlenker (1974) that there is no a priori reason to reject their claim to a scientific perspective. Most scientists assume that they study cause-and-effect relationships that may be discovered and verified by others. Social psychologists may also search for lawlike relationships and rely on objective verification. A social psychologist who shows that mere exposure to a person (just seeing her frequently) produces an increase in interpersonal attraction is also claiming a general cause-and-effect relationship. This result may be objectively verified when other researchers replicate the study and observe similar effects. In fact, the exposure–attraction relationship has been observed and replicated by many researchers at different times and places (e.g., Zajonc, 1968; Moreland and Zajonc, 1982; White and Shapiro, 1987).

• SOCIAL BEHAVIOUR

Social behaviour may be defined as the behaviour of two or more individuals with respect to one another or with respect to a common environment (Skinner, 1953: 297). Many social psychologists have referred to perception, feelings, motivation, and thought in their definitions of their subject matter. These psychological states and processes are usually inferred from behaviour and rely on the researcher's judgment. In order to improve on the subjectivity of this method, we have opted here for a behavioural definition that requires less inference on the part of the observer. If the responses (actions, performances) of two or more individuals are affected by each other's actions, then this is an instance of social behaviour or a **social episode**. An interaction between a speaker and a listener (or audience) is an example of the social episode called communication. According to this definition, social behaviour also occurs when two (or more) people act together (or against each other) to produce some common event, effect, or outcome. Cooperation and competition are specific instances of this kind of social episode.

The definition of social behaviour must apply to examples of human (and animal) behaviour that are commonly regarded as social. Thus, sexual behaviour is social because the partners respond "with respect to one another," and cooperation is social because two or more people must coordinate their responses to meet the requirements of "a common environment." On the other hand, brushing one's teeth to maintain a healthy mouth is a nonsocial response. Although other people may have contributed to this performance, the behaviour of two or more people is not required.

ANALYSIS OF SOCIAL BEHAVIOUR

The complexity of social behaviour makes it appropriate to ask analytical questions. How do evolution and biology contribute to social behaviour? What is the role of environmental experience in the regulation of social conduct? How do biological and environmental conditions combine to produce aggression, altruism, status and power relations, and other forms of social interaction? Is it possible to design a world where people cooperate and are seldom in conflict? Questions such as these imply a scientific strategy to evaluate the role of any particular environmental (or biological) factor.

Social Psychology and Socialization

• THE EXPERIMENTAL METHOD

Social psychologists use the empirical methods discussed in Chapter 2 to answer questions about social behaviour. That is, researchers rely on direct sensory experience that involves observation and measurement. In addition, many social psychologists have relied on the **experimental method** to answer their scientific questions. To show that signs of pain by a victim regulate the level of aggression by an attacker, it is necessary to show that a correlation exists. If the level of aggressive behaviour decreases as the level of perceived pain increases, we speak of a negative correlation. If the level of aggressive behaviour increases as the level of perceived pain increases, we have a positive correlation. Although victim pain and aggression may be correlated, this is not in itself sufficient evidence to claim that pain cues cause (or produce) a less severe or more severe attack. In order to claim causation, the scientist must show that the pain cues occurred before the reduction (or increase) in aggression (**temporal priority** of presumed cause) and that no other condition(s) could have produced the changes in aggressive behaviour (rule out extraneous factors, or **confounding factors**). Experimental and field studies assess the impact of a social stimulus (e.g., pain cues) while ruling out extraneous factors. By designing an appropriate experiment or field investigation, it is possible to show that pain cues preceded the reduction (or increase) in aggression, that pain cues and aggression correlate, and that no other condition caused the changes in level of aggression.

A study of social influence could examine customers interacting with a used-car seller. The behaviour of interest is buying a car; one factor affecting choice is the seller's "pitch." In order to study this interaction, the social psychologist may vary some aspect of the seller's appeal (independent variable) and measure the buyers' behaviour (dependent variable) in terms of the number of cars purchased, the amount of money spent, and so on. Results of the experiment may show that the amount spent on a car depends on the number of benefits to the buyer that the seller mentions during the deal. In this case, the social psychologist can state the relationship between expected benefits and dollars spent.

As the number of expected benefits increases, so does the amount of money that customers spend, but this does not continue endlessly. At some point, additional benefits no longer increase

Box 4.2 UNIT OF ANALYSIS

Although social psychologists often study how individuals respond to social events and stimuli (e.g., appeals by others), the unit of analysis is not always individual behaviour. Some researchers prefer to study social relationships rather than individual actions. Communication may be viewed as a social exchange rather than the behaviour of a speaker and a listener. In this case, the unit of analysis is the interpersonal relationship and an instance of exchange is called a transaction (Emerson, 1974a; 1974b). A transaction is defined by the behavioural responses of *both* participants. Person A asks a question and person B replies. This is one example of an exchange transaction. Social psychologists with a sociological focus are interested in the conditions (social and nonsocial) that regulate the frequency of such transactions over time. They are also interested in how exchanges in one social context or background (e.g., work relations) affect other areas of social exchange (e.g., marital interaction).

As you can see, social psychology has a distinct area of investigation. Social psychologists may study individual behaviour or properties of social relationships as their dependent measures. They attempt to relate these measures to specific aspects of the behaviour of others or to processes of social interaction. These social conditions (social stimuli, social events, etc.) are the independent variables for social psychological research. By studying how a particular social event relates to human action, it is possible to provide an account or interpretation of social behaviour. Such accounts are called theories of social psychology.

money spent. In everyday terms, the more one expects to get, the more one is willing to give — up to a point. Discovery of such a relationship would be important to our understanding of social influence and compliance. With this information, we could predict how much people will give for each additional unit of promised reward. At a practical level, advertisers, fundraising organizations, and religious groups could design more effective campaigns based on this social psychological relationship. An alternative approach would be to study the behaviour of the seller as our dependent variable and show how the buyer's actions (independent variable) affect what the seller says and does.

THEORIES OF SOCIAL PSYCHOLOGY

Chapter 1 outlined sociological theories that try to explain and understand aspects of society (e.g., the distribution of power). Social psychologists have also developed theoretical perspectives and explanatory theories to help organize their research on social behaviour. The theories of social psychology range from those that emphasize general principles of learning to those that stress the importance of human cognition and symbolic behaviour.

• SOCIAL LEARNING THEORY

The **social learning** approach to understanding social behaviour emphasizes three basic processes: classical conditioning, operant conditioning, and observational learning. Each of these learning processes has principles and laws that are used to account for the behaviour of organisms, including human social behaviour. It is not possible to detail these laws and principles in an introductory textbook, but in this chapter you will get a general idea of social learning interpretations.

    Classical conditioning was discovered by the great Russian physiologist Ivan Pavlov (1927), in his research with the salivary reflex in dogs. As shown in Figure 4.1, when food was placed in

Figure 4.1

CLASSICAL CONDITIONING

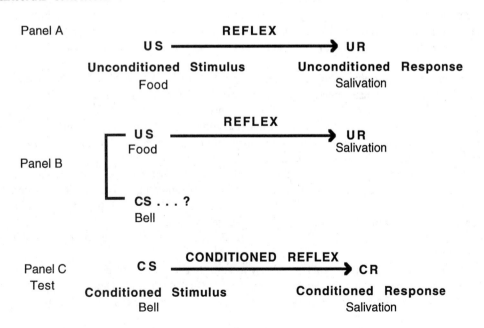

a dog's mouth, the dog salivated to this stimulus. The relationship between food in the mouth and salivation is an example of reflex. A **reflex** is composed of an *unconditioned stimulus* (US) and an *unconditioned response* (UR). Food in the mouth is a US that *elicits* salivation, the UR (i.e., US —> UR). Reflexes are based on the biology of an organism and are not learned. In humans, a knee jerk elicited by a tap on the patellar tendon and pupil constriction in the presence of light are familiar examples of reflexes.

Pavlov's major discovery is the conditioning of reflexes (panels B and C). If a bell sounds just before food is placed in a dog's mouth, then the dog eventually begins to salivate at the sound of the bell. The bell is called a *conditioned stimulus* (CS), and salivation to the bell is called the *conditioned response* (CR). Conditioning establishes a new relationship between an arbitrary event (bell) and the dog's behaviour (salivation) (i.e., CS —> CR). Pavlov's work shows that organisms can learn which features of the environment are associated with positive or negative events. This kind of learning makes biological sense. An animal that runs away when the grass rustles is more likely to survive and reproduce than one who waits to see the predator. Classical conditioning is one way that organisms (including humans) adapt to complex and changing environments.

The principles of classical conditioning have been used in social psychology to understand how people develop likes and dislikes toward others (Byrne, 1971). The idea is that positive and negative stimuli elicit emotional reactions (reflexes). These emotional responses may be conditioned by other objects, features, or events. For example, provision of food and removal of wet clothing are unconditioned stimuli that elicit positive emotional responses for an infant. When a parent supplies nourishment or removes wet diapers, the physical features and behaviour of the parent are associated with the infant's emotional responses. Eventually, the presence of a parent becomes a conditioned stimulus for the positive emotional reactions (CR) of the infant. Of course, parents not only provide "good things," they are also present when "bad things" happen. The current emotional reaction to any person is therefore based on the total conditioning history, involving both positive and negative conditioning episodes.

Although classical conditioning is an important determinant of human attitudes and emotions, most human behaviour is not regulated by associative conditioning. In common speech, we talk about our actions as voluntary, intentional, and purposive. This kind of behaviour is *emitted* in the sense that there is no specific stimulus that elicits the response. B.F. Skinner (1938) described a way to analyze purposive action. He noted that an organism operates upon the environment to produce effects, consequences, or outcomes. These consequences, in turn, change the organism so that the animal or human is more (or less) likely to do this behaviour in the future.

Operant conditioning involves the arrangement of consequences for behaviour. Behaviour designed to produce consequences is called *operant behaviour.* When consequences increase the rate of occurrence of an operant the procedure is **positive reinforcement** (Figure 4.2). Positive reinforcement is an important principle for understanding human behaviour. A parent's approval of a child's derogatory jokes about an ethnic or racial group may act as a positive reinforcement that increases the likelihood of this behaviour in similar circumstances.

Positive reinforcement may also account for the favourable remarks of a child toward ethnic and racial groups. In this case, parents (and others) may present approval and attention when the child makes positive comments. A child (or adult) who has a high probability of stating "liberal views" may be showing the effects of positive reinforcement. Whether a person becomes a bigot or a libertarian may depend on the **contingency of reinforcement** — the contrived or natural relationship between behaviour and its consequences.

Human behaviour is not regulated only by its consequences. A contingency of reinforcement also involves events or circumstances that precede operant behaviour. The preceding event, or *discriminative stimulus,* "sets the occasion for" behaviour that produces reinforcement. Stimulus

Figure 4.2

OPERANT CONDITIONING

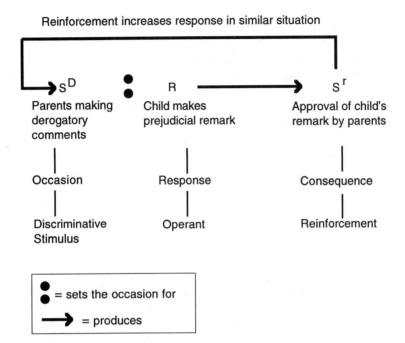

Reinforcement increases response in similar situation

S^D
Parents making
derogatory
comments

R
Child makes
prejudicial remark

S^r
Approval of child's
remark by parents

Occasion

Response

Consequence

Discriminative
Stimulus

Operant

Reinforcement

= sets the occasion for

⟶ = produces

discrimination occurs when behaviour is reinforced in one situation but not in another. A phone's ringing may be a stimulus to answer it by putting the receiver to your ear, which usually results in a conversation with another person. When the phone is not ringing, putting the phone to your ear is not reinforced. After a discrimination is made, the ring of a telephone (discriminative stimulus) may set the occasion for answering it (operant), although the ring does not force you to do so. Similarly, a nudge under the table may prompt a change in conversation, or even silence. Discriminative stimuli may be private or public events. A headache (discriminative stimulus) may result in taking a pill or calling a physician. A mild headache may be a discriminative stimulus for taking an aspirin while a more severe pain sets the occasion for telephoning a doctor.

In social psychology, the idea of group norms may be analyzed as complex discriminative stimuli (Scott, 1971). As Chapter 3 discusses, a *norm* is a rule of conduct that implies sanctions for inappropriate behaviour and rewards for socially acceptable action. It is well known that customary ways of behaving are communicated to new members of a group. Usually, the group members make statements that describe where, when, and how a person should act. These informal statements or rules guide and prompt individual behaviour. Group members monitor the correspondence between the stated rules and what a person does, reinforcing instances of conformity and punishing nonconformity. Generally, many group processes (e.g., conformity, leadership, obedience to authority) may be understood by principles of discrimination and other laws of operant conditioning.

Although operant conditioning is a fundamental mechanism of human learning, people often acquire new responses through observation and imitation (Bandura, 1977; 1986). **Observational learning** occurs when a child watches an adult perform a sequence of actions (the model), and later is able to reproduce the behavioural sequence. Similarly, an adult who wants to operate a computer may advance more quickly by watching a proficient model than by reading instructions or reinforcement by trial and error. Observational learning differs from operant conditioning in that the learner does not perform a response, and usually receives no reinforcement. Instead the learner watches another person's performance and observes the consequences of the modelled action.

A young boy may observe that his older brother showers, styles his hair, and selects appropriate clothes before going out with friends. He probably also notes that his brother receives positive comments from others on his appearance. Based on the observed social consequences, the young boy may anticipate that he will receive similar approval for acting like his brother (imitation). Depending on his language level, the boy may label or symbolically code his brother's behaviour and later recall the sequence of actions. Probably, he will also rehearse aspects of the performance (both publicly and privately). That is, he may try different hairstyles and experiment with clothing. Eventually, the boy acquires a skilled repertoire of "taking care of his appearance." As you can see, observational learning is an important part of human **socialization** (i.e., becoming an acceptable member of society).

The social learning approach suggests that people acquire, maintain, and change their behaviour based on conditioning and imitation. This theoretical view applies to many aspects of social behaviour. It provides a coherent and consistent account of human behaviour generally.

• SOCIAL EXCHANGE THEORY

Social exchange theory is also based on reinforcement principles (Homans, 1961; 1974; Kelley and Thibaut, 1978; Emerson, 1981). In this case, principles of reinforcement are used to analyze the stability and change of interaction between (or among) individuals. Exchange theory states that people choose among a variety of alternatives that provide some rewards and entail some costs. Rewards may involve money, goods, and services, as well as power, status, affection, and attention. Costs include loss of rewards, penalties, sanctions, and other adverse events. The theory assumes that individuals behave in such a way as to maximize rewards and minimize costs. According to this assumption, people select alternatives in terms of the outcomes or profit (rewards less costs) they have received in the recent past. That is, they will select the most profitable alternative more often than an option with moderate payoffs. Additionally, the option with moderate outcomes will be chosen more than the least-profitable alternative.

Exchange theory states that people will establish and maintain a stable social relationship only if they find it profitable. The value of any social relationship is in part due to its current profit relative to past payoffs. This is the *comparison level* — implying that each individual compares current outcomes from the relationship against previous levels. Value also depends on the profit of a specific relationship relative to other options. This is the *comparison level for alternatives* — comparing the profit from one alternative to that of another. To illustrate, in a marital relationship each partner provides sexual reinforcement to the other. Considering only this source of reinforcement, the comparison level is the current rate of sexual contact relative to the rate in the recent past. Using an example of traditional male–female roles, the comparison level for alternatives is the rate of sexual intercourse in the marriage relative to the rate of this reward in extramarital relationships. The husband is a sales representative who has frequent contact with female clients and representatives. His wife does not work outside the home and is the major caregiver for their two children. If the husband has one (or more) extramarital sexual partners available to him, the value of the marriage will be less to him than to his wife who, because of circumstances, may have no sexual alternatives. In this situation, where sexual intercourse is the only reinforcement, exchange theory requires that the husband be unfaithful (i.e., distributing sexual behaviour) and that his wife remain entirely faithful. His degree of infidelity depends on the value of the sexual reinforcement in the marriage compared with the value of the rewards supplied from extramarital sources.

This example also raises issues of **equity** — the perception that rewards received are proportional to costs incurred. Notice the inequity or injustice of this situation for the woman. Assuming equal costs, the analysis shows that the wife's sexual rewards (in terms of variety and frequency) are substantially less than her husband's. Under these conditions, exchange theory holds that people will become angry and attempt to rectify the injustice. To ensure greater fidelity and less inequity, society often arranges legal sanctions for extramarital choices, including loss of income, investments, and family. This procedure may rectify the injustice by having the husband incur greater costs, but it may not solve the problem of extramarital sex. Legal sanctions are often delayed as a result of the time it takes to detect infidelity and mobilize the legal system. Such delays weaken the effectiveness of the legal consequences and usually mean that the husband's sexual choices are regulated by the immediate distribution of sexual reinforcement.

• COGNITIVE THEORY

Cognitive theory is concerned with understanding the processes through which we notice, interpret, remember, and then use information about the social world (Baron and Byrne, 1991: 89). It assumes that all stimuli received by the brain — **perceptions** — are in some way modified to "fit" the predispositions, interests, and feelings of the individual. For cognitive theorists, social psychology has become a science of the "social mind" (Zajonc, 1985: 137) rather than the study of social behaviour. The implication is that stimuli, in and of themselves, make little sense. It is only when placed within a context of interpretation based on beliefs, attitudes, and values that we can decide whether a particular stimulus is relevant for us at any particular moment, and, if so, how to incorporate it into our current thoughts.

Let's take the example of a university student coming into a class on the first day of the term and looking around for friends. Where to sit: Next to a friend, or next to that good-looker in the fifth row? At the back, hoping not to be noticed by the professor, or at the front to demonstrate serious interest? Now the professor walks in. Does she look mean? Will she be helpful during the term? Is she a hard marker? How many term papers is she assigning? Exams? Once the class is over, a decision has to be made. Should the student stay in the class? Find a different section? A class in a different department? There is so much cognitive information to process, based on a very brief introduction. The student can fill in the unknowns with previously acquired information: the difficulty level of other courses in the department; what the rumour mill says about this professor; whether it is a required course; and so on. The ultimate decision — to stay or switch — is based on the best information available, past and present. Of course, one student's decision may be very different from that of someone else in the same class, who has processed the same information in a very different way. Each of us sees the world in a different way, based on our **cognitive sets** — organizations of grouped cognitions that are meaningful to the individual — and our behaviour will reflect those differences.

This does not mean that we do not share cognitions with others. We drive through a city (relatively) secure in the knowledge that (almost) every driver will stop for a red traffic light and proceed through the intersection on a green light. (Amber lights do seem to be somewhat more subject to individual interpretation — some stop, others "floor it" to get through, and a small minority sit in the middle of the intersection, trying to decide what to do.) Traffic lights are part of the complex symbolic system we share with others, including language, gestures, and signs. We can usually agree on the meanings of each symbol or set of symbols within a shared culture; we often disagree, however, on the value that the particular symbol has. Just about everyone in Canada, for example, understands the meaning of the phrase "Right to Life," but there is serious disagreement as to whether this phrase is positive or negative, good or bad, constructive or destructive. This value component — the emotional aspect of symbols — is strongly tied to our cognitive structures.

• ATTRIBUTION THEORY

Attribution theory looks at the processes we use to judge others. It assumes that each of us tries to make sense of our world by attributing others' behaviour to causal factors. Heider (1958), the originator of attribution theory, suggested that we attribute a person's behaviour to either internal or external causes. Internal causes are inherent to the individual: personality, natural abilities, and so on. The professor who says that a student's poor academic performance is due to a lack of ability in his subject area is making an *internal attribution*. If, however, the student's poor performance is explained by a lack of sleep or proper nutrition, that is an *external attribution*. Research indicates that observers are biased toward internal (dispositional) attributions rather than external attributions.

Kelley (1973) tells us that, in making attributions, individuals use information dealing with consistency, distinctiveness, and consensus. For example, if Kimberley responded in a rude manner to Gordon's suggestion that they go out for coffee, it would be relevant to reflect on the *consistency* of her behaviour (has she been rude to Gordon before?), *distinctiveness* (is she rude only to Gordon, or to others as well?), and *consensus* (have others been rude to Gordon?). If Gordon is treated rudely by others as well as by Kimberley, we are likely to attribute the problem to Gordon. From a different perspective, taking these three variables into consideration, we may attribute the incident to the situation or to the individual's disposition. Further, we may take into consideration only those things that occur early, or that are most important to us, in arriving at our attribution.

Our tendency to discount situational events in favour of dispositional factors has been called the **fundamental attribution error** (Ross, 1977). A large number of studies have shown this tendency when explaining other people's behaviour. Interestingly, when explaining our own behaviour, we are much more likely to use situational factors. Thus we may describe someone else as "a grouch" but talk about ourselves as being angry because of "pressures." Our legal system commonly examines the dichotomy between dispositional factors ("he is a naturally evil person") and situational factors ("he had to steal in order to feed his family").

Logically, this fundamental attribution error can be a major obstacle in trying to understand the "true" reasons for the behaviour of others. Our cognitive structures will determine how we relate to others on the basis of limited, initial information. Unfortunately, these structures may prevent us from ever developing a deeper knowledge and understanding of individuals initially rejected on the basis of incorrect attributions.

• ROLE THEORY

As a university student, you probably attend classes, study for and take examinations, party with other students, take advantage of some of the opportunities offered for organizational activities, and complain about the amount of work required by particular instructors. All of these elements constitute what role theorists would call the **social role** of student, a set of behaviours and expectations that distinguish this activity from others you do. The idea of role is drawn from the theatre, where an actor assumes a particular role for a performance but does not play it when she is offstage. The metaphor is faulty in the sense that an actor's role is not "real," whereas the roles that we play during the course of our lives are most assuredly real — both to us and to others who interact with us. In sociology, social role underscores the fact that we behave differently in different situations, responding to the formal and informal expectations and sanctions of others. These significant others also have roles to play in any given social context.

Before one assumes the role of university student preparation is needed. The candidate tries to find out as much as she can about university life, about the expectations for behaviour, and what she may expect to receive in return. The university provides a calendar describing in detail the formal aspects of university life, including course descriptions, the university's code of student conduct, and other matters. These are *role prescriptions* — the codified requirements that set out the role of student. Another set of informal behavioural norms (standards of conduct) will not be set out anywhere, but will be at least as important as the prescriptions. These are the *role expectations* established by our peers at the university. Such informal norms define our rights and obligations toward our friends and acquaintances, and are developed over time through interaction. For this reason, it is virtually impossible to determine the specific nature of role expectations until we actually become involved in university life.

Each of us plays a variety of different roles (student, son/daughter, employer) during our lifetime, and even in the course of a single day. Inevitably, some *role conflict* emerges. Do we attend Aunt Helen's birthday celebration or study for the final exam scheduled for tomorrow? There is a party Friday night that I really want to go to, but my boss wants me to work. Most role conflicts are manageable, but the requirements of one role may have a negative impact on another. The schoolteacher who insists that his children raise their hands before speaking at the dinner table may need to examine his ability to keep his roles of father and teacher separate.

Role theory tells us that social roles regulate not only what we do, but also what we say in terms of our beliefs and attitudes (Michener et al., 1986: 10). Researchers who know the prescriptions and expectations for a particular role should be able to predict an individual's actions and attitudes. However, although there is substantial evidence that much of our behaviour is governed by role prescriptions and expectations, predicting behaviour is difficult. It is not always possible for us to determine the specific expectations that influence an individual at any given time or how each individual will interpret these expectations.

• SYMBOLIC INTERACTION THEORY

One of the more controversial aspects of social psychology deals with the issue of the *self* — the notion that each of us has an image of who we are and how others relate to us. For the symbolic interactionist, the self is central to understanding and explaining human behaviour.

The symbolic interactionist's perspective is based on the work of C.H. Cooley and George Herbert Mead. Cooley (1902) suggested that we imagine how other people see us, and view ourselves from that perspective — the *looking-glass self.* The process involves (1) imagining how we appear to others; (2) imagining how others judge our appearance; and (3) responding to how we imagine others are judging our appearance. Using the concept of the looking-glass self, Cooley explained conformity to others as well as the negative and positive feelings that each of us carries about.

Mead (1932; 1934; 1938) extended Cooley's conceptualizations by discussing the composition of the self and introducing new concepts describing the impact of others on our actions. For Mead, the self consists of the "I" and the "me." The "me" is the objective part of the self, consisting of all of the roles that we fulfil in our daily lives. If asked, for example, to describe yourself, you might respond with words about the various roles you play. They are objective, easily understood, and reflect your "me." The "I," on the other hand, is the subjective part of the self — the *self-concept.* This part of the self embraces the evaluative feelings about the self that are internalized from our interaction with others as we fulfil our roles. When you describe yourself with phrases such as "nice person" or "anxious about my future" you are reflecting the "I" — the self-concept. From the symbolic interactionist perspective, the nature of the "I" will determine how you behave in various social situations. In fact, if your self-concept can be understood, it should be possible to predict the nature of your behaviour in each role or situation.

Figure 4.3 represents the circular development of the self-concept. Each of us, in fulfilling our roles, must behave in a social context. Within that context, others respond to our behaviour

Figure 4.3

MODEL OF SELF-CONCEPT

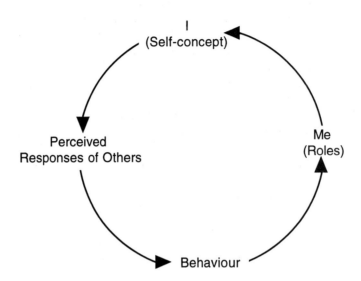

along a continuum ranging from very positive to very negative. As social beings, we have learned to respond to the reactions of others to our behaviour and to modify that behaviour when necessary in order to evoke positive rather than negative responses. It is important to point out here that the responses that we internalize are perceived responses, and may not reflect "reality" — the actual responses of others to us. As the view of self develops, our cognitive sets become established to the point that much of what we perceive is a self-fulfilling prophecy — we see what we want to see. Thus, the shy individual believes that others are actually mocking her, when in fact they may be making every effort to integrate her within the group. Most of us know the opposite kind of character — the one who believes that he can do no wrong, that he is the life of the party, in spite of the "real" reactions of others that are giving him all kinds of signals to back off and not be obnoxious.

Fortunately, most of us have a generally positive self-concept that allows us to perform credibly and accurately in terms of role expectations in most social situations. There are areas in which we believe we cannot succeed — many students shudder at the thought of having to take a statistics course, for example — but as reasonably well-socialized human beings we are able to couple our past experiences and knowledge about a situation with the current reactions of others in order to behave appropriately in most social circumstances.

To be acutely responsive to the reactions of everyone in our social environment at all times would result in a quantity of perceived expectations that would be impossible to satisfy. Instead, we select among all the "others" in our environment those whose reactions are important to us. These people become our *significant others*. For most of us our parents are our first significant others; we add siblings, other family members, peers, schoolteachers, work supervisors, and others as we progress through life. Some significant others are situation specific. Your professor, for better or worse, is a significant other for you while you are taking her course since she has the responsibility for assigning your grade. Her reactions to other aspects of your life, however, are probably of little concern to you. In contrast, your parents are significant others whose opinions about most aspects of your life are probably important, and whose imagined responses will serve to guide your behaviour even when they are not present to witness that behaviour. At the other extreme, the person who drove the bus that brought you to campus will probably not be a significant other at any level (unless he or she is particularly attractive and you would like to establish a relationship).

Often our behaviour is guided by a more generalized set of expectations, which Mead referred to as the *generalized other.* Your decision to wash your face and brush your hair before leaving the house in the morning, even on a Sunday and just to get a newspaper from the 7-Eleven, is probably not based on the expectation that a significant other will see you looking dishevelled, but rather on the fact that people are expected to look presentable when they go outdoors. We stop our car at a red light on a Sunday morning with absolutely no other vehicles in sight in any direction because we would feel guilty about going through. For symbolic interactionists, the generalized other is a kind of conscience that operates at the general levels of behaviour where society has established guidelines. Even at this level, however, the generalized other is not identical for everyone. Some women will shop for groceries with pink curlers in their hair, while others would rather have bamboo shoots inserted under their fingernails than appear in public that way.

For a cognitive theorist, a role theorist, or a symbolic interactionist, each of us is a reflective human being. These theorists assume that our previous learning is internalized, modified, and used along with our assessment of the current situation in deciding how to behave in any social situation. While the final outcome — behaviour — is still of paramount concern, the individual's thought processes and personality are used to explain the resulting social interactions.

SOCIALIZATION

• THE BASIC PROCESS

For the sociologist, "to socialize" means to teach the individual those things that he or she must know in order to live successfully in society. The process of socialization begins at the time the infant is able to respond to the external world; it ends at death. In large measure, however, the skills required for a status in society are learned during childhood — the period from birth to adolescence. The process of socialization is what gives each of us our *humanity* — our ability to lead productive lives within the society — and our *personality* — the unique aspect of oneself expressed in thoughts, feelings, and actions.

Symbolic interactionists emphasize socialization based on learning through role taking. George Herbert Mead believed that children went through *three stages of development* in the role-taking process: imitation, play, and games (Mead, 1954). In the first stage, characteristic of children up to about the age of 3, children do not engage in role taking as such, but instead mimic or imitate. In the second stage, at around 3 years of age, children begin taking the roles of others in their play. By using toys as representations of the real thing, children deal with babies or play "house," "GI Joe," or "Barbie." By the time children reach the games stage in their early school years, they are ready to participate in complex games that require not only an understanding of their own roles, but of the roles of others as well.

Socialization is accomplished through *social agents,* who include family members, peers, teachers, and the media. Each of these social agents has a profound role to play in determining who we are and who we will become. Social agents may express their influence through direct attempts to shape our values, beliefs, and behaviour. This occurs most commonly with parents and teachers, but in some families older siblings and relatives participate in the socialization process. A second type of influence that may have a profound effect on us is the indirect influence of other social agents in our personal lives and in the media. These others unintentionally influence what we do and say through a process called **modelling** (see the section on social learning, above). We observe their behaviour, storing away their actions and consequences for future reference. Social models include those people closest to us — parents, siblings, friends, teachers — but also may include people we have never met. Actors and public figures on television or on a movie screen are also sources of modelling; we listen to them on the radio or on disc, or read about them in books or magazines.

It is important not to confuse knowledge with behaviour. Even though we may have a tremendous repertoire of possible actions at our disposal, we emit only a small sampling of those behaviours during our lifetime. The actions we display are those that mesh with our definitions of self and the requirements set by others.

• THE MEDIA AS AGENT OF SOCIALIZATION

Most of us have seen Arnold Schwartzenegger deal with his opponents in the movies — snapping their necks and blowing them into small pieces with mortars and hand grenades. Although we may cheer Arnie on in the theatre, we are probably not going to emulate his behaviour the next time we get a little annoyed with the neighbour. There is a great deal of controversy in our society surrounding the issue of violence, particularly with regard to television but also focusing on pop music and movies. Many claim that constant exposure to violence through the media will produce not only incidental modelling, but the violent behaviour that ensues from the expression of that modelling. There have, in fact, been some documented cases of real violence where the perpetrator has admitted to getting the idea from some television program. On the other hand, most of us who grew up with the Roadrunner and Wile E. Coyote, Bugs and Elmer, Chuck Norris, Bruce Lee, Arnie, and even Freddy would probably say that we enjoyed the shows for their escapism, humour, and the way they stretch credibility rather than as some behavioural prescription. Recently the chairperson of the Canadian Radio-television and Telecommunications Commission (CRTC) expressed the opinion that there was too much violence on television in Canada, and that government may be required to step in to reduce it. In the United States, the research of George Gerbner (1986) and others has pointed to a "mean world syndrome" among those who watch a lot of television — the feeling that the world, and their society in particular, is a much more dangerous place than is actually the case. Gerbner's work focuses on the cumulative effects of a medium (television) that provides a distorted picture of society in (among other things) its representation of women and minorities, the relative number and lifestyles of people over 65, and the proportion and functions of various occupational groups in society. There is no question that the media, and particularly television, constitute an important *agent of socialization* in our society today, but much research remains to be done in exploring the precise relationships between programs watched and the individual's beliefs, values, and attitudes.

STUDIES OF SOCIALIZATION AND BEHAVIOUR

• PORNOGRAPHY AND VIOLENCE

A topic of current intense interest is the effect of pornography on behaviour. Some feminists have argued that pornography falls into the category of "hate literature" and should be banned in Canada as an illegal form of expression (Alcock et al., 1991). It has been claimed that pornography increases men's callousness toward the plight of women, especially concerning their victimization by rape (Malamuth, 1984), and that pornography causes men to be more violent and coercive toward women. Since much of the pornography can be found in films and videotapes, this topic allows us to explore how social psychologists go about investigating this facet of mass-media socialization.

A very elaborate and carefully designed experimental study was carried out by Linz et al. in 1988 to evaluate the impact of media exposure, especially exposure to pornography, on a person's *sympathy for a rape victim*. At the beginning of their study, the authors offered two general hypotheses: First, they predicted a link between film portrayals of sexual violence and attitudes; specifically, that *prolonged exposure to sexual violence* would cause the viewer to feel less sympathy and empathy for a real victim of sexual assault. Second, prolonged exposure to nonviolent but degrading pornography should cause the viewer to see women as sex objects, to be less supportive of sexual equality, and to be less condemning of a rapist.

The participants were 156 university-age men who were paid for completing the experiment. At the recruitment stage, subjects were told they would take part in a film evaluation study through the Communication Arts Department. Upon coming to the lab, they were shown short excerpts from the films. This preview informed them of the subject matter. Those who were offended could leave at this point. Two left. (This preview ensured that the ethical requirement of **informed consent** was met. That is, the subjects were shown the type of experimental stimuli they were about to receive in greater doses. So informed, they could decide to leave or continue with the study.) Subjects then viewed either two or five films, one every other day. They viewed one of three kinds of films: (1) R-rated violent films (e.g., *Texas Chainsaw Massacre*); (2) R-rated nonviolent teenage sex films (e.g., *Porky's*); (3) X-rated films (e.g., *Debbie Does Dallas*). After viewing their films, subjects were phoned and asked to come to the Law School to watch a documentary. The documentary was a condensed re-enactment of a rape trial. In one version of the documentary, the victim was raped at a fraternity party by an acquaintance who belonged to the fraternity. In the other version, the victim and rapist were strangers to one another.

The *dependent variables* in this study were based on the subjects' responses to a questionnaire given to them before the rape-trial tape and to a second questionnaire given after viewing the tape. The dependent variables were numerous and are listed in Table 4.1. The reason that there are so many dependent variables is to ensure adequate coverage of the concepts being examined. Another practical reason is to have backup measures in case some of the measures are less sensitive to the experimental manipulations.

Before we get to the results, let's look carefully at the experimental or *independent variables*. These are the things that were manipulated by the researchers. First, every subject was exposed to

Table 4.1

DEPENDENT VARIABLES IN LINZ ET AL. (1988)

Pretrial Questionnaire Variables

> Rape Empathy Scale
> Rape Myth Acceptance Scale
> Belief in Conservative Sex Roles
> Force in Sexual Relations
> Women as Sex Objects

Post-trial Questionnaire Variables

> Victim sympathy
> Victim injury
> Victim resistance
> Offender responsibility
> Victim responsibility
> Offender guilt
> Verdict
> Sentence

either two or five films. This is how the dosage or amount of exposure was manipulated. Second, each subject was exposed to only one of the three film types. Third, each subject viewed either the trial tape in which the rapist and victim were acquaintances or the one in which they were strangers. Note that subjects were exposed to a combination of manipulations. For example, some subjects saw the R-rated violent film five times and saw the "acquainted" version of the trial. Others saw the R-rated violent film only twice and the "nonacquainted" version. There were numerous combinations of film types, dosage, and trial tapes. These combinations of manipulated variables allowed the authors to test for **interaction effects**. These are the effects of combinations of variables. For example, we might expect that attitudes would be more profoundly changed if a subject had a greater dosage of the R-rated violent film, whereas the impact of the X-rated film might actually diminish at higher dosages (possibly from boredom).

Of the manipulated variables, only the type of film made a difference. This variable was significant for two of the dependent measures: victim sympathy and rape empathy. Subjects viewing the R-rated violent films were less sympathetic and empathetic toward the victim. This effect was somewhat higher for those receiving higher doses of exposure. Viewing the X-rated or R-rated nonviolent films had no measurable effect on judgments and attitudes. Thus, viewing pornography without violence had no negative impact on the responses of male subjects. Interestingly, the men's score on the Rape Myth Acceptance scale — a scale measuring the conventionality of one's beliefs concerning rape — was a strong predictor of their judgments and attitudes. Since this scale represents beliefs formed during a lifetime of socialization and is not easily susceptible to short-term experimental manipulation, it is clear that fairly recent exposure to mass media — even violent or "pornographic" media — has less impact than prior socialization.

• OBEDIENCE TO AUTHORITY

A classic study in socialization is Stanley Milgram's (1963) study of obedience. **Obedience** is defined as whether or not a person complies with someone else's order. If you are in a restaurant and a person dressed like a fireman bursts through the front door carrying an axe and dragging a hose and asks you to leave because there is a fire in the kitchen, you will probably put down your fork and leave. You have "obeyed." You may not have wanted to leave your delicious meal, which surely will be too cold (or too crisped) when you return. You may not have been convinced there was a fire, since you saw no smoke. Nevertheless, the fireman looked as if he was in charge and knew what he was doing, so you went along with his order. Acts of harmless or beneficial compliance take place every day. Milgram, however, was interested in more *antisocial forms of obedience* — e.g., soldiers blindly following the orders of their superiors to massacre civilians during wartime.

Milgram's experiment to test the extent to which we obey antisocial directives was, on the face of it, very straightforward. A naive subject was engaged by the experimenter, an authoritative-looking male in a white lab coat, to be a "teacher" and help a "learner" with a memory task. The learner, a middle-aged male (actually a confederate of the experimenter) was taken into an adjacent room and hooked up to the electrodes of a device that provided electric shocks. The learner's job was to listen to a series of word pairs and try to memorize which two words belonged together, or were "associated." On a series of trials, the learner was given one word from a pair and then had to guess which of four multiple-choice possibilities was the correct association. If a wrong answer was given, the teacher-subject was to motivate the learner by punishing the learner with a shock. Shocks were delivered from a shock generator with thirty voltage levels, ranging from 15 to 450 volts, in 15-volt increments. Verbal designations ranging from "slight shock" to "Danger: severe shock" and then "XXX" for the 450-volt switch were also given. The teacher-subject had a series of switches he could throw to give the next higher shock.

Box 4.3

Ethics and Milgram's Research

Milgram has been criticized for the strong and potentially traumatic experimental manipulations that he imposed on his subjects. For example, a subject may go away from his experiment thinking that he's no better than a Nazi for having mindlessly obeyed and hurt someone else. Milgram has responded to these criticisms (1974) by pointing out that in the debriefing following the experiment subjects were told that they really had not injured anyone and that the deception was necessary for the realism of the experiment and the effectiveness of the manipulations of the experimental variables.

Indeed, most experiments are much milder in their impact than Milgram's. Where deception has been used or where a subject has temporarily been exposed to stressful experimental stimuli, there has been no evidence for long-term deleterious impact on the subject (Alcock et al., 1991: 60). While the "costs" of an experiment may include the dishonesty of deceiving a subject or of creating a mild and temporary state of anxiety, anger, or lowered self-esteem, the payoff is an increased understanding of human behaviour. It is hard to deny that the greater understanding of the dynamics of authority and obedience provided by Milgram has better enabled us to deal with these often very destructive real-life phenomena.

If one shock (e.g., 15 volts) had been given, the subject had to go one level higher (in this case, to 30 volts). To add authenticity, the teacher-subject was given a 45-volt shock as a sample.

As you might have expected, the learner-confederate was not very bright and began giving wrong answers. Consequently, the teacher-subject was placed in the position of having to give increasingly higher and more dangerous shocks. In fact, the learner-confederate was never connected to the shock generator and did not actually receive any shocks. Not a word or sound was heard from the learner-confederate until the 300-volt shock was given; then there was a pounding on the wall. Another pounding occurred at 315 volts. From 330 volts onward, no sound was heard from the learner-confederate and no further answers were forthcoming. When presented with this nonresponsiveness, the teacher-subject was instructed by the experimenter to assume that a lack of response was a wrong answer and to shock accordingly.

The *dependent variable* in this study was whether or not the subject refused to issue the ever-increasing shocks. Behaviour prior to this point of refusal was considered to be obedience. At some point in the experiment, nearly all subjects balked at going on. Milgram's experimenter was pre-programmed to issue four kinds of "prods." The first was "Please continue"; the second, "The experiment requires that you continue"; the third, "It is essential that you continue"; and the fourth, "You have no other choice, you must go on." The experimenter was told to go through these various prods until one of them was successful in evoking obedience, or until no compliance was forthcoming after the fourth was given. In addition, a "special" prod was given if the subject asked if the learner was liable to suffer permanent physical injury: "Although the shocks may be painful, there is no permanent tissue damage, so please go on."

What were the findings? Table 4.2 shows that twenty-six of the forty subjects gave the maximum "XXX" voltage. The minority who stopped were clustered at 300 to 330 volts. Thus, most subjects "complied," suggesting that people will obey antisocial directives. It is less clear from this experiment, however, *why* they obeyed. One factor may have been the authority represented by the lab-coated experimenter and scientific setting at prestigious Yale University. Milgram ran the same experiment again in a run-down office building without any connection to Yale University. Perhaps surprisingly, the level of obedience was only slightly less in the office setting than at Yale. The location did not have a powerful impact on obedience.

Milgram (1974) summarized a number of factors that influence the degree of obedience in the experimental situation, including group pressure and proximity of the authority figure. One of the most important inhibiting conditions is the *immediacy of the victim*. As the victim became more immediate to the subject, the degree of obedience to the experimenter's orders declined sharply.

Table 4.2

Distribution of Breakoff Points

Verbal Designation and Voltage Indication	Number of Subjects for Whom This Was Maximum Shock
Slight Shock	
15	0
30	0
45	0
60	0
Moderate Shock	
75	0
90	0
105	0
120	0
Strong Shock	
135	0
150	0
165	0
180	0
Very Strong Shock	
195	0
210	0
225	0
240	0
Intense Shock	
255	0
270	0
285	0
300	5
Extreme Intensity Shock	
315	4
330	2
345	1
360	1
Danger: Severe Shock	
375	1
390	0
405	0
420	0
XXX	
435	0
450	26

Source: Milgram (1963).

Immediacy of the victim was varied by providing or withholding auditory, visual, and tactile cues of the learner-confederate. In a "no-feedback" condition, the teacher-subject could not see the learner while giving the shocks, did not hear the victim pounding on the wall, and was not exposed to protests by the learner to be let out of the experiment. In the absence of audible sounds and protests, 100 percent of the subjects followed the experimenter's orders fully, giving the maximum level of shock (450 volts).

When the victim pounded on the wall at the 300-volt level ("victim pounds" condition), obedience dropped, so that now 65 percent gave the maximum shock. An "audible protest" condition, in which the victim demanded to be let out of the experiment beginning at the 150-volt level, resulted in only a slight reduction in obedience; 63 percent of the subjects followed the orders fully.

Two other conditions are also interesting. In the "visible victim" treatment, the victim was present in the same room as the subject and began to protest at the 150-volt level. In this condition, the victim gave visual as well as auditory cues. When this happened, obedience dropped again and only 40 percent of the subjects administered the 450-volt shock. Finally, in the "victim touch" condition, the teacher or subject was required to hold the learner's hand on a shock plate and give the shock even though the victim protested. Thus, tactile cues were added to the visual and auditory stimuli presented by the victim. When this happened, only 30 percent of the subjects followed the experimenter's orders fully.

The overall results show that the degree of obedience declines as the immediacy of the victim increases. Social psychological theories of the sort discussed in this chapter may be used to account for such a finding. One way to understand this effect is in terms of response-conflict and social learning. The experimenter's orders lead the subject to increase the level of shock, while the protests of the victim work to decrease it. As more auditory, visual, and tactile cues of the victim are added, the tendency to stop comes to outweigh the tendency to continue. Both of these response tendencies are presumably based on previous moral learning of the experimental subjects.

It is also likely that attribution processes play some role in the immediacy-of-victim effect. When the victim does not protest, the subject may infer that the shocks are not painful and the learner is not suffering. As the protests mount, the subject is likely to reason that the victim is experiencing more and more pain from the shock. Based on this attribution, one obvious solution is to remove the source of the victim's discomfort by refusing to follow the experimenter's orders.

SUMMARY

- Social psychology is a bridging discipline between psychology and sociology.
- The social psychologist views the individual as behaving in a social context.
- Social psychologists may study the behaviour of individuals or aspects of social relationships (e.g., exchange).
- The experimental method is used to establish cause-and-effect relationships between social stimuli or events and individual behaviour.
- Theories of social psychology are either behavioural or cognitive. Behavioural theories (e.g., social learning, social exchange) emphasize the consequences or payoffs of behaviour and social interaction. Cognitive theories (e.g., attribution, symbolic interaction) emphasize thought processes of causal reasoning, language, and conception of self.
- An important problem of sociology is the socialization of people into society. Socialization involves teaching the individual the rules and roles of acceptable conduct in a society. The mass media play an important part in this process through social modelling.
- A recent experiment studying the socialization of violence against women suggests that violent pornography increases men's callous attitudes toward women. However, the effects of violent

pornography are not greater than the effects of exposure to violence alone. Men's attitudes toward women based on years of socialization are the best predictors of their views in a specific circumstance (e.g., empathy in a rape trial).

- The socialization of obedience to authority may result in blind obedience. In Milgram's experiment ordinary Americans were ordered to deliver painful electric shocks to a middle-aged man against his will. The majority of subjects followed the experimenter's orders fully — delivering extremely dangerous levels of shock to the victim. In a series of experiments, Milgram showed that the immediacy of the victim was a critical variable determining the subject's performance. Both social learning and attribution theories may be used to understand the relationship between immediacy of victim and level of obedience.

KEY CONCEPTS

Attribution theory
Classical conditioning
Cognitive set
Cognitive theory
Confounding factor
Contingency of reinforcement
Equity
Exchange transaction
Experimental method
Fundamental attribution error
Informed consent
Interaction effect
Modelling
Obedience
Observational learning
Operant conditioning
Perceptions
Performance expectations
Positive reinforcement
Reflex
Role theory
Social behaviour
Social context
Social episode
Social exchange theory
Social learning theory
Social role

Socialization
Symbolic interaction theory
Temporal priority
Unit of analysis

Review Questions

1. Show that social psychology is a bridging discipline between psychology and sociology.
2. What is the subject matter of social psychology? Give an example.
3. Discuss the importance of the experimental method in the analysis of social behaviour.
4. Outline the social learning approach. Refer to classical conditioning, operant conditioning, and observational learning.
5. Discuss social exchange using the concepts of comparison level, comparison level for alternatives, and equity. Give an example.
6. What is the cognitive perspective? Discuss the basic processes involved in attribution.
7. How does the concept of social role aid in the analysis of social interaction? Give an example.
8. Discuss symbolic interaction and the importance of the self and self-concept in social situations.
9. What is the process of socialization and how do the mass media play an important part in this process?
10. Discuss two experiments on socialization and point to the independent and dependent variables. How do these experiments help answer the researchers' questions? Outline the ethical problems raised by social psychological experiments.

Social Stratification

Kez O. Ugbor

Social Stratification

INTRODUCTION

This chapter is designed to draw attention to key issues and debates of social stratification and the competing ways of doing sociology. Students are encouraged to develop a "sociological imagination." We look first at social stratification, including major concepts, theories, and principles. Rationales for studying social inequality, ideal types of social strata, and mobility within the class system are also examined. Then we focus on stratification and poverty in Canada, drawing attention to the concentration of wealth and power. This chapter ends by reviewing the consequences of class inequality and the role of the political structure in promoting inequality and stratification.

SOCIAL DIFFERENTIATION

We are born into different families and cultural communities as males or females with a range of physical and psychological differences added to our basic similarities. We attain different occupations, live in different locations or circumstances, and pursue a wide variety of educational or leisure activities. Our life progresses from infancy and childhood through adolescence and youth, and on to mature adulthood and old age. These successive stages, no less than all the other differences we have enumerated, entail different socialization influences and role expectations. Thus, social life comes in all shades and colours. The sociological term for such great diversity of positions and functions in human social organization is **social differentiation**.

The idea of social organization suggests the existence of some structure or pattern in both the diverse positions people occupy and the various roles they play. A historical process of increasing complexity in technology, economic organization (i.e., subsistence or production strategies), and the generation of surplus material goods leads to the patterning of social differentiation along lines of inequality in power and privilege. Hunting and gathering societies have no sense of inequality beyond minor individual differences based on personal skills, wisdom, charm, or agility. Division of labour or technology is at an elementary level in tribal societies based on subsistence economies; it does not yet produce surplus wealth to pass on to one's offspring. **Surplus value** (i.e., the value of goods and services in excess of the cost of production or subsistence needs) becomes feasible with greater technological complexity, economic productivity, and the specialization of functions. Greater surplus value was accumulated in the transition from pastoral (herding) and horticultural (gardening) societies to agricultural and industrial (manufacturing) societies (Lenski, 1966).

SOCIAL STRATIFICATION

Stratification emerged out of differentiation. In this process, personal and modest distinctions of rank became attached to social positions involving differential access to social rewards and opportunities (Mayer and Buckley, 1970). In other words, social differences translate to social stratification when they become the basis for assigning people to hierarchical status involving inequalities in power, wealth, and prestige. Social stratification is a pattern of differences (in occupation, gender, age, ethnicity, personal honour, influence, etc.) and inequalities that are closely linked with the institutional arrangements in a given society (Kelsall et al., 1984). By **social stratification,** then, we mean the process by which entire categories of people are layered or ranked into a social hierarchy involving inequalities of various sorts. Social stratification ultimately comes down to "socially structured [i.e., relatively stable and enduring] inequalities and deprivations of various sorts, and from various sources, and *the relationships between them*" (Salaman, 1972: 23). Groups of people occupying positions of similar rank constitute the various social layers or strata. Strata usually pass on the benefits or burdens of their ranks to their offspring through the process of social inheritance (Mayer and Buckley, 1970).

• RATIONALES FOR STUDYING STRATIFICATION

Social life is interwoven with the benefits and burdens of our location in a social hierarchy. However, stratification is not simply a matter of the spread or distribution of attributes such as education, income, or occupation among individuals and groups (i.e., a distributive issue). Perhaps more importantly, it involves social relationships of various kinds (e.g., employer–worker, leader–follower, rich–poor, husband–wife, majority–minority, adult–child), and thus refers to the experiences, opportunities, and constraints to which people are liable (i.e., a relational or structural issue).

Some people occupy the niche of small-town indigent or big-city homeless; others live for generations in ramshackle apartments located in drab neighbourhoods. Some people are accustomed to rickety townhouses, while others live their entire lives in cosy family homes overlooking lush vegetation and radiant lakes. Of those who are accustomed to air travel, there is still the distinction between business-class travellers and coach passengers. It is said to be harder to climb the corporate ladder on high heels (i.e., if you are female) because your *social network* — the direct and indirect webs of relationships linking individuals and/or groups — makes a difference in career opportunities. We can go on and on.

• Life Chances and Lifestyles

Sociologists are interested in the fact that members of the various layers or strata have common **life chances** (probabilities of sharing in the material and cultural goods of a society) and **lifestyles** (preferences in club membership, marriage, consumption, works of art, leisure, etc.). Members of a stratum may even display some collective awareness of themselves. Indeed, our location in the stratification system tends to be consistently and remarkably related to virtually every other aspect of our lives: among others, family size, chances of divorce, life expectancy, health and illness, voting behaviour, IQ test scores, educational attainment, occupational attainment, religious attendance and beliefs, as well as chances of being arrested or imprisoned. Scary stuff, you might say.

• Determinism and Social Actors

People are not simply pawns in the hands of awesome structures or social forces. Far from it. The sociologist's interest in social change obliges him or her to guard against the pessimism that might result from such "sociological determinism." Nevertheless, stratification is primarily a *social* phenomenon in the most profound sense of the word. To adequately and meaningfully explain stratification requires going beyond innate biological or psychological characteristics of individuals and groups. The focus instead is upon people's *social being:* their relationship to the organization and control of economic production, their location in authority and power arrangements, as well as their experience and consciousness of the entire gamut of social and cultural conventions in society (see Abrahamson et al., 1976; Mayer and Buckley, 1970). Thus, while social actors do exercise some options, it is important to realize that they do so in a social and cultural environment that not only constrains the range of choices, but influences the probability of making one choice rather than another.

• Social Change, Order, Politics, and Morality

This brings us to a related sociological interest in the role of stratification in social change, social order, politics, and morality. For our purposes, *revolutionary (or conflict) theories of change* presuppose stratification. These theories assign causal importance to class conflict (between employers and workers), and also to general social conflict or political struggle between men and women, different ethnic or racial groups, politicians and citizens, different age groupings, as well as different regions and countries in the world. The Cold War between the American-led Western alliance and the Soviet-bloc countries was not so much an economic battle between capitalism and socialism as a political and moral conflict over the legitimate sorts and sources of stratification in competing models of the "good society." The *critical approach to social order* emphasizes the role of power and domination as those in the commanding heights of the social hierarchy seek to maintain their privileges through a combination of coercion and ideological control (see Chapter 1).

The politics of stratification also lie in the fact that those in power — economic, political, and/or cultural — use whatever means they can to perpetuate and legitimize the status quo. The moral question here is the possibility that those who are socially deprived to begin with might be further abused by virtue of their limited ability to control and change their circumstances. Although human agents have some **power** (defined as the capacity of A to get B to do something B would not otherwise do) to change aspects of their everyday life, it usually takes something much more drastic and thorough to transform existing structures of **domination** — patterned, recurring, legitimized, or institutionalized relations of power and control. To the extent that stratification makes domination possible, the moral status of socially structured inequality (i.e., its desirability and inevitability) is at issue here. The folk wisdom, "You can't fight City Hall," is both a lesson and a challenge. It may be theoretically and empirically correct today, but is it thereby politically and morally settled? It depends on how you look at it.

MAJOR FORMS OF STRATIFICATION

Empirical evidence reveals many varied forms of stratification from one society to another over time, or, for that matter, within the same society in a given period. For ease of study and description, however, sociologists have identified a few general ideal (pure or abstract) types of stratification systems.

• CLOSED AND OPEN SYSTEMS

As shown in Table 5.1, there are four principal types of stratification systems. First, there is the *slave system* of ancient Greece and Rome, as well as the pre-abolition Americas. Slaves, unlike free men and women, had no legal rights, were condemned to forced labour, and were for all practical purposes the chattels of their masters. Second is the orthodox Hindu *caste system*, perhaps together with the caste-like black/white division, especially in the southern United States in the post-abolition era. The *estate system,* which was born out of feudal relationships in medieval Europe, is the third. These three stratification systems comprise what Kelsall et al. (1984: 3) refer to as examples of "avowed and deliberate inequality between specified groups of people." Societies so affected are relatively **closed** in the sense that the boundaries between strata are rigid and clear-cut, with little or no provision for status change. The caste system is the extreme contemporary form.

At the other end of the scale is the *class system* of stratification. Although it is said to be **open** in the sense that the boundaries are not sharply demarcated and people can move up or down the

Table 5.1

STRATIFICATION SYSTEMS, RELEVANT STRATA, AND DEGREES OF OPENNESS

Stratification System	Relevant Strata	Degree of Openness
1. Slave Relationships	Slaveowners Freepersons Slaves	Closed but partially open
2. Caste System	Pure castes — upper stratum — middle stratum — lower stratum Impure caste Outcastes	Relatively closed
3. Estate System	Nobility (lords temporal) Clergy (lords spiritual) Commoners (peasants, serfs)	Closed but partially open
4. Class System	Upper class (bourgeoisie) Middle classes (petite bourgeoisie) Working class (proletariat) Underclass (lumpenproletariat)	Relatively open

stratification hierarchy through personal talent and effort, the class system has been described as a case of avowed equality yet widespread inequality (Kelsall et al., 1984). The "classless" society of the former Soviet Union did not abolish class inequality, but reconstituted stratification along party-state bureaucratic lines (see Miliband, 1987; Weeks, 1972).

• CASTE SYSTEM

• Caste Principle

Perhaps the best way to understand the orthodox Hindu caste system is to draw attention to the ubiquity of the *caste principle*. The Hindu caste system began as a form of colour discrimination reinforced by conquest (Morrish, 1978). There are many societies in which status is assigned strictly in terms of birth; endogamous (within-group) marriage is enforced formally and/or informally; social contacts between groups are very limited; and certain social positions are restricted to the "right-born." In other words, "whenever status is predetermined by birth, whenever one's colour or ethnic origin or religion or 'name' automatically assigns one special prestige or privilege, or special social handicaps, the *principle* of caste is at work" (MacIver and Page, 1957: 358). The racial division in South Africa under apartheid is an excellent example of the caste principle.

• Pure Castes

The origins of the orthodox Hindu caste system have been traced to the conquest, around 1500 B.C., of the Indian subcontinent by Indo-European tribes who called themselves Aryans. The Aryans were a light-skinned people who prided themselves on their nobility and racial purity. The native Dravidian tribes they met, colonized, and virtually enslaved were for the most part darker in complexion. Through the practical necessities of legitimizing conquest, as well as managing intermixture and settlement, the caste system was eventually entrenched, with the Aryan priestly caste, or *Brahmins,* as the dominant social force. According to the holy books of Hinduism, the *Vedas,* this priestly teacher caste was responsible for upholding the social order under divine guidance. Two other historical castes were formed from the Aryans in this colour-, religion-, and occupation-linked mechanism of control and containment. In descending order, the *Kshatriyas* (the aristocratic warrior caste) saw to the political protection of the social order and the sacred lore, while the *Vaishyas* were the peasant farmers, craftsmen, and merchants. These three castes, which were native to Aryan society, were deemed to be ritually pure, and had the right to wear the sacred thread that symbolized spiritual rebirth.

• Impure Caste, Outcastes

It became the lot of the conquered non-Aryans to form the lowest caste, the *Shudras,* who provided manual and menial services for the three higher castes. They did not enjoy the status or prerogatives of ritual purity. Outside and below the hierarchical caste system was a group (comprising all the tribes excluded from the Hindu spiritual community) variously referred to as untouchables or pariahs; outcastes; or, thanks to the political baptism conferred on them by Mahatma Gandhi, *Harijans,* meaning children of God. Their chief occupation has been that of begging and scavenging, with the proviso that they do not, either by touching or by mere physical presence, "pollute" their benefactors, who would then have to ritually cleanse or wash themselves (for details, see Morrish, 1978; Mayer and Buckley, 1970).

• Ascribed Status, Karma, and Exploitation

The ideal typical caste system is a closed or rigid form of social stratification, with the strata arranged in a fixed order of superiority and inferiority. Caste membership is determined by birth; social position, with its accompanying life chances, is acquired from the parents and cannot be changed through personal effort or achievement. In this sense caste membership is said to be an **ascribed status**. According to Hindu mythology, it is only by living a perfect life in one's present caste condition that one can gradually pay off one's *karmic debt,* enjoy a progressive transmigration of soul to the higher caste(s), or else win the ultimate goal of personal salvation and freedom from the necessity of having to return to pay one's debt.

The present caste system is less a matter of ritual purity and occupational prerogatives than a question of power, domination, and exploitation. It is not an accident that the untouchables or Harijans (about 10 percent of the Indian population) generally live in abject poverty and illiteracy — what Gandhi called "India's sin and shame" — in contemporary Indian society. Although there have been recent attempts to attenuate the deep injuries and deprivations of caste in India by political means (e.g., antidiscrimination and affirmative action enactments in education and employment), the system continues. However, the imperatives of industrialization, urbanization, and bureaucratization have begun to change the caste system in tiny but hopeful ways. It is becoming difficult for higher caste members to avoid physical contacts at work or in public transportation. In fact, women can sometimes raise the caste membership of their offspring by marrying into a higher caste. The bad news is that tradition "dies hard," and so does the symbolic substance of caste in most of India.

• ESTATE SYSTEM

An estate system is a hierarchy of land-based social strata somewhat rigidly demarcated by law and custom. Thus, estates are socially and legally distinct status groups based on *hereditary relationships to landholdings*. An example of an estate system is medieval feudal society, where social life was woven around land held on condition of military service and various other obligations. Feudal relationships emerged in the West European countryside as the major form of social organization in a period so marked by disorder and weak central authority that people sought protection in the hands of powerful warriors on horseback. The region had experienced the collapse of the Roman Empire, the Germanic invasions, and the challenge of Islam. Commerce and transportation were interrupted, merchants virtually disappeared, and towns and cities naturally declined. In their stead emerged a stratification system based on inherited property.

• The Nobility, Clergy, and Commons

The estate system divided society into three distinct hereditary strata or estates: the nobility or lords temporal, the clergy or lords spiritual, and the peasants and some craftspeople, merchants, and professionals, who constituted the commons. Each of these segments of society was separated by custom and lifestyle, together with formally defined legal rights, obligations, and privileges. The *nobility* was a hereditary military aristocracy that took charge of defence and judicial affairs. The learned *clergy* not only ministered to the spiritual needs of the people, but performed important administrative functions. It was the lot of the *peasants* to labour for the upkeep of the nobility and the clergy. As in the caste system, an individual's status or estate (in the two lay estates) was decided at birth — ascribed — and was a legal matter. However, individuals sometimes were able to legally change their estates under rare and exceptional circumstances (e.g., an act of grace from the king, or the marriage of the daughter of a wealthy merchant into the aristocracy). The requirement of celibacy in the priesthood more or less left the lower rungs of the clergy open to talented men of whatever social background (Mayer and Buckley, 1970; Morrish, 1978).

• Merchants, Master Craftsmen, and Capitalist Revolt

The estate system in Western Europe reached its peak between the 12th and 14th centuries, after which feudal society began to disintegrate. Authority was becoming increasingly centralized, the invention of gunpowder was beginning to render the warrior on horseback obsolete, cities and towns were rising again, commerce and transportation returned, and the urban money economy was beginning to divert labour and effort away from the rural, subsistence economy that feudalism represented (Kelsall et al., 1984).

At this point, the bourgeois class of merchants and master craftsmen began to contend as a stratum in the medieval social order. These business owners were determined to free commerce and transportation from the shackles of feudalism. They arranged with princes and nobles to obtain freedom of movement and labour for themselves and others. The **bourgeoisie** formed the leadership of the third estate and in some respects enjoyed a separate status above the commoners but below the nobility and the clergy. The entire system of social estates was later jolted out of balance by a new bourgeois class of manufacturers and industrial entrepreneurs. This capitalist class was to revolt against the feudal aristocracy, abolish its legal privileges, and establish a social order based on personal liberty and equality for all. Thus began the modern class system of stratification in Europe of the late 18th century.

• CLASS SYSTEM

Broadly, there are two views of the class system: the radical position inspired by Karl Marx and the liberal position influenced by Max Weber. The radicals see class as a *relation* among broad aggregates of people rather than a hierarchy of ranks. This means that classes differ in kind rather than degree. For their part, the liberals see classes in terms of the *distributive* properties of individuals or families, such as occupation, education, and income. Liberals equate classes with a continuum of occupations (low to high) that differ in degree rather than kind. This is a graded-status imagery rather than a social relations model of inequality and stratification (for details, see Clement, 1988; Grabb, 1990; Heath, 1990; Hunter, 1986; Ugbor, 1991).

• Occupation, Class, and Social Class

In order to understand the class system, it is important to draw a distinction among the terms *occupation*, *class,* and *social class*. Occupations designate positions within the technical (skill- or activity-based) division of labour — the so-called *technical relations of production*. Class, on the other hand, designates common positions within the *social relations of production* (e.g., employers versus workers as a group). It is within such social relations of power and domination (or simply, management and control) that the technical activities of jobs are performed (Wright and Perrone, 1977; Wright et al., 1982; see also Duke and Edgell, 1987). To illustrate, for two lawyers (i.e., education and profession are identical) in a firm owned by one but employing the other, the "technical content" of their job/occupation remains largely that of providing legal services to clients, but the "social relations content" strictly differentiates the member of an employer class from the member of an employed class. The one that has to report to the other is also the one who could be fired by the other (see Ugbor, 1991: 190–91). It is therefore sometimes misleading to equate classes with occupations, and confusing to use terms such as "occupational classes."

What, then, is social class? The *objective* criterion is based on common positions within the social relations of production. Marx would describe this as merely a "class *in* itself." Second, there must also be the *subjective* criterion of a collective awareness or consciousness of people having similar characteristics and interests. Thus, it is not just common structural position but a collective consciousness and propensity to organize and act as real groups that define social classes. Marx would describe this as a "class *for* itself" (see Cuff and Payne, 1984; Orr and McNall, 1991).

• Achieved Status

The class system is an open form of stratification in the sense that class boundaries are not sharply demarcated. There are no explicit legal restraints on the movement of individuals and families from one class to another. To the extent that people are at liberty to change their class of birth through personal effort and achievement, class membership is an **achieved status**. However, the class system is a case of avowed equality yet widespread inequality (Kelsall et al., 1984). Every class-based society contains pockets of socially inherited inequalities in wealth, power, and prestige.

• Ascribed Status and Self-Recruitment

Class membership, especially where it really matters, is also an **ascribed status,** something we inherit at birth and cannot do much to change. Other examples of ascribed status are gender, race,

Box 5.1

THE CANADIAN ESTABLISHMENT

A study of the members of the Canadian establishment (Newman, 1979, cited in Hunter, 1986) reported that a solid 75 percent of the richest individuals and families inherited businesses that made them instant millionaires. While the richest 20 percent of Canadian families drew 40 percent of the national income, the poorest 20 percent received only 6 percent of the income (Clement, 1988: 9). Insight into the concentration of wealth and power in Canada was first provided by Porter (1965) and in a follow-up investigation by Clement (1975). Briefly, they found that family and social background influenced who became directors of corporations, banks, and insurance companies.

ethnic origin, age, and sometimes religion. Indeed, the upper reaches of the class structure employ family self-recruitment (with grandparents, parents, and offspring remaining at the same stratum), and so are a relatively closed status rank. This is epitomized by the British aristocracy who have survived the transition from estate society to class society and continue to enjoy a high degree of prestige and are characterized by exclusive "lifestyles" of intermarriage, elite clubs, and exotic vacations, as well as exclusive dinners, dances, and receptions. Canadian families such as the Westons, Eatons, and Thomsons are also examples of a relatively closed status rank.

Despite a professed commitment to equal opportunity, the United States of America contains more than 600 000 millionaires and over 32 million people who live below the official poverty line. For all the rhetoric of the American Dream, the 1988 survey of 400 of the wealthiest Americans by *Forbes* magazine reported that 98 family groups had assets ranging between $300 million and $6.5 billion. The interesting thing here is that "all of the 98 families and 154 of the 400 individuals *inherited* all or part of their wealth" (Robertson, 1989: 180; emphasis added). Included in this would be the politically and economically prominent Kennedys, Fords, and Rockefellers.

• Status Consistency and Inconsistency

When an individual or a group occupies a similar position or rank in the three main stratification hierarchies (economic, social, and political) within the class system, sociologists usually refer to it as **status consistency,** or status compatibility. Conversely, when an individual or a group occupies different ranks in different hierarchies, this is known as **status inconsistency,** or incompatibility. Add to all this the three major classes in modern industrial societies (a small and wealthy *upper class;* a large *middle class* of professional, clerical, and allied occupations; and a fairly large *lower class* of skilled and unskilled manual workers) and it is easy to see that the class system is a highly complex stratification structure. Nevertheless, many sociologists consider class societies to be highly competitive and fluid, in the sense that individuals and families move up or down the social hierarchy through personal talent and effort. This idea of "social mobility," together with the mechanism of status attainment, is considered next.

SOCIAL MOBILITY AND STATUS ATTAINMENT

Social mobility refers to the movement of individuals or groups from one social position to another, whether between the classes (vertical mobility), or within a particular social class (horizontal mobility) (Morrish, 1978: 146). Many factors are believed to influence social mobility. They include class background, measured intelligence, educational opportunity and/or attainment, occupation, income, gender, ethnicity, race, religion, language, royalty or title, region, urban/rural residence, migration, financial windfall, rising through the ranks, family size, marriage, character traits, physical appearance, and general social or structural change.

• Mobility Patterns and Their Analysis

A number of concepts and indicators are used in research on social mobility. Research on **intergenerational mobility** examines the present social position of individuals in relation to that of their parents (Blau and Duncan, 1976). The term **self-recruitment** is used if social position remains the same; it refers to the recruitment of new members for the class from within its own ranks. Whether, and how, family members move up or down the social hierarchy from one generation to another defines the rigidity or flexibility of stratification in a given society. Assuming that they do move, the **mobility patterns** may be short-range between adjacent levels or long-range between widely separated levels. **Intragenerational mobility** compares the positions attained by the same individual at different periods in the course of his or her working life (Abercrombie et al., 1984: 196). It is also called *career mobility*.

• Cohort Analysis

There are two major ways of analyzing changes in social mobility. One is to compare surveys that have been carried out at different periods. The other is **cohort analysis,** also known as the "retrospective method." This method takes contemporary mobility survey data, divides the respondents into different age groups (cohorts), and works on the assumption that any alterations in mobility rates between the older and younger cohorts correspond to actual historical changes in social mobility (Kaelble, 1981). However, this method does not separate mobility that is due to the normal operation of society from mobility that is the consequence of changes in the economy, the labour process, or the class structure.

• Structural Mobility and Circulation Mobility

In order to take account of changes in the economic, occupational, or class structure, sociologists sometimes draw a line between structural mobility and circulation mobility. **Structural mobility** is "enforced" by structural changes in the economy. When the economy is booming, more and different jobs are created and opportunities for social advancement are readily available. Conversely, an economic recession entails a slowdown in economic activities, forcing many upwardly mobile people back to their class origins. **Circulation mobility** is the normal trend of movement between, as well as within, different levels of the social hierarchy. The extent to which people circulate between positions depends on how open or closed the society is. Although the basis of circulation mobility — and hence what constitutes an open society — remains unclear, subtracting the rate of structural mobility from the entire mobility rate yields a value for the amount of circulation mobility (Kaelble, 1981). Without structural mobility, it would be business as usual (i.e., "like parent, like child") for the most part, and self-recruitment would be the rule rather than the exception. Despite the impact of structural mobility, radical sociologists (e.g., Althusser, 1971; Apple, 1979; Bernstein, 1977; Bourdieu and Passeron, 1977; Bowles and Gintis, 1976) reject the claims of liberal-functionalists that modern industrial society is fluid, fair, and increasingly middle class.

• The Status Attainment Process: Origins, Entry, and Destination

Status attainment research (see, e.g., Boyd et al., 1985, for work on Canada) tries to specify the processes or mechanisms through which individuals progressively move from one occupational status to another. The basic status attainment model claims that the extent of social mobility, either across or within generations, can be measured in the differences in the status of origin, status of entry, and status of destination. *Status of origin* refers to the occupational status of the individual's parents in the period of childhood and formal education. *Status of entry* concerns the prestige of the first full-time occupation the individual held in the labour force. *Status of destination* is the status of the individual's present or principal occupation (Abrahamson et al., 1976: 206). This is like mapping a three-stage "socio-economic life cycle" of individuals (McRoberts, 1985a), one in which social psychological factors such as measured intelligence, ambition/motivation, parental expectations, value orientation, and significant others affect achieved occupational statuses.

• Conceptual and Methodological Issues

The status attainment research tradition has been greatly commended for bringing technical advances and statistical elegance to bear on sociological research methodology (Li, 1988). It has also been criticized as overly occupationalist, individualist, voluntarist (i.e., astructural), optimistic, and utopian (Knottnerus, 1987). By reducing stratification research to the individual's occupational status attainment process, the relational basis of inequality is excluded from stratification and mobility (Li, 1988; Ugbor, 1991). Conflict sociologists reject the assumption that there is societal consensus about the prestige standings of various occupations. These sociologists dispute that people hierarchically rank the status of occupations in a linear, unidimensional mode (Coxon et al., 1986; Horan, 1978).

THEORIES OF SOCIAL STRATIFICATION

The following theories of social stratification show that the practices in mobility and attainment research, and the criticisms thereof, are not simply technical matters, but rather are disagreements over how to perceive or make sense of social reality. While most mobility and attainment research derives from the idealist functionalist views, most of the criticisms come from conflict or Marxist-influenced sociology (see Chapter 1).

• THE MARXIST PERSPECTIVE

Karl Marx (1818–1883) was not interested in describing the particular stratification pattern (e.g., how many layers or strata there were) in England where he lived or in Germany where he was born. He was concerned with those key groups in society that had either an entrenched interest in maintaining the existing system or a strong interest in changing it. The key groups he identified are the social classes, and Marx's theory of class is tied into his general theory of society and social change (see Cuff and Payne, 1984).

• Class Struggle as a Motor of Change

Together with his long-term collaborator and benefactor, Friedrich Engels, Marx saw class struggle or protracted conflict between the dominant and the exploited classes as the "motor of history." Class struggle is the moving force behind historical change from one type of society to another as defined by the dominant mode of subsistence or economic production. Thus, the conflict between slave masters on the one hand, and free persons and slaves on the other, helped to bring about the decline of the Roman Empire and ultimately the rise of feudalism in medieval Europe. The conflict between feudal lords and serfs precipitated the emergence of a contending bourgeois class of merchants and industrial entrepreneurs that subsequently overran feudalism with capitalism.

• Bourgeoisie versus Proletariat

Marx believed that in the capitalist mode of production, society as a whole splits into two great classes or hostile armies directly facing each other: the **bourgeoisie** or capitalists and the **proletariat** or wage-labourers (Marx and Engels, 1967: 79). The "objective" basis of this acrimonious class division, and hence of inequality, stratification, and exploitation, is the relationship to the means of production. Quite simply, this means ownership or non-ownership of productive property, such as land (a source of food, fuel, or raw materials), machinery, or factories (which turn raw materials into finished products).

Marx used the term **false consciousness** to refer to a situation in which the working class accepts the dominant ideology of the bourgeoisie. A contemporary example might be workers' trade union consciousness, which is limited to fighting for reforms and wage increases rather than basic structural changes. Marx nonetheless saw a ray of hope in the fact that the capitalist system produced *surplus wealth* — goods and services in excess of the cost of production — of which workers received very little while a handful of capitalists received most of the profit. He believed that such exploitation would galvanize the large working class into a political overthrow of the capitalist order.

• Praise, Criticism, and Defence of the Marxist Perspective

Marx has been commended for providing a sociological theory that is based on people's social position, rather than their innate or personal qualities. From a Marxist viewpoint, social position is concrete and formed in the production process (Abrahamson et al., 1976; Bottomore, 1984). However, Marx has been criticized for creating the impression that stratification and inequality come from only one source: ownership or non-ownership of productive property. There seems to be nothing for oppressed women and minorities in such a theory. Max Weber would later try to remedy this drawback.

Critics have also observed that many of Marx's predictions about capitalism made in the 19th century have not been borne out in the 20th century. Extended periods of party–state dictatorship accompanied the rise of socialism in different parts of the world. The former Soviet-bloc countries were anything but classless (defined as absence of inequality), let alone stateless. Instead of the expected polarization of classes, capitalism has evolved a large middle class of professional-managerial, academic, and civil service workers that continues to be a source of headaches and embarrassment for neo-Marxists. Many manual or blue-collar workers receive reasonable wages in advanced capitalist countries. When large corporations are owned by myriad shareholders and controlled by salaried managers, the potentially exploitative powers of *ownership* and *control* of the means of production are no longer in one hand.

Defenders of Marx respond that access to large blocks of shares makes corporate managers and directors something like owner-controllers. New technologies of work and production also are deskilling, devaluing, and proletarianizing otherwise professional and technical personnel. Finally, they argue, capitalist societies have only been buying time through welfare and unemployment measures to curb worker unrest.

• THE WEBERIAN PERSPECTIVE

Max Weber (1864–1920) attempted to improve on Marxist theory by developing a multidimensional approach to stratification and inequality. For Weber, social stratification is really a matter of power, defined as the capacity to realize one's will in spite of opposition. He identified three dimensions of stratification, which he called three phenomena of the distribution of power. These are the class (or economic) dimension, the status (or prestige) dimension, and the party (or political) dimension.

While generally sharing Marx's position that property ownership, or the lack of it, is the defining element of class position, Weber departs from Marx in two subtle ways. First, he focuses more on property or wealth that can be exchanged for money in the market, rather than on economic production as such. Second, his idea of property is not simply physical or material wealth, but, instead, cultural property, such as skills and educational credentials that can also be exchanged for money in the market.

• Praise and Criticism of the Weberian Perspective

Weber's contribution lies in emphasizing the pluralist and complicated nature of stratification in contemporary societies. For example, it is sometimes but not necessarily the case that class inequalities determine inequalities of gender, ethnicity, race, religion, profession, party affiliation, and language. Indeed, it could be quite the opposite, so that the mere socialization or public ownership of the means of production would still leave many relations of domination largely unaffected (Littlejohn, 1972).

Weber has been criticized for separating conceptually what Marx connected theoretically, and for simply leaving the nature of the links between his dimensions of stratification open, subject to particular circumstances (Salaman, 1972; see also Wright, 1991). Weber's fascination with the marketplace often results in an emphasis on "distributive" inequalities at the expense of the "relational" inequalities inherent in the social organization of production under capitalism. It should be obvious, then, that it may not be entirely rewarding to evaluate Weber and Marx in terms of each other's work: they both analyzed stratification and inequality, but from different intellectual assumptions and value positions.

• THE FUNCTIONALIST PERSPECTIVE

Unlike the Marxist perspective in particular, which sees stratification as socially created, class based, conflictual, and exploitative, the functionalist viewpoint assumes at the outset that stratification is natural or inevitable. It sees it as a matter of individual action, equitable in terms of rewards for effort, and socially integrative. Structural-functionalism, as it is sometimes called, also assumes that the social system (i.e., the overall society) has a need for order or equilibrium, and that a major way of meeting this need is the existence of value consensus (general agreement) among all members of society regarding which occupational positions and functions are the most important for society and therefore the most deserving of societal rewards such as power, wealth, income, and, in particular, prestige. (For the general functionalist and other perspectives, see Chapter 1.)

• Parsons: Occupational Status Stratification

For a functionalist like Talcott Parsons, stratification involves the distribution and allocation of social honour to individuals — and hence their families — on the basis of the adjudged importance to society of their occupational status and roles. The resultant stratification system is a gradation or continuum of occupational prestige — that is, a series of strata ranked one above the other in terms of the amount of social honour accorded to them by popular agreement. In essence, the Parsonian model is simply occupational status stratification and the education, income, wealth, and power associated with it.

• Davis and Moore: "Functional Importance" and "Relative Scarcity"

In their elaboration of the above image of society and stratification, Kingsley Davis and Wilbert E. Moore (1945) set out to show the "functional" and "universal" necessity of stratification. Briefly, they argue that if society is to function effectively, it must assign its vital roles or positions to the most skilled and talented persons available. Because various roles or occupations differ both in their functional importance for society and in the relative scarcity of people with the requisite talent and training, society uses unequal material and prestige rewards as the mechanism to motivate people to undergo the rigorous training and sacrifice needed in order to fill the toughest and most vital positions. Thus, a society that values physicians more than janitors, or research scientists more than motor mechanics, will accord higher status and rewards to the positions of physician and research scientist. To the extent that the best candidates fill the toughest positions, this unequal distribution of social rewards is said to be functional (i.e., to have a positive consequence) for society as a whole. Efficiency or effective role performance as well as productivity are the results. And the distribution is somehow equitable, because "what you sow is what you reap": people are responsible for their own outcomes and at liberty to avail themselves of society's opportunities.

• Criticism and Insights of the Functionalist Perspective

The Davis–Moore and general functionalist positions have been criticized for their idealized picture of society and social stratification. It is misleading to claim that all members of society freely agree on all things. If we did, we would not have a multiplicity of laws and law-enforcement agencies telling us what to do and what not to do. Although the roles of hockey player, football player, and boxer are anything but vital or indispensable, it is no secret that people in the business (e.g., Wayne Gretzky, Joe Montana, and Mike Tyson) have generally earned far more than the presidents and prime ministers of the world's leading industrial nations. In cases such as physician versus janitor, the definition of functional importance depends on the criteria used. Is it better to treat a patient for a disease or to prevent that person from contracting a disease to begin with? Indeed, occupational prestige is often a function of gatekeeping and monopolistic practices by associations and unions. This, in addition to the inequalities of access typically suffered by the poor, women, and ethnic/racial minorities, suggests that not all the potentially talented and interested groups and individuals are recruited or trained, let alone rewarded.

However, we must acknowledge that professional skills and technical competencies are a form of cultural property and therefore (even for Marxists espousing the cultural reproduction of class relations) a basis of inequality in power, wealth, and prestige. In postsecondary education, different subject areas ordinarily do not have the same intellectual rigour or average social valuation. Whether on campus or in the world of work, one B.A. or B.Sc. is not necessarily equal to another. All this cannot have been the outcome of ruling-class conspiracy. Children raised in the same home by their biological parents still grow up to be different and unequal in resourcefulness and social accomplishments. There is room for the individual to excel even within a primary group such as the family.

• RECENT THEORETICAL SYNTHESES

Recent attempts have been made to forge some common ground between and amongst the major theories of stratification. Of course, this is risky, because the theories have developed from differing intellectual starting points or ways of seeing the world. In this sense, the theories cannot really be synthesized or combined, only mixed somehow.

• Lenski: A Theory of Conflict and Consensus

Gerhard Lenski (1966) brings together aspects of functionalist and Marxist perspectives in an examination of the ways in which stratification is determined by differential access to power and privilege. He agrees with the functionalist perspective that the survival needs of a society are met by rewarding people in accordance with the adjudged importance of their roles or functions for the collectivity. Beyond this practical necessity, on which most people seem to agree, a society's surplus resources are allocated largely in terms of the Marxist idea of conflict and struggle between different classes or groups. For Lenski, then, social life is a mixture of conflict and consensus.

• Lockwood and Dahrendorf: Convergence of Neo-Marxists and Neo-Weberians

David Lockwood mixes elements of Marx's production relationships and Weber's market capacity in his thesis that class location is a function of *work situation* and *market situation*. The first of these terms refers to the degree of authority and control at work or in the production process. The second deals with source and size of income, degree of job security, and chances of economic advancement (see Haralambos, 1980; Heath, 1990). Ralf Dahrendorf (1959) has probably helped both neo-Marxists and neo-Weberians to begin seriously to find ways of integrating these viewpoints. Beyond describing an expanding new middle class and a differentiated new working class, he spent some time showing that the era of joint-stock, limited liability companies has drastically weakened the link Marx observed between ownership and control of industry. Thus, questions of authority and control by salaried managers or even government bureaucrats are now more important in determining class inequality and stratification than is ownership per se.

• Noneconomic Classes, Nonclass Bases

It has become sociological wisdom that discussion of stratification in modern (post)industrial societies must include people's location in power and authority relations. Such location usually, but not always, is influenced by the possession of special skills or credentials. From this perspective, domination, or the system of institutionalized power relations, becomes a precondition for exploitation. The concept of "domination" applies to economic and "noneconomic" classes (located in economic/production, political/administrative, and cultural/knowledge organizations). Domination is also a precondition for nonclass bases of stratification, such as gender, race, ethnicity, age, language, region, and religion (see, for example, Bowles and Gintis, 1986; Grabb, 1990; Li, 1988; Miliband, 1987; Parkin, 1979; Ugbor, 1991).

STRATIFICATION IN CANADA

One of the longest-running myths about Canada or North America is that of a land of opportunity. All you have to do is go to school and get a job, work hard, earn and save, buy your own property, marry (a beautiful wife or a handsome husband), and live happily ever after! Through the combined influence of the political process, the media, the churches, the school, as well as parents and peers, generations of Canadians have been systematically subjected to heavy doses of this "open" society ideology (see Forcese, 1986). It is only recently that the post–World War II generation of Canadians is beginning to wake up to the fact that poverty, homelessness, and economically generated social conflict are neither an American plague nor a Third World disease encountered only on television. Instead, they are experienced by men, women, and children right here in Montreal, Toronto, Vancouver, Edmonton, and the cities of the Atlantic provinces.

• THE VERTICAL MOSAIC

Porter's (1965) pathbreaking work jolted Canadian intellectuals out of the denial of class inequality. Sociologists began to recognize the salience of classes in Canadian social, political, and economic life (Brym, 1985a). Porter (1965) and, ten years later, Clement (1975) drew attention to the concentration of wealth and power in Canada among a handful of largely Anglo-Saxon (but also francophone) economic and political elites. Other elite members of these two groups could be found in the corridors of leading bureaucratic, media, and intellectual institutions. Both Porter and Clement reported that members of the various elites come disproportionately from upper-class backgrounds, with a large proportion having similar family genealogies.

Myriad formal and informal networks bind together the corporate or economic elite (i.e., those holding multiple and interlocking directorships or executive positions in dominant financial and commercial corporations) and the political elite. These include serving on government commissions and advisory boards, funding political parties, attending private schools together, being an "old boy" of the University of Toronto or McGill University, marrying into each other's networks, as well as belonging to exclusive clubs. The power elite is a closed status group with a tradition of inherited wealth; postsecondary training in engineering, law, or finance; and a background largely British and Protestant (over 90 percent). Whatever their areas of occasional disagreement, the political and corporate elites, just as their counterparts in the United States (see Mills, 1956), form a cohesive brotherhood of power — what Park and Park (1973) would refer to as "those who own Canada" (see also Brym, 1989; Hunter, 1986).

Newman (1979; cited in Hunter, 1986) presents those Canadians known to have in excess of $100 million in wealth by 1979. As Table 5.2 reveals, 75 percent inherited businesses of substantial magnitude, and were made instant millionaires. Only five cases seem to have been virtually self-made members of the Canadian establishment. In 1983, only six families (Weston, Black, Thomson, Demarais, Irving, and Bronfman) and their associates controlled more than 1300 of Canada's largest corporations. The Bronfmans alone controlled more than 700 companies with combined financial assets in excess of $56 billion (Veltmeyer, 1986: 38).

• Distribution of Assets

The next step in documenting inequality in Canada is to examine the distribution of assets in the general population. Assets include liquid financial assets (cash, deposits, Canada Savings Bonds, etc.); nonliquid financial assets (stocks, RRSPs, etc.); owner-occupied homes; vacation homes; real estate held as an investment; equity in, or net value of, businesses, farms, or professional practices; cars, trucks, and recreational vehicles (Oja, 1987: 34). The focus here is on net assets or net worth, meaning total wealth after debts have been subtracted.

Examining the distribution of wealth of Canadian families and individuals living alone in 1970, 1977, and 1984, we find that unattached individuals in all but the poorest and the wealthiest brackets experienced slight gains in their command of the nation's wealth. The wealthiest fell modestly but steadily from 82.7 percent in 1970 to 81.3 percent in 1977, and further to 78.9 percent in 1984. Among Canadian families, the poorest quintile (i.e., 20 percent) remained virtually without any net worth during the period (Oja, 1987: 25). Although the highest family quintile experienced a slight reduction in its share of the nation's wealth between 1970 and 1984 (from 67.7 percent to 65.2 percent), most wealth continued to be owned by this relatively small group. Indeed, the richest 40 percent of Canadian families (the top two quintiles) owned 87.6 percent and 84.9 percent of all net assets in 1970 and 1984, respectively. This barely left 12.4 percent and 15.1 percent of such assets distributed among the least wealthy 60 percent (the bottom three quintiles) in the corresponding periods.

Table 5.2 CANADIANS WITH WEALTH IN EXCESS OF $100 MILLION, 1979

Name	Canadian Headquarters	Probable Present Major Source of Wealth	Business Inheritance
Tomas Bata	Toronto	Bata Ltd. (footwear)	Yes
Samuel Belzberg	Vancouver	First City Financial Corporation Ltd.	Unknown
Poldi Bentley	Vancouver	Canadian Forest Products Ltd.	Unknown
Charles Bronfman	Montreal	Distiller's Corporation — Seagram's Ltd.	Yes
Nelson Davis[1]	Toronto	N.M. Davis Corp. Ltd. (Arrow) Leasing, etc.	Yes
Paul Demarais	Montreal	Power Corporation (Montreal Trust, etc.)	Yes
Eaton Family	Toronto	Eaton's of Canada Ltd., T. Eaton Co. Ltd.	Yes
K.C. Irving	St. John	K.C. Irving Ltd. (oil refining, etc.)	Yes
Maxwell Meighen	Toronto	Canadian General Investments Ltd.	Yes
Molson Family	Montreal	Molson Industries Ltd. ("Molson Golden," etc.)	Yes
Charles Rathgeb	Toronto	Comstock International Ltd. (construction)	Yes
Reichmann Family	Toronto	Olympia and York Developments Ltd. (real estate developer)	Unknown
George Richardson	Winnipeg	James Richardson & Sons Ltd. (securities, etc.)	Yes
Stephen Roman	Toronto	Denison Mines Ltd. (uranium)	No
William Siebens	Calgary	Family sold Siebens Oil and Gas interest	Yes
David Stewart	Montreal	Sold Macdonald's Tobacco ("Export," etc.)	Yes
E.P. Taylor	Toronto	International Housing Ltd. (real estate developer)	Yes
Kenneth Thomson	Toronto	Thomson Newspapers Ltd. (*The Globe and Mail,* etc.)	Yes
Howard Webster	Montreal	Burns Foods Ltd., Quebecair	Yes
G. Van Wielingen	Calgary	Sulpetro Ltd. (oil and gas)	Unknown

1. Deceased, 1979.

Source: Derived from Newman (1979). Reproduced from Hunter (1986: 166).

Note: Since the publication of this table in 1986, certain of the people listed have died. A number of the corporate listings are no longer current, but the fact of business inheritance within family dynasties remains valid.

As a general rule, the wealthiest 20 percent had the largest proportion of net assets, including *over 90 percent of the equity in business.* The poorest 40 percent owned virtually nothing in business and home equity (for details, see Oja, 1987, Table 4: 27). Essentially, the picture that emerges is that of inequality in the distribution of wealth among Canadian families and unattached individuals. Although home ownership has tended to decline, particularly among younger families, real assets such as homes and cars are less unequally distributed than financial assets, particularly holdings of stocks, bonds other than savings bonds, and other rarely held assets (Oja, 1987).

• Distribution of Income

Income is quite concentrated in Canada, but less so than total wealth (Forcese, 1986; Hunter, 1986). The notion of income normally includes wages and salaries, net income from self-employment, cash social benefits, investment income, as well as retirement pensions and annuities (mainly for older Canadians).

A "snapshot" of income distribution in Canada is shown in Table 5.3. Although the average levels of income of all family groupings increased between 1970 and 1985, there were few equalizing changes in the relative gap between the lowest 10 percent and the highest. In other words, a modest improvement in the purchasing power of all families was accompanied by stability in the relative share of incomes.

Major factors underlying the distribution of income are type of occupation, employment (as opposed to unemployment), and labour-force attachment. The pattern of differences in occupational incomes is rather pronounced and tends to be stable over time. It was found (Hunter, 1986: 104) that over a forty-year period (1941–1981), some occupations persistently drew well above average annual incomes relative to the rest (e.g., physicians and surgeons, lawyers and notaries, professors, dentists, and electrical engineers), while others generally remained around or below average in their share of income (e.g., bus drivers, barbers, and hairdressers). Most Canadians depend on their wages, salaries, or earnings as a major source of income.

Males and females are unequally distributed among occupations (see, for example, Li, 1988: 92). Thus, while there have been shifts in the overall labour-force attachment of both sexes between 1971 and 1986, men still control the top-paying managerial-administrative and professional occupations, while women are disproportionately concentrated in clerical and service occupations (notorious for part-time work and low wages), including teaching, nursing, and health (also see Boyd, 1990).

• Occupational Prestige

Most prestigious occupations command high incomes and tend to require extensive formal education. Physicians and surgeons, judges and lawyers, professors and top research scientists, and some others, seem to fit into this picture. As part of the same process, an M.B.A. has become the degree for an upwardly mobile career in business, while a high-school diploma promises to become the entry permit for selling Big Macs or Kentucky Fried Chicken. This phenomenon has been described as "overeducation" and the "diploma disease." As college and high-school graduates apply for every white-collar and service-sector job, employers have to weed out the bulk of candidates by inflating the educational "requirements" of quite mediocre jobs.

Table 5.3

PERCENTAGE DISTRIBUTION OF AGGREGATE FAMILY INCOME AND AVERAGE INCOME PER FAMILY AND PER FAMILY MEMBER, IN CONSTANT (1985) DOLLARS, BY INCOME DECILES, CANADA, 1970 AND 1985

Income Deciles	1970			1985		
	Income Share	Average Income		Income Share	Average Income	
		Per Family	Per Capita		Per Family	Per Capita
	%	$	$	%	$	$
Bottom	1.46	4 350	1 389	1.49	5 650	2 008
Second	3.77	11 248	3 316	3.75	14 173	5 272
Third	5.48	16 354	4 542	5.18	19 615	6 834
Fourth	6.97	20 711	5 596	6.70	25 312	8 287
Fifth	8.20	24 546	6 463	8.13	30 772	9 637
Sixth	9.53	28 365	7 410	9.55	36 124	11 006
Seventh	10.96	32 556	8 502	11.09	41 928	12 621
Eighth	12.60	37 748	9 827	12.94	48 955	14 544
Ninth	15.24	45 522	11 642	15.64	59 147	17 458
Top	25.77	76 472	18 421	25.53	96 596	27 705
Total	100.00	29 803	8 015	100.00	37 827	12 022

Source: Statistics Canada (1990f: 25).

• LEGITIMIZING STRATIFICATION

What purpose does education serve beyond a quick means for eliminating candidates by potential employers? First, education signals the ease with which a person can be trained or socialized toward the technical and social requirements of a job. Such learning or training is acquired mainly on the job. Second, and perhaps more importantly, a major purpose of mass higher education is to legitimize, justify, or rationalize inequality. Education is the means both for social differentiation and the rationalization of such differentiation. Its political-ideological function is to help make failure and inequality the responsibility of the individual rather than that of the system (Bourdieu and Passeron, 1977; Bowles and Gintis, 1976; Curtis, 1984; Collins, 1977; Halsey, 1980; Jencks et al., 1979; Lulat, 1988; Ugbor, 1991; Young, 1971).

• Social Stratification and Distribution of Education

Canada is a welfare state that offers free, compulsory, universal schooling up to high-school completion or the school-leaving age. The period 1950–70 witnessed an incredible expansion of educational institutions in Canada. Government increased its support for education at all levels. Higher education was vastly expanded, and programs such as liberal admission policies and loan facilities were introduced to boost access (Forcese, 1986; Hunter, 1986: 121).

Students from families with higher socioeconomic status are disproportionately overrepresented in the university student population (Porter, 1965). This is only partly a result of greater financial resources, since government student loans are available to lower-income students. A study of over 8000 students in Grades 8 to 12 in Ontario by Porter et al. (1979; cited in Li, 1988: 75) found that high-ability students from higher socioeconomic backgrounds are much more likely to *expect to enrol* in university than are high-ability students from lower socioeconomic backgrounds. Also, Anisef and Okihiro (1982) demonstrated that the educational attainment of children is a function of parental education.

A preliminary analysis by Decore and Ugbor (1991) confirms Li's (1988: 80) finding of an unequal distribution of average years of schooling between different ethnic groups among Canadians aged 35 to 54 (where natives and southern Europeans are slightly disadvantaged). In terms of highest level of schooling, Decore and Ugbor found that 56.7 percent of Canadians aged 15 years and above did not have more than secondary education by 1986. Only 33.5 percent had postsecondary training, while 9.8 percent completed university. Of those who completed university, the order of ethnic concentration is as follows: Jews, Asians and Arabs, northwestern Europeans, Poles, Hungarians (also see Li, 1988).

A subtler form of unequal distribution of education between Canadian males and females is documented in Hunter (1986: 123–24). Over three time periods, 1962–63, 1972–73, and 1982–83, female university students were overrepresented relative to men in the fields of education, arts, nursing, household science, and health programs other than medicine. Conversely, male students were overrepresented in commerce and business administration, science, medicine, and law. As we saw earlier, the latter two specializations are very high in terms of prestige and income. The good news is that overall male–female disparities in these high-status disciplines have begun to narrow.

• POVERTY AND THE POOR

Poverty represents a special case of socioeconomic inequality and stratification. Sociologists usually define poverty in absolute or relative terms. **Absolute poverty** applies to families or individuals living at or below a certain income cutoff point. It is normal in Canada to describe as poor those families or individuals who spend 58 to 70 percent of their incomes on food, shelter, clothing, and health care — the basic necessities of life. This criterion has produced a poverty rate of between 17 and 25 percent of the population. Conversely, **relative poverty** is a matter of the degree to which a family or an individual commands the goods and services — and has access to the living standards — enjoyed by the bulk of the population in a specific time and place. Since poverty as relative deprivation is culturally and situationally based, poverty levels vary within and between societies over time. The average Canadian has a place to live, a colour television set, a car or other transportation, a radio or music equipment, a telephone, a toaster oven, and a microwave oven. However, in 1990, only 7.0 percent of households in the under $10 000 group had a CD player compared to 27.6 percent in the $70 000 and over group. Of households with income under $10 000, 6.1 percent had a boat and only 1.5 percent had a vacation home; meanwhile, for the $70 000 and over group, 23.6 percent had a boat and 10.8 percent had a vacation home (Statistics Canada, 1991c: 12).

Poverty may be correlated with employment, labour-force attachment, number of earners in a family, the presence of children, gender, ethnicity, race, province or region, as well as urban/rural residence. Explanations range from the structural to the cultural and the social psychological. The social psychological explanation blames poverty on the lack of initiative, motivation, and ambition on the part of certain individuals or groups. Related to this, the **culture of poverty thesis** argues that the poor are characterized by negative and substandard family patterns, beliefs, values, and attitudes, which recycle poverty among them and their children. Perceiving these as effects rather than causes of poverty, one version of the **structural explanation** points to capitalism as an exploitative system. This system not only pays most workers subsistence wages, but maintains its squeeze by condemning a reserve army of labour to chronic unemployment and dependence on handouts from governments, churches, communities, or family and friends. Another version draws attention to changes in the economic structure and the labour process: the replacement of well-paying, full-time manufacturing or construction jobs with low-paying, part-time service and clerical jobs.

A third structural explanation points to inequality and discrimination on the grounds of class location, gender, ethnicity, race, and age, among others. Other than the "public" poverty of slum dwellers, the city homeless, wandering derelicts, or "bag ladies," there is a high incidence of poverty among women and children in lone-parent homes headed by a woman. The same holds true for the bulk of Canada's native peoples. Forcese (1986: 70) quite insightfully compares the native condition to that of the outcastes or untouchables of traditional East Indian society. Reminders like this should recover poverty from the myth of the personal economic troubles of individuals, and place it squarely in public issues of morality and politics.

THE CHALLENGE OF STRATIFICATION

Earlier we noted that members of the various strata in a given social hierarchy tend to have common life chances and lifestyles. The term **life chances** refers to the probability of sharing in the opportunities available in society. **Lifestyle** is a matter of the subtle aspects of social standing, such as belonging to exclusive clubs, intermarrying, vacationing in exotic locations, and appreciating prestigious works of art. We also noted that people's location in the stratification hierarchy is remarkably related to important aspects of their lives: health and illness, quality of health care, life expectancy, family size, child-rearing or socialization patterns, chances of being divorced, IQ test scores, educational and occupational attainment, political values and behaviour, religious affiliation, as well as chances of being arrested or imprisoned (see, for example, Mascie-Taylor, 1990; Mayer and Buckley, 1970).

Thus, stratification entails certain types of experiences, opportunities, rewards, and constraints to which people are liable. The costs of stratification — the hidden injuries of class — are disproportionately borne by the less privileged groups in society, and the benefits of stratification — the power and glory of class — are disproportionately enjoyed by the better-off sections of the population. In a sense, the whole of this chapter testifies to the relationships, possessions, and deprivations that are at once the bases and the consequences of stratification. Leaving aside questions of gender, ethnicity, age, and so on, we shall simply sketch in some of the consequences of class inequality.

• DISEASE, ILLNESS, AND HEALTH CARE

In Canada, as elsewhere, the lower social classes have higher rates of preventable diseases or illnesses, including severe mental disorders, than do the better-off classes. The health-care system is more curative than preventative; yet the hard lesson of epidemiology (the study of the origin, distribution, and means of transmission of diseases in the population) is that human health and disease are shaped by social and environmental factors. The poor have higher chances of living in poorly ventilated and squalid homes, working in dangerous and dirty environments (e.g., mines and iron-blasting factories with high risks of dust-induced lung cancer or industrial accidents), eating cheap and rotten or unhealthy food, and so on. All this translates into high rates of people being hospitalized in critical condition and, with predictable regularity, high rates of mortality or permanent physical damage. The availability of flat-rate universal health care is not the same thing as equal opportunity for quality physical, dental, or mental-health care. The upper and middle classes are much more capable of securing such specialized and high-cost treatment through private arrangements or even as the fringe benefits of their high-status occupations (e.g., Forcese, 1986; see also Chapter 14).

• RECREATION, CRIMINALIZATION, AND SOCIALIZATION

The picture is no more encouraging in matters of recreation, criminalization, or socialization. The less-privileged classes have little or no discretionary income after subsistence expenditures are made. They cannot eat out in decent restaurants, nor can they enjoy quality travel, vacation, art, or entertainment. The overall quality of life is thereby reduced. This same group has a higher than average chance of being arrested, prosecuted, convicted, and imprisoned — rather than cautioned or enjoined to get therapy (Lynch and Groves, 1989; see also Chapter 8). Not only are the people in this group incapable of hiring a skilled attorney, but the routines and procedures of the justice system in a class-based society load the dice against them (Liska, 1987).

The socialization patterns in materially impoverished families — unstable, inconsistent, authoritarian, conformist — may also create new problems while trying to solve the basic ones. For example, childhood verbal facility and explorative play are not particularly encouraged, because of the huge costs in time and money. However, such experiences are part of the preparation for dealing with ambiguous situations involving questions of law and order in a middle-class-oriented society. By contrast, the more liberal, consistent, and self-reliant socialization practices in materially well-off homes are believed to be a better preparation for dealing with ambiguous and unfamiliar situations. Needless to say, the class biases among social control agencies structure or saturate such interactions.

• POLITICAL BEHAVIOUR AND RELIGIOUS AFFILIATION

Conservatism, traditionalism, parochialism, fundamentalism — words like these are often used to describe the overall political and religious values or beliefs exhibited in behaviour of the working and rural classes. This is hardly surprising, given their child-rearing stress on conformity in an environment in which the familiar is preferred and nobody can afford or tolerate waste in the name of experimentation. The lower socioeconomic groups are predominantly attracted to dogmatic and fundamentalist religious sects (e.g., Jehovah's Witnesses and the Assembly of God), whose rituals of worship give vent to solidaristic hymns and emotional spontaneity. They are politically withdrawn and apathetic, except for a tendency toward trade union militancy or voting for the New Democrats in recessionary times. The Democratic Party in the United States has also tended to draw a large following from the poorer and middle sections of the population. By contrast, the Progressive Conservatives in Canada and the Republican Party in the United States tend to find sponsorship among the propertied upper class. This class is politically conservative but active in influencing public policy, socially withdrawn but status-loving. The conservative parties also tend to be home to a large mass of somewhat self-righteous, small-town or rural-bred teachers, nurses, technicians, small-business owners, and so on. This lower middle class and the upper class seem to prefer the established churches or denominations. Thus, social stratification seems to have definite consequences — economic, physical, legal, social, political, religious — in the lives of people.

• THE STATE AND STRATIFICATION

Whether the **state** (legal-political institutions of society) should attempt to modify social stratification is a political and moral issue, rather than simply an economic or technical one. There is a sense in which the state is itself a system of stratification. It is a key institution in the shaping of class relations, social citizenship rights (civil, political, and social rights and freedoms), and the social order generally (Esping-Andersen, 1990). Is structured social inequality — as opposed to the personal differences between people — inevitable? If stratification is socially constructed in specific historical conditions (slave, caste, estate, and class relationships), is it not then also politically modifiable? Many sociologists believe that it is. The issue then is whether the state can undertake such a task.

• Contending Viewpoints

There are different ways of looking at whether the state can modify stratification. The **liberal-functional** viewpoint believes that the state is the formal mechanism for planning and directing public social policy. As long as there is a rational basis for action (e.g., the national interest, maintaining public order), the state will constantly fine-tune the nature of inequality and stratification. The **instrumentalist Marxist** position sees the state only as a tool of the ruling capitalist class, or a weapon of class domination, exploitation, and inequality. The **structuralist Marxist** perspective sees the state not as a tool of capital, but as a "relatively autonomous" or independent force in a pattern of relations, only one of which is the requirement that sustained economic growth and the revenue base be maintained under capitalism. To the extent that the state is an arena of social conflict among different competing groups, existing patterns of stratification will be reinforced or modified in accordance with the balance of power between such pressure groups.

The **social democratic** view argues that the state is in its own right a system of stratification. It directly produces and administers the structure of social relations in accordance with either the conservative philosophy (i.e., keeping paternalistic, hierarchical, monarchical, or patriarchal authority), the liberal philosophy (i.e., leaving stratification up to the marketplace — the power to buy or sell), or the socialist policy goal (i.e., the abolition of free-market and conservative stratification). The social democratic welfare state (as in Sweden, Denmark, and Norway) steers a middle course between the liberal and the socialist philosophy. It pursues jointly the ideal and practice of both equality and economic efficiency. The labour movement too in this type of state is concerned not merely with equality and redistribution, but with efficiency and economic growth. The belief here is that the state can restructure or modify existing stratification patterns through the opportunities offered by parliamentary democracy in a market economy. What it needs to do so is a mass-based, coalition-building political party whose heart and soul will have come from a large, politically mobilized trade union movement (for details, see Esping-Andersen, 1985, 1990; Milner, 1990).

• The Canadian Track Record

Canada is a welfare state that lies midway between the Swedish social democratic model and the American liberal capitalist model in the expansion of social citizenship, or social security rights and entitlements (Esping-Andersen, 1990, Table 3.3: 74). Canada's vast system of social welfare — involving federal, provincial, territorial, and municipal levels of government — dates back to the provincial workers' compensation and mother's allowance programs in 1914 and 1916, respectively. In the 1930s, Unemployment Relief Acts were passed, followed by the Unemployment Insurance (1941) and Family Allowance (1945) plans. In 1951, Blind and Pension Allowances, Old Age Assistance, and Old Age Security were introduced. These were followed by the Disabled Pension Allowances (1954), Youth Allowances (1964), the Canada and Quebec Pension Plans, the Canada Assistance Program (1966), the Guaranteed Income Supplement (1967), as well as Child Tax Credits (1978). Up until the end of 1992, all families also received a monthly allowance for each dependent child under 18. Other than these money transfer payments, there is as yet universal health insurance and numerous programs under which assistance in the form of subsidies, exemptions (e.g., for income tax purposes), and rebates is provided (Statistics Canada, 1990f: 46–48).

Thus, the Canadian state "fights" inequality in income distribution by rendering diverse forms of assistance to economically disadvantaged families. In 1985 alone, nine out of ten families with the lowest income received some form of monetary assistance from the federal, provincial, and municipal governments. Nearly two-thirds of the total income of the families in the lowest 10 percent came from government transfer payments (Statistics Canada, 1990f: 56). Nevertheless, poverty continues to affect children and adults, especially in female lone-parent homes. While government transfer payments and subsidies definitely help many of the needy to get by, they tend to address the symptoms rather than the disease itself. The best way to deal with poverty and inequality is probably to confront the issues directly. From the expansion of economic democracy to the pursuit of full employment, to the restructuring of the labour process, to the hiking of the minimum wage, to the enforcement of pay and employment equity — all this is ultimately a political and moral issue, not an economic or a technical matter.

SUMMARY

- Social differences in positions and functions result in stratification when they become the basis for assigning categories of people to hierarchical status ranks involving inequalities in power, wealth, and prestige. These inequalities are associated with different life chances, lifestyles, experiences, and constraints upon people.
- Closed systems of stratification (slave, caste, and estate relationships) have rigidly defined strata; the strata are more flexibly defined in the open class system. Class membership, whether seen relationally or distributively, is both achieved and ascribed.
- Social mobility — the movement of people between and within classes — may be intergenerational (shown in differences between parents and offspring), intragenerational

(career movement by an individual), structural (demanded by changes in the economic structure), or by circulation (routine exchange of positions). The status attainment process maps the socioeconomic life cycle from status of origin through status of entry and on to status of destination.

- Marx explains stratification in terms of the relationship to the means of production: there are those who own and control productive property (the bourgeoisie/capitalists/employers) and those who are propertyless and must sell their labour in order to survive (the proletariat/workers/wage-labourers). Weber sees stratification in terms of three interactive but analytically distinct dimensions of power: class, status, and party. The Parsonian, Davis–Moore position argues that status-role stratification depends on the functional importance of positions and the relative scarcity of qualified candidates. Neo-Marxists and Neo-Weberians are converging toward "noneconomic" classes and nonclass bases of stratification.

- Stratification in Canada reveals not only concentration of wealth and power among a dominant elite, but also unequal distribution of assets, income, occupations, and education among major social groupings.

- Poverty continues to affect children and adults, especially in lone-parent homes headed by a woman. Also disproportionately concentrated in the ranks of the Canadian poor are one-earner, child-raising, unemployed, native, minority, younger, Atlantic, and rural families or persons.

- The consequences of stratification and poverty are diverse and far-reaching. From disease, illness, and health care to recreation, socialization, and criminalization, the dice are typically loaded against the less privileged. These groups also display distinct patterns of political and religious affiliation or behaviour.

- The state, in social democratic terms, is in its own right a system of stratification: a key institution in the shaping of class relations as well as social citizenship rights and entitlements. Structured inequality is at once socially created and politically modifiable.

- The social democratic welfare state — a middle ground between liberal and socialist philosophies — emphasizes not only socioeconomic equity and redistribution, but also productive work and economic growth. So do its labour organizations and class coalitions, which operate within parliamentary democracy.

- The Canadian welfare state — a middle ground between Swedish social democracy and American liberal capitalism — has a vast income security and welfare system that offers diverse forms of assistance to those in need. To deal squarely with the causes and consequences of stratification and poverty, much political and moral work remains to be done.

Key Concepts

Absolute poverty

Achieved status

Ascribed status

Bourgeoisie

Circulation mobility

Closed system

Cohort analysis

Culture of poverty thesis

Domination

False consciousness
Ideology
Instrumentalist Marxism
Intergenerational mobility
Intragenerational mobility
Liberal-functionalism
Life chances
Lifestyles
Mobility pattern
Open system
Power
Proletariat
Relative poverty
Self-recruitment
Social democratic viewpoint
Social differentiation
Social mobility
Social stratification
State
Status consistency
Status inconsistency
Structural explanation of poverty
Structuralist Marxism
Structural mobility
Surplus value

REVIEW QUESTIONS

1. What is social stratification? In what ways can it affect people's life chances?
2. Is the class system of stratification open or closed? Can you support your argument with Canadian evidence?
3. Explain the term *social mobility,* showing its various forms and patterns.
4. Compare and contrast the Marxist and Weberian theories of stratification, old and new.
5. Outline the dimensions of inequality and stratification in Canadian society. Evaluate the explanations that have been offered for some of them.
6. Drawing on competing views of the role of the state, assess the chances of the Canadian state as a social equalizer.

The Organization of Work

Karen D. Hughes and Graham S. Lowe

The Organization of Work

INTRODUCTION

In all societies work is a central activity, ensuring the production and distribution of economic goods and services. For individuals, work is a necessary activity for survival and a potential source of personal fulfilment. For a society, the institutions of work define the organization of economic life.

In industrialized societies like Canada, work refers to a diverse range of activities. But essentially, we can define **work** as any endeavour to transform raw material or knowledge into a product or service that is used or valued by other members of society. While this chapter focuses on "paid work" in the formal economy, it is important to remember that there are other forms of work — such as domestic, volunteer, and informal work — that play an essential role in Canadian society. Domestic work within the household, for instance, though undervalued, ensures that individuals are fed and clothed and able to participate in paid employment.

Above all, the sociological study of work examines the dynamic interaction between individuals and the work institutions they encounter. Sociologists, like economists, are interested in the underlying economic forces that shape particular working conditions. Yet they are equally concerned with the individual's experience of work and the way societies fashion various work arrangements. They consequently draw upon a number of disciplines — such as organizational theory, psychology, industrial relations, labour economics, political economy, and feminist studies — in order to develop a better "social" understanding of work.

Sociologists also draw upon different theoretical traditions in the study of work. As we shall see, a central debate concerns the degree of **conflict** or **consensus** that exists between employers and workers. This debate forms a constant theme throughout the chapter as we explore key issues at both macro and micro levels of analyses.

We begin at the macro level. The questions we explore in this part of the chapter concern the institutions, occupations, and organizations that structure predictable patterns of work. How has industrialization shaped our current institutions of work? Why do labour-market inequalities exist? How have work organizations changed over time? We then turn to micro-level questions about how individuals actually experience work. Are Canadians satisfied with their jobs? What sort of work values do we hold? Does the work we do affect our nonworking lives?

THE CONTINUING EVOLUTION OF INDUSTRIAL SOCIETY

Recent changes in work and society, such as the introduction of computer technologies, have led some observers to proclaim a "third industrial revolution." What does it mean to speak of a "revolution," and what are the consequences for the future of work? A brief look at the changes undergone by industrial society in the 20th century will set the stage for an investigation of these questions.

• THE MODERN CORPORATION AND THE RISE OF MANAGEMENT

During the early 1900s, industrialized societies saw a period of consolidation and growth. From 1890 to 1920 the number of Canadian manufacturing firms shrank from 70 000 to 22 000 as a result of the growing concentration of production in large organizations. This era witnessed a **second industrial revolution** spurred by the development of mass production systems such as the assembly line.

Moreover, the rapid expansion of private-sector and government bureaucracies resulted in the rise of a new managerial elite that made concerted efforts to coordinate and control work through elaborate administrative systems (Lowe, 1987). This early 20th-century quest for greater organizational efficiency and regulation of labour was known as **scientific management**.

• THE RISE OF THE SERVICE ECONOMY

During the post–World War II period, Canada, like many other industrial societies, increasingly became a **service economy**. Economic activity shifted away from manufacturing and toward other activities such as office work and retail sales, as well as educational, health, and social services provided by government. Women's participation in paid work accelerated. In recent decades, the creation of a global economy, greater use of computer and telecommunication technologies, and reliance on more "flexible" production techniques have led some observers to predict a new world of work — a third industrial revolution.

Contemporary sociologists are divided between negative and positive assessments of such change. In the 1970s Daniel Bell (1973) predicted a **post-industrial society** based on the production of information rather than material goods, where highly skilled workers would engage in rewarding and meaningful jobs. A contrasting picture was painted by Harry Braverman (1974), who inspired the **labour-process** tradition. Braverman argued that, regardless of technological developments, work organized under capitalist systems would continue to be deskilled and degraded much as it had been in the industrial age (also see Rinehart, 1987). There is convincing evidence that both Bell and Braverman may have been partly correct. According to research by John Myles (1988), the shift to a service-based economy and accompanying technological changes are resulting in the polarization of employment, as new jobs are created at the top and bottom of the labour market and old jobs in the middle disappear.

THE INSTITUTIONS OF WORK

With the maturing of industrial capitalism came state regulations, unions and professional associations, the educational system, and other institutions that influence how work is organized. Such institutions create *predictable* industrial activity by setting the ground rules for relations between employers and workers and, more generally, regulating labour-market activities (Kalleberg and Berg, 1987).

• THE ROLE OF THE STATE AND EMPLOYMENT REGULATION

In most industrialized countries, the state plays a key role in the economy (Skocpol and Amenta, 1986). In the early days of "unfettered capitalism," the state was much less involved in regulating work activity. Over time, harsh working conditions and the resulting threat of worker unrest made it necessary for the state to oversee employers' practices. Notable examples were late 19th-century restrictions on child labour and hours of work. With the Great Depression of the 1930s and World War II, public pressure grew for state involvement in the economy, paving the way for the emergence of the welfare state (Wolfe, 1989).

Canadian federal and provincial governments have now established the legislative and administrative framework for industry. Specifically, the state mediates between workers and employers and regulates a vast array of conditions such as minimum wages, hours of work, dismissal and hiring practices, human rights, health and safety, unemployment insurance, and training. Recent state initiatives, notably the 1989 free trade agreement (FTA) with the United States (now expanded to include Mexico in the North American Free Trade Agreement), will have major consequences for Canadian industries and workers. The state also has become a major employer within the Canadian economy. Policies such as privatization of government services and deficit reduction have incurred the wrath of its own employees.

• THE ROLE OF UNIONS AND COLLECTIVE BARGAINING

Unions are another important work institution. Poor conditions endured by workers in the late 19th century sparked the first major surge of unionization. Canadian workers had to fight for the right to unionize and until the Trade Union Act of 1872, efforts to organize were deemed "conspiratorial." Many of the pioneers of the Canadian labour movement were skilled craft workers, such as printers and blacksmiths, and consequently **craft unions,** which were organized on the basis of craft, dominated the young labour movement well into the 20th century. It was only in the 1940s that **industrial unionism,** in which one union represents all workers in an industry, became established in Canada. In 1956, individual craft and industrial unions joined forces within the Canadian Labour Congress (CLC), which exists today as Canada's major central labour body.

Over time, the revolutionary aims of unions have been replaced by narrower concerns over the work situations of their members. Typically, the daily activities of unions revolve around defending and improving control over work and job rewards (Crouch, 1982). Despite the popular media image that unions improve their members' interests at public expense, research by Harvard economists Freeman and Medoff (1984) demonstrates that unionization benefits rather than harms the social and economic system. Unions function as managers of discontent, advancing workers' rights and rewards, and boosting productivity by contributing to lower employee turnover, reduced hiring and training costs, and greater labour–management communication and cooperation. In fact, the basic aim of the industrial relations system is to prevent conflict between workers and employers that could result in a strike or lockout.

It is true that unions provide certain advantages to their members in the form of somewhat better wages, working conditions, and job security than would be found among comparable groups of non-union workers. But professional associations have an even greater impact on the distribution of these scarce resources. Medical doctors, engineers, accountants, lawyers, architects — these are the major professions that have a legislated right to restrict access to their specialized expertise and to set the fees for their services (Freidson, 1984). As such, the self-governing professions create "sheltered labour markets," which in turn serve to maintain the power and privileges of their members.

• THE ROLE OF EDUCATIONAL INSTITUTIONS AND TRAINING

In pre-industrial societies schooling was available only to an elite few. However, with industrialization and the greater complexity of work came increased demands for specialized schooling to be provided by the state. Today, most industrial societies have highly developed systems of both *vocational* and *academic education* that prepare people for jobs in the labour market. In recent decades, Canadians have witnessed a dramatic rise in postsecondary education levels, particularly among women, who now are better educated on average than men. Canada's system of vocational, or job-specific, training is weak, however, in comparison to many other industrial societies (Economic Council of Canada, 1992).

Most people believe that education is an "equalizer" within society: the higher your education, the greater the chances of finding a lucrative and rewarding job. The logic of this view is that as educational opportunities increase, society will become more egalitarian. To some extent this is true. **Human capital** and **status attainment** theories demonstrate the importance of education for improved career prospects (Krahn and Lowe, 1993: ch. 4). Yet individual opportunities for education vary according to family background, with children of higher-income families receiving better-quality and higher levels of education. Thus, as theories of social reproduction emphasize, education also perpetuates existing social inequalities across generations.

• LABOUR MARKETS AND SOCIAL INEQUALITY

Many of the work institutions we have discussed feed directly into the labour market: the state, unions and professional associations, and schools all play a role in shaping the demand for, or supply of, workers. Broadly defined, the **labour market** is the economic arena where employers search for qualified workers and potential employees seek satisfactory jobs. Of particular interest to sociologists is the distributive function of the labour market. This refers to how inequalities are generated and sustained. Clearly, some jobs are better than others. But how are workers sorted into good and bad jobs?

Two major theories try to explain this. Human capital theory, which we have mentioned already, claims that workers who have invested more in training and education have higher levels of "human capital" and so receive better jobs. This theory assumes open and equal competition for jobs, where people with highly valued skills and abilities "choose" jobs with higher pay and status. In other words, it is the characteristics of individuals, or the *labour supply,* that determines who gets the best jobs.

An alternative explanation given by **labour-market segmentation theory** suggests that there are *primary* and *secondary labour markets* that separate good and bad jobs (Clairmont et al., 1983). Certain types of workers, such as women and visible minorities, are concentrated in low-paid monotonous jobs in the secondary sector and have difficulty moving out of these "job ghettos" into something better. Furthermore, big corporations and government have the ability to offer relatively attractive employment packages in order to transform their employees into a committed and reliable workforce. Thus, while worker characteristics are important, it is also the structure of the labour market itself, and how employers define the *demand* for labour, that determines where people are employed.

CANADIAN TRENDS

Our discussion so far raises many questions about the specific nature of the Canadian labour market. What are Canada's current employment trends? In which occupations and industries do Canadians work? And how has this changed over time? In order to answer these questions, we draw on statistical data from the Canadian Census and the monthly Labour Force Survey. Both surveys provide valuable information with which to trace the changing contours of the Canadian labour market.

• CHANGES IN LABOUR-FORCE PARTICIPATION

Labour-force participation is defined in terms of paid employment and includes people 15 years and older who are either working for pay (including self-employment or employing others) or actively looking for such work. This means that the *unemployed* are included as part of the labour force, while those working at home raising children and/or keeping house are not. Labour-force statistics also omit workers in the *informal* or *hidden economy,* where work is exchanged for cash or other goods and services, as well as *children's work* done by those under 15 years of age (Qvortrup, 1985).

It is interesting to see how labour-force participation has changed over time. In 1901, 53 percent of Canadians 15 years of age and older were in the labour force. The rate for the same age group rose slightly to 58 percent in 1971. During the next fifteen years growth quickened and, by 1991, 66 percent of Canadians 15 years of age and older were working or seeking work.

The most dramatic change has occurred among women. In 1901, only 16 percent of women were in the paid labour force compared to 88 percent of men. Between 1901 and 1961, female participation slowly rose to 29 percent, after which a combination of factors spurred rates to 58 percent in 1991. In contrast to females, male rates declined to 75 percent in 1991, the result of earlier retirement and longer periods of education for males today (Krahn and Lowe, 1993: 62).

• INDUSTRIAL TRENDS

Industrial classifications reflect the product or service being produced. Generally, industries are grouped into three broad categories: the **primary sector** (e.g., agricultural, mining, forestry, and other resource-extraction industries); the **secondary sector** (e.g., manufacturing and construction), where goods are produced from raw materials supplied by the primary sector; and the **tertiary sector** (e.g., financial and personal services), where services rather than products are offered.

Over the last century, the industrial mix in Canada has shifted. In 1891, 49 percent of workers were employed in primary industries, 20 percent in secondary activity, and the remaining 31 percent in services. With the rise of manufacturing in the early 1900s, the primary sector (mainly agriculture) declined. More recent decades have witnessed a massive expansion of service industries.

This is captured in Table 6.1. In 1951, 23 percent of the labour force worked in the primary sector. By 1990, less than 6 percent was employed in these industries. Manufacturing industries have also declined in importance, employing 26 percent of the workforce in 1951 compared with 16 percent in 1990. In sharp contrast, a staggering 71 percent of employed Canadians now work in services. These trends clearly illustrate that we now live in a *service economy*. A similar pattern of change has been observed in virtually all industrial capitalist societies.

Table 6.1

CHANGES IN THE INDUSTRIAL DISTRIBUTION OF THE TOTAL LABOUR FORCE, CANADA, 1951 AND 1990

Industry	1951 (percent)	1990 (percent)	Net Change 1951–1990 (percentage points)
Primary			
Agriculture	18.4	3.3	- 15.1
Forestry, fishing, and trapping	2.9	0.9	-2.0
Mines, quarries, and oil wells	1.5	1.4	-0.1
Goods producing			
Manufacturing	26.5	16.1	-10.4
Construction	6.8	6.7	-0.1
Service			
Transportation, communication, and other utilities	8.8	7.4	-1.4
Trade	14.1	17.7	+3.6
Finance, insurance, and real estate	3.0	5.7	+2.7
Community, business, and personal service	8.0	33.8	+25.8
Public administration	—	6.4	+6.4
	(100.0)	(100.0)	
Total number in labour force ('000)	5 097	13 681	

Sources: Calculated from Statistics Canada (1980: 92) for 1951; Statistics Canada (1990a: B30) for 1990.

• UNION MEMBERSHIP

In 1989 there were 3.9 million unionized workers in Canada, representing 36 percent of the nonagricultural paid labour force (Coates et al., 1989: 19, 20). Given that only 4.9 percent of all nonagricultural employees belonged to unions in 1911, this is an impressive record of growth. Expansion occurred in three major spurts, the first two coinciding with World Wars I and II respectively, and the third occurring in the 1970s with the rise of public-service unions. Internationally, Canada had one of the lowest levels of unionization in 1961, but has experienced the highest growth since that time. As Figure 6.1 shows, we are roughly in the middle of major industrial nations in terms of our level of unionization.

Union membership in Canada varies by sex, industry, occupation, and province of residence. In 1986, women made up 36 percent of all union members, and the overall rate of unionization for female workers was 29 percent (Coates et al., 1989: 32). While relatively fewer women than men belong to unions, women have been joining unions at a faster rate than men in the past two decades. Women have lower unionization not because they are "passive workers," uninterested in collective bargaining, but because they are concentrated in industries, such as finance and insurance, that historically have lacked union representation (Purcell, 1984; Clemenson, 1989). However, some of the traditionally female professions (notably nursing and teaching) are highly unionized, showing that women are as likely to unionize if opportunities are present and conditions are ripe for collective action.

As we might expect, managers and administrative employees are least likely to be union members. This is largely because labour legislation prevents most of them from even belonging to a union on the grounds that they make career decisions affecting other employees. Union membership also varies by region, with a low rate in Alberta and high rates in British Columbia and

Figure 6.1

UNION MEMBERSHIP IN OECD COUNTRIES, 1986

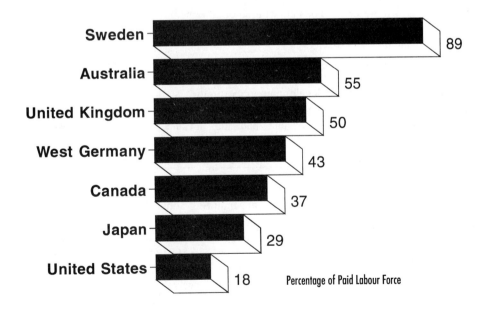

Source: Coates et al. (1989: 21).

Newfoundland. Such variation reflects provincial differences in the industrial base and labour legislation.

• CHANGING CONDITIONS AND FORMS OF WORK

Canadians have witnessed dramatic changes in the conditions and forms of the work they engage in. Weekly hours are one example. In 1870, the average worker put in 64 hours a week on the job. During the next 100 years, weekly hours were sharply reduced as a result of union pressure and productivity gains from new technologies. By the mid-1970s, Canadians were working 39 hours on average. There has been little change since then, with average weekly hours worked standing at 38 in 1990 (Statistics Canada, 1990a: Table 20). However, judging from recent union contracts, there is an emergent trend toward a shorter work week in a number of European countries. The Canadian labour movement is now interested in promoting the same idea.

Any discussion of work hours must account for the dramatic growth of part-time jobs. In 1953, about 4 percent of Canadians worked part time (defined as less than 30 hours a week) (Weeks, 1980). Yet in the last two decades there has been a surge in part-time job creation, and by 1990 just over 15 percent of all jobs were part time (Statistics Canada, *Social Trends*, Spring, 1993: 35).

Certain groups of workers are overrepresented in such work. In 1986, seven out of ten part-time workers were women, with high-school and college students forming the second-largest group. Although women and youth may prefer part-time work in order to balance work and domestic responsibilities, or continue their education, some part-time workers would prefer a full-time job. Indeed, the percentage of workers in *involuntary part-time work* (e.g., those who would take a full-time job if one were available) has risen from 11 percent in 1975 to a much higher level of 22 percent in 1990.

Part-time work reflects a growing trend toward **nonstandard forms of employment**. According to the Economic Council of Canada (1990; see also Krahn, 1991), nonstandard work — which includes part-time, short-term, temporary, and contract work, and own-account self-employment — accounted for one-half of the jobs created between 1980 and 1988. Non-standard work now represents 30 percent of total employment in Canada. It is especially widespread in the consumer service sector, such as retail trade, hotels and restaurants, amusement and recreation, and personal services.

Employers are shifting to nonstandard forms of employment as a way of achieving greater flexibility and reducing costs of labour and fringe benefits. Unfortunately, these jobs are usually low paying and lack training and development opportunities, so the potential benefits to employees of having flexible work schedules is greatly diminished. What this trend may signal is an increasing polarization between "good" and "bad" jobs in Canada's labour market.

THE OCCUPATIONAL STRUCTURE

When we ask someone "what they do," we are inquiring about their occupation. *Occupation* refers to the kind of job that an individual performs or, more specifically, the tasks that she or he carries out in the course of a working day. In industrialized societies, the specialized division of labour gives rise to a complex **occupational structure**. The 1991 Canadian Census, for example, lists close to 500 different occupational categories. To a large extent, our position in the occupational structure determines our living standards, future prospects, and quality of life — in Weber's words, our "life chances." Here we examine how the Canadian occupational structure has changed, and the impact of these trends on social inequality.

• CANADA'S OCCUPATIONAL STRUCTURE

Earlier we discussed the spectacular growth of the service sector in recent decades. Such changes have had an enormous impact on the occupational structure of contemporary Canada. Most workers today are employed in *white-collar occupations,* a broad category including managerial, professional, clerical, and sales jobs. Since the early 1900s, there has been an explosion of such work, with white-collar jobs rising from 15 percent in 1901 to over 50 percent by 1981.

A large part of this expansion comes from the rise of *professions,* such as law and accounting, as well as the poorly paid, nonstandard, consumer service jobs we mentioned earlier. Alongside this growth has been a decline in primary occupations. In 1911, 34 percent of workers were engaged in agricultural work, but by 1991 this had shrunk to less than 4 percent. *Blue-collar occupations,* which include manufacturing and construction, have also declined from 30 percent during industrial expansion at the beginning of the century, and again in the 1950s, to 20 percent in 1991 (Krahn and Lowe, 1993: 72–74).

• INTERNATIONAL COMPARISONS

How does Canada's contemporary occupational structure compare to those of other industrialized nations? In 1981, 8.2 percent of Canadian labour-force participants were to be found in managerial and administrative occupations, compared to 10.8 percent in the United States but only 4.9 percent in Japan, 3.0 percent in West Germany, and 2.3 percent in Sweden. Also, in 1981, 28.6 percent of Canadian workers were in manufacturing, construction, and transportation occupations, compared to 32.9 percent in the United States, 34.9 percent in Japan, 37.3 percent in West Germany, and 33.3 percent in Sweden. Compared to other industrial capitalist societies, then, Canada has a relatively small manufacturing base. It appears that Canadian industry is "overmanaged" given the high proportion of managers (as with the United States) in our occupational structure. This fact should not be ignored when comparing Canadian productivity levels to those of the Japanese and other industrial nations.

• CLASS AND OCCUPATIONAL INEQUALITY

Studying the occupations of Canadians helps to illuminate the class structure of our society (Hunter, 1986). The term **social class** is used in a variety of ways by social scientists and is often used interchangeably with **socioeconomic status** to refer to a higher or lower position in a social hierarchy, as determined by one's occupation, education, and income. Criteria for determining class are usually "occupational" and include **market situation** (e.g., pay, security, opportunity for promotion) and **work situation** (e.g., work tasks, control, social relations of jobs). Congruence often exists between these two factors, with market rewards and working conditions becoming progressively better as one ascends the class hierarchy.

Looking strictly at levels of income, we can see disparities between various occupational groups. Table 6.2 uses 1991 Canadian Census results to document that, among male full-time/full-year workers, 1990 earnings ranged from a high of over $62 026 in medicine and health to about $20 720 in agriculture. Turning to women, we note similar disparities, although overall women's salaries are consistently lower than men's — an issue explored below. Interestingly, the highest-paying female job is teaching ($37 804), which largely reflects the high level of unionization and the fairly homogeneous nature of the profession. The Economic Council of Canada (1990) has reported a decline over the past two decades in the share of the workforce with "middle-level" earnings. This "declining middle class" is largely the result of the polarized "good jobs, bad jobs"

Table 6.2

AVERAGE EARNED INCOME OF FULL-YEAR WORKERS BY SELECTED OCCUPATIONS AND GENDER, CANADA, 1990

	Average Earned Income		
	Women $	Men $	Women's Earnings as a Percentage of Men's
Managerial/admininstrative	32 700	51 258	63.8
Natural sciences	34 409	45 070	76.3
Social sciences	32 817	59 003	55.6
Teaching	37 804	48 279	78.3
Medicine and health	31 557	62 026	50.9
Artistic/recreational	28 089	35 547	79.0
Clerical	23 258	30 829	75.4
Sales	23 328	36 436	64.0
Services	17 231	30 498	56.5
Agriculture	12 956	20 720	62.5
Processing	20 536	33 651	61.0
Machining and related occupations	21 678	33 502	64.8
Product fabricating, assembling, repairing	18 916	32 351	58.5
Construction trades	26 276	35 322	74.4
Transport equipment operating	23 992	33 634	71.3
All occupations	26 033	38 684	67.3

Source: Statistics Canada, (1993a: Catalogue no. 93-332, Table 1).

occupational structure that has accompanied the expansion of the service economy and a transformation of skill requirements (also see Myles, 1988).

• GENDER AND OCCUPATIONAL INEQUALITY

Another source of inequality is the concentration of men and women in different occupations, a phenomenon known as **occupational sex segregation**. A potent combination of gender role socialization, education, and labour-market mechanisms channels women into a limited range of occupations in which mainly other females are employed. In 1986, for example, 85 percent of working women were clustered within "traditional" occupations (such as clerical, health, and manufacturing) that made up only one-quarter of all available occupations (Hughes, 1990). These *job ghettos* typically offer little economic security and very poor opportunities for advancement. Women are not only *horizontally segregated* within the labour market into different occupations than men but are also *vertically segregated* within specific occupations, with men assuming positions of greater authority, remuneration, and benefits.

Figures 6.2 and 6.3 document the gendered structure of the labour market in two ways. First, Figure 6.2 tells us the percentage of all workers in each occupation who are female. While women now make up 44 percent of the labour force, they are underrepresented, in comparison with men, in managerial and administrative jobs, scientific and engineering jobs, and all major blue-collar occupational groups. By contrast, two-thirds of all teachers are female, as are four out of five clerical workers and nursing and health-sector workers. Second, Figure 6.3 examines the distribution of women workers across the labour market. Here we note the high concentration of employed women in clerical and service jobs. In 1989, these two relatively low-status occupations accounted for just under half of all female jobs in Canada.

Figure 6.2

WOMEN AS A PERCENTAGE OF MAJOR OCCUPATIONAL GROUPS, CANADA, 1989

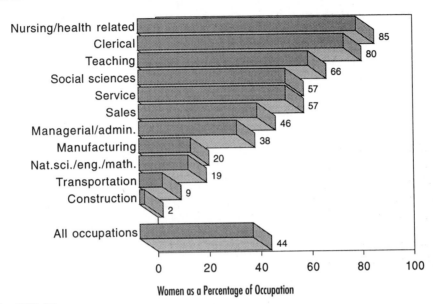

Women as a Percentage of Occupation

Source: Shea (1990: 23).

Figure 6.3

OCCUPATIONAL DISTRIBUTION OF EMPLOYED WOMEN, CANADA, 1989

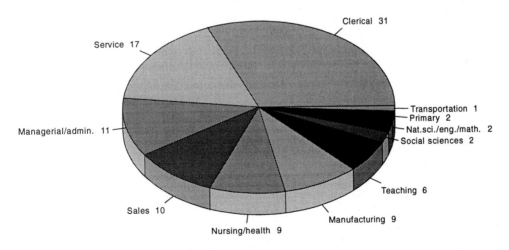

Percentage of Total Female Labour Force in Occupation

Source: Shea (1990: 23).

The origins of gender segregation are multifaceted and deeply rooted, with links to **patriarchy** (systems of male dominance) and the division between paid and domestic work. Women's availability for paid employment has long been constrained by domestic responsibilities, social ideologies of "motherhood" and "femininity," and male unionists wishing to maintain a "family wage." Over time, as social and economic forces have encouraged women's entrance into the labour market, certain jobs, such as clerical work, have become *feminized* (Lowe, 1987).

Despite inroads made by a select group of women into nontraditional managerial and professional occupations (e.g., law and accounting) in the past two decades (Marshall, 1989), the majority of female workers continues to be disadvantaged. The most obvious gender inequality is the **wage gap**. Table 6.2 reveals the gender wage gap. In 1990, women's average income from a full-time/full-year job was $26 033, compared to $38 684 for men. This represents a wage gap of 67.3 percent, meaning that women earn an average of 67.3 cents for every dollar earned by a male. This gap has closed only slightly since 1971, when it stood at 60 percent. There are striking variations in the wage gap across occupations, from 79 percent in the arts and recreation and 78 percent in teaching to 51 percent in health and medicine.

Women also lack opportunities for promotion into higher, more responsible levels of work. Consequently, legislation has now been passed to address these inequalities. Pay equity legislation, which seeks to achieve "comparable pay for comparable jobs," is in place in all jurisdictions except the Northwest Territories, Alberta, British Columbia, and Saskatchewan (legislation is expected in the latter two provinces) (Cuneo, 1990). As well, the 1986 Employment Equity Act seeks to fully open job opportunities for women and other disadvantaged groups within the federal civil service, Crown corporations, and federally regulated firms with more than 100 employees.

• OTHER BARRIERS AND INEQUALITIES: ABORIGINAL PEOPLES, THE DISABLED, AND VISIBLE MINORITIES

While we have focused on class and gender inequalities, other groups — such as the disabled, aboriginals, and visible minorities — also experience inequalities in the workplace. We noted earlier that aboriginal people experience higher unemployment than other Canadians (22 percent in 1986). They are also underrepresented in managerial and professional jobs. So too are the disabled and visible minorities. Given these inequalities, the Employment Equity Act defines them, along with women, as *designated groups.* Under the act, employers must (1) identify and eliminate discriminatory practices, and (2) institute positive policies and practices to ensure that the representation of designated groups is commensurate to their representation within the general workforce. Employers are required to file an annual report with the government outlining the progress of designated groups within the firm (Canada, 1990). However, progress has been slow in increasing the representation of these groups in the organizations covered by the act. A recent parliamentary review of the legislation therefore recommended stricter monitoring and enforcement of the act, broadening it to include more workplaces and requiring greater commitment among employers to achieving equity goals (Canada, 1992).

THE ORGANIZATION

There is little doubt that we live in an "organizational society" (Presthus, 1978). Large bureaucracies touch all aspects of our daily lives. Attending school, negotiating a student loan, searching for a summer job — all these activities bring us into contact with large and complex organizations. Why have bureaucracies become such a defining feature of industrialized societies? And how have organizations, and ideas about them, evolved over time?

• MODERN ORGANIZATIONS

Industrialization has created the need to coordinate, control, and integrate an increasingly specialized division of labour. For managers, the overriding aim is to forge an efficient organization. More than anything, managers continue to believe that this requires a highly motivated and cooperative workforce.

Various "theories of management" have emerged over time advocating different methods for achieving these goals. **Coercive** management techniques favour penalties and harsh discipline; **utilitarian** methods suggest that employees are motivated purely by economic self-interest; while **normative** approaches assume that workers equate their own goals with those of the organization and are thus self-motivated. Here we examine various schools of management that have emerged over time, as well as more critical sociological perspectives on management and organizations.

• MAX WEBER AND BUREAUCRACY

In the early 1900s the first comprehensive "theory of management" emerged, heralding **bureaucracy** as the "one best way" to efficiently coordinate and integrate the multitude of specialized tasks conducted in a large factory or office. Based on the fixed division of tasks, hierarchical supervision, and detailed rules and regulations, bureaucracy was seen to promote speed, precision, clarity, reliability, and efficiency of operations (Morgan, 1986).

German sociologist Max Weber anticipated the spread of bureaucracy, recognizing its growing importance to capitalism. It was, he wrote, a "technically superior" form of organization, without which "capitalist production could not continue" (Weber, 1964: 338). For Weber, the cornerstones of bureaucracy were a detailed division of labour; a hierarchy of authority, rules, and regulations; and recruitment and promotion on the basis of education and ability. Above all, bureaucracies operated according to rational principles. Yet, while acknowledging its merits, he also despaired of the potential of bureaucracy to routinize and mechanize all aspects of human life. On a rather gloomy note, Weber predicted that the spread of bureaucracy would bring "the disenchantment of the world."

• CLASSICAL MANAGEMENT THEORY AND SCIENTIFIC MANAGEMENT

The early management theorists were great advocates of bureaucracy, devoting considerable energy to developing precise principles and methods of management (Pugh et al., 1985). **Classical management theorists,** such as Henri Fayol, concentrated on the design of the total organization, seeking to codify essential ingredients of successful management. Central to his work was the development of "management principles" that could guide the planning, communication, coordination, and control functions within the firm.

A more influential school of thought was **scientific management,** or "Taylorism." Popularized by the engineer Frederick Taylor, it advocated separating the *conception* of work (i.e., the design and planning) from its *execution.* Under Taylorism, managers took over all decision-making aspects of the job and used *time and motion studies* to isolate the most efficient way for workers to execute tasks. Jobs were then redesigned into standardized work procedures, which workers were trained to follow. Production quotas were linked to basic rates of pay, with bonuses and penalties used to motivate workers to produce more.

While the Taylor system of management was influential in North America and, to a lesser extent, in Britain and Europe, employers feared the consequences of its full-scale adoption, instead applying it in piecemeal fashion. Nevertheless, many principles of scientific management became standard features of management practice and can still be seen operating in today's service industries, such as fast food (Reiter, 1991).

• CORPORATE WELFARE AND HUMAN RELATIONS MANAGEMENT

Despite their efficiency, early management techniques created routine, monotonous jobs that robbed workers of decision making and creativity. Employee dissatisfaction was expressed in high turnover, absenteeism, or unionization, and threatened to undermine the machine-like efficiency of the new industrial system.

The need to treat workers as human beings became paramount, and with this, **corporate welfare programs** surfaced. Popular in innovative firms in the 1920s, these programs aimed at reducing the alienating effects of bureaucracy and routine work through a healthier work environment and improved job benefits. Many firms committed to scientific management used welfare measures to gain the cooperation of their staff. Yet it was not until the Human Relations School of management began to systematically examine some of the same concerns in the 1930s that scientific management faced a serious challenge.

The **Human Relations School** originated in a series of studies conducted by Elton Mayo and other Harvard Business School researchers between 1927 and 1932 at Western Electric's Hawthorne Works near Chicago (Krahn and Lowe, 1993: 202–6). Originally the studies focused on the effects of fatigue and monotony on productivity, which were central concerns of industrial psychologists at the time. Experiments with lighting levels, however, led to the unexpected finding that group social relations and employee attitudes had a major influence on productivity. It was with this **Hawthorne Effect** that the workplace came to be recognized as a social, as opposed to purely technical, system.

Human relations emphasized how workers' attitudes, values, emotions, psychological needs, and interpersonal relationships shaped work behaviour. Rejecting the utilitarian assumptions of scientific management, it advocated careful recruitment, effective training, good-quality supervision, and communication.

A common thread in all work reform initiatives is that employees must be treated humanely. But beyond a few minor concessions, these programs tend to gloss over deeply rooted worker–employer conflict. They allow authority to remain firmly in the hands of management.

• THE INFORMAL SIDE OF ORGANIZATIONS

The Human Relations School shifted workplace social relations into the organizational spotlight. Researchers became interested in the *informal* side of organizations. This addresses how employees reinterpret, resist, or adapt to work structures and management directives. Pioneering studies by Roy (1954) of a Chicago machine shop revealed how work groups beat the formal Tayloristic system through their own informal system of production. Dalton's (1959) study, entitled *Men Who Manage,* gave a fascinating account of how managers bend rules and short-circuit bureaucracy in order to achieve their objectives.

• HARRY BRAVERMAN AND LABOUR PROCESS THEORY

Harry Braverman (1974) presented a critical perspective on management practice, not a theory of how to manage, and thereby spawned a renaissance in the sociology of work. Focusing on the **labour process** — the process of production in which labour is applied to raw materials and machinery to produce commodities or services — Braverman argued that modern management continued to rely on Tayloristic methods to increasingly tighten control over, and deskill, worker's activities.

Despite its importance, Braverman's work contained major flaws (Thompson, 1989). In particular, he ignored how workers actively resisted management assaults on their skills and, furthermore, placed too much importance on Tayloristic methods of control. Researchers have since highlighted the continuing resistance of workers and have shown that there is no one strategy of control. Revisions to Braverman emphasize, more than anything, how a critical approach to social relations, power, and control has redefined work research in many countries, including Canada (Rinehart, 1987; Storey, 1991).

• FEMINIST CONTRIBUTIONS

Feminist theory has provided another vital contribution to organizational studies since the early 1970s. Feminist researchers question why men typically occupy positions of authority in organizations. Feminist organizational researchers have challenged the assumptions on which organizations rest, arguing that they are constructed according to male images of society and have been perpetuated as instruments of male power and privilege. This feminist critique has contributed to a growing debate about alternative forms of organization that are more cooperative and democratic, and less hierarchical and structured (e.g., Kanter, 1977; Hearn and Parkin, 1987; Lowe, 1987; Pringle, 1988).

As Kanter argued in her pioneering study, *Men and Women of the Corporation* (1977), understanding gender segregation within the organization is crucial because large corporations act as major employers and reproduce patterns of gender inequality through their own specific management practices. Working on the assumption that "the job makes the person," Kanter revealed how jobs are rigidly "sex typed" and structured so as to create self-fulfilling prophecies about the abilities of women and men. The secretaries in the firm she studied served as "office wives," tied into subordinate and paternalistic relationships with their male bosses. Having little opportunity for advancement, they soon lost motivation and interest in their work. Managers, in contrast, sought to increase trust and conformity within their circle by promoting men similar to themselves. As a result few women reached upper management levels, and those who did faced problems of *tokenism* as the result of their minority status.

An additional contribution of feminist research has been to spark interest in the area of *sexuality and organizations.* Hearn and Parkin (1987) explore the role of sexuality, revealing how it operates both *explicitly* (through sexual relationships or harassment) and *implicitly* (through dress, touch, or jokes) within organizations. Such research has begun to illuminate previously hidden aspects of organizational life such as sexual harassment, discrimination against homosexuals, and the intersection of business and sexual relationships.

• CORPORATE CULTURE AND JAPANESE MANAGEMENT

The rise of Japan as an industrial power has generated enormous interest among managers and social scientists in **corporate culture**. Explorations have revealed how companies rely on shared systems of meaning that are strengthened through language, norms, folklore, ritual, and ceremony. Studies of *Japanese management,* in particular, have highlighted the symbiosis between national and corporate cultures. For example, organizations in Japan mirror strong national values of collaboration, interdependence, and mutual obligation, while firms in the United States reflect a national ethic of competitive individualism (Ouchi, 1981; Pascal and Athos, 1981).

Unlike studies of *informal organization,* which reveal how employees attempt to resist formal culture, literature on corporate culture has focused on the creation of a *dominant culture* that encourages employee conformity and integration (Ouchi and Wilkins, 1985). Here, "ideal" companies are Hewlett-Packard and IBM, whose strong cultures ensure that employees either "buy into" corporate norms or get out. In such organizations, **countercultures** (e.g., trade unions or informal groups), which confront and challenge official rules, are strongly discouraged.

EXPERIENCES OF WORK

How we experience work, whether we dread or look forward to each working day, has enormous consequences for our overall quality of life. In exploring the personal dimension of work, we distinguish between **work values,** which are broad social values about the meaning of work, and **work orientations,** which are the meanings attached to work by specific individuals within society (Blackburn and Mann, 1979). As we shall see, workers do not necessarily share the same work values. Similarly, work orientations are shaped both by larger societal work values and by specific experiences on the job.

• WORK ETHIC

Over the centuries, the meaning of work has changed. According to Max Weber (1958), Calvinist religious principles, which extolled the virtues of hard work and frugality, unintentionally fuelled capitalist development by encouraging individuals to make and reinvest profits. While Weber was exploring a complex set of work values, today we use the term **work ethic** to refer to the willingness to work hard, diligently, and obediently in whatever job is available.

In recent decades, there has been alarm over a supposedly declining work ethic in industrial societies. However, a study of 1985 high-school and university students — the next generation of workers and the usual focus of declining work ethic concerns — found that a large majority of these young people were firmly committed to paid employment (Krahn and Lowe, 1991: 156–57). This echoes the Canadian Work Ethic and Job Satisfaction Surveys of the early 1970s (Burstein et al., 1975). Most respondents said that work was a central part of their lives and agreed that, given the choice, they would prefer to work than not hold a job. Ironically, these same Canadians doubted the work commitment of others.

What about the claim of a superior Japanese work ethic? Despite the prevailing view that Japanese culture creates workers who willingly work long hours and forgo holidays, only 25 percent of Japanese workers are employed within the "high-tech" corporations so admired by North Americans. Instead, the majority of Japanese work in firms providing low pay, poor benefits, and little job security. No doubt, for such workers, long hours and hard work are more a reflection of economic necessity than of different cultural values concerning work.

• MARX AND ALIENATION

Alienation, originally a philosophical concept, was incorporated by Karl Marx into his writings on work and capitalism. Marx believed that the essence of human nature was creative activity, expressed through labour in cooperation with others (see Chapter 1). Marx believed that pre-capitalist society provided work that was creative and fulfilling but that under capitalism, and the extreme division of labour and specialization, work became alienating.

Alienation remains of interest to sociologists, yet its meaning varies for them. Building upon Marx, the **structural perspective** views alienation as a "condition of objective powerlessness" tied to capitalist systems of production. James Rinehart, for example, argues that despite improvements in working conditions, capitalist employment remains alienating because workers lack essential control over their labour (Rinehart, 1987). In contrast, a **social psychological perspective** seeks to measure feelings of "powerlessness," "meaninglessness," and "social isolation" through workers' own self-reports. Researchers here are predominantly interested in the absence of intrinsic job rewards; in this sense alienation comes to resemble job dissatisfaction.

• JOB SATISFACTION

Job satisfaction is a subjective reaction to a particular set of job rewards. Surveys measure job satisfaction with some variation on the question: "Overall, how satisfied are you with your job?" The resulting picture is very positive. For instance, Statistics Canada's 1989 General Social Survey found that 88 percent of respondents were satisfied with their jobs (Krahn, 1992: 130). Does this mean that job dissatisfaction is rare? It may be that more specific and probing questions about job satisfaction are required.

What factors affect job satisfaction? Research has studied both job content and worker traits (Krahn and Lowe, 1993: ch. 10). Frederick Herzberg's (1968) studies of job content differentiated between *extrinsic* (e.g., salary, benefits, work environment) and *intrinsic* (e.g., responsibility, meaningful work) job characteristics, arguing that job satisfaction could be improved only through intrinsic job rewards.

Research on worker characteristics has found that older workers are likely to express more job satisfaction, a finding that may be due to reduced expectations (an *aging effect*), different expectations from younger workers (a *cohort effect*), or greater importance of family and community interests in later life (a *life-cycle effect*). Differences between women and men have also been a focus of interest. While the 1973 Canadian Job Satisfaction Survey found that women were more likely to value good social relationships and be satisfied with intrinsic rewards, most studies suggest that gender differences are a product of the workplace itself.

• STRESS AND WORK

Stress is a multidimensional problem that can lead to serious mental and physical health disorders. Research has distinguished between stressors and individual reactions to them. **Stressors** are objective conditions of work (e.g., noisy work environments, competing job demands, lack of decision-making responsibilities) or events (e.g., disputes with a supervisor, news of job loss) that have the potential to produce a negative subjective response. If stressors are long term and of high intensity, serious diseases can result. **Work-related stress** is thus an individually experienced negative reaction to a job or a work environment. Not only does stress take a toll on workers' health (physical and mental), but it also reduces productivity and therefore should be of far greater concern to employers (Karasek and Theorell, 1990).

Reactions to stressful work depend upon the individual's psychological coping mechanisms as well as social support from family, friends, and co-workers. While home and family may help workers cope with stress, they can also act as stressors. Indeed, many workers, particularly women, face stress from conflicting demands at home and in the workplace (Lowe, 1989).

A common feature of all stressors identified by research is the fact that individual workers have little control over them. Studies repeatedly show that routinized, machine-paced work is extremely stress provoking. Burnout is prevalent among social workers, teachers, and nurses who face huge demands to help people but have very limited resources to actually do so. Work-family stress results from lack of control in either sphere. Combating stress must therefore be carried out on several fronts: through organizational change and job redesign, and a holistic approach to occupational and policy initiatives such as child care, parental leave, and flexible work schedules.

• THE "LONG ARM OF THE JOB"

Many of us believe that people bring work orientations and preferences to their jobs and that these, in turn, influence satisfaction or alienation in the job. However, research shows that it is far more likely for an individual's job conditions to have an impact on her or his subjective experience of work. Participation in routine, closely supervised work fosters **instrumental work attitudes.** In other words, under these conditions workers can expect to derive little intrinsic satisfaction so they end up viewing their job as a means to an end — getting a paycheque. Thus, the nature of work itself is likely to have a large impact on an individual's feelings of satisfaction, alienation, and stress, as well as on his or her work orientations.

Research finds that people who enjoy their work are generally happier with life. Martin Meissner (1971) argued that the "long arm of the job" has an impact on one's life away from work. His study of British Columbia sawmill workers tested whether workers look for leisure activities that offer what is absent from their jobs (**compensatory effect**) or what is similar (**spillover effect**). Meissner found evidence for the spillover effect, suggesting that individuals in jobs with little autonomy are unlikely to engage in leisure activities that require discretion or independent action.

Melvin Kohn's research further explores these issues. Tracing the jobs and personalities of male workers over a ten-year period, Kohn found positive personality changes for those who had "occupational self-direction" — that is, independent, nonroutine work requiring independent judgment. In contrast, jobs with little self-direction more commonly lead to psychological distress (Kohn and Schooler, 1983). Similar studies of female workers, and of workers in different societies, by Kohn and his colleagues show similar results. In short, intrinsically rewarding work, especially work that allows self-direction, has positive consequences for the personalities and careers of those fortunate enough to participate in it.

FUTURE ISSUES

As we approach the year 2000, dramatic changes are transforming the industrial landscape and the experience of work. At the macro level, two powerful forces — microelectronics and industrial restructuring — are reshaping Western industrial economies. Alongside these shifts are growing pressures from individual workers and unions to improve the quality of work through job redesign, greater employee involvement in decision making, and more flexible work arrangements allowing a better integration of work and family. Looking into the future raises crucial questions: Will new technologies and industrial restructuring bring opportunities or problems? What prospects exist for greater industrial democracy? Can environmentalism and industrial growth coexist? How can family and work conflicts be resolved?

• TECHNOLOGICAL CHANGE: "THE AGE OF THE SMART MACHINE"

Advances in microelectronics, computer technologies, and telecommunications have catapulted industrialized capitalist societies into the "information age" (Zuboff, 1988). In Canada, information is now a key resource. An Economic Council of Canada (1987; also see Betcherman and McMullen, 1986) survey of 946 firms shows that the office has become increasingly high tech, with 66 percent of all information technology adoption between 1980 and 1985 being office related. A second major trend is the adoption of automated production systems, such as industrial robots, computer-assisted manufacturing (CAM), and computer-assisted design (CAD), which made up 23 percent of all change.

Given this change, have Daniel Bell's predictions of a highly skilled, post-industrial society come true? Or have Harry Braverman's warnings of deskilled and degraded labour been confirmed? Untangling technological outcomes is difficult given the range of factors that affect the quantity and quality of work. Much research is *technologically deterministic,* ignoring that outcomes depend not on the technology itself but on the manner in which it is adopted (Hughes, 1989; MacKenzie and Wajcman, 1985).

Recent results from the 1989 General Social Survey (GSS) suggest a tentatively positive assessment of technological change, with Canadian workers experiencing boosts to skill levels and the intrinsic interest of their jobs (Lowe, 1991). Yet the GSS report is careful to underline that outcomes vary by industry, occupation, and gender, and that technological change may be contributing to the polarization between good and bad jobs in the labour market. While the GSS offers an overall picture, more focused case studies of specific firms or occupations nonetheless reveal the negative effects of new technologies (Robertson and Wareham, 1987).

• INDUSTRIAL RESTRUCTURING AND GLOBALIZATION

Accelerated technological change is occurring at a time when the economy is undergoing fundamental readjustment. The global oil crises of the 1970s, the recession in the early 1980s, and fierce international competition — especially from the Pacific Rim countries — underlie this economic change. This process of **industrial restructuring** is basic to industrialization. The economist Joseph Schumpeter described it as "creative destruction," referring to breaking down old ways of running industry and building up more competitive, efficient, and high-tech alternatives.

Three strands of change are interwoven through the current processes of restructuring. The first is **deindustrialization:** the decline of so-called sunset manufacturing industries such as automotives, steel, and textiles once central to the economy of Canada and other industrialized societies (Bluestone and Harrison, 1982). Accordingly, the reduction of relatively well paid blue-collar production jobs (often unionized) is contributing to a shrinkage of the middle class. The second strand involves **post-Fordism:** a shift away from "Fordism" (the combination of Taylorist-style work organization with assembly-line technology to mass produce standardized goods) toward "flexible specialization," which utilizes technology to link all aspects of production into a coordinated, skill-intensive system. While there is agreement that the crisis in Fordism — basically, the kinds of economic problems so obvious in the 1980s — has precipitated new approaches to industrial organization, there is considerable debate regarding whether automation, flexible systems, and semi-autonomous work teams have ushered in a new economic era (Wood, 1989). The third strand involves the rise of the **service economy** (Krahn, 1992). Closely linked with these strands of change is the rise of global markets, which will see North America, the European Community, and the Asia-Pacific region form major trading blocs in the 1990s. In Canada, the Canada–U.S. Free Trade Agreement (FTA) has been negotiated to guarantee Canadian–American trade. But there is much debate as to whether the FTA will actually be beneficial for Canadian workers and long-term economic prospects (e.g., Cohen, 1987). Critics argue that hundreds of thousands of jobs, mainly in manufacturing, have been lost since the FTA took effect. Free trade proponents counter that these job losses are a result of the recession, global economic restructuring, and the uncompetitiveness of many Canadian industries (Krahn and Lowe, 1993: 53–54).

• ENVIRONMENTALISM AND SUSTAINABLE DEVELOPMENT

Another challenge in the 1990s is a greater awareness of environmental issues and interest in **sustainable development**. Despite dire warnings in the 1970s that the world has reached its "limits to growth," it has taken time and numerous environmental catastrophes for environmental concerns to work their way up the public agenda (World Commission on Environment and Development, 1987). It is not surprising that environmentalism has emerged only slowly. After all, industrialization has long embraced a belief in "limitless growth," with overextraction of resources, toxic emissions, and industrial pollution as its trademarks.

Public concern over pollution, acid rain, and global warming have now focused interest on the environmental consequences of industrial activity. But are calls for sustainable development and a more competitive global economy compatible? According to Michael Adams, "Canadians believe environmental quality and economic well-being are not only compatible but mutually supportive." Results from the Environmental Monitor (a quarterly survey of 1500 Canadians) show that 80 percent of Canadians believe sustainable development is achievable and should become a major priority for Canada over the next ten years (Adams, 1990). While industry argues that environmental regulations limit its ability to compete globally, the recent proliferation of "green" products suggests that environmentalism may itself become a growth industry.

• QUALITY OF WORKING LIFE AND INDUSTRIAL DEMOCRACY

Pressures for democratic forms of work organization and innovative job design have grown in recent years as employers have struggled to become more competitive and employees have demanded more satisfying work. The **quality of working life** (QWL) movement, which took root in the 1970s, offers itself as an alternative to the legacy of bureaucracy, Taylorism, and Fordist methods of production. Theoretically, QWL claims to combine both humanistic and economic objectives: for employees, challenging, involving, and rewarding work experiences; for employers, increased productivity, quality, and profits. However, QWL advocates have often failed to translate such lofty claims into reality (Rinehart, 1986).

In Canada there has been a smorgasbord of QWL initiatives, using techniques such as job enlargement, job enrichment, job rotation, autonomous work teams, and quality control circles (Nightingale, 1982; Long, 1989). Evaluations of Canadian QWL initiatives document their positive effects, ranging from higher employee satisfaction and commitment to improved earnings, labour relations, and productivity gains. Negative effects such as declining work performance, heightened union–management tensions, and employee dissatisfaction have also been noted (Cunningham and White, 1984).

On the whole, autonomous work teams — where employees are delegated collective authority to decide on work methods, scheduling, and quality control — have the best potential for reallocating decision-making power and creating more interesting, challenging, socially integrated, and skilled work (Rinehart, 1986). However, unions are wary of QWL programs, as management has often used them to circumvent collective agreements (Wells, 1986).

Because QWL addresses more participative management through job redesign, the focus is on task content rather than an overall redistribution of organizational power. In contrast, **industrial democracy** is concerned more broadly with organizational decision making. Based on the principles of representative democracy, it aims to give workers a direct say not only in their own work groups but in the corporation as well through elected representation on the corporate board.

Because industrial democracy challenges traditional management rights, its development in North America has been slow. While one-third of *Fortune* 500 companies have some form of employee participation, it is usually partial (Rothschild and Russell, 1986). Industrial democracy is more advanced in Western European countries such as Norway, Sweden, and Austria. Indeed, Sweden is one of the few countries where industrial democracy is a major national goal, with a tripartite system involving the state, the employers' federations, and the large, centralized Swedish unions representing about 90 percent of the workforce.

• WORK AND FAMILY CONFLICT

Earlier this century, domestic chores excluded most women from paid employment. As women's paid work has grown, work interruptions for childbirth and child rearing have contributed to their concentration in low-paying, non-career jobs. Despite women's recent advances in paid employment, research shows that child care continues to be the primary reason women leave their jobs. Yet women are interrupting work for shorter periods of time. Between 1976 and 1988, the participation rate for women (living with a spouse) with preschool children rose from 35 percent to 62 percent (Statistics Canada, 1990b: 80).

Given women's greater attachment to paid work today, are domestic tasks being shared more equally between women and men? Studies show that employed women now work a "double day" (Hochschild, 1989). According to Finlayson (1989), the average North American working woman spends from 90 to 100 hours per week on domestic and paid work, while working men spend only 37 to 48 hours. Boston University's Balancing Job and Homelife Study found that 74 percent of fathers said they "should" help with child care but that only 13 percent actually did. Yet 36 percent of these fathers said that they experienced "a lot of stress" trying to balance home and work responsibilities (*Newsweek,* 1990). One can only wonder how much stress their female partners feel.

As the number of dual-earner and single-parent families grow, there is increasing pressure for more flexible working arrangements. Indeed, job sharing, home working, and flexible hours and career paths would go a long way to relieving family–work conflict — as would national provisions for parental leave and child care. Such options clearly are consistent with employers' wishes for greater flexibility in order to retain competitiveness; yet steps must be taken to ensure that flexibility benefits both employees and employers alike. Steps must also be taken to ensure that flexible work arrangements are not simply "women's options." Ideally, new work arrangements intended to reduce work–family conflict should be aimed both at men and women, with the intent of reducing the labour-market disadvantages that currently result from worker's participation in the domestic sphere.

SUMMARY

- This chapter looks at the organization of work in historical perspective, examining contemporary issues and venturing some speculations about the shape of work in the future.
- The study of labour processes, labour markets, and work organizations engages the leading theoretical debates in sociology, including the prominent themes of inequality, conflict, power, and change.
- A backdrop to these themes is the dynamic relationship between the individual and society. How much choice can an individual exercise in the labour market, and in her or his job? And to what degree are employees and managers constrained by work institutions, ranging from bureaucratic structures to the elaborate industrial relations system?
- One central point emerges: the ongoing tensions, dilemmas, and compromises characteristic of the workplace provide an ideal laboratory for studying social life.

KEY CONCEPTS

Classical management theory
Coercive approach
Compensatory effect

Conflict
Consensus
Corporate culture
Corporate welfare programs
Counterculture
Craft union
Deindustrialization
Hawthorne Effect
Human capital theory
Human Relations School
Industrial democracy
Industrial restructuring
Industrial union
Instrumental work attitudes
Job satisfaction
Labour market
Labour-force participation
Labour-market segmentation theory
Labour-process theory
Market situation
Nonstandard forms of employment
Normative approach
Occupational sex segregation
Occupational structure
Patriarchy
Post-Fordism
Post-industrial society
Primary sector
Quality of working life
Scientific management
Second industrial revolution
Secondary sector
Service economy
Social class
Social psychological perspective
Socioeconomic status
Spillover effect

Status attainment theory

Stressor

Structural perspective

Sustainable development

Tertiary sector

Utilitarian approach

Wage gap

Work

Work orientations

Work-related stress

Work situation

Work values

REVIEW QUESTIONS

1. What are the current employment trends in terms of the occupations and industries in which Canadians work? How have these changed over time?
2. Discuss the past and present role of trade unions in shaping employment conditions in Canada.
3. Is education an "equalizer" in society? Discuss with reference to theories of human capital and labour-market segmentation.
4. What are the causes and consequences of gender and occupational inequality in the labour market?
5. How important is it to understand the informal aspect of organizations?
6. What factors influence job satisfaction? How important are job conditions for influencing an individual's experience of work?
7. How is industrial restructuring reshaping employment in Canada? What dangers and opportunities does it pose for the future?

Claude Denis and Trevor Harrison

Politics and Society

INTRODUCTION

If you resemble a large number of Canadians, when you hear the word *politics,* you will tune out: you will be bored and somewhat dejected. But politics is not just what the government does and what the opposition parties complain about. Nor is it just the interminable "pseudo-events" — press conferences, political debates, and electoral polls — that intrude on our daily lives. Politics certainly involves failed constitutional accords, Quebec nationalism, Western alienation, aboriginal demands, and debates about trade deals. But politics also is involved when the makers of the movie *Black Robe* think it important for the aboriginal characters to speak their own language (with English subtitles), while at the same time they consider it normal to have the French characters speak English (*Tribute,* 1991: 12; Box 7.1). It is politics when 764 anti-logging protesters at Clayoquot Sound are charged, and many convicted, in the largest mass political trial of civil disobedience in Canadian history (Lee, 1993), while companies breaking environmental laws are regularly served warnings or given minor fines.

In this chapter we will survey the field of politics as it is shaped and reshaped in social relations ("the world out there") and in the heads of sociologists and others who write about politics. And we will explore the relationship between the two: how the sociologists' view of politics is influenced by actual political struggles and how such struggles may be affected by the work of students of society.

First we examine traditional debates in political culture, and how these have differed inside and outside Quebec. Then we look at the political economy debates in English-speaking Canada,

Box 7.1

BLACK ROBE

The case of the film *Black Robe* is interesting for its up-to-date political sensibility. *Black Robe,* a Canadian–Australian co-production, tells the story of the encounter, during the early colonization of New France, of aboriginal peoples and French Jesuit missionaries. The movie was filmed in English, with the French characters speaking English. But the aboriginal characters speak their own language, and subtitles have been added so that viewers can understand what is being said; as well, great care has been taken to portray them in ways that are, if not always flattering, deemed accurate by consultant ethnographers. All this attention to authenticity, which was also prominently on display in the American film *Dances with Wolves,* is most obviously signalled to the viewer by subtitling the aboriginal characters' speech. In addition, the filmmakers insisted in interviews that it is indeed a real aboriginal language that is spoken. But why is it important to be authentic, and to appear authentic when portraying aboriginal peoples? And why is it not important to do the same with the French characters?

Until a few years ago, in English-language films involving "Indians" and other non-English speakers, all the characters spoke English, and the "Indians" were built around any number of cultural stereotypes rather than on ethnographical knowledge. The Indians, in fact,

spoke a form of drunken English, consisting mainly of "How" and "Ugh." Occasionally they spoke an actual Native language, or something that sounded like one. In one case a director simply ran the English sound track backwards to get authentic-sounding Indian "gibberish" (Francis, 1992: 106–7).

But in the last dozen years in Canada, and for another decade before that in the United States, aboriginal issues have acquired an unprecedented degree of prominence on the political scene. It is this political process, including a mounting realization that aboriginal peoples live in appalling conditions (see for example York, 1990), that has changed the image of "the Indian" held by non-natives in Canada and elsewhere, and that has made possible films like *Dances with Wolves* and *Black Robe.*

Politics and Society

which were so important to the rise of its sense of economic nationalism during the 1960s and 1970s. The next section, by contrast, examines the issues of "nation" and "state" that have textured the relations between Quebec and Canada since the 1960s.

We discuss the issue of hegemony in liberal democracies next. Native issues (Box 7.2), the seeming fragmentation of class voting, and the rise and absorption of Social Credit are specifically examined.

"New politics" are important issues such as feminism, social movements, globalization, and state power. We conclude with a discussion of the "mapping" of the political field: how and when some things, and not others, become "political."

STUDYING CANADIAN POLITICAL CULTURE, AMERICAN STYLE

For sociologists, the notion that politics enters into our personal lives in many different ways is a rather new one. It used to be that sociologists with an interest in politics would study such things as governments and political parties, and social behaviour as it related to these institutions. This remains, indeed, the mainstay of the work of political sociologists.

Until the late 1960s in English Canada, political sociologists were chiefly interested in the *cultural* sources of *political behaviour;* in this, they were following the main tendency of American sociology. For many Canadians, definitions of Canada have long involved comparisons with the United States. In the early 1960s, Seymour M. Lipset advanced a theory setting out the historical basis for certain hypothesized cultural differences between the two countries that in turn influenced their respective political development.

Box 7.2

THE SOVEREIGNTY OF ABORIGINAL PEOPLES

Before Europeans ever thought of crossing the Atlantic, indigenous peoples occupied the whole territory of the Americas. As Georges Erasmus and Joe Sanders (1992: 3) write: "Our people decided their own citizenship. They had a wide variety and diversity of governmental systems, almost all of them regulating their activities and the relations among their members with a degree of formality." It is from this standpoint that many of them signed treaties, "nation to nation."

Although aboriginal peoples were gradually pushed into positions of marginality by increasingly strong European institutions and populations, they have never stopped claiming their sovereign right to govern themselves. This is why in recent constitutional negotiations in Canada, representatives of aboriginal peoples have claimed that their *inherent* right to self-government be recognized: the right is "inherent" because they had it before the arrival of the Europeans, and they never gave it up; consequently, they do not need to be given a right, but they do want the fact of their having this right to be recognized.

Until the 1981–82 consitutional debate, however, aboriginal peoples were unable to push their claims onto Canada's political agenda. This debate followed the 1980 referendum in Quebec on sovereignty-association, and involved the patriation of the Constitution (which had officially remained until then a British document) and the adoption of a Charter of Rights and Freedoms. Aboriginal peoples were not invited to the initial negotiations after the referendum, but they forced themselves onto the agenda. They achieved this by, among other things, organizing a mini-conference of their own and lobbying the British Parliament, which had to approve the patriation (Frideres, 1988).

A decade of mounting aboriginal pressure on the Canadian political system followed, culminating in the prominent defeat of the Meech Lake constitutional accord in 1990 and the Oka Crisis of the same summer, which stemmed from the desire of the town of Oka to expand a golf course on land considered sacred by the Mohawk people of the Kanesatake band. This crisis, and the more general struggle of the aboriginal people for the respect of their sovereignty, is starkly symbolized by the picture of the confrontation between a young francophone soldier of the Canadian Armed Forces and a masked Mohawk Warrior.

Lipset's (1963) original thesis, which also included a comparison with Great Britain and Australia, contended that the American Revolution of 1776 resulted in the United States developing a political and civil culture that emphasized individualism, egalitarianism, and universalism. By contrast, said Lipset, the immigration of United Empire Loyalists to Canada at that time reinforced a "counter-revolutionary" ethos that enshrined respect for collectivism, elitism, statism, and deference to established authority. According to Lipset, these respective values had subsequently been enshrined in the two countries' differing religious, political, and other institutions.

For a long time, Lipset's general thesis was widely accepted in the academic community, both in the United States and Canada. It came under increasing attack, however, on several fronts. The most fundamental objection was that although a region's or country's cultural values are important in shaping political life, they cannot be seen as disembodied, or isolated from material circumstances. To paraphrase Marx, people make their own **political culture,** but not just as they please. Rather, political cultures are forged in a dialectic with material circumstances, historically given. This latter aspect of Canadian political life is the focus of **political economy,** to which we will return below.

Sociology in Quebec, meanwhile, developed along largely parallel paths, but with a significantly different emphasis. Quebec sociologists in the 1950s were also under strong American influence, and they too were much interested in the impact of culture on politics. The writings of Pierre Elliott Trudeau during that period, a time when he was a flamboyant intellectual and well before he entered federal politics, provide an excellent example of this trend. In his essay "A Few Obstacles to Democracy in Quebec" (reproduced in Trudeau, 1968), Trudeau argued that since French Canadians had never had to fight for democratic rights — they were handed them by the British Crown — French-Canadian culture remained somehow pre-democratic. Hence the authoritarian bent of Quebec's postwar Union Nationale government. This cultural trait, wrote Trudeau, *had* to change. (We shall see below how this view of Quebec was deeply flawed.) This call for change by an intellectual writing sociology represents a significant difference between the practice of sociology in francophone Quebec and English Canada: starting in the 1940s, sociologists in Quebec saw themselves as participating in a political struggle against the government and the political elites of the time. There was no such involvement in English Canada (Brooks and Gagnon, 1988).

From this obvious involvement in politics (in the usual sense of the word) by Quebec sociologists we get our first overt indication of the political dimension of sociological practice: sociological work has political consequences. This is most obviously so when sociologists issue a challenge to the existing order. But *not* challenging the existing order also has consequences: a non-challenge maintains that order, if only by omission. Neither of these outlooks is a guarantee of quality in sociological work. While we believe that there is plenty to challenge in the existing political order — you will see examples in this chapter — and that much of the best sociological work is animated by a spirit critical of the way things are, there can be a price to pay in sociology for unchecked political enthusiasm.

Quebec sociology in the 1950s is a case in point. This period of Quebec sociology is often seen as fairly heroic: not only were sociologists attempting to establish a new body of knowledge and a new way of acquiring knowledge by giving their discipline a stable place in universities, but in doing so they were actively challenging a political order that seemed all-powerful and as a result they were taking personal risks. Trudeau, for example, was never able to get a university job while the Union Nationale was in power. And the founder of the Faculty of Social Sciences at Laval University, himself a Dominican father, faced a threat from that same government, which appealed to the Pope to have Father Lévesque expelled from the Church on the grounds that he was challenging the only Catholic government in North America; the Pope didn't listen (Fournier, 1986).

From an oppositional point of view, it made sense for writers like Trudeau to paint a very dark portrait of Quebec under the Union Nationale: appalled readers would be all the more inclined to do something to overthrow the old order. Indeed, faced with the might of the Union Nationale, it was easy for these writers to believe that Quebec was indeed a dark place. Moreover, influenced by American sociology, Quebec sociologists naturally looked to culture to explain this ugly state of affairs. But the situation was much more complicated than that. Although the political situation was specific to Quebec, it arose not from some archaic cultural complex, but rather from the tensions stemming from the political economy of post-World War II capitalism. These tensions expressed themselves in many places through nationalism, anticommunism, or both. Quebec sociologists of that era, courageous though they may have been, were blinded by the political struggle and as a result badly misunderstood both the wellspring of their own political predicament and the society that they were portraying (Couture and Denis, 1994).

Anglo-Canadian Political Economy, Old and New

Starting in the 1960s and reaching full strength in the 1970s, a powerful new movement hit Anglo-Canadian sociology: the development of a strong school of political economy, which found inspiration in the earlier works of the Canadian economic historian Harold Innis and more broadly in Marxism. **Political economy** studies "processes whereby social change is located in the historical interaction of the economic, political, cultural and ideological moments of social life, with the dynamic rooted in socio-economic conflict" (Clement and Williams, 1989: 7).

Any examination of Anglo-Canadian political economy must begin with **staples theory,** developed by W.A. Mackintosh and Harold Innis in the 1920s. Mackintosh and Innis were neoclassical economists, influenced by Ricardian notions of "comparative advantages" and international trade. According to neoclassical theory, underdeveloped countries should exploit raw resources ("staples") for export to more advanced countries. With the capital they acquire, the former should then reinvest in technology. Over time, the result is a shift away from labour-intensive, extractive industry to capital-intensive secondary industry and, in turn, an independent and mature economy.

But Innis made a sharp break with both Mackintosh and traditional theory in stating that the colonial circumstances of late-developing countries, such as Canada, placed them on a different developmental trajectory than the European countries about which the classical economists had written. Innis showed how Canada's political economy had been inextricably shaped by its status as, first, a hinterland colony of France and England, and later, an economic and political extension of the United States. The resultant dependence upon a narrow band of staples, whose price was determined on the world market, made Canada's economy, like that of any economic hinterland, particularly vulnerable to boom and bust cycles. More importantly, these cycles supported the existing pattern of hinterland development. While boom times provided the necessary capital for economic diversification, there was little incentive to do so. Instead, this capital was spent on the purchase of manufactured goods from abroad. Conversely, while bust times provided plenty of incentive, the necessary capital was not present (see Watkins, 1963). As a result, even though nominally independent in a political sense, such countries remained colonies, caught in what Innis termed a **staples trap**.

After many years of neglect, interest in Innis's work was revived. This was heralded in 1963 by Melville Watkins's reapplication of staples theory to the circumstances of the modern Canadian economy. Like Innis, Watkins emphasized the necessity for hinterland economies to appropriate linkages to the staple product. Watkins contended, however, that the failure of appropriation in Canada's case had not come about from external forces, but was the result of Canada's internal sociopolitical structures. In particular, he singled out the behaviour of Canada's elites in overconcentrating resources in the country's export sector at the expense of developing Canada's domestic market.

Watkins's work during the 1960s, including a Canadian government report on foreign (mainly American) control of the economy (the Watkins Report), provided the impetus for what became known as the **New Canadian Political Economy (NCPE)**. The first offspring of NCPE was **dependency theory**. Named after an emerging international political economy of the time (see Chapter 1), Canadian dependency theory, as fashioned by Kari Levitt, Robert Laxer, R.T. Naylor, and Wallace Clement, was also influenced by Innis's staples theory and traditional elite theory (à la Gaetano Mosca, Vilfredo Pareto, Robert Michels, and C. Wright Mills).

Levitt's *Silent Surrender* was published in 1970. Describing present-day Canada "as the world's richest underdeveloped country" (1970: 25), Levitt contended that the "old mercantilism" that had restricted independent Canadian growth during the days of colonialism had now been replaced by a "new mercantilism" based on direct control by foreign-based multinationals. Canada's resultant satellite status vis-à-vis the United States hindered genuine economic innovation. More importantly, this dependency was destroying Canada's economic and cultural ties, thus threatening the country's continued political existence.

Similarly, Robert Laxer (1973) argued that foreign ownership and control meant that, as economic conditions deteriorated in the American economy, the Canadian hinterland economy would be gradually shut down. The already small manufacturing segment of Canada's economy would decline. Canada would be, in Laxer's words, **deindustrialized,** possibly leading to Canada's formal political absorption into the United States.

But, if Canada was an American dependency, how had it become so? In answering this question, R.T. Naylor and Wallace Clement looked at the historical role of Canada's elite (see also Chapter 5). In 1972, Naylor presented what came to be termed the **merchants against industry thesis,** whose core was the analysis of Canada's early domination by merchant capitalists. Naylor observed that the great merchants, including financial capitalists, made their profits on the exchange of raw materials produced in the hinterland for manufactured goods, produced in the metropolis (the colonizing power). Therefore, he argued, they intentionally promoted banking and government policies during Canada's formative years that hindered the development of Canadian industry (see also Naylor, 1975).

Although he downplayed Naylor's notion of intraclass conflict, Clement (1975) similarly contended that Canada's elites had inhibited independent development. According to Clement, Canada was ruled by three relatively stable, highly interlocked, and identifiable elites: an **indigenous elite,** controlling Canadian corporations, notably in transportation, finance, and utilities; a **comprador elite,** composed of Canadian-born directors and managers of foreign branch-plant operations; and a **parasite elite,** made up of directors and managers of multinationals, based largely outside of Canada, but operating corporations within the country. Together, these elites managed the Canadian economy to their own advantage but to the continued disadvantage of Canada's development as a whole.

Critics attacked dependency theory on two major counts. First, the notion of dependency ignored important differences between Canada and the former colonies of the Third World. If Canada is a dependency, said critics, its complex political and class structure and blend of both development and underdevelopment surely make it, at the very least, a somewhat unique one. In subsequent years, at least three alternative theoretical descriptions were advanced to account for Canada's relationship to the rest of the world (Williams, 1989). The first variant described Canada as an "intermediary" between more advanced and powerful capitalist states and underdeveloped states (Clement, 1977; Ehrensaft and Armstrong, 1981; Niosi, 1983). A second variant went even further in rejecting the idea of Canada as a dependency, instead suggesting that Canada was now a minor imperialist nation in its own right (Moore and Wells, 1975; Resnick, 1982; Carroll, 1985, 1986). More recently, Williams (1989: 132) has stated that "the Canadian economy may now be usefully conceptualized as a geographically large zone within the U.S. economy." These criticisms, however, do not alter the fact that twenty years after *Silent Surrender,* foreign ownership still dominates the Canadian economy. In 1990, eight of Canada's top ten companies and ten of its top twenty companies were entirely or substantially foreign owned (Table 7.1).

Table 7.1

PERCENTAGE FOREIGN OWNERSHIP, CANADA'S TOP 20 COMPANIES, 1990

Rank by Revenue	Company	Sales or Operating Revenue	% Foreign Owned	Major Shareholder
1.	General Motors of Canada Ltd., Oshawa	18 458 171	100	General Motors, Detroit
2.	BCE Inc., Montreal	18 373 000	10	Widely held
3.	Ford Motor Co. of Canada, Oakville, Ont.	13 706 200	94	Ford Motor, Dearborn, Mich.
4.	George Weston Ltd., Toronto	10 856 000		Wittington Investment 57%
5.	Canadian Pacific Ltd., Montreal	10 499 700	25	Widely held
6.	Imperial Oil Ltd., Toronto	10 223 000	70	Exxon, New York
7.	Alcan Aluminum Ltd., Montreal	10 217 000[1]	46	Widely held
8.	Noranda Inc., Toronto	9 565 000		Brascade Resources 44%
9.	Brascan Ltd., Toronto	7 163 000[2]	20	Brascan Holdings 49%
10.	Chrysler Canada Ltd., Windsor	7 067 000	100	Chrysler, Detroit
11.	Provigo Inc., Montreal (Jan./91)	6 525 700		Unigesco 26%; Empire 24%; Caisse de dépôt 13%
12.	Ontario Hydro, Toronto	6 484 000		Ontario gov't. 100%
13.	Thomson Corp., Toronto	6 259 000[1]		Woodbridge 68%
14.	Seagram Co., Montreal (Jan./91)	5 865 000[1]		C. Bronfman 17%; E. Bronfman 17%
15.	Hydro-Québec, Montreal	5 822 988		Quebec gov't. 100%
16.	Shell Canada Ltd., Calgary	5 508 000	78	Shell Petroleum, Netherlands
17.	Petro-Canada, Calgary	5 317 000		Federal gov't. 100%
18.	Hudson's Bay Co., Toronto (Jan./91)	5 041 733[3]		Woodbridge 73%
19.	Nova Corp. of Alberta, Calgary	4 736 000	17	Widely held
20.	John Labatt Ltd., London, Ontario (April/90)	4 681 000		Brascan 39%; Caisse de dépôt 11%

1. Converted from US$. 2. Includes beneficial interest in gross revenues of consumer products, natural resources, and other operations, but excludes financial services. 3. Continuing operations.
Source: *The Financial Post,* Summer 1991: 94.

A second major criticism of the work of dependency theorists focused on their underdeveloped, or simply inaccurate, treatment of Canada's internal dynamics. In particular, critics attacked Naylor's premise of intraclass conflict. Far from being its competitors, evidence suggested that merchants and bankers both financed and were often directly involved in the development of Canadian industry (Williams, 1979; Richardson, 1982; G. Laxer, 1989). More broadly, critics assailed both Naylor and Clement for their one-sided examination of the role of elites, ignoring the fact that classes act, or fail to act, in relation to other classes and/or other elements of a country's social formation. Considerable research in Canadian political economy after the mid-1970s has involved bringing these elements into the analysis, starting with class and region.

In opposition to dependency theory's assertion of an all-powerful elite, Panitch (1981) contended that the relative power of Canada's proletariat hindered capitalism's accumulation of surplus during the country's early stage of development, thereby resulting in a kind of truncated industrialization. The proletariat's power resulted from the continued survival, well into this century, of the farming class. Because workers remained on the farms, there was little surplus labour available to urban industrialists. Labour scarcity, combined with high rates of unionization, workers' high skill levels, and Canada's proximity to the high-wage American labour market, led to Canada's industrial proletariat being able to demand higher wages than those paid in most developing countries.

By contrast, Gordon Laxer argued that the failure of Canada to set an independent course of development for itself resulted from the relative political weakness of Canada's agrarian class at the key moment when the country's economic policies were being shaped. Had Canada's agrarian class been more politically powerful and organized (like its counterpart in Sweden, for example) Laxer contends that it would have pushed for economic policies such as easier credit and a strong defence, but otherwise frugal expenditures, the unintended consequence of which would have been Canada's independent industrialization. Instead, English–French ethnic and religious divisions combined with the failure to create farm–labour alliances against the monopolists, the country's long-established antidemocratic political culture, and lack of strong nationalism, to allow Canada's elites relatively free rein in setting developmental policy. By the time the agrarians became an organized political force after World War I, their position in the Canadian class structure was already in significant decline. But while farmers lost importance in the east and centre of the country, they remained a very strong presence on the prairies. Such geographical differentiation of Canada's political economy strongly contributed to the rise of regionalism.

Regionalism, or regional alienation, has provided an important backdrop to the rise of numerous political movements in Canadian history, from the Riel and North-West rebellions of the last century to the Progressive movement of the 1920s. Likewise, the historic "development of underdevelopment" of the Maritime region resulted from conflicts between the Maritime's indigenous capitalist class and its counterparts located in Toronto and Montreal (see Acheson, 1972; Brym and Sacouman, 1979). Similarly, the political conflicts of the 1970s and early 1980s between Ottawa and the energy-producing provinces over energy pricing involved, in large part, a dispute between a rising bourgeois class based on the oil and gas industry and located in Alberta, Saskatchewan, and Newfoundland and a traditional Central Canadian elite linked to the manufacturing industries (Richards and Pratt, 1979). In the view of Matthews (1983, 1988) and Brodie (1990), regionalism remains an important source of conflict in Canadian society, a belief substantiated perhaps by the recent rise and triumph in the 1993 election of such regionally based political parties as the Reform Party in the West and the Bloc Québécois in Quebec.

Quebec–Canada: An Obsession with the Nation-State

Use of the term *regionalism* is fraught with problems when speaking of Quebec's place within Canada. If by regionalism we mean the strong sentiment of belonging to a particular area within the country as a whole, an area that is perceived as either actually or potentially aggrieved, then it makes sense to say that Quebec is home to a regionalist movement. But stopping there is insufficient, for it is a particular kind of regionalism that one finds in Quebec, much different from that found, for example, in British Columbia or Alberta: Quebec's regional identity is that of a *nation*.

Given the specificity of Quebec's **nationalism**, when compared to various Canadian regionalisms, many Anglo-Canadian writers have been reluctant to describe it in terms of regionalism. But there is a good deal of confusion in Canadian sociology about how to conceive of Quebec's place in the Canadian polity, stemming from the worldwide dominance of the **nation-state** as the general model for large-scale sovereign political organizations (Denis, 1993). The collapse of the multinational Austro-Hungarian, German, and Ottoman empires at the end of World War I resulted in the triumph of the expectation that sovereign **states** are to be nation-states. This expectation still governs the making and breaking of states as the Soviet Union, Europe's last empire, continues to crumble: to each nation its state, and vice versa. While civil war in the former Yugoslavia provides the grimmest example of this process, the independence of such former Soviet republics as Ukraine, Lithuania, Estonia, and Latvia and the breakup of Czechoslovakia represent peaceful enactments of the "nationalities principle."

The question arises, then: what is a nation? A large amount of work has been done on nations and nationalism over the last twenty years (see Hobsbawm, 1990), out of which emerges the sense that the nation is and will remain a *contested concept*. That is to say, the concept of nation is inherently prone to political dispute. In Canada's case, for instance, if Québécois were to convince other Canadians that the term *nation* properly applies to Quebec, their basic claim to "distinct" treatment within the federation would be greatly advanced. Conversely, the more Canadians are convinced that Canada as a whole is the nation, the more difficult it is for Quebec to win its case without going the way of sovereignty.

A popular way to attempt a definition of the nation has been to ask whether it is an objective or subjective phenomenon. Proponents of the objective view contend that a nation is a community that shares a language, religion, culture, history, territory, and other attributes. One problem with this view is that it is easy to find human groups that are recognized as nations but don't display any number of these traits. The people of Switzerland, for example, are considered a nation, even though there is no unity of language, culture, or religion. Conversely, it is also easy to find groups that display all of them but that are not considered nations. Mennonite communities in western Canada and Amish communities in the United States come to mind. Another problem is that these criteria often turn out to be, in the words of historian Eric Hobsbawm (1990: 6), "fuzzy, shifting and ambiguous, and as useless for purposes of the traveller's orientation as cloud-shapes are compared to landmarks."

Proponents of the subjective view, on the other hand, say that a nation is a group that displays a will to live together. Again, many human communities can be found that fit this bill but that no one would think of calling a nation. Moreover, such a definition would implausibly make nationhood possible for, say, Vancouver Island, if enough of its inhabitants saw themselves as members of a Vancouverian nation.

Both the objective and subjective outlooks, then, are unsatisfactory. One major shortcoming that they share points the way to a more useful understanding: neither of them is sufficiently sensitive to history. Before the 18th century no one talked of "the nation" in the sense that the word is currently used. In world history, the nation is a recent invention. The concept itself, both politically useful and contested, has a history, an element of which is its ability to be linked to various social traits.

In its short history, talk of nation has always arisen in relation to state power. In the 18th century the relationship changed between rulers (the holders of state power) and governed in Europe and the Americas. The kings' divine right to rule was replaced by popular sovereignty: from now on, the right to govern would derive from the will of the people. Hence the key opening sentence in the American constitution: "We, the people of the United States . . . do ordain and establish this Constitution for the United States of America." This is not to say that "the people" would actually rule, in the United States or elsewhere, but rather that whatever social group does rule would have to do so *in the name of* "the people."

In trying to express who "the people" are, nations have formed. In this formation a great variety of *social markers* (ethnicity, religion, etc.) can be put to use, but no particular one is indispensable, save perhaps a common territory — but even that can be aspired to rather than actually shared, as the historical development of the Zionist ideal of a Jewish homeland eloquently shows.

The key point is this: a nation is "an imagined political community — and imagined as both inherently limited and sovereign" (Anderson, 1991: 6). Almost every word in this quotation from Benedict Anderson is a key word. First, it is crucial to keep in mind that a discussion of nations is always one that raises the *political* issue of *sovereignty*. As Hobsbawm has noted, a nation "is a social entity only insofar as it relates to a certain kind of modern territorial state, the 'nation-state'" (Hobsbawm, 1990: 9–10). Also, by saying that the nation is an *imagined* community, we are not suggesting that it is not real. Rather, it is imagined in the two following senses. First, although its members will never know most other members personally or even hear of them, they feel a kind of kinship to each imagined other; they have the sentiment that they do belong together in the same community which, by definition, is *limited:* it excludes others. Second, the social markers that are seen as shared are often invented or uncertain.

One of the most appalling aspects of the war that erupted in the former Yugoslavia in 1991 is what is known as the "ethnic cleansing" practised primarily by Serbs and Croats against each other and Muslims; an area is said to be "ethnically cleansed" when its minority population has been eliminated (Allman, 1993; Ramet, 1992; Ignatieff, 1993). What can be said about the specifically *ethnic* grounding for the deep animosity between Serbs, Croats, and Muslims? Serbs and Croats are, after all, two national groups who share the same historical origin and language. Various regions of their common territory, however, have been controlled by different empires, and different forms of Christianity (Catholicism and Orthodoxy) have taken hold; Yugoslav Muslims once were Serbs and Croats, who converted to Islam under Ottoman rule (Glenny, 1993). It is in this complex situation of shared and divergent social markers, none of which is adequately described as "ethnic," that contending national movements have developed. It cannot be said, in particular, that the war has been caused by ethnicity. Rather, as Michael Ignatieff writes,

> consciousness of ethnic difference . . . only turned into nationalist chauvinism when a discredited Communist elite began manipulating nationalist emotions in order to cling to power (Ignatieff, 1993: 4).

In other cases, social markers have become shared *after* a nation-state's development, as a result of its actions. The French language, for instance, is universally spoken within the borders of France because the French government decided that it should be so. Until the early 20th century, in fact, several regional languages were still spoken in the French territory. But their interdiction in state-run schools, where only French was taught and where attendance was compulsory, brought about their near-complete disappearance. If language can be used as a social marker in identifying the French nation, it is as a result of the French nation-state's policies and actions.

The concept of "nation" is central to the study of politics. There are several reasons for this. One of the first important trends to emerge from the ashes of the Cold War between the Soviet bloc and the advanced capitalist countries is a very strong reassertion of nations and nationalisms. The ex-Yugoslav example makes this clear. Contrary to many predictions, then, nations and national movements would appear to be very much a part — sometimes a disturbing part — of the future. Another reason for emphasizing the nation here is that national issues have been particularly important in the development of Canadian society, as the struggle between French and English — Quebec and the rest of Canada — has reduced the salience of other issues, such as social class.

In Canada the ruling idea that a country is supposed to be a nation-state is problematic because of the presence of more than one group that claims to be a nation. English-speaking Canadians tend to think of themselves as Canadians first, and see Canada as a whole — Quebec included — as a nation. The federal government, in this view, is Canada's national government. But a large majority of Québécois see things differently: for them, Quebec is a nation within a larger, binational or perhaps multinational country. This is why, for instance, the Quebec legislature is called *l'Assemblée nationale*. As well, aboriginal peoples in Canada see themselves as "the First Nations" (Box 7.2).

To the extent that the English-speaking majority in Canada imposes its understanding of "the nation" upon the institutions of federalism (Parliament, the Charter of Rights and Freedoms, etc.), Quebec's attempts to be a nation, and be accepted as one, are thwarted. This type of political dynamic has been called *national oppression*. Applying the word *oppression* to the Quebec–Canada situation may seem excessive to some, considering Canada's democratic institutions and Quebec's share of Canada's considerable wealth. It is hardly a secret, however, that Quebec is not satisfied with its status within Canada, which it has been trying to change for the last thirty years. Even before then, arguments over the Constitution involving Quebec were endemic. Nonetheless, over this whole period the Canadian constitution has never been changed in a way that would meet even some of Quebec's goals. Thus, it is not an exaggeration to say that Quebec's national aspirations within Canada remain unfulfilled, and that this is not for a lack of trying. Those aspirations have been blocked and frustrated as a result of the fact that Quebec is a minority nation within Canada. Had Québécois constituted the majority in Canada, these aspirations would be realized as a matter of course.

Sociologists in English-speaking Canada, with the notable exception of many practitioners of political economy, have had trouble in dealing with the national character of the Quebec–Canada relationship. One popular way to talk of Quebec's place in Canada has been (and remains) to present it as a case of ethnic relations: French Canadians versus English Canadians. But just as many English-speaking Canadians do not have an English ethnic background, many francophones in Quebec are not French Canadian in the traditional sense of the word. Thus, the English-speaking group will come to comprise individuals whose names are Romanow and Messier, for example, while the French-speaking group will include names such as Ryan and Wagner. Also, it is a *Quebec*-centred nationalism that has been asserting itself for all these decades — not a "coast-to-coast" French-Canadian nationalism. The goal of Quebec-centred nationalism has been increased control by Québécois over the social geography of Quebec.

Political economy, by both Québécois and Anglo-Canadian scholars, has been better able to recognize the situation as one of struggle between two national groups who, among other things, strive to absorb outsiders. In fact, the bulk of the work on Quebec and Canada by Quebec political economists has been obsessed with the *national question* — the issue of the relationship between the Québécois nation and Canada's English-speaking majority (Salée, 1983). One of the main debates, for instance, among Quebec political economists during the 1970s was whether there existed a Québécois bourgeoisie, or merely a Quebec branch of the Canadian bourgeoisie. More generally, even when Marxist political economists were studying the class struggle, they were doing so with nation-coloured glasses.

Just as Anglo-Canadian political economy started by studying economic history, so has Quebec's economy been first studied for its history. And here the Conquest of New France by Britain looms large. Indeed, for the large majority of Québécois sociologists and political economists, the Conquest is the dominant social fact in approaching the Quebec–Canada relationship, providing them with the theoretical and historical bedrock for their *national* outlook. In this sense, Québécois scholars see the consequences of the Conquest as still operative in contemporary Canada: Canada is built upon the Conquest, as Christian Dufour (1989, 1992) argues in the context of the constitutional debate. If Canada is seen as dependent upon the United States, Québécois sociology and political economy argue that Quebec suffers a *double dependency:* one relative to the United States and one, quasi-colonial, relative to Canada, which makes Quebec a victim of national oppression.

In this, they have the support of Anglo-Canadian political economists who, for their part, have tended to see Confederation as problematic. Thus, the historian and political economist Stanley Bréhaut Ryerson pioneered the view that Confederation involved, among other things, an "unequal union" between two nations (Ryerson, 1960, 1968). This understanding has been widely adopted by Anglo-Canadian political economists, for whom Quebec is

> a regional homeland for a distinctive national community, the nationalité québécoise. Discrimination, subjugation, and harsh oppression of the members of this community have occurred regularly in the history of Canada (Coleman, 1989: 160).

This oppressed nation, however, has gained control of its own province in the Canadian federation, which has made it possible for sociologists to construct Quebec itself as an object of study, at the expense of Canada. By contrast, the world view of Anglo-Canadian sociology is organized around Confederation in 1867 and its later extension "from coast to coast." (Interestingly, the third coast, the Arctic, has been largely outside the precinct of sociology, left to the anthropologists' study of aboriginal peoples.) As a result, sociologists in Quebec study "Quebec society," whereas sociologists in the rest of the country (and in Quebec's English-speaking universities) study "Canadian society."

Through the work of each of these communities of sociologists, then, two *national sociologies* have constituted themselves: *la sociologie québécoise* and Canadian sociology. This might seem trivial or of interest to no more than a few sociologists and political economists. You may wonder what it has to do with politics. But the fact is that academics do more than write about each other's work: they teach. And each year in Quebec, thousands of CEGEP (junior college) and university students are taught that the society they live in is Quebec and that, by virtue of being a society, it is somehow separate from the rest of Canada. Meanwhile, in English-speaking Canada, students are taught that they live in Canadian society, irrespective of their province of residence. There is no necessary overt political content in either of these outlooks, but both of them foster allegiances that are all the stronger for being apparently obvious. As a result, Quebec nationalism has become the built-in, spontaneous option for the large majority of Québécois educated in French-language colleges and universities since the 1960s. And a Canadian nationalism that is (at least somewhat) dismissive of provincial allegiances, including those of Québécois, is the corresponding option for those educated in English-language postsecondary institutions and exposed to the outlook of their sociologists and other social scientists. Each sociological community, then, is doing its part in building a nation.

HEGEMONY, OR HOW OPPRESSION WORKS IN LIBERAL DEMOCRACIES

Stemming from political economy's interest in social class, a whole literature has developed around the premise that a person's objective class position should influence her political behaviour (see Brym and Fox, 1989: ch. 3). But this premise has been frequently proven wrong in liberal democracies. A liberal democracy is a country "governed by the logic of a capitalist market economy" and "responsive to shifting configurations of class and other (e.g., gender and ethnic), political, industrial and communal struggles" (Stasiulis, 1988: 223). Among political scholars, particularly those influenced by Marxism, the question arises: Why do the poor and/or the working class not seize the citadels of power with their votes? Why do they frequently vote for elite-dominated political parties? The question is particularly relevant to Canada, which, among liberal democracies, has shown a particularly low level of class consciousness (Alford, 1963).

Politically, except for occasional inroads at the provincial and federal level, liberal democracy's dominance in Canada was sustained without a major break until the 1993 election by two political parties, the Liberals and the Conservatives. Why this dominance? Equally interesting, why the occasional inroads?

Recent analyses of the continued dominance of liberal democracy have taken a broad view of what is political. Particularly relevant here is Antonio Gramsci's (1988) concept of **hegemony**. Hegemony refers "to the use by the dominant class of its political, moral, and intellectual leadership to shape the world view of subordinate classes in conformance with its own long-term interests" (Stasiulis, 1988: 232). According to this view, Canada's continued domination by a relatively small elite (see Chapter 5) is less the product of outright coercion — although instances of this are easy to locate — than of compliance by subordinate groups.

In contemporary society, several institutions contribute to producing such compliance. Of particular importance are the family, the educational system, and the media. We have already noted how the teaching of sociology in Canada contributes to the production and reproduction of the two national communities. We have also talked about the role that schools in France have played in the creation of the French nation, through compulsory teaching of the French language. Similar processes are at work in producing, for example, gender and class identities, at school (Russell, 1986) and in the family (Chodorow, 1989). The media also contribute to reproducing hegemony, for instance by promoting certain ideals of femininity and gendered models of behaviour (Wolf, 1990).

The functioning of media, school, and family, then, typically reinforces established power relations, whether these are relations of class, gender, nationality, and so on. These institutions help dominant groups remain dominant; this is what hegemony is all about. For hegemony to be put into question, it is necessary to challenge such institutions with oppositional projects, images, and models. Returning to voting, for instance, the frequent observation that Canada displays a low frequency of class voting (Alford, 1963; Lenski and Lenski, 1974) can be viewed as reflecting the failure of anticapitalist interests to mobilize subordinate groups in support of a viable counter-hegemonic project. Ogmundson (1975), Grabb and Lambert (1982), Johnston and Ornstein (1985), and Pammett (1987) have noted that in many respects Canada's political parties are almost indistinguishable, having assiduously avoided mobilizing voters along class lines. Moreover, as Baer et al. (1987) note, the quasi-political efforts of such organizations as unions have tended to accept and not challenge the basic structures of power in Canadian society (see also Brym, 1989; Langford, 1992). As a result, fundamental conflicts in Canada, as in many liberal democracies, have tended to be neutralized, transformed into "mere differences" (Laclau, 1977).

Occasionally, however, cracks do appear in the hegemonic order through which these conflicts re-emerge. The Winnipeg General Strike of 1919, the Asbestos Strike in Quebec in 1949, the Gainers strike in Edmonton in 1986, and the Oka Crisis of 1990 are a few examples. The case of the Social Credit Party of Alberta (Box 7.3) provides another example of how challenges to the dominant hegemony have emerged and then been contained within Canada.

It is important, however, to reiterate that hegemonies operate not merely in the narrow confines of what we normally view as the political. Rather, hegemonic dominance operates through our everyday experiences and the media that inform those experiences, shaping our world view and informing us of the correctness, logic, and even inevitability of its functioning.

SOCIAL CREDIT

Box 7.3

In 1935, the worldwide Depression was still raging with devastating results. Unemployment and bankruptcies soared. The dispossessed crowded onto trains and into work camps, or stood in long queues outside soup kitchens. The collapse of capitalism seemed imminent, fuelling interest in either extreme authoritarian versions of the same system (e.g., fascism) or contrary systems (e.g., communism). A less extreme, but still radical, response to capitalism's apparent failure was offered by **Social Credit,** an economic theory devised by an English engineer, Major C.H. Douglas.

Although Douglas's ideas received widespread attention throughout the world, notably in England, New Zealand, and Australia, nowhere did they receive more consideration than in Alberta. There, promulgated by a well-known evangelical preacher, William ("Bible Bill") Aberhart, the ideas of Social Credit provided the rallying point for popular mobilization against the existing provincial government. Formally created in 1935, the party went on that year to take fifty-six of sixty-three seats with 54 percent of the popular vote (see Macpherson, 1953; Finkel, 1989; Bell, 1989, 1990).

In its infancy in Alberta, Social Credit espoused an essentially left-of-centre economic doctrine, rejecting the market as the sole arbiter of prices and wages, attacking big business, and advocating such "socialist" policies as state-run medicine. Moreover, during Aberhart's first term in office, the party passed several pieces of legislation — some of them disallowed by the Supreme Court of Canada — that directly challenged capitalism, particularly the banking system.

Following Aberhart's death in 1943, however, Social Credit's leadership was taken over by Ernest Manning. Under Manning, the party was transformed into a socially conservative bulwark of business interests, particularly the oil and gas industry. What had caused Social Credit to lose its radical edge? Manning's leadership, particularly his hostility to anything that smacked of socialism, played a part. Likewise, the practical realities of governing combined with the judicial defeats had no doubt lessened some of Social Credit's utopian zeal. But perhaps equally important was the fact that Social Credit's challenge to Canadian capitalism was contained within one province. No matter what radical ideas or edicts Social Credit might have propounded, the government nonetheless had to interact with the rest of Canada and much of the world within the form of legal, economic, political, and cultural discourse set down by the dominant liberal hegemony.

POLITICS UNBOUND: STATE POWER VERSUS SOCIAL MOVEMENTS AND GLOBALIZATION

• THE FEMINIST CONTRIBUTION

While the study of class voting goes some distance in moving away from the strict association of the political with issues of government, the object of political behaviour tends to remain government or "the state." A more radical break with this conception of politics has emerged, not from the minds of academics but from the women's movement. Indeed, it is this *social movement*, which came on the scene at about the same time as the NCPE, that blew the lid off the usual conception of politics as focusing on government. Specifically, feminism made it clear that *the personal is political:* so-called private relationships between wife and husband, between parents and children, among friends, and so on, are also sites of political struggles and settlements. "Issues related to family structure, domestic labour, sexuality, and psychology" (Adamson et al., 1988: 199), far from belonging to an apolitical private sphere, have to be understood in terms of particular political and social structures.

The study of political economy did not go unaffected by this change in outlook, although it has been slow and reluctant to adapt (see Bakker, 1989). First, feminist political economists have had to "add" women to the world described by their male counterparts; then they have engaged in a redefinition of the field (Fox, in Brym, 1989). For instance, feminist scholars have adeptly catalogued the role of women and paternalistic gender relations in capital accumulation. Van Kirk's (1980) early work showed the economic importance of a "double minority" — native women — to the early development of Canada. Likewise, Cohen (1988) has shown how, in pre-industrial Ontario, the unpaid labour of women and children "freed" men for work in waged labour. At the same time, the products of women's labour also allowed the nascent industrialists to pay male workers less than a regular family subsistence wage. In effect, unpaid female labour "subsidized" Ontario's industrialization. Similarly, Fox (1989) has noted the role of unpaid female labour in the fur trading, farming, and inshore fishing industries, in general. But Fox notes equally the important role that women have increasingly played, either as cheap labour or as surplus labour, in the "paid" sector of the Canadian economy.

The sense that the personal is political and the social movement from which it emerged were outcomes of social changes in North America that began with World War II — first, the increasing participation of women in the paid labour force and then the widespread availability of reliable birth-control methods ("the pill"). Legions of married middle-class women were joining other women already active in the labour market, while retaining their responsibilities in the home as wife and mother. Thus, as Nancy Adamson, Linda Briskin, and Margaret McPhail (1988: 37) have noted: "As the tension between family and work, and between domestic and wage labour, increased, women came to feel that their situation was unjust."

The injustice perceived by women was seen to reside at once in the public world of paid work, in the privacy of their relationships with husbands, *and* in the link between the two worlds. Hence a key original contribution of feminism to politics, as theory and practice: the dissolution of the public/private dichotomy and the corresponding development of the understanding that interpersonal struggles are political issues. To take only one example, if violence against women is now considered an important political issue, it is because of feminism's reconceptualization of politics.

Seen from another angle, feminism is only one of several social movements that have emerged since the 1960s to challenge the old conception of politics as concerned with the state, government, and parties. The Green and aboriginal movements today, the peace movement in the 1970s and 1980s, and the student and antiwar movements in the 1960s have all involved mass mobilization around issues seen as political, but they have done so largely outside traditional party politics.

Also — and this is crucially important to mapping the "changing boundaries of the political" (Maier, 1987) — the geopolitical reach of all these social movements does not follow the pattern of boundaries constitutive of the *state system*: the borders of countries and of social movements don't match. Rather, the political situation defined by contemporary social movements typically embraces at least the bulk of the advanced capitalist countries of North America and Europe, as well as Australia and New Zealand. The geopolitical spread of the aboriginal movement is in this respect a partial exception, covering not only the Americas as a whole and Australia and New Zealand, but also vast regions of Africa and Asia where indigenous peoples have been colonized, usually by Europeans.

• GLOBALIZATION AND STATE POWER

One recent trend in Canadian political economy has been to say that the state is being "decentred." Two types of arguments are made on behalf of this claim. First, the new social movements are "global" movements, which are "redefining the spaces for popular politics" (Magnusson, 1992); moreover, these movements operate on the basis of various logics (fighting patriarchy, or environmental degradation, or racism, etc.), which cannot all be unified under the authority and sovereignty of states. Because of this fundamental diversity, goes the argument, we need

> a re-conceptualization of politics that would de-centre the state as the subject of political analysis, the object of political struggle, and the basic category of political understanding (Magnusson and Walker, 1988: 40).

The second type of argument is that globalization of the economy is rendering states increasingly powerless. Indeed, several transnational corporations today are larger and richer than many states. Moreover, as capital has become increasingly mobile on the international scale, states have to a large extent lost their ability to shape social relations in a variety of spheres of life within their borders. In the industrialized countries after World War II, and in response to memories of the Depression, governments became involved in the management of the macroeconomy. A system of social safety nets and services was provided, and labour regimes (the legislated and/or regulated relationships between workers and their employers) were defined by state policy. Issues such as minimum wages, workers' right to organize and to strike, and the obligation to negotiate collective agreements were now legislated by government. There was considerable variation in such regimes from country to country, contributing to the establishment of political economic situations that were country-specific and interrelated. These situations have been collectively termed **Fordism**[1] by a group of French political economists known as the **regulation school** and who have developed a following in both English Canada and Quebec (see Boismenu and Drache, 1990).

The regulation school is characterized by its attempt to understand the establishment of stable periods in the development of capitalism, whereby capital accumulation proceeds in a sociopolitically regulated way such that social conflicts are contained in a relatively consensual political process. A strong analytical link is thus made between state practices and the functioning of capitalism. The most recent stable period has been that of Fordism, during the thirty years following World War II. Fordism is a form of capitalism

> based on the extension of mass production industries which in turn were dependent upon the extension of markets — primarily domestic markets — for their goods . . . At the same time,

---

1. The description of Fordism presented here is of its application at the macro level. At the micro level, Fordism involved assembly-line work organization leading to mass production. For a further discussion, see Chapter 6.

fordism brought a social compromise — or trade-off — around a wage relation which granted unions collective rights in exchange for leaving production decisions to capital (Jenson, 1989).

In the context of Fordism, states became much more involved in the lives of their citizens (by, for instance, issuing pension or family allowance cheques) and the domain of citizenship grew correspondingly (Cairns and Williams, 1985), resulting in what some authors call the "embeddedness" of the state in society; others write of the fusion of state and society. In any case, this process has led to **politicization:** "the penetration of political considerations into more and more spheres of life," locking "citizens and governments in ever tighter reciprocity" (Cairns and Williams, 1985: 4). It is in this context that the women's movement grew, the fusion of state and society providing much of the material basis for the realization that the personal is political.

Fordism is now dead, following the globalization of the economy and the decisions by governments to emphasize the goal of international competitiveness rather than to achieve some (still conflictual) domestic balance between production and consumption. In doing so, governments claim that they are submitting to international market forces and are accepting "the lead of the world economy while the national economy follows" (Drache and Gertler, 1991: xi). And if the world economy leads, goes this argument, states become largely irrelevant.

But is this argument entirely satisfactory? Admittedly, interpersonal politics and social movement politics are at once much more local and much more global than states are. It is also the case, in Canada as elsewhere, that the importance of political parties in formulating political issues and policy responses has been declining (see Gagnon and Tanguay, 1989), although this trend in Canada will probably be reversed to some degree following the 1993 federal election. And it is true that the ability of governments to manage domestic economies has declined in the post-Fordist period. The fact remains, however, that action by government is a prime target of, for instance, feminists concerned about a woman's ability to control her own body, and environmentalists attempting to reduce industrial pollution. The state remains both the number one target of strategic action in Canadian society (as in many others) and its most powerful political agent.

This is particularly true in Canada because of the recent addition of a potent and destabilizing element to the Canadian state: the Charter of Rights and Freedoms. Adopted as part of the 1982 constitutional reform, the Charter "guarantees the rights and freedoms," including equality rights (Section 15), of everyone in Canada. It thereby forbids discrimination on various grounds: "race, national or ethnic origin, colour, religion, sex, age or mental or physical disability." As such, the Charter represents the culmination of a trend that sees Canadians as individuals becoming increasingly "rights conscious" (Cairns and Williams, 1985: 3). It provides individuals and groups with an instrument to challenge state (and other) practices that are thought to be discriminatory. The women's movement, in particular, has been aggressive in its use of this instrument to further the goal of equality for women (Razack, 1991).

In the very short span of a dozen years, the Charter has considerably transformed the functioning of the Canadian polity, altering the traditional terms of the constitutional debate (Cairns, 1991) and intensifying the relationship between Canadians and their government. It can hardly be said, in this respect, that the Canadian state is becoming "decentred."

The fact that states remain the most powerful political agents and the key focus of political issues is indeed a problem, especially for the environmental movement, but not for the reasons advanced by the "decentrist" authors. The environmental crisis is global, but there are no international institutions endowed with the sovereign political authority to take action against it. International agencies have few powers, and the ones they have depend on the good will of the member countries. States can act, but only within their borders: individual states are not going to solve the crisis. But the fact remains that states are the largest-scale social actors with the sovereign power to *act* upon the crisis — as opposed to pressuring other actors to do something about it, which is basically what a social movement can aspire to.

Also, while many governments claim that their policies are geared to letting market forces operate, their actions do not always match their rhetoric. The negotiations leading to the Canada–U.S. Free Trade Agreement, for example, were marked by American threats to impose protectionist policies against Canada as well as against other countries. And indeed, throughout the 1980s the United States, among other countries, has imposed and threatened to impose any number of punitive policies upon its trading partners in order to force them to assent to the dominant partner's understanding of "free markets."

In this sense, it is not state capacity as such that has been severely reduced under post-Fordism. Rather, it is the sovereignty of weak states that is under attack, not only from "free markets" but also from the governments of strong states — mostly the United States, Japan, and Germany. In this sense, strong states continue to be sovereign. And strong states and global capital are partners in a mutually reinforcing, if sometimes tense, relationship. The difference with the Fordist era, perhaps, is that there were more strong states then than there are now. (For similar points but from a somewhat different conceptual perspective, see Marchak, 1991.) Even then, however, there were weak states, primarily in the so-called Third World. They are still weaker now (Marchak, 1991). Those states tried to carve themselves an independent place in the international economy, only to be "frustrated by the states most strongly attached to the free market ideology, and by policies that persistently favoured authoritarian states" (Marchak, 1991: 233–34).

A major theme in political economy is the idea that *what counts as "politics"* is not always and everywhere the same. This is seen most evidently in the fact that the word *politics* is understood differently in various languages. In French, for example, the word *politique* includes the meanings of the English words *politics* and *policy*.

Also, not every society in world history has had a concept of the political as separate from other spheres of life. In Islamic societies, for example, spiritual power and worldly power are very closely linked. Iran, which since the 1979 revolution has been an Islamic republic, and Saudi Arabia are the best-known contemporary examples of this situation, whose source is the birth of Islam itself in the 7th century A.D. Muhammad was accepted as a prophet by his followers in the same process that he became the ruler of the city of Medina, and then of an ever-expanding empire. The Prophet's successors (in Arabic, *khalifa*), the caliphs, thus inherited a position of religious and community leadership (Hourani, 1991). In this sense,

> the caliphate . . . possessed three elements: that of legitimate succession to the Prophet, that of directing the affairs of the world and that of watching over the faith (Hourani, 1991: 143).

Western societies, on the other hand, where the Christian tradition dominates, have developed a strong distinction between the sacred and the secular, between the government of souls and the government of society. One way in which the Christian tradition expresses the roots of this outlook is to invoke Jesus Christ's admonition to the Pharisees: "Render therefore unto Caesar the things which are Caesar's; and unto God the things that are God's" (Matthew, 22: 21).

In their specific processes of development, then, societies decide for themselves what use, if any, they have for an explicitly defined "political" field, separate from others such as the religious sector. It is often said, in this perspective, that "the Greeks and Romans invented politics" (Finley, 1983: 54). The word *politics* is derived from the Greek word **polis,** meaning "city." They also — especially the Greeks of the Athenian city-state — established a sense of the political that is at the basis of what Western societies understand as "politics." In fact, Aristotle's *Politics* remains a useful guide in making sense of today's seemingly boundless "politics."

In his *Politics,* Aristotle (384–322 B.C.) distinguishes between domestic and civic government, and between despotic and political government. Domestic society is composed of the family and its possessions including, if one is sufficiently rich, slaves; this realm is governed by a man, a patriarch, whose authority is natural. Power in domestic government is that of the master;

that is to say, it is despotic, a kind of monarchy. But, Aristotle noted, families do not live in isolation: several neighbouring and related households will form a village, governed by the patriarch of what we would call an extended family. This is how kingship is born.

When several villages unite, they form a city, a *polis,* where the domestic patriarchal principle can no longer hold. This is where civic, or political, government intervenes, bringing together into a more general self-sufficient society men (despots in their own households) who are free and equal. Among equal free men, government must be based on participation, particularly through *debate.* Indeed, goes Aristotle's argument, it is in order for free men to debate their common government that nature endowed man, and only man, with speech; this is why man is a "civic animal," a "political animal."

The *polis,* then, is defined by the freedom and equality of its members, to the exclusion of inferior non-members (women and slaves, not to mention animals), and by the debatable character of government among equals. Relationships between unequals are not to be debated. By definition they are outside the political field: they are natural, in the order of things. The restricted political field that Aristotle defined is well suited to the maintenance of slavery and gender oppression. However, there was nothing to keep subordinated groups from trying to widen the political field and make inequality an issue; slave revolts did occur, for instance, the best known of which was that led by Spartacus against Rome from 73 to 71 B.C. Dominant groups, on the other hand, could be expected to place barriers of various kinds around the political field in order to keep it from expanding. In the ancient city-states, the basic barrier was indeed to define the political field narrowly and to claim that this was the natural order of things. If this did not convince, force could be brought to bear.

Aristotle's restriction of politics to debate among naturally equal men, and his relegation of issues of inequality to the also natural domestic realm, do not belong to the distant past. Today, as in Aristotle's Athens, dominant groups have an interest in a narrow political field from which debate about issues that challenge their domination is excluded. To take only one contemporary example, inequalities between women and men are still present, and many of the manifestations of women's oppression were defined until recently as outside the political field. It is the women's movement, claiming the equal rights of women, that has widened the political field through relentless pressure; thus the personal became political. "Personal troubles," to borrow from C. Wright Mills (1959), became "public issues," open to debate.

When hegemony succeeds, the political field along with other social relations typically appears to be natural. But hegemony does not always succeed. In this respect, the proliferation of social movements in the last thirty years throughout the advanced capitalist countries has been interpreted by many authors as a failure of hegemony (Habermas, 1975): social movements have expanded the political field by arguing that the existing political order is neither just nor legitimate, making their arguments against gender inequality, the oppression of aboriginal peoples, and other inequities "political."

When hegemony fails and the political field is in danger of being enlarged, dominant groups still have resources at their disposal: they can use force to restrict, or even close completely, the political field. The Spartacus revolt was put down militarily, as was the Chinese student revolt of 1989. When dictatorships or otherwise authoritarian governments put opponents in jail and outlaw political parties, they are forcibly narrowing or closing altogether the field of debate.

In Canada today the field of debate is very wide and shows little sign of narrowing down. The current focus on the politics of everyday life is having several positive impacts. It is encouraging people to look critically upon many of their taken-for-granted practices of daily life and to change deeply ingrained discriminatory practices; but it also has worrisome implications, when criticism takes on overtones of intolerance and censorship. In this sense, what seems to be happening to politics in Western societies is not a dissolution of the dichotomy between private and public, but rather a takeover of the private side of the dichotomy by the public side.

Box 7.4

WHEN HEGEMONY FAILS

Hegemony can fail altogether. People may find that their rulers have lost, if they ever had, the right to rule; that the political regime under which they live has to be replaced. In such circumstances, revolutions may arise that aim at overthrowing the old order, through violence if necessary. The French Revolution, which began in 1789, is often seen as a typical case of such events.

The 20th century has had its share of revolutions, some successful and some not. Among the most important were the overthrow of the Russian imperial regime in 1917 and its replacement by a communist regime — all of which followed an earlier attempt, in 1905, that had failed. Other such upheavals in this century included the communist revolution in China in 1949 and the 1979 Islamic revolution in Iran.

In recent years, peaceful revolutions have occurred, most notably in the former Soviet Union and the countries surrounding it. Armed battle remains an option in several of these, in the shaping of post-communist political regimes — an option, mainly in some of the newly independent ex-Soviet republics, that is already being exercised. But it is remarkable that the overthrow of communist regimes has been done with very little violence.

In China in 1989, however, a nonviolent revolt that initially involved students and quickly grew to include hundreds of thousands of other citizens was crushed when the government used the army to re-establish its authority. This crackdown is widely known as the Tiananmen Massacre, after the name of Beijing's huge city square where insurgents had been gathered. The photograph of the aftermath, circulated the world over, dramatically illustrates the insurgents' determination, as well as their nonviolence, in the face of the military might of the government. Political power, here, could not count on hegemony: as China's premier communist leader Mao Tse-Tung once said, "Political power grows out of the barrel of a gun" (1966: 8).

As a general point, one can be concerned by the all-encompassing character that politics can take in such a situation: when "everything is political," there can be little room left for other criteria (aesthetic, for example) to guide our lives. Unfortunately, there are no simple answers to this problem, for inequality and injustice do permeate every aspect of our lives — and these ought to be treated not as private troubles, but as public issues.

SUMMARY

This chapter began with a comparison of the Canadian and American political cultures, and discussed staples theory, Fordism, and personal politics. After all this, one might be justified to conclude with Warren Magnusson that "politics today is everywhere and nowhere, and this is very confusing for all of us" (1992: 69). It is all the more important, then, to see in what ways all these aspects of politics hang together.

- Politics concerns the processes through which social power is allocated and reallocated. In this sense, politics is related in a basic way to the existence of social inequality. According to the traditional understanding, politics is a matter of strategic action by social agents either to maintain or alter the distribution of power in society — hence the focus on political parties, government, and the state. Thus, political sociologists in Canada have concerned themselves with the political culture of the country (especially as it compares with that of the United States in terms of conservatism versus liberalism) to discover its role in stabilizing the distribution of power in Canada.

- The revival of the Marxist approach and of political economy in Canada introduced an interest in the role played by political power in the development of capitalism, in Canada and elsewhere. In connection with this, interest grew in the struggle of the organized working class, the labour movement. This was followed by a concentration on newly important agents, appearing mostly during the 1960s, that were pushing for radical redistribution of power in society: the new social movements.

- Feminism's view that "the personal is political" made issues of hegemony a key focus of the study of politics. On this understanding, the allocation of social power rests largely upon various processes of hegemony, through which the distribution of power is reproduced as a matter of course, spontaneously, at all levels of social life. This theme first emerged strongly in the "problem" of the lack of class consciousness among the working class and in the insistence by the women's movement that the personal is political.
- What counts as political will vary from society to society and from time to time, according to whether dominant groups are successful in narrowing the scope of politics against possible attempts by dominated groups to expand the field. We used the qualifier "possible" here because subordinated groups do not always challenge the extent of the political field. Hegemony is the process through which such groups accept — without realizing that there might be attractive alternatives — the definition of the field promoted by the dominant groups.

KEY CONCEPTS

Comprador elite

Deindustrialization

Dependency theory

Fordism

Hegemony

Indigenous elite

Liberal democracy

Merchants against industry thesis

Nationalism

Nation-state

New Canadian Political Economy (NCPE)

Parasite elite

Polis

Political culture

Political economy

Politicization

Regulation school

Social Credit

Staples theory

Staples trap

State

REVIEW QUESTIONS

1. How has sociology as practised in Quebec and English-speaking Canada differed?
2. What important contributions has the political economy approach made to our understanding of Canadian development?

3. What is the difference between "nation" and "state"? What problems has confusion over the terms created in Quebec–Canada relations?
4. What is hegemony? How does hegemony work to maintain social and political relations?
5. What does the film *Black Robe* tell us about political sensibilities?
6. Why has class voting not been a factor in Canadian politics?
7. What is meant by "globalization"? What impact is globalization having upon states and politics in general?
8. What is the meaning of the statement, "The personal is political"? What has been the impact generally of feminism upon our view of politics?
9. What factors influence whether or not an issue will be viewed as "political"?

Crime & Deviance

Helen Boritch, James Creechan, James Hackler, Timothy Hartnagel, Leslie W. Kennedy, and
Robert Silverman

Crime and Deviance

INTRODUCTION

This chapter introduces you to many general ideas about crime and deviance. Sociologists recognize that crime is *only one way* of breaking rules, and their discussions about crime often make reference to the general ways that people deviate from social norms. In this chapter, we introduce you to some general ideas about rule breaking and show how crime fits into these general patterns.

First, we will describe how deviance is defined by sociologists. You will learn which characteristics crime shares with other types of rule breaking — and you will see how it is different. Second, we discuss the amount of crime in Canada and show how it is related to several sociological concepts. Sociologists like to measure social events, and they use these measurements to test theories. The study of crime is a good illustration of the strengths and weaknesses of using social statistics. Finally, we describe a broad range of theories that sociologists use to explain rule breaking and crime. We argue that the acceptability of theories is closely linked to our ability to measure deviance and other social factors.

Chapters 3 and 4 showed how people are socialized to internalize and conform to the norms or rules of their society. Without conformity and predictability, society as we know it could not exist. But we also know that social life includes nonconforming behaviour, which is called **deviance** by sociologists. We see people on the street who are "dressed funny" or have strange hairstyles, or we know that some people steal, beat each other up, or even kill. Deviant behaviour occurs in all societies and ranges from serious violations of laws (murder, for instance) to minor infractions of norms (colouring your hair purple). Few people have never been tempted to break socially accepted standards of behaviour — and most of us violate at least one important norm at some time in our lives. A full understanding of society, therefore, must explain how we deviate from social norms as well as how we learn to conform to them. Let us begin with a general overview of all forms of rule breaking.

WHAT IS DEVIANCE?

Deviant behaviour is generally defined as any behaviour that violates a social norm or the standards of society. Underlying this brief and straightforward definition there is a much more complex reality, because deviance, like beauty, is in the eye of the beholder. Although deviance is commonly thought to be inherently bad or evil, sociologists stress that deviance is always relative to what others find acceptable or unacceptable. In North America wearing a skirt is usually deviant for a male, but not for a female. (There are exceptions to this rule: players in traditional Scottish pipe bands wear kilts, for example.) Having two wives is illegal in Canada, but not in Nigeria. As a final example, in North America drinking alcohol is deviant and illegal for adolescents but not for adults. Deviance, therefore, is almost always relative and consists of two parts: one part includes the action or condition attributed to the deviant; the other is the negative societal reaction. Without both, there is no deviance.

The essence of deviance is not only that a person commits an act, but that there is a chance of reaction to it. Deviance is best understood as a social process where *some* people and behaviours are labelled as deviant and are negatively sanctioned. Even murder, which is criminal in all societies, is subject to variations in both definitions and sanctions. The label "murder" tells us that a *particular* taking of life is wrong or wrongly done. But killing may be approved if done for humane purposes, in self-defence, during wartime, or by the police in the line of duty.

If everything is relative, how can we know when an act violates the norms of society? Whether an act is considered deviant is determined by at least three factors: time, social context, and social status.

• TIME

Deviance or crime varies from one time period to another. Using alcohol, cocaine, and marijuana has been regarded as acceptable, deviant, or illegal at various times in Canada. Similarly, tolerance of smoking has varied considerably. In the early 1900s, smoking was banned in parts of the United States; it was considered acceptable and even sophisticated in North America during the 1950s; in recent times, however, laws have been passed to regulate or prohibit smoking in public places, and smoking has taken on a negative image. Consequently, this once-acceptable behaviour increasingly has come to be defined as deviant, and there are anti-smoking activists who do everything they can to see that "offenders" are appropriately punished. In 1993 the federal Minister of Health, Benoît Bouchard, proposed that people who sell cigarettes to minors be fined up to $50 000.

• SOCIAL CONTEXT

An act can be considered deviant depending on the social context in which it happens. Definitions of deviance and crime vary across different societies and political jurisdictions. Solicitation or communicating for the purpose of prostitution is illegal across Canada, but legal in the state of Nevada, and in Denmark, Germany, and France.

Definitions of deviance may vary across groups living in the same society. Simply conforming to the norms of one group may earn intense disapproval from another. Each of the opposing camps in the abortion debate frequently regards the behaviour of the other side as deviant or even criminal. Furthermore, an act may be deviant or conforming depending on the particular circumstances. Talking to yourself occasionally in the privacy of your own home is not deviant, but frequently talking to yourself in public probably would be viewed as deviant.

• SOCIAL STATUS

Social status and power influence what is called deviant. Definitions of deviance do not solely depend on perceptions of the harmfulness of the behaviour; that is because similar acts by people of different social status are not regarded as equally deviant or criminal. In other words, the limits of acceptable behaviour are more elastic for some people than for others. Skid row drunks or drug addicts are routinely sent to jail, while celebrities with substance-abuse problems (e.g., movie star Elizabeth Taylor or hockey star Grant Fuhr) voluntarily enter private facilities such as the Betty Ford Clinic in the United States. A gunman on the street is readily labelled criminal, but the death of hundreds of people exposed to unsafe products, pollution, or hazardous working conditions receives comparatively little attention. Although Canadians face greater risks of dying from work-related causes than by being murdered, corporate executives usually are not regarded or treated as criminal (Reasons et al., 1981; Snider, 1993). In general, behaviour common to the lower classes is more likely to be defined as deviant or criminal and dealt with more harshly than behaviour typically thought of as middle or upper class.

KINDS OF DEVIANCE AND CRIME

Clearly, not all deviant acts should be considered equally bad or receive the same degree of punishment. Deviant acts can be placed on a continuum ranging from those regarded as least to most serious, although in complex societies not all individuals or groups will agree about the seriousness of particular acts. With these points in mind, different types of deviance can be distinguished

Table 8.1

TYPES OF DEVIANCE

Kind of Deviance	Degree of Agreement	Severity of Societal Response	Perceived Harmfulness	Examples
Consensus crimes	Consensus	Severe	Extremely harmful	First-degree murder; armed robbery
Conflict crimes	Conflict	Punitive	Somewhat harmful	"Victimless" crimes (e.g., prostitution, narcotics)
Social deviations	Uncertainty	Indeterminate	Potentially harmful	Mental illness; juvenile delinquency
Social diversions	Apathy	Mild	Relatively harmless	Fads and fashions

depending on three measures of the societal response to the deviance: (1) the level of public agreement about the wrongfulness of the act; (2) the severity of the societal response elicited by the act; and (3) the societal evaluation of the harm inflicted by the act (Hagan, 1984). Table 8.1 illustrates these characteristics and kinds of deviance.

• CONSENSUS CRIMES

Certain rules have a special status in society and are specifically included as statutes in the criminal code. Even though the content of criminal codes varies across different societies and historical periods, there is a high degree of agreement or consensus that certain acts defined by law as crimes are both very serious and harmful to society (e.g., murder, armed robbery, aggravated sexual assault). These consensus crimes are usually severely punished with long prison terms or, sometimes, capital punishment. In any society, consensus crimes are the least common type of deviance.

• CONFLICT CRIMES

Other acts embedded in criminal codes are subject to conflict and debate among individuals and groups in society. Many people regard acts such as prostitution, drug use, pornography, certain sexual acts, and gambling as only marginally serious or harmful, since the "victims" are usually willing participants who do not regard their behaviour as criminal. For these very reasons, "victimless" crimes are more common than consensus crimes and punished less severely. Ultimately, conflict crimes represent the use of the law to impose certain moral standards on society as a whole. Sociologists ask how such acts and persons come to be considered criminal in the absence of societal consensus.

• SOCIAL DEVIATIONS

Many behaviours that are not a part of a criminal code are nonetheless subject to official control. Examples of such social deviations include mental illness, suicide, juvenile delinquency (which is controlled by its own law), and some deviant corporate transactions. Although these deviations appear to be very different, common features unite them. While they are not considered criminal, the stigma they carry is a major aspect of labels such as mentally ill or delinquent. Most of these behaviours are only vaguely defined, perhaps reflecting our uncertainty about what these categories include or how to deal with these behaviours. In the past, some behaviours now considered social deviations were defined and treated as criminal. For example, until 1968, homosexual acts between consenting adults were included in the Criminal Code (and thus were illegal) in Canada. Although such acts are no longer criminal, a majority of Canadians continue to regard them as morally wrong (Stebbins, 1988). The absence of criminal sanctions does not imply that there is no societal response at all. In responding to social deviations, society aims to help or treat "patients" rather than punish them. However, since "treatment" frequently is involuntary, this distinction often is meaningless for those on the receiving end.

• SOCIAL DIVERSIONS

Social diversions represent differences in lifestyle and activities that may strike us as odd or eccentric, but that are generally reacted to with tolerance, amusement, or, more typically, apathy. These are the least serious and most common forms of deviance. In the pursuit of pleasure and excitement, people dye their hair orange, tattoo their bodies, take up bungee jumping, and climb rock faces. The time and energy people expend in pursuing these activities may seem unusual, but these behaviours are seldom considered either good or bad, nor are they treated with anything more than informal disapproval. Instead they are viewed as expressions of individuality, or even as interesting and diverse lifestyles. Still, despite the seemingly benign societal response to most social diversions, public opinion about the seriousness of these behaviours is subject to change. Several years ago the popularity of skateboarding among young people came to be seen by many as both a hazard and a nuisance to the general public. Consequently, skateboarding was increasingly prohibited in both public recreational areas and private parking lots. Responding to these increasing restrictions, the parents of skateboarding enthusiasts sported bumper stickers protesting that "skateboarding is not a crime." Similarly, it is conceivable that the recent injuries and deaths associated with bungee jumping may prompt increasing regulation (or even prohibition) of this recreational pursuit.

PERSPECTIVES ON LAW

Why are some behaviours thought to be so serious that laws are created to prohibit them, while other forms of deviance are not? Two schools of thought provide different answers to this question: the consensus model and the conflict model (Chambliss, 1976; Turk, 1976).

According to the **consensus model,** laws are simple reflections of society's values. Laws are part of society's efforts to regulate harm, and in applying them society takes action to prevent future incidents. The criminal law, therefore, is a rational codification of the "will of the people" and closely represents public opinion. Many consensus crimes have been so labelled because they represent serious threats to individual well-being and must be controlled.

However, other laws might not be explained so easily. The consensus model of law works when there is a unity of opinion and purpose but is inadequate to describe what happens when society has conflicting ideas. It is not just the degree of social harm that determines which acts will be prohibited by law. Why, we might ask, is heroin illegal but not alcohol or tobacco, even though alcohol and tobacco cause more deaths than heroin? In 1992 there were close to 40 000 deaths in Canada related to smoking. Nor is there universal consensus on the threat represented by every act prohibited by law. Although some segments of the population view behaviours such as prostitution, drug use, and pornography as inherently immoral and dangerous, other segments of the population do not share these views.

According to the **conflict model,** these problem areas might become law because one part of society manages to impose its values and definition of crime on everyone. According to this approach, society consists of groups with conflicting values and interests who are struggling to dominate one another. Those with the most power generally succeed in making their definition of crime part of the criminal law. In this case, laws reflect the distribution of power in society. Although there may be instances when the values of the majority coincide with the interests of those with significant power in society, conflict theorists argue that popular opinion is not the driving force behind the creation of laws. Laws, especially those about moral issues, reflect the interests of dominant social groups. Middle- and upper-class people rarely shoot heroin, for example, but they prohibit others from doing it. They do, however, smoke cigarettes and use alcohol (and run huge corporations manufacturing these products); these behaviours are not criminalized.

Laws closely linked to moral issues are not easily enacted, since different groups may have very different opinions about whether certain behaviours should be punished. Some individual or group of individuals must feel strongly enough about an issue to take the initiative to push for the enactment of laws and formal sanctions. Howard Becker (1963) used the term **moral entrepreneurs** to describe individuals who actively advocate official control of some types of deviance and whose efforts are essential to the passing of new laws. Consistent with their belief that the activity is immoral and harmful, moral entrepreneurs may undertake to gain public support for their cause. In these cases, moral entrepreneurs attempt to create a new definition of the activity that would enable them to impose their values on all of society. Whether moral entrepreneurs can succeed in creating a new category of crime depends on their skill in mobilizing central societal beliefs and attitudes. New definitions of crime do not appear in a vacuum but rather require a supportive climate. The best illustration of this process is narcotics control.

• THE ORIGIN OF CANADIAN NARCOTICS LEGISLATION

A historical analysis of the passage of Canadian narcotics legislation during the first decades of the 20th century reveals how cultural beliefs about drug use interacted with intensely hostile attitudes toward Asian Canadians to create a climate that led to a new definition of crime (Cook, 1969; Green, 1979). One important moral entrepreneur who acted to create Canada's first narcotics legislation was Mackenzie King. Before becoming prime minister, Mackenzie King (who was then Deputy Minister of Labour) was sent to Vancouver to supervise compensation to Chinese and Japanese businessmen who had suffered losses during a 1907 anti-Asian riot. While there, King expressed shock and concern at the ease with which opium was available from Chinese manufacturers and merchants. He prepared a report to the government, which led to the enactment of The Opium Act in 1908 prohibiting the non-medicinal use of opiates. In subsequent years, King made a second career out of his moral crusade, attending international conferences and introducing increasingly punitive legislation.

Until King's crusade, the use of opium for either medicinal or recreational purposes was of little concern to the medical profession, the government, or the public. Medications containing opium were routinely prescribed by physicians and were a common ingredient in many over-the-counter cough syrups, health tonics, and infant medications. As a result, a large number of white, middle-class people developed lifelong dependency on opium and its derivatives. For the most part, opium addiction was regarded as a personal misfortune or vice, but not as a general threat to society.

A second and much smaller population of narcotics users consisted of Chinese immigrants to Canada who smoked opium. Initially welcomed as a source of cheap labour during the boom period of the 1860s and 1870s, Asians living in Canada found that the attitude of the dominant white population changed markedly as the economy slowed in the 1880s and jobs became scarcer.

The shrinking job market led to increased racism on the part of white labourers, who argued that Chinese immigrants took away their jobs. They called upon the government to restrict further immigration from Asian countries.

In this social climate of intense hostility, the Chinese came to be singled out as the primary source of a serious drug problem in Canada. Although the majority of drug users were whites, the social reaction concentrated on Asian drug users. This distinction is understandable because of the different ways the drug was used by the two groups. White, middle-class Canadians used drugs, prescribed by a doctor or bought from a drugstore, at home. The Chinese Canadians smoked opium where they lived and worked, making their drug use more visible.

Another central figure in the moral crusade to prohibit narcotics was Emily Murphy, a prominent juvenile court judge in Edmonton. Murphy, in a *Maclean's* magazine article (1920) and in her book *The Black Candle* (1922), promoted a cultural stereotype of the Chinese drug user as a dangerous dope fiend intent on bringing about the downfall of the white race. Exploiting the existing hostility toward Asians, Murphy forged a link among three activities: drug use, sexual promiscuity, and race-mixing. What had previously been regarded as a personal problem of little importance was now redefined as a grave moral threat to the white population. After the drug problem was defined as an Asian-Canadian issue, it required only a small leap of logic for various interest groups to lobby politicians to prohibit further Asian immigration to Canada during the 1920s.

The creation of Canada's earliest drug laws reveals that the target of formal social control often depends on the distance between those who engage in the behaviour and those who seek to redefine it. The success of efforts to create new legislation depends on the social context in which they occur. As long as the use of opium was associated in the public mind with the middle class and respectable elements of the population it was widely tolerated. It was only when opium use was publicly identified with the Chinese population, which was considered to be socially inferior by the dominant white society, that its use came to be widely regarded as a social evil in need of legal reform.

In summary, the factors that predict which rules become part of the criminal code are complex and can only be understood by looking at social factors such as power, influence, and the social climate.

In the next section we turn to the study of the amount of crime in society.

How Much Crime Is There?

A major problem in studying crime and deviance is determining how much crime exists in society. It is important to know how much rule breaking happens and which types are most common. Crime is somewhat easier to count than other forms of deviance; because there is more agreement that it is a harmful form of behaviour, society mobilizes its legal machinery to track it and suppress it. Illegal forms of deviance, then, tend to be counted more carefully than other social problems.

Counts of crime are used to indicate the amount of crime in society; to determine trends (increasing or decreasing) of crime in society; to allocate law enforcement resources by local authorities; to allocate money to law enforcement agencies by politicians; and to test theories about crime by social scientists. Social control of specific kinds of crime is often based on interpretation of statistical trends. Is there more or less drug trafficking? homicide? robbery? Government agencies use statistics at face value and then spend money on that basis.

As you read in Chapter 2, measurement is not a simple problem; statistics must be used with great caution. The case of crime measures is a good example of the problems that can arise. For instance, a Statistics Canada document, *Canadian Crime Statistics, 1991* (Canadian Centre for Justice Statistics, 1992), reports the number of crimes committed in Canada during the year

1990. As we shall see, however, the numbers recorded do not actually represent all the crime that occurred in Canada that year. The "facts" must be used with caution.

This section discusses whether "official crime statistics" (i.e., those generated by the government) indicate the true amount of crime, and looks at how other information sources add to our understanding of crime.

• UNIFORM CRIME REPORTS: OFFICIAL CRIME STATISTICS

The nature of crime statistics necessarily produces an undercount of crime. The only annual crime statistics that are available nationally are compiled by the Canadian Centre for Justice Statistics (CCJS, a unit within Statistics Canada). Crimes that appear in the Statistics Canada documents represent crimes that are *reported to* and *recorded by* police. Each month police departments across the country compile reports about crime in their jurisdictions for Statistics Canada. The CCJS tabulates these results and publishes summary reports. These summaries (like *Canadian Crime Statistics, 1991*) are used by the media; if the reports are not properly interpreted, the public perception of crime may be distorted. In turn, the public perception of crime will affect how governments develop policies to control crime. Consequently, it is important to understand both the strength and the weakness of these official crime statistics.

There are many reasons that explain why some crime incidents are not reported to the police and are not included in official crime records. Several studies prove that a high proportion of even the most serious crimes go unreported (two exceptions being motor vehicle theft and homicide). Crime reporting by the public varies both by *the seriousness of the event* and by *the type of crime* itself. Sexual assault (called "rape" in the Canadian Criminal Code prior to 1982), one of the most serious crimes against the person, has a relatively low reporting rate because victims may be deterred by negative reactions of the police, embarrassment, their relationship to the offender, and other factors (O'Brien, 1985). On the other hand, motor vehicle theft, a much less serious property crime, is highly reported by victims so that they can collect their auto insurance. With few other exceptions, the more serious the crime, the higher the likelihood of a report being filed. When no report is filed or if the police have not discovered the crime, then for statistical purposes no crime has taken place, and there will be *no* indication in the crime reports to show that a crime was committed.

White-collar and corporate crimes are crimes committed using stealth and fraud by those in positions of trust in large organizations, and are much more difficult to detect. This kind of crime

CRIME RATES

Box 8.1

Most reports about crime in society are made in terms of crime rates. The value of using a **crime rate** instead of the absolute number of crimes is that crime rates take account of fluctuations in the population when expressing the amount of crime that occurs. In their generic form, crime rates are simple calculations that describe the relationship between the number of crimes that occur during a given time period in a geographical area and the population base from which the crimes come. When expressing crime rates for large populations (e.g., cities or countries) one usually produces rates per 100 000 population. For instance, the following calculation produces a crude crime rate for Canada in 1991:

$$\frac{3\,438\,379}{26\,999\,442} \times 100\,000 = 12\,735$$

The expression indicates that there were 3 438 379 crimes known to the police in 1991 and there were close to 27 million people living in the country. So in 1991, for every 100 000 people living in Canada, there were 12 735 crimes recorded by the police.

ALL CRIME, VIOLENT CRIME, AND PROPERTY CRIME, CANADA, 1962–1991

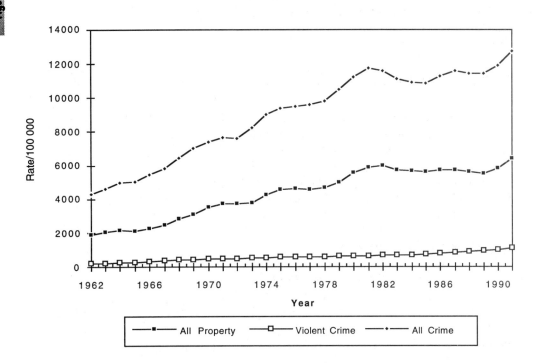

is rarely prosecuted but "cost[s] more money, does more harm and ruins more lives" than any of the street crimes (Snider, 1993). In spite of the level of harm, these crimes are seldom reported in official statistics.

• TRENDS

In the presentation of statistics most specific crime types are grouped into general categories called **indexes**. For instance, murder, armed robbery, sexual assault, and other assaults are all combined to create a violent crime index. Using data from the Uniform Crime Reports it is possible to plot some recent index crime trends for Canada. Figure 8.1 shows the rise and fall of crime rates for *all* recorded crime, *property* crime, and *violent* crime indexes between 1962 and 1991.

Note how much lower the violent crime rate is than either the total crime rate or the property crime rate. In fact, in 1991 less than 10 percent of all crime reported to the police was violent crime. Note as well the general trend. There was a continuing rise in the rate of *all* crimes in Canada until 1981. The rate of all crimes declined until 1987 when it began to rise again. A similar pattern occurs for property crime, with the biggest rise taking place between 1989 and 1991. In contrast, violent crime simply climbs slowly but steadily through the thirty-year period.

It is also possible to look at how *specific* crimes contribute to each overall crime index. Figure 8.2 shows trends for three crimes against the person. Assault (force or threat of force used by one person against another) is the most common type of violent crime. As seen in Figure 8.2 the (nonsexual) *assault* rate has been rising in the last thirty years to a rate exceeding 800 for every 100 000 Canadians. On the other hand, *robbery* (the face-to-face theft of goods by force or

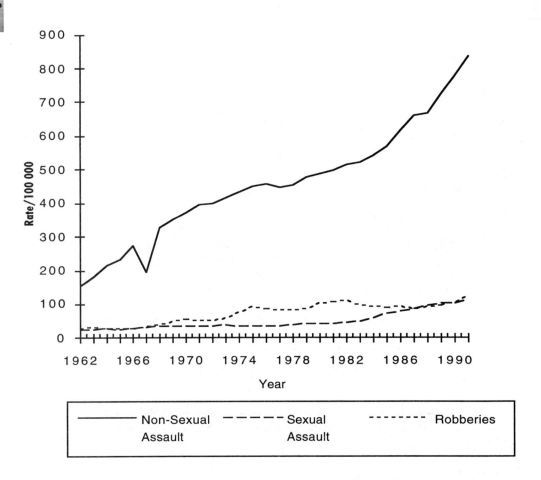

Figure 8.2

All Assault, Sexual Assault, and Robberies, Canada, 1962–1991

threat of force) was relatively stable between the mid-1970s and late 1980s, but rose by 20 percent between 1990 and 1991. Finally, the rate of *sexual assault* (usually forcible sexual intercourse), a relatively rare crime, has risen substantially since 1982. The reason for the rise may have more to do with changes in the legal definition of the act and with women's increased willingness to report the crime than with actual increases in the number of sexual assaults committed. Murder, the crime in which one person criminally kills another, is not illustrated in Figure 8.2; but it is worth noting the rate of murder in comparison to the other violent crimes. The rate of murder in 1991 was about 3 per 100 000 Canadians. It is the rarest of violent crimes, though probably the one that causes most concern.

Figure 8.3 shows trends for three common types of property crimes. Clearly, there is a relatively great amount of *theft* (taking others' property) in Canada. The rate reaches about 3500 per 100 000 in 1982. It then declines somewhat, but between 1989 and 1991 it rises above that rate to reach 3636 per 100 000. Consistent with the legal definition, *break and enter* statistics include any incident of crossing a forbidden threshold. Hence, anyone who illegally enters a house, even if the door is wide open, may be charged with break and enter. Usually, break and enter is coupled with theft (the intent of the crime is to steal). The statistical trends show that Canada had a rising

Figure 8.3

ROBBERY, BREAK AND ENTER, AND MOTOR VEHICLE THEFT, CANADA, 1962–1991

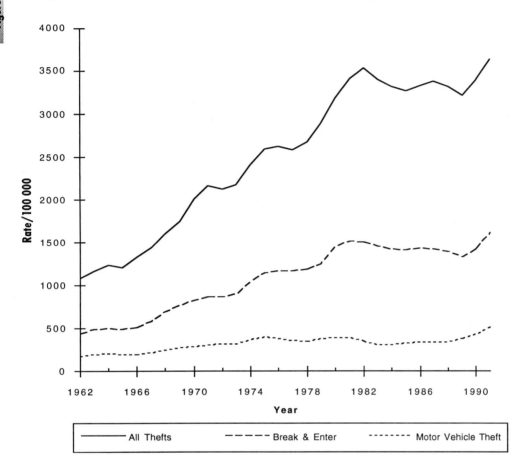

rate of break and enter until the early 1980s and then a decline until the early 1990s. The rate reached about 1500 per 100 000 inhabitants in 1981, a rate that did not occur again until 1991. Finally, *motor vehicle theft* has remained relatively stable since the late 1960s, but rose significantly in 1990 and 1991.

Crime trends vary a great deal by region. For instance, both robbery and motor vehicle theft are much higher in Quebec than in other parts of the country. Quebec also has the highest rate of unsolved murders: gang-related murders, which are not as common in other parts of the country, are responsible.

In the last few years for which data are available, there has been a rise in almost all types of crime shown in these graphs. If the trend continues, criminologists will be busy trying to explain the causes of these new patterns. Trends alone do not tell us much about crime in Canada, but they can be linked to other social conditions to make more meaningful statements. The rise in crime might be related to rises in the birthrate (the baby boom), economic downturns, employment levels, the proportion of women in the workforce, regional variations, and many other variables. Sociologists interested in crime study these issues in much greater detail.

• VICTIMIZATION STUDIES: AN ALTERNATIVE SOURCE OF DATA

As we have seen, the trends presented above do not represent all crime in Canada since they are based on only those incidents known to the police. Victimization studies attempt to create another picture of crime prevalence. Victimization studies track crimes missed in the official statistics (those generated by the CCJS) by asking people about the crimes committed against them. Victimization surveys are very expensive. In Canada there have been only two nationwide victimization surveys — the Canadian Urban Victimization Survey (Solicitor General, 1983) and the General Social Survey in 1988 (Sacco and Johnson, 1990c).

The 1988 General Social Survey interviewed a national sample of approximately 10 000 persons, 15 years of age or older. Interviews were by telephone, providing the most up-to-date information to be assembled yet on victimization for Canada. (The survey results are not directly comparable to police statistics. It is almost impossible to ensure that the same reporting period is included in victimization surveys as in police statistics, and impossible to be sure that crimes claimed in a victimization survey would have been recorded by police investigating the complaint.) The survey estimated that 4.8 million Canadians 15 years of age or older were victimized in 5.4 million criminal incidents in 1987. About one-third of these crimes were violent, while 40 percent were property crimes (Sacco and Johnson, 1990c: 13). These figures are far in excess of the official police reports and provide more information than official statistics about who is victimized by crime.

> Risk of personal victimization is highest for those who are male, young, single, and residents of urban areas and those who are students or unemployed. Rates of household crime are generally greater for households with high incomes, for residences that are rented rather than owned and for those located in urban areas (Sacco and Johnson, 1990c: 13).

Data generated by official means (Canadian Uniform Crime Reports) do not include this information about victim characteristics.

Like official statistics, victimization surveys have methodological flaws. Respondents may forget crimes, or they may bring significant events (such as crimes) forward in time (telescoping) (Nettler, 1984; O'Brien, 1985). Further, the respondent's notion of being victimized may not correspond to a legal definition of crime. Worse, Levine (1976) argued, respondents may invent crime to please the interviewers, and the interviewers may invent crime to please their employers. Researchers have pointed out that victimization data are not directly comparable to official statistics and that there is no precise agreement on how one set of data corresponds to the other (Decker, 1983; Eck and Riccio, 1979; Skogan, 1981).

In this section you learned that measuring crime is not as easy as it may seem. The numbers you read in the newspaper about the amount of crime in a particular area at a particular time are the numbers generated by official recordkeeping and, as you have read, represent only a fraction of crime in Canadian society. It is important to keep these issues in mind, for they influence how people perceive their local crime situation and how politicians spend our money.

In the next section we focus on social and demographic factors related to criminal behaviour. We concentrate on crime because it has been studied more systematically than other types of deviance and because sociologists have collected a great deal of information about criminal deviance.

CORRELATES OF CRIMINAL BEHAVIOUR

Correlates of criminal behaviour are those factors that are related in some systematic way to criminal activity. They are variables that are associated, or vary, with criminal behaviour and become the building blocks for explanations of criminal behaviour. It is probably impossible to draw up a comprehensive list of such correlates. A list of all potential correlates would be a long one; moreover, criminologists debate the inclusion of many of its items. Some have claimed that delinquent behaviour is correlated with subnormal scores on IQ tests; others, that crime is related to poverty. Each of these claims of **correlation** (the association between two variables) has been disputed. Despite the difficulty of the task, however, identifying and describing the correlates of criminal behaviour is an important first step and a necessary one for the explanation of the causes of criminal behaviour. In this section our discussion is limited to a few of the major *social* conditions thought to be correlated with criminal behaviour.

• AGE

Official statistics from many different years and jurisdictions indicate a strong correlation between age and criminal behaviour (Empey, 1982; Steffensmeier et al., 1989). Young persons commit a disproportionate amount of crime. Unfortunately, no official data are published on the age of persons *charged* in Canada, so court statistics for persons *convicted* of only the most serious offences (indictable offences) must be used. (These were last issued in 1973 and do not include data from Quebec or Alberta.) The general pattern in these data is that conviction rates rise with increasing age to 18–19 and then decline as age increases. Thus the highest rates of conviction occur among those 19 and under. These figures undoubtedly understate the amount of crime actually committed in the younger age categories, since youth are less likely to be processed through the criminal justice system and since, until recently, some provinces treated those under 18 as juveniles.

Historical trends in **conviction rates** for indictable offences by age categories reveal a shift in recent years toward the younger ages (Tepperman, 1977). Between 1950 and 1966 the rate of conviction for males aged 16–17 increased by 50 percent, while for older age categories the conviction rate increased only marginally or declined. Tepperman (1977) also points out that the conviction rate for young people has progressively increased since 1891, as their entrance into adult status has been delayed. Major life decisions such as marriage and entry into the workforce are taking place at a later age than previously.

The rapid decline in crime as adolescents move into young adulthood has been termed "maturational reform." This pattern in the age distribution of crime has been attributed to the ambiguous and marginal social position of youth in urban industrial society, which creates a variety of tensions and problems; crime is but one example (Greenberg, 1979; Nettler, 1984). As youth move into adulthood, their social status and integration increase, along with the personal costs of crime. New rewards and costs associated with their new adult status replace those that sustained delinquency in adolescence (Rowe and Tittle, 1977; Trasler, 1980). But Hirschi and Gottfredson (1983) have challenged this interpretation, citing research suggesting that the effects of age on crime do not depend on such life-course events as leaving school, finding gainful employment, marrying, and so forth. So although the correlation of age with crime is one of the least disputed facts in criminology, its interpretation remains open to a good deal of debate.

• GENDER

The crime rate for men greatly exceeds the rate for women. In fact, it has been claimed that gender is of greater importance in differentiating criminals from noncriminals than any other trait (Sutherland and Cressey, 1970). In Canada in 1988, adult males made up 82 percent of adults charged with Criminal Code offences; in addition, over 80 percent of the young persons appearing in youth courts were male (Statistics Canada, 1989a). This gender difference in crime varies somewhat by the type of crime. Thus, males accounted for 90 percent of the adults charged with violent crime, 77 percent with property crime, and 86 percent with other crimes. So violent crime, in particular, is correlated with maleness. To supplement these official statistics, the Canadian Urban Victimization Survey (Johnson, 1986) estimated that males represented 90 percent of the perpetrators of robbery and assault in 1981, a figure reasonably similar to that provided by the official data on males charged with these same two offences — 95 percent. Self-reported delinquency research — a methodology that asks people what crimes they have committed — with juveniles has generally supported this gender difference, though the gap is not as great as in the official data on adults (Hagan, 1985a; Gomme et al., 1984; Hindelang et al., 1979).

Although the male crime rate greatly exceeds that of females, the percentage increase in the female rate has exceeded that for males over the last twenty years and more. Table 8.2 shows the rates of adults charged in Canada, by sex, for the years 1968, 1978, and 1988. Over the twenty-year period, the rate of all Criminal Code offences for males increased by 88 percent, while for females the increase was 261 percent. Females went from 9 percent to 17 percent of adults charged with Criminal Code offences. Similar differences can be observed for violent crimes and property crimes, although 86 percent of the increase between 1968 and 1988 in the number of females charged with Criminal Code offences was for nonviolent offences. In 1988, 13 percent of all women charged were charged with violent crimes, while 60 percent were charged with property crimes. Conclusions about trends in female crime that are based upon official data are, of course,

Table 8.2

RATE OF ADULTS CHARGED[1] BY SEX PER 100 000 POPULATION[2] FOR SELECTED CRIMINAL CODE OFFENCES, CANADA, 1968, 1978, 1988

Offence	1968		1978		1988	
	Male	Female	Male	Female	Male	Female
Homicide	2.4	0.3	4.4	0.7	3.2	0.5
Robbery	26.6	1.6	49.7	3.6	42.6	4.1
Crimes of Violence	270.5	15.0	372.6	34.8	653.3	69.8
B & E	157.6	3.4	308.3	12.9	279.2	12.9
Theft Over[3]	82.4	8.5	77.2	11.3	43.1	7.8
Theft Under[4]	175.0	49.7	369.5	186.8	438.8	215.3
Frauds	105.0	12.8	177.8	53.8	215.1	76.0
Property Crimes	639.7	79.2	1120.3	281.5	1140.5	329.1
Criminal Code	1443.4	152.0	2375.0	415.0	2714.8	549.4

1. Sources: 1968 — Dominion Bureau of Statistics, *Crime Statistics.* Ottawa: Queen's Printer, 1969; 1978 — Statistics Canada, *Crime and Traffic Enforcement Statistics.* Ottawa: Minister of Supply and Services, 1980; 1988 — Statistics Canada, *Canadian Crime Statistics, 1988.* Ottawa: Minister of Supply and Services, 1989.

2. Sources of population estimates: 1968 — Dominion Bureau of Statistics, *Estimates of Population by Marital Status, Age and Sex, Canada and Provinces 1968.* Ottawa: Dominion Bureau of Statistics, 1970; 1978 — Statistics Canada, *Estimates of Population by Marital Status, Age and Sex for Canada and the Provinces, June 1, 1977 and 1978.* Ottawa: Minister of Supply and Services, 1980; 1988 — Statistics Canada, *Postcensal Annual Estimates of Population by Marital Status, Age, Sex, and Components of Growth for Canada, Provinces and Territories, June 1, 1988.* Ottawa: Minister of Supply and Services, 1988.

1968 males = 10 409 900; females = 10 334 100
1978 males = 11 674 100; females = 11 808 500
1988 males = 12 784 600; females = 13 138 700

3. 1968, Theft over $50; 1978, Theft over $200; 1988, Theft over $1000.

4. 1968, Theft $50 and under; 1978, Theft $200 and under; 1988, Theft $1000 and under.

vulnerable to the claim that such data reflect changes in the response to female crime by the criminal justice system at least as much as they indicate real changes in female criminal behaviour.

Criminologists have offered various explanations for the gender difference in criminal involvement as well as for the changes in female participation in crime. A major emphasis has been placed on the importance of different gender role expectations. Most boys are socialized to greater independence and risk taking and are therefore freer to experiment with deviant conduct than are most girls, who are rewarded for compliance and dependence. This provides girls with fewer opportunities to experiment with delinquency (Hagan et al., 1979). Changes in gender role expectations toward greater gender equality may contribute to increases and changing patterns in female crime (Fox and Hartnagel, 1979). Nevertheless, the continued high proportion of women offenders charged with theft or fraud (54 percent of all Criminal Code charges against women in 1988) is consistent with women's traditional domestic roles of shopper and consumer (Johnson, 1987), as well as their continued restricted labour-market participation (Steffensmeier, 1980).

• RACE, CULTURE, AND ETHNICITY

Only limited data are available on the involvement of native people in criminal behaviour. However, it is clear that they are overrepresented in the Canadian criminal justice system compared to their representation in the Canadian population (LaPrairie, 1983; Cawsey 1991a; Hamilton and Sinclair, 1991; Silverman and Nielsen, 1992). The Ministry of Indian Affairs and Northern Development (1980) estimated that while Canadian Indians and other natives constituted approximately 3 percent of the total population, they represented about 9 percent of the national penitentiary population and upward of 40 percent of the jail and penitentiary population in the Prairies and the North. By 1988–89 native offenders accounted for approximately 19 percent of all sentenced admissions to provincial correctional institutions and 13 percent of warrant-of-committal admissions to federal custody, up from 15 percent and 9 percent, respectively, in 1982–83 (Statistics Canada, 1989b).

This overrepresentation of natives varies by offence and by gender. A survey of offenders admitted to Ontario correctional institutions during 1979 and 1980 found that while the total native crime rate for those years was 4.5 times the non-native rate, the native rates for crimes against persons and property were only about 3 times the non-native rates; but the native rate for alcohol offences was 16 times the non-native rate (Hagan, 1985b). This research also discovered that the ratio of native to non-native crime rates was greater among women than among men, and that native crime rates peak later (ages 25 to 35) than non-native rates (19 to 24). Older native women were particularly overrepresented in Ontario correctional institutions, reflecting their extremely disadvantaged position in Canadian society (Hagan, 1985b).

Several possible explanations for this native overrepresentation in the Canadian criminal justice system have been suggested (LaPrairie, 1983; Cawsey, 1991a, 1991b). Natives may actually commit a disproportionate amount of criminal acts and/or commit serious acts to which the public and the criminal justice system are more likely to respond. Alternatively, the agents of the criminal justice system may intentionally or unintentionally discriminate against native people (Havemann et al., 1985). For example, natives in cities may attract police attention by their physical appearance, by their concentration in skid row areas, and by their greater public visibility when drinking, resulting in more frequent arrests (Bienvenue and Latif, 1974; Greenaway, 1980; Frideres, 1988). So police initiative and discretion in seeking out the poor and disadvantaged may be implicated to some extent in the higher frequency of native arrests for certain types of crime. However, despite such well-publicized cases of injustice as that of Donald Marshall, there appears to be little evidence of systematic discrimination by agents of the criminal justice system (Hartnagel, 1987).

Another explanation emphasizes culture conflict through the imposition of the somewhat alien values and rules of the Canadian legal and justice system on native culture (James, 1979; Ross 1992). Finally, overrepresentation of natives within the criminal justice system has been seen as a reproduction of the basic socioeconomic inequalities present in the surrounding society (Verdun-Jones and Muirhead, 1979/80). The social and economic oppression of natives by the dominant white society keeps the majority of natives poor and dependent. This breeds crime, violence, and other social disorders to which the criminal justice system responds, thereby further contributing to the exploitation. Thus, although it is clear that native people are overrepresented in the criminal justice system, the reasons for their overrepresentation remain in dispute.

• SOCIAL CLASS AND SOCIAL STATUS

Social class was discussed at length in Chapter 5. The nature and extent of the correlation between social class and criminal behaviour is a hotly debated question among criminologists. Official statistics seem to support an **inverse** or **negative relationship:** those arrested, convicted, and/or incarcerated are more likely to come from lower socioeconomic categories of the population as indexed by such variables as income, education, and occupational status. A negative relationship indicates that "more" of one variable is found with "less" of another variable. For instance, high socioeconomic status groups have lower official crime rates. However, these official data may underestimate the amount of crime committed by those in higher socioeconomic positions. In fact, evidence from self-report studies, mainly of juveniles, seems to challenge the negative relationship found in official statistics (Tittle et al., 1978). Researchers have attempted to account for this apparent discrepancy between self-report and official data by examining the hypothesis of official discrimination against lower-class adolescents in the enforcement of the law (Nettler, 1984). However, once legally relevant factors such as seriousness of the offence and prior record of the suspect are taken into account, the evidence for such class bias in law enforcement is weak and far from systematic.

Furthermore, recent research using the self-report method has found a negative relationship between class and crime with the introduction of refinements in measurement and analysis (Elliott and Ageton, 1980; Thornberry and Farnworth, 1982). In particular, a negative correlation between class and crime is more apparent for more serious offences and among more frequent and adult offenders, particularly those who are most socially disadvantaged.

Official statistics are notorious for underrepresenting the frequency of those crimes characteristically committed more frequently by the middle class (e.g., employee theft) and powerful elites (e.g., consumer fraud). So official statistics distort the true relationship between class position and criminal behaviour, since the crimes of higher-status persons tend to be less visible (Nettler, 1984) and therefore less likely to come to the attention of the criminal justice system. If we combine this observation with the recent self-report data, therefore, we may find that class position is correlated with crime in something of a U-shaped curve — with higher crime rates at both the bottom and the top of the class hierarchy — depending upon how both class position and criminal behaviour are defined and measured.

• REGION

Geographic region is sometimes said to be correlated with crime (Harries, 1974). When official statistics on crimes known to the police in Canada are examined provincially, an east-west trend can be observed (Lindsay, 1986; Hackler and Don, 1990). The Atlantic provinces have relatively low crime rates while the western provinces experience high rates; Quebec usually displays rates that are somewhat lower than Ontario's, but both are below western rates. The Northwest Territo-

Figure 8.4

RATE PER 100 000 POPULATION OF CRIMINAL CODE OFFENCES, CANADA AND THE PROVINCES/TERRITORIES, 1980 AND 1990

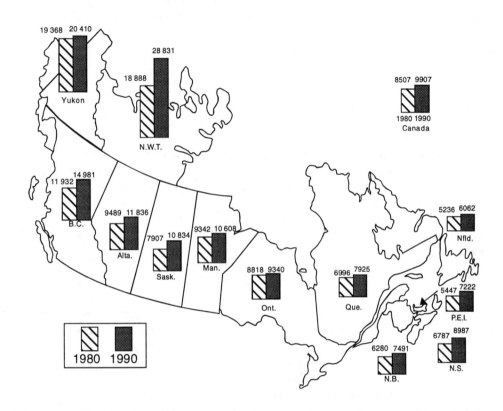

Examination of the provincial/territorial rates for 1990 over 1980 in Criminal Code offences reveals that increases were registered in all provinces/territories. Over this reference period, the Northwest Territories, Saskatchewan, Prince Edward Island, and Nova Scotia recorded the highest percentage increases in the rates for Criminal Code offences (53 percent, 37 percent, 33 percent, and 32 percent, respectively) while Ontario and the Yukon recorded the smallest (less than a 6 percent increase).

Source: Canadian Centre for Justice Statistics, *Canadian Crime Statistics 1990.* Ottawa: Minister of Industry, Science, and Technology, 1991, Catalogue no. 85-205.

ries and the Yukon typically have the highest crime rates (Hartnagel, 1989). These patterns persist over time and for both violent and property crime, with only occasional exceptions. Examining 1984 rates for the major types of violent and property crimes, Lindsay (1986) reported that western provinces filled the great majority of the three highest positions in all categories, while the three lowest positions were filled almost exclusively by the Atlantic provinces. Figure 8.4 illustrates these patterns with data from 1980 and 1990.

Some criminologists have been sceptical of these provincial differences in crime rates because they use official statistics and also may reflect distinctive criminal justice system characteristics, such as the screening practices of different police forces (Hackler and Don, 1990). However, recently published results from the victimization surveys generally confirm the regional patterns revealed in the official statistics (Sacco and Johnson, 1990a, 1990b). The victimization rates for both household property crime and violent crime are highest in British Columbia and the Prairie provinces. But while the Atlantic region has the lowest household victimization rates, the violent victimization rate is lowest, by a wide margin, in Quebec.

There have been few attempts to explain these regional differences in Canadian crime rates. Both demographic composition (age and sex) and urbanization of provinces have been suggested as possible explanations, but with only marginal evidence (Hartnagel, 1978; Giffen, 1965, 1976). Kennedy et al. (1988) have attributed regional variation in homicide to differences in economic conditions, specifically unemployment and income inequality, while Hartnagel (1989) explored the effect of geographic mobility as a potentially disorganizing force. However, a good deal more work examining these regional differences is required.

• URBANIZATION

A correlation between urban location and crime has long been recognized in the criminology literature. Nettler (1978) has stated that official statistics for Canada, as well as for the United States and Europe, reveal a tendency for serious crime to increase with city size. Official statistics for 1988 reveal that both violent and property crime rates generally are higher in large Canadian urban areas than in small cities or towns (Statistics Canada, 1989a). However, the relationship between city size and crime rate is far from perfect: the largest cities do not consistently have the highest rates, and the incidence of violent crime appears to have increased more rapidly in smaller centres in the last decade (Johnson, 1988). Correlations are described on a standard range between 0.0 and 1.0. When there is no relationship between variables, the correlation is zero (0.0). If there is a perfect relationship between two variables, the correlation is 1.0. A 0.5 correlation falls halfway between no relationship and a perfect relationship. Hartnagel and Lee (1990) report correlations of 0.31 and 0.40 between city size and violent and property crime rates, respectively, for Canadian cities with a population of 25 000 or greater. The General Social Survey (Sacco and Johnson, 1990b) found that violent victimization rates were higher in urban than in rural areas. The rate in 1987 among urban dwellers was 88 per 1000 adults, while for rural residents it was 68 (Sacco and Johnson, 1990b). The same survey revealed that all types of household property crime were more common in urban than in rural areas. Overall, the rate for urban areas was 252 incidents per 1000 households in 1987, compared with 146 for rural areas (Sacco and Johnson, 1990a).

Several different arguments have been advanced in an attempt to account for this correlation between urban location and crime (Hartnagel and Lee, 1990). Wirth (1938) developed the idea that urbanization — the concentration of a large and heterogeneous population — leads to a weakening of interpersonal bonds, primary social relations, and normative consensus, thereby undermining informal mechanisms of social control and producing higher rates of crime. Others argue that higher urban crime rates result from the demographic composition of cities rather than from the alleged breakdown of social relations brought on by their size, density, and population heterogeneity (Fischer, 1976). Since urban populations are disproportionately young and childless, the behaviours to which they are especially prone — including crime — should be particularly evident in urban areas. Economic deprivation is a third perspective advanced to explain higher urban crime rates (see also Chapter 5). Both the level of poverty and the degree of inequality in the distribution of income have been suggested as important variables affecting city crime rates (Braithwaite, 1979; Blau and Blau, 1982). Finally, routine activities theory (Cohen and Felson, 1979) suggests that features of urban settings such as the density of potential targets, increased potential for social interaction, greater anonymity, and ease of transportation are particularly conducive to crime.

Hartnagel and Lee (1990) tested these arguments with data from eighty-eight cities in Canada with a population of 25 000 and over. The results provided strong support for routine activities theory: those cities with a greater dispersal of activities away from households thereby provide more opportunities for direct contact, predatory crimes of violence, and crimes against property. This and similar research suggests the importance of shifting the focus away from urban features allegedly shaping the motivation to commit crime — such as disorganization, poverty, and population composition — and toward the structure of *urban opportunities* for crime.

These facts about crime and criminals serve as a starting point for trying to explain the behaviour involved. Correlates are used in complex ways to construct theories. We now turn to a discussion of some of the more popular explanations found in the sociological literature.

EXPLAINING CRIME

From the perspective of the public and the media, probably the most important thing done by sociologists who study crime is to offer explanations of why people commit crimes. Criminologists are constantly asked, Why do they do it? What causes crime? The media like "sound bites" to use on the 6 o'clock news, and the public wants reassurance that it is safe. The truth is that there are many valid explanations for criminal and deviant activity. In this section we introduce some explanations that have been most important in helping criminologists organize their thinking about crime.

Criminologists and sociologists of deviance do not agree on what is the most important explanation of crime. Their theories try to encompass its "root causes." As Nettler (1991) points out, among nominees for "root causes" we find poverty, irresponsible reproduction, disorderly families, inequalities of wealth and power, inadequate schools, insufficient jobs "of the right sort," the low probability of punishment, heterogeneous population, welfarism and its corruption of individual responsibility, "racism, sexism, and classism," messages broadcast by the entertainment and information industries, and more. While the theories discussed below do not include all of Nettler's nominated causes, one can find theories that touch on each of them.

Theories about crime are useful in that they organize our observations in an understandable way. The observations themselves often have more validity than the theories.

For decades criminologists disagreed on how best to study crime. Should the behaviour of *individual* criminals be explained or should certain *groups* of people with higher crime rates be examined? A summary of various attempts to explain crime or deviance must describe theories that usually ask different questions. Scholars usually present schemes for organizing theories into categories or types of explanations that should be thought of as convenient rather than as "true." The theories also reflect the thinking of scholars in a particular culture and time.

• THE STRUCTURAL-FUNCTIONAL APPROACH TO CRIME AND ANOMIE

During the 20th century criminologists constructed many schemes for classifying explanations of deviance. Different disciplines begin by using concepts central to their own tradition: biologists look to inheritance; psychologists look to personality; sociologists look to social class, culture, and organization (Gottfredson and Hirschi, 1990).

The modern sociological explanations about crime and deviance began to be developed in the 1930s. Many different theories had a period of popularity and generated much research. One of the most influential theories was presented by Robert Merton and was based on the earlier work of Emile Durkheim, to whom you were introduced in Chapter 1.

• Anomie

In his book *Division of Labor in Society* (1947 [1933]), Durkheim argued that crime is a necessary part of society. That is, it is functional.

> Crime brings together upright consciences and concentrates them. We have only to notice what happens . . . when some moral scandal has just been committed. People stop each other on the

street, they visit each other, they seek to come together to talk of the event and to wax indignant in common . . . (1947 [1933]: 102).

While it is true that crime might be dysfunctional to society in terms of cost, injury, or disruption, earlier sociologists saw it as functional in that it reminds members of a community about the interests and values they share. Community bonds are strengthened. Deviance also reassures the "good" members of a community that their morality is the acceptable one.

Durkheim popularized the concept of **anomie** to explain crime in advanced and differenti- ated urban societies. Essentially, anomie is a kind of alienation. Heterogeneity and increased division of labour weaken traditional societal norms. The resultant changes diminish social con- trols and allow greater materialism and individualism. Society loses its traditional social control mechanisms such as family and religion and eventually suffers from a high rate of crime.

• Source of Strain: The Gap between Aspirations and Means

Robert K. Merton built on the ideas of Durkheim in his discussion of social structure and anomie (1938). Crime is one symptom of the gap between culturally prescribed aspirations and the socially structured avenues for realizing those aspirations. The culturally prescribed aspirations are the goals held up for all members of society. Merton argues that in America the accumulation of money — and the status (see the discussion of status in Chapters 3 and 5) that results from material wealth — is a universal goal. Socially structured avenues such as schooling are the accepted institutionalized means of reaching these goals. The socially structured avenues to achieve these universal goals may not be a problem for those raised in families that create oppor- tunities for success; but for those raised in disadvantaged families, legitimate means to achieve success may not be readily available. Disadvantaged youngsters will also desire material and social benefits, but have fewer ways to achieve them.

The strain resulting from this gap between the goals and the means to achieve those goals leads to *innovation,* usually deviant in nature. In simpler terms, when society encourages people to want things but makes it difficult for certain groups to get them, they are more likely to steal and cheat in order to obtain the desired goals.

Merton's argument is one type of **strain theory,** and seems to explain many forms of crime in which material gain is the goal. Hence, both street crime, most often committed by the lower classes, and various types of white-collar crime, most often done by business people, can be explained by Merton's conception of anomie and adaptation. Thus, if there is a gap between the desired goals and the means, innovation or illegitimate tactics may be used.

Since human aspirations are boundless, and people cannot always have what they want, people must be persuaded to accept what they receive. When people are not convinced, society becomes anomic, moral guidelines are unclear, social control breaks down, and the norms of those in power may be violated.

Merton's theory does not do as well in explaining crimes with no obvious material motiva- tion. For instance, so-called senseless violence is not explained very well by Merton's theory. But his theory generated much research and inspired other related theories (e.g., Cohen, 1955; Cloward and Ohlin, 1961).

• DEVIANCE AS A GROUP PROCESS

While written in the same era as Merton's anomie theory, Edwin Sutherland's explanation for why people commit crime was very different. Sutherland's theory, one of the most influential explanations of deviance, was presented in 1939 and revised in the following decade (Sutherland and Cressey, 1978). Sutherland argued that criminal behaviour was *like* other behaviour in that it was learned in a social environment; however, the content of the learning can be very different. Criminal behaviour is learned in interaction with others in intimate personal groups. A person becomes delinquent when there is an excess of pro-criminal definitions favourable to violation of the law. These **differential associations** vary in frequency (how often there is contact), duration (how long the contact lasts), priority (whether pro- or anti-criminal sentiments came first), and intensity (the strength of the contact). Learning crime is like other learning. That is, the mechanisms for learning crime are exactly the same as those for learning conforming behaviour; only the content is different (Sutherland and Cressey, 1978).

Differential association theory generated extensive attempts to test these ideas, but they proved difficult to measure and validate. The debates that followed also included attempts to integrate these ideas with other theoretical traditions. Robert Burgess and Ronald Akers (1966) tried to integrate differential association with B.F. Skinner's more general theory, which emphasized rewards, or positive reinforcement, as well as avoidance of punishment, or negative reinforcement (see Chapter 4). The determination of whether the behaviour is conforming or deviant depends on differential reinforcement — that is, the rewards and punishments attached to alternative behaviour. These rewards and punishments come through peer groups, the family, and others in the community.

• Control Theory

Most crime and deviance theories ask why some people do *not* conform, but in social control theories the question is turned around. Why *do* people conform? For Travis Hirschi the question is not why people deviate, but how conformity is explained (1969). His **control theory** is among the most influential of the contemporary period. Hirschi focuses on the **social bond** that ties the individual to society. As the individual's bond to society weakens, delinquent behaviour is more probable. In one sense, deviance is related to freedom. Those who are not attached to their parents, committed to conventional activities, involved with other groups and individuals, and do not share beliefs with law-abiding others are less tied in to the society and are freer to deviate.

Hirschi argued that attachment to peers also reduced delinquency, but Eric Linden points out that the type of peer makes a big difference. His evidence suggests that attachment to *delinquent* peers increases the likelihood of delinquency (Linden and Hackler, 1973). In effect, Linden combines differential association with control theory, claiming that weak ties alone do not explain the *direction* behaviour will take, but that the attractions of deviance are enhanced by like-minded others.

In his later work with Gottfredson, Hirschi suggests that deviant behaviour is reducible to the ability to control oneself. Self-control is directly related to socialization; again, the bond to one's family is evident. He shows that people with low social control not only get into trouble with the law, but are likely to deviate in a variety of other ways as well. Hence, the theory suggests that socializing individuals to control themselves is one of the few ways to control tendencies to become deviant (Gottfredson and Hirschi, 1990).

• Power-Control Theory

Another perspective that focused on family relations was developed by John Hagan, A.R. Gillis, and John Simpson, using data from Toronto high schools (Hagan et al., 1985, 1987). Their power-control theory argues that the relative position of husbands and wives will directly influence the likelihood of their sons' and daughters' delinquency. Positions of power in the workplace are translated into power relations in the household. These power relations, in turn, influence the way boys are controlled and the (often very different) way girls are controlled.

Delinquency is a male-dominated phenomenon and a product of the class structure of modern patriarchal families. A **patriarchal family** has a husband employed outside the family with some degree of authority and a wife who is not employed outside the home. This type of family is likely to reproduce daughters who are like their mothers; it produces females who concentrate on domestic labour and consumption, preparing them to enter a "cult of domesticity" — barefoot, pregnant, and in the kitchen (to paraphrase an old saying). The sons in patriarchal families, however, are expected to prepare for participation in the external labour force.

In contrast, the **egalitarian family** is characterized by households in which both parents work in positions of authority outside the home. Therefore, consumption and production activities are shared by males and females. In egalitarian families, parents will attempt to reproduce both sons and daughters for entry into the production sphere of the labour force.

In the patriarchal family, both father and mother exert more control over daughters than sons, but daughters are controlled even more by their mothers. In egalitarian families parents treat sons and daughters more equally. That is, mothers gain power relative to husbands, and daughters gain freedom relative to sons. The result is that in patriarchal families girls are less inclined to take part in risk-taking activities, although this is acceptable for boys. In egalitarian families risk taking is acceptable for girls as well. Thus, differences in delinquency by gender are greater in patriarchal than egalitarian families.

• Labelling Theory

Labelling theory focuses on how one *becomes* deviant. It does not follow from the theories of Merton or Sutherland but was developed from the perspective of symbolic interaction theory, which you read about in Chapter 4. Labelling theory suggests that one acts toward others and toward things on the basis of what one believes about them, and that belief (or perception) is far more important than the empirical facts. It is often called **societal reaction theory** because other people have great influence on the outcomes. Hence, if teacher Johns tells teacher Smith that Mary is a bad girl, teacher Smith will probably believe the story of teacher Johns without checking it out any further. Mary has been labelled and may be trapped in an assigned role.

Howard Becker (1963), one of the major proponents of the theory, said that "deviant behavior is behavior people so label." This simple statement became the focal point of much of the research that followed. Becker was pointing out that individuals and groups with the power to make a label stick (for instance, through legislation) play a major role in making previously legal behaviour into illegal or deviant behaviour. As discussed earlier, moral entrepreneurs have power to make labels.

Labelling is an interactive process between those being labelled and those who label them. Individuals perform an act that is called deviant, the public reacts to that act, and the individual reacts to the public reaction. One way a person can react is to accept the characteristics of the deviance he or she is accused of and construct a deviant lifestyle around it. The theory projects greater amounts of deviance from those who are successfully labelled (Silverman et al., 1991) and predicts that they will engage in increasingly serious deviant behaviour. This kind of behaviour has been called **secondary deviance** by Edwin Lemert (1951), one of the major figures in generating labelling theory.

A major weakness of labelling theory is that labelling rarely (if ever) explains serious crimes. Today, the major importance of labelling is that it has made sociologists look more carefully at crime from the view of the underdog. Eventually, sociologists began asking broader questions about social reaction and naturally turned to the meaning of rules and how they are made. The next section describes how conflict theorists pursue these ideas in more detail.

• Conflict Theory

The specific theories described earlier in this chapter reflect the consensual model. The **conflict model** represented in critical criminology argues that rules and laws represent the ability of powerful segments of society to impose their values on less influential segments of society. This approach is influenced by the ideas of Karl Marx, which you read about in Chapter 1.

Critical criminology, unlike some of the more conservative theoretical frameworks discussed earlier, is rooted in the study of structural inequality and power. This approach focuses on class relations and the agents of social control, rejects state definitions of crime, and sees the prevention of crime as possible only if current political and economic relations are abolished. Where consensus theoreticians think of "law as legitimate authority, of conflict as unnecessary struggle, and of the state as a neutral mediator," conflict theorists see "law as the exercise of official power, conflict as ubiquitous struggle, and social order as the dynamic equilibrium resulting from a balance of power" (Ratner, 1987: 7).

According to Snider and West (1985), conflict theory also can be characterized by scepticism about individual causation of crime; a belief that legal agencies are motivated by the use of law to maintain a status quo that benefits the powerful; disagreement with the idea that law is representative of community value consensus; and a view that statistics include the biases of the criminal justice agencies that produce them. Critical studies in criminology have focused on explaining why the law discriminates against disadvantaged groups and benefits elite groups; why behaviours that threaten the economic elite are defined as criminal, while the actions of the elite are not; and why harsher sentences are given to the powerless than to the powerful (Snider and West, 1985: 141).

There is a strong element of **praxis** in conflict theory, which is not always found in consensus approaches. That is, criminologists are seen to have a responsibility in creating social change and social justice; they have a responsibility "to promote a revolutionary transformation of society, one that would eliminate the structural causes of deprivation, greed and misery" (Ratner, 1987: 7). There are also many different versions of how social change should be promoted. These will be discussed below.

Left Realism and Links with "Humanist" Criminologists

Most criminologists agree that crime is indicative of a problem in society and reflects the way society is organized, and even conflict theorists admit that there are "bad" individuals. Many of these points of agreement appear in what Jock Young (1986) refers to as "left realism." While not really a theory itself, it does bridge some of the gaps that occur between consensus and conflict theorists. Left realism focuses on crime as experienced by the working class.

Left Realism and the Potential for Reform

Some radical criminologists tend to romanticize crime or assume that the only serious crimes are those committed by the powerful. While income tax evasion certainly involves more stolen money than bank robbery, the majority of victims of crime are poor people victimized by other poor people. Crimes of violence usually involve one poor person hitting another — very often a man hitting his wife. Conflict theorists like Nicole Hahn Rafter (1986), David Greenberg (1981), and Jock Young (1986) criticize some of the left *idealists* (in contrast to the realists) for ignoring the fact that crime really is a problem, particularly for poor people. Brown and Hogg (1992: 200) review left realism in England and Australia and note that it devotes considerable attention to police–community relations. Heavy-handed proactive policing often alienates communities plagued with crime problems, even though these concerned communities can be the most important resource in helping reduce crime. An effective shift in thinking would require that police be both responsible and responsive to those communities.

Left realism does not ignore the impact of crimes of the powerful, but it notes that people who are more vulnerable economically and socially will be caught in situations that create criminals and victims. Although left realism argues that crime illustrates the antisocial fruits of capitalism, it also takes seriously the dangers faced by a woman in a public place at night, the widespread occurrence of domestic violence, and the fears of working-class people in crime-prone areas. Official statistics, despite their flaws, provide insights that help us understand the risk of crime in working-class areas. In general, left realists share with liberal-humanists a practical concern for the day-to-day damage crime does to the most vulnerable part of the population.

• THE NEED FOR A FEMINIST PERSPECTIVE ON CRIME

In the late 19th and early 20th centuries, the dominant theories of both male and female criminality focused on biological factors. By the mid-20th century, explanations of male criminality increasingly shifted toward a greater focus on social, political, and economic factors. However, theories of female criminality largely continue to bear the imprint of the biological legacy. Most such biological theories are premised on the assumption that there are fundamental "natural" differences between men and women that explain their differential involvement in crime. In particular, men are characterized as innately aggressive, while females are naturally more nurturing and passive — which predisposes them toward conformity. Thus, since females are more inner-directed, their deviance is more likely to take the form of mental illness, while males, being more outwardly directed by nature, are more likely to engage in criminal acts. From this perspective, women who do engage in criminal behaviour are seen as double deviants: both "mad" and "bad" (Smart, 1976).

Throughout this century, the few theorists who have concerned themselves with women's criminality have continued to focus primarily on biological and psychological factors to explain both the lesser involvement of women in crime and the nature of their criminal acts. As late as the 1960s, Otto Pollock, in his book *The Criminality of Women* (1961), concluded that menstruation, pregnancy, and menopause were all dangerous times for women because hormonal changes made them more likely to commit deviant acts. In a somewhat different vein, Pollock also argued that although women were less criminal than men, much of their criminality went undetected because of their biologically based, and therefore "natural," deceitfulness. More recent versions of Pollock's ideas continue to link menstruation and crime, most notably the research that suggests that women are most likely to commit crimes just prior to, or during, menstruation. Indeed, in some criminal court cases defendants have successfully used the defence of pre-menstrual syndrome (PMS) to mitigate their punishment (Morris, 1987).

Only recently, largely as the result of the increasing number of women criminologists, has there emerged a feminist perspective in criminology. However, just as criminology is characterized by a diversity of viewpoints, so too is the research and writing of feminist scholars. The dominant thread that ties this body of research together is an increasing awareness of the male bias inherent in traditional theories of female criminality and of the institutional sexism that characterizes the treatment of women in the criminal justice system. To this extent, much of this work can be seen to fit into a conflict theory in that it emphasizes the role of powerful segments of the society imposing their will on those less powerful. In particular, it points to patriarchy, or male domination, to understand both female criminality and the way in which women are controlled through patriarchal structures, including law.

Feminist scholars (e.g., Gavigan, 1983; Heidensohn, 1985; Morris, 1987; Smart, 1976) take exception to theories that centre on stereotypical assumptions about women's sexuality and ignore the importance of women's structural subordination in society in their explanation of both women's conformity and criminality. Some writers, for example, suggest that women's greater conformity is linked to the sexual division of labour within the nuclear family, which has served to make women both economically and psychologically dependent on men (Smart, 1984). This economic inequality, coupled with women's primary responsibility for child care, has acted as an effective form of social control in ensuring most women's conformity.

It is important to note, however, that when women do commit criminal acts they have much in common with male offenders. Most women's crime consists of property crime, and as is the case with male offenders, those who are most overrepresented in official statistics tend to be the most disadvantaged and marginal individuals in society: single, poor, and nonwhite (Hagan, 1985b; Johnson, 1986). Moreover, the increase in women's property crime over the past few decades may well reflect the generally worsening economic position of women in society, or what has been referred to as the "feminization of poverty" (Box and Hale, 1983). To this extent, although gender divisions in society make women less likely to commit crimes, when they do commit crimes the same structural factors that are used to explain male criminality play an important role in understanding female criminality.

In part, then, it is because women are controlled by men through patriarchal structures other than law, such as the traditional nuclear family unit, and as well because of their fear of male violence, that so few ever deviate from conformity and face criminal charges. In addition, the longstanding tendency to view women as more predisposed to mental illness has meant that they are much more likely than men to receive a psychiatric label and be subject to psychiatric control. Indeed, Chunn and Gavigan (1991: 291) argue that "criminalization is the control mechanism reserved for the few women not constrained by fear and medicalization, that is, those who directly attack male power." In this view, the criminal justice system is a form of control reserved as a last resort for females who do not conform to certain traditional expectations. It thus has served to reinforce in the strongest way women's place in a male-dominated society.

It is not surprising, then, that researchers can draw on considerable empirical research to show the ways in which the criminal justice system responds differently to women and men. This is evident, for example, historically in the fact that women who have sought to gain control over their sexuality and reproduction with respect to contraception, abortion, or selling sex have been subject to criminal sanctions. In other ways as well the criminal justice system has institutional-ized sexism through the application of a double standard that criminalized sexual deviance and "immorality" among women but not men (Chesney-Lind, 1986).

More generally, while there has been a longstanding assumption that women are treated more leniently or "chivalrously" than men by the criminal justice system, recent research paints a considerably more complex picture. That is, lenient treatment is conditional on the acceptance of traditional role stereotypes. Women who deviate from these standards of "appropriate" behaviour tend to be treated most harshly (Morris, 1987). Both lenient and harsh dispositions are thus linked to the reliance of the criminal justice system on traditional role stereotypes. To this extent, while the criminal justice system controls both male and female offenders, it seems to control female offenders more by distinguishing among them.

Feminist writings are changing some of our basic thinking about crime. They demonstrate that theories of crime must be able to account for both men's and women's criminality, as well as explain those factors that operate differently on men and women. And while we are as unlikely to see a global theory of female criminality as we are of male criminality, a consideration of gender is of central importance to a comprehensive understanding of criminal behaviour in the same way as are other factors such as social class and race.

• ECOLOGICAL PERSPECTIVES AND ROUTINE ACTIVITIES

Ecological theories — which examine the convergence of space and time to explain crime — tend to be more gender neutral than theories we have described to this point. Early ecological theories concentrated on the geographic and spatial features of an area to explain the distribution of crime. Modern theories — for example, routine activities theory — concentrate on the activities of the population.

Routine activities theory assumes that the ordinary activities of people place them at greater or lesser risk of becoming victims of crime. It proposes that the convergence in space and time of motivated offenders, suitable targets, and the absence of capable guardians increases the probability of being a victim of crime (Cohen and Felson, 1979). Routine daily activities affect the likelihood that property and personal targets will be visible and accessible to potential criminals.

Variations in demographic and structural characteristics such as age, sex, and urbanization create differences in offending rates (Sampson and Wooldredge, 1987). In Canada, the groups most vulnerable to assaults are young unmarried males who frequent bars, go to movies, go out to work, and spend time out of the house walking or driving (Kennedy and Forde, 1990). It appears that it is this public lifestyle that creates exposure to risk. Similarly, young unmarried males who frequent bars and who are out walking or driving around are the most likely victims of robbery (Kennedy and Forde, 1990).

• A GENERAL APPROACH TO CRIME

Criminologists occasionally try to bring ideas together into *a general theory of crime* (Gottfredson and Hirschi, 1990). Gottfredson and Hirschi propose a general theory of crime based on their analysis of the exact nature of criminal acts. They suggest that criminal acts share a great deal with noncriminal acts because they both result from the pursuit of immediate, certain, and easy benefits (1990: 42). For instance, they suggest that "crime and drug use are connected because they share features of criminality. Both provide immediate, easy and short-term pleasure" (1990: 41). These researchers suggest that any theory of crime must explain why these characteristics are similar across behaviours, and they put forward a general theory focusing on the idea of *low self-control*.

Gottfredson and Hirschi begin by defining crime in a very broad way as "acts of force or fraud undertaken in pursuit of self-interest" (1990: 16). They point out that all available data confirm that "ordinary crime requires very little in the way of effort, planning, preparation, or skill" (1990: 16). Further, in the case of property crime, benefit to the individual tends to be small, and by its very nature, gratification from violence can only be short-term. Gottfredson and Hirschi show, on a crime-by-crime basis, how each of the most common crimes fit their description of crime in general.

At the heart of their conception of individual criminal behaviour lies *low self-control*. Low self-control individuals respond to the immediate gratification that criminal acts provide. They are attracted by the effortless nature of the criminal activity (no skills required). The very act of committing a crime is exciting, and these individuals tend to be adventuresome. Individuals with low self-control tend to be self-centred and insensitive to the suffering of others that might result from the crime (Gottfredson and Hirschi, 1990).

The image of the low self-control individual does not imply a specific act but suggests such individuals will engage in some forms of crime or other deviant behaviour. (The notion is a versatility of deviant behaviour.) Low self-control results from the lack of nurturance, discipline, or training (Gottfredson and Hirschi, 1990: 89–95).

NONCRIMINAL DEVIANCE

There are many reasons to suspect that many noncriminal acts are strongly analogous to criminal behaviour. Two such activities identified by Gottfredson and Hirschi are smoking and alcohol use (1990: 91). Studies of why people engage in any rule-breaking behaviour might help us to better understand the meaning of crime.

Consequently, sociologists study both criminal and noncriminal deviance. As shown in Chapter 3 and earlier in this chapter, both result from norm violations. Here, we briefly introduce one type of noncriminal deviance as an example of the way in which sociologists have studied and attempted to explain such behaviours.

• ALCOHOL USE

Drinking alcohol is legal in Canadian society once one reaches the minimum legal age (varying by province), but other mood-altering chemicals remain subject to severe penalties. Alcohol shares pharmacological characteristics with many banned substances that produce depressant effects. It lowers inhibitions and precipitates behaviours that are generally classified as drunkenness. Further, as a drug, alcohol is addictive and produces measurable harm. It is also clear that alcohol causes more societal harm and disruption than any other single drug. Given those few facts, it is no wonder that sociologists have been interested in studying many aspects of alcohol use. Many of the theories used to explain crime have also been used to explain various aspects of the short-term effects of alcohol and long-term addiction to it.

It is clear that there are different drinking patterns in society. Not all groups drink to the same extent, and not all groups get drunk or become alcoholics to the same extent. Subcultural theory is used to explain certain patterns of drinking behaviour. For instance, norms in some religious subcultures (Mormons, some Baptists, and others) demand abstention from alcohol. Other religious groups accept alcohol on religious occasions but abhor drunkenness (for instance, Jews). On the other hand, some nonreligious subcultures find that obtaining and drinking alcohol are the central focus of their subcultural lives (for example, skid row alcoholics). Hence, subcultural theory can be used to explain both high and low drinking patterns.

Both the excessive use and non-use of alcohol can be considered deviant behaviour, depending on the circumstances. In social groups that expect drinking behaviour, refusing a social drink may put one in jeopardy of being called a prude or antisocial, or receiving some other rebuke. On the other hand, getting drunk in many social circumstances will be considered the violation of a norm, and the deviant label may be applied.

One particular form of drinking behaviour that has changed its status in the past twenty years is drinking and driving. The drunk driver who was tolerated on North American roads in the 1950s is much less tolerated in the 1990s. The change in attitude also provides us with a lesson in deterring behaviour. One of the objects of **social control theory** is to make people control themselves. In the case of drunk driving, the advent of a change in public attitude, "checkstops" — random stops of drivers by police to see if they have consumed alcohol — and at least a slight trend toward stiffer sentences have had an impact on arrests.

PUNISHMENT

As you have seen, sociologists who study crime focus on the definition, measurement, and causes of crime. But they also examine the consequences of crime — including attempts to stop offenders from repeating their crimes and attempts to stop potential offenders from becoming actual offenders. Such research often centres on punishment and deterrence.

Deterring crime has been a locus of discussion in studies of society and the law for over 300 years. The debate goes to the very root of our notions of what is right and what is wrong, and brings to our attention the proper and effective use of punishment for those who offend. Very simply, the deterrence doctrine states that the result of effective punishment is that people do not offend again. The effectiveness of punishment depends on restricting the behaviour of the potential offender (specific deterrence) or providing the threat that this restriction will occur (general deterrence).

Specific or **special deterrence** refers to the ways in which individuals will be deterred from offending or re-offending by directly receiving punishment for their actions. For example, if you rob a bank and are caught, the prison sentence that you receive on conviction is viewed as sufficient punishment to stop you from repeating the crime in the future. On the other hand, if you know someone who has robbed a bank and has been sent to jail, it is believed that you (and anyone else who knows of the case) will not want to experience the same punishment. That is **general deterrence**. To be effective, punishment must be meted out swiftly (as soon after the crime as possible), with certainty (punishment *must* follow the crime), and with enough severity to ensure that the offending behaviour is not repeated.

Punishment need not only come from the enforcement of law, however. If potential offenders anticipate that others will disapprove of their arrest for committing a certain act, they may refrain from that activity because they fear the **stigma** of being caught (Williams and Hawkins, 1986). The shame that comes with an arrest (or fear of shaming) may be sufficient to deter the offender. As Braithwaite (1989) argues, shame needs to be used as a reintegrative process into society rather than a means of banning offenders. This adds an extralegal component to the process of deterrence and suggests that the community can play a prominent role in controlling offenders.

Silberman (1976: 443) makes the case that those who are already strongly deterred from involving themselves in a deviant act because they are committed to conform to the norm cannot be further deterred by the threat of punishment. At the same time, the threat of punishment is believed to contribute to the development of morality and respect for the law in the first place. "Social control becomes self-control as the rules of society are transformed into personal standards of action" (Silberman, 1976: 456). Crime persists, however, because much of it is not deterrable through the actions of formal agents of social control (e.g., police). As Silberman points out, the threat of punishment may have differential value for persons with varying perspectives on the law, morality, and the personal costs they will bear because of the punishment.

Summary

- Deviance and crime exist in all societies.
- The general concept that defines deviance or crime is norm violation and, more specifically, society's reaction to the violator.
- Each culture has a set of norms whose violation results in some kind of punishment.
- Norms and punishments will vary as a function of time, social context, and social status. Crimes are a kind of deviance that is enshrined in the Criminal Code of Canada.
- Violation of criminal laws may result in arrest and prosecution.
- Punishments are prescribed by the criminal code. Generally, crimes are more serious than other forms of deviance, and elicit greater public outrage and stronger penalties.
- The measurement of crime is not an easy task. The officially recorded statistics represent only a fraction of the crime that occurs in Canada. Other types of research such as victimization studies help fill the gap.
- Sociologists have been successful in identifying persistent correlates of crime. These are the observations that become a cental focus of our theories.
- Age and gender are the two variables that have been most often linked to crime.

- Region is related to crime in that there is more crime in the western provinces than in eastern or central provinces. This varies by type of crime. There is more bank robbery and gangland killing in Quebec than in any other province.
- Other correlates that have been identified and studied include social class, a hotly debated variable in which the actual relationship between crime and class may be curvilinear, and race — native Indians in Canada are greatly overrepresented in criminal statistics and in jails and prisons.
- Sociology provides a variety of explanations for the occurrence of crime. Theories are a product of the culture in which they are generated and of the training of those who generated them.
- Sociological theory that concentrated on social forces as causes of deviance and crime really began in the late 1930s. These theories indicate that crime is expected in all societies, and they try to explain the specific forces that generate behaviour that is then defined as criminal or deviant.
- Among the precursors to crime are ecological forces — how people are distributed in space and time; alienation from the goals and means of society, which generates a tendency to deviate; the mechanisms for learning crime and the mechanisms for controlling people's behaviour; and opportunities that result in offending against the law. Crime is also explained by how the rules and laws of society represent the influence of the powerful in society imposing their values on the less powerful.
- Tenets of each theoretical perspective were presented in this chapter. None represents *the* explanation for the commission of crime, though some have had more empirical success than others.
- Theories about crime are useful in that they organize our observations in an understandable way. As Nettler pointed out, the observations themselves often have more validity than the theories.
- In addition to criminal forms of deviance, sociologists study behaviours that are deviant but not necessarily criminal.
- Alcohol consumption is legal, but may be a violation of a norm under some circumstances. Both excessive drinking and abstention may be defined as deviant, depending on the social circumstances.
- Sociologists examine the consequences of crime — attempts to stop offenders from repeating their crimes and attempts to stop potential offenders from actually offending. Such research often centres on punishment and deterrence.
- Punishment attempts to deter individuals (specific deterrence) from committing crimes or deviant acts again, and attempts to deter potential offenders from offending in the first place by using punishment as an example of "what could happen to you" if you violate a norm or break a law (general deterrence).

KEY CONCEPTS

Anomie
Conflict model
Consensus model
Control theory
Conviction rates
Correlation
Crime rate

Deviance
Differential association theory
Egalitarian family
General deterrence
Index
Inverse/negative relationship
Labelling theory
Moral entrepreneur
Patriarchal family
Praxis
Routine activities theory
Secondary deviance
Social bond
Social control theory
Societal reaction theory
Specific/special deterrence
Stigma
Strain theory

REVIEW QUESTIONS

1. What major factors determine whether a particular act is considered deviant?
2. What are the major differences between consensus and conflict perspectives on law?
3. What dominant themes underlie the feminist perspective in criminology? From a feminist perspective, why are the issues of women's conformity of central importance to an understanding of women's criminality?
4. What are the assumptions that underlie the following explanations of crime?
   - strain theory
   - differential association
   - control theory
   - power control theory
   - Merton's theory of anomie
5. How does left realism differ from other left-oriented theories?
6. Describe patterns of crime in Canada between 1962 and 1990.
7. When newpapers describe the amount of crime in Canada they use the "officially reported figures." Why are these numbers problematic, and how have criminologists tried to remedy the problems?
8. Define maturational reform and explain its relation to the age distribution of criminal behaviour.
9. Discuss how urban location is correlated with crime and how this relationship may be explained.
10. Discuss the debate concerning the correlation between social class and criminal/delinquent behaviour.
11. Distinguish between specific deterrence and general deterrence. What are the three elements of deterrence that contribute to its effectiveness?

Race & Ethnicity

Baha Abu-Laban and William A. Meloff

Race and Ethnicity

INTRODUCTION

Sociologists concerned with ethnic and minority group relations typically confront a number of challenges. They must design and conduct research into the specific history of different ethnic groups, their way of life, and interrelationships with the larger society; clarify the basic concepts in this area of study; and develop sociological theories of majority–minority relations. To be adequate, such theories must lead to testable hypotheses and assist in explaining the complexity of intergroup relations. Ideally, we would like to be able to determine the conditions under which certain kinds of behaviour may or may not occur.

At a different level of analysis, this area of sociology involves a wide range of practical problems calling for immediate attention and resolution. Hardly a day passes without reports of ethnic prejudice, discrimination, stereotyping and, in the extreme, violence, whether in Canada or in other multiracial/multiethnic societies. At the present time, problem solving is an inherent feature of intergroup relations.

In sociological terms, the problem-solving aspect of ethnic and minority group relations reflects the normative component of this field. It directs attention to community norms and values for the purpose of settling interethnic controversies and conflicts. Much of the Canadian literature on interethnic relations underlines heated public debates involving, for example, immigration policy, individual versus group rights, human rights legislation, and economic equality. These heated debates are evident in recent public discussions of constitutional renewal (e.g., the Charlottetown agreement of August 1992), the Oka Crisis, the turban as permissible headgear for the RCMP, and Canada's policy of multiculturalism. Community opinion was divided on these issues: the position of each interest group involved a statement of preference — a normative approach — regarding the specific issue and how it should be settled.

The two types of challenges embedded in the study of race and ethnicity — research and theory building on the one hand, and problem solving on the other — are not incompatible. In fact, problem solving depends to a large degree on good research and theory. However, it is important to maintain the distinction between the two aspects and have a clear view of what each of them entails.

In the first part of this chapter we will clarify the basic concepts involved in the study of ethnicity and examine the ethnic composition of Canada. This will be followed by an overview of immigration and settlement and an account of the major cultural groupings in Canada: the native peoples, Canadians of British and French origin, and the "other" immigrant groups. Next, special attention will be given to issues of assimilation, cultural maintenance, and multiculturalism, both as a reflection of reality and as government policy. Explanations of prejudice and discrimination will be taken up in the next section, with particular emphasis on sociological and social psychological theories.

THE ETHNIC FACTOR IN CANADIAN LIFE

Ethnicity plays an important and sometimes decisive role in Canadian social life. While it cannot possibly explain every aspect of human behaviour, it exerts considerable influence, either directly or indirectly, on the day-to-day activities of many Canadians. Indeed, it can be argued that very few Canadians are left untouched by the social, economic, political, and moral issues of interethnic relations in contemporary Canadian society.

In the spring of 1989 a group of sixty students, enrolled in a senior course on ethnic and minority group relations at the University of Alberta, recorded their individual responses to the following question: "Step back and reflect upon the ways in which ethnicity has touched your life, the lives of members of your family, and/or the lives of close friends." Typical of university students, the respondents were about equally divided between men and women (with slight overrepresentation of the latter), were young (but with some mature students among them), and were ethnically and racially diverse (including a good number claiming mixed origins). The experiences of these students appear to be consistent with much of the literature on ethnic and minority group relations. And, except for the absence of an extreme right wing in the sample, the results of this survey may be regarded as a microcosm of the larger society.

With reference to ethnic origins, most of the students responded in specific terms, although a number of them indicated that they were simply *Canadian*. The size of the sample does not lead us to expect as wide a range of ethnic origins as is shown in the Canadian Census, but the students were clearly diverse. They included native Indians, British, French, German, Ukrainian, Polish, Yugoslavian, Rumanian, Czechoslovakian, Italian, East Indian, black, Chinese, and "multiple origins." The multiple origins category is interesting because it reflects mixed marriages. In the case of some respondents several ethnic origins were recorded, some so numerous they could not be remembered.

The students who identified themselves as "Canadian" were not unaware of their ethnic origin; rather, they were making a statement of preference. They came from a diversity of ethnic backgrounds including British, oriental, black, East Indian, and multiple origins. It is interesting that some of these respondents sought to detach themselves from ethnicity even in the presence of older relatives (parents and grandparents) for whom ethnic identity was strong. In this respect, these respondents stood in contrast to others who, as third- or fourth-generation Canadians, felt that their ethnic identity had become stronger in recent years.

• ETHNICITY AND ETHNIC IDENTITY

These results draw attention to two important concepts in the study of ethnic relations: ethnicity and ethnic identity. Ethnicity is primarily a matter of self-definition, but others are also involved in how a particular person is defined. For example, an East Indian or a black person whose ethnic self-definition is "Canadian" may be assigned the label East Indian or black by those with whom he or she associates. Sociologically, **ethnicity** is viewed as "an involuntary group of people who share the same culture or . . . descendants of such people who identify themselves and/or are identified by others as belonging to the same involuntary group" (Isajiw, 1974: 122). The most common characteristics with which people identify or are identified by others include culture, language, religion, national origin, and, according to some sociologists, race.

Closely related to the concept of ethnicity is the concept of **ethnic identity**. According to Dashefsky and Shapiro (1976: 5), the term identity is used to "describe an individual's sense of who he or she is." It involves a series of identifications, one of which relates to ethnic categories (as distinct from gender, age, and other important categories). Two processes are involved here: one is to *identify a group* in which the individual places himself or herself socially and the second is to *identify with* that group. As we have discovered from the survey noted above, the strength of ethnic identity may vary from one individual to another, and also over time. For various reasons, some groups may inspire their members to develop a strong ethnic identity, while other groups may not reflect the same tendency.

• ETHNIC COMPOSITION OF CANADA

Table 9.1 shows the population of Canada by ethnic origin, based on the 1991 Canadian Census. In 1991, as in 1981, the Canadian Census determined ethnic origin by the following question: "To which ethnic or cultural group did you or your ancestors belong on first coming to Canada?" The respondents were allowed to indicate single or multiple origins, but no instruction was given on

Table 9.1

ETHNIC ORIGINS FOR CANADA, 1991 CENSUS — 20% SAMPLE DATA

	Number	Percent		Number	Percent
Total Population	26 994 045	100.00	Filipino	157 250	0.58
Single Origins	19 199 790	71.13	Japanese	48 595	0.18
Multiple Origins	7 794 250	28.87	Korean	44 095	0.16
			Pakistani	35 680	0.13
Single Origins[1]			Vietnamese	84 005	0.31
			Other Asian	182 070	0.67
Aboriginal	470 615	1.74	African		
British	5 611 050	20.76	Ethiopian	6 955	0.03
French	6 146 600	22.74	Somali	7 075	0.03
Canadian	765 095	2.83	Other African	22 750	0.08
European			Black	214 270	0.79
Dutch	358 180	1.33	Pacific Islands	7 215	0.03
German	911 560	3.37	Latin, Central and South American	85 535	0.32
Italian	750 055	2.78	Caribbean	94 395	0.35
Jewish	245 840	0.91	Other	14 940	0.06
Polish	272 810	1.01	**Multiple Origins[1]**		
Portugese	246 890	0.91			
Ukrainian	406 645	1.50	British only [2]	1 984 120	7.34
Other European	954 085	3.53	British and French	1 071 880	3.97
Asian			British, Canadian, and/or other	2 673 530	9.89
Arab (incl. N. African)	144 050	0.53	French only [3]	12 065	0.05
Chinese	586 645	2.17	French, Canadian, and/or other	451 295	1.67
East Indian	324 840	1.20	British, French, Canadian, and/or other	707 340	2.62
			Other multiple origins	894 020	3.31

Source: Statistics Canada (1993b). Statistics Canada (1991d: Catalogue no. 93-315, Table 1A, pp. 12–27).

(Note: All figures in this table, including totals, are randomly rounded by Statistics Canada either up or down to a multiple of 5, and in some cases 10. Since the totals are independently rounded, they do not necessarily equal the sum of individually rounded figures in this distribution.)

1. Some of the categories reported in the original table have been combined.

2. The British only multiple category includes persons who report more than one of the following origins: English, Irish, Scottish, Welsh, and Other British not indicated elsewhere.

3. The French only multiple category includes persons who report more than one of the following origins: French, Acadian, French Canadian, and Québécois.

whether to trace ethnic origin through the father's or mother's side. (In the preceding censuses, ethnic origin was determined by reference to the father's side and no provision was made for multiple origins.) Over 71 percent of the Canadian population reported single ethnic origins in 1991, and the remainder reported multiple origins. The Canadian Census requires people to place themselves somewhere in an ethnic niche, but as shown in the preceding discussion, Canadians differ in their attachment to an ethnic label. For those who report multiple origins, it is not clear from the census whether one single origin stands above all others as being important to the individual. Despite these weaknesses, the Canadian Census continues to be a major source of information for sociologists and social scientists in general.

Considering only single origins, it is clear from the table that British (20.76 percent) and French (22.74 percent) are about equally represented in the population, and, combined, these two origins represent about 44 percent of the Canadian population. Other European origins account for 15.34 percent of the population; within this category, numerically large groupings include Dutch, German, Italian, Jewish, Polish, Portuguese, and Ukrainian. The native peoples, including Inuit, Métis, and North American Indian, constitute 1.74 percent of the total population. Although the table has extracted only those data that represent relatively large ethnic groups in Canada, it should be noted that there are in fact over 100 different ethnicities represented, illustrating the tremendous ethnocultural diversity in the Canadian population.

Table 9.1 shows that nearly three out of ten Canadians claimed multiple origins in 1991. The dominant stream in the multiple category is British, reported in four of the seven multiple origins for a total of 23.82 percent. Thus, although Canadians who report single British origins (20.76 percent) are proportionately less than those who claim single French origins (22.74 percent), British origins (single and multiple) are much more pervasively represented in the Canadian population than French.

• RACE

Earlier, we said that one of the common characteristics with which people identify or are identified by others is race. It is important to clarify this term, since it is often used in the context of describing interethnic conflict. Simply defined, the term **race** refers to an involuntary grouping of people who regard themselves and/or are regarded by others to be physically distinct in such characteristics as skin colour, hair texture, eye or hair colour, or facial features. As such, race is ostensibly defined on the basis of biological factors, but the definition and focus of these factors may be socially or politically motivated.

M.F. Ashley Montagu (1960), a leading physical anthropologist, has identified three major races or, as he prefers to call them, ethnic groups: Negroid, Caucasoid, and Mongoloid. Stripped of its details, this classification scheme is simple and hence congenial to lay persons. However, it is important to note that other classification schemes advanced by respected scientists have identified seven, nine, thirty, or even thirty-four races. These differences simply indicate that however we recognize races, it is difficult to draw the line between them. Indeed, Montagu, among others, favours the elimination of the word *race* from our vocabulary because it refers to neither fixed nor clear-cut differences. Moreover, it has been argued that differences within races are as great or greater than differences between them. It is not our purpose in this chapter to provide a detailed critical analysis of the biological or genetic viewpoints on race, but rather to underline the difficulties associated with the existing conceptions of race.

Closely associated with race is the concept of **racism**. At an ideological level, this term refers to a belief in the superiority of one race, usually one's own, over another. Areas of superiority may be moral, intellectual, cultural, or even biological. A good example of this is to be found in Adolf Hitler's statement in *Mein Kampf:* "If we divide the human race into three categories — founders, maintainers, and destroyers of culture — the Aryan stock alone can be considered as representing the first category." Racism may also be reflected in attitudes and/or behaviour, as well as in institutional arrangements designed to create and perpetuate racial inequality.

Perhaps because of these difficulties, sociologists (e.g., Ujimoto and Hirabayashi, 1980) have replaced *race* with the term **visible minorities**. While the focus of Ujimoto and Hirabayashi's work is Asian Canadians, the term visible minorities has been extended, in the literature and in Canadian official documents, to cover a wide range of groupings that may or may not be readily identifiable on the basis of physical characteristics. The defining criteria for visible minority status are essentially social in nature, involving prejudice and discrimination against the group as well as disadvantages in the social, economic, and political domains.

Let us now return to the Alberta student survey. The students' responses included a broad range of direct and/or indirect experiences reflecting prejudice, discrimination, and stereotyping.

Among the experiences most frequently cited are the following: name calling (particularly in public schools), ethnic slurs, offensive statements that reflect negative stereotyping, ill treatment by schoolteachers, ethnic jokes, teasing, and negativism toward "foreign" sounding names. A white female student reported that she had observed prejudice and discrimination at close range when her family adopted a child from a different race. Another student, who worked as a host at a restaurant to help finance her college education, reported with alarm that from time to time patrons asked not to be seated at a table served by a nonwhite waiter. Sometimes young Canadians encounter denial of ethnicity, as in the case of a respondent whose grandfather, an immigrant to Canada, routinely denied his German origin. What these examples suggest is that the experience of ethnicity and some of its effects are more or less universal in the Canadian population.

• PREJUDICE AND DISCRIMINATION

Much of the literature on race and ethnicity attempts to explain why prejudice and discrimination occur. **Prejudice** may be defined as a rigid attitude toward a particular ethnic group, which is highly resistant to change. Such an attitude may be positive or negative, but in either case it reflects an emotional bias. Social psychologists view prejudice as being made up of three components: **cognitive,** which refers to an individual's beliefs and perceptions of a given group; **affective,** which refers to feelings of like or dislike, trust or distrust, admiration or contempt, and so forth; and **conative,** which refers to a predisposition to act in a certain way toward a given group (see Allport, 1958).

In contrast, **discrimination** refers to differential and unequal treatment of people based on their ethnic affiliation. Here, as in the case of prejudice, an individual is treated as a member of a category, regardless of the qualities that the individual may bring into the situation. Although prejudice and discrimination may be highly correlated, the correlation is far from perfect. Sociologist Robert K. Merton (1949) insightfully proposed an interesting typology of prejudice and discrimination that includes the following four types: unprejudiced nondiscriminator; unprejudiced discriminator; prejudiced nondiscriminator; and prejudiced discriminator (Table 9.2).

• STEREOTYPING

The attribution of specific behavioural or moral characteristics to the members of a racial, ethnic, or minority group, positive or negative in nature, is known as **stereotyping**. According to some popular stereotypes Canada's native Indians are seen as drunk and lazy; Jews are shrewd; Ukrainians (or Poles, or Newfoundlanders, depending on which part of Canada you live in) are dumb; Scots are cheap; etc., etc. Even science is used on occasion to "prove" that these traits really exist. A researcher at the University of Western Ontario claims to have "proof" that brain size is related to race and, in a bizarre twist, inversely correlated with genital size and sexual activity. Thus, Asians are portrayed as being the most clever of the races, with the least active sex drive. At the

Table 9.2

MERTON'S TYPOLOGY OF PREJUDICE

	Does Not Discriminate	Discriminates
Unprejudiced	1. Unprejudiced nondiscriminator (all-weather liberal)	2. Unprejudiced discriminator (fair-weather liberal)
Prejudiced	3. Prejudiced nondiscriminator (timid bigot)	4. Prejudiced discriminator (all-weather bigot)

Source: Merton (1949: 99–126).

RACIAL DISCRIMINATION: MYTHS AND FACTS

On March 21, 1989, Canada celebrated the International Day for the Elimination of Racial Discrimination. On this occasion, Multiculturalism and Citizenship Canada distributed a glossy bilingual brochure stating the following myths and facts about Canada:

Myth: There is no racial discrimination in Canada.
Fact: Unfortunately, there is, sometimes subtle and sometimes overt — but most Canadians want to do something about it. They believe in respecting and understanding each other.

Myth: All Canadians have equal opportunity and equal treatment.
Fact: The law says they should. But when it comes to jobs, housing, and services, many Canadians experience prejudice and discrimination because of the colour of their skin.

Myth: There is nothing I can do to make a difference.
Fact: You can do a lot. Start by organizing or taking part in activities for March 21. Join thousands of others in Canada who care. You really can make a difference.

other end of the continuum are blacks, who are the least clever and the most sexually active. Whites fall into the middle category: normal intelligence and sex drive. It has been suggested that this "scientific evidence" underscores the existing stereotype of Asians as being very clever (and thus posing a threat to the white majority in Canada, who cannot compete with them intellectually) and the stereotype of blacks as being a threat not because of their intellectual abilities but rather because of their sexual prowess, which is irresistible to young white men and women.

It would be misleading to give the impression that prejudice and discrimination are evenly distributed throughout the Canadian population. According to our survey, unprejudiced students report that they were aided in their open-minded disposition by their own open-minded parents, by associating with members of different ethnic groups, or by being in close physical proximity to an ethnic enclave — e.g., an Indian reserve. Open-mindedness toward ethnic differences may result in the development of a sense of support for weaker groups. As one student observed: "We may not accept a group's culture or ways, but we must show compassion and understanding."

The student survey results also indicate that some of the factors contributing to open-mindedness do not always give maximum results. For example, some white respondents reported that they were prevented from associating on a regular basis with peers from certain ethnic communities (e.g., Chinese or East Indian) because of those groups' intensive involvement with their own culture. In other words, if the sense of ethnicity is extremely strong in some groups, then the barriers to interethnic friendships are likely to be correspondingly strong. Conversely, the more acculturated members of visible minorities are, the less likely it is that ethnicity will make a difference to others. Another limit on interethnic friendships as reported by white students is perceived oversensitivity on the part of their nonwhite peers to their minority status. Reportedly, such nonwhite students are often on edge, always ready to fight back whether or not offence was intended. Finally, dating outside one's own ethnic or racial group is sometimes negatively sanctioned, as when a white student is called "nigger lover," or a black student is called "white lover."

It is interesting that nonwhite students, according to their reports, face a totally different set of circumstances. For example, they believe that they and their parents suffer from a high degree of prejudice and discrimination. As a result, family and ethnic bonds become increasingly important to them. They often confront a situation in which their parents emphasize the original culture, exhorting their children to avoid westernization and refrain from dating (within or outside their ethnic community). Often they are pushed toward academic achievement. Parental demands for conformity are especially strong if the ethnic group is under severe pressure from the larger society. To be sure, there is emphasis on and pride in being Canadian. As a result, parents may have mixed feelings because, willy nilly, their children are being increasingly assimilated into the Canadian culture. Given the context of their ethnic communities, children also may have mixed emotions as they become increasingly acculturated into the larger society. This is a typical experience among second- or even third-generation Canadians.

Implicit in the preceding discussion is the fact that interethnic relations are usually asymmetrical in nature. That is, one group — the hegemonic majority — tends to stand above all others, and where there is a hegemonic majority group, there is always a *minority* group (or groups). The term **hegemonic majority group** refers to the dominant group in society. It is not a statistical term in that the dominant group may or may not constitute a numerical majority. For example, whites in South Africa are a statistical minority, but are nevertheless the dominant group. Sociologically, this means that they hold power and are socially, economically, and politically in control. Conversely, the South African blacks are a statistical majority, but sociologically they are defined as a **minority group** — i.e., a subordinate group that is disadvantaged socially, economically, and politically.

There are many practical problems to solve in the area of racial and ethnic relations in Canada. Researchers also face the challenge of explaining the causes of prejudice and discrimination. The next section gives a brief account of sociological and social psychological theories of interethnic relations.

IMMIGRATION

• THE EARLY PERIOD

Except for the aboriginal peoples — Indian, Métis, and Inuit — who account for less than 2 percent of the Canadian population, Canadians are immigrants or descendants of immigrants. They have arrived from many different parts of the world, but not in equal numbers. The French were the first to establish permanent settlements in New France (Quebec). However, for most of its history New France had relatively low immigration, and population growth was due largely to natural increase (i.e., excess of births over deaths).

The Conquest (1759–60) marked the start of British and other European immigration to Canada. In the 1770s and 1780s, following the American Revolutionary War, the ranks of anglophones were swelled by the arrival of the United Empire Loyalists from the United States. Most of these arrivals were of British origin, of course, but they also included immigrants from other European origins. The new immigrants settled in Montreal and Quebec City, as well as in the Eastern Townships and the Ottawa Valley. Over time, large numbers of British settlers moved to the Maritime provinces and Ontario (Upper Canada). In the second half of the 19th century they began to move farther west.

From 1871, the volume of immigration to Canada began to increase, albeit with annual fluctuations and also variations in totals recorded for the last three decades of the century. The peak was reached in the 1881–91 period, in which 903 000 immigrants were admitted. The increase in the number of immigrants in the latter part of the 19th century was associated with a push to populate the west and expand agricultural production and local markets. Although the immigrants added to the country's demographic base, it should be noted that in the forty-year period from 1861 to 1901, more people were leaving than arriving in Canada. Most of the departures were to the United States. It is believed that many immigrants used Canada as a stepping stone to the United States.

Box 9.2

SOURCES OF IMMIGRATION, 1980 AND 1988

Since 1980 there have been significant shifts among the source countries of immigration:

• Immigration from Africa and the Middle East doubled from 7 percent in 1980 to 14 percent in 1988.

• Immigration from Asia and the Pacific Islands reached a high of 48 percent in 1980, dropped to about 32 percent in 1982, and then rose to 43 percent in 1988.

• In 1988, immigration from the United States was at a decade low of 4 percent, compared to 7 percent in 1988 (and a decade average of 7 percent).

• Fourteen percent of immigrants in 1988 came from Latin America and the Caribbean. Immigration from this region increased steadily from about 9 percent in 1980 to reach a high of 22 percent in 1986.

• In 1988, immigration from Europe represented 25 percent, compared to 29 percent in 1980. The decade low was in 1985 (22 percent), and the decade average was 28 percent.

Note: The data are based on the immigrants' country of last permanent residence. Total immigration: 143 287 in 1980 and 160 768 in 1988.
Source: Employment and Immigration Canada (1989: 10–11).

• IMMIGRATION IN THE 20TH CENTURY

In international migration studies it is important to maintain a distinction between the terms *immigrants* and *emigrants*. The term **immigrants** refers to those who arrive in a new country for the purpose of settlement. In contrast, **emigrants** refers to those who leave a given country for a new place of abode. Clearly, both types of migrants cross national boundaries. Another important term is **net migration,** which for a given country refers to the difference between the number of persons who arrive (immigrants) and the number of persons who depart (emigrants).

Throughout this century, the volume of immigration to Canada has been relatively large, and net migration has been consistently positive (more immigrants than emigrants). The only exception concerns the period 1931–41, a period of worldwide depression (the Great Depression). In those years, immigration was about 150 000, while emigration reached the 242 000 mark.

Over the course of this century the sources of immigration have become more diverse than ever before, despite the traditional preference for British, American, and northwestern European immigrants. In the period 1901–31 the dominant immigration streams were from central, eastern, and southern Europe. In the post–World War II period, however, and particularly since the 1960s, increasing numbers of immigrants have come from Third World countries in Asia, Africa, the Caribbean, and Latin America. The volume of immigration to Canada has fluctuated during this century. It surged in the 1901–31 and postwar periods. In the latter period, annual immigration has averaged about 130 000 (for more details, see Halli et al., 1990).

A third important feature of immigration underlines change in the occupational and educational qualifications of immigrants. Whereas turn-of-the-century immigrants were minimally qualified, postwar immigrants have included large proportions of university-trained persons, of whom many are in professional occupations and technical fields. The educational and occupational qualifications of some immigrant groups have exceeded the national average. To a large degree, the immigrants' skill level has been related to Canada's manpower needs and economic conditions. Table 9.3 shows the periods of heavy immigration and occupational characteristics of selected ethno-racial-religious groups in Canada.

IMMIGRATION OF SELECTED ETHNO-RACIAL-RELIGIOUS GROUPS INTO CANADA

Table 9.3

Group(s)	Date(s)	Major Occupation(s)
Native Peoples	Pre-1600	All occupational roles of self-contained societies
French	1609 to 1755	Fishing, farming, fur trading, and supporting occupations: military, blacksmithing, etc.
Loyalists from U.S.A.: Mennonites, blacks, Germans, English, Scots, Quakers	1776 to mid-1780s	Farming
English & Scottish	mid-1600s on & 1815 on	Farming, skilled crafts
Germans & Scandinavians	1830s to 1850s & c. 1900, 1950s	Farming / Mining, city jobs
Irish	1840s	Farming, logging, construction
Blacks from U.S.A.	1850s to 1870s	Farming
Mennonites & Hutterites	1870s to 1880s	Farming
Chinese	1855 & 1880s	Panning gold, railway building, mining
Jews	1890s to WWI	Factory work, skilled trades, small business
Japanese	1890s to WWI	Logging, urban service employment, mining, fishing
East Indians	1890s to WWI & 1970s	Logging, service employment, mining, skilled trades, professions, farm work in B.C.
Ukrainians	1890s to 1914, 1940s to 1950s	Farming / Variety of occupations
Italians	1890s to WWI, 1950s to 1960s	Railway building, other construction, small business, construction, skilled trades
Polish	1945 to 1950	Skilled trades, factory work, mining
Portuguese	1950s to 1970s	Factory work, construction, service occupations, farming
Greeks	1955 to mid-1970s	Factory work, small business, skilled trades
Hungarians	1956 to 1957	Professions, variety of other occupations
West Indians	1950s, 1967 on	Domestic work, nursing, factory work, skilled trades, professional service occupations, contract farm labour
Central/South Americans	1970s & 1980s	Professions, factory/service occupations
Vietnamese	late 1970s to early 1980s	Variety of occupations, including self-employment

Source: Cross-Cultural Communication Centre (no date), as quoted in Herberg (1989: 63–64).

The destination of immigrants is a matter of considerable interest to social planners and policy-makers. In the opening decades of this century, large numbers of immigrants went into farming in the thinly populated West. Bloc rural settlements were not uncommon among some immigrant groups, as evidenced by the settlement patterns of the pioneer Ukrainian immigrants, Mennonites, Hutterites, and Doukhobors. In contrast, in the postwar period immigrants tended to gravitate toward Canada's cities and urban centres. Since farming is a highly saturated occupation, few of today's immigrants go into farming. Figure 9.1 shows the pattern of immigration to metropolitan areas for 1988, where the total volume of immigration reached 160 768.

The identification of causes of immigration is another concern of sociologists. The decision to immigrate is a highly personal one, based, at least in part, on a person's experiences, attitudes, and motivation. At the same time, two sets of factors, one operating in the home country and the second in the receiving country, play an important (sometimes decisive) role in the decision to move. Among the factors that push people away from the home country are limited economic opportunities, political instability, restrictions on political or religious freedoms, and prejudice and discrimination. For a country to be attractive as a destination, it must be characterized by positive ratings on these factors. Some people may also be prompted to migrate by a spirit of adventure; the desire for new experiences, career advancement, and social and educational oppor-

Figure 9.1

IMMIGRATION TO METROPOLITAN AREAS, 1988 TOTAL = 160 768

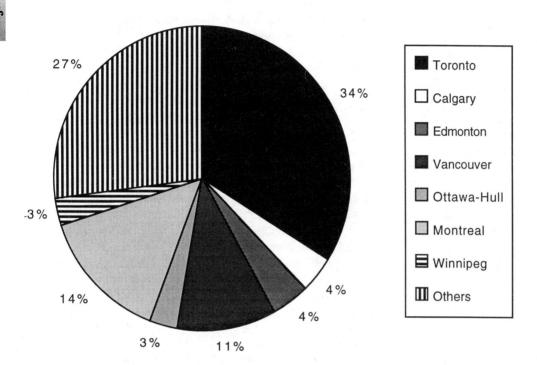

27%

34%

-3%

14%

4%

4%

3%

11%

Legend:
- Toronto
- Calgary
- Edmonton
- Vancouver
- Ottawa-Hull
- Montreal
- Winnipeg
- Others

Source: Employment and Immigration Canada (1989: 19).

tunities for themselves or for their children; and/or the presence of friends or relatives in the receiving country.

• IMMIGRATION POLICY AND CONCERNS

Canada's immigration policy has undergone substantial revision and upgrading. During the period 1861–96 there was no coherent policy and free entry was the norm, except for certain types of immigrants — for example, orientals — who faced restrictions. In the 1896–1914 period (the Sifton era), the policy was selective and favoured immigrants who were destined to till the land. Between the start of World War I and the end of World War II, a large number of restrictive measures were applied. However, a more liberal immigration policy surfaced in the post–World War II period, culminating in the 1967 "points system," which applies universal criteria for immigrant selection. This system, which is still in effect, rates immigrants on education and training, arranged employment, age, personal qualities, knowledge of English or French, and presence of relatives in Canada, among other things. Under this system, all applicants are presumed to receive the same treatment. To qualify for entry into Canada, a candidate must obtain a minimum of 70 points out of 100.

Canada's immigration policy is based on the 1976 Immigration Act, which became law in 1978, and on changes to the act (Bill C-86) that took effect on January 1, 1993. The existing legislation, together with the regulations developed periodically by the minister responsible for immigration, sets the tone for how Canada's immigration policy is to be implemented. The highlights of the policy are (1) respect for family reunification; (2) admission of some immigrants (e.g., refugees) on humanitarian grounds; and (3) integration of immigration and recruitment of immigrants with Canada's economic objectives in mind.

At present, and for the next few years, the Canadian government plans to admit 250 000 immigrants annually. One class of immigrants given high priority is the family class, which consists of immigrants seeking reunification with relatives already in Canada. Other classes of immigrants include refugees; independent immigrants (who can meet Canada's labour-market needs); business immigrants; and immigrants admitted to Canada on humanitarian grounds under special measures. The two immigration classes that will account for the largest proportion of immigration to Canada in the foreseeable future will be the family class and the independent immigrant class, along with their spouses and other dependents.

Let us conclude this section by making a few observations about where Canada stands on the question of immigration and about issues currently being debated in public. First, notwithstanding some reservations and concerns about immigration expressed by certain sectors of the Canadian public, it is commonly recognized that Canada needs immigrants to invigorate the economy and counterbalance the effects of a generally low birthrate. Second, the main sources of immigration at present are Third World countries. The democratization (and economic and political upheavals) in central and eastern European countries may render this region a possible source of immigrants to Canada, but this remains to be seen. Third, immigrants typically face a wide range of adjustment problems, including discriminatory treatment and barriers to full and equal participation. Relevant to this, the Canada Employment and Immigration Advisory Council, in its March 1991 report *Immigration in the 1990s,* has made a number of recommendations for the minister's attention. To quote:

> The recommendations focus on measures to increase the proportion of younger persons in the immigration intake to counterbalance low fertility and an aging population; marketing an educational and race relations program to combat racism and to educate the public on the benefits of immigration; measures to facilitate the integration of immigrants in Canada, including a comprehensive system to evaluate foreign credentials; measures to recruit more French-speaking immigrants; settlement assistance to sponsors who accept genuine refugees; and measures to encourage immigrants to settle in other than major urban centres (Executive Summary).

These recommendations relate to some but not all the issues facing immigrants and immigration. What is clear is that such issues need to be addressed in order to maximize the positive impact of immigration on Canada's social, economic, and cultural fabric.

PATTERNS OF MAJORITY–MINORITY RELATIONS

The cultural diversity Canada encompasses is as old as human history. The aboriginal peoples, whose ancestors formed the first human settlements, were and still are culturally and linguistically diverse. French colonization, the British Conquest, Confederation, and the modern era of international migration have accentuated the ethnic, racial, and cultural diversity that is Canada. The question that has faced and continues to face Canadians is how to deal with this diversity. The answers to this question have been guided by public attitudes and beliefs which, to a greater or lesser degree, have influenced government and especially public-school policies.

Over the years, majority–minority relations in Canada have been governed by three distinct ideologies: assimilation, Anglo-conformity, and pluralism, or multiculturalism. While in practice all three ideologies are simultaneously reflected in the population, at any given point in time only one of them tends to be the dominant ideology. The following is a brief account of these ideologies.

• ASSIMILATION

In popular terms, the ideology of assimilation is known as the "melting pot" ideology. The term *melting pot* has been popular in the United States since the early part of this century, and many Americans today continue to think of their country as a melting pot of peoples. That is, the United States takes as raw material immigrants from other cultures and societies and turns them into full-fledged Americans. Although this term was imported from the United States some eighty years ago to describe the Canadian situation, Canadians have tended to exhibit a milder form of assimilation.

Earlier studies of immigrant communities, particularly in the United States but also in Canada, tended to view assimilation as an inevitable outcome. A general definition of assimilation may be stated as follows: **Assimilation** is a process whereby an ethnic or racial minority adapts itself to the majority group by discarding its separate cultural identity in return for equality of rights and treatment.

Canada's immigration policy was premised on assimilation until the 1960s; the so-called inassimilable types such as Chinese and Japanese were not to be admitted. In many parts of Canada until recently, speaking a non-official language (e.g., Ukrainian or Polish) on public-school premises was subject to corporal punishment. Even the education of native peoples, again until recently, was premised on assimilation into the dominant culture. During this entire period, "foreignness" was feared and deviation from the main idiom was not tolerated. The pressure on immigrants and their children was strong, and the expectation was that ethnicity would and should disappear within a generation or so.

Recent ethnic studies emphasize that neither the United States nor Canada has been a melting pot and that assimilation of immigrants and their descendants has been far from complete (see Driedger, 1989: ch. 2). Ethnic and religious pride on the one hand and prejudice and discrimination on the other have contributed to the perpetuation of ethnic differences. At the same time, sociologists have come to the realization that assimilation is a multidimensional, rather than unitary, process involving many subprocesses. Milton Gordon's (1964) seminal work identifies seven important assimilation variables and directs attention to the need for more research in this area. Among the significant insights emerging from Gordon's work is that structural assimilation inevitably leads to cultural assimilation, but the reverse is not necessarily true. Gordon's assimilation variables are shown in Table 9.4.

Available evidence indicates that immigrants (as individuals and as collectivities) make variable progress on the seven subprocesses of assimilation; in some instances progress may be blocked

THE ASSIMILATION VARIABLES

Table 9.4

Type or Stage of Subprocess or Condition	Assimilation	Special Term
Change of cultural patterns to those of host society	Cultural or behavioural assimilation	Acculturation
Large-scale entrance into cliques, clubs, and institutions of host society, on primary group level	Structural assimilation	None
Large-scale intermarriage	Marital assimilation	Amalgamation
Development of sense of peoplehood based exclusively on host society	Identificational assimilation	None
Absence of prejudice	Attitude receptional assimilation	None
Absence of discrimination	Behaviour receptional assimilation	None
Absence of value and power conflict	Civic assimilation	None

Source: Gordon (1964: 71).

for several generations. While sociologically the term *assimilation* is neutral, at the popular level it has come to be associated with the use of force, unfair treatment of school children, psychological harm, and excessive ethnocentrism, among other things. For this reason, the term is not as frequently used by politicians or liberal-minded Canadians as in the past.

• ANGLO-CONFORMITY

If the melting pot conception of Canadian society is a myth and the policy of assimilation has proven ineffective (given the experience of the United States in particular), then an alternative is to be found in the ideology of Anglo-conformity. This ideology had many adherents during the first few decades of this century when large numbers of non-English-speaking immigrants were admitted to Canada. Echoes of this ideology are heard today expressing fears of the destruction of Canada's British heritage. As the term implies, **Anglo-conformity** demands that all immigrants must act in accordance with the dominant group's cultural and value systems, which are of British origin. Unlike the assimilationist ideology, Anglo-conformity allows immigrants to keep their social distance from the dominant group. This is so because the dominant group, in general, is unwilling to allow wholesale structural assimilation of ethnic, racial, and religious minorities. Unlike the ideology of assimilation, Anglo-conformity makes no promises about equality of rights and treatment. Today, the ideology of Anglo-conformity is considered an inadequate basis for majority–minority relations in Canada.

• MULTICULTURALISM

Generally speaking, the ideology of multiculturalism did not have a substantial following in the first half of this century. However, it began to gather momentum in the 1950s, and its advocates became highly visible in the public arena in the early 1960s. The ascendancy of this ideology has forced the federal government to adopt a uniquely Canadian policy of multiculturalism within a bilingual framework, following the report of the Royal Commission on Bilingualism and Biculturalism. To quote from the prime minister's announcement of this policy in the House of Commons in September 1971:

> It was the view of the Royal Commission, shared by the government and, I am sure, by all Canadians, that there cannot be one cultural policy for Canadians of British and French origin, another for the original peoples and yet a third for all others. For although there are two official languages, there is no official culture, nor does any ethnic group take precedence over any other. No citizen or group of citizens is other than Canadian, and all should be treated fairly.
>
> The Royal Commission was guided by the belief that adherence to one's ethnic group is influenced not so much by one's origin or mother tongue as by one's sense of belonging to the group, and by what the Commission calls the group's "collective will to exist." The government shares this belief . . .
>
> A policy of multiculturalism within a bilingual framework commends itself to the government as the most suitable means of assuring the cultural freedom of Canadians. Such a policy should help to break down discriminatory attitudes and cultural jealousies. National unity, if it is to mean anything in the deeply personal sense, must be founded on confidence in one's own individual identity; out of this can grow respect for that of others and a willingness to share ideas, attitudes and assumptions. A vigorous policy of multiculturalism will help create this initial confidence. It can form the base of a society which is based on fair play for all.

Significantly, multiculturalism is entrenched in the 1982 Canadian Charter of Rights and Freedoms and in the Multiculturalism Act passed by Parliament in 1988. As well, many provinces have developed their own forms of multicultural policies.

Sociologically, there is no one universal definition of **multiculturalism**. On the one hand, it may mean relative autonomy and separate existence of ethnic groups — i.e., institutional completeness (Breton, 1964). At the other extreme, multiculturalism may mean a joint sharing by ethnic groups of a national Canadian culture that represents a synthesis of the "essence" of diverse ethnic cultures, allowing for some ethnic group variations across the country. Between these two extremes, multiculturalism may assume varying degrees of cultural and structural separation from the mainstream Canadian culture and society (see Abu-Laban and Mottershead, 1981). The specific implications of Canada's developing multiculturalism are not altogether clear, mainly because the issues involved have not yet been settled.

The development and growth of multiculturalism in Canada, both as a government policy and a social fact, have been influenced by the co-existence of contradictory social forces and trends (see, for example, Abu-Laban, 1979). On the negative side, the policy of multiculturalism has faced not only political constraints rooted in the attitudes of French and English Canadians, but also some degree of intellectual opposition. It has been noted, for example, that ethnic pluralism detracts from the democratic goal of individual equality and perpetuates ethnic stratification; retards the achievement of consensus; leads to polarization, division, and conflict in the population; causes ethnic prejudice and discrimination; and ignores the trend of convergence of cultures through science and technology.

On the positive side of multiculturalism policy, ethnicity has been a durable element in Canadian society. Also, it has been observed by sociologists and social critics alike that multiculturalism serves a multitude of social and psychological needs: pluralism is good for democracy; ethnicity satisfies an individual's needs for reference group identification, status, and approval; ethnic identification is a source of personal and group pride in the ancestral heritage; and ethnic groups satisfy an individual's need for informal participation.

The debate over the merits and limitations of multiculturalism has been in the public arena for a number of years now. Given that there is no alternative to multiculturalism at the present time, it is important to upgrade the ideology and policy of multiculturalism in order to more effectively accommodate ethnic differences within the context of Canadian unity.

MAJOR LINES OF ETHNIC DIFFERENTIATION

The seeds of conflict are ever-present in ethnically plural societies. The challenge for Canada is to allow ethnic, racial, and religious minorities to flourish while containing interethnic tension and conflict. Special attention needs to be given to three main axes of ethnic differentiation in Canada: "the relationship between natives and non-natives, between English and French and between the colonizing (or 'charter') groups and other immigrants and their descendants" (Breton, 1988: 723). Issues of prejudice, discrimination, and access to resources are major factors influencing ethnic and race relations in all three areas of ethnic differentiation.

• NATIVE PEOPLES

Available evidence indicates that native peoples are one of the most disadvantaged minorities in Canada (Frideres, 1988). Indians, Inuit, and Métis have more than their share of poverty, occupational disadvantage, limited educational opportunities, poor housing and health conditions, and powerlessness. An important area of political and economic contestation between native Canadians and the non-native population is the question of land claims. The native peoples' claim to the land is recognized either by signed treaties with the Crown or by social convention (for more details, see Asch, 1984). Issues facing the native communities across Canada revolve around settlement of land claims, self-government, social and economic development, and cultural preservation. The Oka Crisis in the summer of 1990 underlines the need for a speedy resolution of these issues.

• CHARTER GROUPS (ENGLISH AND FRENCH)

English–French relations have been a point of contention between the two groups ever since the Conquest (cf. Gagnon, 1984). In the postwar period, particularly the 1960s and beyond, French-Canadian discontent has reached crisis proportions. This is why the federal government established the Royal Commission on Bilingualism and Biculturalism in 1963. From Quebec's viewpoint, what is at stake is nothing less than preservation of language and culture, and control of economic and political institutions. The conflict between the two groups involves a multitude of issues. As Breton (1988: 723) notes: "The issues of job distribution, of control of economic institutions, of culture and of the size of their respective populations have been reflected in conflict over policies dealing with matters such as immigration, international relations, industry and trade, education, family allowances, language of education and work, and mass communication." The failure of the Meech Lake accord in June 1990 and the Charlottetown agreement in 1992 — which would have given Quebec a degree of power and autonomy — has aggravated English–French relations. To preserve confederation, it is widely believed that major concessions must be made to Quebec.

• NON-CHARTER ETHNIC AND VISIBLE MINORITIES

The third axis of ethnic differentiation in Canada concerns the situation of those who are neither English nor French in origin. Whether in Quebec or in Canada at large, the concerns of these ethnic and racial minorities revolve around issues of prejudice and discrimination; human rights; and access to employment opportunities, power, and social status. In Quebec, these issues are compounded by legislation restricting their children's educational opportunities in languages other than French and use of English or other languages in public places. The scale of conflicts between these immigrant communities and the larger society (English or French) is potentially large, given that they constitute about one-third of the Canadian population.

This section has touched only the surface of the complex issues that relate to ethnic and minority group relations in Canada. Canada has moved a long way from the relatively culturally homogeneous society that it once was, with its two "founding cultures." On the one hand, the diversity of cultural experience in contemporary Canadian society offers an exciting opportunity. On the other hand, the broad ethnic base of our society presents a variety of social challenges that must be addressed if we are ever to attain a state of harmony (Breton et al., 1980).

Sociological Theories of Ethnic Relations

The sociological approach assumes that patterns of interethnic relations are shaped not so much by individual attitudes as by larger social forces grounded in major institutional areas (such as the economy) and in units of social organization (such as the family, complex organizations, and community). In employing this approach, a sociologist examines how society is organized and how such institutions as the economy and polity regulate interethnic relations and mould individual attitudes. Alternatively, the sociologist may examine how ethnicity and class intersect, thereby conditioning individual attitudes and setting the tone for ethnic and race relations. In addition, a sociologist may focus on the functioning of ethnic institutions and the process of ethnic stratification, and how these are interrelated with similar mainstream units. (See Farley, 1988: 49–73; van den Berghe, 1978.)

• ETHNICITY AND SOCIAL CLASS

A previous chapter showed that inequalities in the economic and political spheres as well as in social status are generated by social class position. Under capitalism, ethnicity and race — in addition to class — may create new divisions and thus widen social, economic, and political disparities. In extreme situations, class structuring may develop along racial lines, as in the case of the slavery system in the United States before the Civil War.

The close relationship between ethnicity and social class has been of considerable interest to Canadian sociologists. In his widely acclaimed book *The Vertical Mosaic*, John Porter (1965: 73) suggests that "immigration and ethnic affiliation have been important factors in the formation of social classes in Canada. In particular, ethnic differences have been important in building up the bottom layer of the stratification system in both agricultural and industrial settings." Using census data over decades, Porter documents the lower occupational status of immigrants and their descendants (which he calls "entrance status") in comparison with the high occupational status of the British charter group. He also shows wide occupational and economic disparities between the French and the British, favouring the latter group. Finally, he shows the economic elite in Canada to be largely of British origin. In an update of Porter's work on elites, Wallace Clement (1975: 233) points out that "it is difficult to distinguish between the effects of social class and ethnic origin for mobility into the economic elite."

Many of the ethnic differences discussed by Porter in 1965 persist to this day, albeit in a narrower form, particularly with respect to income and occupation. The conclusion that ethnicity confers advantage on some groups and disadvantage on others is still valid.

Two theoretical perspectives in social class analysis provide contrasting explanations of differentials in opportunity among different ethnic groups. These are the functionalist and conflict perspectives.

• THE FUNCTIONALIST PERSPECTIVE

In explaining social phenomena, the functionalist perspective assumes that society is made up of many interdependent parts, each of which performs a function that meets a specific need. According to this perspective, social life is a cooperative undertaking, and society tends toward stability and consensus. In emphasizing societal needs for survival, this perspective tends to value social peace over social justice, and hence it is labelled as conservative. Functionalists argue that some jobs are more important than other jobs and require more competent individuals to fill them; therefore, it is essential to provide a system of incentives and differential rewards.

Empirical studies dealing with the intersect between ethnicity and class have repeatedly shown that ethnic and immigrant communities often fill menial and low-paying jobs not so much by choice but because these are the only jobs available to them. In this context, it is interesting that functionalist class theorists explain this pattern in terms of society's survival needs; that is, low-paying jobs, no less than high-paying ones, must be filled in order to contribute their share to the survival of society. The fact that such jobs are often filled by disadvantaged minorities is not as important as the issue of meeting society's needs for stability and survival.

• THE CONFLICT PERSPECTIVE

In contrast to functionalists, conflict class theorists assume that society tends toward conflict more than stability, mainly because of the presence of many groups with diametrically opposed interests. The dominant group in society, capitalists (or whites), holds the reins of power and through legislation and other means appropriates for itself a larger share of economic and social benefits. For theorists of this persuasion, conflict is beneficial because it leads to social change, which in turn leads to more social justice.

According to conflict theorists, patterns of ethnic disadvantage are explained in terms of exploitation of ethnic and racial groups by the dominant group, which has a vested interest in perpetuating the status quo. Indeed, ethnic and racial antagonism in Canada continue to appear in subtle and sometimes not-so-subtle ways. A manifestation of this antagonism is the tendency to blame ethnic and racial minorities for a host of social and economic ills. As Peter Li observes,

> in addition to the class conflicts of a capitalist system, there is racial and ethnic antagonism that is based in part on attempts of higher-paid groups to protect their interests by excluding lower-paid groups from encroaching on their privileged positions, . . . and in part on racist and ethnocentric ideologies that serve to justify their efforts (1988: 50).

Such practices help explain the demands of higher-paid British Columbia workers in the first half of this century for exclusion of oriental immigrants and preventing them from joining labour unions (Moodley, 1981: 10; Li, 1988: 51). It seems clear that the division of the working class along racial/ethnic lines benefits the dominant group. This kind of class fragmentation brings with it racism and intolerance. In turn, "racism and ethnocentrism justify unequal treatment and transform class conflicts into cultural divisions" (Li, 1988: 54).

In contemporary Canadian society, discrimination on the basis of "race, national or ethnic origin, colour, religion, sex, age, or mental or physical disability" is prohibited by the Canadian Charter of Rights and Freedoms and by provincial legislation. Nevertheless, racism continues to surface from time to time. Ethnic and race relations in Canada are shaped to a large degree by the labour market and other institutional arrangements that covertly, and sometimes overtly, favour one group over another. Thus, there is little hope of substantially reducing prejudice and discrimination without restructuring social, economic, and political institutions to eliminate the relevance of race and ethnicity to their functioning.

SOCIAL PSYCHOLOGICAL EXPLANATIONS OF PREJUDICE

The social psychological approach assumes that there is something intrinsic to the individual's personality that causes that person to manifest prejudicial attitudes. A number of explanations of prejudice have been presented, based on this specific assumption.

Anti-Semitism — prejudice against Jews — has been recorded through time. It reached a contemporary peak with the organized and concerted anti-Semitism manifested prior to and during World War II in Nazi Germany. As a contribution to the study of the Nazi phenomenon, a team of researchers at the University of California at Berkeley set out to determine if prejudiced individuals have a unique set of personality characteristics that distinguishes them from nonprejudiced individuals (Adorno et al., 1950).

The researchers, using questionnaires, interviews, and clinical case studies, found that those individuals who expressed anti-Jewish sentiments also tended to express hatred toward other out-groups as well. Further, they found that prejudiced individuals exhibited evidence of insecurity, conformity, and intolerance to others who were different. The measure the researchers developed came to be called the F-scale (F for fascism); people who scored high on the F-scale were described as "authoritarian." The authoritarian personality exhibits the following personality components (Adorno et al., 1950: 255–57):

1. **Conventionalism:** rigid adherence to conventional, middle-class values.

2. **Authoritarian submission:** uncritical acceptance of authority.

3. **Authoritarian aggression:** a tendency to condemn anyone who violates conventional norms.

4. **Anti-intraception:** rejection of weakness or sentimentality.

5. **Superstition and stereotypy:** belief in mystical determinants of action and rigid, categorical thinking.

6. **Power and toughness:** preoccupation with dominance over others.

7. **Destructiveness and cynicism:** a generalized feeling of hostility and anger.

8. **Projectivity:** a tendency to project inner emotions and impulses outward.

9. **Sexual inhibition:** exaggerated concern for proper sexual conduct.

Although the F-scale has been criticized on a number of methodological issues, the fact remains that a great deal of subsequent research in social psychology has consistently demonstrated that prejudice does appear to be correlated with certain specific personality types. Milgram's (1974) research, cited in Chapter 4, is just one example of supportive research in this regard.

Milton Rokeach (1960), while agreeing with Adorno et al. that certain personality types were more inclined to prejudice than others, felt that Adorno and his colleagues had researched only one end of the continuum. Rokeach describes both radical conservatives (the "authoritarians" in Adorno's work) and radical liberals as being narrow minded and likely to be prejudiced toward those who do not fit their ideological mould. Rather than seeing the dimension as a straight-line continuum from least to most prejudiced, Rokeach described a kind of horseshoe continuum, where the people at the ends of the horseshoe were actually closer to one another (ideologically) than either end was to the middle. Rokeach's hypothesis is similar in scale to that of Eric Hoffer (1951), who talks about the **true believer** — the individual who is so sure of his or her beliefs that there is no room for variation, dissent, or alternative belief.

The research of Emory Bogardus (1925, 1959) also supports the notion of a prejudice syndrome — a complex set of prejudices with a broad focus on anything strange or different. Bogardus's research involved a **social distance scale,** which measured people's willingness to interact with specific ethnic, racial, and religious categories on a scale ranging from "would marry" to "would keep out of my country." Bogardus found not only that people tended to express negative attitudes toward more than one category of people when they did respond negatively, but that they also expressed negative attitudes toward categories with fictitious names that were included among the real categories of people. It would seem that people who maintain prejudices seldom confine them to just a single category of people.

Another explanation for prejudice involves the need of some people to blame their failures on others rather than accept the responsibility themselves. This is the process of **scapegoating.** By displacing the anger and recriminations involved in failure from the real source to some imaginary source, a great deal of personal pain can be alleviated. When Hitler blamed the Jews for all the problems in Germany after World War I, he was offering the Germans a scapegoat — an easy explanation for the cause of their problems, as well as an easy solution. By depriving German Jews of their positions, their rights, their belongings, and ultimately their lives, a clear (if irrational) solution was being presented. In the United States after the end of the Civil War, the number of lynchings of black men by whites increased significantly. At least one study found that the frequency of lynchings in some of the counties of the South was inversely correlated with the price of cotton. The inference was that whenever the economy was weak, the frequency of violence against blacks — the scapegoats — increased. In recent years in Canada, Jim Keegstra, a schoolteacher in Eckville, Alberta, was convicted of teaching hatred to his students by denying that the Holocaust ever took place and telling them that Jews were part of an evil conspiracy to take over the world. During the Gulf War, many Canadians of Arab heritage were the subjects of both verbal and physical abuse (Abu-Laban and Abu-Laban, 1991). Gays have been severely beaten on the street by people they had never seen before. Asians have been criticized for "buying Canada out from under us" when they have come here to make investments.

The social psychological orientation, then, treats the roots of prejudice as based in the personality of the individual. A great deal of research has shown that prejudice is acquired — prejudiced children tend to have prejudiced parents. The degree to which that prejudice will be manifested, however, will be a function of the conditions within society at any given time. Where the economy is weak, when politicians reinforce existing prejudices to explain any number of societal ills, we can expect prejudice to be more open than it might be when times are better or when society's norms militate against it.

Summary

- In the Canadian context, research on ethnic and minority group relations has dealt with a wide range of topics. They include the sociocultural characteristics of minority populations and their interrelationships with each other and with the larger society, the salience of ethnic identity in the lives of Canadians, issues of prejudice and discrimination, the impact of ethnicity on employment and income, and the reception and adaptation of immigrants. Research has also focused on public policy: the evolution and implications of multiculturalism as a demographic fact and as a government policy, and policy concerns involving not only immigration but also the management of diversity in Canada.

- For the sociologist, descriptive studies as well as conceptual clarification and theory building in this area are important goals, but there is also the challenge of dealing with a plethora of practical problems involving, for example, human rights legislation and interethnic tension and conflict.

- Ethnicity, in varying degrees, touches the lives of virtually all Canadians, but the strength of ethnic identity varies within and among different ethnic groups.

- Canada is an immigrant-receiving country, with large numbers of immigrants arriving in the first three decades of this century and after World War II. The latter immigration wave has contributed immensely to increasing ethnic diversity in Canada.

- After World War II and up to the present time, Canada's immigration policy has emphasized respect for family reunification, humanitarian concerns, and, increasingly, national economic and labour-market needs.

- The main lines of ethnic differentiation in Canada pertain to three pairs of relationships involving natives and non-natives, the two charter groups (English and French), and charter and non-charter groups — i.e., the other immigrant groups, visible minorities, and their descendants.

- Over the years, three patterns of majority–minority relations have been observed in Canada: assimilation, Anglo-conformity, and multiculturalism. At the present time, multiculturalism (still dominant but somewhat receding) appears to be the only realistic approach to the management of ethnic diversity in Canada.

- Sociological explanations of ethnic disadvantage are advanced in terms of how larger social forces in society (e.g., institutions and the class system) shape individual attitudes and intergroup relations. Thus, occupational and income differences among ethnic groups can be explained in large part by social class position. The two main perspectives in ethnic stratification are the functionalist and conflict perspectives.

- The functional perspective on class emphasizes the status quo, harmony, and social stability. Conflict theorists, on the other hand, view groups as having different self-interests and believe that conflict is essential for a more equitable distribution of desired goods and services.

- In contrast to the sociological approach, social psychological explanations of prejudice single out the individual's personality as the cause. These explanations argue that the individual attempts to alleviate pain or failure by manifesting prejudicial attitudes or by scapegoating.

KEY CONCEPTS

Anglo-conformity
Anti-Semitism
Assimilation
Discrimination
Emigrants
Ethnic identity
Ethnicity
Immigrants
Immigration
Majority group (hegemonic)
Minority group
Multiculturalism
Net migration
Pluralism
Prejudice
Race
Racism
Scapegoating
Social distance scale
Stereotypes
True believer
Visible minority

REVIEW QUESTIONS

1. Discuss three major ways in which ethnicity plays an important role in the lives of Canadians.
2. What do you understand by the term *ethnic identity,* and how does it manifest itself in everyday life?
3. What is the difference between assimilation and Anglo-conformity?
4. What are the main goals of Canada's immigration policy?
5. Do you agree or disagree with the statement that multiculturalism is the most realistic strategy for the management of ethnic relations in Canada? Justify your position.
6. What are the three components of prejudice? What is the relationship between prejudice and discrimination?
7. Compare and contrast the functional and conflict theories of ethnic stratification.
8. Is ethnic-minority origin a resource or a liability? Discuss.

9. How would you explain the differences between sociological and psychological explanations of prejudice?
10. What are the fundamental issues involved in (a) English and French relations, and (b) native and non-native relations?
11. What are the main concerns of Canadians who are neither of British nor of French origin with regard to questions of ethnicity and social justice?

Gender

Sharon McIrvin Abu-Laban, Susan A. McDaniel, and R.A. Sydie

INTRODUCTION

I expect that Woman will be the last thing civilized by Man.

George Meredith, *The Ordeal of Richard Feverel*, Chapter 1

The concept of gender may be both the most confusing and the easiest for students to grasp in a first sociology course. It is confusing because it is laden with misunderstanding, myth, and emotion. It is easy to grasp because it is one of the first concepts we learn as babies, and a basic organizing principle of our society. We all think we understand gender because we live in a society in which gender divisions are a given. Yet gender issues and gender challenges go to the very essence of what a society is and what it means to be social. In this chapter we will focus on the approaches and concepts used in the sociology of gender and how some of these are changing with new knowledge and new perspectives.

First we will discuss the distinctions between sex and gender. **Gender** is a social construct and a continuum. **Sex** is a biological concept typically seen as a dichotomy. Because our society is so gendered, and because sociology, to a large degree, is not an experimental science where biology can be controlled to assess social determinants, it is difficult to separate what is biological and what is social in gender behaviour. This task is often made more difficult by the widespread belief that gender is entirely biological and determines, or at least sets limits on, social behaviour. For example, we may feel confident about checking the "male" category on a form because we are on the university football team or because we are sexually attracted to women. Another person may check the "female" category because she was dressed in pink ruffles as a girl and was whistled at as she passed by a construction site on her way to class. Or, someone may check "male" because he does not wear skirts and is studying to be an engineer. Someone may check "female" because she lacks broad shoulders and is seen as feminine. It does not take much thought to recognize the fallacies in each of these statements. Some males not on the football team, not sexually attracted to women, who study areas other than engineering, and who may wear "skirts" (if Scottish or Malaysian, for example), nonetheless have a clear and unchangeable sense of masculinity. Similarly, some women who were not dressed in pink ruffles, not whistled at by construction workers, who have broad shoulders, and may not be seen by others as feminine may have a strong sense of their womanhood. All of these perceptions and self-images are filtered through social attitudes and beliefs. And many, if not all, vary strikingly across cultures. Yet each group, each generation, each culture, tends to view its own interpretation of gender as anchored in biology.

Gender is so central to our lives — to who we are, what we do, and what we think — that it is almost impossible to imagine a person without acknowledging whether that person is female or male, masculine or feminine. Gender permeates everything we are, every observation we make about society, every hope we dream. It thus becomes a major challenge in sociology to disentangle sociology from other societal forces, to sort out what is social from what is natural. In this chapter we will attempt to sort out some of the approaches and concepts used in the sociological investigation of gender beginning with an examination of theories and research methods. Following that discussion, we will focus on four major challenges to the study of gender issues in sociology: gender identity and sexuality; family and family formations; gender and diversity; and knowledge and cultural constructions.

THEORIES AND RESEARCH METHODS

In most introductory texts sex, age, race, ethnicity, and, sometimes, religion, are taken to be significant variables affecting social interaction. However, until comparatively recently, sex (as well as age) was considered only in association with other variables. Although sex was acknowledged as a basis of difference this did not hinder generalizations to all individuals from single-sex, usually male, samples. For example, Blau and Duncan's 1967 study of the American occupational structure, which concluded with the observation that the stability of American democracy was a function of the "superior chances of upward mobility . . . high standard of living, and the low degree of status deference between social strata" (1967: 439), was based on the occupational figures for males. Women appeared in this text in the role of wife. Not only does this study illustrate a sociological myopia regarding sex, it is also questionable in its conclusions regarding the low degree of status deference when race relations are taken into account. Nevertheless, this study claimed to represent a complete profile of the American occupational structure. In a similar manner, research on different political behaviours and preferences of men and women has tended to take the male activity as the norm and female activity as a deviation.

• SEX STATUS/GENDER

Sex status as a significant variable in its own right usually surfaced in research on marriage and the family. As Ehrich (1971) found in a content analysis of marriage and family sociology texts, the presumed traditional gender division of labour in the family was discussed in these works as "biologically logical and practical," and as the major source of marital harmony as well as being critical to the survival and order of a society. These normative assumptions were presented as *explanations* of gender role differentiation in marriage and family relationships. What is interesting is that the research done by Blau and Duncan as well as the research reported in the texts examined by Ehrich was done just as the women's movement was being rejuvenated and when the number of women in paid labour, irrespective of their marital status, was on the rise. (See figures in Chapter 6 for the changes in women's labour-force participation.) What was problematic and generated the unexamined normative focus in much of the past sociological analysis was the confusion of sex with gender.

Sex status can be determined for most people by their chromosomal, gonadal, and hormonal characteristics. Gender is a social-cultural definition based on sex status. Gender refers to the particular, historically variable characteristics and behavioural expectations for the sexes. For example, in our society we assume that men should be competitive, aggressive, and relatively unemotional, in contrast to women, who are expected to be emotional, passive, and cooperative. These gender expectations are culturally and historically relative. Different societies and historical periods have emphasized different gender expectations. The warrior of medieval Western societies was expected to display courage, fighting skills, and loyalty to a leader. Intellectual abilities were of lesser significance, in contrast to the Renaissance man of later centuries who was expected to display both physical and intellectual strength. Women's characteristics have also varied throughout history. The pre-Reformation Christian idea that women were naturally sinful and, unless rigidly controlled, could lure men into temptation can be contrasted with the 19th-century ideal of the pure, asexual female, the "angel in the home." The various definitions of appropriate behaviours, attitudes, and beliefs about masculinity and femininity are not only culturally and historically variable, they are also variable in relation to class and status.

Whatever the particulars of gender expectations, it is generally the case that the definitions of appropriate gender characteristics and behaviours involve a relationship of power between the sexes that can be summarized by the observation that "Man" stands for human, but "Woman" does not, as the quotation at the beginning of this chapter illustrates. This power relationship between men and women has been recognized as a significant feature by sociologists in the past. Georg Simmel (1984) noted that the identification of man-human concealed the power relationship that defined "inadequate achievements" as "contemptuously called 'feminine,' whilst distinguished achievements on the part of women are called 'masculine' as an expression of praise."

Durkheim believed that civilized women were naturally different from men. Men were "almost entirely the product of society," while women were "to a far greater extent the product of nature" (1966: 385). Consequently, men were more highly socialized beings than were women, and the latter required the regulation of the former for social harmony and stability. Simone de Beauvoir, in *The Second Sex,* also pointed out that it was men who defined women and not vice versa; consequently, "humanity is male and man defines woman not in herself but as relative to him; she is not regarded as an autonomous being" (1952: xviii).

The unexamined assumption in sociology that "Man" stood for all humanity although women were "naturally" different and subordinate to men came under more direct scrutiny in the 1960s and 1970s. The sex/gender relationship became a central problematic in the analysis of social life. In part this was a response to the general questioning of the status quo that coalesced in various protest movements during this period. It also reflected the presence of larger numbers of women in higher educational institutions in contrast to previous eras. This had profound implications for sociological theory and methods — implications that are still being debated and contested in the discipline, as this chapter will illustrate. When taking the sex/gender issue into account, sociologists have used patriarchy to provide a framework for the development of alternative theory and practice.

• PATRIARCHY

Webster defines patriarchy as a "social organization marked by the supremacy of the father in the clan or family in both domestic and religious functions, the legal dependence of wife or wives and children, and the reckoning of descent and inheritance in the male line." Patriarchy is a sexual hierarchy in which men generally have power over all women. Whilst these power relations may vary in their specific characteristics and particular practices, it is usually assumed that they are based on the "natural" fact of women's reproductive capacity. That is, because women reproduce, the natural relationship between the sexes is one of male superiority and female subordination. Women's reproductive role, it is assumed, prevents their full participation in the public world of work, war, and politics. Women's primary identification is with the so-called private world of household and family. For example, most classical sociological theorists assumed that the basic social unit was the mother–child bond. But they also assumed that this was because it was a natural bond, and that the real beginnings of society are to be found when the mother–child relationship is connected with a male, with a father. In other words, patriarchy was the foundation of social life. Thus Weber defined patriarchy as the authority of the master over his household, based on the "natural" superiority of the male's "physical and intellectual energies" (Weber, 1968, vol. 2: 1007).

In general, the construction and maintenance of patriarchy as an everyday experience of men, women, and children is to be found in the structure and relationships within the family household. But the family patriarch is supported by all the other institutional structures of society. For example, the educational system takes it for granted that parents, usually mothers, will monitor and assist their children with homework. As Dorothy Smith (1987) points out, the classroom depends on "good mothering," so that the child of the single parent is at a disadvantage in the school system, especially in the early years. This is a gender issue in that the majority of single-parent households are headed by women. Because the burden of earning a living is confined to one person there is less time available for the single parent to devote time and energy to the work of mothering defined by the needs of the school.

It is in the family (however that institution is defined and structured) that the individual experiences "society" — that is, experiences how the connections are made between social institutions such as schools, corporations, and political structures, and how the individual understands and manipulates these institutions. Understanding patriarchy therefore involves two separate but connecting levels of interaction. As Fox (1988: 176) has suggested, at the structural level, patriarchy frames the political, economic, familial, and ideological arrangements that "handicap the sex that bears children." At the same time, the concept is important in understanding the subjective acceptance of socially constructed gender differences that patriarchy produces and reinforces. Consequently, we can point to the ways in which social structures favour one sex over another, as well as taking into account how individuals react to and change those structures in their everyday lives.

THE SOCIAL CONSTRUCTION OF SEX, GENDER, AND SEXUALITY

> *What are little boys made of?*
> *Frogs and snails, and puppy-dogs' tails;*
> *That's what little boys are made of.*
> *What are little girls made of?*
> *Sugar and spice, and all that's nice;*
> *That's what little girls are made of.*

We shape and are shaped by our social world in an ongoing dynamic between people and society. When we speak of gender, we are addressing major forms and consequences of this interactive process between people and their social world. All human societies make distinctions based on the inborn (ascribed) characteristics of **sex,** the physiological distinctions based on biology and reproductive anatomy that usually group into two categories: male and female. The designation of sex is the most common identification used by and about Canadians, from birth to death. The implications of this are vastly beyond the systematic keeping of records. These physiological sex differences are put to social use. **Gender,** the socially created expectations regarding masculine versus feminine behaviours, arises from the initial categorization of the sexes. At the societal level, gender differentiation is crucial to understanding and explaining the differential distribution of roles and tasks, scarce resources, privileges, and burdens accorded to males and females. At the individual level, the systematic structuring of opportunities and experiences is perpetuated by ideology and maintained by power and tradition. This leads to major inequities between men and women.

• EXPLAINING DIFFERENCES

Few contemporary researchers would hold to a **biological determinist** view that biology produces masculine and feminine behaviours or that "anatomy is destiny." Old debates questioning whether the behaviours of women and men are the result of nature or the result of nurture have been replaced, for the most part, by an acknowledgment that both are influential. In the more traditional, **essentialist** view, sex and gender are seen as innate aspects of the human psyche that develop in early childhood or by biological predisposition to form a core sexual self. This results in a sharply dichotomized view of men versus women, which is the simplest, perhaps most superficial, way of thinking about and explaining differences between males and females. It provides the groundwork for sex stereotypes.

Increasingly, social scientists take a **social constructionist** approach, which views man and woman as ideas or formations that are neither universal nor absolute but emerge historically and are contingent on culture. A social constructionist perspective, ideally, does not discount biology, but instead is sensitive to the interaction between the social and the biological. The focus of a social constructionist approach is on the consequences of societal assumptions and practices regarding sex and gender. Sex and gender then are revealed as more diverse and complexly layered than in an essentialist perspective. Categorizations by sex and gender result in differential access to life chances for men and women. Some of the consequences of this categorization can begin even before birth, when prospective parents and interested onlookers speculate on whether a pregnancy might result in a boy or a girl.

• Sex Assignment and Biology

The categorization into male or female seems the most basic, incontrovertible, biological fact; yet, it will be argued, sex is made up of several components, and the categories themselves reflect social definition. At the earliest phases of development all human embryos appear to be similar. Sex differences can be determined only genetically. The chromosomes provide a blueprint that starts the process of sex differentiation. Both genetic males and genetic females have undifferentiated genitalia, undifferentiated gonads that may develop into testes or ovaries, and both male and female rudimentary reproductive tracts. There is a bipotentiality of the sexes that is dependent on the secretion of sex hormones. The external genitals develop after the third fetal month. Sometimes accidents of development occur that can compromise the development of reproductive structures that are consistent with genetic makeup. Sometimes these are apparent at birth. At other times, their presence is only determined later. Sexual assignment at birth usually results from the process of increasing sex differentiation begun at conception. One of the first, urgent questions asked by the parents of a newborn is likely to be "Is it a boy or a girl?" The answer is critical socially. It is likely to be the child's main descriptor at birth and one of the earliest labels learned with powerful reverberations throughout life, affecting relationships, jobs, finances, safety, choices, and aspirations.

• Biological Variability

There are several components that go into the makeup of biological sex:

1. **Chromosomal sex,** which consists of the chromatic patterns that can be established by skin biopsy or buccal smear and examined under a microscope. This technique is commonly used to test Olympic athletes and has resulted in the exclusion of some anatomical females from the women's competitions;
2. **Gonadal sex,** which includes the presence of ovaries or testes;
3. **Hormonal sex,** which comprises the chemical substances secreted internally by both men and women, but in different proportions (hormonal sex may not be readily apparent until a child reaches puberty and develops secondary sexual characteristics such as breasts, a deepened voice, or facial hair);
4. **Internal sexual organs,** as determined from internal accessory organs, which include the prostate or the uterus;
5. **External genitalia,** which suggest a determination of sex based on outer genital appearance or phenotype (Hampson and Hampson, 1961).

On occasion, sexual incongruities can occur, involving some contradictions among these variables of sex. For example, if an infant is born with an external genital appearance somewhat borderline between male and female, the baby is still assigned to one sex, with all the attendant social implications. The problems with such an initial classification may not be apparent until adolescence, when the child begins to develop secondary sexual characteristics of the opposite sex. The cumulative evidence appears to be that even in cases of "mismatch" between the expected variables of sex, the content of socialization — being taught who we are — is critical in establishing our sense of sexual identity.

• SEX ASSIGNMENT AS A SOCIAL CONSTRUCT

Another way to illustrate the importance of social definitions even in determining sex is to ask "How many sexes are there?" To most Canadians this would appear to be a naive question. As illustrated in Figure 10.1, the understanding and expectations of Canadian society are quite clear — there are two sexes, only. Newborns are either male or female, and the classification is determined by external appearance (phenotype). Each sex has access to a different gender status. Yet each year, an estimated 2 to 3 percent of human infants are born with ambiguous external genitalia. In Canada, such babies receive a sexual assignment of either male or female and, if considered necessary, medical procedures (such as surgical interventions or the administration of hormones) are scheduled to ensure the child's smooth adjustment to the assigned sex status and the gender status anticipated. Historically, there have been other ways of reacting to births of this type.

• The Intersexed

An interesting illustration of societal recognition and acceptance of a third sexual category is found among one of the early aboriginal groups in North America. In the period before contact with Europeans, the Navaho people made their home in the general area of the states of Arizona and New Mexico. They exhibited a wide range of tolerance for sexual diversity. A Navaho newborn could be classified into one of three sex categories: male, female, or nadle. The **nadle** was someone born with ambiguous genitals. The sexual classification was made on the basis of phenotype (observable characteristics). This was not a catch-all, surplus sexual category. The infant born to be a nadle had access to a unique and valued role, with special privileges denied to others. Nadles acted as go-betweens in disputes between men and women. They had special property rights and special religious privileges.

The frequency of supplemental categories for sex assignment in other groups has yet to be systematically assessed; thus far, not many researchers seem to have considered this possibility as a viable research question. Although male and female are treated as polar opposites, biological sex can be seen as more than a dichotomy. The presence of cross-cultural variation in categorization suggests the importance of society in the sex categorization process. The behavioural expectations arising from this categorization into male or female are also social products.

• GENDER ASSIGNMENT AS A SOCIAL CONSTRUCT

To speak of gender is to speak of the social consequences of the initial categorization into male or female. In Canada, differences in the process of gender socialization appear early and, particularly in childhood, the pressures on young boys can be heavy. When children deviate from the rigidities of gender conventions, there is more likely to be bemused tolerance of girls' "tomboy" activities than of boys' activities that might be seen as "wimp" or "sissy." Canadian society expects two sexes and two genders.

• Intersexual Gender

Other societies have allowed for more than two genders. Figure 10.1 illustrates the flexibility of traditional Navaho society with regard to gender. While someone might be born a nadle (an ascribed category) one could also *achieve* nadle status, even where phenotypic sex appeared to be straightforward. The gender status of nadle was accessible to both phenotypic males and phenotypic females. Those who wished to move from a masculine or feminine gender status to an intersexual gender status could do so by undergoing special ceremonies of initiation.

• CULTURAL VARIATIONS IN GENDER CONTENT

Still another example of the diversity of possibilities in defining and allocating gender can be found among a second aboriginal group, the early Mohave peoples, who lived in California and adjacent areas at the time of contact with Europeans. This group, although apparently recognizing only two sexes, acknowledged and accepted *four* different gender statuses (Figure 10.1). Thus a phenotypic male had access to masculine status or, after going through an initiation ceremony, a feminine-like status (alyha). Similarly, a phenotypic female had access to a feminine status or, after an initiation ceremony, a masculine-like status (hwame). These four

DIFFERENTIAL SEX AND GENDER ASSIGNMENT

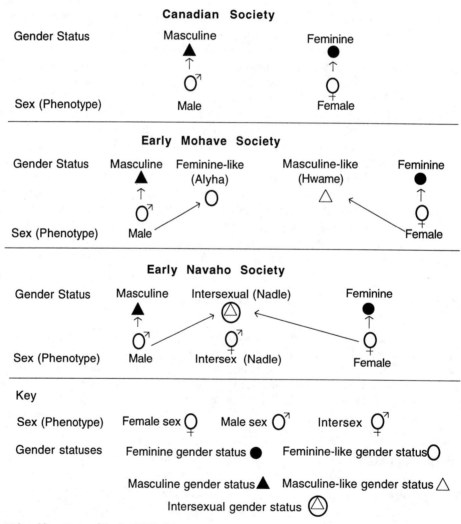

Source: Adapted from Martin and Voorhies (1975: 89).

distinctive statuses allow considerably different behaviours. The **hwame** and **alyha** could cross traditional sex barriers, mediate in disputes, and participate in important spiritual activities that were different from those included in masculine and feminine roles. It is significant that many of the early North American aboriginal groups allocated special privileges, particularly spiritual ones, to community members who were outside male/female, masculine/feminine dichotomies.

While most societies allow for only two gender statuses, the ways in which each society expects men to be men and women to be women can differ considerably. Margaret Mead's classic work (1963 [1935]), which attempts to compare sex and temperament in three different groups in northeastern New Guinea, acts as a corrective. Mead's classic study, based on field work done between 1931 and 1933, found that each of the three groups had contrasting views regarding what constituted an "ideal" male and an "ideal" female.

• The Arapesh

Mead characterizes the mountain-dwelling Arapesh, both men and women, as maternal and gentle. They emphasize that adult members of the community must meet the needs of younger and dependent members. Both men and women value children and the task of caring for children. At the time of delivery, fathers themselves go through the experience of **couvade** (a male ritual simulating pregnancy or delivery). It is a societal ideal among the Arapesh that both women and men emphasize cooperation over competition. According to Mead, in this setting, neither the ideal male nor the ideal female is aggressively sexual, and rape is unknown (Mead, 1963 [1935]: 157).

• The Mundugumor

In contrast to the Arapesh with their emphasis on cooperation and trust, Mead describes the Mundugumor, her second New Guinea group, as aggressive, competitive, and cannibalistic. Mundugumor men and women are similar to each other but quite dissimilar from the Arapesh. In Mundugumor society, children are barely tolerated, often left on their own, and taught, like their elders, to be hostile and suspicious. Neither males nor females are very tender toward children. Women are seen as just as dangerous and aggressive as men, only not quite as strong.

• The Tchambuli

Among the third New Guinea group, the Tchambuli, men and women are seen as temperamentally different from each other — but the traditional sex stereotypes of the West are reversed. Mead describes Tchambuli women as matter of fact and practical. Through their fishing, trading, and weaving, women take care of the business of the community. In contrast, Mead describes Tchambuli men as vain and concerned about personal adornment, and preoccupied with planning ceremonies and festivities and with developing strategies to get the women to notice them (Mead, 1963 [1935]).

Social scientists continue to query cross-cultural variabilities and uniformities regarding femininity and masculinity. As more and more of what we currently understand about gender is examined, the richness and potential of our capacities as humans becomes clearer. The field of sociology of gender is still new, although the continuing questions about masculinity and femininity have a venerable past.

• REASSIGNMENTS OF SEX AND GENDER

Further evidence suggesting the importance of social expectations in shaping our understandings of sex and gender arise out of what may be called "natural" laboratory situations. While, for ethical reasons, we cannot do controlled experiments on infants and young children in order to assess the impact of socialization, we can examine a few unique case studies involving sex and gender reassignment. Two of these cases involve children with anatomical problems. The third example involves transsexuals, people who have "normal" anatomy but a distressing conviction that their anatomy is not right for them.

• Conjoint Twins

A case of conjoint (Siamese) twins at the Hospital for Sick Children in Toronto in 1984 posed challenges to parents and physicians. The infant boys, flown to Canada from Burma, each had a set of legs, but they were joined to one another at the pelvis. The twins shared one liver, common intestines, and common genitalia. After deliberation, surgeons separated the little boys, giving one child the male genitals and doing reconstructive surgery on the second twin to create external female genitalia. This second twin, Win, although genetically male, was thus reassigned at 2-and-a-half years as a female. Win will take female hormones at puberty to effect secondary sexual characteristics such as breast development and feminine voice, but will be unable to bear children and probably will have a compromised sexual response. Once the physicians decided that it was in the best interests of the twins that they be separated, the criteria for selecting which child would be raised as a female are interesting: "The doctors agreed that Lin the *livelier and more aggressive (albeit smaller)* of the two, should keep the male genitals. His sexuality is expected to be fully functional" (*Life*, October 1984; italics added). Follow-up reports on this case have yet to appear; however, an earlier case has been documented over a period of several years.

• Circumcision Accident

This second case of sex and gender reassignment involves an infant born without anatomical malformation. At the age of 7 months, this little boy and his twin brother were scheduled for circumcision. The surgeon used an electrocautery technique, but the electrical current was too strong. It damaged the first baby's genitals and consequently caused the child's penis to slough off, flush with the abdominal wall. After several months of agonizing, the parents consulted John Money, a well-known medical psychologist at Johns Hopkins University. It was decided to reassign the sex of the injured child. At the age of 17 months, the social process of sex reassignment began; *he* would become a *she*. Later, at 21 months, the first of several surgical procedures was performed to progressively construct female-like genitals. The family received guidance on ways to help their child adjust. The early reports by the mother describing differences between her twin children are interesting and suggest the importance of **socialization,** the lifelong process of social shaping by which we all become gendered.

The first changes that were introduced to change the little boy into a little girl began with clothing and hair (the externals to which strangers respond). As described by the mother,

> I started dressing her not in dresses but, you know, in little pink slacks and frilly blouses, and letting her hair grow.

By the time the children were 3 years old, the mother reported that she kept her new daughter almost exclusively in dresses.

I even made all her nightwear into granny gowns and she wears bracelets and ribbons.

By the time they were 4-and-a-half, the mother saw one child as more fastidious and concerned about grooming than the other. She described her new daughter as "neat and tidy."

> I've never seen a little girl so neat and tidy . . . she is very proud of herself, when she put[s] on a new dress, or I set her hair. She just loves to have her hair set; she could sit under the drier all day long and have her hair set. She just loves it.

The mother also reported that her daughter exercised greater sexual propriety than her twin brother and she showed more interest in helping her mother with household chores. In contrast, the mother reported that the other twin rejected housework, liked to copy his father, and was "protective" of his sister. Before the surgical accident, the newly designated daughter had been reported as the dominant twin. After surgery the mother described her as a "mother hen" in relation to her brother.

The future for these identical twins, both genetic males at birth, looks quite different. The ceiling so often placed on the ambitions of girls is illustrated by the mother's early observations, when her newly assigned "daughter" was less than 2 years old, that it was her hope that her remaining son, in particular, would pursue enough education to enable him to have a career: "it's almost essential, since he will be earning a living for the rest of his life" (Money, 1975).

Money reported that by the age of 9, although the situation of the twins was widely known, few outsiders would have judged the reassigned twin as anything other than a girl. However, later research (Diamond, 1982) suggests that as an adolescent she may be confused about gender identity. Several factors might contribute to conflicting feelings as she grows older:

1. the story is widely known by relatives, and she herself knows of her previous status as a male (Money, 1975);
2. she is physically different from other females;
3. she has had to undergo continuing medical procedures in order to approximate female form and function; and
4. her upbringing seems to have been stereotypically female, narrowing her options compared to those of her brother, yet preparing her for a traditional role of biological motherhood (which she won't be able to achieve).

• Transsexuals

The power of the social and of the expectation that the social be in line with the biological is illustrated further by the case of **transsexuals,** people who have the genotype of one sex but are convinced they are in the wrong body; that they are, at their core, the opposite sex. Transsexuals do not describe themselves as "gay." Instead they describe a profound discomfort with their bodies. They feel trapped by the "wrong" exterior. The transsexual's conviction that social role, anatomy, and sexual orientation should be congruent may move him or her to have sex-change surgery to effect reassignment to the desired sex.

Female to Male

After studying to be a Franciscan nun and experiencing much personal turmoil, Maria Martinio (Martinio, 1977) began a long and costly series of medical procedures aimed at making her as much like a man as anatomically possible. In order that she could convincingly live like a man, Martinio began lifelong treatment with male hormones; had her breasts surgically removed; eventually underwent a hysterectomy (removal of the uterus); and had an artificial phallus surgically created. She changed her name to Mario, reassigned herself as a male, and then, for a period, emphasized an *exaggerated* male role.

> Ten years ago, I took a certain pride in being a male chauvinist and this I attribute to my despair in having been born with a female body (Martinio, 1977: 239).

This stereotypical masculinity has apparently been moderated as a result of the post-surgical experience and perhaps because of changes in the general social climate. The new Mario reports that since his sex reassignment, he has become more egalitarian in his relationships with women.

Male to Female

There are more male-to-female transsexuals than there are female-to-male. A well-known case of male-to-female transsexuality is that of the British author Jan Morris who, before sex change surgery at the age of 46, lived life as a male. As James Humphry Morris, he had attended an English boys' school, served as an intelligence officer in World War II, worked as a journalist for the London *Times,* accompanied Edmund Hillary and Norkay Tensing in the first successful conquest of Mt. Everest, married, and fathered five children. All the while he lived in anguish about his sexual identity. After consulting an endocrinologist and undergoing years of treatment with estrogens and progestins, Morris had surgical reconstruction of the genitals and began living a new life as a woman. In *Conundrum* the new Jan Morris reports a very traditional view of male–female roles; the former officer in one of Britain's most "dashing" cavalry regiments reports enjoying having doors opened for her, saying "women who like to feel cherished by a stronger man have every right to their feelings" (1974: 148).

Jan Morris's somewhat idealized image of the traditional female role is qualified by her reflection on whether her personal conflict would have been so difficult had she grown up in an era where the lines between men and women were less rigid:

> If society had allowed me to live in the gender I preferred, would I have bothered to change sex? Is mine only a transient phenomenon, between the dogmatism of the last century, when men were men and women were ladies, and the eclecticism of the next, when citizens will be free to live in the gender role they prefer? (Morris, 1974: 148–49).

It is argued that the dramatic step of surgical reassignment taken by some transsexuals might well be a reflection of the level of societal intolerance. In societies where masculine and feminine are not so rigidly defined, such painful and dangerous medical procedures might not seem necessary. In fact, cross-cultural evidence comparing the incidence and prevalence of transsexuality in Sweden and in Australia suggests these rates are strongly influenced by culture and degree of societal repression over gender choices. Compared to Sweden, Australia, with its more rigid delineations of gender-acceptable behaviour, has a much higher incidence of male-to-female sex reassignment surgery and requests for such surgery (Ross et al., 1981).

• SEXUAL ORIENTATION AS A SOCIAL CONSTRUCT

It is common to think of anatomical sex and gender identity as congruent with sexual orientation. Prior to the pioneering work of Alfred Kinsey, the research literature tended to equate a person's sexual orientation with the essence of that person. Kinsey criticized the rigid dichotomization of homosexual versus heterosexual types in his writings of the late 1940s and early 1950s. Kinsey radically demystified sexuality and challenged dichotomous assumptions of normal versus abnormal sexuality and of homosexual versus heterosexual people. He proposed that individuals and their behaviour could be better understood if viewed on a continuum. Kinsey argued that accounts of sexuality based on either/or categories were not reflective of the complexities of the human condition either developmentally or cross-culturally. Indeed, if we consider the range of human intimacies from infancy to old age, we find that the categories of sexuality are not predetermined or universal. They are subject to social definition and cultural variability. Like explanations of sex and gender, explanations of sexual orientation fall into essentialist and social constructionist approaches.

• Essential Explanations of Sexual Orientation

In an essentialist perspective, a core sexual self develops in early childhood or by biological predisposition. The United Church of Canada, for example, in its recent report on gay clergy, argues that sexual orientation is as beyond personal control as being left- or right-handed. In fact attempts to "explain" the presence of homosexuality have met with little success. To date research evidence on the three distinct essential theories of causation are unclear: (1) there is no strong evidence for the impact of early family experiences; (2) there is some weak evidence for adult hormonal imbalances; and (3) there is somewhat mixed evidence for prenatal hormone imbalance. Ironically, far less research has attempted to "explain" heterosexuality.

• Social Constructionist Explanations of Sexual Orientation

In contrast, a social constructionist view sees heterosexuality and homosexuality as matters of definition that may vary across time and place. Even within the same society, there may be variations over time. For example, in North America same-sex sexual explorations and activity occur between young children, and same-sex "crushes" in adolescence are not uncommon. Canadian society emphasizes heterosexuality and the majority of people classify themselves as heterosexual, yet sexual expression, particularly during childhood, may reflect a degree of overlap between strictly heterosexual versus homosexual activities as part of an evolving process of identifying and labelling personal sexual orientation (Blumstein and Schwartz, 1983).

The proportion of homosexuals in the population has been subject to much discussion. The works of Kinsey and of others suggest some 3 to 4 percent of males identify themselves as exclusively gay while some 2 to 3 percent of women see themselves as exclusively lesbian. There are vested interests in embracing statistics that show greater or lesser incidence of homosexuality in a population. It should be remembered that rates can vary given that there are cultures and epochs that have allowed or promoted controlled homosexual behaviour (never, however, to the exclusion of heterosexual behaviour). For example, among the Azande people of East Africa, a culture where marriage is usually only available to men when they are older and have accumulated wealth, homosexual relationships are sanctioned between young men and boys. This is only one phase in the life of an Azande warrior. He is expected to take on the role of husband and father at a later phase in his life.

For men and women who identify themselves as gay or lesbian, particularly for those who can do this openly in the context of supportive relationships, the evidence indicates positive social adjustment. Among lesbian women a pattern of enduring long-term relationships has been well-established. Statistically, a lesbian couple has better odds for maintaining their partnership than does a heterosexual couple. Gay men, on the other hand, are most likely to have multiple relationships and most likely to experience couple break-up (Blumstein and Schwartz, 1983). However, the tragedy of the AIDS (Acquired Immunodeficiency Syndrome) epidemic and the initial prevalence of its transmission through the gay population in North America has prompted changes in the patterns of gay intimacy, resulting in a shift toward more long-term, monogamous relationships.

• SEXUALITY

An understanding of human sexuality needs to extend beyond the normative baseline of one culture or the single perspective of male-centred (androcentric) perspective. Cross-culturally and historically we find that every society exercises controls over the sexual behaviours of its members. Human sexual behaviour may emanate from biological factors but these are shaped and structured into customs, laws, and rules of sexual conduct. The variety of permissible and forbidden behaviours is large and the distinction between the permissible and the forbidden is changeable. For example, a traditional stereotype in our society is that women have less sexual desire than men. However, until about the 17th century, Europeans believed that women's sexuality needed to be strictly controlled *because it was potentially more insatiable* than men's and if left unrestricted could wreak havoc on hapless males who became the object of a woman's desire.

Michel Foucault (1978) argues that the contemporary view of sexuality arises out of the declining importance of kin and extended family as social controls, a process that began with the Industrial Revolution and progressed through the Victorian era. In the 20th century, sexuality has become the domain of professional and semi-professional experts; the variety and changeability of the advice they have offered illustrates its cultural construction. One feature that remains important in our society is the norm of heterosexuality, preferably practised within the bounds of a marital/family relationship. However, the definition of an appropriate marital/family connection is also culturally variable, as the following section will illustrate.

FAMILY AND FAMILY FORMATION

Family may be the most gendered of social institutions, and yet, strangely, family has only recently begun to be examined through the lenses of the sociology of gender. Family and gender division of labour within the family were treated as givens and linked to the biological. Once the perspectives of the sociology of gender were brought to bear on the family, however, exciting insights became apparent.

Motherhood as an occupation, long presumed to be women's traditional role, is a social convention of late 19th-century Western societies. It was only at that point in history that the family came to depend on men's wages, and domesticity and child care came to be women's exclusive domain. The needs of the new industrial structure for a better-trained and educated workforce redefined women's devotion to childbearing as a serious occupation. Industrialization also contributed to the sharpening of this role division by separating the public from the private for the first time in history. These historical insights have had important theoretical implications. For when what had been presumed to be natural is found to be social, or the convention of a particular historical period, then previously unquestioned assumptions about gender in family are called into question.

Concepts of family have changed too — to become both more and less inclusive. For example, the extended family may no longer comprise only those who are related to us in the traditional sense, but also perhaps stepchildren, an ex-spouse's parents, a new spouse, and a multitude of friends, even same-sex couples. All of these emerging concepts of family call into question the nuclear family with Mom, Dad, and the kids who are biologically and socially theirs. With these new concepts and social changes comes a questioning of gender within the family.

What are some of the changes that have occurred within the family or that have implications for gender in the family? Entire courses and subfields in sociology have been developed to examine these changes. One of the more striking changes has been the phenomenal growth of the two-income family, where both parents work outside the home. Notable here is that the fastest growth in labour-force entrants recently has been mothers of young children. It has been shown with recent Canadian data that families with a second wage-earner contribute in two ways to the Canadian economy: (1) they insulate Canadians from the effects of recession and economic perturbation, and (2) they have increased the overall gross national product substantially, thus decreasing the tax burdens of the welfare state.

A second important change with implications for gender in the family has been the rapid increase in households of unrelated persons (Boyd, 1988: 86). This has been accompanied by growth in single-person households. In part, of course, this reflects increasing numbers of divorced and widowed, but it also suggests a growing diversity in the ways Canadians live in families and a preference to live outside traditional families at some point in life. For women, this change has meant a greater diversity of options than ever before in history. But most Canadians do marry at some time, so the greater diversity of family life does not suggest any end to the family.

A third change is the tendency among Canadians to live common-law. Preliminary findings from the 1990 General Social Survey (McDaniel, 1991) suggest that 28 percent of women and men report having lived common-law at some time, compared to 17.3 percent of women and 15.6 percent of men in 1984. It is not clear why common-law unions are growing in popularity, but this could be a sign of dissatisfaction with traditional marriage.

• Family Formation

In much but not all of Canadian society, family formation occurs in the context of romantic love and sexuality. This means that gender issues of attractiveness, career aspirations, and how adolescents see the family come into play. All of this is ideologically defined and determined. So, for example, if young women are taught that their futures lie in being the wife of "Prince Charming" and making him happy, then they will be less likely to strive for careers that require postponement of marriage and family. Similarly, if boys are taught that girls will grow into women who put their husbands' needs and aspirations ahead of their own, then they may come to expect that women will be secondary to them in the family. In Canada today girls tend to expect to marry, stay married, never face poverty or violence in the family, and always be happy, while at the same time having some sort of career (Baker, 1985). Boys value their own looks more than they used to, but still far less than girls, suggesting that they still get fewer rewards from society for their appearance than do girls. Some of the preoccupation girls have with body image (discussed elsewhere in this chapter) may contribute to health problems such as bulimia and anorexia nervosa.

Family formation often occurs in the environment of an active interest in sexuality, an interest that for adolescent males is often shaped partly by pornography. Women and women's bodies are portrayed as existing for men and men's pleasure, often with an explicit connection between sex and violence. At the same time, the media emphasize to women the importance of being glamorous and alluring. It may not be surprising, then, that school achievement of girls (typically higher than boys in the early years of school) drops in high school. The message that many young girls are getting from society is that it is more important to be popular than to excel academically. This leads to a differential achievement level for women than for men, which, when compounded by wage and occupational mobility gaps, means that women have less opportunity to earn, and hence be independent, than men. In marriage, this differential means a gap in power, as it is most often the person who makes the most money who continues to work when the children are young, and who makes the basic decisions about the family.

• PATRIARCHY IN THE NUCLEAR FAMILY

In many ways, the nuclear family is among the most patriarchal of social institutions. Despite changes, it is an institution where male domination receives society's cultural and legal sanction. It is only within the past decade and a half that children can take their mother's name legally at birth without the mother having to declare that the father is unknown. The nuclear family is where male/female differences in earning power tend to be very pronounced, and it can be a place of violence directed largely at women and children.

But patriarchy comes into play at another level as well, in the ways the nuclear family serves society. Two illustrations will suffice here. First, men's often tedious and boring work in modern industrial society can be more easily justified in their eyes if they are the breadwinners for the family. This role gives men a sense of power over and within the family, which compensates for their powerlessness in the larger society. Men who justify working in meaningless jobs "for the good of the family" are less likely to cause trouble for employers, thus maintaining social order. In this sense, the nuclear family, premised as it is on gender divisions of labour in the wider world, can be seen as a stabilizing institution in society. Women's public work roles can be seen as threatening to this basic reward structure, and thus women's work outside the home may be resented and undervalued. The threat may be less to men's jobs, per se, given the occupational ghettos most women work in, and more to the fit between the gender-structured nuclear family and the work world.

A second example comes from the theories of Dorothy Smith (1977), a Canadian sociologist. Her essential idea is that in corporate capitalism, the nuclear family is a vital extension of the corporate sector. In a workplace where evaluations no longer depend on production measures (i.e., of material goods), images become the means by which status is obtained; how a corporate executive lives affects his prospects for promotion up the corporate ladder. Thus, it becomes important for him to pick the "right kind" of wife who attended the correct schools, knows the social graces, and can run a home and raise children to be a credit to their father and, by extension, their father's corporation. Women's abilities to organize social events, dress well, and speak with assurance but not too much assertiveness become the means by which Dad's soundness as a corporate leader is assessed. Children are part of the picture as well, as they are carefully taught, usually by Mom, that it is important to the family that they achieve, and under no circumstances do anything to embarrass the family. Smith argues that this is another way in which nuclear families are structured by gender in patriarchal society and contribute to political and economic stability.

• HOUSEWORK AND CHILD CARE

The provision of housework and child care in the family is one of the many benefits that accrues to society from the nuclear family. Moreover, these fundamental services presumably are provided out of love since there is no visible remuneration. This does not imply that child care and housework are not very rewarding, but rather that if the same services were provided by the open market they would be costly indeed.

Housework is perhaps the most invisible type of work. Cooking and cleaning are supposed to be labours of love. This perception is very strongly upheld by TV advertising, which tells us that housework is generally women's work and that women are better mothers and wives if they use the right kind of laundry detergent and fabric softener, bake the right cake, and make the right cocoa. Housework is done in the privacy and isolation of the nuclear family, and once done, it requires redoing almost immediately. John Lennon once remarked during his period of heavy involvement with raising his son that it is better to make records because then you get the royal-

Box 10.1

BRAVE NEW BABIES

Not many years ago, test-tube fertilization, frozen embryos, and cloning were science fiction, beyond the realm of anything but our imaginations. In the 1990s in Canada, sex selection, artificial insemination, "in vitro" (test-tube) fertilization, embryo replacement/transfer/freezing, and surrogate mother contracts are commonplace. In 1989 the government of Canada set up a Royal Commission to examine all aspects of the new reproductive technologies (NRTs). Plagued with controversy and politics, the new Commission will deliver its findings in late 1992.

How new are the new reproductive technologies? Surrogate motherhood dates back 4 000 years, to the book of Genesis. Rachel, Jacob's infertile wife, had her maid Hagar bear two children for them. The first recorded artificial insemination occurred in 1884 in Philadelphia at Jefferson Medical College, where an unidentified woman, infertile because of her husband's lack of sperm, was injected with the sperm of a medical student by Dr. Pancoast as his medical students looked on. The woman, anesthetized under the pretense of a routine medical examination, was not informed of this procedure, even after she gave birth to a baby boy — but her husband knew. Between 1978 and 1988, a number of firsts occurred: first test-tube baby (Louise Brown, born 1978); first test-tube twins, triplets, quintuplets born; first baby born entirely unrelated to its womb mother; first grandmother giving birth to her own granddaughter; first legal case involving inheritance rights of frozen embryos; first legal case involving custody dispute between biological father and surrogate mother; and first cloning of domestic mammals.

Many questions are raised about the NRTs, among them gender questions. While infertility for some couples and some women not in couples may be difficult and even painful, questions arise as to whether NRTs increase choices or not. Failure rates for in vitro fertilization range from 80 to 90 percent. Eligibility criteria for infertility treatments often range beyond the medical and into the social including marital status, sexual orientation, doctors' perceptions of the appropriateness of the couple and of the woman, and the decision to seek in vitro, and priority systems that place couples with no natural children as a couple ahead of those with natural children from previous marriages or relationships, or those with adopted or stepchildren. Control and access are determined almost completely by the medical profession, without any legislation to guide or govern use. In several provinces, the procedures are not convered by health insurance, meaning that only the better-off can afford access. The gender implications are many. Reproduction takes on factory production terminology: failure rates, production levels, successful outcomes, candidates for procedures, etc. Mothers are no longer mothers per se but genetic mothers, gestation mothers, surrogate mothers, rented wombs, etc. Fathers are no longer fathers, but sperm donors, contractors with surrogate mothers, biological fathers, etc. Emphasis is placed less on the joys and social responsibilities of parenting than on the biological child as output, as product. And, only perfect embryos are "harvested."

The NRTs are many things, but they tend toward aspects of Margaret Atwood's Republic of Gilead in her 1985 novel *The Handmaid's Tale*, where sexuality and reproduction are sharply controlled to raise a low birthrate and to quell social unrest, notably women's demands for equal rights. A whole class of women exists in Gilead whose sole purpose in life is reproduction — they are otherwise hidden and cannot see the world they live in. They exist as reproductive robots.

ties, whereas when you bake bread for the family, they eat it up and you must bake more! Such is the nature of housework. It is thus not surprising that it is undervalued and unseen by many, even those who could not live without its being done for them.

Housework has another vital element in structuring the relationship between women and men in society. Women are expected, more often than men, to patch up, keep things going, settle everyone down, and generally absorb tensions — all the while denying needs of their own. This places women in the social position, even outside the family, of caring for others as though it were their natural role. Within the family, women tend to be the shock absorbers for the wider society. Children and men are nurtured and made ready to enter the worlds of school and work without anxiety about unclean toilets and whether they will eat dinner.

Child care has some of the same elements of invisibility and presumed naturalness as housework, but more ideological baggage. Motherhood is seen as a central feature of women — natural, a full-time occupation, and a Noble Calling. As we saw earlier, the concept of motherhood as a lifetime occupation is very new in human history, but we act in our society as if it has always been so. These beliefs may push women into motherhood whether or not they as individuals think they would make good mothers. They also tend to deny the role of fatherhood in children's lives. It is interesting that the term *mothering* is taken to mean child rearing, while *fathering* is most often taken to mean the act of insemination. This example shows how deeply ingrained in our language is gender differentiation in family. Today this model is all the more obsolete in that the new reproductive technologies have the potential of redefining the meaning and practice of motherhood.

• VIOLENCE ON AN INTIMATE FRONTIER: GENDER ASPECTS

Family is portrayed as a warm, friendly place where one can be oneself and be safe. Yet overwhelming evidence exists that family can be a distinctly unsafe place, in fact the place most likely to be violent in all of society. More murders occur in families or among friends than among strangers. Family violence is not random — it is gendered. Women more than men are the victims, and children are very often victims, too.

In the past, the violence of men within the family was seen as their prerogative, a means of disciplining unruly wives, children, and animals. Legal history documents how much violence by men over women and children is acceptable. The term *rule of thumb* originated in a law permitting a husband to beat his wife without society being concerned, provided he used nothing wider than his thumb! Laws to protect animals from abuse preceded those to protect children from abusive family members.

The origins of family violence have been traced in many recent books. A significant factor is that children and women are considered to be possessions of the man to do with what he will. Many vestiges of this point of view continue into the present — for example, the belief that wives should be dutiful to husbands and, if they are not, can be disciplined. Similar is the belief that children are the private possessions of fathers to be treated as they see fit. Related to these notions are others such as the belief that reports of family violence are exaggerated by women and children seeking revenge against husbands; that violence cannot (and does not) occur in families; and that violence is justified when provoked. All these beliefs (and there are many others) seem to underlie the idea that the family and relations in it are rather like feudal relations between a master and his serfs — that family members are expected to be subservient to the master (husband/father).

More enlightened attitudes toward family violence and the profound harm it does to victims are beginning to develop. That these attitudes exist and have begun to affect public policies testifies, in no small part, to sociology's insights on gendered aspects of family life and how these tend to encourage violence. However, the ingrained understanding of gender difference that takes for granted the superiority of the male and provides the normative basis for violence remains a problem, as the recent findings on date rape illustrate (Box 10.2).

What do these studies reveal about gender? They suggest, first, that there is an area of sexual violence that is to a significant degree not highlighted nor well understood by research or by the general public. That date rape is widely experienced and yet not acknowledged fully is telling indeed. It is yet another hidden problem, like violence against wives (MacLeod, 1987) and sexual assault generally, that has been largely denied by the wider society, with the costs and the pain borne disproportionately by the women experiencing it. That date rape is so commonly explained away with the line "Boys will be boys," or as "young men sowing their wild oats" is to deny women the risk and pain they experience, in favour of a male definition of "fun" and adolescent experience. It further suggests that women are to be without choices in the matter of sexuality, that they are to be compliant in a dating script written totally by men, so that their "No" is not to be taken seriously.

Box 10.2

DATE RAPE/VIOLENCE

Recent attention to violence in dating relationships, including a November 1992 article in *Maclean's* ("Campus Confidential") on incidents on Canadian university campuses, reveals that society and the media are beginning to take seriously a gender issue of power and control. Publicized incidents have occurred at the University of Prince Edward Island, where an alleged rape of a woman student in the student residences was not made known by the university administration until some time after it had occurred, and at Queen's University, where signs appeared on a male student residence in response to a 1989 "No Means No" campaign to combat date rape on campus, saying, "No means kick her in the teeth," and "No means tie her up" ("Campus Confidential," 1992: 44).

It is now known (Aizenman and Kelly, 1988; Check and Lacrosse, 1988; Ward, 1991) that these incidents are far from isolated. One-fifth of high-school girls interviewed in Toronto in a 1988 survey (Check and Lacrosse, 1988) reported victimization in a dating relationship, and a 1987 survey of 1000 high-school girls in Nova Scotia (Mercer, 1987) found that 19 percent were forced into sex against their will. Ward (1991) reports that 34 percent of a U.S. sample of college women report having experienced unwanted sexual contact, and 20 percent have experienced unwanted sexual intercourse. Ward finds that unwanted sexual encounters occur most frequently in dorms (student residences), in off-campus apartments, and in fraternities, where 28 percent report having experienced unwanted sexual contact. It is further estimated that 1 in 10 high-school students experience violence in dating relationships (Flynn, 1987), and 2 to 3 out of 10 young women are involved in a relationship in which violence occurs (Volinets, 1989).

A significant proportion (84 percent) of women who had experienced sexual assault in college or university knew their attacker ("I Never Called It Rape," *Ms.*, 1988), with some 57 percent of the assaults occurring while on a date. Strikingly, date rape is among the least well reported of crimes, with only an estimated 1 percent of those assaulted reporting the assault to authorities. In approximately 75 percent of date rapes, the assailants had been drinking or taking drugs at the time (Ward, 1991).

Some fascinating studies have been done on the acceptability of sexual assault among university men. Malamuth (1981) found in a 1981 study of university and college students in Winnipeg and Los Angeles that an average of 35 percent of these young men would, indeed, force sexual relations on a woman, provided they could be assured of not being caught.

• THE FUTURE: GENDER IN THE FAMILY

Everything still encourages the young girl to expect fortune and happiness from some Prince Charming rather than to attempt by herself their difficult and uncertain conquest.

(de Beauvoir, 1952: 153)

The last two decades have seen profound changes in individual experiences of family life in Canada. Similarly, there have been changes in gender roles, expectations, and beliefs. The question posed here is what some of these contemporary changes hold in store for the future. This is not an abstract question; it is *your* future that is at stake. We all have some say in creating a future that we want. This process of creating our own futures works at both the individual and at the societal levels, and is fraught with serious constraints. Individuals are not entirely in charge of their own destinies, as they discover with age and wisdom, but very much shaped by the society in which they live.

At the level of society, family and gender are highly contested grounds. Far from being private, these issues and the challenges they pose are a source of policy concern and of emotional public debate. There is the contest between how we live and how some think we should live. There is the contest between the rights of individuals within families and the collective rights of families. There is the contest between family as ideal and family as lived reality. There is the question of what kinds of families are best, and for whom.

Making the process of looking into the future more difficult is that we really have remarkably little information about how people actually live in families — how they organize themselves, how housework and child care are delegated, who pays for what, and how power is actually structured. With this fundamental lack of basic information, it is difficult to challenge persistent myths about the family, and even more difficult to look toward the future.

It seems that the future, for the most part, holds more of the present. Quests for more egalitarian families are not likely to stop, or even diminish, despite the hopes of some advocacy groups that we return to the "old-fashioned" family of the past, where men were in charge and women were kept in their places. We are equally not likely to see a decline in the labour-force participation of women and of mothers of small children, since most families need the income of two wage-earners. Yet despite moves toward more egalitarian families, it is likely that people will continue to value family, as indeed they always have. Some extended family ties might be more strained as a result of increasing geographical mobility, but phones, faxes, and postal services allow maintenance of family ties, even at a distance. Families are likely to become even more contested on gender grounds in the future than they are now, as gender aspects of family become more widely understood. Issues like day care, elder care, domestic work, intimacy and sexuality, and reproductive choice will continue to be debated. Perhaps we shall move closer to a recognition that families matter to people, even if they also work. Our hope for shaping the future is to build on the firm understanding of how families are gendered and the implications of that understanding. Certainly the need to connect the family with the world of paid labour is essential for any understanding of the gendered nature of our social world.

GENDER AND DIVERSITY

Canadian society is complex and diverse, and this diversity extends to gender. It is abundantly clear that there are no "generic" women or "generic" men. There are, in fact, substantial differences among women and substantial differences among men. These differences are socially constructed, stratified, and therefore sociologically relevant.

Other chapters in this text examine the implications of these socially constructed differences on class, race and ethnicity, and age. How do these distinctions relate to gender? Patriarchal societies are by their very nature hierarchical; they involve the rule of some over others. Under patriarchy, males are generally superordinate to females and male privilege is preserved, but as well, *older* males are generally superordinate to *younger* males; and some *groups* are superordinate to other groups. Consequently, there are *many* inequities and a complex of superordinate and subordinate relations in patriarchal societies (Abu-Laban, 1993). These socially created and socially legitimated disparities intersect with one another. Thus, gender inequities interact with other social constructions/identities such as race and ethnicity, class, and sexual orientation. As a consequence, gender prerogatives as well as gender burdens are differentially experienced. Ageism, racism, classism, heterosexism are not simply added to the oppression of sexism, incrementally layering into doubled or tripled oppression. Rather, these are interactive. To experience racism is to experience a *distinctive form* of subordination and oppression. When racism interacts with gender, a quite different pattern emerges (Abu-Laban, 1993). The following examples illustrate the importance of this variability.

• GENDER AND RACE/ETHNICITY

For people who experience multiple forms of oppression, there may be competing identifications and divided loyalties. During the widely televised 1991 U.S. Senate confirmation hearings regarding the appointment of Judge Clarence Thomas to the Supreme Court, the conflict between race and gender was apparent. Professor Anita Hill charged Thomas with sexual harassment. Both Hill and Thomas are African-American. Hill was criticized by some African-Americans for pushing a "woman's issue" and "pulling a brother down" (Gillespie, 1993: 80), instead of closing ranks against the (white) oppressor and supporting Thomas's case for confirmation, regardless. In this example, the hierarchies of race and gender are seen as competing. Giving support to "our men" is often emphasized by oppressed ethnocultural or national groups, and women who push "their" issues may be seen as devaluing issues important to "the race" or "the nation," as these are defined by patriarchy.

Another issue faced by women generally is the objectification of their bodies through the mass media and the tyrannical presentation of a culturally standardized notion of "beauty." This airbrushed, sometimes computer-redesigned ideal sets physical standards that are unobtainable by most women. But there is also an ethnic/racial bias in this authoritative beauty ideal, which compounds the problem for visible minority women. Caucasians are a privileged racial group in Canadian society, and the predominant advertising imagery reflects the status of the dominant group with idealized models who are tall and slim, with fair skin and light hair and eyes. This sets an ethnocultural racial standard that is northern European and excludes most of the world's women. Women frequently diet, groom, and purchase products to imitate this consumer icon. Visible minority women, specifically, may use hair straighteners, skin lighteners, or cosmetic surgery (to alter epicanthic eye folds, body shape, or nose) in order to partially "erase" signs of racial or ethnic origin that are implicitly discredited by the media.

The interaction between sexism and racism is reflected painfully when considering minority and majority racial or ethnic relations in Canadian society. For example, aboriginal women can experience forms of sexual harassment provoked by their dual visibility as women and as a distinguishable minority. "As victims, we carry the burden of our memories; of pain inflicted on us, of violence done before our eyes to those we loved, of rape, of sexual assaults, of beatings, of death" (Sugar and Fox, 1990: 8). The devastating interaction of sexism and racism is illustrated in the tragic case of a young Cree high-school student in The Pas, Manitoba. In 1971, Helen Betty Osborne was abducted by four men, sexually assaulted, and murdered. The Report of the Aboriginal Justice Inquiry of Manitoba notes that these men had been cruising for sex — purportedly looking for a "squaw." Helen Betty Osborne was kidnapped because she was a woman *and* native. The Justice Commission notes, "She fell victim to vicious stereotypes of ignorance and aggression — it is evident the men who abducted Osborne believed that young Aboriginal girls were with no human value beyond sexual gratification" (Manitoba, 1991: 52). This callous attitude seems evident in the fact that although the identity of the murder suspects was widely known in the white community of The Pas by the fall of 1972 (Manitoba, 1991: 95) there was a *sixteen-year delay* before these suspects were ever brought to trial. The Manitoba Aboriginal Justice Inquiry concluded that this unprecedented delay was attributable to both sexism and racism.

In sum, gender is not static, but intersects with other social constructions/identities. These intersections take place in a shared arena and produce complex effects that are only beginning to be explored (Abu-Laban, 1993). Both dominant and oppressed groups are affected by the intersecting and interacting nature of gender, race/ethnicity, class, age, and sexual orientation. The resulting differences must be acknowledged at the same time that similarities of experience are recognized. There is a reality in these claims that needs to be addressed and explained at the larger level by theory itself (see Chapter 1).

KNOWLEDGE/CULTURAL CONSTRUCTION

What is known about society is filtered by who is doing the observing and by the means used for observing. This may perhaps seem obvious, but it is quickly forgotten when knowledge is seen as "scientific." Gender is a social construct, as well as the means by which sociologists conceptualize the social world so that it becomes comprehensible. Yet people act as if the social construct were real, and they give it reality by their actions. This is what sociologists call a self-fulfilling prophecy. At the same time, sociology may help cement that prophecy by "scientifically" endorsing as unchangeable what is in fact socially and historically variable.

Socially constructed concepts grow out of the need of society and of sociologists, theorists as well as researchers, to understand particular social phenomena. What attracts the attention of sociologists may be something that is important in a particular historical period, or something that they think matters. Gender has mattered in our society in the past, and still does. Thus, it is not surprising that gender has received a good deal of attention in sociology — not all of it valuable by today's standards.

• WHOSE KNOWLEDGE?

Those with the opportunity and freedom to spend their lives thinking and writing have been largely male. This is still true today. Clearly, not all males in the past have been sufficiently well off that they could afford not to grow crops or raise animals, make goods or produce services. Only those in an elite group have had the chance to think full time, to write, and to publish their writings. It is, then, the elite males in society who have asked questions about society and about how gender works in society. Not surprisingly, their questions may not be those posed by members of other socioeconomic groups or by women, in the past or today. For example, many of the sociologists at the turn of the 19th century accepted the idea that because a woman's brain was smaller than a man's her mental abilities would be poorer and college education, for example, would be wasted on a woman. Indeed, advanced education as well as paid labour could be dangerous to the woman and the nation's health because the mental and physical effort required would drain her strength and make her less fit reproductively. U.G. Weatherly (1909) published an article in the *American Journal of Sociology* entitled "How Does the Access of Women to Industrial Occupations React on the Family?" His answer was that the reaction was negative, in fact possibly producing "race suicide" as a result of their weakened reproductive capabilities.

What we see, how we interpret it, and how that knowledge ultimately fits into a larger framework is coloured by a number of factors, patriarchy among them. If, for example, males are thought to be the creators of art, science, and society, it is unlikely that women's roles in creativity and in society will be noticed. So, when sociologist Jessie Bernard asked scientists to name the top ten scientists in each of their fields, almost all named men. When Bernard, who knew many of the leaders in these fields, mentioned the names of several leading women scientists, the respondents agreed that they should be included, but that they had not thought of them. Similarly, artistic genius is thought to be a male attribute, so that when the work of a woman artist is brought forward as great art, it is usually judged as good "for a woman" but not, of course, approaching the greatness of her male contemporaries or male artists of the past. In addition, a woman's artistic work is often seen as a substitute for maternity. As the sculptor Reg Butler suggested "I am quite sure that the vitality of many female students derives from frustrated maternity" (quoted in Parker and Pollock, 1981: 7).

• FEMINIST QUESTIONS

Because knowledge is socially constructed, it is not static. New questions are posed by new scholars and people with different vantage points on society. Feminist sociology examines how knowledge, particularly our understanding of gender, needs constant reassessing in light of new perspectives, data, and theories. Feminist sociology has emphasized that the production of knowledge of any sort, but perhaps social science knowledge even more, is not distanced from society, does not exist in an "ivory tower." The questioning of received wisdoms on the part of feminist scholars and activists has had interesting spinoffs for men, as the fledgling men's movement attests (Box 10.3). Feminists themselves have subjected their own work and understanding to questioning and revision. The current discussions of the "white" characteristics of feminist knowledge production and the criticisms of the structural reforms sought by feminists that have often been more beneficial to educated, white, middle-class women than to women generally, illustrate this approach. For example, Ng (1988: 202) points out that the demand for equal rights for work of equal value was "defined in terms of white middle class women's perspective and priority" and as "immigrant women's locations in society are different as a result of their unequal treatment under the law and in the labour market, their demands have been different." In reality, ideas and knowledge are important tools in serving the interest of those who have power. For example, if girls are taught, on the basis of what is supposedly known about women's abilities, that they cannot do mathematics or physics as well as boys, they may not try as hard and thus not do as well. Academic disciplines that assume that women cannot perform as well as men may be less

Box 10.3

THE MEN'S MOVEMENTS

The development of women's movements in the 1960s was followed by the formation of men's movements in the 1970s. The beginnings of the men's movements were tentative and concentrated initially on thinking about what it means to be a man in our society and what this also means for women. Like the beginnings of the women's movements, the initial focus was on consciousness raising, supplemented by academic books and articles on the nature of the male role (see, for example, Fasteau, 1974; Pleck and Sawyer, 1974). Pleck (1989: 591) indicates that many of the men involved in the movements in the early years were criticized as "inadequate in their masculinity, guilt-ridden dupes of feminism, or discontented homosexuals." The first National Conference on Men and Masculinity was held in 1975.

In the 1980s two separate perspectives in the men's movements became apparent. Fiebert (1987) describes the two perspectives as the "promasculinist" and the "profeminist" camps. The promasculinists focus on the personal lives of men and especially on the harmful stereotypical traits socially assigned to men in our society. Men, like women, are seen as victims of gender role prescriptions, and the focus is generally on supporting men's rights, especially fathers' rights in relation to the legal system. Generally, the promasculinist groups support changes that would end sexism, but they also tend to see feminists as male-bashers and they give the issue of homophobia little attention.

A more recent promasculinist spinoff has been the "wild man" movement. The focus here is on spiritual healing achieved through the release of the primal "wild man" buried inside civilized man. Mythology, such as the Iron John story in poet Robert Bly's (1990) work, is an important part of the therapy and rituals the groups use to heal the alienation men experience because of the absence of fathers, the attacks of feminists, and the generally oppressive nature of the occupational world. A key feature of the movement is the belief that only men can initiate men into manhood. This is an interesting return to the idea of the "men's house" and the various warrior cults and their initiation ceremonies.

The profeminist groups, exemplified by the National Organization for Changing Men, formed in 1983, are "profeminist and gay-affirmative," open to men and women, and committed to the "broad goal of social and personal change" (Kimmel and Messner, 1989: 597). The focus of the profeminist groups is on the social and cultural structures of patriarchy that reward a few privileged men (white, educated, heterosexual) but penalize women and other men. Although the profeminists endorse personal change as important in the eradication of sexism, they are also more concerned than the promasculinist groups with promoting revolutionary change in the structure of society. These groups align themselves with the feminist movements and point out that joining together for change is essential, because as long as patriarchal structures remain intact, no amount of consciousness raising on the part of men will effect significant, permanent change. As Brod (1989: 603) points out, "male problems are the other side of the coin and are inseparable from male privilege" so that an awareness of the limitations of the male role should promote a "feminist political identity" among men.

Whatever the stance taken on the question of men's gender roles, it is clear that effective change for an equitable society must include the efforts of both women and men. It is also clear that changes will occur, albeit slowly, perhaps, because no one who has had a taste of freedom willingly turns back the clock.

attractive to women, thus seeming to substantiate the belief in women's lesser abilities. Similarly, if sociology accepts without question the idea that the family is women's natural area of specialization, then the fact that men may put less energy into family and more into work is seen as natural and right and, again, the "justness" of this division of labour is supported. These ideas were, however, propagated at a particular time in history when it seemed that they served the needs of society best. But it is easy to forget that such ideas are to a large extent ideological rather than real, and that they are not necessarily universal.

• CULTURAL CONSTRUCTION

Ideas are taken to be real, especially by those not in a position to assess their scientific merit, because of the way in which they are embedded in cultural constructions. **Culture** refers to collective normative understandings and beliefs, which are symbolized in cultural constructions. Such constructions involve the artifacts of everyday life as well as those that are set apart from the everyday and labelled "Art" or "Culture." One of the important ways in which the symbolic representation of beliefs and values is effected is through images.

• IMAGES AND GENDER

The production of images has always been closely connected with the exercise of power. It is no accident that some of the most significant images in the Western art tradition are religious. Church hierarchies have always known about the power of the image as a means to legitimate the power of the church and to control the ideas and values of the faithful. (One of the forms of protest against the dominance of the Catholic Church on the part of Protestant dissidents was the destruction of images in the churches. "Images," whether in the form of videos, film, books, or art remain targets of religious groups. However, the ability to wipe out the offending motes is considerably more difficult in our society than it was for the Luthers and Calvins of previous eras.)

We are a society that is inundated with images. Advertising is a prime example. The advertising industry is in the business of persuasion and their product is designed to break down consumer resistance. It is because of this that the manner in which gender is portrayed in the images produced is important. In general, advertising images of women and men reinforce the cultural assumptions of a patriarchal society.

A key to the relationship between images and power rests with the fact that in our society it is the masculine gaze that is socially permitted. Berger (1972) maintains that the masculine gaze is a voyeuristic gaze that looks at women as Other, as possessions. The depiction of women is thus related to masculine desire, but women very often will "watch themselves being watched" and seek to conform to the needs and desires the image presents to them. That is, there is complicity on the part of women in their symbolic representations. Many women look at images of women in terms of what they mean to men and what, therefore, their own conformity to the image might mean in their relationships with men. Men confront their images in a different manner. It is not primarily how they appear to women that is important, but how they situate themselves in regard to other men. There is a different relationship of power that operates in the imaging of men as opposed to women.

• GENDER AND STEREOTYPES

Images, especially advertising images, are constructed stereotypically. Stereotypes are the broad, composite, normative depictions of particular types. As such, stereotypes are not necessarily negative. For example, stereotypes are important in childhood socialization. Stereotypes become problematic when they encourage persistent inequities and where subordinate groups have little or no control over their own stereotypical depiction — that is, the fixed, general patterns are constructed and interpreted in power terms. A brief examination of the nature of masculine body images in recent advertising illustrates this point.

The images of men in our society have to do with their economic/political status. In this context the body image is important. Traditionally, the association of power and status has been represented by the degree to which the individual male could distance himself from the muscular body of the working man. George Orwell, in his essay "The Lower Classes Smell," points to the important class division that the muscular, working man's body represented. More recently it would seem that the difference has been eliminated with the emphasis on personal fitness and body care. But the lean, mean machine of the corporate manager is very different from the muscular body of the construction worker. The high-status masculine body is a designer-built body that takes shape outside the occupational context.

The presentation of self is accomplished through our attention to stereotypical images. This applies to both men and women — but women have generally been obliged to devote more attention to their presentation than men because of the relative power imbalances in a patriarchal society. Women have been encouraged to make external conformity to a fashionable norm a central part of their existence. And women have often been enthusiastic about meeting the fashionable norm — for example, rib removal for the fashionable Edwardian hourglass figure, and, more recently, liposuction and, of course, the range of possible transformations that plastic surgeons can offer.

THE FUTURE SOCIOLOGY OF GENDER RELATIONS

• WOMEN'S MOVEMENTS

A sociology of gender relations developed out of the resurgent women's movements of the 1960s. The gender issues addressed in the academic context had, and continue to have, their origin in the pragmatic realities of women's lives. In other words, it was not the specialists in social relations who realized the significance of gender, but grassroots activists who provided the basis for the subsequent theoretical and empirical investigations of gender relations in sociology as well as other academic disciplines. While the relationship between academic feminists and grassroots activists has not always been congenial, the ongoing connection of scholarship and pragmatic politics has produced an impressive body of interdisciplinary research and significant practical advances toward gender equity. However, the advances on both the practical, day-to-day front as well as in the academic context remain fragile gains as long as women are excluded from social power. As Dorothy Smith (1987: 19–20) has pointed out, the "making and dissemination of the forms of thought we make use of to think about ourselves and our society are part of the relations of ruling and hence originate in positions of power." Generally, women are excluded from these positions of power and the result is that the "concerns, interests, and experiences forming 'our' culture are those of men in positions of dominance whose perspectives are built on the silence of women (and of others)."

• ANTIFEMINISM

The silence of women can no longer be taken for granted. In fact, women have been extremely vocal in the last decades of the 20th century, much to the chagrin of some men and also some women. An example of the latter is the organization that calls itself R.E.A.L. Women, which maintains a "separate but equal" position on gender relations and insists that women's unique biology fits them for child care and housework, just as men's superior intellectual abilities and physical strength fit them for the domination of the public sphere. As a result, the movement opposes any measures that would increase gender equality in the public sphere and adopts what it calls a "pro-family" position. It insists that homosexuality is a threat to the family and publicly subsidized day care should be replaced by child care tax credits to assist women to stay at home and care for their children. The antifeminism of this organization is an important part of the backlash that may jeopardize the gains made by feminists in the past, but a more significant aspect of a backlash is represented in the violent reactions of antifeminist men who resent what they see as women's usurpation of their rights and privileges. With the cry that "You're all a bunch of feminists, and I hate feminists," a gunman shot fourteen women engineering students in Montreal in December 1989. This act may have been the act of a demented mind, but it was nurtured in the patriarchal context of gender inequity and oppression.

• A FEMINIST FUTURE

Future progress toward an egalitarian society, the general goal of the women's movements, requires both the maintenance of practical gains — such as legislated pay equity, the inclusion of gender equality rights in the Canadian Charter of Rights and Freedoms, the establishment of rape crisis centres and battered women's shelters — as well as the maintenance of a general commitment to feminism that will ensure continued progress toward the goal of equality. In this regard, a troubling issue is the reaction on the part of many young women summed up in the phrase "I am not a feminist, but . . ." Many of the gains of the women's movements are taken for granted by those who fail to realize the need for a continued struggle. For many women this is because they have yet to confront what Steinem (1983: 17) called the "four big, radicalizing experiences of a woman's life: joining the labour force and discovering how it treats women; getting married and discovering it is not usually an equal partnership; having children and finding out who takes care of them and who does not; and aging."

Whatever the particular features of future gender relations, it is clear that the sociological descriptions and explanations can no longer ignore gender and assume that the "world according to Man" includes women. One of the strengths of academic feminism is its interdisciplinary character and the ties many of its practitioners hold with community-based organizations. It is these characteristics that help to maintain both the relevance of the research to the movements' general emancipatory intentions and ensure that any future sociological work must take gender into account.

In order to fully incorporate gender into sociological research the first, fundamental step is, in Dorothy Smith's words, "to begin where women are in society, with the everyday worlds of our experience, and to be prepared to reconceptualize the accepted concepts, frameworks, and theories" (1987: 4).

SUMMARY

- Gender has often been stereotypically presented in the classic sociological accounts. This is partly a result of confounding biological status with culturally developed ideas about masculinity and femininity.
- Patriarchy refers to the social assumption of the supremacy of males over females. It is a concept that involves both structural features as well as subjective, psychological understandings.

- Sex, gender, and sexuality must be analytically distinguished in order to understand the range of behaviours and beliefs that generate masculinity and femininity for any society or culture.
- The case of transsexuality illustrates the complex interactions between social constructions of gender and biological sex markers.
- The investigation of family types and formations taking gender into account provides a clearer exposition of the nature of family relationships and their changes over time.
- In examining family while taking gender into account, the importance of the division of labour with regard to housework and child care for women and men is made clear.
- The social assumptions about family power relations and power relations between men and women provide the basis for understanding the nature of violence and date rape.
- The culturally and historically specific assumptions made about paid labour and gender provide insights into the gendered inequities of the world of work.
- The social construction of knowledge and the production of stereotypical images in a variety of contexts illustrate both the pervasiveness of gender stereotyping and the cultural relativity of such constructions and images.

KEY CONCEPTS

Alyha

Aphenotypic

Arapesh

Biological determinism

Child care

Couvade

Culture

Essentialism

Family formation

Gender

Hwame

Nadle

Sex

Social constructionism

Socialization

Transsexual

REVIEW QUESTIONS

1. What is patriarchy and how does this concept relate to our understanding of family and family formations?
2. What are some of the examples used in this chapter to illustrate the social constructionist approach to the study of gender?
3. Why are housework and child care the major responsibilities for women in our society? What are the possibilities for any change in this division of labour?

4. What do you think the future holds in Canada with respect to change in gender relations? More equity? Less?

5. What roles do you think new movements such as the men's movements or the fathers' rights movement might have on future gender relations?

6. How are stereotypical gender relations normatively perpetuated? What are the possibilities for change in this regard?

7. With so much upheaval in the workforce in Canada today, what do you think might be the future of equity policies in the workplace and in public policy?

Age, the Aged, & An Aging Society

Sharon McIrvin Abu-Laban, Susan A. McDaniel, and Herbert C. Northcott

Age, the Aged, and an Aging Society

INTRODUCTION

Age is a key component of social structure and a basic organizing principle in all human societies. Age has always been a variable in sociological analysis and theory, but only recently has aging been analyzed as a process, important both in the individual's life cycle and in society itself. Why is interest increasing in the sociology of aging? There are several answers. One is the increasing awareness of how little we know about people's lives in the older years: how people adjust to the death of a spouse; what roles the aged play in families; whether retirement provides welcome leisure time. Furthermore, there are many more questions than answers. What is the relationship between population aging and demands on the health-care and pension systems? Are the challenges of aging different for men than for women?

In addition, the Canadian **age structure** (the proportional distribution of different age groups in the society) is changing. The proportion of people aged 65 and over has shifted from 4 percent of the population in 1910 to 11.6 percent in 1991. The proportion is projected to continue to increase well into the 21st century. This shifting of the age structure has implications for a wide range of concerns. As the proportion of elders in a society increases, so does the incidence of chronic health conditions, raising issues regarding health-care practice and policy. There are also implications for labour-force participation, economic security, pensions, and the general distribution of resources and opportunities between the younger and the older. As families have increasing numbers of aged members, new issues emerge concerning family dynamics, the status of elders, and responsibilities between the generations.

This chapter gives an overview of age as an organizing principle in society, together with selected concepts, theories, and methodological issues in research on aging. It examines major demographic characteristics of older Canadians and selected implications of the changing population structure, and discusses some of the important social policy implications.

AGE: AN ORGANIZING PRINCIPLE AND SOCIAL CONSTRUCT

Age differentiation refers to distinctions made on the basis of age, which then become the basis for differences in the allocation of social roles and resources. Socially created age distinctions (e.g., adult versus child; teen versus adult; aged versus middle-aged; or older versus younger) can reflect important differences in power, privilege, and prestige. Specialists in the sociology of aging are particularly interested in examining the social construction of age and the social consequences of age differentiation.

Our culture is regulated by clocks and calendars, yet the meanings of age and of aging are not clear-cut. We have multiple, changing, and sometimes conflicting conceptions of age. Age is not simply a biological phenomenon; rather it is both a biological and a social process. Old age to a justice of the Supreme Court may be very different from old age to an athlete (see Box 11.1). Further, even **biological aging** itself can be influenced by social variables. For example, in Canada, since the turn of the century, the average age at the onset of menarche has *decreased* from age 16 to 12, while the average age at menopause has *increased* from age 45 to 52. In other words, sociohistorical factors have affected biological aging, and this is reflected in an extension of the potential childbearing years of the average Canadian woman.

In Canada, as in other industrialized societies with systematic recordkeeping, there is a preoccupation with **chronological age,** the passing of calendar time. Most official forms in Canadian society require information on chronological age or date of birth. Age is of such importance in Canada that when older people do not have official proof of age (because records were never kept or the records are missing) **age tribunals** may be established to assign approximate age by hearing historical evidence and personal testimonies. Through this technique, government officials can formally assign a birthdate to satisfy bureaucratic routine and document age eligibility for

Box 11.1

THE TIME OF THE HEAVYWEIGHT CHAMP

Our definitions of age and old age are socially created. As such they can vary by time, place, and circumstance.

At the end . . . the man who would be king forever [three times World Heavyweight Champion] slumped on his stool, both eyes swollen slits, . . . what had once been a redwood . . . was just an old, dead shell, rotting and lifeless on the inside, rendered impotent by the termites of age . . . just a burned out old fighter who, like so many before him, didn't know when his time had run out . . . Muhammad Ali [age 38] had, at last, accepted the inevitable.

Source: Bill Lyon, "Battered Ali Ushered Out," *The Edmonton Journal,* October 31, 1980, p. D1.

special benefits. Age tribunals have been of particular help to some foreign-born elders, as well as to people born in more remote parts of Canada.

• AGE CATEGORIES

Conceptions of relevant age groups reflect specific cultural and historical contexts. Social historian Philippe Ariès (1962) argues that the conception of childhood is relatively recent.

> In medieval society the idea of childhood did not exist; this is not to suggest that children were neglected, forsaken or despised. The idea of childhood is not to be confused with affection for children; it corresponds to an awareness of the particular nature of childhood, that particular nature which distinguishes the child from the adult, even the young adult. In medieval society this awareness was lacking. That is why, as soon as the child could live without the constant solicitude of his mother, his nanny or his cradle-rocker, he belonged to adult society (Ariès, 1962: 128).

Similarly, Frank Musgrove (1964) argues that only from the mid-17th century on has there been a conceptualization of a period *between* childhood and adulthood. The social creation of the period known as adolescence has resulted in the increasing *exclusion* of youth from the world of adults. Musgrove argues that adolescence results in adolescents being denied adult rights and responsibilities, obligated to undertake years of training in segregated institutions (i.e., schools), and faced with a deferral of adulthood and with reduced opportunities to move into responsible leadership positions in society.

In contemporary developed societies, somewhat arbitrary definitions of old age have emerged. Age 65, designated in 1889 by the German chancellor Bismark as his determining point for receipt of old age pensions, is still a common convention in industrialized nations today (Myles, 1989). Mandatory retirement at a specific age is now being challenged in the courts as an example of age discrimination and a violation of human rights.

For researchers, it is increasingly common to differentiate between the **young-old** (aged 65 to 74), the **middle-old** (aged 75 to 84), and the **old-old** (85 and older) (Chappell et al., 1986). It is the old-old that is the fastest-growing age group in Canadian society. One consequence of this is that increasingly, among Canada's senior citizens (those 65 and over), there are many families where both parent and child are over the age of 65.

• AGE ADVANTAGES AND DEFERENCE

Advanced age or being the oldest can be of societal advantage. For example, the **rule of primogeniture** was a feudal European rule of inheritance whereby the property or title passed on to the first-born son or eldest child. While practices of primogeniture are rare in contemporary industrialized societies, in some developing societies relationships are structured on the basis of birth order. Traditionally, among the Yoruba people of southwestern Nigeria, **age deference** practices require respectful language to be used to recognize seniority.

Sometimes the cumulative advantages of the aged result in gerontocracy. **Gerontocracy** refers to rule by the old. Some societies (e.g., the indigenous peoples of Ethiopia, Kenya, and Australia) have been characterized as gerontocracies. But in fact, even in these societies patterns of control by elders are not evenly distributed. They often reflect the rule of *some* old men, and not many old women. Thus the dynamics of power reflect interpersonal political competition and selection as well as the intersection of the systems of age stratification and gender stratification.

Western industrial societies have elements of gerontocracy in that some spheres, such as judicial and ecclesiastical hierarchies, tend to be dominated by the aged, generally aged men. The average age of a justice on the Supreme Court of Canada is 59 (Canadian Parliamentary Guide, 1990), while the average age of a man selected to be Pope in this century is 61 (*World Almanac,* 1991). An interesting exception to the pattern of age and political leadership is that revolutionary leaders are often much younger. For example, Cuban leader Fidel Castro was in his early 30s when he took power in the Cuban Revolution in 1959, and Métis leader Louis Riel was in his mid-20s when he emerged as a central figure in the Red River Rebellion that led eventually to the creation of the province of Manitoba.

Although Canadian society emphasizes equality of opportunity, nevertheless, the advantages of seniority for some aged persons co-exist with disadvantages for many others. The obverse side to advanced age and advantaged status is found in attitudes of ambivalence and even hostility toward the aged. Such attitudes are neither historically new nor culturally unique. Ancient Egyptian hieroglyphic drawings document ambivalent attitudes toward the aged and the process of aging, as do early Roman plays and the Old Testament.

Ageism refers to attitudes, beliefs, or practices that favour or disadvantage one age group over another, or ascribe purported group characteristics to individuals, simply because of their chronological age. These prejudicial attitudes or discriminatory behaviours may be directed toward individuals in any age group. For example, both the young and the old can find themselves excluded from educational or training opportunities (see Box 11.2), housing, employment, or marriage opportunities ("look at that cradle snatcher").

AGE NORMS: INTERNS AND PILOTS

 Box 11.2

Faculty of Medicine Admission and Academic Regulations

Personal requirements. While admission to the M.D. program is granted mainly on the basis of academic standing, the lack of essential *personal qualities* in an applicant may be deemed sufficient cause for refusal of admission.

Age is a consideration for admission to the Faculty. Students who will be *28 years of age or older* at the time of application for admission are advised to consult with the Dean before starting pre-medical studies.

Source: *80–81 Calendar,* The University of Alberta, p. 122.2.1 (italics added).

Air Canada Admits Young Pilots Sought

Toronto (CP) — Air Canada prefers not to hire anyone over 27 because older pilots are less adaptable and less competent, an airline executive said Thursday . . . [Captain Keith] Sanderson said that while the airline didn't deny jobs to older applicants, it "has shown preference to younger pilots when available. We found it enhances safe operations."

Source: *The Edmonton Journal,* February 22, 1980.

Ageism, like racism and sexism, reflects closed thinking and perpetuates inequalities and stereotypes. In our youth-oriented culture, ageism is reflected in beliefs that the aged are typically senile, live in nursing homes, or are uneducable ("you can't teach an old dog new tricks"); or that aging employees are prone to accidents, sickly, and often absent. In fact, research evidence points to the errors of all of the above beliefs. The vast majority of Canadians 65 and over — 91 percent — live outside institutional settings. Older employees are *more* reliable and less accident prone than other employees. Elders do have problems, but these are usually overemphasized. Given the prevalence of negative attitudes toward older age, it is not surprising that many studies have documented a reluctance on the part of adults to identify themselves as "old." In essence, by avoiding age labels the aging person may attempt to "pass" as younger in our rather ageist society.

Interestingly, some of the negative views regarding older people may be linked to hostility to older women — an interaction of ageism and sexism (see Box 11.3). Part of this interaction may be associated with the cultural emphasis on physical appearance, particularly for women (see Chapter 10). The particular emphasis on the appearance of youth for females is reflected in television programming, where research has shown an underrepresentation of middle-aged and older women in key roles and a typical pattern of age-asymmetric romantic liaisons where the male character is considerably older than the female.

Thus, in many ways, aging is less socially damaging to men than to women. This has been characterized as part of the **double standard of aging**. Women's appearance, status, and self-concept are more dependent on a youthful image, while for men power and money are more likely to take precedence (Abu-Laban, 1981, 1984). As will be seen throughout this chapter, gender differences are important considerations in the study of aging.

Box 11.3

AGEISM AND SEXISM: A DOUBLE BIND

Women often bear a heavy burden in old age. Ageist attitudes affect younger women as well. The double bind of ageism and sexism is illustrated in the following court cases.

September 2, 1976, Ontario Provincial Court. Judge Vincent McEwan attributed the unreliability of a 48-year-old woman's testimony to female menopause. Barbara Szabo had brought charges against Paiva Cabral for indecent exposure. In questioning during the trial, the Judge asked the complainant about her age. Later he dismissed the charge on the basis of a mistake in identifying Cabral. "There comes a certain stage in a woman's life, some point around that age, where the evidence is not too reliable."

September 2, 1977, British Columbia Provincial Court. Upset because his longtime girl friend, aged 23, had broken off their relationship, Anthony Tourangeau kicked in the back door of her house. Palming a knife, he forced her into a bedroom and locked the door, later ripping out the telephone cord after [her] terrified friend had tried to call the police. His previous record included breaking and entry, theft, possession of stolen property, possession of a narcotic, driving while disqualified, fraud, common assault, and forcible seizure armed with a knife. Judge Les Bewley sentenced him to six months.

> I could give him five years but I don't think under the circumstances of this case I'd be entitled to . . . he got mixed up with a silly little bunch of girls . . . a bunch of clucking females running around and they're all so scared they have to call the police . . . they're a free-floating type of female, young for their age, very nubile, very attractive surely, but . . . still impressionable, still stupid. You know women don't get much brains before they're 30 . . .

Source: *Chatelaine*, March 1978, pp. 58, 118.

• AGE NORMS AND EXPECTATIONS

Chronological aging has social ramifications. Although children may be asked "How old are you?" this is not a polite question in adult society. While children may tend to *overstate* their age, adults in middle age are more likely to *understate* their age. People middle-aged or older are generally pleased to be told that they look younger than their chronological age; children and adolescents often like to be told they look older. In general, youth and middle age are valued more than old age.

Bernice Neugarten (1968) has argued that people operate with internal **social clocks,** socio-cultural expectations regarding the appropriate timing and sequencing of life transitions. It is these internal clocks that tell us whether we or others are "on time" or "off time." This sense of social timing is implied by such statements as "She married young," "He's a late bloomer," or "She's so young to be a professor." Self-assessments can be profoundly influenced by social judgments such as these. People may be told "It's time to settle down" or asked "You're still single?" To be too early or too late is to be "off time." The pressure to conform to age-based societal expectations can sometimes be onerous.

Age norms refer to generally agreed upon societal expectations regarding the behaviour appropriate for specific ages. Neugarten and her colleagues (1965) did a classic study in this area. Using a range of samples, they found a high degree of agreement on issues relating to the timing and sequencing of life events. The responses in the earlier study are an interesting contrast to the response from a replication study done twenty years later (Table 11.1). The wording of the origi-

Table 11.1

AGE RANGES FOR THE TIMING OF AGE-RELATED TRANSITIONS, LATE 1950S VERSUS LATE 1970S

Age-related transitions and events	Age range	Late 50s study: Percent who agree		Late 70s study: Percent who agree	
		Men	Women	Men	Women
Best age for a man to marry	20–25	80	90	42	42
Best age for a woman to marry	19–24	85	90	44	36
When most people should become grandparents	45–50	84	79	64	57
Best age for most people to finish school and go to work	20–22	86	82	36	38
When most men should be settled on a career	24–26	74	64	24	26
When most men hold their top jobs	45–50	71	58	38	31
When most people should be ready to retire	60–65	83	86	66	41
When a man has the most responsibilities	35–50	79	75	49	50
When a man accomplishes most	40–50	82	71	46	41
The prime of life for a man	35–50	86	80	59	66
When a woman has the most responsibilities	25–40	93	91	59	53
When a woman accomplishes most	30–45	94	92	57	48
A good-looking woman	20–35	92	82	33	24
A young man	18–22	84	83	29	22
A middle-aged man	40–50	86	75	41	47
An old man	65–75	75	57	52	37
A young woman	18–24	89	88	41	25
A middle-aged woman	40–50	87	87	49	50
An old woman	60–75	83	87	50	44

Source: Patricia M. Passuth, David R. Maines, and Bernice L. Neugarten, Age Norms and Age Constraints Twenty Years Later. Paper presented at the annual meeting of the Midwest Sociological Society, Chicago, 1984. As cited in Diane K. Harris, *Sociology of Aging*, 2nd ed. New York: Harpers, 1990.

nal questionnaire reflects biases prevalent in the United States in the late 1950s and is an example of sexism in research design (see Chapters 2 and 10). For example, the respondents were asked about the prime of life for a man, but there was no corresponding question regarding a woman. Similarly, respondents were asked the "best age" for men to be settled in careers, but this question was not asked for women, either. Finally, respondents were queried about a "good-looking" woman, but were not asked an equivalent question regarding a man. The contrasting responses from the late 1950s to the late 1970s suggest an increase in norm flexibility and illustrate that age norms vary by sociohistorical context. That is, people's assessments of a so-called best age to accomplish tasks in family, career, or other areas of life are contingent on the sociocultural context.

As people are exposed to an increasing proportion of elders, the diversity of the aging experience is likely to challenge many of the traditional stereotypes and normative expectations. Conversely, since aging has some disadvantages, increased exposure to the aged may generate further ambiguity and mixed feelings regarding aging and the aged. Age norms may be becoming more flexible and the boundaries between age groups more muted. However, norm change is not norm abolishment. Instead, society may be in the process of shifting from one set of age norms to another.

Research Design

Although the research methods used in the study of age, the aged, and aging are similar to those discussed in Chapter 2, the topic does raise some characteristic methodological issues, particularly the issue of the study design. Research that focuses on aging implies an examination of change over time. The question is which of two major research approaches to change and time best provides information about age and aging: the examination of alterations over time (**age change**), or of comparative characteristics at a common point in time (**age differences**)? An awareness of this question is critical to understanding and evaluating research evidence in aging.

Most research on aging is based on **cross-sectional research** that compares older people to younger people at the same point in time and often infers that differences between them are the result of age. Cross-sectional research is like a snapshot in time. A study on attitudes toward retirement conducted in the year 1994 with people in different age categories — comparing 20-year-olds, 40-year-olds, and 60-year-olds — is an example of cross-sectional research. Cross-sectional evidence can give information on age differences — "20-year-olds watch more rock videos than do 40-year-olds" — but it does not necessarily tell us about age *changes* because it does not follow the actual aging of a group of people as they move from ages 20 to 40 to 60.

In contrast, a **longitudinal** approach follows the same group of people over time and studies them systematically as they move from one chronological age to another — for example, from an initial study at age 20 to a restudy at age 30 and another at age 40. Longitudinal research is more expensive and time consuming, provides delayed rewards to researchers, and presents problems in keeping in contact with participants and in the interpretation of the findings. For these and other reasons it is done less often. However, longitudinal research is an improvement over cross-sectional research; it starts to give researchers an idea about **age effects** — emerging characteristics that can be traced directly to the effects of advancing age. Despite their problems, more longitudinal studies are being initiated today than in the past.

There are two other important considerations that researchers need to take into account: cohort differences and period effect.

Age, Cohort, and Period Effects

Age effects are the consequences of aging. **Cohort effects** refer to the consequences of membership in a particular cohort. The concept of **cohort** is important in the study of aging. It refers to a group of people who share a particular characteristic, usually that of being born in the same time period — for example, between 1970 and 1980.

Cohort effects, then, are usually seen as the consequences of being born at a certain time in history. Cohorts are arbitrary, researcher-created designations that have proven very useful as an aid to understanding age-linked phenomena. For example, Canadians born between 1900 and 1910 can be characterized as a specific cohort. If we compare the aging experiences of this group of Canadians with a second cohort, those born between 1930 and 1940, we find that the average timing of the typical sequences in their lives — formal education, marriage, birth of children, last child leaving home, widowhood — differs. Birth cohorts reflect the consequences of shifts in such things as values, opportunities, and environmental factors, as well as the effects of their own composition. The **baby-boom** cohort (those born between 1946 and 1966) has been disadvantaged because it has so many members in the labour market at the same time competing for an insufficient number of jobs. In contrast, Canadians born during the 1930s, a time of harsh economic circumstances when people had fewer children, found a more receptive labour market when they became young adults. This group had a much smoother transition from school to paid employment. The cohort concept alerts researchers to the distinctive characteristics and histories of each group. These are critical in understanding their aging.

The term **period effect** refers specifically to how historical periods influence age or a person's experience of a particular age. To be a young person in times of war may be very different from being young in times of peace. In addition, the social context of each war may differ. Canadians born between 1915 and 1924 were in their teens and 20s during World War II. In contrast, the cohort born between 1945 and 1954 was in its teens and 20s during the Vietnam protests. In both periods there were wars, but the degree of popular support and the level of popular dissent differed. Furthermore, during the Vietnam War, younger people were more likely to express dissent than were middle-aged or older persons. In other words, the period effect can be different for different cohorts.

Age, cohort, and period effects are difficult to untangle. Generally, cross-sectional data are ambiguous in that they fail to separate age and cohort effects. Longitudinal data are more useful in allowing age and cohort effects to be untangled.

THEORIES OF AGING

Theory and research are informed by one another. Evidence without explanation is insufficient, as is theory without supporting data. Theories attempt to explain aging, to answer when, how, and why. The sociological study of aging aims not only to describe but to explain the social patterns of aging. The complexity of age-linked issues has resulted in multiple theoretical approaches that are usually aimed at partial explanations rather than the totality of aging. Some of these theoretical approaches are derived from general sociological theory, and some are unique to the study of aging.

To give an overview of the attempts to understand and explain age-related social patterns, six theories will be discussed: activity theory; disengagement theory; continuity theory; the aged as a minority group; modernization theory; and the political economy of aging.

• ACTIVITY THEORY

The early research in social gerontology focused on questions regarding adaptation to the process of aging and to retirement. A key concern revolves around the question of what characterizes successful adjustment in older age. Researchers' attempts to define the well-adjusted elder were associated with two contrasting, yet similar theoretical approaches: activity theory and disengagement theory. Both were influenced by structural-functionalist theory (see Chapter 1). In the 1940s the noted sociologist Ernest Burgess characterized aging as a "roleless role." In his view, social roles are undefined in older age. There are no ground rules, implicit or explicit, for being a retired person, a widow, or widower. Since there are few shared conceptions of appropriate agedness, the process of aging is without signposts and is fraught with difficulties. Burgess's characterization of old age as a roleless role became a popular aphorism. Since there was an absence of normative guidelines, how could elders live well-adjusted lives? *Activity theory* (sometimes called *the substitution approach*) was the first scheme that seemed to answer this question. Havighurst et al. (1968) suggested that unless there are health problems, the older person and the middle aged have similar inclinations and social needs. Where age-related changes disturb health, income, occupation, or family relationships, replacements are needed and roles need to be realigned. Proponents of the activity approach argue that the best way for individuals to adjust to older age is to keep busy, carrying on the activities of the middle years.

Research evidence, however, doesn't lend full support to activity theory. The evidence is mixed, and the activity approach is criticized for failing to deal with the issue of the meaning of activity or inactivity. For instance, there is evidence to suggest that some older people value some decrease in activities (Kelly et al., 1987; Cutler and Hendricks, 1990). This approach also tends to ignore ways in which the aged may be blocked from social participation by finances, physical change, discrimination, or death of peers and kin.

• DISENGAGEMENT THEORY

Disengagement theory was first articulated in 1961 in *Growing Old: The Process of Disengagement,* a landmark book by Elaine Cumming and William E. Henry. Disengagement refers to a process of withdrawal from social involvements as an adaptation to age-related changes. Like the activity theory, disengagement theory is concerned with roles and activities, but it argues that it is beneficial for both society and the elder if an aging individual decreases levels of activity. In this perspective, society withdraws and curtails investment in those members who are closer to the end of their lives, starting the process of adjustment to the eventual loss of a member. Conversely, the individual who is aging, and thus presumably closer to death, reduces activity and finds more time to reflect, be introspective, and make meaning out of the years that have been lived and the few years remaining. The aging individual is preparing for the extinction of the self. Thus, the elder who reduces personal involvement is more likely to have a successful old age.

Disengagement theory has undergirded many research projects. As a functionalist approach it emphasizes equilibrium, tends to accept the status quo, and does not examine the extent to which the individual may be forced to disengage. Nor does it fully examine the cross-cultural applicability of its arguments. It is asserted that, at base, disengagement theory is untestable because it cannot be falsified (Hochschild, 1976) and, like activity theory, it neglects the importance of meaning. Behaviour that looks like disengagement to the researcher may be defined by the actor as engagement. Thus an older woman who takes an early retirement from paid employment may see this move less as withdrawal from social activity and more as freeing her time to pursue other active interests.

Much of the early research in gerontology focused on the micro (or individual) level of analysis using disengagement or activity frameworks. More recent research has moved from a focus on elder adjustment to an examination of issues relating to elder power or powerlessness.

• CONTINUITY THEORY

Continuity theory takes a position between the more extreme and opposing positions represented by activity theory and disengagement theory. Continuity theory, like disengagement theory, suggests that people often make changes in their lifestyles due to advancing age. Nevertheless, like activity theory, continuity theory suggests that people tend to maintain an interest and involvement in meaningful activities. Changes with advancing age are made as necessary, but these tend to be minimal or involve change from one related area to another. An aging person might have to give up competing in marathons, for example. However, rather than disengaging to the rocking chair, this person might take up walking and hiking.

• THE AGED AS A MINORITY GROUP

The early arguments suggesting that the aged could be seen as a minority group (see Rose, 1965) raised issues of discrimination and prejudice against the aged. In the sociological definition of the term, a *minority group* is a "group of people who because of their physical or cultural characteristics, are singled out from others in the society in which they live for differential and unequal treatment and who therefore regard themselves as objects of collective discrimination" (Wirth, 1945: 347). Comparing the aged with other deprived groups such as members of a visible minority, the economically disadvantaged, or the physically challenged, signals compassion as well as concern about righting wrongs (Abu-Laban and Abu-Laban, 1977). Early arguments focusing on the disadvantages of the aged compared the position of the aged to that of women in patriarchal societies (e.g., both are objects of prejudice and stereotyping, both are physically identifiable) and debated whether the social psychological aspects of subgroup membership and "sense of consciousness of kind" held by seniors were sufficient to qualify them as members of a minority group. More recently, these concerns have broadened from examining the disadvantages experienced by the aged to analyzing age-related benefits and the potential of **grey power**.

• MODERNIZATION THEORY

Modernization theory is a macro-level (societal) approach that looks at the relationship between societal change, modernization (or selected indicators of modernization such as industrialization and urbanism), and the position and status of elders. Cowgill and Holmes (1972) developed the first major articulation of the approach arguing that the status of older people declines with modernization and urbanization. They presented evidence to support their hypothesis from a comparative analysis of several different societies. Subsequent research has challenged these findings. For example, countries not yet "modernized" may have citizens who are "modern," yet researchers have not found that modernized individuals have more negative views on aging. Several researchers have suggested that modernization theory assumes a romanticized "before and after" vision of societal change (i.e., in times past and places distant elders fared better) that isn't supported by the research evidence. In other words, the status of the aged may be relatively unaffected by modernization. Alternatively, it has been suggested that the relationship between elder status and modernity may not be linear but instead curvilinear. That is, elders may have high status at rudimentary stages of societal development, lose status with industrialization, and rise in status with post-industrial development. The assumptions undergirding modernization theory, although sharply challenged by the research evidence, continue as part of popular and, in particular, political discourse.

• THE POLITICAL ECONOMY OF AGING

The *political economy of aging* looks at the larger political, economic, and historical processes that produce age inequities (see Chapter 1). It reflects a conflict approach that asks which age group, class, or interest group benefits, directly or indirectly, from social policies such as mandatory retirement. By looking at age-related policy, prioritization of needs, and allocation of government resources in the context of social, political, and economic forces, the political economy approach argues that the dependencies and inequalities of older age are more often socially created than biologically inevitable (Myles, 1989).

The issue of retirement can be used to illustrate the political economy perspective. Retirement is a relatively recent phenomenon, occurring in economically developed societies. The political economy approach suggests that the practice of retirement was institutionalized in order to displace older and often more costly workers (given that salaries tend to reflect seniority) from the labour force. Thus the practice of retirement benefited younger persons who sought entry into the labour force, younger workers who sought promotions, and employers who sought to maximize the profit margin. Finally, it benefited the capitalist system by providing a mechanism for capital accumulation (i.e., pension funds) and for labour-supply control. The retired worker gained a life of "pensioned leisure" but lost the right to work and the right to a full wage. In short, the political economy perspective challenges conventional assumptions and explanations. Things are not always as they seem, and the real reasons are not always the reasons given.

There is no single theoretical perspective that can account for all areas of concern in the sociological study of aging, nor can any one approach explain or predict all outcomes. A range of theories have been developed. Different interpretations and explanations often compete to explain the same situation.

THE AGED: A DEMOGRAPHIC VIEW

The age distribution of a population affects the social structure — the regular, predictable patterns of social interaction. In reciprocal fashion, the social structure has an impact on the characteristics of the population. The dynamics of a population age structure — that is, the shifting proportions, composition, and geographical distributions of people in different age categories — are influenced by rates of fertility, mortality, migration, and a variety of sociohistorical events such as wars and plagues. Some understanding of the interrelationship between population and social structure is critical to an understanding of the sociology of age and aging.

• POPULATION AGING

Individual aging and population aging are two very different concepts. **Individual aging** refers to the passage of time since an individual's birth and the changes that come with the accumulation of birthdays. Generally, we tend to think of the 65th birthday as officially marking entry into "old age." **Population aging,** on the other hand, does not refer to the passage of time but rather to the increase in the proportion of the population that is "old." According to the United Nations (1956), a population is "old" when 8 percent or more of its members are 65 years of age or older.

Population aging is influenced by three variables: mortality, fertility, and migration. Declining mortality means increasing life expectancy — that is, more people survive to reach "old age." Many assume that this trend is the prime determinant of population aging. However, while it is certainly a factor, the major determinant of population aging tends to be declining fertility. That is, as families have fewer and fewer children, the proportion of children in the population declines and seniors consequently make up an increasing proportion of the population. The third variable — migration — can also affect population aging. The proportion of seniors in a population will tend to increase either when seniors are moving in or non-seniors are moving out, leaving resident seniors behind.

Population aging is most evident in the so-called developed nations (Population Reference Bureau, 1992). In 1992, Sweden was the "oldest" country, with 18 percent of its population made up of seniors. The United Kingdom and Germany stood at 16 and 15 percent respectively, while the population of Europe as a whole was 14 percent seniors. The United States had reached 13 percent. By contrast, Africa had 3 percent and Latin America 5 percent seniors in their populations.

In comparison, Canada in 1991 had 11.6 percent of its population who were seniors (Statistics Canada, 1992). Alberta had the lowest proportion of seniors of any province in Canada (9.1 percent), in large measure resulting from the heavy in-migration of non-seniors during the oil boom years of the 1970s. Saskatchewan had the highest proportion of seniors of any province in Canada (14.1 percent), in large measure a result of the heavy out-migration of non-seniors seeking jobs in other provinces. Projections for the future, using various assumptions about future trends in fertility, mortality, and migration, estimate that by the end of the first third of the next century Canada's elderly percentage of the population will peak somewhere in the low to mid-20s (McDaniel, 1986: 106; Denton et al., 1986).

• POPULATION PYRAMIDS

A **population pyramid** is a bar chart that indicates the proportions of males and females of various ages in a population. The population pyramids for Canada in 1991 and 1891 and for Saskatchewan and Alberta — the "oldest" and "youngest" provinces — in 1991 are shown in Figure 11.1.

A comparison of the bars on each side of the population pyramid indicates the **sex ratio** for each age group — that is, the ratio of one sex to the other. At the youngest ages, there tend to be more males than females, while at the older ages there are more females than males. Indeed, the sex ratio becomes quite discrepant for Canada's aging citizens. These differences exist because more male babies are born than female babies, but males have a lower life expectancy than females.

The population pyramid also visually represents another ratio of interest, the **dependency ratio**. This statistic combines the older and younger segments of the population and compares them to the remaining age groups. The assumption behind this comparison is that the old and the young are "dependent" on those who are of working age. A common assumption is that an aging population implies an increasingly burdensome dependent population, as measured by the dependency ratio. Note, however, that an aging population implies an increasing proportion of seniors but a decreasing proportion of youth. Because the "dependency" of youth is different from the "dependency" of seniors, some separately calculate a **seniors dependency ratio** (the number of seniors aged 65+ compared to the number of persons aged 20–64, for example) and a **youth dependency ratio** (the number of youth aged 0–19 compared to the number of persons aged 20–64). Actually, because age is a rather crude measure of "dependency," one might wish to calculate the **labour-force dependency ratio** that compares the number of persons outside of the labour force to the number of persons in the labour force.

Returning to the population pyramid: the bulge in the middle (made up of the baby boomers born in the 1946–66 period) is working its way upward. In 2011 the oldest of the baby boomers will begin to turn 65 years of age, beginning a **seniors' boom** that will exaggerate, for a time, the population aging trend.

A comparison of population pyramids over time (Figure 11.1) shows that the population aging trend affects the population pyramid by constricting the base (as a result of declining fertility) and expanding the top, as seniors make up an increasing proportion of the population. The modern population pyramid is increasingly bottle-shaped rather than pyramidal in form. As the top of the pyramid increases in size it becomes increasingly important to distinguish among the young-old, middle-old, and old-old. An inspection of population pyramids over time suggests that not only are seniors an increasingly large proportion of the population, but the old-old are an increasingly large proportion both of the population as a whole and of the population of seniors.

Figure 11.1 POPULATION PYRAMIDS FOR CANADA 1891 AND 1991, ALBERTA 1991, AND SASKATCHEWAN 1991

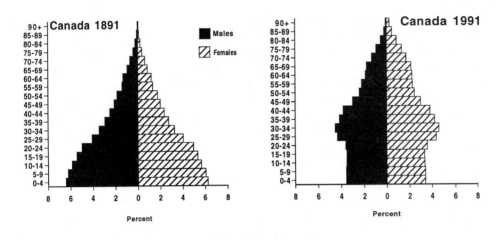

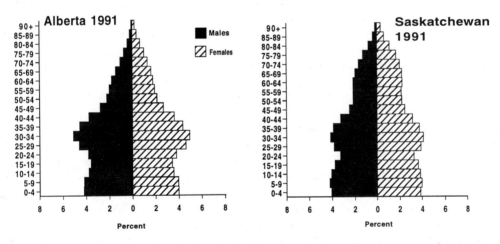

Source: These pyramids were constructed using data from Canada, Bureau of Statistics, *Census of Canada, 1890–91* (Volume IV). Ottawa: S.E. Dawson, 1897, Table G, p. 404; Statistics Canada, *The 1991 Census of Canada: Age, Sex and Marital Status* (Catalogue no. 93-310). Ottawa: Supply and Services, 1992, Tables 1 and 3, pp. 6, 14, 15, 32, 33, 48–51.

That is, a person in Canada today has a better chance than ever before of living past the age of 80 or 85, for example.

• DISTRIBUTION OF SENIORS

The number of seniors living in a given location and the proportion of the population of that location that is seniors are two different things. A relatively small number of seniors, for example, live in either Yukon or Prince Edward Island. However, while seniors in 1991 made up 4.0 percent of the population in Yukon, they made up 13.2 percent of the population of Prince

Edward Island (see Table 11.2). A relatively large number of seniors live in Ontario, where in 1991 they constituted 11.7 percent of that province's total population.

In Canada, some 80 percent of seniors reside in urban settings. In Alberta in 1991, for example, over half of all seniors resided in either Edmonton or Calgary, the province's largest cities. Another 10 percent lived in the medium-sized cities of Lethbridge, Medicine Hat, Red Deer, Grande Prairie, and Fort McMurray. Over three-quarters of older Albertans lived either in or near these major cities. On the other hand, the concentration of seniors on the farms and in the sparsely populated northern portion of the province was relatively low.

While most of Canada's seniors live in urban settings, there are wide variations in the elderly proportion of local populations. Among Canada's largest cities in 1991, Calgary had the lowest percentage of seniors (7.8 percent), while Victoria had the highest (18.6 percent). In 1991 in Alberta, seniors made up 12.2 percent of the population of Medicine Hat, 8.5 percent of Edmontonians, 7.8 percent of Calgarians, and only 0.8 percent of the population of Fort McMurray. Delivery of services for seniors tends to be more economical and more effective where seniors are concentrated in both large numbers and high proportions. Low numbers and low proportions impede the delivery of services.

• ETHNICITY

Ethnicity and aging in Canada has been examined by Driedger and Chappell (1987). They report (1987: 47) that in Canada in 1981, the population that was 55 years of age and older was 48 percent British in ethnic origin, 24 percent French, 5 percent German, 3 percent Ukrainian, 3 percent Italian, and 2 percent each of Scandinavian, Polish, Jewish, and Dutch origins. The remainder represented a diverse variety of ethnic origins. In 1986, about 1 percent of persons 65 years of age and older were of native ancestry. Finally, in 1991, 24 percent of seniors living in Canada had been born in another country and were therefore classified as immigrants.

Changing patterns of immigration imply future changes in the ethnic composition of seniors, given sufficient time for successive waves of immigrants to reach old age. Nevertheless, while

Table 11.2

THE PERCENTAGE OF THE CANADIAN POPULATION THAT IS SENIORS, BY PROVINCE, 1991

Province	Percentage 65 Years of Age and Older 1991
Newfoundland	9.7
Prince Edward Island	13.2
Nova Scotia	12.6
New Brunswick	12.2
Quebec	11.2
Ontario	11.7
Manitoba	13.4
Saskatchewan	14.1
Alberta	9.1
British Columbia	12.9
Yukon Territory	4.0
Northwest Territories	2.8
Canada	11.6

Source: Adapted from Statistics Canada (1992: Catalogue no. 93-310, Table 1).

immigrants often come to Canada as young adults, some do arrive as senior citizens. Indeed, in 1986, over 1 in every 100 persons 65 years of age and older in Canada had migrated to Canada during the previous five years.

It is important to take ethnicity into account when considering service delivery for seniors. Native or eastern European seniors will tend to have different cultural, linguistic, religious, and nutritional preferences than seniors of British or Chinese origin, for example. Furthermore, recent immigrants who are seniors will have had less time to adjust to the Canadian context and may be ineligible for certain services, such as Old Age Security, that depend on long-term residency in Canada.

• MARITAL STATUS

The proportion of the population that never marries is generally quite small (under 10 percent). Most people marry and those who divorce often remarry. The likelihood of being married in one's old age, therefore, is primarily a function of whether or not one's spouse is still alive. Because women have a longer life expectancy than men (currently about seven years longer, on average) and because women usually marry men who are older, it follows that older women are more likely to be widowed than are older men. Indeed, in 1991 in Canada, about 75 in every 100 elderly men were currently married, in comparison to 40 in every 100 elderly women (Statistics Canada, 1992).

The only two ways to exit widowhood are through remarriage or death. Widowed women are much more likely to remain widows until death than are widowed men (Northcott, 1984). In other words, widowed men are more likely to remarry than are widowed women. This is in large part due to the fact that widows outnumber widowers by about 5 to 1 (in Canada in 1991). When the pool of those seniors who are eligible for marriage (i.e., the widowed, divorced, and never married) is considered, the excess of eligible females creates a "**marriage squeeze**" such that even after all the eligible men are "taken," there is a substantial number of eligible women left unmarried.

There is a tendency to think of widowhood as problematic. However, more than one widow has stated that she appreciates her new "freedom" and is unconcerned about her limited opportunities for remarriage. Nevertheless, the absence of a spouse may mean the absence of a pension and/or the absence of a person who might provide needed care. Older males are more likely to have both the pension and a spouse to care for them. Older females, who are more likely to outlive their spouses, are at greater risk of poverty and being institutionalized, in part because of the lack of a spouse to care for them at home.

• LIVING ARRANGEMENTS

Most seniors live in their own homes. About one-quarter live alone. Some rent their accommodation and the likelihood of renting increases with age. Similarly, the likelihood of institutionalization increases with age. Women are more likely than men to either rent or live in institutional settings, in part because they are more likely to be widowed. In 1991, 8.1 percent of Canada's seniors lived in collective dwellings (primarily lodges, nursing homes, and hospitals). While there is a tendency to assume that the majority of seniors, or at least the majority of the older elderly, reside in institutions, even for Canadians 75 or more years of age in 1991 only 1 in 9 males and 1 in 5 females resided either permanently or temporarily in collective dwellings (Statistics Canada, 1992).

Age-Related Social Policy

Population aging is introducing major changes in Canadian society. The increasing proportion of senior citizens and the rapid increase in the number of old-old necessitates reassessment of services and resources, raising a variety of social policy issues in health care, financial security, protective services, and housing and the built environment (public buildings, sidewalks, transportation).

Social policy analysis takes place in a theoretical context, and the theoretical perspective used influences the conclusions drawn. Two theoretical perspectives of relevance to the discussion of aging and social policy — the political economy perspective (see Chapter 1) and a feminist perspective (see Chapter 10) — are highlighted here.

Three social policy considerations will be discussed in the following sections: pension politics and challenges, retirement, and selected problems that put older women, on average, at greater risk.

• PENSION POLITICS AND CHALLENGES

The history of pensions in Canada has three overriding political components. First, the mainstream political parties (Liberals and Conservatives) have used pension reform as a tool to retain their power against left-wing movements and parties. Two examples of this are the Old Age Pension Act of 1927 (when a number of left-wing parties were agitating for social reform) and the Old Age Security Act of 1951 (when the Mackenzie King government was determined to preserve the free enterprise system from the popular left-wing Co-operative Commonwealth Federation, or CCF, now the New Democratic Party, or NDP) (Granatstein, 1975). The same kind of "structural incentives" were at work when the unemployment insurance program (Cuneo, 1979) and universal health-care insurance were implemented (McDaniel, 1988a; Naylor, 1986). The political economy perspective enables us to see the economic and political forces that operate beneath the surface of public policy. It analyzes pension policy in Canada as the result of a struggle among competing interests in terms of power, dominance, and control, with profit and ideology at its core.

Second, federal–provincial disputes have plagued the history of pension policy in Canada, as is true for most social policies (Ismael, 1985; Myles, 1989). The British North America (BNA) Act, by default, gave control over pensions to the provinces. However, as pensions took on increasing importance, the provinces were left with the responsibility, but not the finances, to cope. Over the years the federal government generally has wrestled control of public pensions from the provinces, but not without compromise. The best example of compromise concerns the **Canada Pension Plan (CPP)**. In order to obtain provincial agreement to implement the CPP, a deal was struck whereby the provinces could borrow from the CPP fund at favourable rates of interest. The provinces have borrowed so much from the CPP that they are now borrowing the interest they repay on the original loans, and it is not clear whether they will ever be able to pay back what they owe (Finlayson, 1988). In addition, large provinces such as Ontario retain veto power over CPP reforms.

Third, there has been tension between the public and private sectors over the provision of pensions. Generally, the private sector has been reluctant or slow to provide pension coverage. Indeed, the private pension system currently excludes more than one-half of all Canadians and more than two-thirds of Canadian women. Certain elements in the private sector, particularly the insurance industry, have a vested interest in the expansion of private pensions. Similarly, federal government policy in the late 1980s also focused on improvements in the private system. However, continuing inadequacies in private pension coverage have motivated the National Council of Welfare (1990a) to bring the issue of expanding CPP benefits to the fore again — pointing out that a large proportion of elderly persons, particularly women, who receive CPP still qualify for the **Guaranteed Income Supplement (GIS),** which they require to make ends meet. Supporters of reform have argued for a public pension that replaces 37.5 percent of earnings at the average wage and from 37.5 percent to 50 percent of earnings below the average wage. It is not known yet whether this proposal will receive enough public support to bring the issue of CPP reform to the front of the pension arena. Again, it is through the political economy perspective that the interests of business and those of public policy can be seen as overlapping and mutually supporting.

One important new initiative regarding pensions is the declaring of pension credits to be marriage "property," much like a home or car. In 1978 equal splitting of CPP credits on divorce was introduced, a step toward addressing financial difficulties of older women. Equal splitting is not automatic — application must be made. Further, women (and men) may forfeit this right in divorce/spousal agreements, and forfeiture of this right for immediate cash or property may seem like the only viable option for many women at the time of divorce. Pension credit splitting is low; between 1978 and 1989 fewer than 21 000 applications had been submitted and approved, while approximately 500 000 divorces took place (National Council of Welfare, 1990a). Clearly, this reform is not bolstering women's pension income. A reformulation of the process of pension credit splitting is required and should be, but is not, high on the agenda of women's interest groups. Nonetheless, a feminist theoretical perspective has introduced the concept of shared assets in a marriage and pointed out some of the inequities that result when men typically see pension and other assets as theirs alone. Important also to the concept of shared assets is the often undervalued, and sometimes unpaid, contribution of women to the family.

• The Spouse's Allowance

Sometimes one spouse has reached age 65 and qualified for **Old Age Security** while the other spouse is still under the age of 65 and is therefore ineligible. To cover this situation for retired couples with inadequate pension income, the **Spouse's Allowance (SPA)** provides an income supplement (where the spouse of the old age pensioner is 60 to 64 years of age). There is also an income supplement for widowed persons who are 60 to 64 years of age. The Spouse's Allowance is being challenged in the courts as a violation of the Charter of Rights and Freedoms in that it covers only legally married, heterosexual couples. The outcome of these court battles will probably not be known for a few years, but if the challenges are successful the SPA could be abandoned altogether for reasons of cost. This could have very negative consequences for the pension incomes of poor older people and the widowed. The restrictive definition of family relied on for Spouse's Allowance reflects a traditional image of family. Feminist sociologists have argued (see Chapter 12) that the definition of family should be broadened to include more kinds of caring and sharing long-term relationships, including common-law and same-sex relationships.

• The Private Pension System

The private pension system is not as "private" as it might appear (Myles, 1988). First, many of the private pension plans involve the government as the employer (and thus involve civil servants whose employers also make policy about pensions); second, private plans are regulated by both federal and provincial governments and must meet certain minimal standards; and third, both private pension plans and RRSPs (Registered Retirement Savings Plans — which are individual savings plans for retirement) receive large tax concessions (Statistics Canada, 1988e; National Council of Welfare, 1989). Both the political economy and the feminist theoretical perspectives would argue that the policy distinction between private and public is often too sharply drawn. For example, government incentives to encourage private pension savings might be said to blend the public with the private.

In recent years government policy has emphasized reform in *private* pension plans rather than changes in the public pension system. The federal and provincial governments have agreed on a number of changes in **vesting** (qualification for benefits), **portability** (taking pension credits from an old job to a new job), **survivor benefits,** and coverage for part-time employees. While the changes in rules regarding vesting and portability, in particular, could improve the private pension system, the crucial problems of who is eligible for pensions and how pensions are or are not adjusted for inflation (this is called **indexation**) remain.

Only 52 percent of men and 37 percent of women in the paid labour force are even covered by a private pension plan. That is, the majority of Canadians have no private pension coverage at all. The percentage of workers with private pension coverage actually decreased in the 1980s (Statistics Canada, 1988e).

Indexation of private pensions to the cost of living has been a hot issue in recent years. Most pensions are *not* adjusted for inflation (or cost of living), which is why one hears sometimes about pensioners who live on "fixed incomes." Among public-sector pension plans, 29.9 percent are fully indexed to inflation and 37.0 percent are partially indexed (National Council of Welfare, 1989). Although indexation is crucial to ensure adequate income in later life (and retroactive compensation is important for current retirees whose incomes have been severely eroded by inflation), the interest of business and industry is to maintain the status quo. The Ontario government is pushing for mandatory private pension plan indexation, but employers and the pension industry are staunchly opposed. Some employers have threatened to change their plans drastically or to terminate them altogether if they are forced to provide cost-of-living protection or retroactive compensation (Finlayson, 1988). The key issue in the indexation debate concerns control of pension assets. It is clear that employers do not want to lose control of the enormous pension funds that accumulated in the 1960s and 1970s — money that many employers have used as company capital. A *lot* of money is at stake. In the first quarter of 1987, private pension plan assets were in the order of $130 billion. In that quarter, they earned $5 billion and netted, after expenditures, $3.4 billion (Finlayson, 1988). No wonder the question of who controls these funds — employees or employers — is such a heated issue!

The political economy and feminist theoretical perspectives enable us to see that power and control over monies substantially determine whose voice is heard in the political policy debate over pension indexation. Seniors generally, and particularly older women, often have limited power over the pension system under which they must live day to day.

Another example of the emphasis on private pensions in the Canadian pension system is increased government support for private savings plans such as RRSPs. Until recently, self-employed individuals and persons without private pension coverage could contribute up to $7500 annually. In the case of persons with pension funds at work, the maximum was $3500, minus their contribution to their own plan. New, more complicated, and administratively costly rules recently have been implemented. The overall thrust of the changes is to make it possible for Canadians to contribute *more* to RRSPs. The message is clear — policy-makers see individuals as responsible for their retirement income.

Plans such as RRSPs serve to perpetuate economic inequality. Only Canadians with extra disposable income (or the ability to take out a bank loan) can benefit from RRSPs, both in the short run (tax write-off) and in the long run (retirement savings). Approximately 19 percent of Canadians purchase RRSPs in a given year: among high-income earners, the figure is about 60 percent; among low-income earners, it is approximately 5 percent (National Council of Welfare, 1989). Accessibility to RRSPs is clearly linked to income, and the better-off are the winners. Another aspect of inequity in RRSPs relates to tax savings, with the largest tax savings going to persons with the highest incomes. RRSP contributions are handled as tax deductions;

the federal government refuses to convert RRSP deductions to tax credits (which are more equitable). These tax deductions represent a substantial government subsidization of well-off Canadians. It is not known how much this subsidization costs Canadians in general, as the federal government will not release this information.

The current politics of pensions represents many competing interests and forces. The federal government is playing a curious game: on the one hand, the taxing back of Old Age Security payments (phased in from 1989–91) hits well-off retirees; on the other hand, policies regarding RRSPs subsidize those with higher incomes. Overall, it appears that the federal government wants no substantial changes in the public pension system (except for taxing back pensions, or "clawback"), and is encouraging reforms in the private system. The corporate sector is resisting major changes, particularly indexation, and faces a major battle with the province of Ontario on this issue. Canadians appear to be caught in a political fight over control of pension capital on the one hand, and a trend toward privatization on the other, almost losing track of the issue of ensuring income security for older Canadians.

• RETIREMENT

The concept of not working while still able to do so is new in human history, and exists only in advanced capitalist countries. For the individual, retirement marks the end of one's primary work life and the beginning of a new phase of life, less clearly defined by society. For society, retirement means having a proportion of older adults who are not working and contributing in that way to society.

When age 65 was instituted as the age of retirement by Bismarck in the late 19th century, very few people lived that long. Today, men in Canada can expect to live 18 years after age 60, and women 23 years (Statistics Canada, 1985), making the post-retirement years a significant portion of life. Retirement is now the rule, the expectation for most Canadians. Among specific groups in Canadian society, most notably native people and working-class men, retirement in good health is less certain and shorter in duration, given their lower life expectancies (Table 11.3). Differential life expectancy by class reveals that life chances are determined in Canada by economic factors, with highest-income men outliving lowest-income men by almost 6 years (the comparable difference for women is almost 2 years). This kind of analysis is part of a political economy perspective.

• Retirement as a Social Process

In Canada's past, few people actually experienced retirement (McDonald and Wanner, 1990: 17–26). In part, this was a function of lower life expectancy and unavailability of pensions. As well, the concept of living without working was neither viable nor imaginable in the past. Work

Table 11.3

LIFE EXPECTANCY FOR MEN AND WOMEN BY CLASS, CANADA, LATE 1986

	Male	Female
Overall	73.8	80.4
Income Level		
Lowest	70.4	79.1
Middle	74.4	80.7
Highest	76.1	80.9

Source: Adapted from Russell Wilkins, Owen Adams, and Anna Brancker, "Changes in Mortality by Income in Urban Canada from 1971 and 1986." *Health Reports* 1989, Vol. 1, Table 3 , p. 146.

was an essential part of living for all those whose status and income did not allow them to escape it entirely. The kinds of work people did in the past — from farming to small businesses to hunting and trapping — did not lend themselves to the concept of retirement.

Myles (1989) suggests that two changes led to the development of the concept of retirement. The first was the emergence of the **retirement principle,** the concept that at a given age a person leaves paid work and lives on a pension. The second is the growth in the **retirement wage** — the income provided from the public purse on retirement. The new idea here is that people capable of working, both mentally and physically, no longer work but are still paid. Widespread support for these new concepts came from both private and public sectors. The private sector was permitted, in adopting the retirement concept, to have worker turnover, hiring younger workers at lower wages. The public sector supported the retirement idea because it allows a graceful exit from work, without the necessity of individual merit assessments.

Although retirement became more widespread after World War II, it was not institutionalized as a phase of life until very recently. Myles (1989: 21) states, "By 1980, the institution of retirement had been consolidated and old age had become a period of the lifecycle defined and sustained by the welfare state." This development was parallelled and reinforced by the idea that a working wage ought to be continued in retirement with provision of a pension.

Despite the importance of pensions to retirement as a life phase in Canada, scholarly writings on retirement and pensions have followed very different tracks and been driven by different questions. Retirement research has focused largely on individuals coping with the transition from work to leisure. Pensions have been analyzed largely in terms of economic policies and socioeconomic considerations, with little attention given to the interrelatio nships of pensions and retirement, or to the individual experience with pensions.

As a social process, retirement is not governed as directly by public policy as are pensions. Conventions such as retirement at age 65, workplace practices, and legal precedents determine retirement. Pensions, by contrast, are determined by layers of public (and to a lesser extent, corporate) policy. Pension policy determines the age at retirement more than any legal statute.

• WOMEN AND AGING

Women are a particular focus of the sociology of aging for a number of reasons. As seen earlier in this chapter, there is a complex interplay between ageism and sexism (Box 11.3). Population aging is the result of a declining birthrate, which is related to changes in women's lives, preferences, and greater opportunities for work outside the home. As well, women tend to outlive men, with the result that the proportion of women is greatest among the oldest populations. Women are also more likely to live longer with chronic illnesses, partly as a function of longer life expectancy, and tend to spend more of their older years in poverty (Figure 11.2). It may be that aging tends to accentuate gender inequalities that occur throughout the life cycle, as discussed in Chapter 10. These insights are informed by a feminist theoretical perspective. This focus on women does not, in any way, suggest that many older men do not also experience challenges.

Women's family roles and their caring for others pose particular challenges to women in aging families (Box 11.4). Given their longer life expectancy, women are more likely than men to be in need of care in their older years, and are most likely also to be the ones who do the caring, as much feminist sociology has shown. Often, this places middle-aged women in a kind of "sandwich" between the needs of a younger and an older generation (Schwartz, 1979; McDaniel, 1988b; Kaden and McDaniel, 1990). Catchy as the phrase "warehousing the elderly" may be, Canadian families do *not* send their older relatives to nursing homes, except as a last resort (less than 8 percent of seniors reside in nursing homes and most are *very* old and sick). Rather, older relatives are cared for at home by their families, typically meaning wives, daughters, and daugh-

Figure 11.2

POVERTY RATES FOR PERSONS 65 YEARS OF AGE AND OLDER, BY MARITAL STATUS AND SEX, CANADA, 1990

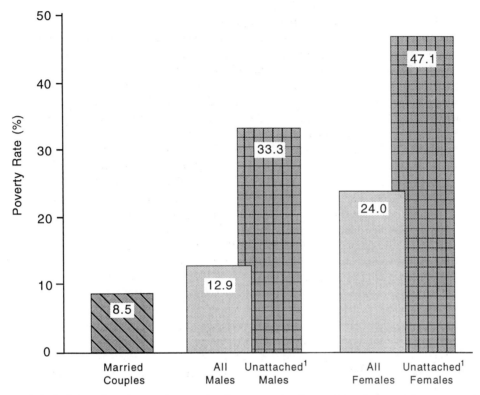

1. Unattached individuals are those who are neither married nor living common-law. Their actual marital status might be never married, widowed, separated, or divorced.

Source: The data on which this figure is based are from National Council of Welfare, *Poverty Profile, 1980–1990*. Ottawa: National Council of Welfare, 1992, pp. 12, 14, 67, 69.

ters-in-law. Indeed, the 1990 General Social Survey of 13 345 Canadians found that the overwhelming majority of older people rely on family and friends for any assistance they need.

Who are the caregivers? The case studies in Box 11.4 illustrate some of the realities women can face as principal caregivers to the dependent aged. A divorced woman who provides care to her former mother-in-law and an aging daughter who is a primary caregiver first to her dependent father and then her dependent husband illustrate the plight of the "woman in the middle" (Rush, 1975). These middle-aged people (mostly women), members of the "caught" generation (Vincent, 1972), have been characterized as "hidden patients" (Fengler and Goodrich, 1979). The workloads they carry are often heavy and insufficiently recognized by society, despite the enormous contributions they make. It is estimated that some 80 percent of the health care given to the aged comes from the informal sector of society, largely family. Some middle-aged women are so torn between their commitments to work and family (particularly the growing needs of their elderly relatives) that they are forced to quit their jobs or retire prematurely. Women, told throughout their lives that caring for others, particularly family members, is a natural activity and that they will harm their family's interests by getting sick themselves, may be putting their own needs aside to take on increasing loads. In the long run, these women may face their own older years less well off in both health and economic resources. These observations are highlighted by the feminist theoretical perspective, which makes the structure of familial caring more visible.

Given demographic changes in Canada over the past decades, particularly the declining birth-rate, families now tend to be smaller than they used to be. This means that women today who are caring for older relatives may have many more relatives in their parents' and husbands' parents' generation than they have siblings to assist them in the caregiving. It is as if the shape of families has become like a big oak or apple tree, with a wide top (the larger families of parents and grand-parents) and a narrow trunk or base (the smaller families of today). There are fewer and fewer younger family members now, with the birthrate in Canada so low. (Those now in their teens and 20s are called the "baby-bust" generation.) When the parents of the baby-bust generation get old and need help, there will be fewer siblings than ever to share the load.

A feminist theoretical perspective further indicates that women are in a kind of sandwich also with respect to caregiving in the paid labour force. Geriatric or chronic care is among the lowest paid and lowest status health-care work, and it is done mainly by women. Despite its importance, caring for older people for pay is often stressful, unrecognized, and relatively unrewarded. Risks are high among elder care workers for burnout and stress-related illnesses: female caregivers are expected to *care* as part of the job, thus both justifying low pay ("it is done out of love") and adding to job stress (caring behaviours such as listening and talking may not seem to one's super-visor to be work, raising the question of how "caring" is to be evaluated on the job). This is more of a kinship model than a work model. Often, women who caregive on the job then go home to more of the same kind of work and stresses in their families, working double or even triple "shifts."

Economic challenges also exist for older women in Canada. Although many presume that they will have access to pensions in old age either through a spouse's pension plan or through one of their own, all too often the assumption is incorrect. Public pensions in Canada, such as the

Box 11.4

AGING WOMEN AND CAREGIVING

Daughter, Wife and Mother: Life in the Sandwich Generation

After her mother's death, Carla D. invited her aged father to move into the relatively small home she shared with her husband and four children. Carla's father had urinary problems, which meant that he had to use the bathroom several times through the night. He was given the largest bedroom, the only one with an adjoining bath. As a consequence, for seven years, during most of their children's adolescence, Carla D. and her husband slept each night on the living room sofa. Years passed. Carla D.'s father died, and her children moved out of the home. In her late 50s, Carla D. has re-entered the labour force as a secretary, but caregiving responsibilities continue as she deals with age-linked issues. Her husband has severe emphysema, is housebound, physically dependent, and on a disability pension. In addition, two of the adult children make periodic return moves to the family home as they try to cope with troublesome issues in their own lives. Some factors have changed, but Carla D. has been and continues to be a woman caught in the middle.

A Daughter-in-Law and Post-Divorce Commitments

A high-school graduate with little experience in the paid labour force, Pat K., the mother of three grown children, was married for nearly three decades to a well-paid professional. Through the years of her marriage, Pat K. reassured her aging, blind mother-in-law that she could be counted on to help the older woman avoid institutionalization. Now divorced and working at a minimal wage, Pat K. finds that her former mother-in-law has had to have surgery, is bedfast, and needs several months of assistance in order to remain in her home during her recovery period. Irrespective of the fact that these women are no longer (legally) related, Pat K. closes up her own home, moves out of province and gives her former mother-in-law the support and care she promised her so long ago.

Source: Adapted from S.M. Abu-Laban, 1982.

Canada and Quebec Pension Plans and Old Age Security, are not intended as pensions on which people can actually live — i.e., meet their basic requirements. When instituted, they were intended as incentives to the private sector to develop private pension plans, as a political economy perspective suggests. Although most large employers in Canada do have some sort of pension plan for their permanent employees, many Canadians (particularly women) do not work for large employers and may, therefore, have no access to private pension plans. Another catch for women is that they more often work in jobs that are part time, non-union, temporary, informal-economy jobs (farm work, babysitting, working in the family business, etc.), for which they receive no benefits package. The presumption, to a large degree, has been that women will be provided for by the pension of a husband — a presumption that is often not borne out.

Some women, however, have never married, and thus cannot get pensions as wives. Others are married to men with no private pensions of their own. Among those who are married to men *with* private pensions are many who will benefit for a limited time: only about one-quarter of private pension plans have any survivors' benefits, meaning that the woman can depend on the husband's pension *only as long as he is alive.* Given differential life expectancies of men and women, the probabilities are high that women will outlive their husbands and thus spend many years without *any* private pension income. A woman who depends on a husband's pension should do some careful checking before assuming that her husband's pension will ensure her a secure retirement. Figure 11.2 reveals that women over the age of 65 often live below the poverty line in Canada, and of those who are not currently married, almost one-half live in poverty.

The prevailing model of distribution/redistribution of resources among people in Canada is one of competition among groups, with political factors determining who gets what in terms of pensions and benefits. Of interest here is the idea that young and old are competing for the same scarce resources, including social policy benefits (see Gee and McDaniel, 1992). In these days of government deficits, there is considerable concern about the economic consequences of population aging. The resulting image is one of a Canada that may no longer be able to afford its social programs — programs that create debt, so the argument goes, for both old and young today, but will leave debts for the young to pay. This is seen as an issue of intergenerational equity. The aptness of this interpretation can usefully be analyzed through the political economy perspective.

Population aging does not by itself create a social policy crisis. Nonetheless, the Canadian population is aging at a time when social policies are being called into question. Consequently, population aging and social policy challenges are intertwined. The interconnections of policy issues are underlined by both the political economy and feminist theoretical perspectives. For example, pension and retirement policies affect and are affected by the economics of aging and by women's situations in an aging Canada as both family members and workers/retirees. Further, informal caregiving affects women's capacities to contribute economically, which in turn relates to their demands for pensions and ultimately health care.

It seems clear that gender issues will continue to play a prominent role in social policy developments of the future. Once the issues of gender inequities of aging and social policy are raised, it is no longer possible to suppress them. Many policies of concern to an aging Canada are of central concern to women, even if at first glance the issues seem only indirectly related to aging. Pay equity and day care are but two of these issues. Working women who are paid fairly for their work and can work knowing that their children are being cared for are more likely to have access to pensions when they are older, because they will have fewer job interruptions. In short, the interconnections of social policy and aging throughout the life cycle are many and complex.

THE FUTURE OF AGING

As we move into the 21st century not only will there be increasing proportions of aged people but there will also be dramatic social changes influenced by our expanding understanding that aging is more than biological, that agedness is plastic and not fixed, that the biological is influenced by the social, and that the social is massively important to the quality of our lives and our aging. Population aging is likely to provide growth in occupational opportunities as well. The delivery of services to older people has been described as "one of the fastest growing areas of employment in the Western World" (Atchley, 1991: 401). The sociology of aging now attracts lively research interest and growing numbers of students. The Network of Excellence Program sponsored by the Canadian government in 1990 funded only one social science program in Canada — for research on aging. In recognition of the national importance of the aging of the Canadian population, other special funding efforts and monies have been earmarked for research, centres, and programs. While researchers may study aging from traditional disciplinary perspectives (e.g., from the perspective of biology, sociology, psychology, economics, or social welfare), much of the research on aging is *interdisciplinary* in fact or in spirit. Maddox (1987: 5) suggests that today's researchers are engaged in the process of "inventing the future of aging" — not only increasing our understanding about age and agedness but adding to the *quality* of the additional years of human life that will be available in the next century.

SUMMARY

- The aging of Canada's population is expected to continue and then accelerate as the baby-boom generation reaches old age. As a result, family dynamics, the status of elders, social programs, and the general distribution of resources and opportunities between younger and older Canadians will also change to meet the needs of an evolving age structure.

- Aging is both a biological and social process. Age categories may reflect chronological age differences or socially constructed definitions of age. Gender issues cut across the aging process, leading to a double standard of aging. As a result, in Western societies there are multiple, and sometimes conflicting, attitudes toward aging, ranging from deference toward the aged to ageism. Many of the stereotypes about the elderly are not supported empirically (i.e., not borne out in fact).

- Various theories of aging reflect diverse societal responses. Activity theory stresses continued activity as necessary for adjusting to aging and retirement. Disengagement theory highlights a particular form of adaptation, that of gradual withdrawing from social activity and reflecting upon one's life in preparation for its end. Continuity theory recognizes necessary changes in lifestyle, but suggests a tendency to substitute activities that maintain a meaningful existence. Other theorists see the aged as a minority group subject to discrimination, as losing status as society becomes more modern and urban, or (in the political economy approach) in conflict with the interests of other age groups.

- The aging of a population is a function of a declining birthrate, an increase in individual longevity, and geographic mobility, particularly the in-migration of older people and the out-migration of younger people seeking opportunities elsewhere. Canadians worry about an inflating dependency ratio but, to some extent, the expanding number of seniors is balanced by the diminishing number of dependent youth.

- Canadian senior citizens live mainly in cities and in their own homes, although the likelihood of institutionalization increases with increasing age. Women live longer than men, and elderly women are more likely than elderly men to be widowed and live alone or in an institution. At the same time, many aged women lack an adequate pension income and live in poverty.

- Pension policy in Canada has changed over time and has been influenced by competition among political parties, various levels of governments, and public and private economic interests. While Old Age Security is universally paid to Canadians from age 65 on, other government payments, such as the Guaranteed Income Supplement and the Spouse's Allowance, depend on the individual's personal or family income and personal circumstances.

Benefits from the Canada Pension Plan and from private pension programs are proportional to a person's wage history and his or her payments into the particular plan. On average, pensions benefit those with a history of higher earnings and tend to benefit elderly men more than elderly women.

- Retirement and pensions are relatively recent concepts that developed with the advance of capitalism. As life expectancy has increased, retirement has come to constitute a significant portion of people's lives.

- Aging presents challenges to both men and women. However, gender inequalities may be accentuated as people live longer and begin to require care by others. The responsibility for caregiving in our society is disproportionately assumed by women, usually wives and daughters, often at the expense of other commitments to work and family. In the long run, their own health and economic resources for old age may suffer. With family size decreasing, the burden of caring for larger numbers of elderly people will fall upon fewer potential caregivers.

- Population aging has become a focus for research in an attempt to understand and predict societal change and to guide changes in social policy. Employment opportunities are expected to change with the growth of service delivery for older people.

KEY CONCEPTS

Age change
Age deference
Age differences
Age differentiation
Age effects
Age norms
Age structure
Age tribunal
Ageism
Baby boom
Biological aging
Canada Pension Plan (CPP)
Chronological age
Cohort
Cohort effect
Cross-sectional research
Dependency ratio
Double standard of aging
Gerontocracy
Grey power
Guaranteed Income Supplement (GIS)
Indexation

Individual aging
Labour-force dependency ratio
Longitudinal research
Marriage squeeze
Middle-old
Old Age Security (OAS)
Old-old
Period effect
Population aging
Population pyramid
Portability
Retirement principle
Retirement wage
Rule of primogeniture
Seniors' boom
Seniors dependency ratio
Sex ratio
Social clock
Spouse's Allowance (SPA)
Survivor benefits
Vesting
Young-old
Youth dependency ratio

REVIEW QUESTIONS

1. How does existing social policy increase or decrease inequalities between young and old?
2. In what ways is caregiving to elders structured by gender?
3. Why is social policy such an important issue for aging women in Canada?
4. What are the demographic causes, demographic characteristics, and social policy implications of population aging in Canada?
5. Compare and contrast various theoretical perspectives on individual and population aging.

Marriages & Families in Canada

Wayne McVey, Lyle Larson, Charles Hobart, and Cathy Krull

Introduction

Family Diversity and Change

Defining Marriage and Family

Theories of the Family

Premarital Patterns

Marital Patterns

Family Patterns

Contemporary Family Issues

Summary

Key Concepts

Review Questions

Marriages and Families in Canada

INTRODUCTION

This chapter is an introduction to the sociological study of marriage and family relationships. Several important dimensions of family study will be emphasized, including key concepts, relevant theories, cross-cultural and subcultural variations, the characteristics of premarital, marital, and family relationships in Canadian society, and divorce and remarriage. In addition, the chapter will cover selected issues in family change and social policy relevant to families.

• THE FAMILY AS BASIC UNIT

For most of us, the **family** is the most basic unit of human organization. Most of us are born into and raised in families. Most dwellings are occupied by families with children at home, married couples who haven't yet had children, or married couples whose children have left home. The majority of us expend more time, effort, and emotion in our families than in any other social domain — including paid work, education, religion, or politics. Few people are able to escape (nor do they wish to escape) the pervasive influence of their own families, past or present. The family, whatever form it takes, is more important in fulfilling most individuals' basic needs than any other social institution.

FAMILY DIVERSITY AND CHANGE

The concept or idea of the family exists in all cultures. The specific social arrangements that are defined as family, however, depend on the culture and the society in which people live. There is both commonality and diversity in most societies of the world. Although **monogamy** (one husband and one wife) is the predominant marital form in all societies, there are two major types of **polygamy** (plural marriage) that are acceptable in many societies. **Polygyny** involves one husband and two or more wives, while **polyandry** refers to one wife and two or more husbands. The **nuclear** or conjugal family (composed of a father, mother, and their children) is the predominant family structure in many societies of the world, although various forms of **extended** families (families in which at least three generations share the same household) are very prominent in nonindustrialized societies. Patterns of authority and regulation within family systems (typically referred to as *descent patterns*) also vary among societies. There are three basic types of descent: matrilineality, patrilineality, and multilineality. **Matrilineality** is tracing descent through the line of mothers, and recognizing one's relatives as those who trace their descent through the same line of mothers. **Patrilineality,** the most common pattern, involves tracing descent through the line of fathers. The Canadian system is **multilineal** in that we trace descent through two lines (mother's and father's) at the parental level, through four lines at the grandparental level (maternal grandmother and grandfather, paternal grandmother and grandfather), through eight lines at the great-grandparental level, and so forth. Our own system, however, has been influenced by patrilineality in that most of us get our surnames through the line of our fathers.

Canada, like most contemporary industrialized societies, is a monogamous society. However, given our rates of divorce, our marriage pattern is sometimes dubbed **serial monogamy** (two or more monogamous marriages over the life span). The nuclear family has likewise remained the most common family structure in our society. As Nock (1992: 27) points out, the family unit that consists of a man and a woman and their own and adopted children is referred to worldwide as a nuclear family. It is apparent, however, that there are a variety of family structures and patterns within Canadian society. Many societal changes have had profound effects on traditional marital and family forms; they include the erosion of religious authority, the growth of individualism, a trend toward higher educational attainment, and the movement toward greater equality and independence for women. These and related factors have contributed to a significant increase in the average age at first marriage and in the number of divorces, remarriages, births outside of marriage, and common-law unions. A significant decrease in the number of births has also occurred (Grindstaff et al., 1989; McDaniel, 1990). In response to these social patterns, a variety of couple and family forms have emerged, including common-law couples, single-parent families (never-married, or single as a result of separation, divorce, or widowhood), and remarried couples and families. There is also a movement to include same-sex couples as a family form.

DEFINING MARRIAGE AND FAMILY

• A UNIVERSAL DEFINITION

The purpose of a universal definition of the family is to identify the basic, predominant, and most widely approved family form in all known societies. Murdock (1949), using the World Ethnographic Sample, concluded that the basic family type in all societies for which data were available was a nuclear family with four functions (reproduction, socialization of children, provision of legitimate sexual relations, and economic cooperation between spouses). Follow-up research concluded that several societies did not fit this definition (Reiss, 1965). There were a few societies, for example, where the predominant family form was a single-parent family with strong kinship ties. In several other societies, moreover, several of the functions were not performed by the nuclear family. Murdock, Reiss, and other scholars were searching for that *minimum* "set of relationships" in all societies that could be identified as the predominant social institutions of marriage and family. It is argued that a universal definition would ensure that researchers are studying the same social phenomena.

Universal definitions of marriage emphasize approval by society, intentions of permanence, and sexual relations between *at least* one male and one female. Legitimate marriage is also seen as the social location where children *may* be conceived.

Marriage is a normatively defined relationship between at least one man and at least one woman, established with the intention of permanence, and as the primary sexually based bond in which the reproduction of children is expected to occur.

This definition emphasizes that society has a significant stake in what marriage means. Social norms indicate what marriage is and what it is not; the social institution of marriage defines eligibility for the conception and birth of legitimate children (Davis, 1939; Gough, 1960; Radcliffe-Brown, 1959; Stephens, 1963). The majority of men and women in a particular society will enter a relationship that is publicly recognized as acceptable. It may be a matter of law and may include requirements such as a licence, a public ceremony with witnesses and verbal pronouncements, and perhaps a blood test. Typically, however, most societies do not have written laws. Indeed, the practice we think of as common-law relationship with recognized stable intentions is the standard form of marriage in many societies.

A universal definition of the family involves a kinship group normatively defined to carry out the nurturant socialization of dependent children. In this definition, the term **kinship group** means a social network of people related by common ancestry, adoption, or marriage (Robertson, 1987: 349). The term does *not* specify the number of parents or children. The type and number of parents are not defined because the form or structure of the social unit varies from society to society. Most cultures require a biological father and mother, others only a mother or a grandmother, or both. Universal definitions are the most commonly used in introductory family textbooks on the family.

• INCLUSIVE DEFINITIONS

Inclusive definitions emphasize the diversity of structures, functions, and relationships in sexuality, intimacy, and child rearing. Although research on marriage and family employing a universal definition has been influential, it has also been strongly criticized, particularly regarding its applicability to the United States and Canada. The critics reject the existence of a universal family because there are so many variations (Baker, 1990; Boyd, 1988; Eichler, 1988a; McDaniel, 1988c; Vanier Institute of the Family, 1981; Veevers, 1991). Viewing the family strictly in terms of which family is being analyzed enables sociologists to see families as constantly changing as society changes, as varying even within a single society, and inclusive of many kinds of caring, long-lasting unions, including common-law and same-sex relationships (McDaniel, 1988c, 1990). Indeed, Scanzoni (1987: 407) argues that the concepts of "family" and "marriage" should be abandoned altogether and be replaced by the concept of **close relationships**. He defines close relationships as social arrangements involving "strong, frequent, and diverse interdependence that endure over relatively lengthy periods of time."

Eichler (1988a: 6) argues that "as soon as we put forward a conception that there is such a thing as 'the' family, we are by implication ruling out other similar kinds of groupings as nonfamily." She advocates what she calls a *multidimensional approach* to the family, which would recognize all possible family forms and interactions that are generally recognized as families to some degree (Box 12.1). She proposes that there are six important dimensions of family interaction: the procreative dimension, the socialization dimension, the sexual dimension, the residential dimension, the economic dimension, and the emotional dimension. Within each of these dimensions, familial interaction varies. Consequently, many different family forms can be derived. For example, the traditional nuclear family can be characterized by the following: the couple have child(ren) together only, both spouses are involved in parenting, the couple have sex together only, all family members live in the same residence, one member is totally responsible for the support of all family members, and there is mutual positive involvement. Interaction in any of the dimensions can vary independently. Thus, a couple may be low on the procreative dimension (i.e., they are childless) but high on the emotional dimension (i.e., they have mutual positive involvement).

Family scholars are evaluating the merits of these two types of definitions. Those who use universal definitions emphasize societal norms that prescribe the nature and meaning of the social institutions of marriage and the family and proscribe deviations from them. It is argued, for example, that not all relationships are marriages because not all relationships (e.g., friendships, roommate relationships) are social institutions. Similarly, not all adult–child relationships are families. Theorists and researchers in this tradition, however, are also interested in studying the variations and changes in family forms and functions. Scholars who use inclusive definitions differ in that they believe that social institutions are changing *radically*. The inclusive model, it is argued, permits greater flexibility in defining and explaining patterns and trends. The definitions of family or marriage employed will probably continue to vary depending on organizational purposes, ideological persuasions, the type of research, or the theoretical approach being used.

THEORIES OF THE FAMILY

Sociologists divide the various conceptual approaches into two basic levels of study: *macro-sociological* and *micro-sociological*. The macro level of analysis focuses on societal and cultural issues. Research and theory on this level emphasize the study of the family cross-culturally, historically, or through a single society. Societal structures and processes (such as government,

Box 12.1

DIMENSIONS OF FAMILIAL INTERACTION

1. PROCREATIVE DIMENSION
   —the couple have child(ren) together only
   —one spouse has child(ren) by other partner & couple have child(ren) together
   —both spouses have child(ren) by other partners & couple have child(ren) together
   —both spouses have child(ren) by other partner, no joint child(ren)
   —one spouse has child(ren) by other partner, no joint child(ren)
   —both childless

2. SOCIALIZATION DIMENSION
   —both spouses involved in parenting
   —one spouse only involved in parenting
   —neither spouse involved in parenting or irrelevant

3. SEXUAL DIMENSION
   —couple have sex together only
   —couple have sex together and one of them has sex with other(s)
   —couple have sex together and both of them have sex with other(s)
   —one of them is celibate, the other has sex with other(s)
   —both of them have sex with other(s) only
   —both are celibate

4. RESIDENTIAL DIMENSION
   —all family members live in the same residence only
   —all family members live in the same residence but one has an additional separate
      residence
   —all family members live in the same residence but more than one have additional
      separate residences
   —one family member lives in a separate residence only
   —all family members live in separate residences only

5. ECONOMIC DIMENSION
   —one member is totally responsible for the support of all family members
   —one family member is totally responsible for the support of some but not all
      family members
   —one family member is partially responsible for the support of all family members
   —one family member is partially responsible for the support of some but not all
      family members
   —each family member is totally responsible for own support

6. EMOTIONAL DIMENSION
   —mutual positive involvement
   —mutual negative involvement
   —one-sided positive involvement
   —one-sided negative involvement
   —lack of any emotional involvement

Source: Eichler (1988a: 8–9).

urbanization, technological or social change, and social policies) are examined in the study of family patterns and processes. Two macro-level conceptual approaches in family study are discussed on the following pages.

• MACRO-LEVEL CONCEPTUAL APPROACHES

• A Functionalist View of the Family

The **structural-functional approach** focuses on the interdependency of the many parts of a society (Parsons and Bales, 1955; McIntyre, 1981; Kingsbury and Scanzoni, 1993). Each part is assumed to make a contribution to the whole — to perform an important function for each other part and for the maintenance of the social system. The family fulfils many requirements in meeting a society's basic needs, such as "giving birth to new members, teaching them how to behave appropriately, inculcating ethical and moral principles shared by society, producing and/or distributing goods and services, and maintaining social order" (McDaniel, 1988d: 103). Because the family is primarily responsible for at least one or more of these functions in all societies, the family is also assumed to be a functional requirement for the stability and survival of society. Critics, however, have pointed out that although all of these functions are necessary for the survival of the social system, the family is not necessarily the only plausible agency that can fulfil them (McDaniel, 1988d; Robertson, 1987: 350).

It is also argued that the family is like a miniature society. Family survival is thus dependent on the fulfilment of several functions including economic cooperation, goal orientation, interpersonal affection, and a common value system. *Functions, dysfunctions,* and *eufunctions* (the integrative social consequences of a social or cultural phenomenon) in systems and subsystems are emphasized. Dysfunctional patterns refer to behaviours or values that undermine societal well-being. Eufunctions, in contrast, refer to behaviours or values that have nothing to do with societal stability. A typical research question for a structural-functional theorist would be, "Why does the family exist in most societies of the world?" Chapter 1 provides a general summary of structural-functionalism.

• A Conflict View of the Family

Karl Marx, the father of the **conflict approach,** emphasized the economic inequities between the upper class and the working people. He argued that women, wives, and mothers were exploited because they received lower pay when employed, and no payment as housewives or mothers. Patriarchy was promoted by the capitalist system, and systematically reinforced in families through socialization processes and the maintenance of a traditional division of labour (Farrington and Chertok, 1993).

Canadian scholars, particularly those with a feminist perspective, argue that the economic arrangements between men and women in the workplace and in the household are determined by systems of *power* designed to maintain the status quo (Maroney and Luxton, 1987). Smith (1977: 18) argues that the separation of public and private spheres furthered the oppression of women by designating women exclusively to the private sphere and excluding them from the public domain where "history is made to happen." She brings together Marx's concept of the alienation of labour with that of women's relations to the family and to the mode of production (see Chapter 1 for an overview of the alienation of labour). The survival of corporate enterprise, the stronghold of contemporary capitalist society, is dependent on the portrayal of the home as a domestic haven in which women are the executives. Women are responsible for providing a retreat for their husbands when men are not at work, and for raising the next generation of workers. Women's work becomes nothing more than a "private service" to their husbands, which facilitates corporate capitalism. The oppression of women is not easily addressed by a structural-functionalist approach, which focuses more on how a natural division of labour is constructive in meeting societal needs.

Although this approach grants that marriage and the family are essential to the survival of both individuals and societies, it emphasizes that competition, aggression, conflict management, negotiation, and bargaining are natural processes in human relationships. Continual confrontations among individuals and among societies are thus seen as necessary to growth and change. A typical research question for a conflict theorist would be, "How do family members avoid or cope with conflict when it is natural to initiate and maintain conflict?"

The conflict approach at the micro level assumes that people are more self-oriented than other-oriented and are therefore inclined to pursue their own interests at the expense of others. The unequal distribution of power within families leads to the use of power (and resistance to power) to keep things as they are (Szinovacz, 1987; Farrington and Chertok, 1993). As participation in family life is both necessary and involuntary, two conflicting demands are always present: to continue to participate in order to survive more effectively, and to compete with spouses and other family members for individual autonomy, authority, and privilege.

• MICRO-LEVEL CONCEPTUAL APPROACHES

The micro level of family study deals with interpersonal relationships among individuals within families and relationships between families. Psychologists, social psychologists, and micro-sociologists examine questions that ask (for example) why we feel, think, and do the things we do to and with each other. Relationships are examined between husbands and wives, and parents and children; the multiple relationships connected with the establishment and breakdown of marriages and families are studied. We will briefly examine two micro-level approaches. (Chapter 4 provides a more detailed summary of social-psychological theories.)

• The Symbolic Interactionist View

The **symbolic interactionist approach** emphasizes the role of individual *interpretations* of reality and role definitions in marital and family interactions (Charon, 1985; Burr et al., 1979). Perhaps most basic to symbolic interaction theory is that people think about their actions and the actions of significant others. When intimate partners, spouses, or family members interact, they interpret the situation and consider the consequences of their actions for themselves and others. A symbolic interactionist would ask a question such as, "How do your perceptions influence the way you behave in response to the actions of other family members?"

• The Exchange View

The concepts of costs and rewards are central tenets of the **exchange approach** (Blau, 1964; Chadwick-Jones, 1976; Nye, 1979). Exchange theorists argue that individuals evaluate the relative costs and rewards of entering, staying, or leaving a marital or family relationship. If the relationship is perceived to provide a higher profit than other relationships available to an individual, he or she is likely to stay. The evaluation process involves two comparisons. The **comparison level (CL)** refers to a person's evaluation of rewards and costs based on what that person has received before from the relationship. Each person compares current profit with the profit in the recent past. When profits fall, people become discontented with the relationship. The **comparison level for alternatives (CLalt)** refers to what a person perceives can be gained in an alternative relationship compared to what is gained in the present relationship.

Family exchange theorists often emphasize the significance of duties, rights, and equities in marital and family relationships (Scanzoni, 1970, 1978). This is often referred to as the *principle of reciprocity*. People are obliged to help those who help them and should not be unfair to or undermine those who have helped them. Exchange theorists simply ask husbands and wives to list the costs and rewards, as they see them, for staying in or leaving a degrading relationship. Exchange theory is one of the more precise theories in the family field, in that it defines specific conditions that regulate interpersonal sexual, premarital, marital, and family phenomena.

PREMARITAL PATTERNS

For some, "going out together," serious courtship, sexuality, or even cohabitation may not lead to marriage. The purpose of this section is to examine briefly the nature of premarital activities and their links to mate choice and marriage.

• DATING

Prior to the 1920s, dating in Canada and the United States was quite restricted and regulated by parents. Dating was often interpreted as a preliminary commitment to marriage. Between 1920 and 1960, in contrast, dating patterns were influenced by the automobile, urbanization, the telephone, and co-education (Murstein, 1980). Beginning with the 1960s, dating standards included three changes: more freedom for females in initiating dates, greater informality, and an increase in group dating activities.

There are typically four major reasons for dating: recreation, socialization, status, and mate choice (Skipper and Nass, 1966; Wells, 1984). Socialization involves learning how to interact with persons of the opposite sex. Persons who date for status try to date those who are popular, who are attractive, or who might enhance one's own worth. Some people who date are deliberately looking for a person to marry, whereas recreational dating (which is often associated with an interest in sexual interaction) may simply involve having a good time. Peters (1980) found that the majority of Canadian high-school students date for the purposes of recreation or socialization. Although dating is a prominent activity among both high-school and university students in Canada, Herold (1984) found in a study conducted in the early 1980s that 33 percent of high-school students were not dating; among university students, 15 percent of females compared to 33 percent of males were not dating.

Research has documented that the pathway from dating to mate choice and eventual marriage seems to move through a set of phases or stages (Wells, 1984). The first stage is attraction (e.g., physical attraction and discovery of similar interests). It is followed by attraction perpetuators (such as rapport and the favourable reaction of significant others). The third stage involves *deeper* attraction perpetuators (such as value compatibility and a *mutual* level of physical attractiveness). The decision stage emphasizes role compatibility, empathy, and increased commitment. As will be seen in the next section, sex is increasingly common in several phases of dating.

• SEXUALITY

Research shows that there have been dramatic changes in both premarital sexual standards and sexual behaviour (Reiss, 1960; Hobart and Grigel, 1990; Hobart, 1990). Traditionally there were two standards: the abstinence standard, which prohibited sex before marriage, and the double standard, which stated that sex before marriage was acceptable for men but not for women. In principle, religious morality forbade all premarital sex, but popular morality tended to expect that "boys would be boys," and would "sow wild oats," while girls were expected to be "good," and remain virgins until marriage. Kinsey's famous studies estimated that by the late 1940s about 92 percent of American men and about 50 percent of women reported having had premarital sex (Kinsey et al., 1948, 1953).

The birth-control pill, which became easily available by the early 1960s, largely freed women from the fear that pregnancy would result from premarital sex and so helped popularize two new sexual standards. The "love standard" stated that premarital sex was not wrong if the parties *loved each other*. The "fun standard" accepted premarital sex as moral if *both parties wanted it,* regardless of whether love was present.

Hobart (1990) examined changing premarital sexual standards in three studies of Canadian university and trade-school males and females between 1968 and 1988 (Table 12.1). Hobart's results show that there has been a sharp decrease in the abstinence standard for both English- and French-Canadian young adults. The shift has been most dramatic for women (from 45 to 13 percent for anglophone women and from 48 to 2 percent for francophone women). Similarly, support for the love (sometimes known as "permissiveness with affection") and fun ("permissiveness without affection") standards has increased. The love standard increased more sharply among English-Canadian women than men (an increase of 20 percent compared to 10 percent). There was little change in the love standard among francophone men, but a sharp increase among women (an increase of nearly 30 percent). As Table 12.1 shows, the sharpest rate of increase was in the fun standard, particularly among francophone females (by about 34 times — from 1.1 percent in 1968 to 37.1 percent in 1988).

Premarital sexual intercourse (one or more times) has likewise increased over these two decades (Hobart and Grigel, 1991): from 59 percent to 73 percent among anglophone males, compared to an increase from 39 percent to 76 percent among anglophone females. Francophone women have become more active sexually than anglophone women, increasing from 30 percent in 1968 to 84 percent in 1988. One of the interesting shifts is that in 1988, students who *professed* a certain premarital sexual standard were also likely to *practise* this standard. Consistency in sexual attitude and behaviour increased between 1968 and 1988 (Hobart and Grigel, 1991). Hobart and Grigel argue that these shifts may be due, in part, to the decreasing influence of religious norms in Canadian society. The seeming rejection of the church in Quebec may be a salient factor in the dramatic shifts of attitude and behaviour among young francophone women. Premarital sexual behaviours have become a regular feature of dating, particularly among couples who believe they are in love. However, as documented above, sexual activity for its own sake (the fun standard) is an increasing feature of dating.

• COHABITATION

Living together before marriage, often referred to as **cohabitation,** is an alternative form of "going steady" and an intermediate stop on the pathway to marriage. For a small minority, it is seen as an alternative to marriage.

The acceptance of cohabitation has increased in Canada. A national study of high-school students found that 88 percent thought that living together is acceptable (Bibby and Posterski, 1992). Among post-secondary English-Canadian students, only 10 percent considered cohabitation as "definitely bad," while 20 percent said that cohabitation is "definitely good" (Hobart and Grigel, 1992). French-Canadian students, in contrast, held much more liberal attitudes: only 2 percent described cohabitation as "definitely bad," while 71 percent thought that cohabitation is "definitely good."

The Canadian Census now collects data on cohabiting relationships, referred to as common-law. Census data for 1991 show that 6.7 percent of the population over the age of 15 were living

Table 12.1

Premarital Sexual Standards Professed by Anglophone and Francophone Males and Females in 1968 and 1988 (Percentages)

	Males		Females	
Years	1968	1988	1968	1988
Professed standards, anglophones				
Abstinence	27.5	12.8	45.3	13.0
Double standard	3.6	2.0	6.7	1.6
Engagement standard	11.6	10.5	11.9	16.8
Love standard	29.5	39.1	29.5	48.9
Fun standard	22.4	36.4	3.3	19.7
Other	5.3	0.0	3.3	0.0
Total number	335	845	360	834
Professed standards, francophones				
Abstinence	26.1	4.4	48.4	1.9
Double standard	5.3	0.0	8.6	0.0
Engagement standard	16.5	9.8	19.4	13.6
Love standard	36.2	33.9	18.3	47.4
Fun standard	12.2	51.9	1.1	37.1
Other	3.7	0.0	3.2	0.0
Total number	188	183	186	213

Source: Hobart (1990: 25).

in common-law relationships on the day of the census (Statistics Canada, 1992). Nearly 16 percent of never-married persons were living common-law, compared to 41 percent of divorced persons. These data may indicate that divorced persons hope that by living together they may improve their chances of making a wiser choice of mate the second time around.

Survey research on the incidence of cohabitation provides a somewhat different profile. In the 1988 research study by Hobart and Grigel (1992), 18 percent of the English-Canadian males and 21 percent of the females had cohabited. About 23 percent of French-Canadian students had cohabited. Cohabitation continues to be more popular among young people between the ages of 15 and 25 than it is for older people, although the median age of cohabitation has increased about three years since 1981 (Stout, 1991). Most cohabiting relationships tend to be short term and result in either marriage (about 63 percent) or separation (35 percent) (Burch and Madan, 1986). As young Canadians continue to accept nonmarital unions as viable, along with continuing high divorce rates, cohabitation will likely gain in importance as an alternative living arrangement.

Marital Patterns

• Mate Choice

Most people in Canada have broad freedom to choose whom to marry. Of course, how their marriage works out affects their children and thus the society as well. So far the Canadian government has not tried to restrict who may marry whom (assuming that the bride and groom are each at least 18 years of age). Nor does it seem likely that the government will try to interfere in the near future, although society is burdened when children are inadequately raised and become destructive members of society.

How well does the dating process work? Do individuals choose partners with whom they are compatible? These issues are strongly related to the concepts of propinquity and homogamy. **Propinquity** refers to proximity or accessibility. People typically marry others from the same country, region, often the same "part of town," church, university, or workplace. These places are where people encounter and become acquainted with eligible, appropriate marital partners. The result of propinquity is often **homogamy,** the tendency for people to marry others like themselves, in terms of age, race, ethnicity, education, religion, and social class. Age homogamy is one way of increasing similarity. The age spread between husbands and wives averaged 1.9 years in 1991 (Statistics Canada, 1991d). Religious homogamy, in contrast, is less apparent. The number of interfaith marriages in Canada has more than doubled between 1981 and 1990 (from 22 percent to 49 percent) (Heaton, 1991). Religious homogamy is highest among Jewish and non-Christian faiths, and lowest among mainline Protestant faiths. Research on ethnic homogamy, although somewhat out of date, shows that in 1971, 86 percent of French Canadians married within their own ethnic group. The average degree of ethnic homogamy for all Canadians, however, was 63 percent (Richard, 1991). Education, social class, and religion also continue to play a role in homogamous marriage (Eshelman, 1991). The evidence seems to indicate that background homogamy continues to have less influence in mate choice, while relational compatibilities are becoming more important.

Several other factors influence the dynamics of the mate selection process. Clearly, the ratio between males and females in the relevant age groups influences marriage opportunities. The relevant age groups in this instance would be in accordance with the prevailing **mating gradient,** which is the normatively supported age difference between the sexes at the time of marriage. When the relevant age groups are in imbalance — that is, when the number of either males or females is deficient — the frequency of marriage is likely to alter. If the social pressures to marry at a certain age are very strong, individuals caught in such a **marriage squeeze** may have to deviate considerably from the mating gradient in order to conform.

Veevers (1988) calls attention to a continuing marriage squeeze on women. She points out that because of **hypergamy** (the expectation that women will marry men of higher social class standing than themselves), bachelorhood, homosexuality, and the significantly longer life expectancy of women in contrast to men, the pool of eligible wives far exceeds the pool of eligible husbands.

Veevers argues that this marriage squeeze will have a number of consequences. These include an increase in those who will remain single (singlehood), the growth of an **ideology of singlehood** that emphasizes the advantages of remaining unmarried, increased independence among women as the number who do without husbands increases, and increased single parenthood among women who, though they have no husbands, still want to be mothers.

• AGE AT MARRIAGE

The average age at both marriage and first marriage steadily declined for brides and bridegrooms between 1941 and 1966, indicating an increasing societal tolerance for younger marriages. The urgencies of the war period, as well as the immediate postwar economic prosperity, probably contributed to this tendency. The distorting influence of remarriages on this statistic was minimal because of their low incidence at this time. Age at first marriage declined until 1972, when brides married at an average age of 22.2 years and grooms, 24.7 years.

Both average age at marriage and average age at *first* marriage have increased over the past two decades. The rise in remarriages has undoubtedly affected the average age at marriage; the increase in age at first marriage is more complicated to explain. Societal prohibitions may dictate a lower age at first marriage that becomes a social limit, thereby discouraging further declines for either males or females. It is not likely that this threshold had been reached in 1972 — in fact, other evidence suggests that there has been greater social acceptability of younger marriages in Canada — yet the average age at first marriage has increased steadily to a record high in 1990 of 26 and 27.9 years for brides and bridegrooms, respectively. The pursuit of higher levels of education, particularly among females, and the popularity of cohabitation among young people have contributed to the rise in the age at first marriage.

• CANADIAN MARRIAGE RATES

Although the absolute numbers of marriages have increased from the 71 254 recorded in 1921 to 187 737 in 1990, it is interesting to note that the marriage rate has declined slightly from 7.9 to 7.1. The **marriage rate** is defined as the number of marriages per 1000 population in a given calendar year. As can be seen in Figure 12.1, low marriage rates were recorded during the economic depression of the early 1930s — the lowest ever recorded in Canada was 5.9 for 1932 — reflecting the hesitancy of the eligible population to take on the additional responsibilities of marriage. Marriages that had been postponed because of the Great Depression and, later, wartime absences helped stimulate a peak rate of 10.9 per 1000 in 1942 and 1946, respectively. This period of high marriage rates generated large cohorts of women for childbearing. One consequence of the resultant baby boom appeared about twenty years later in the form of high marriage rates commencing in the early to mid-1970s.

Since reaching a post-1950s high of 9.2 in 1972, the Canadian marriage rates continued to decline to the low 6.9 rate recorded in 1986; they marginally recovered to 7.1 in 1990. Shrinking cohorts of eligible men and women (produced by the lower birth rates of the 1960s), coupled with increasing economic uncertainty, job competition, and changing values relating to marriage, seem likely to sustain lower marriage rates.

Figure 12.1

MARRIAGE RATE TRENDS: ALBERTA, QUEBEC, AND CANADA, 1921–1990

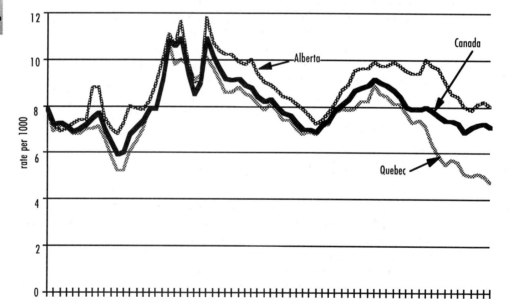

Sources: Statistics Canada (1975: Catalogue no. 84–205, Table 11; 1980: Catalogue no. 84-205, Table 10; 1984b: Catalogue no. 84–204, Table 10; 1989d: Catalogue no. 82–003s, Table 1; 1990g: Catalogue no. 82–003, Table 1, p. 58; 1990h: Catalogue no. 82–003S16, Table 1).

• MARITAL ADJUSTMENT

Marriage is a social institution. This means that the nature and intentions for marriage are defined by society and by socialization processes within our families of orientation (the families into which we are born). One of these expectations is that we marry because we are "in love." Indeed, most studies show that married persons like their marriages — over 60 percent are very happy and more than 80 percent are happy (Glenn, 1991). In spite of this high level of satisfaction, there are often areas of disappointment, disagreement, and conflict. Larson (1987) found that husbands and wives often see their relationship quite differently. Only 42 percent of the couples agreed in their responses to the statement "My spouse helps me feel important." Over 60 percent of the wives felt taken for granted by their husbands. Husbands and wives gave the same response among only 24 percent of the couples. Indeed, gender differences often play a part in the evaluation of one's marriage. In a recent review of the literature on women and men in marriage, Thompson and Walker (1991) conclude that wives are not satisfied with the degree of emotional intimacy in their marriages. Wives want their husbands to be more expressive and are more likely to alter their sexual desires and actions to please their husbands. Wives tend to assume more responsibility for trying to change or resolve relationship problems and conflicts than do their husbands.

Recent research shows that the resolution of differences and the making of joint decisions on matters of importance are more likely to occur (1) with husbands who are cooperative in conflict situations; (2) when spouses have equitable economic resources; (3) with wives whose communication styles are less coercive and demanding; and (4) with spouses who are able to mutually influence each other (Godwin and Scanzoni, 1989). A recent Canadian study found that a nonmasculine orientation among husbands was strongly related to less conflict over the expression of affection and fewer episodes of insulting/swearing or stomping out of the house (Harrell, 1990). An increased level of education among wives was also correlated with reduced conflict.

The same study (Harrell, 1990) found that husbands were less satisfied with their jobs and family life if their wives earned higher incomes than they did.

It seems apparent that making and building a strong, healthy marriage takes work. The ongoing attraction to one's partner is typically based on positive affect and compatibility. The intimacy connected with living together with intentions of permanence demands much more. It typically involves establishing mutually acceptable ways of being love-partners, building trust, practising effective communication, making decisions, resolving important differences, performing household tasks, maintaining boundaries between one's marriage and other relationships and responsibilities, and many other skills and attributes. The probability of divorce is greater for those who fail to make the key adjustments.

• WOMEN'S PARTICIPATION IN THE PAID WORKFORCE

Labour-force participation rates for women have more than doubled over the past forty years, from about 24 percent in 1951 to almost 60 percent in 1991. As can be seen in Table 12.2, women's participation in the labour force has increased in every age group, with the exception of the oldest, from 1951 to 1991. The most significant increases in female labour-force participation are noted in the younger childbearing ages from 20 to 34, which partially accounts for the decline in fertility since 1959. It is also evident that there have been considerable increases in the later age groups, as women either continue to work through the childbearing years or re-enter the workforce after their children have matured.

Few developments have been more important in recent years in modifying the roles and relationships of family members than the increasing number of working wives and mothers.

Table 12.2

Female Labour-Force Participation Rates by Age, Canada, 1951–1991

Year	15–19	20–24	25–34	35–44	45–54	55–64	65+	Total
1951	37.8	46.9	24.2	21.8	20.4	14.5	5.1	24.1
1961	34.2	49.5	29.6	31.1	33.4	24.4	6.7	29.7
1971	36.9	62.5	44.5	43.9	44.5	34.4	8.2	39.9
1976	42.6	67.6	53.9	53.7	49.3	33.9	6.9	45.0
1981	44.3	77.1	65.7	64.1	55.7	35.4	5.5	51.0
1986	45.4	80.7	73.5	72.0	62.4	36.0	4.3	55.0
1991	47.5	81.1	78.5	79.6	71.9	39.2	5.6	59.9

Source: Based on 1971 Census of Canada, *Economic Characteristics*, 1976 Census of Canada, Catalogue no. 94-805; 1981 Census of Canada, Catalogue no. 92-915; 1986 Census of Canada, Catalogue no. 93-111; 1991 Census of Canada, Catalogue no. 93-324 ,Table 1.

Indeed, the dual-income family has become the dominant family type in Canada. Of all husband–wife families in 1986, the majority (61 percent) were dual-income families, while only about one-third were traditional-earner families (Moore, 1989: 24). Of married women, 63.2 percent participated in the labour force in 1991 compared to 11.2 percent in 1951 — a more than fivefold increase. Moreover, the presence of young children in the family has not deterred married women from working outside the home. Between 1981 and 1991 the participation rate of married women increased from 49.4 percent to 68.4 percent. It is clear that Canadian women have gained a significant position in the labour force and are preparing for and pursuing work careers throughout the life cycle in much the same manner as men.

This trend toward two-income families resulted not only from women's changing attitudes toward a career, but also because by the 1970s a husband's salary could no longer maintain a family's economic position (Boyd, 1988). Gelber (1972: 7) argues that "the vast majority of women, particularly married women with young children, who double their work burden by going out to work, are employed because of economic need." Similarly, Ostry (1970) maintains that the need for two incomes is the strongest force determining married women's participation in the workplace. Changing marital and fertility patterns have also influenced the participation of women in the labour force. Women are likely to have completed training and be established in the pursuit of their work or professional careers before marrying, and will be unlikely to leave the labour force after marriage. In contrast to earlier times when children were highly valued for their economic contribution to the family, the married working woman has become the new economic asset to the contemporary family.

Women have also been pulled into the labour force because they are an extremely attractive commodity in the marketplace. Women not only tend to be better educated than men, but they are a cheap source of labour (Ostry, 1970; Wilson, 1991). On average, women working full time earn only about 60 percent of what men earn. In 1985 the average female salary was $18 136, in comparison to the average male salary of $27 675 (Wilson, 1991: 94). Women who work full time and who have a university education earn approximately 67 percent of what men with similar qualifications earn. Moreover, university-educated women earn only about $1600 more per year than men with only a high-school education (Wilson, 1991: 97). Job segregation is central to understanding this wage gap. The labour market continues to be segregated by sex so that women tend to be concentrated in sales, service, and clerical positions. In 1986, almost 60 percent of female employees worked in these three sectors. Indeed, Marshall (1987) found that only twelve of the forty-six professional occupations were not male-dominated. Moreover, women's paid work is often characteristic of women's traditional domestic roles. De Koninck (1991: 237) argues that "these typically female jobs are different expressions of the mothering function that women exercise in our society. The expected prerequisites for these jobs, like those for mothering, are regarded not as skills but rather as attributes of feminine socialization." Segregation in the labour force by sex and the related pay differential have consequences beyond the workplace. They also reinforce gender inequality in the home.

• MARITAL ROLE EQUALITY

Husbands and wives tend to share household roles before children arrive, but this is not the case after children arrive. Research in both the United States and Canada continues to indicate that when wives are employed outside the home they take on two jobs — the job for pay, and continuing major responsibility for the unpaid household job. Kalleberg and Rosenfeld (1990), for example, in a review of the division of labour in four countries, found that the average woman was employed 35.2 hours per week and yet performed an average of 78 percent of the household tasks in the United States and 80 percent of such tasks in Canada. Lupri and Mills (1987) found that the average employed mother in Calgary with children 6 years of age and older worked 7.2 hours per weekday in household and child-care duties, while the husband/father of the children averaged 2.5 hours per day. Fathers with children under 6 put in an additional hour per workday compared to fathers with children over 6 years, but their wives put in an extra 3.4 hours per workday. In families where all the children were under 6 years, employed mothers averaged 6.6 hours per day in paid work and 10.6 hours per day in household and child-care duties. Lupri and Mills also found that there was no difference between the father's domestic work in dual-earner households and single-earner households.

> A 1981 study of Canadians showed that women who were in the labour force spent twice as much time on child care as did men, nearly five times as much time on housework, and were more likely than men to do the shopping. Men in the labour force spent more time than did women on household maintenance and home-based leisure such as watching T.V. . . . The emphasis placed on women as responsible for caregiving causes many to resolve their child-care crises by leaving the labour force. . . These exits can curtail the occupations and incomes of women by reinforcing employer stereotypes about women being intermittent employees and by causing women to suffer reduced or lost seniority-related benefits (Boyd, 1988: 93–94).

Husbands were found to be more involved in household tasks such as cleaning and cooking if they had a nontraditional view of masculinity and their wives had a higher level of income in a 1980 study of 138 couples (Harrell, 1985). Traditional husbands were less likely to perform household tasks and to perceive more conflict between work and family life. Blair and Lichter (1991), in an American study, demonstrated that female income and both male and female education decrease the level of inequality in household labour between employed mothers and fathers. Even so, they conclude that the average well-educated male would have to reallocate about 50 percent of his time to family work before sex equality in the division of labour would be achieved. As suggested in Box 12.2, these differences are increasingly considered unjust and unfair.

Despite the inequality that exists in marital roles, Blumstein and Schwartz (1983: 115–20) argue that a new perspective of an egalitarian, two-paycheque couple is emerging. This new family form would have both husband and wife gainfully employed full time and both sharing equally in the household responsibilities.

• MARITAL DISSOLUTION AND REORGANIZATION

Marital dissolution refers to the dissolving of marital unions through divorce, separation, and death. Although divorce is the official indicator of marital breakdown in Canada, there is also an intermediate stage of separation that a couple enters before legally terminating a marriage. Not

Box 12.2

WORKING MOTHERS TAKE ON TWO JOBS

The double burden borne by women is a central dimension of the family crisis provoked by our rapid move to new family forms. As the Canadian husband/wife family has come to rely on two earners, women have been forced to assume two jobs. The resulting stress and resentment have in no small part contributed to the rising rate of marriage failure. Men's general failure to accept a fair sharing of domestic and child care tasks has presented many women with a hard choice: either accept the double burden in order to sustain the family or opt for divorce and a period of single parenthood. More and more women are making the second choice.

Source: Conway (1990: 107).

all separated persons end this status with a divorce; however, all divorced persons have experienced a separation of varying duration. Separation status does involve emotional and physical termination of a marriage. A study of separation based on self-reported data from the 1976 Census of Canada found that the proportion of the population in this status equalled or exceeded the proportion divorced for every five-year age category over the age of 15 (McVey and Robinson, 1981: 353). This finding suggests that relying on divorce statistics alone to monitor marital dissolution may underestimate the magnitude of family disruption in Canada.

The **divorce rate** — the number of recorded divorces per 100 000 population in a calendar year — increased dramatically from 6.4 in 1921 to 294.0 in 1990 (Figure 12.2). Significant increases in marriages tend to generate high numbers of divorces a few years later. The first peak divorce years of 1946 and 1947 reflected the marital disruption experienced by the large marriage cohorts of the World War II period. A second notable upswing in divorce began in 1969, with a rate of 124.2 demonstrating the impact of the 1968 divorce legislation. Broadening the grounds for divorce to include marital breakdown determined by specified years of separation in the 1968 Divorce Act stimulated this unprecedented increase in marital dissolution. With the implementation of the second major divorce legislation in 1985, the divorce rate increased to a record 355.1 in 1987 — the consequence of further changes in divorce procedures that included a reduction in the period of separation required prior to petitioning for divorce, provisions for more equitable property disbursement between the spouses, and a time limitation on alimony payments.

As can be seen in Figure 12.2 the divorce rates in Alberta have been consistently higher, reaching a peak of nearly 400 divorces per 100 000 population in 1987. The rate of divorce in Quebec, in contrast, remained lower than the overall rate for Canada until 1968. After the change in divorce law of 1968, divorce rates in Quebec climbed rapidly and have become similar to the Canadian average, reaching a peak of just over 300 in 1990.

Marital stability is often publicly questioned in the light of the high divorce rates in recent years, and many people quickly conclude that the outlook is dismal for marriage and the family in Canada. It is important to recognize, however, that the high rates since 1969 and again in 1987 probably reflect the final dissolution of many marriages that have been disrupted for some time. The liberalization of divorce grounds permitted separated couples and partners maintaining "empty-shell" marriages to resolve their marital discord.

Although it is likely that the Canadian divorce rate will long remain higher than it was before 1969, the yearly increases will probably not be as dramatic as they were between 1966 and 1976. Higher rates of divorce will be sustained in future years because of (1) the relative ease in obtaining divorce as a means of resolving marital discord; (2) the increased economic independence of women; (3) the alternatives to marriage conveyed through the mass media; (4) the declining birthrate, which allows less complicated divorces; and (5) the fact that children raised in divorced families are more likely to obtain a divorce in their own marriages. Nearly a quarter century of high divorce rates has left its imprint on remarriage patterns in Canada.

Figure 12.2

DIVORCE RATE TRENDS, ALBERTA, QUEBEC, AND CANADA, 1921–1990

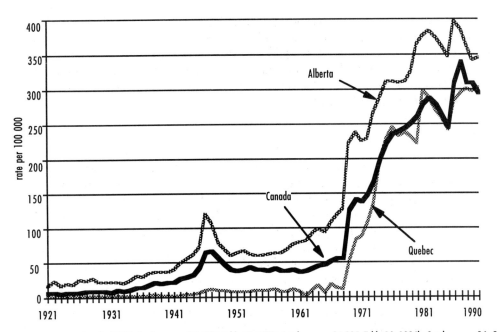

Sources: Statistics Canada (1975: Catalogue no. 84–205, Table 11; 1980: Catalogue no. 84–205, Table 10; 1984b: Catalogue no. 84–204, Table 10; 1989d: Catalogue no. 82–003s, Table 1; 1990g: Catalogue no. 82–003, Table 1, p. 58; 1990h: Catalogue no. 82–003S16, Table 1).

Marriages involving at least one partner who had been previously married increased sharply with the implementation of the 1968 Divorce Act; these remarriage rates are higher for men than for women. Remarriage accounted for almost one-third (32.2 percent) of all marriages in 1990, as divorce became the dominant factor in producing men and women eligible for remarriage. Of all previously married Canadians, divorce accounted for 87.8 percent, while death of a spouse accounted for only 12.2 percent.

Most divorced women are awarded custody of the children, consequently resulting in more female-headed lone-parent families. The mother's financial status correspondingly deteriorates as she experiences reduced family income, thus encouraging her entry into the labour force.

FAMILY PATTERNS

• VOLUNTARY CHILDLESSNESS

Voluntary childlessness refers to the decision by married couples not to have children. Such couples may have made a decision not to have children at all, or they may have simply postponed having children for the time being. Childlessness is on the increase in Canada. The proportion of childless married women (women aged 15 to 44 years who are or have been married and have not yet borne any children) was 14 percent in 1961, 18 percent in 1971, and 23 percent in 1981 (Ram, 1990). It may be emphasized, however, that in each of these years as many as 1 in 10 women may have been biologically incapable of having children — often referred to as involuntary childlessness. It is likely that the *proportion* of the involuntarily childless has decreased as a result of medical advances in the effort to reduce infertility, while more women are probably making the choice to remain childless. It is also likely that the shifts between 1961 and 1981 have become more apparent in the 1980s and 1990s.

The reasons for an increase in voluntary childlessness include the availability of more effective methods of contraception and relatively easy access to abortion. These factors have also been accompanied by increased employment opportunities for women — another incentive to put off having children, perhaps permanently.

• FAMILY SIZE AND FERTILITY

Average family size is getting smaller. The average number of children aged 0 to 24 in the Canadian family dropped from 1.9 in 1961 to 1.3 in 1991. Fertility rates have likewise dropped to below the replacement level of 2.1 children per family. Quebec's total fertility rate, for example, dropped to 1.4 in the mid-1980s, although the rate climbed to 1.7 in 1990. Government incentives in Quebec may partially explain this increase. Even so, the long-term outlook is for a continuing decline in fertility rates. Between 1961 and 1981 childlessness increased from 14 percent to 30 percent among females aged 25 to 29 years (Romaniuc, 1989). As women spend more time preparing for and participating in the labour force, and increasingly opt for singlehood and nonmarital living arrangements such as cohabitation, the likelihood of eventual marriage and childbearing may decrease.

• PARENTHOOD AND FAMILY LIFE

Just as most people marry, most who marry will also have at least one child. The majority of families will be two-parent families — either in a first marriage or through remarriage. Some people will become never-married single parents, and others will become single parents through widowhood, divorce, or separation.

In a recent Canadian survey (Finlayson, 1987), 77 percent of the respondents ranked family ahead of career or religion; 92 percent of the respondents who have children at home said that the family was becoming more important to them. This evidence indicates that Canadians continue to be pro-family in their orientations. Nonetheless, parenthood had an early tradition of being defined as a *crisis* (LeMasters, 1957). It was assumed that marital quality was undermined and that couples were shocked by the demands of an infant on their time and energy. Studies in the 1960s tended to focus on parenthood as a *transition,* emphasizing that most couples were pleased to be parents despite the increased and disruptive workload (e.g., Dyer, 1963). A more recent longitudinal study (Belsky et al., 1985) shows that marital conflict increases as a result of perceived in-equities between the new mother and father in infant care. New mothers in particular are dissatisfied with the failure of the husband/father to also become actively involved in infant care. A follow-up study of 128 families (Belsky and Rovine, 1990) indicates that the characteristics of couples before the birth of their first child significantly affect the ways in which they relate to each other after the birth. Marital quality improves for about 30 percent of couples and deteriorates for about 16 percent, with the balance of the couples either experiencing no change or continuing husband–wife conflict.

It is argued that early parent–child patterns of interaction influence individual development and parent–child relationships throughout the lifespan (Bowlby, 1982; Ainsworth et al., 1978). In general, the research evidence indicates that support and control are the key dimensions of parental behaviour that influence child development. Children reared with optimum levels of support and control (guidance, discipline, punishment, and encouragement of autonomy) tend to have more positive self-views, attitudes, and behaviours (Devereux, 1970; Pratt et al., 1992; Roberts, 1989).

Parent–teen relationships are often seen as a period of storm and stress. Parents apparently consider the period of adolescence the most difficult stage of parenting. Scott and Alwin (1989) found that both mothers and fathers experience parental strain but that mothers experience more parental strain, role demands, and life strain than do fathers. There is little difference in stress and strain between mothers who work outside the home and those who do not. Even so, the research of the 1980s indicates that for most adolescents, relations with parents are more positive than negative, and most adolescents both like themselves and identify with and like their parents (Gecas and Seff, 1990). Offer et al. (1988) found that these patterns characterized adolescents in ten countries. However, suicide rates among 15-to-19-year-old males are high, compared to other countries, in both the United States and Canada (Leenaars and Lester, 1990). Although the suicide rates tend to be five to six times higher among teenage males than teenage females, females are much more likely to *attempt* suicide than males. While suicide is a distinctly rare event, it clearly indicates that adolescence is a painful struggle for a significant minority.

• LONE-PARENT FAMILIES

As divorce dissolves husband-wife families, the fastest-growing family type is the **lone-parent family,** usually a woman living alone with her children. Since 1981, lone-parent families have increased by 34 percent; they accounted for 14 percent of all families in 1991. The divorce reforms of 1968 and 1985 contributed significantly to the increase of lone-parent families headed by women — 82.4 percent in 1991. Divorce has replaced death as the major vehicle in creating lone-parent families in Canada (McVey and Robinson, 1985).

It is estimated that nearly 60 percent of children will experience the single-parent family living arrangement at some point (Wargon, 1979: 26). High divorce rates mean that children today are socialized in mixed milieus, in that there are multiple sets of parents, grandparents, live-in friends, as well as other untested (and often short-term) living arrangements.

The effects of divorce on children appear to be more negative than positive. Amato and Keith (1991), in a review of 37 research projects involving over 81 000 respondents, reported that adult well-being was significantly lower among adults who experienced divorce as a child compared to adults who had never experienced divorce. Depression, health problems, unhappy marriages, higher rates of divorce, and lower levels of educational achievement, income, and occupation were the primary sources of difference. Even so, as demonstrated in longitudinal studies, about one-third to one-half of children, depending on their age at the time of divorce, do better by escaping dysfunctional family situations (e.g., Wallerstein and Blakeslee, 1989). Some family scholars argue that the negative effects of divorce may be exaggerated (e.g., Wells and Rankin, 1991).

In addition to divorce, two other sources contribute to the growing numbers of lone parents: teenage pregnancy and single adult women opting to have a child. The proportion of divorced lone parents increased from 7.6 percent in 1966 to 39 percent in 1986; at the same time the proportion never married increased from 3.8 percent to 17.4 percent (Ram, 1990). Census data show that in 1976 there were 29.5 pregnancies per 1000 never-married teenage females (15 to 19 years old), including those terminated by abortion as well as those resulting in childbirth. By 1986 this figure had increased to 32.3 per 1000 (Ram, 1990). The increase in sexual activity among teenagers and the failure to use contraception is of growing concern. There is a small but growing number of mature single women who deliberately decide that, although they do not have or want husbands, they do want to have a child. It appears that many of these are middle-class career women earning good salaries, who are able to afford child-care services that enable them to be mothers and continue their careers.

The lone-parent family form will continue to be a significant nontraditional family living arrangement owing primarily to increases in divorce, separation, and never-married parenthood.

• REMARRIED FAMILIES

Remarried families vary in complexity. Remarriages that occur after the children leave home, so that the new marriage is without residential children, are considered the least complex. In contrast, remarried families where both parents bring one or more children to the new family are considered the most complex. The greater the complexity, the greater the problems in remarried families (Hetherington and Camera, 1985). There is often confusion about new roles such as stepfather, stepmother, and stepchild, as well as about family boundaries (Cherlin, 1979; Brown and Hobart, 1988). When a remarried couple gives birth to a *shared* child, bonding is facilitated between the parents regardless of the presence of children from previous marriages. Remarried families with shared children have the lowest risk of divorce (Griffith and Koo, 1984). About 60 percent of remarriages end in divorce.

• FAMILIES AND OLD AGE

As mortality levels decline, the obvious effect is that Canadians enjoy more years of life than ever before in history. Households headed by people aged 65 or older will continue their above-average rate of increase, as Canadians live longer and continue to live alone rather than move in with relatives. Improvements in health behaviours, diagnostics, and health services have extended the number of years that people can maintain such independent lifestyles.

The life expectancy of women, at almost 80 years, is 7 years greater than the life expectancy for men. In addition to this mortality differential, men tend to marry somewhat younger women, thus extending their wives' number of years of potential widowhood and living alone. Widows have fewer opportunities for remarriage in accordance with the prevailing mating gradient in Canada, because they greatly outnumber eligible males (McVey and Kalbach, 1994). With improved longevity and expanded pension and retirement benefits, increasing numbers of the elderly, especially women, will be able to maintain their own households into the 21st century.

Improvements in longevity will produce a different situation for extended families. Grandparents will still be living while the grandchildren are becoming adults. Increasing numbers of elderly will depend upon their children for survival, since existing (and projected) social services are not likely to meet the demand. Although many elderly parents insist on maintaining independence by living in their own homes or apartments, they still may require assistance on a regular basis. Middle-aged female children are now faced with a social problem for which there are no guidelines. This **sandwich generation** will have to satisfy the caregiving demands not only from their children, but from their aging parents as well. With a continued decline in fertility, there will be fewer children in families to meet these role obligations in future years. Elder family members require frequent social contact, usually by telephone or visits, require assistance for grocery shopping and medical visits, and may have to be assisted in maintaining their home. The dual-carner family will be especially challenged, because the time and energy of both adults are already fully committed. There have already been some instances of "grandparent dumping," where families have abandoned their dependent elderly members at hospitals or in public places to be cared for by others. Compensatory strategies such as extended-care services and visiting or live-in professional caregivers and health professionals, or income and care subsidies, may prove costly.

Contemporary Family Issues

Scholars in the family area hold a variety of perspectives concerning the meaning and quality of family life in the 1990s. There is often strong disagreement, and even controversy, in attempting to describe the changes and their implications for child, adult, and family well-being. A few scholars argue that the family is in a period of significant *decline* (e.g., Popenoe, 1993). A larger group of scholars believe that the family is in a period of *adjustment* and will adapt in positive ways (e.g., Blankenhorn et al., 1991). Several scholars have adopted a rethinking perspective in which it is argued that current changes are inevitable, are necessary, and will eventually produce an acceptable *diversity* of lifestyles that will serve the needs of individuals more effectively (e.g., Scanzoni et al., 1989). Many specialists in the family area, however, have adopted a *don't know* perspective (e.g., Furstenberg and Cherlin, 1991).

The issues often debated include divorce rates, individual rights, the needs of children, family violence, sexually transmitted diseases, recreational sexuality, teenage pregnancy, changing definitions of marriages and families, reproductive choice, and related contemporary patterns. We will briefly discuss three of these issues and conclude with a note on preventative policies in support of families.

• FAMILY VIOLENCE

The contemporary issue of greatest concern is probably family violence. Since the early 1970s the literature on physical aggression and/or violence has exploded. Major cross-national studies have been conducted in the United States. In addition, several regional studies have been carried out in Canada (Brinkerhoff and Lupri, 1988; Kennedy and Dutton, 1989; M.D. Smith, 1987). Hundreds of articles and books have been published detailing the frequency and meaning of violence in dating relationships, marriage, and parent–child relationships. Most of us think of the poorly lighted street on a dark night as the place of danger. In fact most violence occurs within the marital or family context. An estimated 6 of every 10 women murdered in Canada are killed by husbands or boyfriends (Carreiro, 1990). Destructive or abusive families — involving some degree of physical, sexual, or emotional abuse — represent 20 to 25 percent of all families (Larson, 1985). They are also often characterized by the intentional neglect of their children (Garbarino et al., 1986).

Physical aggression is a significant reality in intimate relationships. Although we do not attempt to define the causes of violence in families, it is apparent that this issue cannot be ignored.

• Dating Violence

One would think that while dating, men and women would be more likely to treat each other with respect. However, research has indicated that this is not necessarily the case. In a study of 202 male college students (Barnes et al., 1991), 42 percent had committed *one* or more of the following violent acts against the female they were dating: threw something at her (4 percent); pushed, grabbed, or shoved her (15 percent); wrestled with her (12 percent); slapped or spanked her (5.5 percent); bit or scratched her (0.5 percent); threw her (1 percent); or physically forced her to have sex (only one student admitted to doing this). About 25 percent reported more than one incident of abuse. Males whose fathers had been violent to their own mothers and/or who had been drinking were more likely to commit abuse. Studies have found that the amount of abuse in dating relationships is even higher in the United States. Studies of cohabitation have also reported higher rates of violence among cohabitors than among married persons (Stets and Straus, 1989; Stets, 1991). In a recent study (Stets, 1991) approximately 14 percent of cohabitors admitted to hitting, shoving, or throwing things at their partner during the past year, compared to only 5 percent of married people. It is argued that cohabitors experience less social support and less social control as a result of the less committed nature of their relationship.

• Marital Violence

Studies of marital aggression typically distinguish between verbal, minor, and severe violence. Stets (1991) found, in a study of 1089 married men and 1547 married women, that more women than men committed acts of verbal violence such as sulking, insulting, doing something to spite the other, or stomping out of the room. Acts of minor or severe physical violence, however, are more common among married men. Kennedy and Dutton (1989) found from a survey of over 1000 households that husbands threw something (4.2 percent), pushed, grabbed, or shoved (9.2 percent), or slapped their spouses (1.7 percent). These are all examples of "minor" violence. Acts of severe violence (kicking, hitting, beating up, threatening with a knife or gun) were committed by 2.3 percent of husbands. These data represent the incidence of one or more acts of violence in the previous twelve months. Lupri (1989), in a study of 1834 Canadian men and women, found that 18 percent of the men had committed at least one of eight listed violent acts in the past year. Moreover, 10 percent of the men had committed at least one severe violent act. These rates of violence are quite similar to findings in the 1985 cross-national survey in the United States (Straus and Gelles, 1986). The incidence of lifetime severe violence against wives is about 13 percent (Strauss et al., 1980). However, it should be emphasized that research on violence is based on *reported* acts of violence. It is likely that actual violence exceeds reported violence. Some have suggested that actual physical violence may be as high as 25 percent to 30 percent. According to a recent study by Silverman and Mukherjee (1987), there were 126 cases of intersexual homicide between 1976 and 1982 in the cities of Edmonton, Winnipeg, and Calgary. Over 45 percent involved daters, common-law, divorced, separated husbands and wives, or legally married spouses still together at the time of the homicide.

• Child Violence

Similar data have been collected on parents and their children. In the 1985 U.S. study (Gelles and Straus, 1987), about 55 percent of parents slapped or spanked their children, and 31 percent grabbed, pushed, or shoved them in the previous twelve months. Ten percent hit or tried to hit their children. Another analysis of these data examined aggression by teenagers against their parents (Gelles and Cornell, 1987). Eleven percent of adolescent sons were found to have committed acts of violence against their mothers and 8 percent against their fathers. About 9 percent of mothers and 4 percent of fathers were treated violently by their daughters. Most of these actions represented acts such as slapping or hitting. Like adults, teens also kill. A recent Canadian study by Meloff and Silverman (1992), based on 990 cases of homicides committed by youths under the age of 17 between 1961 and 1983, found that about 14 percent were committed against parents and 20 percent against other family members.

• CHILD CARE

The effective nurturant care of children has always been a priority for families and the larger society. Recent data indicate that the adequacy of child care has become a national issue. Statistics indicate that 60 percent of Canadian teens who became pregnant in 1989 kept their babies. Nearly 80 percent of these teenage mothers were the sole providers for their children; at least 25 percent have reported abuse and 20 percent have been treated for substance abuse (Fullton, 1993). Many of these young mothers were on welfare and barely able to survive.

In 1988, 58 percent of young mothers with children under 3 years of age were employed outside the home (Statistics Canada, 1989c). As pointed out by Zigler and Ennis (1989), the

Box 12.3

THE ISSUES IN DUAL-INCOME FAMILIES REQUIRE RESOLUTION

In fact, the dual-income, dual-career family is the most significant variation among the new emerging family forms ... A traditional male can avoid or rationalize the new economic reality, and given the continuing advantages enjoyed by men in the world of work, he can even to some extent insulate himself from increasing female competition. But such insulation is more difficult to carry off if a man's wife works outside the home. Even if the woman earns significantly less than her husband, and therefore her income can be seen as merely secondary or supplementary; even if she agrees to put her husband's career first; even if she continues to carry the full childcare and housekeeping load, the new domestic reality forces even the most traditional of men to make adjustments and concessions ... Historically, women's oppression was inseparable from their economic dependence within the patriarchal family. It follows that women can never achieve liberation until the patriarchal family is dismantled and replaced by a family form that deliberately seeks to reconcile women's economic independence with fairly shared marital and parental obligations.

Source: Conway (1990: 183–84).

driving force in the massive movement of mothers into the workforce is economic — the continuing decline in median family income. Some young mothers choose to stay home with their children, economic hardship notwithstanding. The June 1992 issue of *Transition* is devoted to the many trade-off issues for stay-at-home and workplace mothers. The title of this focus issue is apt: *The Pain of Choice, the Agony of None*. Career women, often late childbearers, also seem to be weighing the pros and cons of their careers and motherhood. Barsky (1992) refers to career-oriented mothers who have opted to stay home until their children are in school as "neohomemakers." The choice to stay at home with a young child is often very difficult financially. There is little if any incentive for those mothers or fathers who strongly prefer to stay with their children for a year or two. Extended maternal or paternal leaves are seldom available, and there are no government-funded financial incentives for home child care.

Young mothers who must work, as well as those who prefer to work, do not have adequate licensed day-care services available. According to Burke et al. (1991), the mothers of 1.3 million preschoolers (under the age of 6) were in the labour force in 1990. In the same year, however, there were only 321 000 licensed spaces. Just 18 percent of these children were in licensed family day care or day-care centres. Most of these small children, therefore, were in unlicensed care facilities or being looked after by relatives. Feminists strongly advocate universal day care to ensure the right of *all* mothers to work or pursue their careers. They reject policies that undermine that goal (Prentice, 1988). There is little question that public day care must be available, accessible, and of *high quality*. Given the high cost of universal day care, however, other options might include temporary job sharing to permit fathers or mothers to obtain half-time employment, tax credits for stay-at-home young fathers or mothers, and related considerations. Children, it is often said, get short shrift in modern society.

Another salient dimension of child care arises from the apparent inequities between mothers and fathers in dual-work households. Dual paid work is *the* new struggle for many Canadian families (Box 12.3). An equitable household division of labour is essential to build and/or rebuild strong marital bonds. These concerns will need to be creatively resolved by both families and those social institutions that support families in Canada.

• REPRODUCTIVE TECHNOLOGIES

The quest for medical solutions to involuntary childlessness has recently turned to several new reproductive technologies, including artificial insemination, in vitro fertilization (IVF), and embryo transplants. In 1990, Bryant reviewed the new reproductive technologies and concluded that the success rates were unacceptable and the techniques too experimental. The Canadian Advisory Council on the Status of Women recently released a sharp critique of these new technologies, emphasizing that the rights of women are being undermined (1991). The uncertain meanings of ovum donor, gestational mother (surrogacy), social mother, sperm donor/genetic father, and social father, it is argued, represent a premature renegotiation of the meanings of maternity and paternity (1991: 5). Surrogacy — a host woman carrying an embryo to term for a price — although not new, is now a source of significant revenue for some women. According to one recent estimate there were 2000 such births by 1990 (Kantrowitz et al., 1990). The typical birth mother is paid about $10 000 for "womb time," although the price has reached nearly $75 000 in a few cases (Benokraitis, 1993: 298).

To some feminist scholars, reproductive technologies are a subset of issues relating to the woman's rights in reproductive choice. McDaniel (1988c: 180), for example, argues that differences in allocation of these technologies involve "issues of reproductive control always [being] more closely linked to the broader issues of sexual, moral, social, and political power than to family size per se." Martin (1989: 57) likewise maintains that because we focus so much on the technology that is involved in reproduction decisions, our attention is diverted from the "power and domination" that is involved. In the light of this, the critique continues, an infertile woman has the choice of either remaining childless in a society that defines her in terms of her reproductive functions or, if allowed by the medical profession, she can use the various reproductive technologies, which are invasive, expensive, and experimental, and which have extremely low success rates (Hubbard, 1990; McDaniel, 1988c; Corea, 1985, 1991).

These issues are of obvious significance to women as individuals. They are also central to intimate relationships, marriages, families (siblings, grandparents), and to both women and men as potential parents. Recreational sexualities, contraception, abortion, and recent bio-technologies influence and are influenced by marital and family bonds.

• PREVENTATIVE FAMILY POLICY

There is considerable disagreement among family scholars about the meaning and implications of contemporary sexual, relationship, marital, and family patterns. Even so, most advocate policies and programs that will both *reduce* dysfunctionality, inequities, and poverty, and *enhance* child, adult, relational, marital, and family well-being. Preventative actions have already been implemented in the control of unhealthy behaviours and lifestyles (e.g., smoking, diet, and stress reduction). Although the analogy is self-evident, it is apparent that similar principles apply to societal conditions, family pathologies, dysfunctional relationship traditions, unhealthy ways of relating to women (and to men), and pervasive inequities in domestic labour. Priorities are the enhancement of marriage and the family, an unequivocal commitment to the welfare of our children, and the special and increasingly unique needs of our aging men and women. The need for a caring, supportive society in the 1990s seems even more apparent in a period of escalating deficits, increasing unemployment, and continuing interpersonal uncertainty.

SUMMARY

- There are diverse marriage and family forms and patterns, both cross-culturally and within societies such as our own. In Canada, most marriages are monogamous, and most families are nuclear.

- Universal and inclusive definitions of marriage and the family were provided in this chapter. Universal definitions emphasize the basic commonalities among cultures; inclusive definitions emphasize the diversity in structures and the characteristics of relationships.
- There are several basic conceptual approaches in family study, four of which were briefly summarized: the functionalist, conflict, symbolic interactionist, and exchange approaches.
- Premarital relationships continue to involve various phases and types of dating. Sexuality before marriage is increasingly more common among youth and college/university students. Cohabitation has become a more common pathway to marriage.
- The age at marriage is continuing to increase, while the rate of marriage is decreasing.
- Although most couples believe that they are happily married, the evidence indicates that more is expected of marriage. Inequities in domestic labour seem to be becoming more apparent as wives and mothers have entered the paid workforce. Divorce rates peaked in 1987, and although they have decreased slightly since, it is expected that rates will probably increase in the 1990s.
- Childlessness is on the increase in Canada, while average family size is getting smaller. Even so, bearing and rearing children remain important to most Canadians. The complexities of parenting, however, have increased as a result of paid employment by both mothers and fathers and inadequate child-care arrangements.
- Other than widowhood, there are three major sources of lone parenthood: divorce, teenage pregnancy, and single motherhood by choice. Although many children do quite well in lone-parent families, well-being is significantly lower among adults who experienced the divorce of their parents when they were children.
- This chapter emphasized several contemporary family issues in Canadian society: violence, child care, reproductive technologies, and the importance of preventative family policies.
- Social scientists view family issues in the decade of the 1990s in four differing ways: a period of "further decline," "adjustment and adaptation," a "continuing and necessary diversity of lifestyles," and a "wait-and-see" perspective.

KEY CONCEPTS

Close relationships
Cohabitation
Comparison level (CL)
Comparison level for alternatives (CLalt)
Conflict approach
Divorce rate
Exchange approach
Extended family
Family
Homogamy
Hypergamy
Ideology of singlehood
Inclusive approach

Kinship group
Lone-parent family
Marital dissolution
Marriage
Marriage rate
Marriage squeeze
Mating gradient
Matrilineal
Monogamy
Multilineal
Nuclear family
Patrilineal
Polyandry
Polygamy
Polygyny
Propinquity
Sandwich generation
Separation
Serial monogamy
Structural-functional approach
Symbolic interactionist approach
Universal approach

REVIEW QUESTIONS

1. Review the differing types of marriages and families.
2. Identify the similarities and differences in the four conceptual approaches to the macro- and micro-sociological study of families.
3. What are the major shifts in premarital patterns in Canadian society?
4. Review the major patterns and trends in mate choice, marriage, wife and mother participation in the workforce, divorce, and remarriage.
5. Identify the trends in childlessness, fertility, research on parenthood, and child development. Outline the issues pertaining to lone-parent and remarried families.
6. Review the issues that individuals and families are facing in the 1990s.

Religion & Society

Stephen A. Kent and Charles Hobart

Religion and Society

INTRODUCTION

As a social phenomenon both in culture and in people's lives, religion often plays unique and dramatic roles. Religious beliefs and attitudes may influence behaviour and beliefs in a multitude of direct or indirect ways. Social psychologists have paid close attention to these subjective and emotional elements of human life. Other sociologists concentrate on religion's institutional dimensions, realizing that these organizational structures hold varying degrees of power among other institutions and over vast numbers of people. Consequently, this chapter discusses religion both as a social psychological set of experiences and as an organizational or institutional force in society and the world. Moreover, it highlights five important perspectives in the study of religion: structural-functional theories, dysfunctionalism and conflict theories, social exchange theories, attribution theories (as part of social psychology), and typological theories.

Neither sociology nor any other science can make statements about the existence or nonexistence of God or any other supernatural beings or forces that religions worship. Furthermore, social scientists cannot comment on any powers or actions that these supernatural figures or forces allegedly possess or perform. Science has these limitations because it can study and draw conclusions about the natural world only. Religion, in contrast, presupposes the existence of a supernatural realm — a realm (if it exists) whose contents are beyond scientific scrutiny. Nonetheless, people's *beliefs* about deity are empirical phenomena that can be studied, as are the organizations that propagate such beliefs. Likewise, sociologists are able to learn about the beliefs held by people in different kinds of societies and how these belief systems and their related symbols, myths, and rituals affect individual and collective lives.

SYMBOLS, MYTHS, AND RITUALS IN RELIGION

Emotions and feelings play a key role in religion; they range from awe and reverence to fear and dread. When we talk about such emotions, we use **connotative language,** which is the language of feeling and of poetry (Fromm, 1951). "[L]ay up for yourselves treasures in heaven" (Matthew, 6.20; references are to the Authorized Version) for example, is a connotative statement, since it uses arbitrary symbols whose meanings are *evocative* and emerge out of the rich complex of meanings and feelings that these words (*treasures* and *heaven*) bring to mind. In contrast, **denotative language** involves precise definition and is the type of communication that we use in scientific discourse. It utilizes signs, symbols, arbitrary sounds (words), and marks (writing) that have precise meanings — as, for example, in scientific formulae.

The distinction between the two types of language is important for identifying the power of religious imagery, such as occurs, for instance, in the Christian statement that "Christ died on the cross to save us from our sins." While many Christians take this statement to be factual, its evocative significance is even more important for the sociologist of religion.

When religions use objects and images in rituals and myths, these objects and images gain emotional significance. To use more Christian examples, the cross for Protestants and the crucifix for Catholics evoke the connotations of the sacrificial death of Christ, who is their tradition's central religious figure. For Catholics, the image of the Virgin Mary connotes feelings of purity, compassion, understanding, and the hope of supernatural intercession in times of need. The Protestant immersion baptismal font symbolizes (1) the grave in which the old self is buried; (2) the womb, from which a new "saved" self is born; and (3) the purification of a person thought to be spiritually cleansed by the water (Eliade, 1958: 120; Warner, 1961: 265–340).

These religious symbols (the cross or crucifix, the Virgin Mary, the baptismal font) derive their emotional significance from religious accounts that sociologists call "myths." A myth is not a fairy story. Rather, it is a nonhistorical account whose emotionally dramatic content addresses questions that are fundamental to a culture and its people. For Jews and Christians, for example, the early chapters of Genesis provide a myth that answers questions concerning the origins of the universe, animal and plant species, humankind, suffering, and death. Specifically for Christians, the first four books of the New Testament answer additional questions about the nature of God and humanity, sin, and salvation.

Other traditions use objects and images in rituals that hold powerful meanings for their adherents. For Moslems on pilgrimage to Mecca, the large, black cube-shaped structure called the Ka'ba represents the tradition's connection to Abraham, who they believe built the edifice (Koran 22.26; see Lewis, 1976: 45). Devout Jews are powerfully moved by praying and reciting Torah at the Wailing Wall in Jerusalem, which is the remnant of the Temple begun by King Solomon and destroyed by the Romans in A.D. 70 (Noss, 1969: 410). Sri Lankan Buddhists undertake ritual pilgrimages to a mountain called Adam's Peak, where they venerate an alleged footprint of the Buddha, which is "a trace of his mythic visit to the sacred island" (Smart, 1977: 36–37). Tibetan monks spin prayer wheels as visible symbols of the Buddha's message, which supposedly "set the wheel of the Law in motion" (Smart, 1977: 93). Eastern Orthodox Christians often kiss holy pictures or icons as a means of showing "affection and respect . . . to the visible representation of the unseen, angelic world" (Smart, 1977: 94). As these diverse examples suggest, sacred symbols derive their significance from religious myths of which they are important components.

Rituals that use sacred symbols also derive their significance from the religious myth system that they partially re-enact. Catholicism provides recognizable examples in its Mass. The Mass both celebrates and symbolically re-enacts what many believe was the sacrificial death of Jesus on the cross in order to atone for humanity's sins. Catholic theology claims that this mythic sacrifice and atonement make possible the opportunity for repentant people to go to heaven. The priest who conducts the Mass says, "Christ is crucified again," and the Catholic doctrine of transubstantiation holds that the wine and bread of the communion wafers are transformed miraculously into the actual blood and body of Christ (see Warner, 1961, for a fuller discussion).

Contemporary analyses of rituals emphasize the extent to which participation in them empowers participants. Put succinctly, "ritualization is first and foremost a strategy for the construction of certain types of power relationships effective within particular social organizations" (Bell, 1992: 197). The logic behind this insight is that "the person who has prayed to his or her god, appropriating the social schemes of the hegemonic order in terms of an individual redemption, may be stronger because these acts are the very definitions of power, personhood, and the capacity to act" (Bell, 1992: 218).

Not to be neglected, however, are examples of rituals that actually disempower participants to the extent that they reproduce socially sanctioned patterns of domination, subservience, passivity, and sexism. Moreover, on interpersonal levels, ritual leaders may use their claims of ceremonial superiority or hegemony to manipulate or abuse fellow participants in the name of a higher, religious justification.

The use of rituals to empower or disempower indicates that after religious symbols come into existence they can be used for a variety of purposes. They can comfort the dying or bereaved; they can attempt to ward off evil; and they can claim God's support during war or election campaigns. Likewise, they can increase people's confidence in the likely success of a venture, as when a bishop blesses either a fishing fleet at the beginning of the season or an army on the eve of a battle. In short, the humanly constructed nature of religious symbols allows us to (re)mould or (re)assign them in arbitrary ways, even when they contradict the meanings assigned to them by other authorities and traditions.

DEFINITIONS AND DIMENSIONS OF RELIGION

Sociologists use various definitions of religion, and these definitions allow researchers to examine a wide range of groups, activities, and behaviours. Common to most of the definitions is

Religion and Society

recognition that religion claims to be involved with a supernatural realm. Any definition that speaks about this (presumably) supernatural realm is a **substantive** one, since it claims that the *substance* or essence of religion is its members' belief in some form of otherworldliness. Thus, a basic example of a substantive definition is the one that the British anthropologist E.B. Tylor offered more than a century ago: religion is "the belief in Spiritual Beings" (Tylor, 1871: 8). Contemporary substantivists often expand the definition to say that religion is "belief in spiritual *forces*" (which, of course, would include beings), since not all belief systems that people generally agree are religions (such as Theravada Buddhism) postulate heavenly entities of any kind (Spiro, 1967).

Other types of sociological definitions of religion examine the functions provided by religion in society's creation and maintenance of meaning and order. These are called **functional definitions,** and they do not necessarily make supernatural claims about religious phenomena. Under these definitions, any activities that provide participants with large, embracing systems of meaning and order are, at least in a sociologically functional sense, religious. In this spirit, such mundane activities as hockey watching (Sinclair-Faulkner, 1977) and such secular groups as motorcycle gangs (Watson, 1982) are functionally religious because of the overriding importance that some participants place on them.

The most useful definitions of religion, however, combine substantive claims about the nature of religion (that it allegedly involves supernatural forces or beings) with discussions about how religions serve (or function) to provide meaning and order to their adherents. These definitions emphasize the collective nature of religion, but in addition they recognize that religion allows people to place their joys, sorrows, and uncertainties in a comprehensive framework (as we are about to see).

An influential definition of religion appeared in the work of French sociologist Emile Durkheim, who argued that religion was "a unified system of beliefs and practices relative to sacred things, that is, things set apart and forbidden — beliefs and practices which unite into one single moral community called a church, all those who adhere to them" (Durkheim, 1965 [1912]: 62).

This definition implies three things. First, **the sacred** is anything that society (or some of its members) believe is antagonistic to the profane world and superior in dignity and power. Second, religion comprises a social system that integrates beliefs and practices. Third, religion is a social (and not merely an individual) phenomenon. That is to say, a group of people adhere to a particular set of beliefs and practices in a setting that (for convenience) Durkheim called a "church," but which includes any formal social organization (such as a synagogue, mosque, temple, etc.).

Broad definitions of religion such as Durkheim's are adequate for much sociological research, but studies into the range, depth, and scope of religiosity have caused researchers to highlight different aspects in their definitional preferences. Charles Glock (1962), for example, specified five dimensions to religiosity or religious belief; these dimensions are especially useful for researchers who want a definition that provides measurable traits. The first dimension is *experiential* — the extent to which a person either claims to have direct knowledge of a deity or supernatural force, or experiences profoundly religious emotion. (Keep in mind, however, that perceptions and identifications of religious emotion differ from religion to religion.)

The second dimension is *ideological* — the extent to which a person holds certain beliefs. Thus, religions usually have basic sets of beliefs or creeds that members profess; researchers can measure the degrees of agreement with them. The third dimension, which is closely related to the second one, is *intellectual* — the extent to which a person is informed and knowledgeable about the basic beliefs of the religion and its reputedly sacred scriptures.

The fourth measurable dimension of religion is *ritualistic* — the extent to which a person performs those specifically religious practices that are expected of the faithful. Rituals of this nature often include prayer, offerings, religious fasting, ceremonies at birth, marriage, and death, and so on.

The fifth and last dimension is *consequential* — the effects of religion on the behaviour of people and the extent to which it *makes a difference* in their lives. Sociologists are able to measure the extent to which religious beliefs affect secular activities, such as choice of occupations, levels of income, selection of marriage partners, and political orientations.

In Canada, for example, geographer Al Hecht concluded that "the [religious] influence works itself through in part on where people decide to live; what kind of occupations they pursue or don't pursue; to what extent they pursue education; whether they speak English at home, and a whole host of things" (cited in Simone, 1992: C8). Specifically regarding his own religious group, the Mennonites, Hecht determined that "religion does have an impact on income, and that impact was most pronounced in the Mennonite group, which tended to be lower than average, even after other variables such as education and area of residence were worked into the statistical analysis" (cited in Simone, 1992: C8). To Mennonites themselves, however, their tendency "to have lower income is not necessarily a bad thing — it may simply reflect the group putting its priorities on other areas of life" along with their "attitudes about the afterlife and the relationship between the accumulation of earthly wealth and the afterlife" (cited in Simone, 1992: C8).

THEORIES OF RELIGION

As a human enterprise, religion has existed in virtually all societies over a vast expanse of human history. Its pervasiveness suggests that it serves important and often vital functions for societies and the people who live in them.

• STRUCTURAL-FUNCTIONALISM

Structural-functional theory assumes that religion and other major structures (groupings or organizations) of society have important, perhaps necessary, functions or consequences for the survival of society. According to this theory, society could not survive without the structures of family, government, economic organizations, and religion, because all of them contribute to the survival of society as a unit. Structural-functional analyses have led sociologists of religion to identify at least six functions of religion in society. Together they help explain why religion has operated so widely throughout the world's cultures.

The broadest, and probably the most important of these vital functions is that *religion makes life meaningful* to many people because it addresses issues that are central (if not basic) to their lives. Many religious teachings, for example, include **cosmologies** that explain the origins of the world as well as its ultimate fate. Included in these cosmologies are directives about the manner in which individuals (and sometimes the groups to which they belong) are supposed to live their lives. Believers in each religious tradition are then able to view their lives as part of a grand divine plan, thereby feeling part of a vast and sometimes personal unfolding of cosmological forces.

The second and next most important function of religion involves the *comfort* that it provides to the sick, bereaved, suffering, aged, and poor. The ability of religion to provide comfort is the result of its attempt to answer fundamental human questions that involve life, death, and suffering. Such questions appear in the forefront of people's minds in times of crisis or despair, such as when loved ones are hurt or die. Such crises may make people wonder about the purpose or value of human life, so all successful religions must deal with the threats to meaning posed by suffering and evil in the world. Thus, one researcher concluded that "what a religion has to say about suffering reveals, in many ways more than anything else, what it believes the nature and purpose of existence to be" (Bowker, 1970: 2). The answers to these and similar questions of meaning are called **theodicies** (see Weber, 1956 [1922]: 138–39), and their interpretations allow people to continue experiencing life as meaningful and desirable.

Different theodicies operate among the world's religions, and they may vary in different historical periods or cultural settings within the same religious traditions. Jewish, Christian, and Islamic theodicies, for example, include the expectation that a messianic figure soon will arrive to alleviate worldly distress, along with other beliefs that people will attain their appropriate eternal rewards in heaven or hell (see Weber, 1956 [1922]: 138–44). Moreover, some Christian traditions (most notably those related to Calvinism) additionally claim that God has predestined or "decreed not only human fate on earth but also human destiny after death" (Weber, 1956 [1922]: 143).

In contrast to these varied Western theodicies, both Hinduism and Buddhism assert that people's current life situations are a direct result of what they earned while living during *previous* lives (called karma), so that persons who suffer misfortunes are paying for deeds that they committed in other lifetimes (Weber, 1956 [1922]: 145). Finally, some dualistic religious traditions (such as Zoroastrianism, Jainism, and forms of Gnosticism) explain evil as the product of dark forces that compete in the world for dominance against the forces of goodness and light (Weber, 1956 [1922]: 144–45).

Prominent and specially trained religious figures in each religious tradition put believers in touch with their tradition's cosmologies and interpret their theodicies to adherents in ways that provide solace and comfort in difficult times. These activities fall within the realm of pastoral care, which (in basic terms) is "the religious cultivation of the individual" (Weber, 1956 [1922]: 75). In essence, providing followers with both meaning and doctrinal interpretations are **priestly functions,** since they involve persons with special training (such as is received by priests, ministers, rabbis, imams, etc.).

In contrast to religion's priestly or comfort functions are the third type, **prophetic functions,** which are carried out when religious leaders criticize or condemn people or entire societies for their alleged moral or religious transgressions. The term *prophet* comes from the Hebrew Bible/Old Testament figures who condemned the political, moral, and religious conditions of the societies in which they lived. They based their condemnations upon values that they believed were divinely inspired, thereby elevating their criticisms to the level of godly directives. Weber's classic analysis of religious figures distinguished between an "ethical prophet" such as Zoroaster and Muhammad who claimed to be "an instrument for the proclamation of a god and his will," and an "exemplary prophet" such as the Buddha "who, by his personal example, demonstrates to others the way to religious salvation" (Weber, 1956 [1922]: 55).

A fourth function that religion serves is that of *providing communities* in which people involve themselves. These communities provide social settings for people to acquire friends and social contacts among fellow members who supposedly share the same basic values. Were it not for religion, for example, immigrants or rural migrants to cities probably would become members of what David Reisman called *The Lonely Crowd:* isolated urban dwellers with few if any local family or friends.

Religion's provision of community is aptly demonstrated by the functions of some religious organizations in Alberta during the first part of the 20th century. Numerous sectarian groups in Edmonton and Calgary "assisted in the adjustment of people of rural background to an urban environment" (Mann, 1955: 154). More broadly, "in both urban and rural areas, the sects' interest in newcomers, and their many weekday activities and status conferring offices, enabled them to draw marginal people into a fairly close-knit socio-religious community. In a province characterized by a high incidence of social marginality, this sectarian function contributed significantly to social integration" (Mann, 1955: 155). Similarly, in a sweeping study of the role of religion in Canada from 1760 to the late 1940s, S.D. Clark concluded that "the religious institution as an integral part of the whole institutional complex of the community served as one of the means of entering into social relationships and of becoming a part of a recognized group life" (Clark, 1948: 433).

A fifth important function that religion serves for some people is that it *provides a source of identity*. People may see themselves as inseparable from the religion to which they belong. Close identifications of this kind are especially likely to occur either when people have to make important sacrifices to remain members of the faith or when they are isolated from mainstream society in significant ways. Religions such as the Hutterites, Jehovah's Witnesses, and Mormons are obvious examples of groups that demand sacrifices from members who in turn identify strongly with their respective religious traditions.

Hutterite commitment to their colonies, for example, is based on the principle of the "community of goods," which

> governs not only the production and distribution of resources so that "one person must not have abundance and another suffer want," but also the control of the natural appetites. Carnal desires are believed to express themselves in the adornment of the body and in activities that cater to gratification — "the lusts of the eye" — such as movies, television shows, dancing, recreation in public places, excessive drinking, and worldly music. Curling, a common form of recreation in Canadian towns, and skiing are also viewed as a great waste of time and money and are forbidden. Such manifestations are not legitimate "needs" and are not part of the consumption pattern of either the individual or the colony (Hostetler, 1974: 194–95).

Avoidance of these habits and activities combines with isolation from the secular community and extensive communal activities in order to form religiously based self-identities among Hutterite members.

Contemporary Mormons, in contrast, rarely live in colonies, but their identity formation (especially for men) involves sacrifice and distance from the outside world. As do members of some other religious organizations, devout Mormons give 10 percent of their incomes to the church (Gottlieb and Wiley, 1984: 97). Mormon men (and increasingly, women) usually serve as missionaries for two years under the strict control of church officials, with their families paying their expenses. Persons whose missionary plans require language training may attend the Missionary Training Center (originally called the Language Training Mission [LTM]) in Provo, Utah. The diary of one young man from that program recorded that the training he underwent there "meant a transition to a new kind of identity." "I was the creature of the LTM," he wrote. "It had created me. Outside it, my existence had no context, no purpose, and no meaning" (quoted in Gottlieb and Wiley, 1984: 130). In essence, his religious organization had formed for him a new identity.

   operate within the doctrinal confines of (what one sociologist called) "ideological absolutism," which teaches the Witnesses "to owe exclusive loyalty" to Jehovah as revealed through the corporate body. If members adhere to the ideology as the organization intends, then it "is able to prescribe detailed moral regulations for them" (Beckford, 1975: 199). Behavioural prescriptions dictate that a member

> must not join a political party, vote for public officials, perform jury duty, attend bull fights, fence, stand for the national anthem, salute the flag, offer toasts, smoke, chew tobacco, use hallucinogenic drugs, celebrate holidays, engage in improper sexual relations (as defined by the [organization]), accept a blood transfusion, or . . . participate in certain types of dancing or listen to certain types of music (Penton, 1985: 280).

In sum, many religions provide identities for their members that require individuals to commit themselves to the adherence of organizationally prescribed and proscribed attitudes and behaviour, usually involving substantial sacrifices of time and resources.

Finally, society itself also may utilize religion *to legitimize its collective identity*. National mythologies, for example, often connect the origins of countries with the will of a divine figure. The most readily available examples come from the experience of the United States, whose earliest permanent European settlers, the Pilgrims, envisioned their efforts in the so-called New World as a covenant with God. A respected modern historian of the Pilgrims, Perry Miller, surmised, "this much is indubitable, that when New England was settled the two covenants, the religious and the political, had become one in the minds of the leaders. No political writing of seventeenth century Massachusetts and Connecticut can be fully understood without reference to the whole system" (Miller, 1939: 414). Perceptions of the United States as "the promised land" continue to permeate that country's national thinking through the modern period, and appear in conceptions of America as "one nation, under God" in that country's pledge of allegiance to its flag.

• CIVIL RELIGIONS

Closely related both to religion's legitimation of collective identities and to its frequent sanctification of existing structural arrangements in society is its use as *a justification for the actions that nations undertake*. Throughout history societies have seen their activities as the performance of God's work on earth. In essence, civic actions may become religious in the eyes of society's members and leaders. Robert Bellah (1967) termed this phenomenon **civil religion,** in which societies mix religious and patriotic symbols and impute divine support to the purposes and officials of the state.

Currently nations from a variety of religious backgrounds — Jewish, Christian, and Islamic — invoke the blessings of their respective deities for their social and political actions. The United States, for example, prints the words "In God We Trust" on its coins, and many of its politicians' speeches are laced with religious language. President John Kennedy's inauguration speech in 1960 even had the tone and phrases of a religious sermon:

> Now the trumpet summons us again — not as a call to bear arms, though arms we need — not as a call to battle, though embattled we are — but a call to bear the burden of a long twilight struggle, year in and year out, "rejoicing in hope, patient in tribulation" — a struggle against the common enemies of man: tyranny, poverty, disease and war itself . . .
>
> Finally, whether you are citizens of America or citizens of the world, ask of us here the same high standards of strength and sacrifice which we ask of you. With a good conscience our only sure reward, with history the final judge of our deeds, let us go forth to lead the land we love, asking His blessing and His help, but knowing that here on earth God's work must truly be our own (reproduced in Copeland and Lamm, 1973: 741–42).

Sociologists have recognized how easily civil religion can sanctify economic colonialism, and one particularly socially conscious academic, C. Wright Mills, protested to his fellow American citizens that people "of religious congregations do evil; [and] ministers of God make them feel good about it" (Mills, 1958: 200).

Although researchers seemingly have discovered civil religions in several countries (Bellah and Hammond, 1980), by no means does one exist for Canada. Unlike its southern neighbour, Canada never rebelled from its parent country, and so Canada never had the need to sanctify national acts of revolution. Nor has it had a national crisis on a scale with the American Civil War that might have forced it to mythologize its past. Furthermore, different regional histories and economies fostered in the country a staunch regionalism that mitigates the appeal of national symbols. Some commentators, however, argue that the solemnity of Remembrance Day services in all cities across the country indicates at least a minimal level of civil-religious attitudes.

Most fundamentally, early Canada's two very different religious cultures of French-speaking Catholicism in Quebec and English-speaking Anglicanism in Upper Canada shared only the broadest dimensions of Christian symbolism, clouded by different ethnic and historic allegiances. Even after World War II, Quebec's Catholicism "encouraged, legitimated, and sustained state conservatism, authoritarianism, and reaction even to the point of flirtation with neo-Fascism" (O'Toole, 1982: 184). Nineteenth-century Anglicanism's political agenda was very different, proclaiming:

that the Anglo-Saxon burden of [British] Empire, monarchy, aristocracy, and British constitutionalism were part of a sacred scenario; and by the same token, its condemnation of mass democracy, egalitarianism, republicanism, and revolution as the work of the devil, left an indelible mark on English-Canadian political life (O'Toole, 1982: 185).

Consequently, each culture may have formed largely incompatible regional civil religions, and in the process produced few religiously based symbols that politicians could appropriate on a national scale. Nevertheless, nostalgic lamentations for return to the mythic "virtues of the British tradition" (Blumstock, 1993) occasionally appear in some contemporary Canadian discourse and even may colour the political positions taken by the Reform Party (see Harrison, 1993: 133–44).

• CONFLICT THEORY

Mills's lament about ministers sanctifying allegedly evil acts by the American nation suggests that religion can contribute to societal or global dysfunction just as readily as it does to society's smooth and necessary operations. The challenge to structural-functional theory comes from **conflict theory**, whose assumptions trace back to the work of Karl Marx, who coined the memorable phrase that religion is "the opium of the people" (Marx, 1964 [1844]: 42). Whereas structural-functionalists see religion as essential to human survival, conflict theorists see religion as a powerful social vehicle for subjugating and exploiting populations. From a conflict perspective, religious doctrines about a heavenly afterlife are merely tools of oppression used by the powerful to ensure obedience to self-serving authority.

Historical examples of religion's oppressive functions are easy to find. They include the alliance between the Czar and the Orthodox Church in Russia that sanctioned the power and wealth of the royal family while most of the population remained peasants (see Ziryanov, 1988: 166–67). Similarly, the Roman Catholic Church signed "concordats" or treaties with two dictatorial regimes earlier in this century — Mussolini's Italy and Franco's Spain (Hanson, 1987: 43, 93). In present times, some commentators see the forces of conservatism at work in the efforts of Pope John Paul II to restrain the "liberation theology" movement within the Latin American Catholic Church.

As conflict theorists insist, powerful social groups can use supernatural claims to control people's behaviour in manners that preserve social and political privileges. These social groups will claim either that their privileges are divinely ordained or that people should minimize the importance of worldly affairs and seek rewards in an afterlife.

One of the most famous examples of religion sanctifying the social privileges of the elite in a particular society occurs in the ancient Indian scriptures called the Rig Veda, in which one hymn (10.90) portrays society as having emanated from various parts of a god's sacrificed body. The social and religious elite (called Brahmins or priests) emanated from the god Purusha's mouth; the warriors from his arms; the peasants from his thighs, and the serfs from his feet (see Bose, 1966: 285). This hierarchy of privilege and social tasks forms the basis for India's caste system, and the system's claim of supernatural origin has contributed to its fundamental stability over countless centuries. As the renowned Indologist A.L. Basham deduced, "By the end of the R[i]g Vedic period [at approximately 1000 B.C.] society was divided into four great classes, and this fourfold division was given religious sanction and looked on as fundamental" (Basham, 1959 [1954]: 35).

Not only have religious hymns and myths sanctified what might best be called class position and power, but they have also sanctified male patriarchy in the major religions of the world. The noted religious comparativist Geoffrey Parrinder observed that "in all living religions, and many ancient and prehistoric religions, men have been dominant, because physically stronger, and women have been subordinate" (Parrinder, 1980: 244). Scholars certainly would dispute his interpretation of male domination based upon average differences in physical strength, and others might point out a few "new" religions that seemingly practise equality or female dominance, but no one would dispute Parrinder's central observation concerning the prevalence of patriarchy.

These examples suggest that religion's *sacralizing* or *legitimizing power* may receive both functional and dysfunctional interpretations, depending upon one's set of values. Sacralization or legitimation means that people are able to justify their actions through divine claims and to sanctify their behaviours by asserting divine guidance or destiny for them. Thus, Weber (1930 [1920a]) realized that certain Puritan groups in 17th-century England felt that worldly success was a probable sign of their eternal salvation. Likewise, royalty, especially in earlier periods of history, argued that their hegemonic position was divinely sanctioned. As elaborated in the British theory of the Divine Right of Kings, monarchy claimed to be "a divinely ordained institution" whose kings were "accountable to God alone," thereby making "resistance to a king . . . a sin" (Figgis, 1965 [1914]: 5, 6).

Additional dysfunctions of religion may occur in the area of community involvement, in direct contrast to the experience of persons who see religion's provision of a community in a positive, functionalist light. Persons may feel constrained and constricted by their religious communities, even to the point that they denounce the restrictions and controlled lives that they had lived for years. For example, two former Canadian Jehovah's Witnesses, Heather and Gary Botting (1984), launched a bitter attack on their former religious community, equating their lives in it with George Orwell's description of totalitarianism in his novel, *1984*.

Not only may religious communities become restrictive social environments, but also they may develop attitudes toward persons outside of their communities that are hostile, demeaning, and racist. A recent study of Canadian racism, for example, isolated the role of religion in the constellation of racist and anti-Semitic attitudes, behaviours, and organizations that the author identified across the country:

> Theological racism not only supposedly explains why whites are superior and non-whites are inferior (God made us that way) but it also has the capacity to accommodate all the other significant strands in the white supremacist's belief system: communism is anti-Christian, homosexuality is an abomination before God, and the white man's Western civilization is coterminous with Christian civilization. Furthermore, there is a specific strand in the white supremacist's belief system, intrinsically linked to Christianity, that is the most potent of all: anti-Semitism. Jews are said to be Satan's children, the killers of Christ. Interracial mixing, communism, drugs, abortion, social change

Box 13.1

RELIGIOUS DYSFUNCTION

No example in Canadian history more dramatically illustrates religious dysfunction than the case of Roch Theriault. By the late 1970s, the charismatic and dynamic Theriault had gathered around him a small band of followers. In 1978 he ordered them to escape to a remote valley in Quebec so that they would survive the impending Armageddon (end of the world). After arriving there, he declared himself to be God's emissary, and ordered his followers to sever contacts with the outside world and assume biblical names.

Living in almost complete social isolation, the group fell under Theriault's abusive control — a control that entrapped members by his divine claims and drunken rages. For over a decade his followers suffered severe beatings, exhausting labour, sexual exploitation, child abuse, abuse of a corpse, and medical violence. His botched medical operations cost the lives of two members, while a third person lost an arm. Even after he pleaded guilty to second-degree murder while serving time on other charges, several of his former communal wives remained devoted to him. Recently one gave birth to another of his many children, conceived during a conjugal prison visit.

Source: Kaihla et al. (1993).

in general — all of these are supposedly promoted by Jews, providing evidence of the insidious international conspiracy . . . Anti-Semitism constituted the radical right's theoretical system or paradigm (Barrett, 1987: 337).

All of the religiously based anti-Semitic themes that Barrett identified swirled into public view during the two trials of Jim Keegstra (in 1984 and 1992), whose charges (and eventual conviction) stemmed from having taught high-school students in Eckville, Alberta, "paranoid fantasies about a Jewish world-conspiracy bent on controlling, and then destroying, Christianity" (Bercuson and Wertheimer, 1985: x; see Mertl and Ward, 1985; Barrett, 1987: 215–60). As Barrett concluded, however, "the single most important factor . . . that makes Keegstra tick [is] his orientation to religion" (Barrett, 1987: 215).

Religious ideology, therefore, often plays a primary role in the propagation of attitudes and behaviours that probably are dysfunctional to major segments of society or significant numbers of people. Religious institutions, moreover, may provide social opportunities and social networks that unequally advantage some members of society at the expense of others. Evidence for religion's role in the perpetuation of social inequality appears in Clement's (1975) groundbreaking study of Canada's corporate elite. When analyzing their religious backgrounds, he discovered that a disproportionate number of the elite (25.3 percent in 1972) were Anglican, despite the fact that Anglicans made up only 11.8 percent of the population (Clement, 1975: 240). Presbyterians, who were 4 percent of the population, also were overrepresented among the elite at 8 percent. Baptists and "other" Protestants, however, were underrepresented among the elite (2.6 percent), although they constituted almost 8 percent of the population. Likewise, Catholics were poorly represented among the elite (at 12.7 percent), although they were 46.2 percent of the population.

Clement realized the difficulty of interpreting these findings since, for example, the low Catholic percentage may reflect combinations of religious, ethnic, and educational factors. Regarding the high percentage of Anglicans among the elite, however, Clement suggested that the role of educational institutions was central to the explanation. Realizing the fundamental role played by "private schools" (along with private clubs) in "maintaining class opportunities in favour of the privileged" (1975: 7), Clement observed that quite a number of private schools were Anglican affiliated. Attendance at these schools

promotes association and friendships among the upper class based on common social experiences. It is because Anglican institutions have been established as class institutions and exclusion mechanisms that a disproportionate number of Anglicans appear in the elite and not because there is some "ethnic" [group] associated with this denomination which creates elites (Clement, 1975: 240).

In sum, institutional religion can contribute to social disparity and selective privilege by fostering social elitism and class exclusion through educational structures.

• SOCIAL PSYCHOLOGICAL THEORIES

Traditionally, psychology has stressed the importance of examining the feelings, experiences, and cognitive processes of individuals. Sociology, in contrast, has insisted that the significant focus of research must be the groups and other social influences that provide the cognitive and emotional contexts that limit and direct individuals' feelings, perceptions, and life possibilities. A common ground between the disciplines is **social psychology,** which acknowledges that individuals' experiences are important to research partly because they are heavily influenced by their social environments. In the study of religion, significant promise lies in insights provided by social psychological interpretations of humanity's claims concerning experiences of the supernatural or divine (see Hunsberger, 1980).

Social psychological examinations of religion have addressed such diverse phenomena as children's religious socialization, drug and meditational experiences, possible relationships between religious dogmatism and authoritarianism, religion and sexuality, religion and the fear of death, and religious motivations for secular behaviour (see Argyle and Beit-Hallahmi, 1975). We shall concentrate on one aspect of religious experience — conversion — in order to show the interpretive power of social psychology.

Sociologists realize that diverse patterns exist regarding the processes by which people adopt a belief system. Not only are individuals' experiences frequently different regarding conversion to the same group, but also the groups themselves have distinct requirements that converts must follow. For example, evangelical Christians emphasize an emotional experience involving "the acceptance of Jesus into the heart" as a "born-again" experience. Conversion to either Judaism or Jehovah's Witnesses involves doctrinal acceptance that occurs throughout extended periods of study (Wilson, 1978: 503; Lofland and Skonovd, 1981). Other conversion experiences are sudden and dramatic, occurring after participation in emotionally charged ceremonies or services requiring behaviours and actions outside the boundaries of normal life. Such behaviours include "speaking in tongues" (or *glossolalia*), when people allegedly speak in languages that are spiritual rather than human) or rapid chanting, often in foreign languages that the chanters do not understand. Some religions require people to reveal emotionally uncomfortable and painful events from their lives. All of these groups attain deeply committed converts, usually after participation in such emotionally charged and culturally unique social activities.

Social psychological theories about **attribution processes** help explain why these emotionally charged forms of conversion take place. Attribution theories (for there are more than one) examine the processes by which individuals assign or *attribute* meaning to events that affect their emotions, their self-perceptions, and their motivations (see Proudfoot and Shaver, 1975). Religious ideologies — with their explanations for suffering, death, and the purpose of life — provide meaning systems that individuals use to interpret their lives. Conversions frequently occur, therefore, after emotionally charged religious services because the groups' religious ideologies provide participants with supposedly supernaturally based interpretations that make sense out of events for which they have no interpretive framework. In essence, religion provides meaning to otherwise meaningless situations (see McGuire, 1992), even when religious groups create the otherwise meaningless events in the first place.

Attribution theories also may explain why some people become more religious in response to various life crises. Religious groups design events and experiences for which potential converts have no interpretive context; life crises present situations that people may not be able to integrate into their existing personal interpretive frameworks. Common to all life crises — such as facing death, struggling with disease, mourning the loss of loved ones, or entering new phases of life — is the breakdown of ordinary cognitive systems of action and rules for the resolution of conflict. Religious systems are particularly attractive at such times because they are total systems, providing comprehensive interpretations of experience. Consequently, these systems pre-empt, and thus render relatively insignificant, the conflicts and cares of mundane life (Proudfoot and Shaver, 1975: 325).

As an interpretive system, therefore, religion is unique among ideologies in its ability to provide untestable, unverifiable, and supposedly supernatural answers and explanations for many of life's fundamental questions. Its explanations include assertions about the supernatural that are difficult if not impossible to *dis*prove, thereby giving adherents an overriding sense of certainty concerning the explanations.

Not all conversions, however, occur simply because people misattribute supernatural powers to groups or their leaders. Many individuals' decisions to join groups are influenced significantly by the quality of social bonds that they have with group members in comparison to those that they have with people who are not part of the group. If family or friends already are members, then a person's chances of converting increase dramatically. These chances increase even further for people who are personally predisposed to value religion in their lives. Conversion, in short, occurs because religiously predisposed people meet groups at appropriate periods in their lives.

Two sociologists, John Lofland and Rodney Stark, clarified the relationship between predisposing factors and what they called the "situational contingencies" of conversion in a study that they carried out in a city on the American west coast in the early 1960s. Their work took on an unforeseen importance since the group that they studied contained the first members of the Unification Church (i.e., the Moonies) in North America. For a conversion to take place, Lofland and Stark argued, the three following *predisposing factors* must apply. Individuals must

1. be experiencing enduring, acutely felt tensions in their lives;
2. have the perspective that theirs is a religious problem (as opposed to merely a psychological or economic problem, for example); and
3. see themselves as *religious seekers*.

In addition, the three following *situational contingencies* must occur. Individuals must

4. meet one or more group members at turning points or crises in their lives;
5. develop strong attachments to them; and at the same time
6. diminish if not eliminate nongroup (often family) relationships.

Unless individuals progress through each of these stages (although not necessarily in this order), they are unlikely to convert (Lofland and Stark, 1965).

As Lofland and Stark's study implies, conversions almost never take place spontaneously, but are the result of people working to make them happen. Evangelists are specialists at this type of "conversion work," and the most successful of them is Billy Graham. As a study of the 1974 Billy Graham Crusade in Phoenix, Arizona, makes clear (Altheide and Johnson, 1977), the conversions that he achieves are not solely a result of his preaching effectiveness.

Planning for the Phoenix crusade took a full year, and perhaps 6000 people were involved in various parts of the project (Altheide and Johnson, 1977: 325). These volunteers included 3000 choir members and 1500 counsellors; the latter filled out information cards on the people who responded to this call. These counsellors were scattered throughout the auditorium, and when Graham instructed people to come forward and accept Jesus into their hearts they stood up and slowly walked to the front. By doing so they created the impression that they were responding to Graham's call, thereby making it much easier for nonvolunteers to come forward (Altheide and Johnson, 1977: 332). The size of this evangelical organization is indicated by its 1974 budget, which was over $20 million (Altheide and Johnson, 1977: 324), and it maintains offices in many countries around the world.

One might think that most people join evangelical or conservative churches because they are converted to that form of Christianity. A study of new members joining twenty conservative churches in Calgary (Bibby and Brinkerhoff, 1973) found, however, that the largest number of "converts" (72 percent) were people who transferred their memberships from other conservative churches. Those who had been born to parents who were members of conservative churches constituted 18 percent of the "converts," and only 9 percent were new to the conservative tradition. The reason for joining was unknown for 1 percent. Conversion to conservative churches, therefore, primarily involved a circulation of members rather than an infusion of new people.

Beginning with William James's psychological classic, *The Varieties of Religious Experience* (1902), many investigators have explored the diversity of situations that give rise to religious feelings and experiences. Earlier in our discussion of attribution theory, we mentioned one set of circumstances in which groups create religious feelings by giving people supernatural interpretations of otherwise meaningless or unique occurrences and events. People have religious feelings, however, in a wide variety of circumstances and under a vast array of situations. Social psychologists would stress in each one the importance of people's cultural backgrounds in influencing their experiences and then their supernatural interpretations of them. In addition to the socially constructed attributional situations that we already have discussed, five sources of religious experience are worth noting.

First and most basic is people's reaction to dramatic sights in the natural or social world. When many contemporary and sophisticated people see something awesome (like an incredible sunset or a sudden view of majestic mountain peaks) or awful (like a vast natural or social disaster), then they may attribute the event to a divine figure or force. Certainly we know that many elements of nonliterate religions were awed responses to events or natural phenomena.

A second source of religious feelings is people's beliefs that they have had a mystical or supernatural experience in which they claim to directly touch, enter, or feel God or the meaning of the universe. Greeley (1974) reports that in a well-conducted survey of a large and random sample of Americans, 76 percent said that they had had some kind of mystical or supernatural experience. James (1902) concluded that the more intense religious experiences typically have four characteristics in common. They are

1. **ineffable** — people cannot describe adequately what the experience was like;
2. **noetic** — people have a feeling of *clarity of understanding* such as they never have had before;
3. **transient** — usually (but not always) the experience or feeling is brief; and
4. **passive** — the experience is *something that happens to people,* but is not something that people can bring about.

Recent debates about alleged mystical accounts insist that they must be understood and interpreted in their appropriate historical and cultural settings, and cannot be viewed as obvious examples of humanity's direct and clear perceptions of God or divinity (Kent, 1987a, 1987b, 1989a).

A third source of religious feelings is the phenomenon of getting "swept up" or "carried away" in ecstatic group experiences that sociologists would examine as collective behaviour. In these circumstances people may lose their sense of individual identity and therefore engage in behaviours that otherwise they would not do. Distressing examples of "getting lost in the crowd" occur in riots, panics, and mobs. In religious contexts, people may get "carried away" in religious services that involve crying, shouting, dancing, and enthusiastically singing, as occurs in Christian Holiness groups (which earned them the nickname "the Holy Rollers"). These emotionally charged collective experiences can be so powerful that Durkheim (1965 [1912]: 249–50, 424–27) believed they constituted the original religious experiences among nonliterate peoples.

Somewhat related to feelings that develop out of collective ecstasy is a fourth source of religious experience, which involves feelings that emerge from a sense of *community*. Particularly for people who are lonely or alienated, the process of being warmly and lovingly accepted into a community may be a religious experience. When, for example, reporters spoke of the Unification Church (i.e., the Moonies) "love-bombing" potential converts in the 1970s, they were acknowledging that the sense of belonging to a caring community often is interpreted in religious terms.

An account from a Moonie convert about recruitment practices in Oakland, California, illustrates the point. The member reported that Onni Durst, who was one of Oakland's directors

> emphasizes not so much the truth at first, but that you must really love people. You must "love-bomb" them. Onni has a staff of about twelve people who are the best "love-bombers" in the whole world. Sometimes when I would be having trouble with one of my guests — they were not responding — I could give one of them a look and they would come over. Their ability wasn't anything they said but it was in loving that person. Finally the person's heart would melt and he or she would sign up for a training session (reproduced in Barker, 1984: 174).

If this account is accurate, then it seems that recruiters heavily influenced many people's conversions to the Oakland branch of the Unification Church by making them feel loved. Analogous processes occur for people converting to other groups.

Fifth and finally, symbols, music, or rituals can stimulate religious experience. As suggested earlier, however, people must be socialized or conditioned to respond to the connotative language with appreciation or awe, or they must be given religious interpretations of otherwise meaningless events and activities. Such things as pilgrimage shrines, relics, and music are not *automatically* inspirational in a religious sense. People must be conditioned or socialized previously into interpreting these items as sources of religious feelings.

• EXCHANGE THEORIES

After individuals have converted to particular faiths, the groups that they have joined face the problem of maintaining the converts' participation for an extended period of time. Converts bring into groups an array of wealth, talent, and enthusiasm that contribute heartily to their new organizations' lives, so they are valuable resources that groups hope to cultivate and use.

Exchange theories postulate that people calculate the probable costs involved in receiving rewards and avoiding punishments for their actions. In a religious context, they assess the likelihood of receiving both the immediate rewards as well as the divine ones supposedly received in heaven or the next life. At the same time, however, they also are trying to avoid parallel sets of immediate and posthumous divine punishments.

Religious groups are uniquely able to motivate and maintain membership because they rest their policies and practices upon *claims of supernatural legitimacy*. No other social institution is able to legitimize its policies in this manner, which helps to explain why so many people throughout history have been willing to sacrifice themselves in the name of their faith. These people believe that the costs they suffer on earth will be amply rewarded in the supernatural realm that they enter upon death (Stark and Bainbridge, 1985: 5–8, 1987). Conversely, they probably also believe that they risk intense punishment on earth, and perhaps after death, for failure to follow the divine principles of their faith while they still are living. With these claims in mind, we shall examine the unique social control systems that religious groups impose on their members (Kent and Mytrash, 1990).

Social organizations, including religious ones, offer members a range of *rewards,* or *relatively immediate benefits,* in exchange for participating in them. People may receive rewards of *purpose* — they may feel good about their actions or feel that they are working toward a larger goal; *affective* rewards — emotional ties with others, secure images of self-esteem in relation to other members, high status either within the secular community or among other participants; rewards of *wealth* — money, property, subsidized food or shelter; or *bodily-sensual* rewards of sex, sumptuous food, or entertainment. The ability of religious groups to offer these rewards differs little from that of many other social institutions.

Parallel systems of *punishments,* or *relatively immediate inflictions of undesirable sanctions,* exist for most social systems as well, including religious ones. Thus, a group can punish members by charging that they fall short of the group's purposes (e.g., by allegedly being "selfish" or self-centred). Groups may restrict *affective* social contact between deviants and other members or remove items of *wealth* from them as punishment for deviant acts. Finally, groups can inflict pain, fasting, or other forms of *bodily-sensual* restrictions or impositions as harsh forms of punishment for transgressions. To greater or lesser degrees, all groups engage in social forms of punishment such as these.

Religion, however, introduces an entirely unique dimension of rewards and punishments in exchange for various commitments by the devout. By convincing their members that spiritual or supernatural realms exist, religious groups have at their disposal a vast array of motivators and threats that other social groups cannot devise. In essence, religious groups can promise their members the eternal rewards of an afterlife or the endless punishments of divine retribution.

These supernaturally asserted rewards and punishments cannot be either proven or disproven by ordinary scientific tests, so members must accept them on faith. They are not expected to occur relatively soon (as are earthly rewards or punishments), but in an unverifiable future (i.e., heaven, hell, rebirth). These supernaturally sanctified promises and punishments have real consequences in people's lives, regardless of the objective reality of their existence. In essence, they *compensate* for immediate rewards and punishments by promising eventual fulfilment in a supposedly inevitable supernatural realm. Thus, these compensatory reward and punishment systems parallel the immediate reward and punishment systems that are commonplace for most secular groups.

In *purposive* areas religion can promise the compensation of heaven or higher rebirth, or threaten the compensatory punishment of eternal separation from God or lower rebirth. In *socioemotional* areas religion can promise the eternal bonding of loved ones or threaten the eternal loss of cherished friends and relatives. In areas related to *wealth,* religion can promise either an eventual reversal of a disprivileged economic position ("Blessed are the meek, for they shall inherit the earth" [Matthew 5.5]) or a divine justification for socioeconomic privilege. Conversely, it can threaten one's offspring and progeny with repeated economic hardship. Finally, religion can offer unverifiable promises in *bodily-sensual* areas such as perfect bodies in heaven or an abundance of heavenly foods, or threaten deviant members with divinely based eternal pain (in, for example, a fiery hell). In the face of these promises and threats, we begin to understand why people are willing to exchange their time, wealth, health, and independence for the demands of a religious life.

• MESSIANISM AND CHARISMA

Many devout people (especially in Western countries) are willing to commit enormous resources to religious groups if they believe that they are living in the final days before the occurrence of a religious event of profound importance. Most commonly, the devout may expect the imminent return of the messiah, who then supposedly will reign for an eternity. In some historic and contemporary instances, however, groups become convinced that the messiah has already arrived. In both cases, social scientists use the term **millenarianism** to mean *the imminent collapse of existing society and social order and their replacement with a divinely directed one.*

Millenarianism has five characteristics for its adherents that appear (with slight variations) in nearly all of its expressions throughout history. It is (1) "collective" (rather than merely to be experienced by an individual); (2) "terrestrial" (as opposed to heavenly); (3) "imminent" (occurring "soon and suddenly" if not already begun); (4) "total" (in the sense that it will completely transform life on earth); and (5) "miraculous" (in the sense that it is to be accomplished by, or with the help of, supernatural agencies) (Cohn, 1976: 5).

The supernatural being who believers expect to rule during the millennium is a messiah or saviour, and as a figure in Western religious traditions he (the sexist pronoun is deliberate) first appeared in the prophetic books of the Hebrew Bible/Old Testament and then in the apocalyptic Book of Daniel (7.13–14). From these sources, messianism entered both Christianity and Islam. Christianity, for example, is messianic to its core, believing that Jesus was the messiah who, as Christ, will return again to subdue Satan and judge the eternal fate of the living and the dead. Along similar lines, many Shi'ite Muslims believe that the twelfth successor of Muhammad (the Twelfth Imam) is in occultation or concealment from people's eyes, waiting "until the day when he will manifest himself again by God's permission" (Momen, 1985: 165) and vanquish his foes in an apocalyptic battle (Momen, 1985: 166).

Some devout Jews wait expectantly for the messiah, and the translation of their belief into political actions concerning the state of Israel is having dramatic and damaging effects on the Israeli–Palestinian problem (see Friedman, 1990). Some believe, for example, that their messiah will rebuild the Temple in Jerusalem, but before he will return and do so they must remove two Islamic holy sites, the Al Aksa Mosque and the Dome of the Rock, which stand on the Temple's ruins (Friedman, 1990: 41). The situation is explosive, since damage to these two Islamic sites could ignite the entire region in war.

Adherents of Hinduism and Buddhism have comparatively minor traditions involving the return of their respective religious leaders. Tradition records that Vishnu's final incarnation will be Kalki or Kalkin (see O'Flaherty, 1975: 235–37), and the Buddha apparently predicted his own return as Maitreya (*Cakkavatti-Sīhanāda Suttanta*, trans. in Rhys Davids, 1965 [1921]: 73–74). Neither of these messianic figures, however, receives much attention in these traditions, probably because of the emphasis that both religions place upon suffering as an inevitable part of existence from which one should attempt to escape by asceticism or devotion.

Messianic claimants, who themselves claim to provide escape from suffering, have appeared throughout Western history. They are the most dramatic examples of what Weber (1956 [1922]) called **charismatic leaders**. Charismatic leaders claim to have unique qualities as the result of allegedly possessing special, supernatural gifts, and as a result of their alleged possession of these gifts they attract a devoted following. As Weber offered,

> the term "charisma" will be applied to a certain quality of an individual personality by virtue of which he is considered extraordinary and treated as endowed with supernatural, superhuman, or at least specifically exceptional powers or qualities. These are such as are not accessible to the ordinary person, but are regarded as of divine origin or as exemplary, and on the basis of them the individual concerned is treated as a "leader" (Weber, 1978 [1968]: 240).

Charismatic leadership, therefore, contains three aspects: (1) leaders who claim to possess divinely bestowed gifts and (2) followers who believe the claim, and who (3) continually reinforce one another's devotion (see Cartwright and Kent, 1992: 335–36 n. 19). History is replete with examples of charismatic, often messianic, leaders attracting around themselves hundreds if not thousands of followers.

As the Moon example (Box 13.2) illustrates, charismatic leaders can motivate extraordinary acts of commitment and devotion in followers, especially when these leaders make messianic claims that their followers believe.

• TYPOLOGICAL THEORIES

Except perhaps for belief systems in isolated cultures, religions in every society undergo development and change. As one would expect, therefore, all the world's great religious traditions have complex, often schismatic, histories. For example, Buddhism emerged out of Hinduism and in turn eventually divided into Hinayana and Mahayana. Out of Judaism (which now has at least three major branches) evolved Christianity and Islam. Christianity divided into Catholicism, Eastern Orthodoxy, and various forms of Protestantism, and Protestantism itself gave rise to innumerable offshoots. Islam divided into Sunni and Shi'ite traditions. Sociologists have tried to bring some order to this confusing religious variety by creating logical **typologies** or sets of classifications for religious organizations, although, regrettably, most of them are based upon Western religious examples. Among the most basic typologies is one that distinguishes among churches, denominations, sects, and cults.

A **church** enjoys universal support in a society and claims to be inclusive of all society's members. It is conservative, which means that it supports the social order, and accommodates

Box 13.2

MESSIANIC CLAIMANT SUN MYUNG MOON

A current example of a religious leader whose messianic claims serve as the basis for his charisma is Reverend Sun Myung Moon, founder of the Unification Church. Although Unification teachings stop short of stating his messianic status, "there is . . . no doubt in the minds of the overwhelming majority of Moonies that Sun Myung Moon is the Messiah" (Barker, 1984: 83). Moon himself probably believes that he is, since in a 1982 court case he testified that "he had met and had conversations with Jesus, Moses and Buddha. 'I have the possibility of becoming the real Messiah,' he said" (Chambers, 1982: A1). On the basis of charismatic claims such as this one, many Moonies who were engaged in activities for their church (such as fundraising) worked (according to disgruntled former members) "frenetic hyperactive eighteen-hour days" (Bromley and Shupe, 1979: 122). Indeed, U.S. District Court Judge Richard Owen allowed Moon to testify in the 1982 case because he realized that members' commitment to Moon and his organization derived from their belief in his charismatic assertions:

> I have heard testimony during this trial from college graduates who said they spent two to three years fundraising on the streets, who have been told that the witness here [Reverend Moon] is their personal Messiah and that he is responsible for their well-being on this earth and the hereafter.
>
> It is on the basis of this that these young people follow him, doing incredible acts of almost self slavery, selling flowers from buckets from 8 A.M. to 11 P.M. year after year. Mr. Galen [the alleged abductor and "deprogrammer" who was on trial] has been charged with trying to interrupt this life. And so we want to know whether this is a bona fide religion or not (quoted in Chambers, 1982: B8).

itself to the secular world. Examples of churches include Islam in many Arab countries and European Catholicism throughout much of the Middle Ages.

A **denomination** is an organization that operates in a society among religious competitors and has relinquished claims to inclusiveness. Consequently, it acknowledges the validity of other religious groups. Like the church, the denomination has accommodated to society. Examples include most contemporary Protestant churches, since they agree that salvation may be achieved through many religious bodies and are generally supportive of the values of their host countries.

A **sect** is a religious organization composed of persons who aspire to spiritual perfection and fellowship with other members. Members think of themselves as "saved." Typically, the group is indifferent or hostile to the rest of society, which its members see as spiritually decadent and "lost." A sect claims that it alone of all the competing religions in society practises the true religion. By this claim it excludes most of society's members. Examples probably would include groups such as the Jehovah's Witnesses and the Mormons.

A **cult** is a loose association of persons with a private, eclectic (borrowed from many sources) sets of beliefs and practices. Typically, cults are not exclusive, and they do not object if their members belong to other religious bodies. Examples include the Theosophical Society and Self Realization Fellowship, both of which claim to facilitate people's inner spiritual development. (Note that this sociological definition differs from the pejorative connotation that the term *cult* has in the popular press, where it is applied to a group that observers consider to be destructive or harmful.)

From a related perspective, Glock (1964) classified religious organizations according to the human needs that he felt they served. He claimed, for example, that people who are economically deprived establish *sects*. Those who are socially deprived or alienated join *churches*. When people have persistent illnesses or bodily handicaps they tend to join groups emphasizing faith healing. Similarly, people who have psychic problems (which Glock [1964: 212] defines as being "without a meaningful system of values") may be attracted to the "new ideologies" that *cults* allegedly offer. Finally, when people are preoccupied with ethical issues they are most likely to join or establish reform movements in their own religious organizations and attempt to modify them from within.

An early attempt to extend Weber's original study of sectarian Puritanism was H. Richard Niebuhr's *The Social Sources of Denominationalism* (1929), which discussed the impact of race and ethnicity, social class, war, and the frontier on the development of American religion. His analysis was especially insightful about the effects of social class on the origins of sects and their evolution into denominations. He described, for example, how middle-class Protestant denominations, which emphasized "Sunday best" appearance and "good taste" in worship style, felt alien to lower-class people. The lower classes responded by establishing their own "store-front" religions. These sects chose ministers from among their own congregants, and they preached messages that sanctified their own class and criticized the wealthy. Consequently, these lay preachers would emphasize such New Testament passages as "Blessed are you poor, for yours is the kingdom of God" (Luke 6.20) and "it is easier for a camel to go through the eye of a needle, than for a rich man to enter the kingdom of God" (Matthew 19.24). Moreover, these sects had emotionally charged ("enthusiastic") sermons and ceremonies, in contrast to the restrained and unemotional services of their wealthier counterparts.

Over time, however, external, secularizing influences and internal developments pressured these sectarian congregations to diminish their hostility toward wealth and worldly success. Some of the original members, for example, became relatively successful in the secular world (which occurs in societies that allow social mobility) and contributed significant sums to the sectarian group. Likewise, the group was likely to systematize its doctrines in an attempt to transmit them to the children of first-generation members (see Niebuhr, 1929: 19–20). In response, preachers toned down their diatribes against the rich. "Blessed are you poor" (Luke 6.20) was replaced with "Blessed are the poor in spirit" (Matthew 5.3), because preachers did not want to alienate members who were covering significant amounts of their groups' expenses. Moreover, the preachers themselves faced pressures to institutionalize and obtain formal training in an effort to ensure that they possessed the theological and educational skills necessary to digest, interpret, and transmit their group's formalizing doctrines (see Niebuhr, 1929: 20).

If, over time, many members rise in class position as the organization itself formalizes, then the enthusiastic sect probably will evolve into the kind of middle-class denomination against which it initially had separated. As this transformation occurs, however, a new group of socially disadvantaged people will feel alienated from the restrained forms of worship and will break away and form a new enthusiastic sect. As this happens, the cycle of "denominationalism and sect formation" continues.

Recent work on sects, cults, and new religions in Canada focuses on the intense debates that occur among religious groups and their opponents attempting to have themselves defined as societally tolerable and their opponents considered intolerable (Kent, 1990; see also Kent, 1993a). This perspective realizes that many religions are outside of Canada's historically normative faiths (Catholicism, Anglicanism, and the United Church); thus they must carve for themselves a niche in the country's religious landscape. Many of these same groups, however, hold doctrines or engage in activities that are controversial, so they find themselves in pitched public-relations battles with opponents. In these battles, both sides engage in "efforts to get . . . opponents socially labelled as intolerably deviant through allegations of illegal, immoral, and unethical practices" (Kent, 1990: 396). These positive and negative labels greatly determine the kind and amount of resources (wealth, tax benefits, members, status, etc.) that religious organizations obtain (Kent, 1990: 408).

THE EFFECTS OF RELIGION ON SOCIETY

Max Weber and many other sociologists have been aware of the intimate interweaving of religion and politics throughout history. The potent combination of religion's supposedly supernatural rewards and punishments with the polity's immediate incentives and retributions makes them formidable partners. In essence, people can strive for worldly, political power in the name of God.

• HISTORICAL EFFECTS

When identifying religion's effects upon society, sociologists often refer to the most widely read study in the sociology of religion — Max Weber's *The Protestant Ethic and the Spirit of Capitalism* (1930 [1920a]). Weber examined particular forms of Protestantism in an attempt to determine what factors contributed to the appearance and development of rational, systematic money making (called "rational capitalism") in the West rather than in other parts of the world. He concluded that unique, religiously driven attitudes toward work and living held by various English Puritan groups unintentionally provided the mental and emotional discipline as well as comportment that early modern capitalism later would require among its workers and entrepreneurs. Puritan groups, particularly Calvinists and Quakers, cultivated frugal, honest, hardworking lives among their members, who often laboured in small businesses and trades. Weber characterized their lives as ascetic (i.e., self-denying) yet *inner-worldly* (i.e., they held occupations in society, in contrast to the monastic lives of Catholic monks and nuns). The **inner-worldly asceticism** of the Calvinists grew out of the psychologically stressful theological doctrine of predestination, which stated that God, at the beginning of time and creation, had selected only a few people for eternal salvation while damning all others. Because (as the theology insisted) mere mortals could not know the will of God, no one could be certain about one's eternal fate.

Traumatized by this uncertainty, Calvinists sought some relief from the severe psychological stress of predestination by believing that they probably could receive signs about their eternal fate by their degree of worldly success. In what today we would call a self-fulfilling prophecy, Calvinists worked hard, reinvested their profits into their businesses, practised honesty in their business dealings, and avoided drunkenness and idleness in an effort to create the very occupational success that they interpreted as favourable signs of their eternal state.

Groups such as Quakers, in contrast, rejected the doctrine of predestination. Nonetheless, their religion motivated them to demonstrate their (presumed) salvation to their Calvinist contemporaries, and this motivation, along with their desire (shared with Calvinists) to glorify God, also drove them to live inner-worldly ascetic lives (see Kent, 1983, 1989b).

From the asceticism that these groups practised, which stressed the godly value of work in a calling or occupation, a new ethic evolved in society at large that rewarded industriousness and prized job commitment. Puritans had no way of imagining that these same work values would be essential for the development of early modern rational capitalism, which first emerged in the Puritans' homeland, England. Tawney (1928) and others have argued against Weber that additional, nonreligious factors contributed significantly to the rise of capitalism, but Weber himself made this point in some of his writings.

Having determined religious bases for behaviours that were to contribute to the rise of early modern capitalism, Weber also examined religious bases for the hindrance of early capitalist development in other world cultures. He concluded that countries (most notably India) that were dominated by Hinduism and/or Buddhism did not develop attitudes about life and work that could have aided early capitalist development because their primary religious ideals involved **other-worldly** (in contrast with Puritan inner-worldly) **asceticism**. Buddhist monks aspired to escape the cycle of rebirth, which in a practical sense diminished worldly activities as mere distractions from spirituality. Moreover, the Hindu doctrines of karma and rebirth provided ordinary people little hope of social mobility or worldly progress in *this* life. The most one could hope to achieve was a life that earned good karma by strictly following caste regulations about purity and appropriate behaviour. Consequently, the culture stifled innovation of any kind among the masses by cultivating among them the hope of higher rebirth (and eventual worldly release) as the result of

Box 13.3

THE EFFECTS OF RELIGION ON CANADA: THE SOCIAL GOSPEL MOVEMENT

Around the period of World War I, a religiously based social movement began growing in Canada. Known as the Social Gospel, it emphasized "one aspect of Christian belief — the responsibility of each person for his neighbours and for the development of just social and political institutions" (Crysdale, 1976: 426). To establish these just institutions required "a fundamental change in the social structure, namely the transfer of ownership of natural and capital resources from private into public hands" (Crysdale, 1976: 426). The movement became especially strong in Saskatchewan, where its political expression, the Co-operative Commonwealth Federation (CCF), was voted into power in 1944. Its articulate and skilful leader, Tommy Douglas, was a Baptist minister who redirected his considerable oratorical and campaigning skills into politics. The CCF's most lasting social legacy may be the creation of the continent's first program of universal medical coverage. Subsequently the CCF gave birth to the New Democratic Party. The CCF's influence still is felt among many contemporary religious groups that involve themselves in political justice issues (see Hewitt, 1993: 258).

strict adherence to caste constraints. As Weber concluded, "the orthodox or heterodox Hinduistic and Buddhistic educated classes found the true sphere of their interests quite outside the things of this world. This was the search for mythic, timeless salvation of the soul, and the escape from the senseless mechanism of the 'wheel' of existence" (Weber, 1958 [1920c]: 338).

China's Confucianism, Weber concluded, also stifled the development of attitudes toward the world that could have fostered early modern capitalism. Its emphasis on "propriety" in all aspects of life (see Weber, 1951 [1920b]: 156) combined with ancestor worship (see Weber, 1951 [1920b]: 168, 229) to bind people to traditionalism. Consequently, the possibility of economic innovation was eliminated, since worldly activity had value only to the extent that it reproduced reputedly timeless, Confucian-valued patterns. In this culture, Weber concluded, "there was no leverage for influencing conduct through inner forces freed of tradition and convention" (Weber, 1951 [1920b]: 236). Weber concluded, therefore, that religion had facilitated economic development in parts of the West while inhibiting it throughout the East. It is notable that one of Asia's most technological countries, Singapore, is trying to re-emphasize Confucianism as providing foundational principles upon which to build a modernized social ethic (Pan, 1989).

● MODERN EFFECTS

The recent worldwide upsurge in religious fundamentalism dramatically illustrates the dynamism of the combination of religion and politics yet at the same time hints at some of the limitations on religion in the political sphere. Diverse in its particulars, **fundamentalism** is

> the affirmation of religious authority as holistic and absolute, admitting neither criticism nor reduction; it is expressed through the collective demand that specific creedal and ethical dictates derived from scripture be publicly recognized and legally enforced (Lawrence, 1989: 27).

Fundamentalist movements exist among (to name a few groups) American Christians; Latin American Protestants; Israeli Jews; Egyptian and Sudanese Sunni Muslims; Iranian, Iraqi, and Lebanese Shi'ite Muslims; Indian Hindus and Sikhs; Sri Lankan Buddhists; Malaysian and Indonesian Muslims; and Japanese Shintoists (see Marty and Appleby, 1991). Adherents to these movements around the world tend to be

> (1) minority advocates of scriptural idealism who are (2) oppositional to the dominant ethos . . . Their leaders and followers tend to be (3) secondary-level male elites who are bound to one another by (4) a religious ideology that relies on insider, technical language (5) [the adherents are] only to be found in the Technical Age as tenacious opponents of modernist ideologies that challenge their scriptural ideals and spiritual loyalties (Lawrence, 1989: 236).

Despite a "divinely driven" fervour that adherents feel, the secular demands of the world inevitably dampen or destroy the religious doctrinalism of fundamentalist groups in power. Indeed, one student of fundamentalism predicts that "in the long run, fundamentalists will not be able to control the tone of discourse or activity in the public sphere of any major nation-state" (Lawrence, 1989: 240). A segment of Canadian political history bears this out.

In the 1930s a political party in Alberta known as Social Credit gained office on a platform that combined economic and political policies with religious doctrinalism. Based upon ideas developed in the early 1920s by an English engineer, Major C.H. Douglas (1859–1952), Social Credit argued that a discrepancy existed between workers' purchasing power and the higher total of production costs. Consequently, workers were unable to buy all that they produced, thereby requiring (so the argument went) governments to distribute money to citizens in order to extend their ability to consume (see Elliott and Miller, 1987: 98; Irving, 1959: 5; Morley, 1988: 2024). Alberta's fiery radio preacher William Aberhart (1878–1943) became attracted to Social Credit in the autumn of 1932, proffering it in his weekly broadcasts as the province's means to escape the Great Depression.

Aberhart's involvement with and preaching about Social Credit was "a radical departure from his previous theology, a theology that can best be described as highly sectarian, separatist, apolitical, other-worldly, and eschatologically oriented" (Elliott and Miller, 1987: 118). Nevertheless, he saw his new emphasis solidly within a religious context. In a 1933 letter Aberhart stated, "One thing that appeals to me and I believe will appeal to every thinking Christian, in the Douglas system of Economics [i.e., Social Credit], is the fact that from beginning to end it was based on the principles of God's great economy" (quoted in Elliott and Miller, 1987: 116). In 1934 he went further, boldly pronouncing that "one of the finest and greatest exponents of Social Credit was Jesus Christ Himself. His one mission in life was to feed and clothe His people . . ." (quoted in Elliott and Miller, 1987: 167).

As public interest grew and no existing political party would embrace the ideology, Aberhart formed his own movement and was elected provincial premier in 1935. Once in office, however, Aberhart was able to translate almost no Social Credit doctrines into viable policies, and by 1939 "Social Credit was quickly disappearing from the government's agenda" (Elliott and Miller, 1987: 283). Aberhart remained in office until his death in 1943, at which time his protégé, Ernest Manning, assumed the premier's office. He held it until 1971 (Morley, 1988: 2024).

• SECULARIZATION AND THE EFFECTS OF SOCIETY ON RELIGION

Much of Social Credit's appeal stemmed from Aberhart's ability to weave religion into politics and economics. As an early study of the movement observed, "Aberhart had no hesitation in presenting Social Credit to Albertans as a Divine Plan for the salvation of society, the parallel in the economic sphere of the Divine Plan for the salvation of the individual" (Irving, 1959: 338). The party remained in power for such a long time, however, largely because it abandoned both religious and economic doctrinalism and replaced them with "conservative financial and social policies which even bankers could applaud" (Morley, 1988: 2024). This loss of religious ideology within the polity after pressure from secular institutions is one example of what sociologists call **secularization** — a general term covering all forms of religion's decline in influence in the modern world.

Religion is unique among social institutions in its ability to motivate human behaviour through a combination of secular and allegedly supernatural promises and threats, but considerable evidence exists that fewer and fewer people in Canada allow religion to provide primary meaning to their lives. A twofold decline of religion seems to be occurring, both of whose elements are indicators of secularization. First, according to survey research conducted by University of Lethbridge sociologist Reginald Bibby, a clear trend exists regarding Canadians' decreasing involvement in religious institutions. Using a standard measure of religiosity as "weekly church attendance," Bibby's research indicates that fewer Canadians (28 percent as opposed to 67 percent) attended services in 1981 than in 1946 (Bibby, 1983: 15). Second, only a small percentage of people use religious interpretations when trying to answer life's "mysteries" (notably, death, the meaning of existence, the purpose of suffering). As Bibby concluded, Canadian "life is increasingly not meaningful in terms of religion but rather in terms of tangibles such as money and career, family and friends, recreation and entertainment, social and personal causes" (Bibby, 1983: 15).

In contrast to Bibby's second finding, other researchers argue that the advance of secularization in industrialized societies is self-limiting, with new religions or "cults abound[ing] where the churches are weak" (Stark and Bainbridge, 1985: 471). These new religions provide new sets of meaning and order to people who have little contact with traditional denominations. Bibby, however, insists that membership in these new religions is small, and that the existence of such groups does little to mitigate the overall secularization trend. "As the century draws to a close," he concludes, "people in greater and greater numbers are drawing upon religion as consumers, adopting a belief here and a practice there. Additionally, they are calling on clergy to perform various rites of passage relating primarily to birth, marriage, and death" (Bibby, 1987: 80).

An earlier study in which Bibby was involved indicated that the patterns of religious consumerism among adults was being replicated, through socialization, among teens. "This general pattern of 'polite detachment' yet ongoing identification with and consumer-like use of religious organizations mirrors dramatically the nature of adult religion in Canada" (Bibby and Posterski, 1985: 127).

Within this general pattern of secularization, however, specific patterns of affiliation and religious preference appear. In 1981, 47 percent of the Canadian population reported *affiliation* (which is different, of course, from attendance) with Catholicism, and this figure grew to 50.5 percent of the population by 1985 (Mori, 1987: 13, 14). Also in 1981, 40 percent of Canadians were affiliated with Protestant denominations, which indicated a proportional decline from previous years (Mori, 1987: 13). Significantly, the data also indicated that "the secularization trend which first became evident in the 1971 Census also showed no sign of letting up in the early 1980s." Between 1981 and 1985, "the percentage of the population aged 15 and over reporting no religious preference increased from 7 percent in 1981 to 10 percent in 1985" (Mori, 1987: 14). Canadian religion, in sum, is becoming another consumer item for which increasing numbers of Canadians have little use, except perhaps at transitional moments in life.

It seems doubtful that Canadian immigration patterns will have any long-term effects on the general secularization trend. Mullins (1989) identified cultural and structural assimilation patterns of Japanese churches and their members in Canada and concluded that "without new immigrants to replenish the ethnic membership base, the probable end of the minority church life-cycle appears to be either organizational dissolution or transformation into a multi-ethnic church" (Mullins, 1989: 179). Quickly scanning evidence about the fate of other ethnically based churches in the country, he added that "these findings alone demonstrate that assimilation takes its toll upon the ethnic churches of other minorities in Canada" (Mullins, 1989: 182). Since the pattern of ethnic churches involves either transformation into multiethnic denominations or assimilation into existing non-ethnic religious bodies, we can surmise that within three generations people from ethnic backgrounds will find themselves replicating the general pattern of secularization.

DEVELOPING ISSUES IN THE CANADIAN SOCIOLOGY OF RELIGION

In spite of the secularization of Canadian society — itself a topic in the sociology of religion — the religious scene in Canada continues to present an expanding field of sociological study. Long-established mainstream religions as well as recent arrivals have been held up to scrutiny. They have been joined by newly publicized quasi-religious manifestations seen as deviant. The evolution of the Canadian state and constitutional practice has raised the issue of government intervention in religious matters. Finally, the social activism of religious bodies has attracted research attention, especially at a time of economic and social uncertainty.

First, regardless of the eventual fate of ethnic religions, the fact remains that Canada is likely to see the appearance of many new faiths on its shores, all of which require study. The appearance of these faiths will have significant implications for Canada, each of which presents sociologists and other researchers with unique research opportunities.

Canadians should expect an influx of religions from Hong Kong as immigrants leave in anticipation of the colony's repatriation to China in 1997. Transplanted faiths such as these often bring in their theologies unresolved social and political issues, as well as implicit cultural patterns of behaviour that reflect life in the home country. Consequently, Canadians are likely to find that some of the country's newest members are embroiled in issues that heretofore seemed distant or remote.

A dramatic example of a social and political agenda being interwoven with theology occurred among Canada's Sikh community, in which a substantial number of fundamentalists — concentrating in British Columbia (Mulgrew, 1988: 105) — "began to use Canada as an overseas base for their fight in India" for a homeland (Mulgrew, 1988: 106). As money and personnel flowed back to the Punjab, many Canadian Sikh temples became embroiled in bitter disputes between moderates and fundamentalists. Sometimes the results were deadly (Mulgrew, 1988: 104, 107). Even moderate Sikhs, however, encountered problems with the Canadian establishment, as some turban-wearing men were barred from Canadian Legion halls and others fought for (and eventually received) permission to wear their religiously obligatory turbans while serving as members of the RCMP (*The Edmonton Sun,* 1990: 16) and carry their ceremonial knives (called *kirpans*) in school (*The Globe and Mail,* 1990: A16). Other clashes of (religious) cultures seem likely as immigration patterns continue to reflect world crises.

Second, the convictions of Catholic priests for sexual assaults against children (see Harris, 1990) and the exposure of physical and sexual abuse at residential schools for native children sponsored by numerous mainstream religious organizations (York, 1989) provide tragic research opportunities for studying the ways agents of social control contribute to deviance and societal dysfunction. For example, the commission that inquired into sexual abuse of children by some members of the clergy of St. John's, Newfoundland, placed joint blame for the abuse on both the offenders and the Catholic Church organization:

> The Commission thus concluded that the events which occurred in the Archdiocese cannot be passed off as the manifestation of a disease: both the offenders and the Church management must be held accountable. The Church administration in the archdiocese chose to deny the abuses and discount the victims' disclosures of criminal activity. Rather than reporting the allegations to civil authorities, the Archdiocesan administration chose to accept repeated denials of the allegations and allowed the abuses to continue (Winter, 1990, 1: 138–39).

Almost certainly the perpetrators and their denominational sponsors must share the blame for the abuses in residential schools. In both cases, normative religious institutions permitted deviance on an astounding scale. There is much here to be sociologically explored, partly as an attempt to prevent the recurrence of similar abuses.

Third, researchers in Canada and elsewhere in the Western world will continue to debate the puzzle of allegations concerning satanism and ritual crimes. Allegations of ritual crimes received national attention in the mid-1980s in relation to an eighteen-month trial held in the Hamilton-Wentworth Unified Family Court. Beginning in October 1985, the custody battle raged over two young sisters who had disclosed allegations of sexual abuse, pornography, cannibalism, and ritual murder to their foster mother. Children's Aid Society officials concluded that the children were telling the truth, but police failed to uncover any evidence to substantiate criminal charges against the alleged perpetrators. As in similar cases throughout the Western world, opinions were divided over the truth of the girls' satanic accounts.

Kevin Marron, a reporter who covered the story, concluded that

> in the absence of other credible explanations, we cannot afford to dismiss the possibility that these allegations point to the activities of groups engaged in satanic ritual, or pornography, or both, and that there may be some communication or connection between such groups (Marron, 1988: 239).

Yet another writer, who also attended the trial, heard the same evidence and concluded that "what is really at issue here is not that children are being abused, but that a plethora of out-of-context facts and figures distorts our legal and psychological perspectives and leads inevitably to the institutionalization of injustice" (Kendrick, 1988: 137). In essence, two investigators heard the same evidence and drew opposite conclusions about the reality of satanic crimes.

The debate over the reality of satanic abuse continues into the 1990s. Research has carefully separated the flourishing practices of paganism and various occult groups from the satanic debate, since these groups claim inspiration from non-Christian sources rather than from the anti-Christianity alleged to lie behind much satanic activity (Marron, 1989). Even within these more precise boundaries, sociologists still disagree over the reality of satanic abuse claims. The widely accepted sociological article that reviewed Canadian newspaper articles on the subject during the 1980s concluded that

> the construction of Satanism as a social problem in Canada has been made possible by various claims-makers, particularly American experts and the Canadian news media. The efforts of these and other dominant claims-makers can be seen as a symbolic crusade against perceived threats to their conservative ideology and way of life (Lippert, 1990: 436).

This "moral panic" position is challenged by another sociologist who argues that many of the intergenerational abuse accounts (involving children, their parents, and possibly their grandparents or other relatives) may be true. In essence, social deviants may "either develop satanic rituals from material that exists in easily accessible mainstream religious texts, or sanctify their violence by framing it within passages in otherwise normative scriptures" (Kent, 1993b: 231; see Kent, 1993c).

Fourth, increasing sociological attention should be paid to debates between the regulatory state and various religious denominations. Issues involving health care for children in groups such as Jehovah's Witnesses, fundamentalist Mennonites, and Christian Science spring up periodically across North America. The spate of American cases involving these and other groups suggests that Canada will see additional delicate legal battles over the limits of religious freedom and practice. Currently, for example, cases before Supreme Court of Canada will decide the extent to which a noncustodial parent has the right to teach his or her children religious beliefs about which the custodial parent disapproves. On another religious topic related to the law, Canada may become a haven for Mormon-affiliated polygamists, since legal experts apparently concluded that "the section of the Criminal Code of Canada pertaining to polygamy was unconstitutional" (Hunter, 1992: 1). Finally, sociologists of religion are well advised to pay continued attention to the uncomfortable relationship between religious broadcasters and the Canadian Radio-television and Telecommunications Commission (CRTC), since continued advances in telecommunications, reception, and delivery are likely to lead to a repetition of the recent war between the Commission and Christian "pirate" stations (Cernetig, 1991: A1).

Fifth and finally, sociologists of religion should continue to monitor the extent to which religious bodies mobilize on social issues. Cuneo's (1989) study of Revivalist Catholics in the antiabortion movement provides a blueprint for scholarship of this kind. We may see greater mobilization in the years to come on issues involving day-care facilities, government expenditures on religious and private schools, care of AIDS patients, homosexual marriages and adoptions, and the right to die.

Secularization may be an inexorable force in Canadian life. Nonetheless, religion is alive in multifaceted forms throughout the country, and its study remains a challenging and demanding sociological enterprise. Researchers discover that the sociology of religion may be the most eye-opening field in the entire discipline, especially when they do qualitative research involving interviews with the faithful. Certainly the religious topics that these researchers examine are among sociology's most unusual, since all manner of human actions are undertaken in the name of God.

Summary

- Connotative language — the language of feeling and poetry — uses images in myths to evoke strong feelings and emotions about religion.
- Rituals partially re-enact myths through the use of sacred symbols. Depending upon the circumstances, rituals may either empower or disempower participants.
- Substantive definitions of religion claim that some form of otherworldliness (a being or a force, for example) is central to members' beliefs; functional definitions claim that religion creates meaning and order in society.
- Sociologist Charles Glock identified five dimensions of religiosity as

  1. experiential — the extent to which a person either claims to have direct knowledge of a deity or supernatural force, or experiences profoundly religious emotion;
  2. ideological — the extent to which a person holds certain beliefs;
  3. intellectual — the extent to which a person is informed and knowledgeable about the basic beliefs of the religion and its reputedly sacred scriptures;
  4. ritualistic — the extent to which a person performs those specifically religious practices that are expected of the faithful; and
  5. consequential — the extent to which people's lives are affected by their religious beliefs and practices in such secular activities as the selection of marriage partners, political orientation, and so on.

- Structural-functional theory assumes that religions (along with other major social structures) have important if not necessary functions or consequences for societies. These functions or consequences include

  1. making life meaningful through cosmologies;
  2. comforting people in distress by providing theodicies or answers to questions about why suffering exists in the world (the priestly functions of religious leaders include providing meaning through doctrinal interpretations);
  3. providing outlets for religious leaders to criticize people or entire societies for their alleged moral transgressions through religion's prophetic functions;
  4. providing communities in which people involve themselves; and
  5. providing a source of identity.

- Society itself may use religion to legitimize its collective identity, especially through civil religions that claim divine support for the purposes and officials of the state. A civil-religious tradition, however, is very weak in Canada.
- Conflict theory views religion as a powerful social vehicle for subjugating and exploiting populations. Subjugation and exploitation come through

1. myths that sanctify social inequality;
2. patriarchal mythologies and theologies;
3. claims of the supposedly divine origins of one's own social position or the position of royalty;
4. restrictions and constraints placed on people by authoritarian religious communities;
5. theologically based attitudes toward persons outside the religious community that are hostile, demeaning, and racist; and
6. provision of social opportunities in areas such as education that advantage some members of society at the expense of others.

- Social psychologically based attribution theories argue that religious conversions occur in emotionally charged settings. The groups' religious ideologies provide participants with supposedly supernatural interpretations of events for which participants have no interpretive framework.
- Sociologists have identified conversions that occur at the end of a multistage process, in which religiously predisposed individuals encounter specific situations for religious involvement with particular groups.
- The numerous conversions to conservative Christian churches actually involve large numbers of transfers from other churches rather than recruitment of many new people from other traditions.
- Religious feelings can be inspired by such conditions as

1. dramatic natural or social events;
2. experiences that people define as mystical, but which are located in appropriate historical and cultural settings;
3. intense involvement in ecstatic and highly charged group experiences;
4. participation in a community, especially after periods of loneliness or alienation; and
5. experience of highly evocative symbols, music, or rituals.

- Exchange theories propose that religious behaviour involves calculating the likelihood of receiving immediate rewards as well as supposedly divine ones in heaven or the next life, and at the same time attempting to avoid immediate and otherworldly divine punishments.
- Religions are unique among social institutions in their ability to motivate and maintain membership by claiming supernatural legitimacy.
- Millenarianism is "the imminent collapse of the existing society and social order and their replacement with a divinely directed one."
- Various religious traditions (especially Western ones) expect messiahs or saviours to rule during the millennium.
- Messiahs are the most dramatic examples of charismatic leaders who claim to possess divinely bestowed gifts and have followers who believe the claims and continually reinforce one another's devotion.
- Typological theories classify religious organizations (especially Western ones) into

1. churches, which include all of society's members;
2. denominations, which see themselves operating amidst other groups;
3. sects, which comprise persons who aspire to spiritual perfection and fellowship with other aspirants; and
4. cults, which are loose associations whose members borrow eclectically from many traditions.

- Particular Puritan sects inspired among their adherents inner-worldly ascetic behaviour that became crucial for work attitudes in England's development of rational capitalism.
- Religious fundamentalism around the world probably will fail in its efforts to offset global and national secularization trends (at least in industrialized countries).

KEY CONCEPTS

Attribution processes
Charismatic leader
Church/denomination/sect/cult typology
Civil religion
Conflict theory
Connotative language
Cosmology
Denotative language
Exchange theories
Functional definition
Fundamentalism
Inner-worldly asceticism
Messianism
Millenarianism
Other-worldly asceticism
Priestly functions
Prophetic functions
Ritual
The sacred
Secularization
Social psychology
Structural-functional theory
Substantive definition
Theodicy

REVIEW QUESTIONS

1. What are the necessary elements in substantive definitions of religion, and what are the necessary elements in functional definitions?
2. What types of functions does religion serve for its followers?
3. How would you define "theodicies"? Give examples for various world religions.
4. How would you distinguish between religion's priestly functions and its prophetic functions?
5. Why is the civil religion tradition so weak in Canada?
6. What uses of religion cause conflict theorists to criticize it as a tool of oppression?

7. How would you describe religion through the eyes of an exchange theorist?
8. How are the concepts "messianism" and "charisma" related?
9. How would a typologist define churches, denominations, sects, and cults?
10. How did Weber describe the emergence of the so-called Protestant work ethic?
11. What evidence can be cited to support secularization claims?

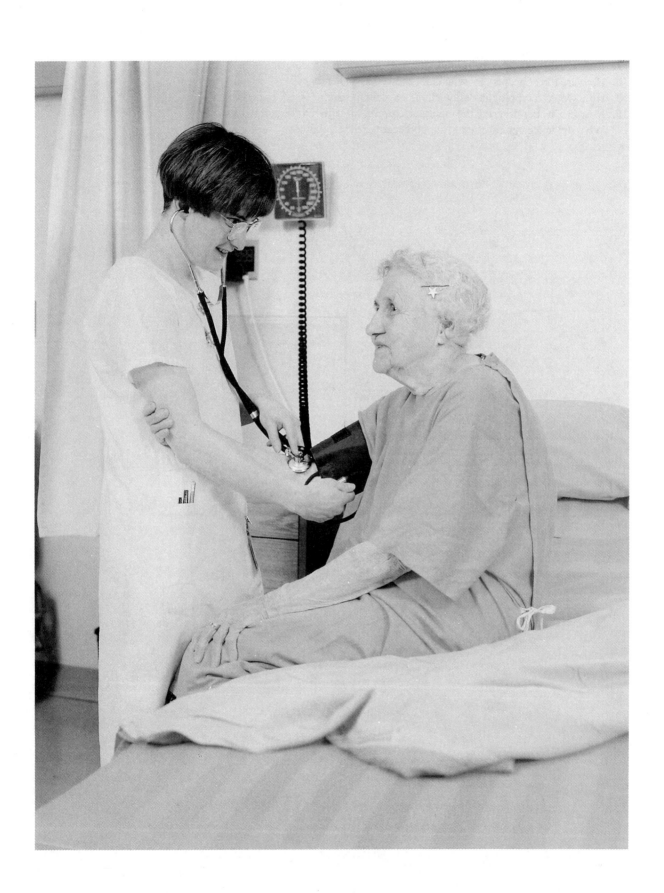

Health, Health Care & Dying

George K. Jarvis

Health, Health Care, and Dying

INTRODUCTION

Throughout history humanity has been concerned with its health and with the ever-present risk of death. In the Middle Ages alchemists sought the elixir of life; explorers sought the elusive fountain of youth. Today, to prolong life and well-being, the health food business, the health appliance business, and the vitamin business bring in billions of dollars and find a ready market among an increasingly aged population. Many wealthy societies consider the provision of basic health care to be a right for every person. The rights of the individual to health and adequate health care have been extended to include the rights of the dying person. To die with dignity and under conditions of one's choice have become goals of many people in today's individualistic, consumer-oriented society.

HEALTH

Only in recent years has sociology become concerned with health, health care, and death. The number of scholars studying these topics and the number of classes offered in colleges and universities have increased rapidly (Fulton, 1976).

• DEFINITION OF HEALTH

The definition of health has changed through the years. It used to be thought that health was the absence of disease. The World Health Organization replaced this with the following: "Health is a state of complete physical, mental and social well-being and not merely the absence of disease or infirmity" (Kelman, 1975). This definition brings mental health into focus as an important aspect of health. After all, a person may be seriously ill but feel that life is meaningful and tolerable, and even consider herself healthy compared to others. It is also possible that a person with no measurable physical or emotional illness may feel unhealthy. Sutherland and Fulton (1990) define health as "a reasonably optimistic, contented state of mind." This definition emphasizes the subjective dimension of health. It is often more important to feel healthy than to be objectively healthy.

The definition of health has in recent years been amplified to include the ability to lead a socially and economically productive life. This allows us to consider the functional side of health and to hope that it may be achieved for all segments of the population. Dubos (1968) has said that health is not an idealized state of well-being but a way of living that enables "imperfect men [and women] to achieve a rewarding and not too painful existence while they cope with an imperfect world." In this sense, health may be defined as being physically and emotionally healthy enough to perform the most important daily tasks.

• DECLINE IN MORTALITY

In the past the major causes of shortened life were infectious and parasitic diseases. These have largely been overcome as causes of death in developed countries through a combination of better nutrition, personal hygiene, clean water, sewage disposal, food hygiene, healthier lifestyles, and medical advances. Most experts put medical advances late in this process (McKeown, 1978; Razzell, 1974).

Prior to the 18th century conditions of life for the average European were loathsome. Sanitation was nonexistent. Cities stank from the offal, urine, and house slops thrown into the streets. Dwellings were crowded and poorly heated. Water in the cities was dangerous to drink.

The decline in English **mortality** was due mainly to the decline of **infectious diseases**. Airborne infections such as tuberculosis, bronchitis, pneumonia, and influenza accounted for

40 percent of the decline between 1848 and 1971. Lesser reductions were due to declines in scarlet fever, diphtheria, whooping cough, and measles (McKeown, 1978). Water-borne and food-borne diseases such as cholera, diarrhea, dysentery, nonrespiratory tuberculosis, typhus, and typhoid also diminished.

Declines in these diseases were not attributable to medical discoveries, treatments, or practices. Mortality was often falling long before treatments or preventions were discovered. In 1850 tuberculosis was the single largest cause of death in England and Wales, yet the death rate from this disease was already decreasing by 1850. It was not until 1882 that the tubercle bacillus was identified and isolated.

Medical treatments existed in the 19th century and throughout human history, but they were often ineffective. In the 1820s Rachel Jackson, the wife of United States President Andrew Jackson, was diagnosed as having tuberculosis. Her doctor prescribed smoking tobacco. Doctors at that time often prescribed doses of toxic chemicals such as mercury compounds. Patients were bled, which weakened them, or were given purgatives that caused them to vomit. Surgical standards were low and infection was rampant in hospitals. Brown (1979: 62–63) notes that by the middle of the 19th century, "cholera victims were given an even chance of being done in by the disease or by the doctor." As one 19th-century writer said, "Cured last night of my disease, died today of my physician."

In time medical improvements began to contribute to a lower death rate. The first disease for which vaccination became available was smallpox (Lyons and Petrucelli, 1987). Although there is evidence of experimentation with smallpox inoculation in ancient times in Africa and Asia, this innovation first began to lower the smallpox death rate in the first half of the 19th century in England. According to Thomlinson (1965), medical improvements, especially the development of **antisepsis** and **asepsis,** were responsible for a further mortality decline, but this decline occurred in the late 19th century. Until then women in England who had their babies in the hospital suffered a greater risk of death than women who stayed home to give birth.

What factors caused the death rate from infectious diseases to drop? The declines in Europe and America were primarily due to environmental factors. In the 18th century better nutrition began to prevail in England as a result of greater production and distribution of food. This led to increased resistance to infections. The increased food supply was due to the **agricultural revolution,** more efficient use of land, and the scientific breeding of animals. Widespread acceptance and adoption of new crops such as the potato and maize (corn) contributed to the food supply. The potato was particularly valuable as a nutritious crop. In Norway as well the mortality decline between 1735 and 1865 was due to an improved food supply. Dysentery and typhus deaths in Sweden and Norway were closely associated with harvest failures.

Razzell (1974) claims that hygiene may have done more than nutrition to reduce disease before 1850. Before then the English were dirty (as were others). Even among the rich, it was very uncommon to take a bath. We read in the diary of a middle-class American that she "withstood a shower bath better than expected, not having been wet all over once for 28 years." Washstands that held soap began to be used in the 1770s, but bathtubs did not become a regular part of the bathroom until the late 19th century. Even as late as the 1920s there were more automobiles than bathtubs in Muncie, Indiana (Lynd and Lynd, 1929). Soap consumption per person doubled during the first forty years of the 19th century. The increased use of cotton clothing allowed more frequent washing than wool or linen, which also improved cleanliness.

Public health and sanitation made major contributions in the latter half of the 19th century. Water was purified; sewage began to be treated and disposed of properly. Foods were more hygienically prepared. Pasteurization of milk began to be practised late in the century. These advances were of special assistance to infants. As the infant mortality rate began to drop, life expectancy of the population began to advance.

The U.S. mortality rate fell in the 20th century. There was a strong decline between 1900 and 1950, mostly because of reductions in eleven major infectious diseases: typhoid, smallpox, scarlet fever, measles, whooping cough, diphtheria, influenza, tuberculosis, pneumonia, diseases of the digestive system, and polio. In 1900, 40 percent of deaths were due to these causes, which are now responsible for a much smaller proportion of deaths. They have been replaced by heart disease, cancer, stroke, and other chronic diseases of middle and older age. This change is called the **epidemiological transition** (see Chapter 15).

Most of this decline in infectious disease was not due to medical practices and therapies. Penicillin is the accepted medical treatment for scarlet fever. It was introduced to the public in 1946, but only 1.75 percent of the decline in the scarlet fever death rate came after 1946. Tuberculosis shows a similar history. It declined as a killer throughout the 19th century. Not until 1947 did streptomycin provide effective chemotherapy, although by then death rates due to tuberculosis were only one-sixth what they had been a century earlier.

Only the death rates of influenza, whooping cough, and polio showed substantial declines (over 25 percent) after the date of effective medical intervention. Thus only 3.5 percent of the decline in the general death rate since 1900 can be explained by medical intervention in the major infectious diseases. Medical measures contributed little, usually being introduced after a marked decline had already set in. The demographic consequence was that most people, avoiding death from infectious diseases of early life, lived into middle and old age. The major threats to life began to be from the previously mentioned chronic diseases.

Only in the last half generation has another deadly infectious disease begun to take an increased toll of human life in North America as AIDS has spread through the young adult populations of the continent's major cities. Serum hepatitis has also become a danger to North Americans, as cases have been imported through immigration and travel from parts of the world where the disease is prevalent. Recent outbreaks of drug-resistant strains of tuberculosis have caused concern in the United States. Each year in Canada about two thousand cases of tuberculosis are identified, many in small, isolated native communities. As drug-resistant strains migrate to Canada, the treatment and containment of this disease will be more difficult, especially among the poorer parts of the population and those with impaired immunity. Millions of Canadians as well have been infected with sexually transmitted diseases. Most of these conditions have been successfully treated by existing drugs. Yet some diseases — herpes, HIV infection, and a few others — are not curable at this time. Previously curable diseases such as gonorrhea are now beginning to emerge in drug-resistant strains. Greater efforts are needed to combat the spread of these diseases.

During the past twenty-five years in Canada, progress has been made against death from heart disease, respiratory disease, stroke, and certain forms of cancer. For the first time in this century male life expectancy is increasing faster than female life expectancy. The death rates of persons in middle and older age are beginning to drop. This has resulted in a great increase of the population over 85 years of age.

For many years death rates in the developing world have declined. The great killer, smallpox, ceased to be a threat. Though the eradication of smallpox was largely achieved through vaccination, the decline in other diseases came through improved nutrition and socioeconomic conditions, mosquito control, and the availability of at least rudimentary medical care. In the less-developed countries, infectious diseases still cause many deaths. Malaria, diarrhea, measles, tuberculosis, and other diseases claim millions of lives each year. Much of the population does not live to be old enough to fall prey to heart disease, cancer, and other diseases of the developed world. Uwe Brinkmann, a Harvard epidemiologist, has said that more than half of the 300 million urban poor in the developing world are in a permanently weakened condition because they carry one or more parasites.

Recently, the resurgence of malaria, tuberculosis, and cholera has caused concern. The cholera epidemic that hit Latin American cities in 1992 hospitalized more than 400 000 people and killed at least 4000 in a few months. The infection of millions with human immunodeficiency virus (HIV) casts a pall on the future. All of those currently infected are potential AIDS victims. In addition to the impact of its own symptoms, AIDS lowers the immunity to other diseases such as tuberculosis. The poverty of some nations makes it difficult to maintain the status quo against these killer diseases, as does the increasing resistance of organisms to agents of control used successfully in the past.

The fragmentation of states and loss of effective civil order cause breakdowns in public health and food supply, and may cause many deaths through violence. Somalia has provided a recent example of this terrible process. Long racked by civil war, the government of the country has deteriorated. Warring clans and other armed private groups steal available food and sell it at high prices, thwart efforts at food relief and public health, and themselves kill many persons. Ominous signs of the fragmentation process are seen in other parts of the world and portend health difficulties for persons in affected countries.

Declines in the health of populations in developing nations inevitably pose a danger to the health of Canadians. The world is increasingly linked by travel and the transportation of goods. As a result of the severe outbreak of cholera in Latin America, several Canadian tourists were stricken with this severe gastrointestinal disease. Malaria kills about two million people a year and is thought by some to be the biggest current disease problem in the world. Each year about five hundred Canadian travellers contract malaria and a few of them die. The health of the population in developing nations is increasingly a concern of Canadians.

• FACTORS IN GOOD HEALTH

Good health is one of life's most desirable goals. To achieve this, more people are taking an interest in the factors that lead to a healthy life. Many universities and secondary schools in North America have developed health courses aimed at increasing awareness of healthy lifestyles and encouraging students to take control of their health. The effort at health promotion is a major emphasis of government as well. Not only may sickness and suffering be reduced, but a healthier population benefits us all through lower health costs.

• Lifestyles

The styles people adopt in their lives — the ways they choose to live — are sometimes called **lifestyles**. These habits and customs of life are influenced by socialization throughout life. The extent to which people engage in preventive health practices, exercise, good sleep, good nutrition, and satisfying social relationships are important facets of a healthy lifestyle. Not only are some lifestyles markedly healthy, but some are much more likely than others to be unhealthy, tending to more illness and earlier death. For instance, careless driving habits, lack of seatbelt use, risk taking, smoking, immoderate use of alcohol, lack of proper rest, and poor diet are elements of an unhealthy lifestyle.

• Health Promotion

Governments and other large organizations are increasingly encouraging their members to adopt healthy lifestyles. This is called **health promotion**. Emphasis on preventive health and health promotion is shifting as the threats to life and health are changing. In less-developed countries, emphasis is on good nutrition and cleanliness, and prevention, discovery, and treatment of infectious diseases. In other countries emphasis is on taking control of one's health and improving nutrition and lifestyle to avoid chronic diseases.

In the past medical research looked for a "magic bullet," a specific cure for each illness. A miracle inoculation or a drug effective in treatment was sought. For many of today's most deadly diseases and conditions such an approach seems ineffective. For instance, heart disease and cancer seem to have multiple causes. They resist the search for single, simple cures. To reduce the risk from these killer conditions, one needs to alter many aspects of one's life.

• Preventive Health Practices

Certain actions people take can protect them from serious illness or injury. Other actions can identify illness early so that treatment is more effective. These are called **preventive health practices**. Examples of these actions are the pap smear and breast self-examination for women and the testicular self-examination and prostate examination for men. For both genders the monitoring of blood pressure and the wearing of seatbelts may prevent injury or death. Those who are convinced that they have responsibility for their own health are more likely to undertake these possibly life-saving procedures.

Women are more likely than men to engage in preventive health practices. Fifty-six percent of all women in Canada have regular pap smears to detect cervical irregularities. Breast examination, important in the detection of breast cancer, is frequently done by doctors but less often performed by self-examination. According to a recent survey, 65 percent of all adult Canadian women had a doctor or nurse examine their breasts during the previous year. About 75 percent of women have been shown how to examine their own breasts, but only 38 percent examine their breasts each month (Health and Welfare Canada, 1988). Men are less likely to have regular prostate examinations or to perform testicular self-examinations to detect cancer in these locations. Efforts are currently being directed at encouraging men to be more active in preventive health.

Another important preventive health practice is to check blood pressure. High blood pressure is a major risk factor in heart disease, kidney disease, and strokes. The 1981 Canada Fitness Survey reported that 29 percent of men and 18 percent of women exceed 140/90, considered the borderline for high blood pressure (Stephens et al., 1986). Many individuals, especially men, are unaware that their blood pressure is too high. Blood pressure can be reduced by lifestyle modification such as diet and exercise, or by medication. The majority of Canadians (57 percent) have their blood pressure checked at least every six months (Health and Welfare Canada, 1988). Women, the more educated, and persons over 45 years of age are more likely to undergo regular monitoring.

The wearing of seatbelts can protect against injury and death in motor vehicle accidents. Road safety received the highest priority of ten health topics considered in the Health Promotion Survey of 1985. Over the past fifteen years seatbelt use has increased to about 4 in 5 drivers in Canada as a result of seatbelt legislation and education about its benefits (Health and Welfare Canada, 1988). An even greater proportion of adults say that they always insist that children use restraint systems. Women use seatbelts more than men. The more educated the person, the more likely he or she is to use restraints. The category that uses seatbelts least is young males; this is also the group that has the most serious motor vehicle accidents. Those who drink and drive or who drive under the influence of marijuana also use seatbelts less than the average. Their lack of regard for their own safety and that of others is alarming. This suggests a serious need for education and enforcement among these high-risk categories.

• Smoking

As early as 1915, Japanese researchers identified a relationship between the substances in cigarette smoke and lung cancer. In 1936 Alton Ochsner, a chest surgeon working in the United States, noticed that all the persons in his practice who developed lung cancer were heavy smokers. This led to much research that has established a strong linkage between smoking and cancer at respiratory sites. More recent studies have shown that smoking is related to cancer at other sites as well, and is also related to heart disease and chronic respiratory diseases such as emphysema.

Cigarette smoking reached a peak during the 1950s and 1960s, when at least half of all adult Canadians smoked. Now only 31 percent of Canadians aged 15 and over smoke regularly (Health and Welfare Canada, 1991). Although this proportion has not changed since 1985, smokers now smoke fewer cigarettes per day. Thirty years ago about twice as many men as women were smokers. Now men and women smoke in roughly equal numbers. Young women (aged 20 to 24) and men aged 25 to 44 are most likely to smoke (38 percent of each). Adults 65 years of age and over smoke least (21 percent for men; 16 percent for women). Older smokers smoke fewer cigarettes per day. Newfoundlanders are most likely to smoke (36 percent); residents of British Columbia are least likely (28 percent). Education is the most important variable distinguishing smokers from nonsmokers. University graduates are about half as likely to smoke as Canadians with high-school education or less. Current drinkers of alcoholic beverages are five times as likely as abstainers to be heavy smokers (Health and Welfare Canada, 1991).

Secondary smoke is also dangerous. All of us smoke to a limited degree by inhaling others' tobacco smoke. The wives of heavy smokers, even when they themselves do not smoke, are twice as likely to develop lung cancer as nonsmoking wives of nonsmokers. Evidence like this has brought about a revolution in the restriction of smoking to limited areas in buildings. Repeatedly, expert committees on smoking at the World Health Organization have said reduction in cigarette smoking is the single most cost-effective way to reduce mortality in the world.

• Alcohol

Alcohol is a popular drug, usually consumed in a social context. In a 1988 study, 83 percent of men and 75 percent of women in Canada reported drinking at least once in the past year. But the majority (69 percent) of Canadians who drink say they do so once a week or less (Health and Welfare Canada, 1989b). Governments are heavily involved in the sale of alcoholic beverages and regard it as a major source of revenue. In 1985–86, provincial and federal government revenues from alcoholic beverages in Canada were $3.78 billion. Yet alcohol abuse is recognized as one of the most serious public health problems in Canada. Alcohol abuse was estimated to have cost Canada $5.25 billion in 1985–86 (Health and Welfare Canada, 1989a).

From 1950 to 1980 there seems to have been a long and consistent increase in alcohol consumption by Canadians. During the 1980s this pattern reversed with declines in sales, fewer drinkers, and less consumption. Among students the proportion who drink is decreasing even more rapidly than in the general population. Still, in a survey done in the late 1980s, 1 in 5 students reported becoming drunk in the previous month. This is most likely to occur at parties (Health and Welfare Canada, 1989a).

Drinking is not uniform across the population of Canada. Men, who are more likely to drink than are women, also consume more than do women of similar age. Consumption is highest in the north and west of Canada. Young adults (aged 20 to 44) are most likely to be drinkers, but the higher a person's education or income, the more likely that person is to report drinking within the last month. On the other end of the social scale, those not in the labour force and those at lower educational levels are the least likely to be drinkers.

Alcohol consumption is correlated with tobacco consumption, marijuana and hashish use (Health and Welfare Canada, 1988), and other dangerous habits such as drinking while driving. In Canada the Criminal Code forbids the operation of a motor vehicle if the concentration of alcohol in the driver's blood is more than 0.08 grams of alcohol per 100 millilitres. One study showed that 79 percent of fatally injured drivers were legally impaired (Donelson et al., 1986). This may exaggerate somewhat the effect of alcohol in that alcohol-related accidents are not necessarily caused by alcohol. But it is clear that alcohol is a major factor in motor vehicle accidents. Despite this, in a recent survey, 17 percent of Canadian adults (aged 16 to 69) — about three million people — reported driving in the past year after having at least two drinks in the preceding hour. Men (26 percent) were three times more likely to do this than were women (8 percent) (Health and Welfare Canada, 1989b). Over 25 percent of Canadian adults believed they could drive safely after having four or more drinks in a three-hour period (Health and Welfare Canada, 1989a). Almost surely drinking so much in so short a time would result in driving with more than the legal limit of alcohol in the blood. More than half of all instances of drinking and driving can be blamed on a small minority (3 percent) who repeatedly drive after drinking. They are also likely to use cannabis (Health and Welfare Canada, 1988).

Heavy consumption of alcohol has direct effects on health. When taken in excess, alcohol contributes to a wide variety of illnesses, including alcoholic liver disease, pancreatitis, gastric discomfort and bleeding, short-term memory loss, **Wernicke-Korsakoff syndrome, alcoholic cardiomyopathy, fetal alcohol syndrome,** and anemia. Some of these conditions are life threatening. The amount of alcohol needed to bring on these conditions varies with the individual, but the more alcohol that is consumed, the more likely is the person to experience negative consequences.

• Nutrition

The kind and amount of food eaten also affect the risk of contracting serious disease. Conditions such as **beriberi, scurvy, kwashiorkor,** and **rickets** are the result of nutritional deficiencies. Other illnesses such as cancer and heart disease are related to the type of food eaten as well. Cholesterol is generated by the body in response to the amount of cholesterol in various foods. Fat in the diet is related to elevated risks of cancer and heart disease. The eating of foods or supplements containing beta carotene, vitamin C, possibly vitamin E, and the metal selenium is thought to reduce the risk of cancer, as is the eating of cruciform vegetables such as broccoli, brussels sprouts, cauliflower, and cabbage.

In Canada, as in other industrialized countries, problems of eating are often due to eating too much rather than too little. Over 66 percent of adults in Canada believe that they can improve their health by changing their eating habits. People think that certain foods should be avoided, including those high in fat (35 percent of respondents), cholesterol (27 percent of respondents), and sugar (24 percent of respondents). Canadians would like to eat more fruits and vegetables.

In a recent study reported in the prestigious British medical journal *Lancet,* healthy eating was found to reverse coronary artery blockage. The study was conducted on 41 heart disease patients in Sausalito, California. The 22 patients in the experimental group followed a low-fat vegetarian diet, took regular exercise, attended stress management classes where they meditated, and did not smoke. Eighty-two percent showed a reversal of blockages in the coronary arteries. Although the control group did not smoke either, pursued moderate exercise, and ate a diet with 30 percent fat calories (which is a moderate level), 53 percent of this group experienced worsening of artery blockages. More research must confirm these findings, but the study offers hope that lifestyle, including healthy diet, may prevent heart disease.

More than 50 percent of Canadians want to change their weight, primarily through weight loss. "Fat busting" is a multibillion dollar international industry that feeds on society's obsession with slimness. In Canada alone, people have been spending more than $300 million annually to lose weight. About 350 000 Canadians, 90 percent of them women, have been signing up for franchised diet clinics each year. Usually dieting is ineffective. Within three years 95 percent of people who lose weight by dieting regain it. Many gain weight beyond their starting point. Dieting can trigger eating disorders such as anorexia nervosa, a compulsive illness in which victims starve themselves. Rapid weight loss can in itself be dangerous. Muscles and organs are weakened, including vital organs such as the liver, kidneys, and heart. Prolonged and dangerous low protein levels can lead to irregular heartbeat, dehydration, low blood pressure, fatigue, and dizziness. Some researchers believe that low-calorie diets can cause gall bladder disease. About 70 percent of women at a "good weight for their height" want to lose weight, and 23 percent of women who are underweight want to lose more weight (Health and Welfare Canada, 1988). This suggests that many people, particularly women, have unrealistic, perhaps unhealthy, images of their bodies.

• Exercise and Sleep

Exercise, though it increases risk from joint and other traumatic injury, is related to better cardio-respiratory fitness, better self-image, and somewhat longer life. Adequate sleep is also related to longevity. Enstrom (1989) followed a sample of Mormons for ten years and found that those who actively participated in their religion, avoided smoking and alcohol, and had adequate exercise and sleep lived substantially longer than others in the United States population. Average female life expectancy under these conditions was 86 years, and males who participated similarly in healthy lifestyle lived an average of 84 years (Enstrom et al., 1989).

Canadians do not think they exercise enough. Fifty-eight percent of adults believe they exercise less than they should. Yet Canadians are actually rather active. Over half (54 percent) of Canadian adults engage in exercise three or more times per week. Younger persons are most likely to be regular exercisers, but the decline with age is gradual. There are no consistent differences between men and women in level of exercise. Persons of higher education are more likely to exercise than others in the population. Those who exercise report better health and say they are happier than those who do not exercise.

Only about one in four Canadians can be called "sedentary" — engaging in no regular exercise. Inactive Canadians are not very motivated to change, although they are aware of the benefits of a more active life. (A minority of sedentary people do not exercise because their health does not permit vigorous activity.) Over five million persons in Canada are at risk of health problems that could be avoided or reduced by increased exercise (Health and Welfare Canada, 1988).

• Social Relations

There is evidence that healthy social relations predispose people to longer life and that loneliness, personal distress, and other social difficulties may lead to more illness and early death. Those who are married tend to live longer than those who are not. The reasons for this are complex. Those who marry are healthier to begin with than those who do not. Sometimes sickness puts a strain on marriage, causing the marriage to dissolve, and causing as well the untimely death of one of the partners. Apart from this, there is evidence that the presence of a supportive marital relationship is a major resource in withstanding the crises of life. The same is true for other close, caring relationships.

There are many ways in which friends and family may affect a person's health. They may intervene directly to protect others from bad habits or dangerous behaviour. Seventy-six percent of respondents in the Health Promotion Survey claimed to have intervened to prevent others from driving while impaired. People may protect those for whom they are responsible — for example, preparing themselves by learning resuscitation and first aid techniques should they be needed by a loved one. People also intervene to prevent behaviour that is a threat to *themselves* from others, as did the 45 percent who said they had asked someone not to smoke around them (Health and Welfare Canada, 1987).

In other ways, the presence of close relationships makes us vulnerable. The loss of a prized relationship is itself one of life's great trials. The death of one's spouse or a close family member, or the loss of a close relationship is related to higher rates of sickness and death during the period immediately following the loss. Part of this risk may be due to changes in lifestyle adopted as a result of the stress of life adjustment. While fewer than one in three Canadians smokes, one of every two separated or divorced persons is a smoker. Most serious, violent acts and abusive relationships occur between those who are linked by a close relationship. Along with the benefits, there is risk in intimacy.

Our family and friends influence us in lifestyle choices. Users of tobacco and alcoholic beverages tend to find friends and spouses among those like themselves (Health and Welfare Canada, 1988). This is true as well for heavy drinking, drinking and driving, use of marijuana, and use of tranquillizers. It is also true for exercise and other positive lifestyle choices (Health and Welfare Canada, 1987). Alcoholics Anonymous for many years has promoted a most successful technique for reinforcing and maintaining sobriety among alcoholics. It provides a support group and spiritual meaning to the recovering alcoholic. Network therapy is now being used with considerable success in the treatment of addictions. This technique uses existing relationships to build and sustain the addict as he or she recovers.

• ENVIRONMENTAL HEALTH

Environmental health is concerned with everything in the environment of humans that exerts an influence on health and well-being. Concern with the environment's effect on health is of ancient origin. Pliny (A.D. 23–79) knew that lead-based paints were associated with lead poisoning. The medieval guilds understood that some trades were hazardous and warned their members accordingly. In the 13th century the king of England made laws to reduce the smoke from cooking pots in the city of London. These laws were widely ignored, as are many environmental concerns today.

Mexico City stands in a ring of mountains. It has had a tremendous increase in the number of automobiles, often driven without adequate pollution control. When the wind is not blowing, the level of smog may rise to a level four times as high as the level considered unsafe in California. Healthy people can be injured by such poor air quality, while persons with respiratory problems die in increased numbers.

The city of Tokyo generates about 20 000 tonnes of trash per day, despite efforts to recycle and incinerate the refuse. Tokyo has been running out of dump sites. The city has been building artificial islands in Tokyo Bay to hold garbage. To continue this practice will threaten fishing and shipping industries.

People around the world face risks from polluted air, contaminated water, deposits of solid waste, food contaminants, and toxic substances created by industry. More than 4 000 000 chemicals have been identified. Over 60 000 are commonly used in industry, about 700 new ones every year. There is often a casual attitude toward the disposal of waste chemicals, which are sometimes allowed to leak into storm sewers or out of tanker trucks. The risks from these substances need to be evaluated.

In more-developed countries risks are monitored by epidemiologists who map regional cancer incidence and relate it to environmental contaminants. They have discovered rare cancers occurring more frequently among asbestos workers and those who work with vinyl chloride. Risks of higher cancer incidence and increased mortality were identified for those exposed to radiation living downwind from atomic testing facilities in Nevada and living near a nuclear power station at Sellarfield in England. At Minamata Bay in Japan 1200 cases of neurologic disease and birth defects occurred among people eating fish contaminated with methyl mercury. Large areas of forest and lakes in Canada and the United States are being contaminated by acid generated by sulphurous and nitrogenous industrial air emissions.

Though much remains to do, some successes have been registered in the reduction of environmental risks in industrialized countries. Efforts to improve air quality have succeeded in many industrial cities. Indoor air quality is improving as rules limiting smoking are implemented. Water quality is usually adequate, although standards for new contaminants need to be developed. Some improvement of water quality in the Great Lakes has been achieved.

In the less-developed world, concern with the environment is often considered a luxury. Economic development is the primary interest of planners. Jobs are the first consideration. Often, high-residual pesticides such as DDT are still used, and rain forests are cut down and burned. Air and water quality are often very poor.

It is in the interest of all the world's peoples to manage the environment for the future. Pollution problems cross political boundaries, as Canadians and Americans have seen with the acid rain problem. Solutions to environmental problems are slow in coming. In some cases they involve government spending and regulation, including taxing companies that pollute, monitoring elevated risks and relating them to environmental contaminants, and encouraging citizens to recycle and reduce pollution. Some promising suggestions, such as proposals for drawing heat from sewage and other solid waste, hope to address more than one environmental problem at a time.

HEALTH CARE

• ILLNESS AND ILLNESS BEHAVIOUR

Not all segments of the population have benefited equally from the decline of mortality. Age, gender, race and ethnicity, and social class are related to mortality and **morbidity**.

• Age

Most of the decline in mortality throughout the world has been effected by reducing the toll of infant death. Infancy is a most dangerous time of life. Even today in a few countries such as Afghanistan and the poor countries of East and West Africa approximately 15 percent of infants die in the first year of life. In Canada only 7.2 infants under 1 year of age die per 1000 births, a figure that amounts to less than 1 percent of Canadian infants.

The control of infant death has led to an increase in life expectancy for a Canadian infant at birth from 47 years in 1900 to 77 years today, a 64 percent increase. This change, with the decline in fertility, has led to a great increase in the number of the aged. Though people are living longer, they also face more years of disability at the end of life. The poor especially experience more disabilities in old age than the wealthy (see Chapter 11).

The fastest growing segment of the aged is the population 85 years of age and over. These people often require special types of health care, oriented to the long-term treatment of chronic diseases. Health and nursing care are continuing to grow more expensive. As the aged use more of these services, the increase in the number of elderly persons will put greater pressure on the health-care system in future years. As tomorrow's elderly will have smaller families upon which they can rely for assistance, they may place still greater demands on community services (Cockerham, 1992). Despite these special needs, older persons of tomorrow are likely to remain healthy longer than in the past.

Health is the single most important determinant of the quality of life for an older person (Cockerham, 1991). It affects the capacity to pursue chosen activities and take part in all other areas of life as well. Studies in Canada and Israel find that those who rate their health highly tend to live longer than those who do not (Mossey and Shapiro, 1982; Kaplan et al., 1988), other things being equal. Although health declines with age, older persons rate their health positively (Stoller, 1984). Older persons have fewer **acute conditions** than do younger persons and so miss fewer days of work (Atchley, 1985). But they do have far more long-term or **chronic conditions** such as cancer, heart disease, arthritis, and rheumatism, which require special care. Older persons appear to adjust their definition of what good health is: they may rate their health positively because they do not have as demanding a level of activity as younger people and because they feel at their age they are lucky to be alive. Their health has not deteriorated as seriously as they had expected (Stoller, 1984).

If death does not intervene first, eventually all old persons become unhealthy. In addition to the chronic conditions of old age, they suffer from poorer general physical condition, and diminished stamina, hand and eye coordination, hearing and vision, and capacity to recover and to heal.

• Gender

Gender differences in mortality and in health are extremely significant. The most obvious difference is that females outlive males in almost all countries of the world and throughout most of the life cycle. Even prenatal deaths are more likely to be male than female. In this we are like most nonhuman species; their females also live longer than males.

In Canada male life expectancy at birth in 1986 was approximately 73 years, while that for females was approximately 80 years, a difference of almost 7 years (see Chapter 15). At the turn of the century the difference in life expectancy was only 2 to 3 years. Much of the male disadvantage was due to hazardous conditions at work, though this was partly offset for females by the greater risk that they experienced in childbirth than they do today. In the years since 1900 both dangers have decreased.

Before and during World War I, males in large numbers began to smoke cigarettes. Soldiers were encouraged to smoke, as they received cigarettes as part of their rations. Approximately 20 years later, differences in cancer and heart disease rates for males and females began to create a **sex mortality differential**. The differential increased until smoking began to affect female death rates and health. Females began to smoke cigarettes during and after World War II (Retherford, 1976). Since the 1980s male life expectancy has begun to increase more rapidly than that of females. For the first time in this century the gap in mortality is shrinking. Females have begun to feel the effects of cigarette smoking at the same time as males have quit smoking in larger numbers than women have. Other male lifestyle risks are beginning to be shared by women as they enter previously segregated male occupations and experience stresses and risks that were once felt only by males.

Although females live longer than males, they report more illnesses, miss more days of work, spend more days sick in bed, stay more days in the hospital, and make more visits to the doctor. These differences are diminished but still persist when exclusively female conditions such as childbirth and difficulties in menstruation are subtracted. At least part of this difference is due to female socialization, which encourages more seeking of help than male socialization. Women are also more likely to engage in health-protective behaviours such as regular check-ups and self-examinations.

In some ways the health of men and women is not very different. When asked to rate their health, they give almost identical answers (Health and Welfare Canada, 1987). When one considers health expectancy — years of disability-free life — the difference between men and women is small. Much of the extra life expectancy of women in Canada is plagued with major disabilities (Wilkins and Adams, 1983).

Women have not always been treated equally by the health establishment. Doctors in North America have typically been male, upper-middle-class persons who interact with patients much as a traditional father would interact with his family — particularly with his children. Women, as health consumers, are today demanding more equal treatment. Many doctors, to their credit, are responding to this with less authoritarian, more informative treatment of patients. Patients are coming to be seen as responsible for their health and in need of more complete information.

• Race and Ethnicity

In Canada major differences in mortality and health are associated with race and ethnicity. Although systematic studies of mortality and health by ethnicity have not yet occurred in Canada, the longest-lived groups in Canada seem to be those of Asian background, followed by Caucasians. The group with the shortest life expectancy in Canada is native Canadians. At last reckoning native people could expect to live ten fewer years than other Canadians at birth. These differences in longevity are thought to be due to lifestyle.

Native people also report more chronic and acute illness than other persons (Gartrell, 1986; Jarvis, 1988a, 1988b). Surveys on eight Alberta Indian reserves show that Indians report more emotional disorders (such as depression), more arthritis and rheumatism, more dental problems, and more migraine headaches, and are at greater risk of visual disorders than the Canadian population as a whole. Studies in Manitoba and Alberta (Kashuba et al., 1992) find that native persons experience higher rates of hospitalization and are more often recorded as medical patients than the rest of the population. Tuberculosis rates are still higher among Indians than the rest of the population, though deaths seldom occur from this disease. Although new cases of tuberculosis are declining among Indians, the registered Indian rate in 1982 was still nine times that of the Canadian population (Lithwick et al., 1986).

Alcoholism is also more prevalent among Indians than others. The Canadian government estimates alcohol abuse levels between 35 percent and 40 percent for the adult population and between 10 percent and 15 percent for adolescents (Health and Welfare Canada, 1989a). The reasons for this are not clear. The pattern of drinking for Indians is also different from other Canadians. Caucasian heavy drinkers tend to drink almost constantly. Indian heavy drinkers go on frequent episodic binges. This pattern of binge drinking begins for some Indian youth when they are still in junior high school. Because of heavy alcohol consumption, Indians experience high levels of cirrhosis of the liver, a deadly condition in which the liver deteriorates. Fetal alcohol syndrome is much higher among natives than other Canadians. This is a form of retardation among children, much more common among children whose mothers have consumed alcohol during pregnancy.

Indians, more than any other Canadian ethnic group, die of violent causes. Indians are from three to five times more likely than other Canadians to commit suicide. Most of the suicides occur among young Indians. By the time young Indians have entered secondary school, as many as one in six have attempted suicide. Indians also suffer from high rates of homicide and from accidental death. Accidental deaths common among Indians include motor vehicle accidents, drowning, death by fire, firearms, overdoses, and exposure. Some of this is due in part to the isolation of many Indians in places where most households have guns, home heating may be faulty, medical care is remote, and safety instruction is inadequate. Unfortunately, violent death is made more likely by excessive drinking.

One study used autopsy, police, medical examiner records, and interviews with families to examine each death that occurred on thirty-five reserves and colonies in Alberta. Almost half of the deaths had violent causes. For 80 percent of violent deaths alcohol consumption was a strong contributing factor (Jarvis and Boldt, 1982).

In the past, Indian infant mortality was about twice that of other persons in Canada. The Indian infant mortality rate in Canada was 12.3 in 1990, higher than the 7.6 per 1000 rate for the country as a whole, but not by as much as in the past. The Canadian health-care system provides health care for those with official Indian status through the Medical Services Branch, Health and Welfare Canada; the provinces cover native persons without Indian status.

On a different note, there are ethnic differences in how people respond to symptoms and pain, and in how much they trust health-care personnel. For instance, an American study showed that those of Italian and Jewish origin are more sensitive to pain than Irish and "old American" groups. Jewish persons have less trust in doctors than do Italians and "old Americans." Their sensitivity to pain is linked to concern over what the pain means for their general health. Italian sensitivity focuses more on the pain itself. If given pain killers, Italians are content; Jewish patients continue to be concerned with the underlying condition that caused the pain (Zborowski, 1952).

• Social Class

Social class differences in health and mortality are dramatic. Throughout history poor people have lived shorter lives with greater rates of sickness, especially serious illness. This is true also in Canada, where the poor have shorter life expectancy than others. They also become sick and experience disability more often than other Canadians.

In the past, the rate of health-care utilization was lower for the poor. National systems of health-care insurance have allowed greater utilization by the poor, although the state of their health suggests that they should ideally be using even more health care than they do. The reasons for this underutilization are not perfectly clear, but probably are more related to system barriers than to lack of finances. System barriers include social distance and lack of communication between middle-class health-care personnel and poor patients, as well as intimidation and strangeness experienced by poor people when they enter doctors' offices and hospitals.

Over thirty-five years ago Koos (1954) studied a small city in New York and found that the poor people in that community were less likely to recognize symptoms or to obtain medical aid for conditions that would lead middle-class persons to seek health-care assistance. There is evidence that this is still true. The poor, the less educated, and the elderly are more acquiescent in health-care situations, demanding less of caregivers, and questioning less often what is done to them.

• MENTAL HEALTH

Good mental health is a state of mind that permits the individual to develop abilities, pursue goals, meet needs, and cope with life's problems without undue stress (Sutherland and Fulton, 1990). It is a state that allows the individual to function well within his or her capabilities and feel happy while doing so.

Mental health services have been severely neglected in the past and are only slightly less neglected today. In 1960, four of every thousand Canadians were in **mental hospitals**. Half these mental patients had been in hospitals for more than seven years. By the 1980s two of three psychiatric admissions lasted less than two weeks (Sutherland and Fulton, 1990). People were less often sent to hospitals, and when they were placed in hospitals it was for a short time. During these years, many hospitals were abandoned or reduced in size. Mental patients were often treated in the psychiatric wards of acute-care hospitals or as outpatients.

There are four types of people who may seek mental health services (Sutherland and Fulton, 1990):

1. the long-term and significantly disabled (chronic psychotics);
2. the short-term seriously disabled (acute psychotics or those experiencing situational reaction);
3. the distressed (significantly neurotic, poor copers);

4. the dissatisfied (the bored, alienated, and unhappy, neither disabled nor ill).

Of these categories, mental health services in Canada spend the most time on chronic psychotics. Although chronic psychotics today are less likely than in the past to be housed in mental hospitals, they need constant support. This group constitutes about 1 to 2 percent of the population. Yet Sutherland and Fulton (1990) estimate that 25 percent of the Canadian population have inadequate mental health. Some distressed are noticed today and receive help, though in the past they did not. The dissatisfied, perhaps the most numerous category, receive little formal mental health assistance. Our services concentrate on the most seriously ill and offer little help to the much larger number of those who are distressed or dissatisfied. Usually mental health services receive low priority in funding and do not easily attract trained personnel.

• HEALTH-CARE PROFESSIONALS

Health care in Canada is provided by a variety of professionals, including physicians, nurses, and many other ancillary professionals (Table 14.1). During the decade 1971–81 the largest health-care occupational group was registered nurses with over 200 000 workers by 1981, followed by licensed nursing assistants (88 000) and physicians (over 45 000). No health-care occupation grew by less than 38 percent in this decade. The more established occupations (physicians, nurses) were among the slowest growing, while some newer types of worker grew the most rapidly (respiratory technologists, dietitians, medical radiation technicians). Health-care workers are extending into new specialties that are becoming recognized as valuable services.

CANADIAN HEALTH-CARE WORKERS: 1971–1981

Table 14.1

Type of Worker	1971	1976	1981	% change
Audiologists/Speech Therapists	0	1 047	1 633	56
Chiropractors	1 076	1 424	2 100	95
Dental Nurses and Assistants	1 522	2 928	2 169	43
Dental Hygienists	849	1 936	1 424	68
Dentists	7 453	9 401	11484	54
Dietitians	1 713	2 654	4 191	145
Health Record Administrators	1 397	2 055	2 287	64
Health Service Executives	0	1 198	1 654	38
Medical Laboratory Technicians	10 202	16 368	18 649	83
Medical Radiation Technicians	4 627	8 012	9 660	109
Registered Nurses	145 683	179 567	206 184	42
Licensed Nursing Assistants	48 716	71 641	88 344	81
Occupational Therapists	1 062	1 505	1 852	74
Opticians	1 404	2 303	2 726	94
Optometrists	1 575	1 879	2 224	41
Orderlies (in hospitals)	11 447	14 901	17 456	52
Pharmacists	11 330	14 687	17 039	50
Physicians	32 942	40 130	45 542	38
Physiotherapists	2 287	3 591	4 453	95
Respiratory Technologists	466	1 309	1 929	314
Social Workers	4 966	5 112	6 936	40

Source: *Canada Health Manpower Inventory 1982.*

• Physicians

Physicians have by far the greatest power and prestige among health-care occupations. They also are the most highly rewarded. This was not always the case. One hundred and fifty years ago the physician was not as well trained, nor did medicine offer much to cure disease. Most doctors lacked special training, often entering the profession as ship's surgeons, apothecaries, or clergy who had obtained familiarity with medical knowledge. At this time the best medical training was to be found in Europe. By 1900 this had begun to change. During the latter half of the 19th century, medicine realized an impressive list of scientific achievements. Pasteur's work on the germ theory of disease; the development of the stethoscope, anaesthetics, and the X ray; the identification of organisms that caused tuberculosis and cholera; and knowledge of the human endocrine system were just a few of the advances.

Medical schools in North America began to improve their training. Large philanthropical foundations began to pump money into American scientific research. As a result, research in North America came to equal and even surpass the outstanding work being done in Europe. The medical profession developed a service orientation and a body of scientific knowledge, two of the important components by which they increased their power as a group (Goode, 1957, 1960).

The next step in the growth of physicians' power was due to the formation and growth in power of medical associations. In Canada health care is mostly organized under provincial jurisdiction; national physician groups such as the Canadian Medical Association tend to be relatively unimportant. Every province has a college of physicians and surgeons. These groups license physicians and discipline members of the profession as needed. Provincial medical associations are responsible for negotiating collective agreements with government. They also lobby government and seek to improve the quality of medical practice. Occasionally provincial medical associations have experienced conflict with the provincial colleges of physicians and surgeons, usually over issues of the quality of medical practice. By lobbying government and influencing public opinion, physicians gained control over their profession, the practice of medicine, the prescription of drugs, the level of fees that could be charged, licensing of new doctors, disciplining of physicians who violated rules, and the training of new doctors. These were all important steps in developing medical practice as it stands today in Canada.

Most physicians in Canada are in private practice. This means that physicians perform services and bill a fee for those services. What they can bill is determined by a negotiated schedule of services within each province. Medical practice in Canada and the United States is based on the fee-for-service system. The main difference between the two countries' systems is that most United States physicians bill the patient or the patient's private insurance provider directly, while in Canada the physician bills the provincial health-care insurance system.

Physicians evaluate their own work. They also control their practice to a considerable extent. This results in some problems for the medical consumer. First, there is an uneven geographic distribution of physicians in Canada. They tend to live in the larger cities and leave many rural areas somewhat untended. Second, certain types of services, such as house calls and counselling, are largely unavailable. Third, at certain times of the day and the week services are inadequate. Finally, there is a lack of input from the public or any other agency outside the medical profession about medical practice, particularly its quality (Sutherland and Fulton, 1990).

In the past physicians have been upper middle class in orientation and background. They also enjoyed considerable autonomy over the terms of their medical practice. Today, this autonomy is decreasing as younger physicians are less authoritarian, other health professions require more say in the health-care team, government expands its watchdog role, and medical consumers demand more consultation in matters of their health.

Doctors are becoming less conservative, more willing to listen to others, and more amenable to the team concept of medical practice. As these changes occur, the medical profession should become more sensitive to the needs of the entire population.

Women have in the past been important occupants of health careers but have been segregated into female-dominated occupations such as nursing. Within medical practice segregation is also evident, as women physicians are most often family practitioners or occupy such specialties as pediatrics. They are seldom surgeons, the highest-status medical specialty. Today the medical profession is recruiting more broadly than in the past. More minorities and more women are becoming physicians. Within the ranks of physicians, the specialties are becoming somewhat less segregated.

• Nurses

Nurses are the largest health-care worker group and second only to physicians in authority in the hospital. As with physicians, the professionalization of nursing is a development of the past 150 years. Before professionalization nursing was a low-prestige occupation carried out by persons of low status and little training. Hospitals were practically deathhouses, where treatments and conditions were often dangerous.

Florence Nightingale, an Englishwoman from a middle-class family, played a major role in upgrading the nursing profession. Having experienced a vision in 1837 that God had called her to his service, she received nursing training in Germany. The Crimean War (1853–56) in Russia gave her a platform to demonstrate that nursing could provide motherly care to the afflicted, that it could be an honourable profession, and that hospitals could be clean, orderly, and staffed with trained personnel. She proved in her treatment of the wounded that the survival rate could be greatly increased. For her efforts she became a national hero and wielded great influence in the reform of the nursing profession, establishing many schools of nursing that carried on her ideals. Although the nurse learned to be a disciplined mother figure and housekeeper, she also learned to be obedient to doctors and to perpetuate the subordinate role of women in the hospital (Strauss, 1966).

Even though nurses are many and powerful, they lack formal autonomy over the conditions of their work. This is a principal grievance in recent labour disputes involving nurses in Canada. Because they are under the direction of doctors and hospital administration, they are required to tend too many patients and work hours they do not select, and are not rewarded in income and prestige according to their training. On them falls responsibility for organizing much of patient care in hospitals and supervising other personnel who deal with patients.

Under these conditions nurses have developed techniques by which they can accommodate doctor authority and yet make suggestions for the benefit of therapy. Leonard Stein (1967) has called this set of techniques the "**doctor-nurse game**." This style of interaction allows the nurse to be assertive and make recommendations about patient care and yet not seem to instruct the doctor. The doctor can ask for recommendations without appearing to do so, by asking about what has helped this patient in the past in the same circumstance. The nurse replies with the recommendation. The doctor makes out the prescription order and thanks the nurse.

There is good evidence that nurses and doctors are moving away from such one-sided relationships and toward team responsibility for patients, along with other health professionals. Reduced physician dominance is an important part of this change. Rank and Jacobson (1977) attempted to replicate a study from the 1960s in which an experiment at a hospital showed that 21 of 22 nurses were willing to comply with a doctor's order to give a nonlethal overdose of Valium to a patient. In the 1970s, by contrast, 16 of 18 nurses refused to comply with the request. Nurses are not only gaining greater autonomy but are beginning to face the threat of lawsuits for their actions.

A further difficulty for nurses has been the nature of their training. Many nurses are trained in hospital diploma programs from which they graduate as registered nurses. Others are trained in university programs from which they graduate after somewhat longer training with a Bachelor of

Science in Nursing (B.Sc.N.). The hospital program offers shorter, more practical training in contrast with the longer, more academic training of the university. Fragmentation and disagreement about standards have not presented a clear image of nursing training in Canada. Nurses are clearly different from doctors in that they specialize in interactive patient care whereas doctors specialize in scientific aspects of treatment. Instead of emphasizing the difference in responsibility in nurse training, many programs have attempted to increase the level of scientific training, blurring the distinction with physicians and reducing nursing's claim to an autonomous area of expertise (Edginton, 1989). Nursing as a profession is currently grappling with training issues such as these, attempting to integrate nursing education while improving standards and upgrading the profession.

Although most nurses today work in hospitals, there are future opportunities in other settings. Public health nurses are active in health promotion and in monitoring health in schools and communities. Nurses will continue to practise medicine in the isolation of northern and other remote communities. The less developed countries also require nurses to help in providing health to areas of special need. In Canada there seems to be a need for nurses to function as nurse practitioners, with greater autonomy than in the past, to provide assistance to physicians in dealing with a wide array of illnesses. If this system were adopted costs could be cut and physicians could be freed for other duties. Nurses would get greater autonomy, greater financial rewards, and increased personal satisfaction.

• HEALTH-CARE INSTITUTIONS

Cockerham (1992) details the evolution of hospitals from centres of religious practice to poorhouses, to deathhouses, to centres of medical technology. Society has always had institutions for those the family could not or would not help. Travellers, the sick, the insane, and the old were cared for during the Middle Ages at hospices, often operated by the church. These early institutions offered more humanitarian care than curative treatment. As the power of the church waned and fragmented, as in England, what were originally institutions of the church became homes for the indigent, functioning as virtual poorhouses. As quality deteriorated, the hospital became a place where people went when they were ill and no one would care for them — a place where people went to die. Eventually, in the 20th century, hospitals have become centres of medical technology, factories for medical care.

Health care is carried out in a variety of institutions, including large, acute-care hospitals, chronic or auxiliary hospitals, mental hospitals, nursing homes, and in the home itself. There are over 1200 hospitals in Canada employing more than 476 000 full- and part-time workers. Hospitals are major employers, employing more persons than many primary and secondary industries. Most hospitals in Canada are not operated for profit.

Hospital ownership is of five types: religious, municipal, provincial, federal, and proprietary (for profit). Religious hospitals are governed by a hospital board selected by the church that operates the hospital. They are decreasing in number. Municipal or community hospitals have become the most common type of hospital. They are owned by one or more communities, but are not operated by them. Deficits are not usually assumed by the sponsoring municipality, although in a few instances this has happened. Most provincial hospitals are institutions for the mentally ill. The federal government operates hospitals for the military and the native population, a few remaining veterans' hospitals, and specialty institutions such as leprosariums and quarantine stations. Unlike the United States, Canada has only a few proprietary hospitals. They tend to be small institutions and provide either mental health or addiction services.

Hospitals have a dual authority structure: administrative and professional. The hospital provides a workplace for large numbers of self-employed professionals, loosely administered according to service, and an administrative hierarchy that keeps track of patients, manages the physical plant, receives and makes payments, and attends to other mundane matters. The two hierarchies have different purposes, different styles, and frequently suffer from a gap in understanding. For instance, the doctor is expected to make autonomous judgments about the patient's health and treatment. The administrative hierarchy makes judgments according to bureaucratic rules and practices. The physician is encouraged to use every means possible to save a life; the administrator may point out that some means are not available to everyone. The physician may order tests whenever they seem likely to benefit the health of the patient; the administrator may point out that the laboratory is closed. Administrators are seeking to assume greater control over the activities of physicians who are affiliated with their hospitals. Some groups, such as nurses, are subjected to conflicting expectations of the two hierarchies, a confusing and sometimes frustrating state of affairs.

Once admitted to the hospital, the patient is subject to its rules and its restraints. The process has been referred to as "**stripping**" — the stripping of the person's past statuses as he or she becomes a patient. Clothing is removed and replaced with standard garb. Mobility is restricted. Access to family and possessions is limited. The patient's person is violated at the hospital's convenience when tests or schedule require. The recent tendency is to modify these dehumanizing customs to make the hospital a more humane, psychologically satisfying environment. Patients recover better if they are happy with their environment. Still, a recent study of hospital decisions regarding patients in Manitoba showed that 90 percent of these decisions were made without consulting the patient (York, 1987).

• Acute-Care Hospitals

Acute-care hospitals have become the focal point of medical practice. Expertise of great profundity and equipment of the costliest type are gathered at these locations. The public travels long distances to receive complex diagnosis and treatment. Emphasis is on the specialized, bureaucratic treatment of large numbers of individuals. These hospitals include major education and research institutions. They are institutions of hope for the afflicted, but they are also very costly to operate. To reduce costs governments are requiring the reduction of beds in use and are encouraging shorter stays by patients.

• Chronic-Care Hospitals

Auxiliary hospitals for chronic care treat those patients who require long-term care. Fewer dramatic interventions are made in such hospitals, but patients can be treated around the clock. Costs are much less per day than in acute-care hospitals. Beds and patient days in these facilities are increasing.

• Mental Hospitals

Mental hospitals are treatment facilities for individuals with serious mental illness that requires hospitalization. Thirty years ago there were far more of these facilities, and patients stayed a much longer time. Now the average patient stays only two weeks. Today many patients with mental illness are treated in psychiatric wards of acute-care hospitals and released speedily to the community where they are treated as out-patients.

• Nursing Homes

Older persons, those who are disabled, and those who have no other place to live but still do not require around-the-clock nursing care often live in **nursing homes**. These are less expensive than chronic-care hospitals. They are usually publicly owned in Canada, although many in the United States are proprietary.

• Home Care

Many sick, disabled, or elderly persons who need support from nurse visits or who need meals, housekeeping, physiotherapy, and other similar services can receive these services in their homes. Budgets for **home care** are increasing as experience shows that it may bring cost savings. Patients usually prefer service in their own homes. They can live in familiar surroundings, be in control of their circumstances, and receive help to remain independent.

• HEALTH-CARE SYSTEMS

Health not only results from the absence of disease, but also from healthy lifestyle choices. It is dependent on the structure of health care in the nation, the province, and the community in which people live. More-developed nations have increasingly come to regard a measured level of access to health care as a fundamental right of residents in the country. If infectious diseases are controlled and modern facilities and highly trained personnel are provided, the individual has a much better chance of survival and of remaining healthy and productive. The whole society benefits from the health of its people and from the absence of serious health defects in the population. So nations expend much effort to devise health-care systems that are appropriate to their needs and operate inexpensively.

• The Canadian Health-Care System

The first era of European-style health care in Canada was the period from 1608 to 1867. It began in the initial French settlements on the St. Lawrence. In 1639 the first hospital was established, in Quebec City, run by the Catholic Church. In this period much responsibility for health care was left to the individual; the government tried to manage epidemics. There were high rates of mortality and especially infant mortality, and many accidental deaths. By the 1850s medical schools were established in Upper and Lower Canada. Unlike medical schools in the United States at this time, they were affiliated with universities.

The British North America Act of 1867 ushered in a new era, lasting through World War II. The BNA Act divided responsibilities for health care between the provinces and the federal government. The provinces had responsibility for asylums, hospitals, and all matters of local and private health. The federal government was responsible for quarantine, marine hospitals, and native health.

Saskatchewan was an innovator in cooperative health programs. In 1914 the first publicly financed system for payment of physicians was initiated in Regina. Also during World War I, Saskatchewan began the union hospital plan. Municipal hospital-care plans were begun during the war as well to enable thinly populated areas to tax their populations to build hospitals. This was an important precursor of later government involvement. Five years later, in 1919, the federal Department of Health was formed. Saskatchewan implemented the first publicly financed hospital insurance program in North America in 1946 and 1947. Other provinces soon joined Saskatchewan in funding hospital insurance.

The Canada Sickness Survey was taken in 1951, the first country-wide investigation of health and health care. It found that high-income groups were more than twice as likely to visit doctors as low-income groups. Yet the poor were more often seriously ill than the well off. On the assumption that the poor did not have adequate access to hospitals, in the late 1950s governments oversaw the construction of many new hospitals. The Hospital Diagnostic Services Act, passed by the federal government in 1957–58, split the costs of building the new hospitals equally between the provinces and Ottawa.

Mr. Justice Emmett M. Hall of Saskatchewan chaired the Royal Commission on Health Services in 1961. It found that among the problems in Canadian health care were high infant mortality, high incidence of sickness, few trained personnel, gaps in health insurance, and inequality in health care for the poor. It recommended federally subsidized, publicly administered, tax-supported, and compulsory provincial health insurance for all. In 1962 Saskatchewan enacted the first provincial medical-care insurance program, and the doctors in Saskatchewan went on strike — also a first.

In 1966 the Medical Care Act brought about a national medicare program, implemented in 1968. When Yukon Territory was enrolled in 1972, the plan became universal across Canada. The principles of the plan were as follows:

1. **universality** — all Canadians should be covered, unless already covered by the federal government;
2. **comprehensiveness** — it was to cover a broad range of medical services, which differs from province to province;
3. **portability** — coverage carries over from province to province;
4. **public administration** — to be operated on a nonprofit basis without involvement of the private sector;
5. **accessibility** — all citizens are to have reasonable access to services without barriers of cost and remoteness.

The plan supported private practice of physicians and the fee-for-service system. Doctors were to be paid by the insurance program according to the services they billed based on a negotiated fee schedule.

Since the 1960s there has been a shift in the availability of hospital beds, with an increase in long-term care and a reduction in beds for short-term care. The aging population and subsequent rise in chronic diseases of older age require long-term hospital care. There has also been a shift in outlook. Since the 1974 report *A New Perspective on the Health of Canadians* published by Health and Welfare Canada, the emphasis has been increasingly on prevention of disease, promotion of healthier lifestyles, and increase in noninstitutional care. Increased costs have led the federal government to review its programs and further emphasize environment and lifestyle. Responsibility for health care is to be shifted to the individual and the family and away from government and the health-care system. Responsibility for health care has come full circle. It began with the individual, was put into the hands of the health-care institutions and governments, and is returning to the individual who has again been given responsibility for his or her health.

In 1984 the Canada Health Act did away with **extra-billing** by doctors and user fees for hospitals. Those who most need such services are those who can least afford them; those most likely to be deterred by user fees are the aged, the poor, and the sick (Northcott, 1982). Surveys taken since then in both Canada and the United States have shown public satisfaction with Canadian-style, public-sponsored health insurance. Although there are continuing problems with health-care labour disputes and increasing costs threatening services, the Canadian health-care system is an aspect of Canada that most residents appreciate.

• Costs of Canadian Health Care

Latest estimates indicate annual expenditures of $51 billion per year for health care in Canada. This represents over $1800 for each man, woman, and child in the country, and has doubled in the last decade. In recent years hospitalization costs have risen more sharply than any other aspect of medical care. Today a person's expenses in a Canadian acute-care hospital may be more than $1000 per day. Dying persons use more health-care dollars in the last year of life than in their entire previous lifetime. Provincial governments are looking for ways to reduce the heavy burden of escalating costs. As services are threatened, rationing and user fees have been proposed. The public will become well educated on these issues during the next few years.

Although it is the perception of many Canadians that they have a national health-care program with equal access for all, there are great variations across Canada in the amount paid per person by the provinces and territories. There are also wide differences in emphasis, with one province focusing on one aspect of health care and another province emphasizing something else.

More is paid for hospital care than for any other expense, followed by amounts paid to physicians. The territories pay more per capita to hospitals than other sections of the country, followed by Nova Scotia and Alberta. Provinces paying the least are Saskatchewan, Prince Edward Island, and British Columbia.

Wealthy provinces such as Ontario and British Columbia pay the most to physicians; poorer provinces such as Newfoundland and Prince Edward Island pay only about half as much per person to doctors. Alberta joins Ontario and British Columbia in paying dentists and other health-care professionals the highest amounts per capita. The Atlantic provinces and the territories pay the least (Health and Welfare Canada, 1990).

Payments for home care are a new expense. Programs are popular with those who receive them yet are vulnerable to cost cutting. Most experts think that home-care programs are desirable and should be expanded. Manitoba funds home care most generously, followed by British Columbia, Ontario, and Saskatchewan. Quebec, the territories, and New Brunswick hardly give these programs any funding at all.

Ambulances are most costly in the territories. With the great distances to cover this does not surprise. Small provinces such as New Brunswick and Prince Edward Island pay very little for ambulances. Alberta also pays a small amount considering its size and wealth.

Prescription drugs are those sold through a retail outlet at the specific order of an authorized practitioner. Nova Scotia residents pay more than twice the national average per person. Ontario and New Brunswick residents also spend more than the national average. Estimates of nonprescription drugs — those not needing an order from a practitioner — show that those living in Saskatchewan and Manitoba pay the most. The territories pay far less for both prescription and nonprescription drugs than Canada as a whole.

Public health expenditures are made for the prevention of disease, the protection of health, and the general administration of health departments. The territories pay far more per person than other areas for public health. This is probably due to the large number of community health units per population. Ontario pays the most for health research per capita, followed by Quebec and Manitoba. The territories, New Brunswick, and Prince Edward Island pay the least (Health and Welfare Canada, 1990).

With widely differing amounts paid for different types of health care in the various parts of Canada, the quality and the style of health care differ as well. It should be said, though, that quality of health care does not always follow large health-care expenditure. Some areas may be doing more for innovative programs than other areas. Some parts of the country are less wealthy than others. If general earnings are lower, it may be easier to contain some health costs. Finally, some areas have special problems of remoteness that make health care more costly.

Dying

• Attitudes Toward Death

Woody Allen has said, "I don't want to achieve immortality through my work. I want to achieve immortality through not dying." All men and all women have to confront the reality of death. We realize that those we love will die. Their aging reminds us of death. The death of friends and family members puts in our minds that each of us will eventually pass through this experience.

In the past hundred years changes have occurred in society that allow us to distance ourselves from death. First, there has been a general reduction of death rates. Most of the extension of life expectancy accomplished in this century has been from reduction in the risk of death for young persons. Second, people today tend to die of diseases of longer duration than in the past. Treatment is usually conducted by trained personnel and more often occurs in hospitals where the family is separated from the dying individual. Third, the younger generation often relocates to places far from parents. They are less likely to be near their parents when they die. Fourth, life is often extended by new technologies that prolong life beyond the wishes of patients and family. These technologies serve to isolate dying persons from those close to them. Fifth, when death occurs, the dying and the dead are cared for by specialists who make every effort to hide death from survivors.

These factors have worked together in the 20th century to insulate North Americans from natural death; it is no longer a part of daily life. Operas and plays of the 19th century usually had a death scene. The audience was familiar with death and considered it part of the life cycle. Today, most young persons have never seen anyone die, not even a close family member. While death is taking place and until the final disposition of the body, survivors are shielded by specialists from the reality of death. When they see the body of a loved one, it has been carefully prepared so that it appears to be peacefully asleep.

Natural death is ignored and avoided. Still, the public is preoccupied with two forms of death: death from violent causes and the deaths of famous persons. Much of modern news is concerned with violent deaths. Movies and television dramas often depict death, usually in its violent forms. In particular, youthful audiences are attracted to the details of death, including blood and the breaking of bones.

Celebrity death is also fascinating to the public. Special interest is paid to stars and other famous individuals who die younger than average. Ten years after the death of Elvis Presley, large crowds gathered at his home in Memphis to commemorate his death. Details of his death and his life continue to be of interest. Part of the fascination is that he died suddenly and "before his time."

• Death Education

Death education has become popular. In 1964 a list of publications about death would have held only about four hundred references. In 1975 Robert Fulton, a pioneer death educator, estimated that there were ten times that many references. Since then, the list of publications about death has increased even more rapidly (Despelder and Strickland, 1992). In 1963 Fulton taught the first regular course on death education in North America, at the University of Minnesota (Pine, 1977, 1986). Today it is estimated there are several thousand courses on death and dying taught in North America (Despelder and Strickland, 1992).

• DEATH AS SEEN THROUGH THE LIFE CYCLE

Children are not born with an adult view of death. They get their understanding of death gradually from a variety of sources. Parental messages directly and indirectly convey ideas about death. If parents are afraid of death, they will often have difficulty talking about it. Parents may tell their children not to look at a dead animal on the road, and thus communicate their unwillingness to examine dead things. Many children receive the idea that death should be neither examined nor talked about. Cultural influences such as the educational system and the mass media also give messages to children about death.

Children who have some close experience with death are forced to develop an opinion of death at an early age. They may encounter death when a person close to them dies. Even the death of a pet may turn a child's thinking to death. A child's questions at such times are important, and may lead to a more mature understanding of death.

It is good to speak with children about death at the time they raise questions. It is not as desirable to wait until there is an emergency and the discussion must be conducted under the stress of loss. After the person explaining death has concluded, he or she should ask the child what the child understands. Then corrections can be made.

Some children must contend with the idea of death because their lives are threatened. The most common causes of death among children are accidents and cancer. Accidental death usually occurs quickly. The child will typically not have the time to confront his or her own death. In contrast, death from cancer is more gradual and affords time for the child victim to interact with health-care personnel, other children similarly afflicted, and family members. Bluebond-Langner (1978) studied children in a cancer ward. The children, mostly between the ages of 3 and 9 years, found it easier to talk to other children than to anyone else. From crying, avoidance, and other indirect cues from their families and health-care personnel, children were able to assess the severity of their illness even if no one had told them directly how seriously ill they were (Bluebond-Langner, 1978).

Often, as children's conditions become worse, they grow more distant from parents. This is painful for loved ones who visit. Modern care attempts to combat excessive distancing by encouraging more family contact, sometimes even providing for the child to return home to die. This is difficult for families, but reduces grief and guilt in survivors after the death.

As adults age, they have more frequent contact with death. They lose their parents, friends, and other family members, and may perhaps lose a child. These losses are stressful, as are other changes such as the loss of a relationship. Holmes and Rahe (1967) have listed the major events that cause stress in life, with a rating of the stress that each event produces (Table 14.2).

If too many stressful events occur in a short time, the individual's immune system may be affected and illness may result. Illness is yet another stressful event and perpetuates the pattern of deterioration.

• FACING DEATH

Most people fear death less than they fear the process of dying. They fear losing their capabilities, suffering pain, experiencing separations, and becoming dependent. When a patient enters a hospital, the type of care called for is influenced by three things: the patient, the institution's administrative and organizational patterns, and the staff.

Care in emergency wards may depend in part on patient characteristics. Sudnow (1967) observed patients entering emergency wards in the United States for treatment of life-threatening conditions. He saw that if choices had to be made, the poor and the old were put aside while the young and the wealthy were treated more aggressively. It is not known whether this type of treatment is as marked in countries such as Canada, where all the population has health insurance.

Table 14.2

SOCIAL READJUSTMENT RATING SCALE

Rank	Life Event	Mean Value	Rank	Life Event	Mean Value
1	Death of a spouse	100	22	Change in responsibilities at work	29
2	Divorce	73	23	Son or daughter leaving home	29
3	Marital separation	65	24	Trouble with in-laws	29
4	Jail term	63	25	Outstanding personal achievement	28
5	Death of close family member	63	26	Wife begins or stops work	26
6	Personal injury or illness	53	27	Begin or end school	26
7	Marriage	50	28	Change in living conditions	25
8	Fired at work	47	29	Revision of personal habits	24
9	Marital reconciliation	45	30	Trouble with boss	23
10	Retirement	45	31	Change in work hours or conditions	20
11	Change in health of family member	44	32	Change in residence	20
12	Pregnancy	40	33	Change in schools	20
13	Sex difficulties	39	34	Change in recreation	19
14	Gain of new family member	39	35	Change in church activities	19
15	Business readjustment	39	36	Change in social activities	18
16	Change in financial state	38	37	Loan less than $10 000	17
17	Death of close friend	37	38	Change in sleeping habits	16
18	Change to different line of work	36	39	Change in number of family get-togethers	15
19	Change in number of arguments with spouse	35	40	Change in eating habits	15
20	Mortgage over $10 000	31	41	Vacation	13
21	Foreclosure of mortgage or loan	30	42	Christmas	12
			43	Minor violations of the law	11

The **death trajectory** is the planned outlook for a death. When a patient is diagnosed as having a terminal condition, a plan is laid out so that hospital and medical facilities can be allocated. A trajectory made up of life expectancy, needs for care, and institutional support is drawn up. When the death trajectory is altered, the staff need to make adjustments. For instance, if an individual dies earlier than expected or lives longer than expected, schedules need to be revised.

Generally, persons born today in Canada can expect to live 77 years, as we have seen. But not all persons live exactly 77 years. The death of children may be seen as a departure from the generalized death trajectory. These deaths seem out of season. Sometimes hospital personnel will cry over the death of a child although they have witnessed death often in their jobs. The death of older persons does not usually evoke such emotions.

Most deaths in Canada occur in hospitals. Modern, acute-care hospitals are very much like factories. Bureaucratic organization predominates. The organization is impersonal, oriented toward the many rather than toward the few. But the dying person does not wish to be treated impersonally; the patient wants to be treated sensitively, as a human being should be treated. Instead, dying patients are often avoided, sometimes treated as though they are dead even before the last breath has been drawn. Bystanders may talk about the patient as though the patient is not there or cannot hear them. Sometimes, however, the patient does hear them and is affected by what they say.

The hospital is organized to preserve life. Death, when it occurs in such a setting, is an embarrassment, an acknowledgement of failure. It is to be hidden, to be kept secret. People are asked to leave the room when death seems imminent. This is so that emergency, heroic measures to prolong life may be performed — but also to disguise the risk of failure from bystanders. The dead are prepared privately by hospital personnel. Sometimes there are special elevators to transport dead bodies to the basement.

Care of the dying takes place in different types of circumstances. The dying patient can be put with other patients and given no special treatment, or the care can involve specially trained personnel and relaxed rules oriented to the dying person. This is called **palliative care**. Palliative care takes place throughout the hospital but may be coordinated at a central location, in palliative care wards, in **hospices** (special hospitals for the dying), or at home. Palliative care emphasizes management of pain and providing company for the patient, as opposed to crisis care, which emphasizes high technology intervention.

• THE DYING PATIENT

Reactions to one's own fatal illness are varied but often follow a familiar pattern. Some patients assume they are responsible in some way for the disease. Perhaps their actions have brought it upon them. Perhaps they could have done something that would have prevented it. There is a sense of helplessness in the face of poorly understood forces, of being betrayed by one's own body. The patient is likely to feel a stigma for having acquired the disease. Many persons avoid the patient, not knowing what to say or how to act.

When a person first hears that he or she has a life-threatening illness, the reaction is often to deny or disbelieve this fact. Then that person may become angry and resentful. The person wonders why this has happened when others are living their normal lives, effortlessly unaware of tragedy in their midst. Young, healthy people may excite anger in the dying person. He or she is tempted to bargain with God for a cure, a remission, relief. When this does not occur, the next stage is one of depression and sadness. The person grieves for all the good things in life about to be lost. He or she also may feel loneliness and abandonment. Finally, resignation and acceptance complete the process (Kübler-Ross, 1969).

Patients do not always follow these stages. They may skip stages or may go back and forth between them. Some people may never reach a resigned acceptance of death. They may "rage, rage against the dying of the light." The everyday world of the patient is banal, unexciting, even boring. The patient may feel low-grade anxiety about pain and loss of competence. There may be fear of the unknown, interspersed with hope that comes and goes.

Communication between health personnel, the dying patient, and family members is not always direct. In the past doctors and nurses have felt uncomfortable at being completely open about the patient's condition, instead resorting to evasion and pretence. Some doctors believe that hope is therapeutic; they are unwilling to take that away from the patient. Some patients do not want to know details of their condition or hear any negative predictions. Still, the preference of most patients is for frankness. Today doctors and nurses are more likely than in the past to give an honest evaluation of the patient's condition, even if the news is bad.

Family and friends also feel uncomfortable visiting a dying person. They do not know what to say, how to avoid platitudes, how to keep from saying something that is out of place. Because of this, they choose different styles of interaction with the patient. These have been called styles of awareness (Glaser and Strauss, 1965). There are four different styles of awareness between patient and visitor: closed awareness, suspected awareness, mutual pretense, and open awareness.

In **closed awareness,** the dying person does not know that death is near, although others may be aware. Communication is generally not possible about the fatal illness or impending death.

Suspected awareness occurs when the patient suspects that death will occur, but this has not been confirmed by those who know. The patient may try to gain information by testing visitors. Despite efforts to withhold information, visitors are not able to keep the patient from observing his or her condition. There may be disruption of family life and lack of composure in those who visit. Sometimes the patient has guessed it all and is distraught because he or she cannot get information. The patient may be relieved to finally hear the truth.

In **mutual pretense awareness** both patient and visitor know that the patient is terminally ill but both pretend that it is not so. There are complicated, unspoken rules that allow avoidance of direct discussion about the patient's condition. The illusion that the patient is getting well is fostered. Talk follows routines, such as "What lovely flowers!" "Nice weather outside," "How are we today?" "Oh, I'm OK." This approach gives privacy and dignity but leads to isolation. The dying person usually controls the discussion. If he or she feels the visitor cannot handle a topic, the subject will be changed.

If **open awareness** is in place, both patient and visitor can talk frankly about the patient's illness, impending death, arrangements for the funeral, or other matters that may need to be discussed. Patients often have unfinished business they would like to wrap up. Sometimes one session is enough. An open question may be all that is needed to start the discussion — for example, "Have you been thinking about dying?" Patients may enjoy planning their funeral or dividing up their assets, or otherwise planning to use their remaining time.

• THE RIGHT TO DIE

How can one's last days be lived with dignity? Modern death can be a degrading experience. Medical technology preserves life without patient or family consent. Sometimes patients are kept alive in pain and at great expense when there is no hope for recovery. Today many seek greater patient control of the treatment process, including the way people die.

Living wills were developed so that people would not be kept alive artificially when they did not want it. Such advance directives may indicate that no heroic measures be taken to sustain life when there is no realistic chance of recovery. This has been called passive euthanasia and is widely practised in Canada. A living will also protects health-care personnel from lawsuits if they do not resuscitate a person.

Originally, living wills lacked force in law. This is still true in Canadian jurisdictions, where they have only the force of recommendation to the doctor in charge. However, by the end of 1989, thirty-eight states and the District of Columbia in the United States had passed some type of living will legislation. Living wills are controversial. Proponents argue that they give the patient some control over the patient's style of death. Opponents say that they may lead to such practices as arbitrarily withdrawing treatment from patients who are close to death. They claim that living wills are a step toward active euthanasia.

• EUTHANASIA

Euthanasia is literally the "good death." One type of euthanasia, **assisted suicide,** or helping patients end their own lives when they express the desire, has been growing in popularity. For years assisted suicide has ended the suffering of many terminal patients. Sigmund Freud, suffering from incurable cancer, persuaded a friend in 1939 to inject him with a lethal dose of morphine. He had said of his remaining life, "Now it is nothing but torture and makes no sense." Doctors in the Netherlands are informally allowed to instruct patients in the means to commit suicide. The doctor prescribes a large dose of barbiturates that the patient takes with or without the physician in attendance. Dr. Jack Kevorkian, a retired pathologist from Royal Oak, Michigan, has assisted a number of people who wanted to die because of terminal illness or intense suffering. Such active assistance to suicides is usually illegal in North America. Yet many persons, faced with a hopeless, long-term illness, wish to exercise what they call their "last right" and end their lives. "Why should we have to suffer interminably and expend every last dollar we have saved through our lives in a hopeless struggle?" they ask. In answer, some cite the religious taboo against suicide, based on the idea that life is given and must be taken by God. In this view, your life is not your own. Others reply that just as people cannot steal from themselves, they cannot murder themselves. Their life, as their belongings, is their own to do with as they please.

Under certain circumstances physicians may also provide active euthanasia — that is, they may take the life of a consenting patient. This is usually done by a large dose of barbiturates to bring on coma, followed by an injection of curare to stop breathing and heart action. Current law in the Netherlands calls for twelve years' imprisonment for anyone who takes the life of another "at his or her explicit and serious request," but no doctor has been penalized for this violation in more than two decades. Prosecution is withheld because the practice has wide public support and is regulated by physicians who have developed certain conditions. The patient must request death explicitly, be fully conscious, and must see another doctor independently. Physicians in the Netherlands will apply euthanasia if the patient is terminally ill, has no hope for improvement, and is undergoing physical or great mental suffering. Estimates are that up to 3000 persons a year end their lives this way, about 2000 at home and 1000 in clinics and hospitals. About 40 percent of requests are denied. Most who die in this fashion (85 percent) are cancer patients in the final weeks of life. Others include patients with AIDS, multiple sclerosis, or other paralytic diseases. Patients are usually in their 60s; progressively fewer persons request euthanasia as age increases.

Opponents to euthanasia say that there is always hope for a cure or a spontaneous remission from illness. Also, the fear is expressed that euthanasia cheapens life and may lead to the legal killing of large classes of socially unproductive or undesirable people.

According to a recent poll of 1007 persons, Canadians strongly favour the legalization of euthanasia. Seventy-seven percent of Canadians believe that doctors should be allowed to perform active euthanasia on a patient who has requested it in writing and is undergoing great suffering from an incurable disease. A smaller majority of Americans (65 percent) agree with legalized euthanasia. Support for euthanasia is greater among young people than among older persons, but a majority of respondents of all ages favoured euthanasia under these circumstances. In 1968 a survey in the United States found that only 45 percent were in favour of legalized euthanasia (Bozinoff and Turcotte, 1992). It appears that euthanasia is a problem legislators will have to wrestle with during the next few years.

• DONATION OF ORGANS

Another idea growing in popularity is the donation of organs at the time of death. This has occurred because of the development of techniques for transplantation of organs. Blood transfusion on a large scale began with World War I. Skin grafts began in the late 1920s. But these transplants involved parts of the body that could regenerate. They did not raise the ethical questions that transplantation of irreplaceable body parts raised.

Shortly after the turn of the century, Carrel and Guthrie developed a technique to sew blood vessels. Yet before transplants could occur, the typing of blood and knowledge of the immune system were required for successful organ transplantation. Peter Medawar and others experimented with rabbits in the 1940s and discovered that organisms could recognize tissue as friendly or foreign by the antigens, or markers, on the surfaces of cells. If the cells are recognized as foreign, the body rejects them. This led to tissue typing, a process that examines the antigens on cells of the donor and of the recipient. The higher proportion of markers that are similar, the greater the chance the tissues are compatible and rejection will be unlikely. New drugs have also lessened the ability of organisms to develop antibodies, reducing the likelihood of rejection. In 1983 cyclosporine was approved for use. This drug, though costly, reduces the risk of rejection but permits the user some immunity to viruses and bacteria. It must be taken throughout the life of the transplant recipient to prevent rejection. There may be long-term risks in this, but they are outweighed by the advantages of the functioning organ (Varga, 1984).

These developments have greatly increased the frequency of organ transplantation. Kidneys began to be transplanted in 1951, and are commonly transplanted today. Other organs transplanted successfully include the heart, the liver, pancreas, lung, bone marrow, bone, ovary, testicle, and brain cells. This has produced a major demand for donor organs — many of which can be given only by a donor who is dead. Many donors are youthful individuals who have sustained fatal head injuries, though the rest of their body is in good shape.

Accidental death is usually sudden and not planned in advance. If individuals want to donate their organs they must sign a formal permission. In some jurisdictions such a form is attached to the driver's licence. If they wish the procedure to be carried out smoothly they should notify their family in advance so that the family does not oppose the donation.

The strong demand for organs has led to illegal "harvesting" of organs in some parts of the world. Defenceless people such as mental patients and children without parents are particularly likely to be victimized, but the list of victims has included drunks and even unwary tourists. Poor people in Third World countries have also been known to offer their organs for sale.

• THE DEFINITION OF DEATH

It is said that a former law in Canada required repetition of the question, "Are you dead?" three times, each time shaking the person presumed to have died. Traditionally, death has been determined by the doctor or by the family. Cessation of breathing and stoppage of the heart have been the normal indicators that death has occurred. That is, the body's capacity to move its fluids has determined whether the person is alive or not.

Before this century people were buried quickly after death. Many persons were afraid they would be buried alive — which accounts for the legal questioning of the supposed corpse.

With increased demand for transplantable organs, improvement in resuscitation techniques, and sophistication in machinery, death is increasingly determined by the cessation of electrical activity in the brain. Neurological indications, such as pupillary responses and reflexes, are routinely sought. Certain American states now require more than one flat EEG (electroencephalograph) reading over a given period along with other standard indications of death before organs can be removed for transplantation.

• LAST RITES

Last rites are socially important for two conflicting reasons: they emphasize that the dead person is truly gone and they generate the support of others on behalf of the survivors. On the one hand, separation is made clear; on the other, connection is emphasized. Similarly, the much-criticized custom of preparing the dead person for viewing by the family and friends is said by funeral directors to assist in the realization that the person is actually dead.

When death occurs, the body must be disposed of in some reasonable way. In Canada, the most common form of disposition is burial; the next most common is cremation. Cremation is gaining as a form of body disposition. The farther west in Canada, the more likely cremation is to be used (Turchnyiak, 1979). British Columbia is the province where cremation is most favoured. Other, less common forms of body disposition include encryptment, donation to science, cryonic preservation, and burial at sea.

• BEREAVEMENT

Bereavement comes from a root word meaning "shorn off" or "torn up." It is the event of loss. **Grief** is the emotional response to the loss. **Mourning** is the adaptation process people experience as they incorporate the loss into their lives.

Bereavement brings increased stress, as does any change in life. The most stressful of life's experiences are bereavements. The death of a spouse, a child, or any other close family member is particularly hard to bear for most people.

Bereavements differ in how much grief they produce in survivors. Conditions that lead to especially deep grief are

1. the death of a person out of season (for instance, the death of someone young);
2. a sudden, unexpected death;
3. strong attachment to the person who has died;
4. a death leaving unfinished business;
5. violent death (suicide brings strong guilt, and homicide intense anger);
6. a survivor with poor networks of support;
7. a survivor with little death experience;
8. a survivor who is less mature and more dependent;
9. some particular social roles (a soldier is allowed less grief, a spouse or parent more);
10. elements in the survivor's value structure (belief in life after death or eventual reunion may reduce grief; views that life is futile and meaningless may increase grief).

Those who survive and experience grief are victims. Theirs is often the heaviest burden of suffering. Death from a broken heart is a reality. The chances of heart disease increase after a bereavement. Death rates among widows in the first year following the death of the spouse may be as much as seven times higher than for others of the same sex and age (Rees and Lutkins, 1967). Some of the sensations associated with grief include sleeplessness, loss of appetite, tightness in the chest, difficulty breathing, intermittent crying, stomach ulcers, asthma, and other physical symptoms. Serious social consequences may include the divorce of the parents following the death of a child, inadequate performance at work, and increased risk of accidents from lack of attention when driving.

Children have special grief problems, as do the parents of children who die. Parents whose infant has died of sudden infant death syndrome can often provide special support for others who have experienced a similar loss. The same is true for survivors of the suicide of a close friend or family member. Sometimes police and executioners have feelings of isolation and special guilt feelings about the persons they have killed in the line of duty.

Grief passes through stages. It is most intense at the beginning and slowly retreats with time. However, it may recur at anniversaries and other times that remind survivors of their loved one. Gorer (1965) has identified three stages of grief: shock, intense grief work, and re-establishing physical and mental balance. At first the person left behind is shocked and may deny the event. The funeral, viewing the body, and the words of others help the survivor realize that the death has happened. The second stage, intense grief work, is very difficult and often takes place without much social support. Friends who have not experienced grief do not realize how long it takes to work through grief. Yet time brings lessening of pain, and the survivor begins to build a new life. No relationship will ever replace that with the dead person. The widow may idealize the departed husband; later marriages must contend with the ghost of the idealized husband. Nevertheless, most people attain the third stage and replace relationships and re-establish themselves in a satisfactory mental and physical condition.

Those who work with the bereaved find the following principles to be of help:

1. total care of a dying person needs to include contact and rapport with survivors-to-be;
2. contact should begin as soon as possible after the tragedy, within the first seventy-two hours if possible;
3. survivor-victims seldom resist your approaches;
4. negative emotions toward the deceased, including irritation, anger, envy, and guilt need to be explored, but not at the very beginning;

FALLACIES AND FACTS ABOUT DEATH

Box 14.1

There are several common fallacies about dying patients. This list presents ten of them accompanied by corrective statements of fact.

1. **Fallacy** We think they no longer need social contact and physical love.
   Fact They may well want these things, although there is some withdrawal as death approaches.

2. **Fallacy** We think they cannot hear us if they are unconscious.
   Fact Sometimes they can be and are affected by our comments.

3. **Fallacy** Only suicidal and psychotic people are willing to die. No one wants to die, even when death is inevitable.
   Fact Many people reach a state in which death is welcome.

4. **Fallacy** Fear of death is the most natural and basic fear of humankind. The closer one comes to death, the more intense the fear becomes.
   Fact Fear is different from person to person and may change from day to day as the illness progresses.

5. **Fallacy** Reconciliation with death and preparation for death are impossible. Therefore, say as little as possible to dying people. Turn their questions aside and use any means to deny and avoid open discussion.
   Fact Open discussion may be necessary to clear up unfinished business and may be therapeutic.

6. **Fallacy** Dying people do not really want to know what the future holds. Otherwise they would ask more questions. To force a discussion or to insist upon unwelcome information is risky. The patient might lose all hope and might commit suicide, become very depressed, or even die more quickly.
   Fact For some patients this may be true, but they are in the minority. Most persons are better able to focus their efforts if given realistic information.

7. **Fallacy** After speaking with family members, the doctor should treat the patient as long as possible. Then, when further benefit seems unlikely, the patient should be left alone. He or she will then withdraw, die in peace, without further disturbance and anguish.
   Fact The dying person may take comfort from sympathetic, understanding conversation at all stages of illness.

8. **Fallacy** The relief of pain is valuable but substances should not be given in amounts and frequencies that may cause the patient to become addicted.
   Fact The patient's well-being, including relief from pain, should be the first goal of medicine. Controlled addiction is not consequential if the patient is dying. It is reckless, if not downright cruel, to inflict unnecessary suffering upon the patient or his or her family.

9. **Fallacy** The patient is doomed; nothing can really make any difference. Survivors should accept the futility, but realize that they will get over the loss. The patient is not responsible; he is ignorant and complacent.
   Fact The modern patient often feels responsibility for his or her health. This is healthy and leads to longer and healthier life. Patients are given greater discretion in the type of treatment they will accept.

10. **Fallacy** Physicians can deal with all phases of the dying process because of their scientific training and clinical experience. The emotional and psychological sides of dying are vastly overemphasized. Consultation with psychiatrists and social workers is unnecessary. The clergy might be called upon, but only because death is near. The doctor lacks further obligation after the patient's death.
    Fact Other professionals may be needed, experts in the very important spiritual, emotional, and psychological aspects of dying. After the patient's death the survivor-victims need care from all available professionals so that their stress does not lead to a break in their health and so they can healthily reconstruct their lives.

5. the worker is not the conscience but the quiet voice of reason;

6. medical evaluation of survivors is crucial (Shneidman, 1984).

• NEAR-DEATH EXPERIENCES

Forty-three percent of persons who have a cardiac arrest have an out-of-body experience (Sabom, 1981). Typically these experiences share certain characteristics. These people have the feeling that they have left their bodies. The body is seen below them as they float in the air. Many have the experience of passing through a tunnel. They often hear a noise, such as a buzzing or a ringing. They see a light at the end of the tunnel. They are conducted through a review of their life by a being of light.

There is controversy over whether these experiences are real. Those who do not believe in the reality of these events attribute them to the process of cell death, the release of endorphins as death occurs. Those who believe that these are real events cite the powerful changes in the lives of those who have near-death experiences that, they say, demonstrate that these are not dreams or hallucinations. Often the person learns facts when out-of-body that he or she could not have known otherwise. People will often hesitate to recount the experience, as they do not want to be misunderstood. Near-death experiences have been reported in many countries. Those reporting them are from all social categories, with believers in an afterlife not reporting proportionally more such experiences than nonbelievers (Sabom, 1981).

SUMMARY

The following are some of the main points covered in the chapter.

- Health is not just the absence of disease but includes feelings of well-being and the ability to lead a socially and economically productive life.
- From the 18th century to the present, infectious disease mortality has declined, at first because of better nutrition, hygiene, and clean water, and later through medical advances. Political fragmentation and new strains of disease have led to a recent increase in infectious disease. In the more-developed nations, most persons live to old age and become subject to chronic diseases such as heart disease and cancer.
- Good health is increasingly the responsibility of the individual and the product of lifestyle choices. Some harmful choices are tobacco use, excessive use of alcohol, harmful foods, and social isolation. Healthy choices include preventive health practices, healthy nutrition, appropriate exercise, adequate sleep, and satisfactory social relations. The efforts of large organizations, especially government and business, are increasingly significant in that these bodies may engage in health promotion and safeguard health from environmental risks.
- An increasing proportion of the health-care dollar is absorbed by the aged in an aging population.
- Women live longer than men but experience more sickness, hospitalization, and a longer period of disability at the end of life.
- Racial and ethnic groups in Canada have different health-care patterns. Native people report more illness and live shorter lives than any other major group.
- Social class differences in health and mortality continue to favour wealthy and middle-class Canadians over the poor.
- Mental health is often overlooked as a health problem in Canada. It receives comparatively few resources; therefore, only the most obviously sick can be treated.
- Nurses are the largest health-care profession in Canada, but work under the direction of physicians, who over the last 150 years have secured control of the health-care institution.

Today physician authority is waning, and new types of health-care workers are increasing in number.

- Hospitals have evolved to become modern factories for health care. They have a dual authority structure and manage patients in a bureaucratic way. In Canada most health-care institutions are publicly owned and include acute-care facilities, chronic-care hospitals, mental hospitals, and nursing homes. Home care is an increasingly popular alternative.

- The Canadian health-care system evolved from a system that relied on individual responsibility to one that insured hospitalization and medical services for residents of all provinces. Under the jurisdiction of the provinces, it stressed the five principles of universality, comprehensiveness, portability, public administration, and accessibility. In later years there has been a shift back to individual responsibility for one's own health care, stressing promotion of healthy lifestyle choices.

- Costs are the principal difficulty facing the health-care system; hospitalization costs are rising the most rapidly.

- In the last hundred years changes in society have distanced the average person from death.

- Death education is increasing rapidly in North America.

- Children develop a mature concept of death as they have experiences related to death.

- Care for the dying depends on patient characteristics, on the type of facilities, and on the training of the staff. A death trajectory is developed that guides care of the patient.

- Reactions to one's own fatal illness generally follow five stages: denial, anger, bargaining, depression, and acceptance.

- Four styles of awareness may be adopted between patient and visitor: closed awareness, suspected awareness, mutual pretense awareness, and open awareness.

- Living wills are advance directives barring heroic treatments and resuscitation for those who are seriously ill. Assisted suicide and active euthanasia by request also give the patient control over his or her own death, but are legally forbidden in some locales.

- Organ transplants prolong healthy life for many, but the demand for organs has forced changes in the definition of death.

- Some deaths bring greater grief than others, especially those that are youthful, sudden, or violent; those where there is strong attachment or unfinished business; and those where the survivor has poor support, little death experience, or is less mature, or has a role or values that increase grief.

- Grief follows three stages: shock, intense grief work, and re-establishment of physical and mental balance.

- Almost half of those who survive a cardiac arrest report an out-of-body experience.

- Fallacies about death are common and widespread. Some of these are reported in this chapter along with corresponding facts about death.

KEY CONCEPTS

Acute-care hospital
Acute condition
Agricultural revolution
Alcoholic cardiomyopathy
Antisepsis
Asepsis
Assisted suicide

Bereavement
Beriberi
Chronic-care hospitals
Chronic condition
Closed awareness
Death trajectory
"Doctor-nurse game"
Epidemiological transition
Euthanasia
Extra-billing
Fetal alcohol syndrome
Grief
Health promotion
Home care
Hospices
Infectious diseases
Kwashiorkor
Lifestyles
Living will
Mental hospitals
Morbidity
Mortality
Mourning
Mutual pretense awareness
Nursing homes
Open awareness
Palliative care
Preventive health practices
Rickets
Scurvy
Sex mortality differential
"Stripping"
Suspected awareness
Wernicke-Korsakoff syndrome

REVIEW QUESTIONS

1. What factors were responsible for the decline of mortality in Europe and North America? What is happening to mortality in the developing world today?

2. List the most important lifestyle choices that can protect health.

3. How does health vary over the life course and by gender, ethnicity, and social class in Canada?

4. How have the roles of physician and nurse developed over the past 150 years? Explain the dominance of the physician role.

5. What are four types of people who may seek mental services? Which of these have received the most attention in the past?

6. What five principles underlie the national-health care program in Canada?

7. What changes have removed natural death from the average person's attention?

8. When a person has a life-threatening illness, that person goes through stages of coping. What are these stages?

9. How have changes in the transplantation of human organs altered the definition of death?

10. Some deaths bring greater grief than others. What conditions lead to a "high-grief" death?

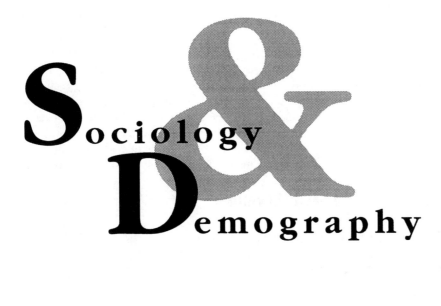

Sociology & Demography

Frank Trovato

Sociology and Demography

INTRODUCTION

Demography is the science of studying what happens to populations in terms of growth, stability, or decline on the basis of the interplay among fertility, mortality, and migration. The term **demography** derives from the Greek word *demos,* which means people. Thus, demography is the scientific study of population. In a broader sense, students of population are also involved in the study of how populations are distributed geographically and compositionally in terms of age and sex structure, ethnic origin, language, education, and other such characteristics. The numerical aspect of scientific demography is often complemented by analyses of population dynamics, because demographic phenomena are ultimately the result of individual and social behaviours.

DEMOGRAPHY AND INDIVIDUAL BEHAVIOUR

Much of our behaviour is inherently demographic. We are born into this world and some day we shall die — two inescapable realities of our existence. In between these two fateful events we get on with the business of life: we may enter school, graduate, find a place in the labour market, possibly marry, change residence, raise a family, divorce and remarry, witness the marriage of our children, and eventually retire from working life. Some of these events in the life cycle are repeatable, as in the case of migration, childbearing, and remarriage.

The regularity in the quantity and timing of demographic events in the lives of individuals is interesting. For example, the timing of marriage tends to coincide for many persons in a given birth **cohort** (generation), a regularity which reflects the influence of powerful sociological forces.

A similar observation can be made in connection with many demographic phenomena. For example, the probability of changing residence is highest among persons aged 20 to 39. What are the factors that induce so many individuals to form this aggregate phenomenon? Why do death probabilities increase during the adolescent and young adult years? Why are males more likely to die at a younger age than females? Answers to such questions require both statistical demographic analysis and sociological interpretation.

DEMOGRAPHY AND SOCIOLOGY

Demographers typically ask "How many people, of what kind, are where?" (Yaukey, 1985), while sociologists are predisposed to ask "How come?" and "So what?" Demographers may confine their scope to quantifying population phenomena, computing the degree of change in population size over some period of time for a given society, or documenting how the age-sex composition of the society has changed over time; they may quantify how the population is distributed and how its compositional characteristics are distributed in the population (e.g., proportion married, single, widowed, separated). Thus, while demographers are interested in a variety of statistical and quantifiable aspects of population change, sociological studies of population phenomena are based on the premise that there are social antecedents and consequences of population dynamics.

As a way of demonstrating this point, Kammayer and Ginn (1986) propose three classes of studies in the investigation of population phenomena: (1) Formal demographic studies; (2) Type I studies, and (3) Type II studies. Table 15.1 demonstrates their classification scheme. Formal demography's objective is to study how demographic independent variables affect other demographic dependent variables. An example of this would be how the birthrate (independent variable) causes changes in the age composition (dependent variable) of society. Type I studies relate nondemographic independent variables to demographic dependent variables, as in the relationship between socioeconomic status (independent variable) and mortality (dependent variable). Type II studies are concerned with demographic variables as predictors of nondemographic phenomena, such as the effects of age composition on voting behaviour. In fact, research tends to incorporate both demographic and nondemographic variables as both predictors and consequences of population phenomena.

DEMOGRAPHIC COMPONENTS: FERTILITY, MORTALITY, AND MIGRATION

Human populations grow, stabilize, or decay in their numbers as a function of the interaction among **fertility, mortality,** and **migration**. One way to demonstrate this fact is with the demographic balancing equation: $P_2 - P_1 = (B - D) + (IN - OUT)$, which tells us that the difference in population size between two points in time (P_1 and P_2) for a given area or country is a function of what happens to fertility (B = births) and mortality (D = deaths) between the two points in time and the net population exchange during the same interval (IN = the number of in-migrants, out = the number of out-migrants). The component (B – D) is called **natural increase,** while the difference (IN – OUT) represents **net migration.** Therefore, in a strictly numerical (formal) sense, a population will change only as a function of the interplay of these components.

A more elaborate presentation of how these three variables interact is given in Table 15.2. The typology outlines hypothetical outcomes as a function of change in fertility, mortality, and migration levels. In cell number (1), net migration is positive, which means that more people enter the society than leave it. In this same cell, however, natural increase is negative because mortality levels are higher than fertility levels, meaning that more people die than are born into this society. Notwithstanding these differences, the outcome in cell (1) can be one of three: increase, decrease, or stability in population size. Increase would result if net migration gains compensate for the negative natural increase. Decrease in numbers would occur if net migration gains are not sufficient to offset the negative difference between fertility and mortality. Stability

Table 15.1

CHARACTERISTICS AND EXAMPLES OF FORMAL DEMOGRAPHY, POPULATION STUDIES TYPE I, AND POPULATION STUDIES TYPE II

Type of Study	Independent Variables		Dependent Variables
Formal demography	Demographic Variables		Demographic Variables
		Examples	
	Age composition		Birthrate
	Birth rate		Age composition
	Sex composition of in-migrants to a community		Sex ratio of the total population of the community
Population study, Type I	Nondemographic Variables		Demographic Variables
		Examples	
	Social class (sociological variable)		Death rate
	Attitude toward motherhood (soaial psychological variable)		Number of children
	Annual rainfall (geographic variable)		Population density
	Economic opportunities (economic variable)		Migration
Population study, Type II	Demographic Variables		Nondemographic Variables
		Examples	
	Age composition		Voting behaviour (political variable)
	Migration		Social change (sociological variable)
	Birthrate		Need for infant and children goods and services (economic variable)

Source: Helen Ginn Daugherty and Kenneth C.W. Kammayer, *An Introduction to Population.* New York: The Guildford Press, 1993, p. 19.

Table 15.2

HYPOTHETICAL MODELS OF POPULATION CHANGE

Net Migration (IN − OUT) is:

Natural increase	(+)	(−)	(zero)
Mortality > Fertility	(1) I.D.S.	(2) D	(3) D
Mortality < Fertility	(4) I	(5) I.D.S.	(6) I
Mortality = Fertility	(7) I	(8) D	(9) S

Note: I = Increase in population size; D = Decrease in population size; S = Stability in population size
Source: Goldscheider (1971: 10).

would result if natural increase and net migration were exactly the same. The remaining cells in the table can be understood by considering net migration and natural increase components interacting in similar ways as described for cell (1).

WORLD POPULATION: PAST, PRESENT, AND FUTURE

The history of the human population can be divided into two broad periods: one characterized by a very long era of slow growth (from about 1 million B.C. to about A.D. 1850) and another that is best described as a brief period of rapid growth (from about 1850 to the present). If this trajectory of population change were to be displayed graphically, the graph denoting population would be very close to the base (along the time dimension) from 1 million B.C. to approximately A.D. 1850, at which point it would increase exponentially to unprecedented levels.

• PAST

According to estimates reported by Ansley Coale (1974), prior to the industrial revolution the earth's population was quite small and its rate of increase very low. Between 1 million B.C. and 8000 B.C., the average population size of the world was only 8 million, with a corresponding average rate of increase at 0.01 percent per year. For the period 8000 B.C. to A.D. 1, the average population at the end of the period was 300 million with an average annual rate of increase of 0.036 percent. For the period A.D. 1 to A.D. 1750, the average population at the end of the period is estimated to have been 800 million and the rate of growth 0.050 percent per annum (Table 15.3).

World population reached its first billion between A.D. 1750 and A.D. 1800. The second billion of population was actualized around 1930, approximately 130 years later. By 1960 the earth was inhabited by three billion people. The fourth billion occurred in 1975 and the five billion mark was reached only ten years later, in 1985.

• PRESENT

Current statistics show that the world's population is over 5.3 billion (Population Reference Bureau, 1990). The crude birthrate stands at 27 per 1000 population, and the crude death rate is 10 per 1000 population. The rate of natural increase (rounded) is 1.8 percent per year. At this rate of increase, the globe's population would double every 39 years (Table 15.4).

Table 15.3

HISTORY OF WORLD POPULATION

	Estimated Average Population at End of Period	Average Annual Rate of Growth (%) at End of Period
1 million B.C.–8000 B.C.	8 million	0.01
8000 B.C.–A.D.1	300 million	0.036
A.D.1 –A.D.1750	800 million	0.056
1750–1800	1 billion	0.40
1800–1900	1.7 billion	0.54
1900–1950	2.5 billion	0.80
1950–1974	3.9 billion	1.7–2.0
1975–present	5.3 billion	2.0–1.8

Source: Adapted from Coale (1974); Population Reference Bureau (various years).

If the annual rate of increase were 0.5, 1.0, or 1.5 percent respectively, the world's population would double in approximately 140 years, 70 years, and 47 years, respectively. Rates of increase of 2.0, 2.5, and 3.0 percent per annum would engender a doubling of the current population within 35 years, 28 years, and 23 years, respectively. At the current rate of increase (1.8 percent), the number of people being added to the population of our planet each year is over 95 million! This gain is greater than the combined populations of Canada, the United Kingdom, Sweden, and Norway.

North America (United States and Canada), Europe, and other industrialized parts of the world have relatively low rates of population growth (natural increase). Other regions, especially those in sub-Saharan Africa, are growing more rapidly, primarily owing to their very high fertility levels in conjunction with moderate but declining death rates.

• FUTURE

The most important factor responsible for the current situation is the large-scale reduction in mortality that began around the turn of the century in the Western world and spread shortly thereafter to the developing world. Western nations experienced high fertility until the beginning of this century. Since the late 1920s, the developing countries have contributed an overwhelming portion of the world's growth in population. For this part of the world, fertility rates have been high while death rates have been declining rapidly, causing very high rates of natural increase. Current figures indicate that the Western world is experiencing very low rates of population increase, while the less-developed world has much higher levels of increase. Future projections of the globe's population are therefore dependent on this fact: one region is characterized by low growth potential, and the other is typified by high rates of natural increase. Fertility is the critical factor determining future population trends, as mortality is relatively low and is expected to continue declining in the future. Projections are also dependent on this important fact.

Depending on the fertility assumptions we introduce into our projections, the globe's population in the year 2020 could range anywhere from 6 to 9 billion. In the more distant future, say, 2100, our global situation may vary by a population in the excess of 50 billion to a low of 6.5 billion. It depends on what happens to fertility: will it remain high (TFR of 3.5 or higher) or will it decline? Of course, no one can say for certain what will be the eventual size of the earth's population. Projections can fail terribly. Projections are only tentative scenarios for the future based on assumptions concerning fertility and mortality (Table 15.5).

Table 15.4

POPULATION CHARACTERISTICS OF WORLD REGIONS, 1990

Region	Population (Millions)	CBR	CDR	RNI	Population Doubling Time
World	5321	27	10	1.8	39
More developed	1214	15	9	0.5	128
Less developed	4107	31	10	2.1	33
Less developed (excluding China)	2987	35	11	2.4	29
Africa	(661)	(44)	(15)	(2.9)	(24)
North	144	38	10	2.8	25
West	206	47	17	3.0	23
East	199	47	17	3.0	23
Central	68	45	16	3.0	23
South	45	36	9	2.7	26
Asia	(1997)	(31)	(10)	(2.1)	(33)
West	132	36	8	2.8	24
South	1192	35	12	2.3	30
Southeast	455	29	8	2.1	34
East	1336	20	6	1.3	52
China	1120	21	7	1.4	49
North America	(278)	(16)	(9)	(0.7)	(93)
Canada	26.6	14	7	0.7	96
U.S.A.	251.4	16	9	0.8	92
Latin America	(447.0)	(28)	(7)	(2.1)	(33)
Central	118	32	6	2.5	27
Caribbean	34	25	8	1.7	40
Tropical S. America	247	29	8	2.1	33
Temperate S. America	49	21	8	1.4	51
Europe	(501)	(13)	(10)	(0.3)	(266)
North	84	14	11	0.2	286
West	159	12	10	0.2	326
East	113	14	11	0.3	215
South	145	12	9	0.3	250
U.S.S.R.	(291)	(19)	(10)	(0.9)	(80)
Oceania	(27)	(20)	(8)	(1.2)	(57)

Note: CBR = Crude Birthrate; CDR = Crude Death Rate; RNI = Rate of Natural Increase
Source: Adapted from Population Reference Bureau (1990).

Table 15.5

PROJECTED FUTURE WORLD POPULATION*

| Period | Assumptions Regarding Fertility (TFR) | | |
	TFR = 3.5 (Current)	TFR = 3.0	TFR = 2.0
1990	5.3	5.3	5.3
2000	7	6	5.5
2020	9	8	5.6
2040	14	10	5.7
2060	25	13	5.9
2080	35	16	6.2
2100	53	21	6.5

* Figures are approximations, in billions. Note: TFR = Total Fertility Rate
Source: Adapted from Population Reference Bureau (1988).

The growth rate of the human population will certainly return to zero or close to it in the future. The question is how such a state will be attained. If future population size reaches very large numbers, we may witness an increase in death rates as a consequence of resource depletion, poverty, sickness, and political instability. The most desirable scenario, therefore, would be continued reductions in fertility levels with accompanying low mortality conditions.

THEORIES OF POPULATION CHANGE

There are a number of theoretical formulations central to demography and population studies. We will review three of the most influential ones: the demographic transition theory, the Malthusian principles on population, and the Marxist view on human population.

• DEMOGRAPHIC TRANSITION

Prior to the industrial revolution society was predominantly rural-agrarian. In general, people did not have the capacity to control their environment in any significant manner; society was characterized by a harsh and unpredictable environment, with frequent wars, pestilence, high rates of disease, and famine. Mortality rates must have been very high, and yet the population did grow. It grew at very low rates of natural increase, primarily resulting from the very high levels of human fertility accompanied by radically fluctuating high rates of mortality. This stage of human demographic history is referred to as Stage I of **demographic transition**. Birth and death rates in the ancient world probably fluctuated between 35 and 45 per 1000 population (Table 15.6).

As Western society progressed through the Middle Ages, the Renaissance, and subsequent stages of development, humanity's capacity to master and predict the environment improved significantly. Standards of living were raised considerably owing to better food supply and innovations in agriculture. The uncertainty that characterized human life in the ancient world gave way to a more comprehensible and predictable environment. People began to explore new frontiers in scientific, technological, political, and humanistic endeavours. These advances ultimately contributed to improvements in the social structure and the dramatic reduction of mortality levels (McKeown, 1972).

With the advent of industrialization in Western Europe during the mid-19th century, mortality rates declined even further, but fertility remained high. This situation may be described as a stage of disequilibrium, characterized by explosive rates of natural increase. This state is known as Stage II of demographic transition.

HYPOTHETICAL STAGES OF DEMOGRAPHIC TRANSITION

Table 15.6

Stage	Type of Society	Crude Birthrate	Crude Death Rate	Natural Increase
I	Rural-Agrarian	High: 35–45/1000	High: 30–50/1000	Low: +, –, zero
II	Transitional-Developing	High: 35–50/1000	Moderate Low: 15–25/1000	Very High: +
III	Contemporary-Modern	Low: 10–15/1000	Low: 7–10/1000	Very Low: +, –, zero

Source: Adapted from deVries (1988).

Stage III of demographic transition was accompanied by continued increases in industrialization and rapid urban growth. Modern medicine had made great strides after discovering germ theory during the 1920s. The development of penicillin and other antibiotics contributed significantly in the fight against disease. By the turn of the century, most nations in the Western world had embarked on their final stage of demographic transition, characterized by low mortality and fertility levels and hence low rates of natural increase.

The vital revolution in Western Europe took approximately 150 years to evolve. Demographic change was accompanied by profound alterations in the society, as a result of social, economic, technological, medical, and social psychological developments generated by society over many years. This is a fundamental difference between the European experience and that of the contemporary developing nations. For the latter, the opportunity for economic development and infrastructural change is relatively limited. For this reason, developing nations must often rely on help from the industrialized nations of the world.

Will Third World countries go through a similar experience to that of Western Europe (Teitlebaum, 1975)? There are crucial differences between the demographic situations of the West and the developing nations of today. European society had many years to adjust to the explosive growth rates during Stage II. Europeans had the opportunity to leave their continent and make their fortunes in the New World countries such as Canada, the United States, and Australia. Furthermore, the surplus population in the rural areas of Europe was absorbed by the emerging industrial centres within Western Europe. Unfortunately, the developing nations do not have recourse to massive out-migration to relieve population pressure, as geopolitical boundaries are now in place and are strictly enforced by the industrialized countries of the world.

Another important difference between the demographic experience of Western Europe and the contemporary developing nations has to do with the mechanisms responsible for demographic change. In the West, change occurred as a function of internal forces, such as industrialization, science, technology, and mortality reductions, which occurred gradually over a long period of time. In the developing nations, the pace of mortality decline has been occurring much faster than was the case in Europe during its transition. Public health, medical measures, and family-planning programs, largely sponsored by the West, have helped to curtail mortality levels in a matter of a few decades. However, fertility has been more resistant to change and is still quite high. In general, societies readily adopt the technologies and means for reducing mortality, but tend to lag behind in their acceptance of the means to control fertility (e.g., contraception) due to the prevalence of strong traditions, norms, and values that favour large families (Caldwell and Caldwell, 1990). Consequently, many countries in the Third World are now in their second stage of demographic transition, characterized by high fertility rates, declining mortality levels, and high rates of natural increase. The doubling time of such populations is much shorter than that of those in the industrialized countries of the world.

Within the last two decades or so, some transitional countries have been experiencing significant declines in their fertility levels, and are therefore approaching the final stage of demographic transition. According to Coale (1983), the declines have tended to be most rapid in island nations (e.g., Singapore, Cuba, Hong Kong, Mauritius, Taiwan, Sri Lanka, Puerto Rico) and in countries with a Chinese origin culture, where vigorous family-planning programs have been in place for some time. A related development in such nations is that age at first marriage has been increasing in recent years.

There has been little sign of fertility declines in Africa (excluding South Africa, Egypt, and Tunisia), as well as Haiti, Honduras, Nicaragua, Bolivia, Burma, Laos, Vietnam, Nepal, Bangladesh, Pakistan, Iran, and other areas in south central Asia and the Arab countries. The absence of significant declines in family size (and in some cases there is evidence of recent increases) in these relatively poor parts of the world is a cause for concern.

• THE MALTHUSIAN THEORY OF POPULATION

A substantial body of demographic literature deals with population thought that can be traced back to Confucius and the early Greeks (see for example, Overbeek, 1974). Perhaps the best-known and most controversial theory of population is that of Thomas Malthus (1766–1883), who was a professor of political economy in England during the late 18th and early 19th centuries. His most famous work, *An Essay on the Principle of Population,* was first published in 1798. All subsequent theoretical works on human population have been influenced in one way or another by this important treatise.

At the time Malthus wrote his *Essay,* a number of scholars had already contributed their thoughts on the matter of population. Some of these authors, such as Rousseau and Condorcet in France, and Godwin in England, viewed population growth as a positive development. Adam Smith felt that a growing population would help stimulate economic growth and settlement of colonies overseas. Malthus reacted strongly to utopian views of population growth. He was pessimistic about man's capacity to keep a balance between the available resources (e.g., food supply) and the number of mouths to be fed. He set out to warn humanity about the dangers of unchecked population growth.

Malthus assumed that there is an inherent tendency in humans to increase in numbers beyond the means of subsistence available to them. Mankind, he argued, lives at the brink of subsistence. He warned that population when left unchecked doubles once every generation; it grows at a geometric rate (e.g., 1, 2, 4, 8, 16, 32, . . .) while the food supply grows at an arithmetic rate (e.g., 1, 2, 3, 4, 5, 6, 7, 8, 9, . . .). In the long run, this situation would result in the population surpassing the food supply.

To understand Malthus's views, it is important to recognize that for him sustenance and sexual passion are in constant opposition. He felt that the latter is stronger and therefore humans will always tend to reproduce beyond the carrying capacity of their environment, ultimately resulting in an increasing death rate as a consequence of inadequate food supply and disease. In this way, human population would ultimately be checked by the undesirable outcome of increasing death rates, or by what he termed "vice and misery" (also called **positive checks**).

The alternative to this disastrous scenario is for individuals to exercise "moral restraint" (also called **preventive checks**) — that is, the imposition of the human will to deliberately curtail reproduction by practising celibacy, postponed marriage, and abstinence from sexual intercourse before marriage.

As one might suspect, these views have sparked ardent and vociferous criticisms by many scholars ever since the *Essay* first appeared in print. One criticism is that Malthus may have failed to appreciate the resilience of humanity in its ability to control and manipulate the environment and to respond in constructive and innovative ways to the problems we face. Advances in science and technology are often the consequences of needs created by a growing population. Some writers have argued that the agricultural revolution, and later the industrial revolution, were partly a function of the demands created by a growing population (Boserup, 1965).

Critics have also indicated that Malthus failed to specify what is an acceptable level of subsistence for humans and what would be an optimum population size. Of course, this is a difficult issue because social standards for the basic necessities in life change from epoch to epoch. For example, in our own society everyone is expected to have not only food, shelter, and clothing as basic necessities, but also access to good health care and an education. Subsistence level is culturally determined: the society decides what is to be defined as "basic necessities" in life; there is no constant standard. It seems that the more societies develop economically and socially, the higher the standard for "basic" necessities. Therefore, Malthus may have been wrong in insisting that it is the biological drive of sex that induces mankind to subsistence levels because he disregarded the role of culture and society in defining what is an acceptable standard of living.

Malthus thought birth control was immoral, which is certainly inconsistent with his advocacy of human motivation to control human fertility levels. In actuality, people throughout the centuries have always resorted to some means of birth control at one time or another. More recently, since the early 1950s, contraception and family-planning services have been used extensively in both the West and many developing countries in order to control fertility. In the Third World, family-planning programs have contributed significantly to keeping rates of childbearing below what they might have been otherwise. The positive checks (vice and misery) are more likely to occur in the more deprived areas of the world. Therefore, the use of birth control is crucial in slowing down fertility and helping to minimize population pressure and the concomitant human suffering such as poverty and famine. These problems are rarely a function of humans' inability to exercise control over their sexual desires.

Insofar as Malthus identified human motivation as a key determinant of population control, he made an important contribution. He placed the onus on the individual to do something about the population problem. This is now recognized as an important principle. We, as individuals, are expected to make our own decisions concerning family matters and family size. This idea is gaining acceptance in the developing countries as well.

• THE MARXIST VIEW OF POPULATION

Marxists have severely criticized Malthus's principles of population. Marx contended that the population problem would take care of itself if disadvantaged people were given equal access to the wealth and resources available in capitalist societies. According to this perspective, the Third World's population predicament is largely a function of relative economic deprivation. The root of the problem is not overpopulation, but poverty and inequality. Writers such as Engels maintained that even though population may indeed grow geometrically, as Malthus contended, science and technological solutions in society also tend to progress at a geometric pace. Therefore, the key is how the benefits of scientific progress are distributed. If they are distributed more equitably throughout the nations of the world, population will cease to be a problem.

Marx's contribution to our understanding of population dynamics lies in his idea that inequality is at the roots of social problems, including overpopulation. This is an important insight that must be considered seriously in any analysis of population.

Canada's Population: An Overview

Our population is relatively sparse in relation to its geographical vastness — the second-largest country in the world. As shown in Table 15.7, in 1990 the estimated population of Canada was 26.4 million. In 1851, this country's population was a mere 2.4 million. It was not until 1931 that we reached the 10 million mark; by 1966 the population was slightly over 20 million. Approximately one-third of this increase in numbers can be attributed to immigration and the remainder to natural increase (Beaujot and McQuillan, 1982).

Components of Population Growth

• MORTALITY

Demographers monitor changes and differentials in human mortality by computing measures such as the crude death rate, **age-specific death rate,** cause-specific death rate, **life expectancy,**

Table 15.7

POPULATION GROWTH, CANADA, 1851–1990

Period	Pop. ('000)	% Change from Previous Period	Interval	Natural Increase ('000)	Net Migration ('000)
1851	2 436	—			
1861	3 230	24.58			
1871	3 689	12.44			
1881	4 325	14.71			
1891	4 833	10.51			
1901	5 371	10.02			
1911	7 207	25.48			
1921	8 788	17.99			
1931	10 377	15.31			
1941	11 507	9.82	(1931–41)	1 222.00	-91.92
1951	14 009	17.86	(1941–51)	1 972.39	+168.96
1956	16 081	12.88	(1951–56)	1 473.21	+598.15
1961	18 238	11.83	(1956–61)	1 674.89	+482.47
1966	20 015	8.88	(1961–66)	1 517.89	+258.74
1971	21 568	7.20	(1966–71)	1 089.39	+464.04
1976	22 993	6.20	(1971–76)	931.02	+493.28
1981	24 221	5.07	(1976–81)	978.24	+310.00
1986	25 274	4.17	(1981–86)	988.00	+264.34
1990	26 440	4.41	(1986–90)	751.76	+479.28

Sources: Grindstaff (1981: 48); Dumas (1990: 46–52); Dumas (1987: 64); Urquart and Buckley (1983: A1–14, A339–350); *Canada Yearbook 1990*, Catalogue no. 11-402E/1990, pp. 2–20; Statistics Canada (1990e: 49–51).

and infant mortality rate. The crude death rate is defined as the number of deaths in a given year divided by the midyear population, usually expressed per thousand. There are significant variations in this measure of mortality across world regions and subpopulations. In 1990 the highest crude death rates in the world were found in Africa (particularly the sub-Saharan region), while the lowest rates predominated in industrial nations such as Japan, the nations of Western Europe, Australia, New Zealand, Canada, and the United States.

Life expectancy at age zero (i.e., the average number of years left to live for a newborn) and the **infant mortality rate** are regarded as very sensitive indexes of overall standard of living. When infant mortality (the number of deaths to infants in a given year divided by the number of live births in that given year) is high, life expectancy at age zero will be relatively low.

Table 15.8 demonstrates regional variations in the three measures for 1980 and 1990. The most notable generalization that can be gained from these data is that since the early 1980s there has been a general improvement in mortality conditions in virtually all major areas of the world. However, wide disparities still exist and will probably continue for some time. Particularly in the case of infant mortality, many developing nations have a long way to go before they attain the low levels characterizing countries such as Canada (IMR in 1990 = 7.3 per 1000). Many countries in the African continent have infant mortality rates above 100 per 1000 births.

• Age Pattern of Mortality

Although human mortality rates are not constant over age, there is a general age pattern of mortality that is basically invariant across human populations. The level of death rates varies across societies, but the graph tends to be characterized by a J-shape. The probability of dying is high in infancy, and it gradually reduces until about age 10 when it increases again, but to a much lower

Table 15.8 — CRUDE DEATH RATES, LIFE EXPECTANCY AT AGE ZERO, AND INFANT MORTALITY RATE BY WORLD REGION, 1980 AND 1990

Region	1980 CDR	1980 IMR	1980 E_0	1990 CDR	1990 IMR	1990 E_0
World	11	97	61	10	73	64
LDCs	12	110	57	10	81	61
MDCs	9	20	72	9	16	74
Africa	17	140	49	15	109	52
N. Africa	42	121	54	10	87	59
W. Africa	49	159	46	17	119	48
E. Africa	19	132	47	17	116	50
Mid. Africa	45	167	45	16	118	50
South Africa	39	101	59	9	61	62
Asia	28	103	58	9	74	63
S.W. Asia	40	117	56	8	71	64
Mid-South Asia	37	137	51	12	101	57
S.E. Asia	13	96	53	8	70	61
East Asia	6	51	65	6	35	69
China	6	56	64	7	37	68
Hong Kong	5	12	72	5	7.4	77
Japan	6	8	75	6	4.8	79
North America	8	13	73	9	9	74
Canada	7	12	73	7	7.3	77
United States	9	13	73	9	9.7	75
Latin America	8	85	64	7	54	67
Middle L. America	7	72	64	8	57	68
Caribbean	8	72	65	8	57	68
Tropical S. America	9	98	62	8	59	65
Temperate S. America	9	44	68	8	28	71
Europe	10	19	72	10	12	74
North Europe	11	13	72	11	9	75
West Europe	11	12	72	10	8	76
East Europe	11	23	71	11	16	71
South Europe	9	24	71	9	14	68
U.S.S.R.	10	31	70	10	29	69
Oceania	9	42	69	8	26	72

Note: CDR = Crude Death Rate; IMR = Infant Mortality Rate; E_0 = Life Expectancy at Age Zero; LDC = Less-Developed Countries; MDC = More-Developed Countries
Sources: Excerpted from the Population Reference Bureau (1980 and 1990).

level than in the case of infancy; then the risk of dying starts a gradual rise with advancing age, and by age 65, the odds of dying surpass the risk established in infancy. To provide a concrete example of this pattern of mortality, we may examine the **life table** probabilities of dying within certain specified age groups in Table 15.9, and its graphic representation in Figure 15.1.

• Sex Differential in Mortality

The fact that males are less advantaged in survival probabilities in comparison to females was established many years ago (Madigan and Madigan, 1957). Considerably less is known about the

Table 15.9

LIFE TABLE PROBABILITIES OF DYING BY SPECIFIED AGE GROUPS, CANADA, 1981 AND 1986

Age	1981		1986	
	Male	Female	Male	Female
0	10.68	8.27	8.58	6.78
1–4	2.39	1.83	1.94	1.59
15–19	6.39	2.26	5.09	1.95
20–24	7.85	2.31	6.78	2.06
40–44	13.60	8.04	11.91	7.04
65–69	144.11	73.94	142.04	71.40
85–89	570.82	447.66	766.46	539.71

Note: Probabilities expressed per 1000.
Sources: Nagnur (1986: 205, 214); Statistics Canada, Health Division, Vital Statistics and Disease Registry, *Life Tables, Canada and Provinces, 1985-1987.* Ottawa: Minister of Supply and Services, 1989, pp. 16–19.

Figure 15.1

DEATH RATES BY GENDER AND AGE, CANADA, 1988

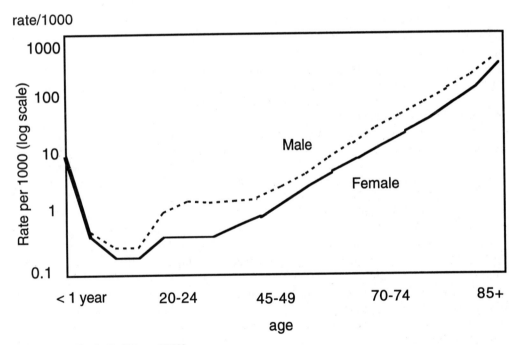

Source: Statistics Canada, Catalogue no. 82-003s.

causes of this differential (Nathanson, 1984). The literature has tended to emphasize two perspectives: (1) environment and (2) biology. The environment perspective basically argues that the causes of males' excess mortality in relation to females is due to men's risky lifestyles and work patterns, and their lower disposition to seek prompt medical care when illness strikes. The second perspective is difficult to test directly, but there is general agreement in the literature that the sex differential in mortality cannot be wholly attributed to environmental conditions. Biological factors have some relevance. For example, studies on fetal deaths reveal that spontaneous abortions are predominantly male fetuses. Moreover, early **neonatal mortality** (death within the first week of life) is considerably higher among male babies. If we examine the Canadian case in 1987, out of 100 000 babies born, 304 males die within the first day of life, while only 241 female babies succumb to death by the time their first day of life is completed (Dumas, 1990: 32). This fact may reflect a biological superiority of females over males. The influence of environment cannot possibly be of major relevance in causing such a discrepancy in risk so early in life. This sex differential in the early phases of human experience is most likely an innate one (Waldron, 1986).

It is doubtful, however, that biological differences between the sexes account for much of the variability in the mortality discrepancies between men and women beyond the very early phases of life (Nathanson, 1984; Waldron, 1986). For example, male rates in the age group 15–29 are typically three times greater than those noted among females. Motor vehicle accidents, violence, and suicide account for most of the sex differential, suggesting that lifestyle differences between the sexes are at the root of this phenomenon (Lopez and Ruzicka, 1981).

At ages beyond 29, men tend to suffer an elevated risk of coronary heart disease and other cardiovascular complications, which are leading causes of death in contemporary industrial nations. An important risk factor for heart disease is elevated cholesterol levels, particularly low-density lipoproteins (LDL) — often termed "bad cholesterol." In general, men have higher levels of LDL, while women possess higher levels of the "good cholesterol," high-density lipoproteins (HDL). Why this difference? Some medical analysts believe that the higher level of estrogen in females has something to do with their higher levels of HDL (see Nathanson, 1984 and Waldron, 1986 for a review of this literature). Others look to behavioural differences for the higher LDL cholesterol in men, arguing that perhaps it is a function of poorer diets, obesity, lack of exercise, smoking, and male proneness to develop Type A personalities — that is, hard-driving, competitive, aggressive, and task-oriented behaviours that characterize many men in our society. This explanation would predict that personality differences in men and women account for the stress differential in the sexes, which in turn affects cholesterol levels and mortality variations by sex (Nathanson, 1984).

Waldron (1976) has interpreted the available medical, epidemiological, and demographic evidence surrounding sex differences in mortality and concluded that about three-quarters of the observed differential is accounted for by male–female differences in causes of death that are thought to be overwhelmingly social in their etiology: coronary heart disease (M/F ratio 2:1), lung cancer (M/F ratio 6:1), emphysema (M/F ratio 5:1), motor vehicle accidents (M/F ratio 3:1), suicide (M/F ratio 3:1), and cirrhosis of the liver (M/F ratio 2:1). Walter Gove (1973) reached similar conclusions in an earlier study. Thus, the widening sex mortality differential that has been documented for most countries since the early 1930s is largely due to men's higher death rates from leading causes of death that are largely associated with differences in environmental conditions facing the sexes (Omran, 1971; Lopez and Ruzicka, 1981; Preston, 1976).

The recognition that the gender gap in mortality can be narrowed by promoting behavioural changes among men is appealing, since lifestyle is more amenable to change than are biological differences. If men reduce their cigarette consumption and the intake of fats in their diet, exercise more, drive more carefully, take better care of themselves when ill, and reduce Type A orientations and stress in their lives, they can live longer (see Chapter 14).

It has become clear, however, that in recent decades women are increasingly taking on "masculine" patterns of behaviour: they smoke more, drink more, and are involved in occupational pursuits that engender stress and Type A orientations typically associated with males. Will women's superiority in longevity slow down as these processes intensify in the future? One indication that this may be happening is reflected in their increasing rates of lung cancer (mostly explained by increased smoking) over the last two decades or so. However, it also is important to realize that although females' lifestyles have been changing significantly in society, the gap in male–female death rates will probably narrow in the future rather as a consequence of improvements in males'

Table 15.10

Life Expectancy at Age Zero and Female Excess in Life Expectancy at Age Zero in Canada, 1921–1986

Sex	Period 1921	1931	1941	1951	1961	1971	1981	1986
Male	58.44	60.00	63.04	66.40	68.44	69.40	71.88	73.04
Female	60.60	62.06	66.31	70.90	74.26	76.45	79.06	79.73
Difference: M–F	(-1.76)	(-2.06)	(-3.27)	(-4.50)	(-5.82)	(-7.05)	(-7.18)	(-6.69)

Sources: Nagnur (1986: 70–71); Dumas (1990: 93, Chart 13).

mortality conditions. Males have much further to go in increasing their longevity, while females may have already reached a level of life expectancy that is close to the maximum. Although too small to make any definite generalizations, some indication of a recent narrowing in the male–female gap in life expectancy at age zero is given in Table 15.10.

• THE EPIDEMIOLOGICAL TRANSITION

In contemporary Canada and other advanced nations, most deaths occurring in a given year are due to a small but influential number of causes, such as **cardiovascular diseases,** cancers, accidents, and violence. Infectious and parasitic diseases such as typhus, cholera, smallpox, and tuberculosis are now rare causes of death. In the past, the situation was quite different, as these ailments predominated over the chronic, degenerative, and man-made causes of death (Omran, 1971). The leading killers were predominantly infectious and parasitic diseases. For example, in 1931, out of 104 514 deaths in Canada, malignant neoplasms and cerebrovascular and cardiovascular diseases combined to account for 32.2 percent. In 1981, out of a total 167 799 deaths, these same **chronic diseases** claimed 72.3 percent (Nagnur and Nagrodski, 1991). (See Table 15.11.)

The historical shift in the cause-of-death distribution is largely a function of society's ability to combat infectious and parasitic diseases through improved nutrition, sanitation, refrigeration, public health, better food processing (e.g., pasteurization of milk), and enhanced medical sophistication (vaccines and antibiotics to fight off diseases). Consequently, during the last sixty years or so, infant mortality has declined significantly at a rapid pace, and life expectancy has increased dramatically. We have made tremendous improvements in longevity by postponing death to older and older ages. In the future the leading causes of disability and death will be increasingly associated with old age (Fries, 1980; Manton, 1982).

• Fertility

Fertility is the most critical component of population change. To a large extent it determines how rapidly a population grows and, conversely, whether it will decline in numbers. In the industrialized countries of the world, fertility has been below replacement levels since the early to mid-1970s. In the developing countries, fertility is quite high, which means that the prospects for a slowdown in future population growth rates are significantly attenuated. Paradoxically, in the industrial nations there is now an orientation toward the possible implementation of policies to promote fertility. In the Third World, if there is a sense of concern, it is to reduce fertility levels (e.g., China's emphasis on family planning to reduce population growth).

AIDS IN CANADA

Box 15.1

AIDS (acquired immune deficiency syndrome) is a mortal illness that strikes terror in the late 20th century, and is caused by the HIV (human immunodeficiency virus). It does not yet have a strong presence in mortality statistics. In fact, the first HIV deaths were not published by Statistics Canada until 1987. Between 1987 and 1988, AIDS increased by 26 percent.

According to the Bureau of Epidemiology and Surveillance, Federal Centre for AIDS, Health Protection Branch, National Health and Welfare, since the first case of AIDS was reported in Canada in 1982, there have been over four thousand cases among Canadians. AIDS is the result of gradual destruction of the immune system after infection by HIV. Death caused by HIV can occur without the development of AIDS, but most people who die with HIV infection die as a result of AIDS. At this time, given our current understanding of the natural history of HIV infection and AIDS, it is probably true that everyone who becomes infected with HIV, who survives long enough, will develop AIDS. However, the incubation period for AIDS can be long. Some studies have determined that within eleven years, only 50 percent of people with HIV will have developed AIDS.

It is, in part, because of the difficulty of recognizing an HIV-infected person that AIDS cases are counted instead. The case definition for AIDS, developed at the Center for Disease Control in Atlanta, Georgia, is the one adopted by the Federal Centre for AIDS at Health and Welfare Canada.

For the moment, it is safer to confine the inquiry to counts of these cases. Rates that could be calculated, even age-specific ones, would not be very revealing because the populations compared are heterogeneous and the subpopulations at risk within the groups are impossible to measure quantitatively. This disparity is particularly evident when Alberta and British Columbia are compared. With almost identical population numbers, there were 114 deaths in one province in 1988, and only 32 in the other. Statistics at the national level clearly show enormous male excess mortality. They also show a concentration of deaths in the 30–44 age group. In 1987 this concentration was 58 percent, and in 1988 it was 57 percent.

However frightening it may seem for the future, AIDS is not yet among the leading causes of death. In 1989, such deaths amounted to only 17 percent of deaths attributed to suicide, itself a minor cause.

AIDS is still one of the most important causes of death for men in their 20s, second only to accidents. In the light of the number of years of young adult life that are lost, it remains an issue of great public concern. In a communication, Dr. G. Wells, LCDC, at the 1990 Joint Statistical Meeting, Anaheim, California, said that between 1983 and 1988 AIDS became the largest contributor to potential years of life lost for men between 20 and 49 years of age.

The exact number of Canadians infected by HIV is unknown. At this time, the number is estimated to be between 20 000 and 30 000. This number, however, does not have a high level of statistical significance. It might be more fruitful to develop a demographic model that takes into account entries into and exits from this illness as a way to evaluate, all other things being equal, the future evolution of the disease.

Source: Dumas (1990: 33–35).

Measures of Fertility

The most basic measure of fertility is the **crude birthrate,** which refers to the number of births in a given year divided by the midyear population times 1000. In Canada the current crude birthrate is 14 per 1000 population, which is the lowest ever recorded in the history of this nation. Since 1921 this rate has declined considerably, but some of the highest crude birthrates have been recorded during the peak years of the **baby boom,** which began after World War II and ended in the early part of the 1960s. Since the early 1970s, Canada has embarked on what some demographers have termed the "baby-bust" phenomenon (Grindstaff, 1975, 1985; Romaniuc, 1984), characterized by sharp and continued declines in childbearing (see Chapter 12).

Table 15.12 shows these patterns of fertility change over time. The **total fertility rate** (TFR) is given along with the crude birthrate because the former is a more refined index of reproduction.

Table 15.11

CHANGE IN THE CAUSE-OF-DEATH STRUCTURE, CANADA, 1900–1930 TO 1980s

Period	Major Causes of Death	Approx. Percentage of Total Deaths
1900–1930	Bronchitis, Influenza, Pneumonia,	85
	Cardiovascular-renal diseases	5
	Other	10
Late 1980s	Heart disease	35
	Cancer	21
	Stroke	10
	Accidents	7
	Respiratory	7
	Other	20

Source: Adapted from Warren Kalbach and Wayne McVey, *The Demographic Bases of Canadian Society.* Toronto: McGraw-Hill Ryerson, 1979, pp. 85–86, and from Vital Statistics publications.

Table 15.12

CRUDE BIRTHRATES AND TOTAL FERTILITY RATES, CANADA, 1921–1991

Year	CBR ('000)	TFR
1921	29.3	3.54
1925	26.1	3.13
1931	23.2	3.14
1935	20.5	2.82
1941	22.4	2.87
1945	24.3	2.93
1951	27.2	3.26
1955	28.2	3.29
1961	26.1	3.15
1965	21.3	2.89
1971	16.8	2.19
1975	15.8	1.85
1981	15.3	1.70
1985	14.8	1.67
1990	15.3	1.86

Note: CBR = Crude Birthrate; TFR = Total Fertility Rate
Sources: Romaniuc (1984: 121–22, 130–32); Vital Statistics for 1985. Ottawa: Minister of Supply and Services, 1986; Statistics Canada, *Health Reports*, Ottawa: Canadian Centre for Health Information, 1992, p. 76 for 1990.

The TFR gives an indication of the average number of children a woman would bear if she were to experience the prevailing age-specific fertility rates over her reproductive years. A TFR of 2.1 is needed in order for the society to ensure replacement of the generations. Out of the 2.1 children it is assumed that, on average, one will be a daughter who will eventually bear children herself when she reaches maturity. As we can see from Table 15.12, total fertility levels in Canada were well above replacement until the early 1970s, at which point there began a rapid slide toward below replacement levels.

Fertility and Public Policy: The Quebec Case

The low fertility rate in Quebec has prompted a revaluation of the family's place in provincial government priorities. A series of clearly pronatalist policies have been implemented over the past few years. Between 1987 and 1990, budgetary measures were enacted to make living conditions more comfortable for families with children. These measures involved income tax breaks, subsidized day care, and baby bonuses. For the 1988–89 fiscal year, the Quebec government offered a bonus of $500 for the birth of first and second children and a bonus of $3000 for third and subsequent children. In effect, this consists of $375 paid quarterly over two years. The bonus system was changed for the 1989–90 fiscal year so that for second children the family receives not only the initial $500, but an additional $500 on the child's first birthday. For the third child, families receive the quarterly $375 over three years rather than just two (for a bonus of $4500). In the latest amendment (1990–91) bonuses for the first two children will remain the same, but parents of third and subsequent children will receive quarterly payments of $375 over four years.

How these measures will affect fertility remains to be seen. When there is an increase in the birthrate, the contribution of financial incentives in relation to other factors, such as changing attitudes, is not easy to gauge. In the case of Quebec, it is difficult to establish a relationship between the 1988 birthrate and the pronatalist policies of the same year, whereas the policies of the previous year were too modest to have any lasting effect. There has been, however, an increase of almost 10 percent in first-order fertility for all age groups in Quebec that has not occurred in the rest of Canada. As for higher-order births, especially the closely observed third order, levels are very low and continue to drop, both in Quebec and in the rest of Canada. The 1988 results show that even though the national rate remains stable at 1.7, it is rather precariously situated. Two rather uncertain movements — a slight increase in Quebec and a slight decrease in the rest of Canada — are confusing. The provisional count for 1989 is 91 315 births for Quebec. This would mean a very significant increase of 10 percent over two years.

Source: Dumas (1990: 21–25).

• Baby Boom and Baby Bust

The rise of fertility in Canada and other industrial countries after World War II is a complex phenomenon that cannot be easily summarized by "quick" explanations. It is clear that social, psychological, economic, and demographic factors all played key roles.

Demographically, the baby boom was precipitated by changes in **intermediate variables** (Davis and Blake, 1955), which are a number of variables through which societal and biological factors operate in affecting reproductive levels. For example, demographers have documented that marriage rates increased after the war years and that people tended to marry at a relatively early age in comparison to previous decades. Fertility increased partly because of rising marriage rates and early age of marriage (Romaniuc, 1984).

Economically, the years following World War II were characterized by a new prosperity in economic productivity and development. During the early 1950s, wages began to rise significantly, unemployment was quite low by today's standards, and opportunities in the market world looked promising. According to Easterlin (1969, 1980) these factors, in combination with a relatively small cohort of young workers (due to the low fertility of the 1930s), induced young couples not only to marry early, but to have children at an early point in their marital careers and to continue to have, on average, more children than their parental generation. There was a prevailing sense that material aspirations could be actualized even in the presence of three or more children in the household. Moreover, Easterlin argues, these new couples did not have particularly strong materialist preferences because during their childhood and adolescence they had been socialized in a context of economic restraint.

The sociological factors of the baby-boom phenomenon go beyond childhood socialization for material tastes. During the 1950s and 1960s, people married in large numbers because they generally placed a strong value on the institution of family and marriage. The war had merely frustrated people's desire to comply with the strong allegiance to such a central institution. The cultural context after the war favoured high marriage rates and early entry into this institution. Marriage was also seen as an escape from the authority of the parental household, particularly for the young women of that time. With increasing **urbanization** and **urbanism,** lifestyles and attitudes began to change, people began to seek personal freedom to carry out a more existential life unencumbered by the watchful eyes of authority figures. Marriage was therefore seen as an attractive proposition for many young couples during the 1950s (Caldwell, 1982).

An important sociological factor in this development was what Betty Friedan (1963) called the "Feminine Mystique." She outlined the tendency of women in the 1950s to be preoccupied with marriage and motherhood, a new home in the suburbs, and a successful husband who ensured a comfortable standard of living for the household. The male role was essentially one described by Davis (1984) as "breadwinner." What concerned men was work, success, and providing for their families.

In many respects, the developments that took place during the baby boom period led the way to the subsequent baby-bust phenomenon. Sociologically, a number of important changes evolved in the early 1960s and unloaded their full impact during the 1970s and 1980s. With increasing urbanism, and the sex role revolution spearheaded by Frieden's *Feminine Mystique,* women's roles changed radically. One of the most significant barometers of this change is the dramatic surge of women's participation in the paid labour force. Starting with the early 1960s, women began to participate in the economic and educational spheres of society. By the mid-1970s, in Canada and other industrial countries, marriage rates plummeted and the average age at first marriage rose significantly for both men and women — a trend continuing to this day.

During the early part of the 1960s effective contraceptive technology became readily available, facilitating the sexual revolution: men and women no longer had to enter into legal matrimony to engage in sexual play, as unwanted births could be easily averted. Declining marriage levels coupled with effective contraceptive technologies and a general sense that a new liberalism had arrived contributed to the rapid slide in the overall birth rate.

Easterlin (1969, 1980) proposed a cyclical theory of fertility based on the interplay of economics, demography, and sociology. The baby bust is really a natural sequence in a self-regulatory phenomenon: a period of high fertility is followed by a subsequent period of low fertility, which in turn is followed by a new cycle of high fertility. The driving forces for this cyclic pattern include how well the economy performs in meeting the material aspirations of young adults, the proportionate numbers of young workers in the age structure, and the childhood socialization for material tastes among persons of parental age.

The baby bust is also a function of other more pervasive and fundamental forces in our society that have evolved over time and are likely to stay with us indefinitely: (1) the rise of individualism as a dominant aspect of our culture, which emphasizes detachment of the individual from traditional sources of regulation such as religion; (2) the rise of a consumerist ideology emphasizing strong material preferences over familism; (3) the increasing levels of divorce and alternative living arrangements to legal marriage; (4) the sex role revolution and the movement toward increasing levels of emancipation of women and men from traditional roles, taking people further away from the centrality of traditional family and marriage as sources of self-fulfilment; and (5) a general sense among men and women that alternative sexual orientations are legitimate (Westoff, 1983; Preston, 1987; Davis, 1987; Keyfitz, 1987; Romaniuc, 1984; Beaujot, 1986; Trovato, 1988a).

Implications of Falling Fertility Rates

The sociological, economic, and demographic trends observed in the Western world during the last three decades provide no indication that the current course of fertility is likely to change in any significant manner in the foreseeable future. It is unlikely that contemporary society will revert to the fertility levels of the baby-boom era.

The most significant demographic impact of declining fertility will be felt through the aging of the population. Low fertility translates into a greater proportion of the population that is 65 years of age and older. With declining mortality rates overall, particularly among the senior sector of society, an important challenge facing us will be the provision of economic, social, and medical care for a growing senior citizen component.

• MIGRATION

Migration represents the third and final component of population change. We usually distinguish **internal** from **international migration**. The former pertains to movements within a given territory or country, while the latter refers to the crossing of international boundaries for the purpose of permanent resettlement.

• International Migration

Canada is known as a country composed of **immigrants** and their descendants. Currently, about 16 percent of our population consists of first-generation immigrants. The other significant, but numerically small, sector of the Canadian population is the aboriginals. During the formative stages of this country their contact with the Europeans resulted in their conquest and subordination (Lieberson, 1961), which is one of the least celebrated aspects of this country's immigration experience. This fact has had far-reaching consequences for our native peoples, as reflected in their high rates of poverty, illness, and mortality.

The extent of **international immigration** to Canada has fluctuated significantly over the years (Figure 15.2; see also Chapter 9).

Provincial Distribution of Newcomers

Unquestionably, most newcomers to this country prefer to settle in the largest metropolitan areas of Ontario (about 50 percent), British Columbia (15 percent), and Quebec (15 percent). This rank order of preference has not changed much over the years (Dumas, 1990). This situation is largely a reflection of the varying economic and social pulls characteristic of the regions in Canada, with the more advantaged areas receiving the majority of immigrants. Over 60 percent of new Canadians settle in Toronto, Montreal, and Vancouver. There is relatively little movement out of these attraction poles once settlement has been established (Trovato, 1988b). This phenomenon is due not only to the economic and social advantages the large city offers a new immigrant, but also to the strong pulling effects of the ethnic communities prevailing in the large cities. For newcomers, the presence of others with the same ethnic, cultural, and religious origins is a source of comfort and support, both psychologically and materially (Trovato and Jarvis, 1986; Trovato, 1988b).

• Factors of Migration

The permanent resettlement of people from one part of the world to another is a phenomenon of great magnitude involving factors associated with the country of origin of immigrants and factors

CANADIAN IMMIGRATION, 1900–1990

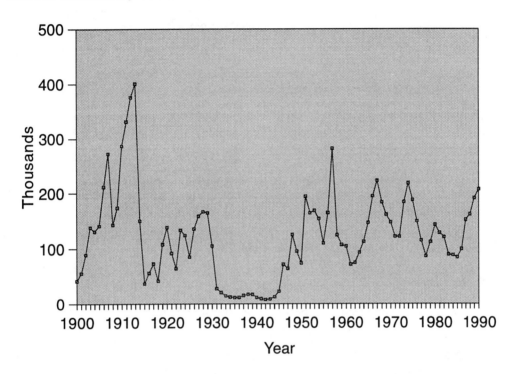

associated with the receiving country (Goldscheider, 1971). Lee (1966), in his "theory of migration," refers to **"push" and "pull" factors** to describe these origin and destination effects on the individual. The decision-making process involves the individual's assessment of the pluses and minuses in the intended destination as opposed to his or her place of origin. For example, one may perceive that resettlement in Canada will permit greater economic opportunities for oneself and one's family, while remaining in the home country will limit opportunities for upward mobility. At the same time, the potential migrant may also project that settling in Canada will result in difficulties such as having to learn the language, customs, and culture of a new society. Remaining in the home nation will prevent such difficulties. Thus, the decision to move is largely a function of adding up the perceived benefits and disadvantages in the context of the information one has about conditions in both origin and destination countries. If the positives outweigh the negatives, the decision will be to move; otherwise, the motivation to migrate will be low.

Even when one's overall assessment is to change residence, the act of moving is dependent on the presence and extent of "intervening obstacles." Examples of intervening obstacles are restrictive immigration policy in the intended country of destination, the distance that would have to be travelled, and the financial costs of moving.

Although Lee's theory is inherently micro, it does recognize the importance of macro factors, but only as they are perceived by the actor. Macro theories of migration abound in literature (see Shaw, 1975 for a review).

• Age Pattern of Migration

Migration is more likely to occur during certain stages of the life cycle such as graduation, first permanent job, marriage, divorce, and retirement. One of the most persisting migration differen-

Table 15.13

IMMIGRATION TO CANADA BY COUNTRY OF BIRTH, 1945–1986

Area	Period (% shown)				
	1945–50	1951–60	1961–70	1971–80	1981–86
Europe	79.75	84.31	68.04	36.16	28.57
Africa	0	0	3.15	5.28	4.58
Asia	0.73	1.80	9.89	30.11	42.16
U.S.A.	12.55	5.58	10.57	11.04	6.54
South and Latin America	0	0	1.52	6.31	9.23
Caribbean	0	0	4.63	9.20	7.46
Australia	0	0.79	20.27	1.03	1.37
Not Stated	6.97	7.51	0.32	1.21	0.07
Total	100.00	100.00	100.00	100.00	100.00

Source: Samuel (1990: 384).

Box 15.3

CANADA'S ETHNIC PATTERNS CHANGING: IMMIGRANTS' ORIGINS SHIFT

The Globe and Mail

The percentage of Canadians who are immigrants has remained almost exactly the same since the Second World War, but their cultural backgrounds have not.

Figures published yesterday by Statistics Canada show that the ethnic diversity of new Canadians has increased dramatically, especially in the past decade . . .

Ellen Gee, a sociologist at Simon Fraser University in Burnaby, B.C., said the changes in immigration patterns have taken place so rapidly that the result is a recipe for social unease. "Survey after survey shows that people are very negative about immigrants. I'm very pessimistic. Basically, what we're dealing with . . . is racism."

The new numbers extracted from the 1991 census show that Canada is now home to at least 4.3 million immigrants, who Statscan defines as people not born in Canada but granted the right to live here permanently. They represented 16.1 per cent of the population — a figure that has remained virtually the same since the late 1940s but is substantially lower than the 22 per cent or so recorded early in the century.

But the source of this immigration has changed greatly. In 1961, 90 per cent of immigrants came from European countries; between 1981 and 1991, this figure had plunged to 25 per cent.

The portion of Canada's immigrant population born in Asia rose from 14 per cent in 1981 to 25 per cent in 1991. Asian-born people comprised almost half of all the immigrants who came to Canada between 1981 and 1991.

The impact of this trend can be seen most clearly in big cities. In Toronto, which has the highest proportion of immigrants of any metropolis, 38 per cent of the population is immigrant. This works out to nearly 1.5 million people. Of these, the greatest proportion have come from Britain (12.4 per cent), followed by Italy (10.5 per cent).

But the picture for recent immigrants, those who arrived between 1981 and 1991, is vastly different. During this period, the greatest proportion of immigrants came from Hong Kong (10.2 per cent) followed by India (6.9 per cent).

In Montreal, more immigrants have come from Lebanon (10.1 per cent) over this same period than from any other country. Quebec has greater control over its immigration practices than other provinces and attempts to attract French-speaking immigrants.

Prof. Gee said opinion surveys consistently show the public disapproves of immigrants, particularly in the large urban areas that receive most of them.

cont. on page 399

cont from page 398

Fifty or 60 years ago, she noted, Canadians vowed not to let more Chinese immigrants into the country because they were deemed to be unable to be assimilated into Canadian society. The prejudice is more sophisticated now, she said, but it is just as potent: "You can't go along assuming that if you just do some sort of ad campaign, all of a sudden it's all going to be better, because it's not."

She said it is unrealistic to expect the tension created by an influx of visible minorities to simply disappear. "It did when they were Italian, German and Portuguese in the fifties. But this is different."

The current level of immigration — roughly 250,000 a year — has rarely been seen since the First World War, and is intended, in large part, to bolster the country's population.

Since the early 1970s, Canadians have not been bearing enough children to replace themselves. Demographers predict that if the birth rate stays the same and immigration declines, the population will drop over time — a prospect that makes policy-makers blanch because they fear for the country's economic stability.

Also, the population is aging rapidly. In the next 20 years, the first wave of baby boomers will start drawing pensions, and many policy-makers fear there will be too few workers to support the added demands on government programs.

The government's answer has been to maintain high levels of immigration, despite the policy's unpopularity. Some demographic pundits have argued that to ensure true population growth, the annual immigration target ought to be 600,000 or more.

However, Christopher McAll, a sociologist at the University of Montreal, said yesterday he believes much of the resistance to immigration is the result of Canada's tough economic times, rather than latent racism.

Last month the unemployment rate hit 11.8 per cent, the highest in almost a decade, fuelling widespread anxiety about job security. But Prof. McAll, the author of a report on the impact of immigration in Quebec, said there is no evidence that newcomers take many jobs away from Canadian-born citizens. In fact, he said, there is no evidence immigration affects the economy one way or the other.

He said the answer to the growing discomfort Canadians feel with immigration is not to reduce the numbers admitted, as several vocal organizations have argued, but rather to improve the country's capacity to absorb them by creating more support programs.

He noted that since its birth Canada has built its population by opening its doors to newcomers. "I see no real reason why Canada should cease to be a country based on immigration."

Source: Alanna Mitchell, *The Globe and Mail*, December 9, 1992, pp. A1, A9.

tials in the literature is associated with age, a variable that is highly correlated with life-cycle stage. The theoretical graph shown in Figure 15.3 identifies this relationship.

During childhood the predominant basis of relocation is due to family migration, and one's chances of changing residence at a young age are tied to the family's exigencies. During the late teens up to the early 30s, there is a heightened propensity to move. This is a life-cycle stage that involves a number of important firsts: graduation, university, entrance into the labour force, and possibly marriage. The likelihood of migration diminishes considerably after the late 30s and early 40s. During this stage of life, the emphasis for most people is to establish a household and family. Most individuals in this segment of their lives are settled in a permanent job, and the necessity to relocate is not preeminent.

In many industrial countries, including Canada, there is a typical retirement age migration phenomenon, resulting in another peak, albeit of lower magnitude than that observed in young adulthood. A large number of people retire at around the age of 65 and seek residence in locations more desirable to seniors. In the United States, the retirement flow is mostly to Florida, California, and the other southern states. In Canada, retirement migration is largely directed toward British Columbia (Northcott, 1985).

AGE PATTERN OF MIGRATION

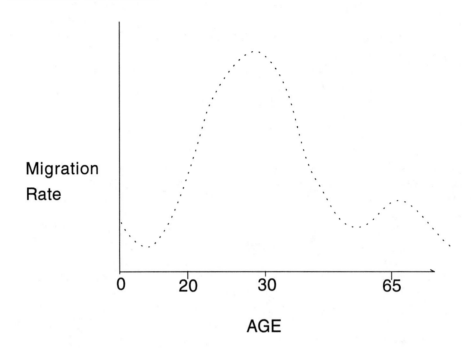

Migration Rate

0   20   30   65

AGE

• Interprovincial Migration in Canada

In Canada, the flow of migration can be described as being predominantly from economically disadvantaged areas to economically advantaged regions. Much of the interprovincial exchange is economically driven. Historically, the Atlantic region of Canada has been a net loser in that more people leave than enter this region. Depending on the period of observation and the economic context, the net migration balance for a given province will be either positive or negative and its magnitude will also vary.

Table 15.14 shows the Canadian interprovincial migratory balance for the last four decades. Between 1951 and 1989, over thirteen million people changed residence. British Columbia, Ontario, and Alberta, in that order, have shared an overall positive net migration over the forty-year period, while the remainder of Canada has tended to suffer net losses. These three leading areas are the most economically advanced provinces in Canada, and have been therefore successful in attracting migrants.

AGE AND SEX STRUCTURE

The age-sex composition of society can provide important clues about mortality, fertility, and migration. For example, if the population pyramid is narrow at the base, we know that fertility is low and declining. A wide base would indicate high fertility. The width of the pyramid at advanced ages reflects mortality conditions. A very narrow top suggests high mortality levels. If disproportionately more women than men are present in the older ages, then we have evidence of sex-selective mortality at such ages. Since migration occurs mostly between the late teens and early to mid-40s, irregularities in the age distribution in this part of the pyramid may signify extreme in- or out-migration levels.

Table 15.14

INTERPROVINCIAL MIGRATORY BALANCE FOR FOUR DECADES, CANADA

Province	1951–1960	1961–1970	Total 1971–1980	1981–1989	1951–1989
Newfoundland	-9 816	-34 557	-20 840	-26 900	-92 113
Prince Edward Island	-7 938	-5 732	2 927	780	-9 963
Nova Scotia	-28 851	-43 521	4 165	2 200	-67 987
New Brunswick	-25 360	-45 277	6 441	-3 233	-67 429
Quebec	-72 877	-142 594	-234 163	-108 867	-558 481
Ontario	148 036	236 081	-96 391	200 369	488 095
Manitoba	-40 587	-64 161	-68 977	-29 880	-203 607
Saskatchewan	-87 938	-123 492	-50 603	-53 815	-315 848
Alberta	32 858	30 022	244 991	-82 746	225 125
British Columbia	93 075	192 713	216 486	107 919	610 193
Yukon and Northwest Territories	-600	519	-4 036	-5 827	-9 944
Total Interprovincial Movements	2 962 004	3 660 061	3 849 741	2 868 282	13 340 088

Source: Unpublished data from Family Allowance Files, Estimates Section, Demography Division, Statistics Canada. See Dumas (1990: 106).

From the age composition we can determine whether society is aging and to what degree this may be occurring over time. In 1881 Canada had a relatively young population, with a large proportion of its people under the age of 15. In 1987 the proportion of persons aged 15 and under was 21 percent, while those aged 65 and over represented 11 percent. In 1951 seniors accounted for only 3 percent of Canada's population.

The proportions of the population that are below age 15 and above age 65 give an indication of a society's dependency burden. In many less-developed countries, the youth **dependency ratio** (population <15/population 15–64) is quite high. The major challenge for such societies is to provide adequate care for a large and growing youth segment of the population. Unfortunately, in such countries the working-age sector of society is disproportionately small and economically the society would have difficulties in providing adequate care and resources for the population as a whole.

In the industrial world we are witnessing the development of the opposite problem: the old-age dependency ratio (population 65+/population 15–64) is relatively large and will continue to grow as a result of the low fertility levels prevailing in these societies. A major challenge facing industrial countries like ours is to ensure adequate economic, social, and health-care provisions for a growing senior citizen component of the population. Since the youth dependency ratio is relatively low, a large part of the country's resources may have to be redirected toward fulfilling the growing needs of the old (Preston, 1984).

Fertility is the strongest determinant of age composition. Mortality, while not unimportant, accounts for relatively less in determining age structure. Sex structure, however, is more a function of mortality and to some extent migration. In general, there are 105 males per every 100 females at birth. This **sex ratio** declines with advancing age, and by age 55 it favours females. The underlying mechanism for the reversal is the excess mortality of males at all age groups: as the sex-mortality differential intensifies with advancing age, the masculinity ratio declines.

There are varying types of age-sex structures. Figure 15.4 provides a visual indication of this fact. The "wide pyramid" type, as reflected by Kenya, is characteristic of populations with a very high level of reproduction. In such societies, the proportion of the population that is below age 15 can be as large as 45 percent. Sri Lanka in 1985 may be defined as a "modest pyramid" because the wide base extends beyond the very young ages, making the pyramid somewhat less pyramidal

Figure 15.4

AGE-SEX PYRAMIDS

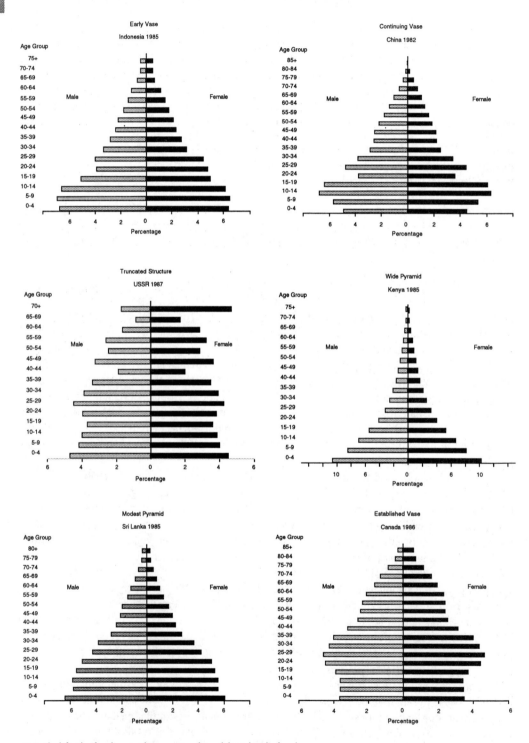

Note: The left side of each pyramid represents males and the right side, females.

in appearance and indicating a high-fertility society. Indonesia provides an example of an "early vase" — a situation arising from recent fertility declines after a relatively long period of high fertility levels. China is a continuation of this process, where fertility has been declining for a longer period of time. Therefore, its population structure is becoming increasingly representative of a vase.

As fertility declines intensify into the next century, some developing nations will enter a stage in which the shape of their population structure will be more like that of the industrialized nations of today. They will move into the "established vase" phase, as characterized by Canada in 1986. The significant alteration in our nation's population structure since the early 1960s is a function of sustained fertility declines. Eventually, Canada will begin to exemplify the "truncated structure" of the U.S.S.R. in 1987. This last phase of the evolution of age-sex structure will become increasingly prevalent in the countries of the industrial world as their populations continue to age.

SUMMARY

- Demography is the study of human populations — a matter of central concern to sociology.
- All demographic phenomena are the result of individual and social behaviour. Numerically, population can change only as a function of the interplay between fertility, mortality, and migration.
- World population has reached unprecedented levels of growth since the turn of this century. The major factor responsible was natural increase — a high rate of fertility and declining mortality.
- Today, Western societies have low rates of natural increase with low fertility and mortality, while the developing nations possess high rates of growth that are due to rapidly declining death rates coupled with high birthrates. The world's future will depend largely on how humanity copes with this demographic reality.

KEY CONCEPTS

Age-sex pyramid
Age/sex-specific death rate
Age structure
Baby boom
Cardiovascular diseases
Chronic diseases
Cohort
Components of population growth
Crude birthrate
Crude death rate
Demographic transition
Demography
Dependency ratio
Epidemiological transition
Fertility

Immigrant
Infant mortality rate
Intermediate variables
Internal migration
International migration
Life expectancy
Life table
Migration
Mortality
Natural increase
Neonatal mortality
Net migration
Positive checks
Preventive checks
"Push" and "pull" factors
Sex ratio
Total fertility rate
Urbanism
Urbanization

REVIEW QUESTIONS

1. How would you describe the historical evolution of the human population? What is atypical about our current stage of demographic history in comparison to premodern times?
2. What is the role of individual behaviour in demographic processes?
3. Describe how the theories of Malthus and Marx differ in relation to the population issue.
4. Compare Canada's fertility and mortality levels and patterns of the past with those of today. How have these population variables changed? Why have they changed?
5. What determines one's probability of changing residence?
6. What determines the age-sex composition of society?

Collective Behaviour

William A. Meloff

INTRODUCTION

A variety of social phenomena that are of significance to the total study of human society are not subsumed by studies of group behaviour or by studies of organizations, societies, or cultures. These are **collective phenomena,** which include, according to Herbert Blumer (1951), "collective excitement, social unrest, crowd behaviour, riots, manias, crazes, fads, mass alarms, mass hysteria, public revolts, protest movements, rebellions, primitive religious behaviour, reform movements, and revolutionary movements." Collective behaviour, according to Gerth and Mills (1953), is "obviously a catchall for various phenomena that do not readily fit into conceptions of institutional order."

Current work in the area of collective behaviour is leading us to a different view from the one expressed by Gerth and Mills. At least some researchers now approach this area from a perspective that compares, rather than contrasts, the behaviour of collectivities to other areas of social life. This is particularly true for social movements. When Milgram and Toch (1969) listed the factors that differentiate collective behaviour from social institutions within society — spontaneity, planlessness, and relative lack of organization — it is reasonable to assume that they were addressing those phenomena such as mob behaviour, fads, and crazes that clearly do happen without the benefit of much organizational planning. Other phenomena that come under the classification of collective behaviour are, in fact, as carefully planned and organized as any other aspect of the social structure. The differences in type will become apparent as this chapter progresses. Irrespective of organization or structure, the behaviour and organizations that constitute collective behaviour are extremely relevant to society because they profoundly affect the society in which we live.

The first part of the chapter looks at nonaggregate collective behaviour, where the individuals involved are not in physical proximity but nonetheless engage in similar behaviour along a particular dimension. Fashions, fads, and crazes are all representative of social phenomena of this type that have captured the attention of large segments of the society, usually for relatively brief periods of time.

The second section deals with congregate collective episodes, involving people in close physical proximity who behave in non-normative ways for brief periods of time. Subcategories under this heading include audiences and mobs; a typology of the various types of mobs encountered throughout history is presented.

As with any observed behaviour, sociologists are interested in explaining collective episodes through the application of theory. The third section of this chapter examines the theories that have attempted to explain the various types of collective behaviour.

The fourth and final section of this chapter examines social movements — those aspects of collective behaviour that have arguably had the most profound effects on the direction and growth of a society. Social movements have been viewed from an organization perspective as well as a collective perspective; the various theoretical orientations in this regard are examined.

NONAGGREGATE COLLECTIVE BEHAVIOUR

• FASHIONS, FADS, AND CRAZES

Some types of collective behaviour do not require the individuals involved to be in physical proximity. Rather, they are mass expressions of acceptance of new forms of behaviour — most likely disseminated through the mass media. When glue sniffing, for example, became a major substance abuse problem in North America, it was determined that its occurrence was directly related to the appearance of articles dealing with glue sniffing in the local newspapers — articles that generally provided detailed descriptions of methods of using glue for obtaining a "high."

Fashions are defined as socially sanctioned norms showing continual change (Sargent and Williamson, 1966: 535). It is expected that fashions will change, and the more a society is characterized by social change generally, the more rapidly we may expect fashions to change. Fashions are reflected in many areas of our life: clothing styles, architectural designs, popular music, slang expressions, automobile designs, and so on. Even such stable aspects of society as religion and morality are susceptible to the introduction of fashion from time to time. (The question whether a man should offer a cigarillo to a woman was, for a time, one of the great moral dilemmas of our society — at least according to the media.)

Being "fashionable" involves conformity, and those categories within the social structure that are under the greatest pressure to conform tend to be the ones most concerned with fashion. Advertisers and manufacturers have known for a long time that adolescents provide one of the best markets for fashion innovation since they are subject to extreme pressures to conform on the part of their peers, and because they are highly susceptible to change. Senior citizens, on the other hand, are much more resistant to the attractions of a new fashion, being generally more content to retain the clothes or the automobile that they currently own. Fashion is also linked to social class, with those individuals who enjoy high social standing being most likely to adopt new fashions as a symbol of their success and prestige.

Fashion is transitory, cyclical in nature, and generally unpredictable. The one thing of which we can be sure is that fashions will change, not only because change is expected, but because it means profits for manufacturers and their advertising agencies. The direction of change, however, is usually unclear. The length of women's skirts and dresses moves up and down in a cyclical manner, but there is seldom much warning as to which direction they will move in any given year. In the same context the lapels on men's jackets widen and then narrow; double-breasted jackets are in, then out, then in again. Blue jeans were originally designed for hard physical work, but now constitute a fashion statement if they have the correct label on the back, are pre-washed with rocks or acid, or, in the most recent incarnation, have a number of random holes accomplished by a shotgun at some stage in the manufacturing process.

Utility is not a significant factor in the selection of clothes. Men have been tying pieces of patterned cloth tightly around their necks for years, in spite of the discomfort involved; women have spent endless hours styling and blow-drying their hair in conformity with the current fashion (as have men, since crew cuts disappeared from the fashion scene). Nor does sexual desire have any apparent leverage in the determination of fashion. In fact, the opposite seems to hold true; whatever is fashionable is considered sexy.

The motivation for fashion is seen as having its roots in the desire for conformity and the desire for prestige. Other motives that have been mentioned include the psychoanalytic suggestion that fashion serves as a sublimated outlet for exhibitionist or aggressive tendencies (Flugel, 1930: 414) and the sexist theory of Thorstein Veblen (1912) that a well-dressed woman symbolizes her husband's success and prestige, thus satisfying both husband and wife. From an interactionist perspective, clothes are seen as an extension of the wearer's self, designed to give others the messages that the wearer desires to provide. In this context, it is felt that clothes and other fashionable items are selected as a reflection of the individual's self-concept. (The yuppie automobile of choice according to the wisdom of the 1980s was the BMW, and not a pickup truck.)

Fashions, then, are an integral part of contemporary society, where change is an expected, everyday occurrence, and the lack of change is equated with stagnation and even death.

Fads are closely related to fashions, but tend to be of shorter duration and often generate a higher intensity of emotion. Fads may be local, national, or international in scope, and may appeal to rather specialized groups.

Sargent and Williamson (1966: 540) differentiate between "cultist" and "spasmodic" fads. The **cultist fad** involves an ideology dealing with the benefit of the fad for the individual participants. Weight-loss plans enjoying brief periods of glory such as the drinking (alcohol) diet and the grapefruit diet, a variety of exercise machines and gadgets, isometric exercise, jazzercize, and even nudism have all been justified as increasing health and happiness.

In contrast, the **spasmodic fad** offers no particular benefit other than fun. It catches on rapidly and dies away just as rapidly. Rubik's Cubes, yo-yos, hula hoops, disco, and the lambada have come and, mercifully, left just as quickly. Other fads such as bingo and bridge have been retained in the culture and are now institutionalized forms of recreation. Once again it is in the adolescent subculture that fads are found most frequently. Teenagers have worn dog collars on their ankles, nickels in their "penny loafers" to indicate they were going steady, T-shirts with customized messages, and army jackets autographed by all their friends. At the university level, raccoon-skin coats, goldfish swallowing, Volkswagen "beetle" and telephone-booth stuffing, marathon shower sessions, and teach-ins have all had their moments of glory.

Aguirre et al. (1988) list seven characteristics of fads:

1. **Homogeneity:** Fad behaviour tends to be consistent across place and time.
2. **Novelty:** Fads offer new forms of behaviour, dissimilar to anything that has gone before.
3. **Oddness:** In the context of existing societal norms, fads seem strange, if not dangerous, ridiculous, or even deviant by those who do not participate.
4. **Nonutility:** Although fad behaviour is important in the context of its presence in many areas of life, its consequences for the individual tend to be seen as frivolous or superficial.
5. **Suddenness:** Fads appear on the basis of impulse rather than planning, appearing suddenly and unexpectedly.
6. **Rapid spread:** Fads may originate in any social stratum and spread very quickly among a relatively limited segment of the total population.
7. **Quick acceptance and short lifespan:** Fads are accepted quickly and die out quickly. Generally speaking, they do not return, at least not in precisely the same form.

Crazes are more emotionally intense than fads and tend to reflect a greater degree of self-involvement and personal commitment to an ideology. In the 1960s the Beatles generated a craze that involved a great many adolescents in collecting records, buying various "Beatles" items, actively participating in fan clubs, and attending concerts where a very high level of emotional response to the music was expected. Other crazes have included the paranoia over witchcraft in the 16th and 17th centuries, the near-hysterical reaction to communism in the United States in the 1950s, and some short-lived but highly intense religious cults in the 1960s and 1970s.

CONGREGATE COLLECTIVE BEHAVIOUR: THE CROWD

When a large number of people are in physical proximity — congregate — they constitute a **crowd**. The crowd is generally too large for the people who compose it to engage in meaningful interaction in the manner of a social group. Rather, the individuals in a crowd become **polarized:** there is a common focus of attention on some activity or phenomenon. The nature of the activity engaged in by the members of the crowd will determine its type. In the case of an **audience,** people congregate for the purpose of learning, being entertained, or witnessing an event. Audience participation will range from the generally passive behaviour manifested by people in a movie theatre or lecture hall to the active behaviour manifested by those at a rock concert or religious revival. In all cases, the lifespan of the audience is relatively short, the members will disperse when the event is over, and in all probability the particular composition of the audience will never be exactly duplicated.

Another kind of crowd constitutes, or becomes transformed into, a much more active collectivity — the **mob**. Mobs tend to be more emotionally intense than audiences and may manifest behaviour that is destructive — to the members of the mob, to other individuals, or to things. Roger Brown (1954) has suggested three broad categories of mobs: aggressive, acquisitive, and escape.

The **aggressive mob** involves hostile behaviour on the part of the mob toward one or more individuals. When the action is essentially one-way and is directed against one or a very few individuals, we have a **lynching**. One-way aggression toward a large number of people — destroying an entire village, for example — constitutes a **terrorization**. Aggression involving two identifiable mobs constitutes a **riot**. In many instances, a true riot as defined here takes place only when the police move in to disperse a large assembly of people and violence ensues. The task of specially trained riot squads within a police department is to prevent a riot from breaking out, rather than instigating one through violent action.

An **acquisitive mob** involves an uncontrolled, often destructive attempt on the part of a crowd to acquire something of value. Members of an audience at a rock concert may transform into an acquisitive mob when they surge toward the stage to get closer to, or try to touch, the stars. Individuals have been trampled at concerts and sporting events when the crowd surged forward in a struggle for seating. In many of the civil rights riots during the 1960s in the United States, at least some of the individuals present were busy breaking store windows and stealing the merchandise within while others were battling the police — our definition of a true riot.

An **escape mob** involves individuals who are trying to get away from a situation that they perceive as dangerous. A fire in a theatre may transform a passive audience into an escape mob —

Box 16.1

CASE STUDY: A RIOT IN EDMONTON

In 1984 the Edmonton Oilers won their first Stanley Cup. The city of Edmonton hosted a civic reception and parade for them three days after the series ended. Some 100 000 people assembled to watch the parade and see the players and coaches introduced in front of City Hall. When the official celebrations ended at 6:30 p.m., about 2000 fans congregated at the corner of Jasper Avenue and 101st Street. The chanting fans forced the closure of Edmonton's major downtown avenue between 101st and 102nd streets. Edmonton's police force reacted by bringing in reinforcements and two trucks to try to open the avenue to traffic.

According to *The Edmonton Journal* (May 23, 1984), the crowd began to get violent about 8:30 p.m., when beer bottles were thrown at the police. At the height of the violence just after 9:00 p.m., some seventy-five police officers charged the mob, trying to arrest the bottle-throwers. A fire department truck arrived and fire fighters began to hose down members of the crowd who refused to disperse. According to *The Edmonton Journal*, "about 9:25 p.m., someone in the crowd yelled 'There they go' and a squad of uniformed officers, truncheons raised, charged into the crowd and began hitting people and chasing those who ran."

A police information officer denied that police had provoked the crowd. "These people aren't Oiler fans, they are troublemakers who have taken advantage of the situation," he said.

There were minor injuries and a few arrests. The incident resulted in a review of police procedures with regard to mob violence. Subsequent Stanley Cup celebrations in Edmonton were much more peaceful, largely as a result of better preparation on the part of the city and its police force.

It was generally accepted that many of the people involved that evening were looking for the opportunity of "acting out" in a destructive and violent manner. Other members of the crowd may have been drawn into the activity because of the high emotions manifested. A great many others, it should be noted, did nothing more than observe the destructive behaviour of the violent members of the crowd. Thus, in any crowd we may expect to find some who are caught up in the emotion of the situation, some who elect to do nothing more than observe, and some who may decide to depart the scene in order to avoid any involvement. Each of the theories of the crowd helps us to explain the behaviour of some — but not all — of the crowd members. They are not mutually exclusive as analytic tools.

attempting to escape without regard to the safety or welfare of others. The resulting **panic** may bring about a loss of life and personal injury that would not have taken place if successful leadership to control the panic had been present.

EXPLANATIONS FOR COLLECTIVE BEHAVIOUR

The earliest explanations of collective behaviour derived from observation of destructive mobs engaged in attempts to overthrow, or at least significantly modify, the existing social structure. Subsequent explanations tended to be somewhat more objective in tone but were still grounded in the assumption that collective behaviour was at best random and unplanned, and at worst extremely dangerous and at least potentially lethal. The following section details the major theories of collective behaviour that have been used to deal with phenomena as varied as fads on the one hand and lynch mobs on the other. As noted, some of the theoretical approaches are more useful than others in attempting to understand what has taken place.

• CONTAGION THEORY

A French physician, Gustave LeBon, witnessed the destructive and frightening behaviour of mobs and attempted to explain it using a concept borrowed from medicine. In discussing his "law of mental unity of crowds," LeBon (1960) said:

> Whoever be the individuals that compose it, however like or unlike be their modes of life, their occupations, their character, or their intelligence, the fact that they have been transformed into a crowd puts them in possession of a sort of collective mind.

LeBon based his analysis of crowds on a metaphor from his medical practice. The behaviour of people in active crowds, he felt, cannot be explained by their behaviour in normal situations, when they tend to be law abiding and restrained. In a crowd a process of emotional **contagion** takes place, he felt, which strips away people's veneer of socialization and turns them into animal-like beings, highly susceptible to emotion and violence. This "collective mind" is a dangerous manifestation of the contagion process.

Much of LeBon's writing is characterized by unscientific and emotional portrayals of people who seemed to be under some sort of spell. Nevertheless, there is certainly some validity in the observation that emotionally intense situations seem to sweep normally rational people up in the heat of the situation and provoke behaviour that is less than rational.

• CONVERGENCE THEORY

Diametrically opposed to contagion theory is the theory that like-minded people **converge** — come together — to engage in mob behaviour. The implication is that these individuals are already predisposed to violence and are simply awaiting the opportunity that the anonymity of a large crowd offers.

• EMERGENT NORMS

Although a crowd is generally too large for face-to-face interaction to take place among all the participants, there is a tendency on the part of everyone in the crowd to determine what is happening and to act accordingly. Through the process of **rumour,** information is passed through the crowd on two levels: first, regarding the nature of the problem or situation, and second, pertaining to possible responses. Since we have been socialized to look in every social situation for norms — standards of behaviour — and to act accordingly, it is normal and natural that we would look for these norms within the crowd as well. If the norms as defined are compatible with our self-concepts we will probably decide to participate. If the norms are not compatible — if they seem to require behaviour that would be uncomfortable for us — we will probably not participate. Thus, **emergent norm theory** helps explain the diversity of behaviour within any crowd, without negating the presence of emotional contagion or predispositional convergence.

Box 16.2

Case Study: The Los Angeles Riot

In March 1991 the world viewed with horror a video of the brutal beating of Rodney King by members of the Los Angeles Police Department. The video, taken by a resident of a housing complex close to where the beating took place, showed King receiving fifty-six blows after being hit with two electrified Taser darts. The video was played and replayed on network and local television. Four white members of the Los Angeles Police Department were charged in the assault on King, an African-American. In addition to the video, transcripts of conversations between three of the police officers were obtained in which they talked about "a Big Time use of force." One remarked, "I haven't beaten anyone this bad in a long time." At the trial, the fourth police officer testified against the others.

The defence lawyers were successful in having the trial moved to Simi Valley in Ventura County, 56 km northwest of downtown Los Angeles. It is an overwhelmingly white community of a hundred thousand people, most of whom moved there to escape the violence, crime, gangs, minorities, and housing prices of the city. On the afternoon of May 29, 1992, the jury (ten whites, one Hispanic, one Asian, no African-Americans) returned a not-guilty verdict for most of the charges and declared themselves undecided on one additional charge against one of the officers. Within hours, violence erupted in Los Angeles leaving forty-four dead, two thousand wounded, and over $1 billion in damage to buildings and property. Additional disturbances were recorded in San Francisco, Seattle, Atlanta, and New York.

In Los Angeles, within hours of the announcement of the jury's verdict, television helicopters showed a massive mob building at the intersection of Normandie and Florence avenues in the South-Central neighbourhood. At first, teenagers began throwing rocks and bottles at passing cars. Then two motorists were hauled from their cars and beaten. At 6:30 p.m., Reginald Denny, driving his gravel truck through the area, was hauled from his truck by five men who kicked him, hit him on the head with a fire extinguisher, and stole his wallet. He lay on the street for almost an hour until an African-American, who witnessed the beating on television, drove to the area and with the help of three other African-Americans took the badly injured man from the cab of his truck to a hospital.

Newsweek magazine described what happened next: "The violence rippled outward. Drivers jumped from cars and fled. Shouting kids smashed windows, tromped on hoods and roofs, torched the abandoned vehicles. Then they turned to a liquor store, small shops, a gas station. Before long, flames and black smoke engulfed the neighborhood. And the LAPD was nowhere in sight."

Ultimately, the violence was not limited to the South-Central neighbourhood. Downtown, angry mobs vandalized the police headquarters, an adjacent hotel, and other buildings in the area. A department store was looted and torched, and adjacent apartment buildings were set on fire. Firefighters responding to the many blazes wore flak jackets to protect themselves from attack. The next day, 2000 National Guard troops and hundreds of California highway patrol officers were dispatched to restore order. The day after, 4500 federal troops were sent in. Curfews were enforced throughout Los Angeles. After seventy-two hours, the violence was reduced to minor incidents.

The initial tendency was to equate this riot with the infamous riot that took place in the Watts area of Los Angeles in 1965. There were some significant differences, however. First, the 1965 riot was contained in the Watts area — a black ghetto — and did not move out into the rest of the city. In 1992 violence occurred in areas stretching from the predominately white, upper-class areas of Beverly Hills and Westwood in the north to Santa Monica in the west, to the downtown area of the city, and to the predominately black area known as South-Central. Further south, a motorcyclist was shot and killed and fires were set in Long Beach. Second, there was little use of firearms in 1965. In 1992 guns were openly used both by rioters and by people protecting their property. Finally, the Watts situation was essentially a race riot; the 1992 event was described as a "class" riot, where the rioters were Hispanic and white as well as African-American.

From Smelser's (1962) theoretical perspective, there is no doubt that the jury's verdict in the Rodney King trial served as the precipitating incident. The structural conduciveness and structural strain, however, can be traced to the social structure of a city that provides vivid differences between the "haves" and the "have-nots." The wealth and luxury of Los Angeles's upscale areas exist in striking counterpoint to the urban ghettos. The Los Angeles Police Department has had a long history of violence in its dealings with visible minorities, evidenced by the millions of dollars paid out over the years by the city to citizens who were the victims of police brutality. Racial tensions have been exacerbated on many occasions by verdicts that appeared to favour whites and Asians over African-Americans. Los Angeles, like most of North America, was in the grip of a severe recession in 1992; unemployment was at a record high, and social programs had been significantly reduced.

An equally significant factor is the role of the media in fanning the flames of violence. Live television broadcasts brought scenes of violence into the homes of Los Angeles residents instantly. The value-added determinant of generalized beliefs, as Smelser presents it, no longer requires information to be passed by word of mouth through the rumour process. All one needs to know about what is happening can be presented live and in colour by television helicopters. There is no doubt that the vivid scenes presented on television served to encourage large numbers of people to emulate the violent behaviour of those who had already joined the mob while at the same time instilling a sense of panic and a defensive reaction among those who feared for their personal safety and their property.

Finally, the response of the police was inadequate at best. Social control is based on the premise that societal norms will be respected and that adequate enforcement will be exercised. There were a great many heroes in Los Angeles during those seventy-two hours of turmoil, mostly private citizens representing all races, ethnic groups, and social classes who put their own safety on the line to protect life and property. Unfortunately, the most critical element of social control — the police — was absent for a prolonged period. Established law-enforcement procedures that can contain and restrict mob violence were not, for reasons still undetermined, immediately employed by the Los Angeles Police Department. By their inactivity and lack of presence the police gave tacit support to the rioters, thus exacerbating a situation that, theoretically at least, could have been significantly reduced if not entirely eliminated.

The Los Angeles riot of 1992 was a frightening, remarkable display of the kind of collective behaviour that can be expected in contemporary society given the appropriate variables and when the response from law-enforcement agencies violates established principles of fast and effective control.

Sources: *Time*, May 11, 1992; *Newsweek*, May 11, 1992.

• VALUE-ADDED DETERMINANTS

In his book entitled *A Theory of Collective Behavior*, Neil Smelser (1962) provides a framework for the analysis of collective episodes. He presents six **value-added determinants** for collective behaviour — factors that must be present, one logically following and building upon the previous one, in order for collective behaviour to occur. They are (1) structural conduciveness, (2) structural strain, (3) generalized belief(s), (4) precipitating factors, (5) mobilization for action, and (6) social control.

• Structural Conduciveness

Before a collective episode can take place, the social structure must be conducive — it must be set up in such a way that what is about to happen can in fact happen. The separatist demonstrations in

Box 16.3

CASE STUDY: VIOLENCE IN TORONTO

To the family and friends that Joel Richards left behind, the cause of his death was painfully obvious: he was simply in the wrong place at the wrong time. But that fatalistic explanation defies the ugly reality of life for thousands of young urban Canadian blacks. Scarred by poverty and racial animosity, they occupy a social and economic no man's land in a country that proclaims itself a haven for people of every race, creed and colour. To be sure, many of Canada's 500,000 blacks enjoy quiet lives in secure, prosperous surroundings. But others are trapped in a world apart at the bottom of society. Poorly educated, deprived of conventional job opportunities and hardened by repeated skirmishes between blacks and whites and among blacks themselves, they are caught in a maelstrom of frustration, rage and despair.

Last week, these toxic emotions boiled over on the streets of downtown Toronto. Angered by the acquittal of four white Los Angeles policemen in the savage videotaped beating of black motorist Rodney King, black activists in Canada's largest and most ethnically diverse city had organized a protest rally in front of the local U.S. Consulate. Several similar demonstrations against racism have passed without incident, but this time there was an additional, and highly volatile, ingredient: after the announcement of the rally, but two days before the actual event, a white policeman shot and killed a 22-year-old black man after a late-night chase on foot through dark alleys and backyards in a violent, drug-infested west Toronto neighborhood. The victim was Raymond Constantine Lawrence, an illegal immigrant and casual labourer who moved to Canada from Jamaica in July, 1990. According to police, plainclothes Const. Robert Rice shot Lawrence, an alleged crack dealer, twice in the chest at close range after the suspect approached the officer with a knife.

Within hours, reports of Lawrence's death had spread throughout the 250,000-member black community in the Toronto region. The resulting anger was in clear evidence at the protest rally two days later: organizers reminded the thousand demonstrators that Lawrence was the 14th black victim of a police shooting in the city since 1978, and the fourth black fatality.

But the orderly protest soon dissolved into an uncontrolled rampage. As more passive members of the crowd stared in helpless disbelief, scores of young men and women — including skinheads, street kids and fashionably dressed suburban high school students — stormed through the heart of the city's central retail district, smashing windows, looting stores and pelting police with rocks and empty bottles fished out of sidewalk garbage cans. Police eventually quelled the violence, but later in the week there were several more outbreaks of vandalism and tense standoffs between crowds of young people and riot-ready officers on Yonge Street, Toronto's seedy commercial strip.

As cleanup crews lined downtown streets, replacing shop windows and sweeping up debris, merchants and civic leaders issued urgent appeals for an even stronger police presence. But in the midst of the debate over public safety, few people spared much thought for the root causes of last week's senseless violence. Rightly or wrongly, the participants themselves seemed convinced that their actions represented a justifiable response to the poverty and racism that define black urban life. Among them was Denzel, a 17-year-old high-school dropout who says that he lost his job at a fast-food restaurant last year because of the recession. Born in Toronto to a Jamaican woman who subsequently put him up for adoption, he ran away from his foster parents when he was 15. He now lives with friends in a two-bedroom townhouse in Regent Park, a concrete jungle that is home to 10,000 of the city's poorest residents. Standing with three friends outside the downtown Eaton Centre, a popular hangout where street kids mingle with middle-class teenagers and an often bizarre assortment of pedlars and cult followers, Denzel talked openly about the damage that he and his cohorts had inflicted on the white business establishment. "Something that costs them money — that's the only way to get their attention," he asserted. His friend, Mark, 20, said that he was proud of breaking store windows and stealing merchandise. "All those broken windows can be replaced with insurance money," he added. "The black people who were killed cannot be replaced."

Source: *Maclean's*, May 18, 1992, pp. 24—26.

Quebec in the 1960s took place in a Canadian society that, while obviously not oriented to riots, did permit freedom of expression and assembly. The likelihood of a similar demonstration taking place in a totalitarian country is very small by comparison, since the citizens of that country are not provided with the liberties that exist in Canada. From a different perspective, we are not likely to find evidence of continually changing fashions in clothing in the anthropological accounts of small tribal societies that have not changed substantially for hundreds of years. In Canada, on the other hand, the social structure is oriented strongly toward social change of every kind, and fashion changes are expected annual events.

• Structural Strain

The fact that a social structure may be conducive to the manifestation of a collective episode is obviously not enough. Beyond that, there must be conditions within the structure that create strain, presenting disharmonies of sufficient importance that individuals within the structure recognize them and want to do something about them. Thus, to return to our Quebec example, the demonstrations and violence that occurred in the 1960s did not take place simply because of structural conduciveness within Canadian society. The perception on the part of francophones in Quebec that they were being discriminated against in language rights, job opportunities, and other areas created the structural strain necessary under Smelser's framework. Depending on the type of collective episode with which we are dealing, the strain may be as minor as the need for new styles in automobiles or as major as the need for radical change in the political system. Whatever the situation, there is a disjunction within the social structure, with the concomitant desire on the part of at least some people within that structure to rectify the situation.

• Generalized Belief(s)

Once conditions of structural conduciveness and strain are present, one or more generalized beliefs emerge as a precondition to the mobilization of people for collective action. The generalized beliefs are tied strongly to the rumour process, which facilitates the spread of beliefs among the individuals concerned. They are, in general, attempts to reduce or remove the ambiguities inherent in situations of strain by providing explanations — in many cases attributing blame, in other cases focusing the problem. Smelser delineates five major types of generalized beliefs:

1. hysteria, which transforms an ambiguous situation into an absolutely potent, generalized threat;
2. wish fulfilment, which reduces ambiguities by positing absolutely efficacious, generalized facilities;
3. hostility, which involves removing some agent or object perceived as a generalized threat or obstacle;
4. norm-oriented beliefs, which envision the reconstitution of a threatened normative structure; and
5. value-oriented beliefs, which envision the reconstitution of a threatened value system.

• Precipitating Factors

Following the determinants listed above, some event or set of events must trigger the collective episode. The precipitating factor may be innocuous in and of itself, but in the context of the other determinants it will serve as the next link in the collective chain. Crazes have swept the country after the actions of a few people were reported by the media; the conspicuous arrest of a minority group member proved to be the precipitating factor in a major race riot; a panic may be created by someone shouting "Fire!" in a crowded theatre.

• Mobilization for Action

Once the first four determinants are in place, it remains only to mobilize the prospective participants. Panic may be averted if leadership can be established; panic can be created if someone in a conspicuous position runs for the exit, for example, or jumps overboard. Riots have begun when a speaker at a rally was successful in mobilizing the audience.

Box 16.4

CASE STUDY: THE OCTOBER CRISIS OF 1970

On Monday, October 5, 1970, James Cross, the senior British trade commissioner in Quebec, was kidnapped from his home by four men who identified themselves as members of the FLQ — the Front de libération du Québec. The FLQ emerged during Quebec's Quiet Revolution, the evolution of the province from domination by the Catholic clergy and the government of Premier Maurice Duplessis to the emergence of a strong francophone identity and the independence of its culture and commerce. For the FLQ, as for many others, the tide of change was far too slow. Bolstered by a Marxist philosophy, particularly as interpreted by the guerilla hero Che Guevara, the FLQ engaged in a variety of violent acts beginning in 1963. Buildings were torched, mailboxes blown up, banks robbed, and explosives stolen. Until the kidnapping of Cross, however, the FLQ was perceived as troublesome, but not as a major threat.

Five days later, on October 10, Quebec Minister of Labour Pierre Laporte was kidnapped by four men belonging to a different FLQ cell. Earlier, he had described the kidnapping of Cross as "a wind of madness blowing across this province" (*The Edmonton Journal*, September 30, 1990).

On October 12, members of the Canadian military moved into Ottawa to protect government and public figures. In an interview the following day, Prime Minister Trudeau responded to a reporter who questioned the propriety of the armed troops around Parliament: "Well, there are a lot of bleeding hearts around who just don't like to see people with helmets and guns. All I can say is go on and bleed."

"How far will you go?" asked the reporter.

"Well, just watch me," was Trudeau's reply.

On October 15, Premier Robert Bourassa asked the federal government to impose the War Measures Act. Introduced originally during World War I, the act allows for the suspension of civil rights, unrestricted search and seizure, the imposition of censorship, and the right to hold people in jail without trial. Declaring a state of "apprehended insurrection," the Commons approved the act the following day, on a vote of 190 to 16, with the dissent coming from the NDP. Opinion polls showed that the people of Canada overwhelmingly supported the action. Within the powers of the War Measures Act, the FLQ was outlawed and a series of pre-dawn raids by the Quebec police resulted in the jailing of more than 450 people. Most were subsequently released without being charged.

On October 17, the FLQ telephoned a radio station to say that Laporte had been killed. His body was found a day later in the trunk of a car, strangled. No word on James Cross had been received since the original ransom note demanding $500 000 in gold, safe transport out of the country for the kidnappers, and publication of the FLQ manifesto.

On December 3, negotiators worked out an arrangement with the kidnappers of Cross, guaranteeing them and their families safe conduct to Cuba. Early the following day, after assurances from the Cuban consul that the kidnappers had arrived safely in Cuba, James Cross was released.

Although the details of the 1970 October Crisis are murky in the minds of many Canadians today, the experience was a keystone in the process of examining the relationship of Quebec to the rest of Canada. A decade later, Québécois rejected the concept of sovereignty-association, largely on the promise of constitutional reform. Subsequently, the failure of the Meech Lake and Charlottetown accords has resulted in a continuing sense of uncertainty and a lack of resolution of the issues underscored by the October Crisis more than twenty years ago.

• Operation of Social Control

Social control is not, strictly speaking, the last determinant in the chain. Rather, it has an important effect on each of the others, in that social control may impede, speed up, or set parameters for the resulting collective episode. During the campus disturbances of the 1960s and 1970s it was not unusual to find various agencies of social control — police, administration, faculty — in conflicting positions over how to handle the situation. This lack of cohesiveness served to encourage the students and probably created more problems for the universities concerned than there would have been had a unified stand been taken by all concerned. On the other hand, even severe riots have been contained within specific areas, and highly vocal demonstrations may not result in physical aggression.

By applying Smelser's value-added determinants in the analysis of a collective episode, we can systematically describe what took place and, if desired, work out a plan to preclude similar episodes in the future.

• THE RATIONALITY OF CROWDS

Beginning with the work of LeBon in 1895 and continuing for over fifty years, the crowd was treated as an entity characterized primarily by hysteria. Many writers have claimed that individuals will behave in a crowd situation in a manner that is totally foreign to their behaviour in the presence of friends and family. Freud (1922) suggested that in a crowd the superego — the conscience — is stripped away, and individuals are reduced to behaving according to the demands of their leader. Some historical accounts of the behaviour of crowds emphasized the villainy of the members, while other accounts extolled the virtues and the sacrifice of the same people, acting on behalf of an exalted cause. The truth appears to be somewhere in the middle, as exemplified in George Rudé's *The Crowd in the French Revolution* (1959). Rudé examined the records from 1787 to 1795, a period that encompassed the early fighting between the crowds and the police, the fall of the Bastille, the march on Versailles, the fall of the monarchy, the Reign of Terror, and the counter-revolution. He found that the participants were neither low-life thugs nor lofty idealists. The main motivation of the people involved seemed to be their need to obtain a steady and inexpensive supply of bread and other essentials.

In a similar manner, Hobsbawm (1959) described the appearance of "Robin Hood" figures in various countries who symbolized the frustrations of the peasants and who, in creating difficulties for the authorities, provided some measure of gratification to the downtrodden. Again, the motivations of the people involved appear neither criminal nor righteous, but rather the expression of a rather pragmatic discontent with their inability to subsist at a reasonable level.

The assumption of rationality is given further support in the political perspective of Charles Tilly (1978) and his associates. According to this approach, collective violence is seen as a means whereby people are able to attain a valued end or goal; as such it is both rational and intentional. Furthermore, collective violence is not unique or abnormal behaviour. It is simply the natural extension of normal social interaction, which is frequently characterized by conflict. In this regard, violence is seen as a natural aspect of the social relations that arise between competing factions in any society.

The political perspective also argues that participants in collective violence are the ones who are the most committed to societal institutions, and not the alienated, anomic people that writers like LeBon would have us believe.

Finally, this perspective holds that collective violence often represents an attempt on the part of those in power to retain that power, or alternatively an attempt by other groups to gain power. Tilly and his associates point out that the issues may be general as well as specific and that some of the goals may not be spelled out with any more clarity than the rather vague recognition of the need to attain power.

While this type of analysis encourages a reconsideration of the stereotypical view of crowd behaviour, it does not suggest that all crowds act in an absence of hysteria and maliciousness. The world watched in horror as innocent victims were dragged from their vehicles and beaten in the Los Angeles riots (Box 16.2); countless riots over history have been accompanied by the same apparently irrational behaviour. This framework suggests, however, that the manifested behaviour is not unique, nor is it characteristic of some inferior class of people lurking in the background and waiting for a riot to happen. To dismiss collective episodes by categorizing them as unique occurrences with no relationship to the ongoing social structure suggests that they are merely aberrations and not worthy of inclusion in the mainstream of sociological analysis.

SOCIAL MOVEMENTS

In the history of most societies — particularly those that are characterized by rapid social change — attempts are made from time to time to "improve" the existing social structure. This change almost always comes from outside the power structure, since the power structure must by definition struggle to maintain the status quo and in so doing retain its own power. Social movements may be categorized as reactionary, conservative, reformist, revolutionary, escapist, and expressive (Goode, 1992: 410).

Reactionary social movements are those devoted to bringing some aspect or aspects of society back to an earlier, more comfortable, "better" state. Organized efforts to repeal the Young Offenders Act, bring back the death penalty, or reinstitute the prohibition of abortions represent reactionary, or **regressive,** social movements in the sense that they have tried to impress on their followers the desirability of returning to older styles of behaviour.

Conservative social movements are interested in retaining the status quo — opposing changes that are proposed by other movements. The controversy over employment equity, for example, pits those who seek to ensure equity in the workplace irrespective of gender, race, or religion against those who believe that the present system works and should not be tampered with.

Reformist social movements are devoted to changing one or just a few aspects of society. The Women's Christian Temperance Union (WCTU) was largely instrumental in banning the sale of alcohol in Canada from 1918 through 1919, and for a time thereafter in individual provinces on the basis of local plebiscites. The Greenpeace Foundation has been successful in garnering publicity in its attempts to stop the annual seal hunt in Canadian waters, while the Moral Majority's campaign to remove sexuality and violence from television programming in the United States has had implications for Canadian television viewers.

A **revolutionary social movement** has as its goal broad-based change throughout an entire society. Many revolutionary social movements have had a religious base. The Protestant Reformation is perhaps the best example of a wide-ranging social movement that emerged, took hold, and ultimately became institutionalized in many societies around the world. Other religious-based social movements have not enjoyed the same success, although many have existed for years.

Canada has seen the emergence of revolutionary social movements in the political arena. Some have held on so tenaciously that they have become institutionalized. The Social Credit Party in Alberta began as a social movement, proposing a radical change to the economic system and a "back to the roots" fundamentalist Protestant theology. When it did manage to gain power in Alberta under William Aberhart the party abandoned many of its original precepts and established itself as a conservative government in the province. The New Democratic Party began as the Cooperative Commonwealth Federation (CCF), a social movement devoted to a broader sharing of Canada's wealth than was envisioned by the established parties of the day. The CCF arose out of the Great Depression in the prairies, where it promised the farmers something better than they had received at the hands of the Liberals and Conservatives. From those early roots, the party gained national status; the CCF and its successor, the NDP, have formed the government in Saskatchewan, British Columbia, Manitoba, and Ontario.

Escapist social movements seek to remove their members from the mainstream of society, working for individual rather than societal change. For this reason, there is some controversy as to whether these groups should actually be considered social movements (Goode, 1992: 412). The ill-fated People's Temple, its membership led to the jungles of Guyana by Jim Jones and ultimately coerced to commit mass suicide, represents one of the most notorious examples of this type, but many religious groups, particularly sects and cults, tend to fall within this category.

Expressive social movements are involved with changing the psychological state of their members rather than the larger society. The emphasis of these movements is on changing attitudes rather than behaviour. If, for example, we learn to define world hunger as a non-issue, as one group advocated, then no actions are necessary to eradicate it. As with escapist movements, there is serious question as to whether this category is an appropriate one when studying social movements.

The emergence of a social movement, then, is the result of factors within society that are perceived by a segment of that society to require change, which, for whatever reason, is not forthcoming from the existing institutional structures. Clark et al. (1975) delineate two broad categories of conditions that are necessary for a social movement to develop: the perception of institutional deficiency and mobilization.

• THE PERCEPTION OF INSTITUTIONAL DEFICIENCY

There are, within most societies, inconsistencies between various normative structures as well as inconsistencies between the goals and the means to attain those goals (Merton, 1957) within any single normative structure. Where these deficiencies are perceived — and the idea of **perception** is a central one here, since without recognition there will be no dissatisfaction — the individual in society will be faced with having to deal with potentially troubling inconsistencies. For example, a major norm in Canadian society is the accumulation of wealth. People are expected to succeed and to exhibit their success in normative ways — possession of homes, automobiles, clothes, and so on. When factors within society make it impossible to succeed in spite of the normative expectation for success, it creates an inconsistency that demands resolution. Canada's poor have always existed with that inconsistency, but it has been rationalized by the power structure — and often by the poor themselves — in terms of the individual's inability or unwillingness to succeed, rather than society's failure to ensure that the means for success are available. When the economy falters, however, and people who are used to at least a modicum of success find themselves unable to succeed any longer, the situation is ripe for a social movement that will promise to resolve the perceived inconsistencies.

The critical factor, then, is the differentiation between expectations, on the one hand, and achievements, on the other. The fact that virtually everyone in Canada today enjoys a much higher standard of living than their ancestors of 100 years ago means little when the expectation standard is not geared to what it was then, but rather to what it is today.

• MOBILIZATION

"By itself, a perception of institutional deficiency does not cause a social movement. People must not only recognize that something is wrong; they must be collectively activated to do something about it. The activation of human resources for collective participation in a social movement is called **mobilization**" (Clark et al., 1975: 12). The three elements necessary for the mobilization of a social movement are as follows:

1. An ideology on which potential members can be united. "An ideology does two concrete things. First, it provides a common perception of the institutional deficiency. It identifies what is wrong, who is responsible for it, and who are the victims . . . Second, an ideology provides a remedy for the deficiency. It tells people what they have to do and what changes must take place in society as a whole, if the deficiency is to be overcome" (1975: 13).
2. Willing and able leadership. "The chances of mobilization are greatly increased if a charismatic leader is available . . . The success of the Social Credit movement was, in large measure, due to Aberhart's charismatic qualities: 'his imposing physical presence, his performance, and as orator and organizer, his resource and inflexible will, his infinite resourcefulness, his ability to hypnotize people by his voice [and] his contagious belief in himself' " (1975: 15).
3. Channels for communication and a network of cooperative relationships. These "permit the dissemination of views and norms. In fact, it is through a back-and-forth flow of communication among supporters, and between supporters and leadership, that values and norms get formulated. In addition, channels for communication facilitate what could be called the **mechanics** of mobilization" (1975: 17).

• Resource Mobilization

Clark, Grayson, and Grayson's perspective on social movements is a significant departure from the orientations discussed earlier in this chapter on noncongregate and congregate collective episodes. Resource mobilization theory does not emphasize the presence of social strain or deprivation as a fundamental aspect of the development of a social movement. On the contrary, it argues that social strain is almost always present in society, but that strain in and of itself will not create a social movement. Nor, it says, are the activists in social movements necessarily those who are most affected by the issues. The various movements established to erase poverty and homelessness, for example, tend to involve activists who are not suffering from economic deprivation; both pro- and antiabortion groups contain many individuals for whom abortion will never be a personal issue; the movements on behalf of homosexual rights have many "straight" members. The key to understanding social movements from this perspective is to examine the **social movement organization (SMO)** — the structure of the movement. The success of the movement will be less a function of the intensity of the emotions surrounding the issue than a function of the effectiveness of the movement's leadership and its ability to mobilize the resources that are available within the social structure. These resources may include the support of politicians, the assistance of government and private agencies, the financial contributions of corporations and businesses, and favourable publicity via opinion gatekeepers and the media.

The model for resource mobilization theory lies in the classic theories of bureaucracies and organizations presented by Max Weber and others. As a "rational" model of social movements, it traces their development in terms of leadership (from charismatic to legal-rational) and organization to the point where there are few differences between a fully developed social movement and any established aspect of society. It assumes that the members of a social movement organization remain committed on the basis of **incentives,** which may be material, solidary, or purposive in nature. Material incentives involve the receipt of money or other tangible rewards; solidary incentives include prestige, respect, and the friendships that can be found within the organization; and purposive incentives relate to the fulfilment of the goals of the movement. It is generally agreed that purposive incentives are most commonly involved in membership retention, and that they are manifested through activity-oriented events such as demonstrations, fundraising drives, and so forth (Miller, 1989: 317).

While resource mobilization theory addresses many of the weaknesses of the other theoretical orientations presented earlier in this chapter insofar as they attempt to explain the success or failure of social movements, it is not without its own critics. There is the suggestion, for example, that the assumptions of rationality and structure are not realistic in trying to explain some social movements that appear to be far more spontaneous and unstructured than this theory would allow. When we loosen some of the assumptions to embrace these "exceptional" cases, we run the risk of working with definitions that are so broad as to be virtually meaningless. (The same argument has been applied to Smelser's use of "strain.") Ultimately sociologists will probably develop a synthesis of the resource mobilization and value-added perspectives, using the best points of each. Such a synthesis will allow us to understand the mechanics of social movements in terms of both their similarities and their differences in the context of other types of collective behaviour.

SUMMARY

- Collective behaviour subsumes a tremendous range of human behaviour, including fashions, fads, and crazes; various types of mob behaviour; and social movements.
- Although much of collective behaviour takes place outside the regular parameters of society's standards, the consequences for society tend to be extremely important.
- Even though fads, fashions, and crazes may be relatively trivial, their economic consequences are anything but trivial. Even the introduction of an item as minor as the Cabbage Patch Doll can determine the fate of a large corporation and the economic success of thousands of retailers.
- Aggregate collectivities have profoundly changed the course of societies' development in the past, and can be expected to do so in the future.
- Events known as "riots" can differ significantly. While the "riot" in Edmonton was a minor glitch in the smooth operation of the city, the Los Angeles riot continues to take its toll on the psychological well-being of the city's residents and the economic well-being of the city itself. The Los Angeles riot's relationship to racial unrest in other centres such as Toronto is only now beginning to be explored.
- Social movements arguably constitute the most important aspect of collective behaviour insofar as they involve a concerted, organized effort on the part of citizens to bring about changes in the social structure that will profoundly affect society.
- Social movements have been instrumental in bringing peaceful and orderly change to society, but some have been the motivators for collective incidents such as riots and other types of mob behaviour.
- The October Crisis of 1970 was an example of the complex relationships that obtain between social movements and collective episodes.
- The original conceptions of irrationality and deprivation as key explanatory factors in the analysis of social movements are less than adequate.
- Although the concept of structural strain is important, structural strain is far too prevalent to allow us to predict a collective episode or the emergence of a social movement strictly on the basis of its presence.
- The resource mobilization perspective on collective behaviour appears to be the most useful orientation for explanatory purposes, despite its shortcomings.

Key Concepts

Acquisitive mob
Aggressive mob
Audience
Collective behaviour
Collective phenomena
Congregate collectivity
Conservative social movement
Contagion
Convergence
Craze
Crowd
Cultist fad
Emergent norm
Escape mob
Escapist social movement
Expressive social movement
Fad
Fashion
Generalized belief
Incentives
Lynching
Mob
Mobilization for action
Panic
Perception
Polarize
Precipitating factors
Reactionary social movement
Reformist social movement
Regressive social movement
Resource mobilization
Revolutionary social movement
Riot

Rumour

Social control

Social movement

Social movement organization (SMO)

Spasmodic fad

Structural conduciveness

Structural strain

Terrorization

Value-added determinants

REVIEW QUESTIONS

1. What are the factors that differentiate fashions, fads, and crazes?
2. Distinguish an audience from a mob.
3. What are the essential differences between lynchings, terrorization, and riots?
4. Differentiate between aggressive mobs, acquisitive mobs, and escape mobs.
5. What elements of the Edmonton, Toronto, and Los Angeles riots support the contagion perspective?
6. What are the similarities and differences among convergence theory, emergent norm theory, and the value-added determinant perspective?
7. Should crowds be considered rational or irrational? What theory or theories would you use to support your position?
8. What are the six categories of social movements? How would you differentiate between them?
9. How would you categorize the October Crisis of 1970 in terms of the perspectives presented in this chapter? What was its impact on Canada?
10. What are the three elements required for the mobilization of a social movement?
11. What are the strengths and weaknesses of the resource mobilization perspective?

References

Abercrombie, N., S. Hill, and B.S. Turner 1984. *Dictionary of Sociology*. Harmondsworth, England: Penguin.
    1988. *The Penguin Dictionary of Sociology*, 2nd ed. Harmondsworth, England: Penguin.

Abrahamson, M., E.H. Mizruchi, and C.A. Hornung 1976. *Stratification and Mobility*. New York: Macmillan.

Abu-Laban, Baha 1979. "East Europeans and the Politics of Multiculturalism in Alberta." In *Language and Society*, edited by William C. McCormack and Stephen A. Wurm. The Hague: Mouton, 605–15.
    1985 [1980]. *An Olive Branch on the Family Tree: The Arabs in Canada*. Reprint, Toronto: McClelland and Stewart.

Abu-Laban, Baha, and Donald Mottershead 1981. "Cultural Pluralism and Varieties of Ethnic Polities." *Canadian Ethnic Studies* 13: 44–63.

Abu-Laban, Baha, and Sharon M. Abu-Laban 1991. "The Gulf War and Its Impact on Canadians of Arab and Muslim Heritage." In *Beyond the Gulf War: Muslims, Arabs and the West*, edited by Baha Abu-Laban and M. Ibrahim Alladin. Edmonton: MRF Publishers, 120–42.

Abu-Laban, Baha, and Sharon McIrvin Abu-Laban 1992. "Primary Education and National Development: The Case of Arab Society." *Arab Studies Quarterly* 14 (2-3): 19–37.

Abu-Laban, Sharon McIrvin 1981. "Women and Aging: A Futurist Perspective." *Psychology of Women Quarterly* 6: 85–95.
    1982. "On Strengthening Interpersonal Supports." In *Proceedings of the Alberta Symposium on Aging*. Edmonton: Alberta Social Services and Community Health, 62–68.
    1984. "Les femmes âgées: problèmes et perspectives." *Sociologie et Sociétés* 16(2): 69–78.
    1993. Traversing Boundaries. Unpublished manuscript. Department of Sociology, University of Alberta.

Abu-Laban, Sharon McIrvin, and Baha Abu-Laban 1977. "Women and the Aged as Minority Groups: A Critique." *Canadian Review of Sociology and Anthropology* 14(1): 103–16.

Acheson, T.W. 1972. "The National Policy and the Industrialization of the Maritimes, 1880–1910." *Acadiensis* 1(2): 3–28.

Adams, Michael 1990. "Sustainable Development." *Inside Guide* 4(6): 51–52.

Adamson, Nancy, Linda Briskin, and Margaret McPhail 1988. *Feminist Organizing for Change: The Contemporary Women's Movement in Canada*. Toronto: Oxford University Press.

Adler, Patricia A., Peter Adler, and John M. Johnson, eds. 1992. Special edition. *Journal of Contemporary Ethnography* 21(1): 3–132.

Adorno, Theodor W., Else Frenkel-Brunswick, D.J. Levinson, and R.N. Sanford 1950. *The Authoritarian Personality*. New York: Harper and Row.

Agger, Ben 1979. *Western Marxism: An Introduction: Classical and Contemporary Sources*. Santa Monica, Calif.: Goodyear Publishing.

Aguirre, B.E., E.L. Quarantelli, and Jorge L. Mendoza 1988. "The Collective Behavior of Fads: The Characteristics, Effects, and Career of Streaking." *American Sociological Review* 53 August: 569–84.

Ainsworth, Mary, M. Blehar, E. Waters, and S. Wall 1978. *Patterns of Attachment*. Hillsdale, N.J.: Erlbaum.

Aizenman, Marta, and Georgette Kelly 1988. "The Incidence of Violence and Acquaintance Rape in Dating Relationships among College Men and Women." *Journal of College Student Development* 29(4): 305–11.

Alcock, J.E., D.W. Carment, and S.W. Sadava 1991. *A Textbook of Social Psychology*, 2nd ed. Scarborough, Ont.: Prentice-Hall Canada.

Alford, Robert R. 1963. *Party and Society: The Anglo-American Democracies*. Chicago: Rand McNally and Company.

Allen, Richard 1973. *The Social Passion*. Toronto: University of Toronto Press.
    1988. "Social Gospel." In *The Canadian Encyclopedia*, 2nd ed. Edmonton: Hurtig Publishers.

Allman, T.D. 1993. "Serbia's Blood War." *Vanity Fair* March: 96–118.

Allport, Gordon W. 1958. *The Nature of Prejudice*. Garden City, N.Y.: Doubleday Anchor Books.

Altheide, David L., and John M. Johnson 1977. "Counting Souls: A Study of Counselling at Evangelical Crusades." *Pacific Sociological Review* 20(3): 323–48.

Althusser, Louis 1971. *Lenin and Philosophy, and Other Essays,* translated by Ben Brewster. New York: Monthly Review Press.

Amato, Paul R., and Bruce Keith 1991. "Parental Divorce and Adult Well-Being: A Meta-Analysis." *Journal of Marriage and the Family* 53: 43–58.

Ambert, Anne-Marie 1976. *Sex Structure*, 2nd ed. Don Mills, Ont.: Longman Canada.

Anderson, Benedict 1991. *Imagined Communities. Reflections on the Origin and Spread of Nationalism*. London: Verso.

Anisef, Paul, and Norman Okihiro 1982. *Losers and Winners*. Toronto: Butterworths.

Apple, Michael W. 1979. *Ideology and Curriculum*. London: Routledge & Kegan Paul.

Argyle, Michael, and Benjamin Beit-Hallahmi 1975. *The Social Psychology of Religion,* 2nd ed. London: Routledge & Kegan Paul.

Ariès, Phillippe 1962. *Centuries of Childhood: A Social History of Family Life*, translated by Robert Baldick. New York: Knopf.

Aristotle 1975. *The Politics of Aristotle,* translated by E. Barker. London: Oxford University Press.

Arnold, S., and D. Tigert 1974. "Canadians and Americans: A Comparative Analysis." *International Journal of Comparative Sociology* 15: 68–83.

Arnold, Tom 1992. "Rats Rule behind WEM's Glitz." *The Edmonton Journal* May 24: 1–2.

Asch, Michael 1984. *Home and Native Land: Aboriginal Rights and the Canadian Constitution.* Toronto: Methuen Publications.

Atchley, R. 1985. *Social Forces and Aging.* Belmont, Calif.: Wadsworth Publishing.

1991. *Social Forces and Aging: An Introduction to Social Gerontology.* 6th ed. Belmont, Calif.: Wadsworth.

Avishai, Bernard 1985. *The Tragedy of Zionism: Revolution and Democracy in the Land of Israel.* New York: Farrar Straus Giroux.

Baer, Douglas, Edward Grabb, and William Johnston 1987. "Class, Crisis, and Political Ideology in Canada: Recent Trends." *Canadian Review of Sociology and Anthropology* 24(1): 1–22.

1990. "The Values of Canadians and Americans: A Critical Analysis and Reassessment." *Social Forces* 68(3): 693–713.

1992. Orientations to Elitism and Equality in Four English-Speaking Democracies. Paper presented to the Annual Meeting of the Canadian Sociology and Anthropology Association in Charlottetown, P.E.I.

1993. "National Culture, Regional Culture, and the Values of Americans and Canadians." *Canadian Review of Sociology and Anthropology* 30(1): 13–36.

Baker, Maureen 1985. "What Will Tomorrow Bring? A Study of Aspirations of Adolescent Women." Ottawa: Canadian Advisory Council on the Status of Women.

1990. "Introduction: Theories, Methods, and Concerns in Family Sociology." In *Families: Changing Trends in Canada,* 2nd ed., edited by Maureen Baker. Toronto: McGraw-Hill Ryerson.

Bakker, Isabella 1989. "The Political Economy of Gender." In *The New Canadian Political Economy,* edited by Wallace Clement and Glen Williams. Montreal: McGill-Queen's University Press.

Bandura, A. 1977. *Social Learning Theory.* Englewood Cliffs, N.J.: Prentice-Hall.

1986. *Social Foundations of Thought and Action: A Social Cognitive Theory.* Englewood Cliffs, N.J.: Prentice-Hall.

Barker, Eileen 1984. *The Making of a Moonie: Choice or Brainwashing?* London: Basil Blackwell.

Barley, Stephen R. 1986. "Technology as an Occasion for Structuring: Evidence from Observations of CT Scanners and the Social Order of Radiology Departments." *Administrative Science Quarterly* 31: 78–108.

Barnes, Gordon E., Leonard Greenwood, and Reena Sommer 1991. "Courtship Violence in a Canadian Sample of Male College Students." *Family Relations* 40: 37–44.

Baron, Robert, and Donn Byrne 1991. *Social Psychology: Understanding Human Interaction,* 6th ed. Needham Heights, Mass.: Allyn and Bacon.

Barrett, Stanley R. 1987. *Is God a Racist? The Right Wing in Canada.* Toronto: University of Toronto Press.

Barsky, Lesley 1992. "Our Families Come First: Why More Mothers Are Choosing to Stay at Home." *Chatelaine* February: 49–53, 102.

Basham, A.L. 1959 [1954]. *The Wonder that Was India.* Reprint. New York: Grove Press.

Beaujot, Roderich P. 1986. "Dwindling Families." *Policy Options* September: 3-7.

Beaujot, Roderich, and Kevin McQuillan 1982. *Growth and Dualism: The Demographic Development of Canadian Society.* Toronto: Gage.

Becker, Howard S. 1963. *Outsiders: Studies in the Sociology of Deviance.* New York: Free Press.

Beckford, James A. 1975. *The Triumph of Prophecy: A Sociological Study of Jehovah's Witnesses.* Oxford: Basil Blackwell.

Bélanger, Yves, and Pierre Fournier 1987. *L'entreprise québécoise: Développement historique et dynamique contemporaine.* Ville de La Salle: Hurtubise-HMH.

Bell, Catherine 1992. *Ritual Theory, Ritual Practice.* New York: Oxford.

Bell, Daniel 1973. *The Coming of Post-Industrial Society: A Venture in Social Forecasting.* New York: Basic Books.

Bell, Edward 1989. "The Petite Bourgeoisie and Social Credit: A Reconsideration." *Canadian Journal of Sociology* 14(1): 45–65.

1990. "Class Voting in the First Alberta Social Credit Election." *Canadian Journal of Political Science* 23(3): 519–30.

Bella, Leslie 1992. *The Christmas Imperative: Leisure, Family and Women's Work.* Halifax: Fernwood.

Bellah, Robert N. 1967. "Civil Religion in America." *Daedalus* 96: 1-18.

Bellah, Robert N., and Phillip E. Hammond 1980. *Varieties of Civil Religion.* New York: Harper and Row.

Belsky, Jay, M. Lang, and M. Rovine 1985. "Stability and Change in Marriage across the Transition to Parenthood: A Second Study." *Journal of Marriage and the Family* 47: 855–65.

Belsky, Jay, and Michael Rovine 1990. "Patterns of Marital Change across the Transition to Parenthood: Pregnancy to Three Years Postpartum." *Journal of Marriage and the Family* 52: 5–19.

Benokraitis, Nijole V. 1993. *Marriages and Families: Changes, Choices, and Constraints.* Englewood Cliffs, N.J.: Prentice-Hall.

Bercuson, David, and Douglas Wertheimer 1985. *A Trust Betrayed: The Keegstra Affair.* Toronto: Doubleday Canada.

Berger, J., B.P. Cohen, and M. Zelditch, Jr. 1972. "Status Characteristics and Social Interaction." *American Sociological Review* 37: 241–55.

Berger, John 1972. *Ways of Seeing.* Harmondsworth, England: Penguin.

Berger, Peter 1963. *Invitation to Sociology: A Humanistic Perspective.* New York: Doubleday.

Bernstein, Basil 1977. *Class, Codes and Control,* Vol. 3. London: Routledge & Kegan Paul.

Betcherman, Gordon, and Kathryn McMullen 1986. *Working with Technology: A Survey of Automation in Canada.* Ottawa: Economic Council of Canada.

Bibby, Reginald 1983. "Religionless Christianity: A Profile of Religion in the Canadian 80s." *Social Indica-*

tors Research 13: 1–16.

1987. *Fragmented Gods.* Toronto: Irwin.

Bibby, Reginald W., and Merlin B. Brinkerhoff 1973. "The Circulation of the Saints: A Study of People Who Join Conservative Churches." *Journal for the Scientific Study of Religion* 12: 273–83.

Bibby, Reginald W., and Donald C. Posterski 1985. *The Emerging Generation: An Inside Look at Canada's Teenagers.* Toronto: Irwin.

1992. *Teen Trends: A Nation in Motion.* Toronto: Stoddart.

Bienvenue, R.M., and A.H. Latif 1974. "Arrests, Disposition and Recidivism: A Comparison of Indians and Whites." *Canadian Journal of Criminology and Corrections* 16: 105–16.

Billings, Dwight B. 1992. "Critical Theory." In *Encyclopedia of Sociology,* edited by Edgar Borgatta and Marie Borgatta. New York: Macmillan.

Blackburn, R.M., and M. Mann 1979. *The Working Class in the Labour Market.* London: Macmillan.

Blair, Sampson L., and Daniel T. Lichter 1991. "Measuring the Division of Labor: Gender Segregation of Housework among American Couples." *Journal of Family Issues* 12: 91–113.

Blankenhorn, D., S. Bayme, and J. Elshtain, eds. 1991. *Rebuilding the Nest: A New Commitment to the American Family.* Milwaukee: Family Service America.

Blau, J.R., and P.M. Blau 1982. "The Cost of Inequality." *American Sociological Review* 47: 114–29.

Blau, P.M. 1964. *Exchange and Power in Social Life.* New York: Wiley.

Blau, Peter M., and Otis Dudley Duncan 1967. *The American Occupational Structure.* New York: John Wiley and Sons.

Blishen, B.R., and H.A. McRoberts 1976. "A Revised Socioeconomic Index for Occupations in Canada." *Canadian Review of Sociology and Anthropology* 13: 71–79.

Bluebond-Langner, M. 1978 *The Private Worlds of Dying Children.* Princeton: Princeton University Press.

Bluestone, Barry, and Bennett Harrison 1982. *The Deindustrialization of America.* New York: Basic Books.

Blumer, Herbert 1951. "Collective Behavior." In *Principles of Sociology,* edited by A.M. Lee. New York: Barnes and Noble.

Blumstein, Philip, and Pepper Schwartz 1983. *American Couples: Money/Work/Sex.* New York: William Morrow.

Blumstock, Robert 1993. "Ideology, Civil Religion and Generational Interests." In *The Sociology of Religion: A Canadian Focus,* edited by Ted Hewitt. New York: Butterworths, 173–91.

Bly, Robert 1990. *Iron John: A Book about Men.* Reading, Mass.: Addison-Wesley.

Bogardus, Emory S. 1925. "Measuring Social Distance." *Journal of Applied Sociology* 9: 299–308.

1959. *Social Distance.* Yellow Spring, Ohio: Antioch Press.

Boismenu, Gérard, and Daniel Drache, eds. 1990. *Politique et régulation: Modèle de développement et trajectoire canadienne.* Montreal and Paris: Editions Méridien and Editions L'Harmattan.

Bose, Abinash Chandra 1966. *Hymns from the Vedas.* Bombay: Asia Publishing House.

Boserup, Ester 1965. *The Conditions of Agricultural Growth.* Chicago: Aldine Press.

Botting, Heather, and Gary Botting 1984. *The Orwellian World of Jehovah's Witnesses.* Toronto: University of Toronto Press.

Bottomore, Tom 1984. *The Frankfurt School.* Chichester, England: Ellis Horwood.

Bourdieu, Pierre 1984. *Distinction: A Social Critique of the Judgement of Taste,* translated by Richard Nice. Cambridge, Mass: Harvard University Press.

Bourdieu, P., and J.C. Passeron 1977. *Reproduction in Education, Society and Culture.* London: Sage.

Bouvier, Leon F. 1980. "America's Baby Boom Generation: The Fateful Bulge." *Population Bulletin* 35(1).

Bowker, John 1970. *Problems of Suffering in Religions of the World.* Cambridge: Cambridge University Press.

Bowlby, John 1982. *Attachment and Loss,* 2nd ed., Vol 1. New York: Basic Books.

Bowles, S., and H. Gintis 1976. *Schooling in Capitalist America.* New York: Basic Books.

1986. *Democracy and Capitalism.* New York: Basic Books.

Box, S., and C. Hale 1983. "Liberation and Female Criminality in England and Wales." *British Journal of Criminology* 23: 35–49.

Boyd, Monica 1988. "Changing Canadian Family Forms: Issues for Women." In *Reconstructing the Canadian Family: Feminist Perspectives,* edited by Nancy Mandell and Ann Duffy. Toronto: Butterworths, 85–110.

1990. "Sex Differences in Occupational Skill: Canada, 1961–1986." *Canadian Review of Sociology and Anthropology* 27: 285–315.

Boyd, M., J. Goyder, F. Jones, H. McRoberts, P. Pineo, and J. Porter 1985. *Ascription and Achievement: Studies in Mobility and Status Attainment in Canada.* Ottawa: Carleton University Press.

Bozinoff, L., and A. Turcotte 1992. "Majority of Canadians Continue to Support Legalized Euthanasia." *The Gallup Report.* November 23.

Bradley, Harriet 1989. *Men's Work, Women's Work: A Sociological History of the Sexual Division of Labour in Employment.* Cambridge, England: Polity Press.

Braithwaite, John 1979. *Inequality, Crime and Public Policy.* London: Routledge & Kegan Paul.

1989. *Crime, Shame, and Reintegration.* Cambridge: Cambridge University Press.

Braverman, Harry 1974. *Labor and Monopoly Capital.* New York: Monthly Review Press.

Breton, Raymond 1964. "Institutional Completeness of Ethnic Communities and the Personal Relations of Immigrants." *American Journal of Sociology* 70: 193–205.

1988. "Ethnic and Race Relations." In *The Canadian*

Encyclopedia, Vol. 2. Edmonton: Hurtig Publishers.

Breton, Raymond, Jeffrey G. Reitz, and Victor Valentine 1980. *Cultural Boundaries and the Cohesion of Canada.* Montreal: The Institute for Research on Public Policy.

Brinkerhoff, Merlin B., and Eugen Lupri 1988. "Interspousal Violence." *Canadian Journal of Sociology* 13(4): 407–34.

Brod, Harry, ed. 1987. *The Making of Masculinities: The New Men's Studies.* Boston: Allen & Unwin.

——— 1989. "Fraternity, Equality, Liberty." In *Men's Lives,* edited by Michael S. Kimmel and Michael A. Messner. New York: Macmillan.

Brodie, Janine 1990. *The Political Economy of Canadian Regionalism.* Toronto: Harcourt Brace Jovanovich, Canada.

Bromley, David G., and Anson D. Shupe, Jr. 1979. *"Moonies" in America: Cult, Church, and Crusade.* Beverly Hills, Calif.: Sage Publications.

Brooks, Stephen, and Alain G. Gagnon 1988. *Social Scientists and Politics in Canada.* Kingston and Montreal: McGill-Queen's University Press.

Brown, David, and Charles Hobart 1988. "Effects of Prior Marriage Children on Adjustment in Remarriage: A Canadian Study." *Journal of Comparative Family Studies* 19: 381–96.

Brown, David, and Russell Hogg 1992. "Essentialism, Radical Criminology, and Left Realism." *Australian and New Zealand Journal of Criminology* 25: 195–230.

Brown, E.R. 1979. *Rockefeller Medicine Men: Medicine and Capitalism in America.* Berkeley: University of California Press.

Brown, Roger 1954. "Mass Phenomena." In *Handbook of Social Psychology,* edited by G. Lindzey, Vol. 2. Cambridge, Mass.: Addison-Wesley, 833–76.

Bryant, Heather 1990. *The Infertility Dilemma: Reproductive Technologies and Prevention.* Ottawa: Canadian Advisory Council on the Status of Women.

Brym, Robert J. 1985a. "The Canadian Capitalist Class, 1965–1985." In *The Structure of the Canadian Capitalist Class,* edited by Robert J. Brym. Toronto: Garamond Press, 1–20.

——— ed. 1985b. *Regionalism in Canada.* Toronto: Irwin.

——— 1989. "Canada." In *The Capitalist Class: An International Study,* edited by Tom Bottomore and Robert J. Brym. New York: Harvester Wheatsheaf, 177–206.

Brym, Robert J., and R. James Sacouman 1979. *Underdevelopment and Social Movements in Atlantic Canada.* Toronto: New Hogtown Press.

Brym, Robert J., with Bonnie J. Fox 1989. *From Culture to Power: The Sociology of English Canada.* Toronto: Oxford University Press.

Burch, Thomas K., and Ashok K. Madan 1986. *Union Formation and Dissolution.* 1984 Family History Survey. Ottawa: Housing, Family and Social Statistics Division, Statistics Canada, Catalogue no. 99-963, November.

Burgess, Robert G. 1984. *In the Field: An Introduction to Field Resarch.* London: Unwin Hyman.

Burgess, Robert L., and Ronald L. Akers 1966. "A Differential Association-Reinforcement Theory of Criminal Behavior." *Social Problems* 14: 128–47.

Burke, Mary Anne, Susan Crompton, Allison Jones, and Katherine Nessner 1991. "Caring for Children." *Canadian Social Trends* Autumn: 12–15.

Burr, Wesley R., Geoffrey K. Leigh, Randall D. Day, and John Constantine 1979. "Symbolic Interaction and the Family." In *Contemporary Theories about the Family,* Vol. 2, edited by Wesley R. Burr, Reuben Hill, F. Ivan Nye, Ira L. Reiss. New York: Free Press.

Burstein, M., N. Tienharra, P. Hewson, and B. Warrander 1975. *Canadian Work Values: Findings of a Work Ethic Survey and a Job Satisfaction Survey.* Ottawa: Information Canada.

Byrne, D. 1971. *The Attraction Paradigm.* New York: Academic Press.

Cairns, Alan 1991. "Constitutional Change and the Three Equalities." In *Options for a New Canada.* Toronto: University of Toronto Press, 97–100.

Cairns, Alan, and Cynthia Williams, eds. 1985. *Constitutionalism, Citizenship and Society in Canada.* Toronto: University of Toronto Press,.

Caldwell, John C. 1982. *Theory of Fertility Decline.* London: Academic Press.

Caldwell, John C., and Pat Caldwell 1990. "High Fertility in Sub-Saharan Africa." *Scientific American* May: 118–25.

Canada 1980. *Indian Conditions.* Ottawa: Ministry of Indian Affairs and Northern Development.

——— 1992. *A Matter of Fairness.* Report of the Social Committee on the Review of the Employment Equity Act. Ottawa: House of Commons.

Canada Employment and Immigration Advisory Council 1991. *Immigration in the 1990's.* March.

Canadian Advisory Council on the Status of Women 1991. *Brief to the Royal Commission on New Reproductive Technologies.* March, no. 91-L-174. Ottawa.

Canadian Centre for Justice Statistics 1988. *Relative Trends: Microcomputer Application and Database.* Ottawa: Statistics Canada.

——— 1989. *Relative Trends: A Statistical Package for Generating Crime Trends.* Ottawa: Statistics Canada.

——— 1990. "The Future of Crime Statistics from the UCR Survey." *Juristat* 10(10).

——— 1992. *Canadian Crime Statistics, 1991.* Catalogue no. 85-205. Ottawa: Minister of Industry Science and Technology.

Canadian Parliamentary Guide 1990. *Canadian Parliamentary Guide.* Toronto: Info Globe.

Canadian Sociology and Anthropology Association 1992 [1985]. "Code of Professional Ethics." *Society: Newsletter of the Canadian Sociology and Anthropology Association* 16(3): 13–19.

Carr, Lowell J. 1948. *Situational Analysis: An Observational Approach to Introductory Sociology.* New York: Harper and Brothers Publishers.

Carreiro, D. 1990. "Violence Haunted Slain Woman's Life." *Winnipeg Sun* August 2: 3.

Carroll, William 1985. "Dependency, Imperialism and the

Capitalist Class in Canada." In *The Structure of the Canadian Capitalist Class,* edited by R. Brym. Toronto: Garamond Press.

— 1986. *Corporate Power and Canadian Capitalism.* Vancouver: University of British Columbia Press.

Cartwright, Robert H., and Stephen A. Kent 1992. "Social Control in Alternative Religions: A Familial Perspective." *Sociological Analysis* 53(4): 345–61.

Cawsey, A. 1991a. Task Force on the Criminal Justice System and Its Impact on the Indian and Metis People of Alberta. *Justice on Trial,* Vol. 1. Main Report. Edmonton: The Task Force.

— 1991b. Task Force on the Criminal Justice System and Its Impact on the Indian and Metis People of Alberta. *Justice on Trial,* Vol. 3. Working Papers and Bibliography. Edmonton: The Task Force.

Cernetig, Miro 1991. "Pirate Stations Spread the Gospel." *The Globe and Mail* October 8: A1, A7.

Chadwick-Jones, J.K. 1976. *Social Exchange Theory.* New York: Academic Press.

Chambers, Marcia 1982. "Moon on Stand, Tells of His Religious Beliefs." *New York Times* May 28: A1.

Chambliss, William J. 1976. "Functional and Conflict Theories of Crime: The Heritage of Emile Durkheim and Karl Marx." In *Whose Law? What Order?* edited by W.J. Chambliss and M. Mankoff. New York: John Wiley and Sons.

Chambliss, W.J., and M. Mankoff, eds. 1976. *Whose Law? What Order?* New York: John Wiley and Sons.

Chandler, Alfred D., Jr. 1977. *The Visible Hand: The Managerial Revolution in American Business.* Cambridge, Mass.: Harvard University Press.

Chapin, Vincent J. 1990. *Work Life and Personal Needs: The Job-Sharing Option: A Background Paper.* Ottawa: Labour Canada (Women's Bureau).

Chappell, Neena L., Laurel A. Strain, and Audrey A. Blandford 1986. *Aging and Health Care: A Social Perspective.* Toronto: Holt, Rinehart and Winston.

Charon, Joel M. 1985. *Symbolic Interactionism,* 2nd ed. Englewood Cliffs, N.J.: Prentice-Hall.

Check, James P., and Victoria Lacrosse 1988. "Attitudes and Behaviour Regarding Pornography, Sexual Coercion and Violence in Metropolitan Toronto High School Students." Toronto: LaMarsh Research Programme Reports on Violence and Conflict Resolution.

Chen, L.C., E. Huq, and S. D'Souza 1981. "Sex Bias in the Family Allocation of Food and Health Care in Rural Bangladesh." *Population and Development Review* 7(1): 55–70.

Cherlin, Andrew 1979. "Remarriage as an Incomplete Institution." *American Journal of Sociology* 84: 634–50.

Chesney-Lind, Meda 1986. "Women and Crime: The Female Offender." *Signs: Journal of Women in Culture and Society* 12: 78–96.

— 1989. "Girls' Crime and Women's Place: Toward a Feminist Model of Female Delinquency." *Crime and Delinquency* 35: 5–29.

Chodorow, Nancy 1989. *Feminism and Psychoanalytic Theory.* New Haven: Yale University Press.

Chunn, Dorothy E., and Shelley A.M. Gavigan 1991. "Women and Crime in Canada." In *Canadian Criminology: Perspectives on Crime and Criminality,* edited by Margaret Jackson and Curt Griffiths. Toronto: Harcourt Brace Jovanovich Canada.

Clairmont, Donald, R. Apostle, and R. Kreckel 1983. "A Segmentation Perspective as a Middle-Range Conceptualization in Sociology." *Canadian Journal of Sociology* 8: 245–71.

Clark, S.D. 1948. *Church and Sect in Canada.* Toronto: University of Toronto Press.

— 1962. *The Developing Canadian Community.* Toronto: University of Toronto Press.

Clark, Samuel, J. Paul Grayson, and Linda M. Grayson, eds. 1975. *Prophecy and Protest: Social Movements in Twentieth Century Canada.* Toronto: Gage.

Clemenson, Heather A. 1989. "Unionization and Women in the Service Sector." *Perspectives on Labour and Income* Autumn. Ottawa: Statistics Canada.

Clement, Wallace 1975. *The Canadian Corporate Elite. An Analysis of Economic Power.* Toronto: McClelland and Stewart.

— 1977. *Continental Corporate Power: Economic Elite Linkages between Canada and the United States.* Toronto: McClelland and Stewart.

— 1983. *Class, Power and Property.* Toronto: Methuen.

— 1988. *The Challenge of Class Analysis.* Ottawa: Carleton University Press.

Clement, Wallace and Glen Williams 1989. "Introduction." In *The New Political Economy,* edited by W. Clement and G. Williams. Montreal: McGill-Queen's University Press.

Cloward, Richard 1959. "Illegitimate Means, Anomie, and Deviant Behaviour." *American Sociological Review* 24 (April): 164–76.

Cloward, R., and L. Ohlin 1961. *Delinquency and Opportunity.* New York: The Free Press.

Coale, Ansley J. 1974. "The History of the Human Population." In *Scientific American, The Human Population.* San Francisco: W.H. Freeman and Company, 15–28.

— 1983. "Recent Trends of Fertility in Less Developed Countries." *Science* 221: 828–32.

Coates, Mary Lou, David Arrowsmith, and Melanie Courchene 1989 *The Current Industrial Relations Scene in Canada 1989: The Labour Movement and Trade Unionism Reference Tables.* Kingston, Ont.: Industrial Relations Centre, Queen's University.

Cockerham, W.C. 1991. *This Aging Society.* Englewood Cliffs, N.J.: Prentice-Hall.

— 1992. *Medical Sociology,* 4th ed. Englewood Cliffs, N.J.: Prentice-Hall.

Cohen, Albert 1955. *Delinquent Boys: The Culture of the Gang.* Glencoe, Ill.: Free Press.

Cohen, L.E., and M. Felson 1979. "Social Change and Crime Rate Trends: A Routine Activity Approach." *American Sociological Review* 44(4): 588–608.

Cohen, Marjorie 1987. *Free Trade and the Future of Women's Work: Manufacturing and Service Industries.*

Toronto: Garamond Press and the Canadian Centre for Policy Alternatives.

———. 1988. *Women's Work, Markets, and Economic Development in Nineteenth-Century Ontario.* Toronto: University of Toronto Press.

Cohn, Norman 1976 [1957]. *Pursuit of the Millennium.* Revised and enlarged, 1970. Reprint, New York: Oxford University Press.

Coleman, William D. 1989. "The Political Economy of Quebec." In *The New Canadian Political Economy,* edited by Wallace Clement and Glen Williams. Toronto: McGill-Queen's University Press, 160–79.

Collins, Randall 1977. "Functional and Conflict Theories of Educational Stratification." In *Power and Ideology in Education,* edited by J. Karabel and A.H. Halsey. New York: Oxford University Press, 118–36.

———. 1988. *Theoretical Sociology.* New York: Harcourt Brace Jovanovich.

———. 1992. "Conflict Theory." In *Encyclopedia of Sociology*, edited by Edgar Borgatta and Marie Borgatta. New York: Macmillan.

Collins, Randall, and Michael Makowsky 1989. *The Discovery of Society*, 4th ed. New York: Random House.

Conway, John F. 1990. *The Canadian Family in Crisis.* Toronto: James Lorimer.

Cook, Judith A., and Mary Margaret Fonow 1990. "Knowledge and Women's Interests: Issues of Epistemology and Methodology in Feminist Sociological Research." In *Feminist Research Methods,* edited by Joyce McCarl Nielson. Boulder: Westview Press.

Cook, Shirley 1969. "Canadian Narcotics Legislation, 1908-1923: A Conflict Model Interpretation." *Canadian Review of Sociology and Anthropology* 6(1): 36–46.

Cooley, Charles H. 1909. *Social Organization.* New York: Scribner.

———. 1964 [1902]. *Human Nature and the Social Order.* Reprint, New York: Schocken Books.

Copeland, Lewis, and Lawrence W. Lamm, eds. 1973. *The World's Great Speeches,* 3rd ed. New York: Dover.

Corea, Gena 1985. *The Mother Machine: Reproductive Technologies from Artificial Insemination to Artificial Wombs.* New York: Harper and Row.

———. 1991. "How the New Reproductive Technologies Will Affect All Women." In *Reconstructing Babylon: Essays on Women and Technology,* edited by H. Patricia Hynes. Bloomington and Indianapolis: Indiana University Press, 41–60.

Coser, Lewis A. 1977. *Masters of Sociological Thought: Ideas in Historical and Social Context.* New York: Harcourt Brace Jovanovich.

Couture, Claude, and Claude Denis 1994. "La captation du couple tradition-modernité par la sociographie québécoise." In *Canada: Discours theoriques/Theoretical Discourse,* edited by Terry Goldie, Carmen Lambert, and Rowland Lorimer. Montreal: Association for Canadian Studies Association/Association d'études canadiennes.

Cowgill, Donald O., and L. Holmes 1972. *Aging and Modernization.* New York: Appleton-Century-Crofts.

Coxon, A.P.M., P.M. Davies, and C.L. Jones 1986. *Images of Social Stratification and Mobility.* London: Sage.

Craib, Ian 1992a. *Anthony Giddens.* London and New York: Routledge.

———. 1992b. *Modern Social Theory: From Parsons to Habermas,* 2nd ed. Brighton: Harvester Press.

Crothers, Charles 1987. *Robert K. Merton.* Chichester and London: Ellis Horwood/Tavistock.

Crouch, Colin 1982. *Trade Unions: The Logic of Collective Action.* Glasgow: Fontana.

Crysdale, Stewart 1976. "The Sociology of the Social Gospel: Quest for a Modern Ideology." In *Religion in Canadian Society,* edited by Stewart Crysdale and Les Wheatcroft. Toronto: Macmillan of Canada, 423–33.

Cuff, E.C., and G.C.F. Payne, eds. 1984. *Perspectives in Sociology.* London: Allen & Unwin.

Cumming, Elaine, and William N. Henry 1961. *Growing Old: The Process of Disengagement.* New York: Basic Books.

Cuneo, Carl J. 1979. "State, Class and Reserve Labour: The Case of the 1941 Canadian Unemployment Insurance Act." *Canadian Review of Sociology and Anthropology* 16(2): 147–70.

———. 1990. *Pay Equity: The Labour-Feminist Challenge.* Canada: Oxford University Press.

Cuneo, Michael W. 1989. *Catholics against the Church. Anti-Abortion Protest in Toronto, 1969-1985.* Toronto: University of Toronto Press.

Cunningham, J.B., and T. White, eds. 1984. *Quality of Working Life: Contemporary Cases.* Ottawa: Labour Canada.

Curtis, Bruce 1984. "Capitalist Development and Educational Reform." *Theory and Society* 13: 41–68.

Curtis, J.E., E. Grabb, N. Guppy, and S. Gilbert, eds. 1988. *Social Inequality in Canada.* Scarborough, Ont.: Prentice-Hall.

Cutler, Stephen J., and Jon Hendricks 1990. "Leisure and Time Use across the Life Course." In *Handbook of Aging and the Social Sciences,* 3rd ed., edited by Robert H. Binstock and Linda K. George. New York: Academic Press, 169–85.

Dahrendorf, Ralf 1959. *Class and Class Conflict in Industrial Society.* Stanford: Stanford University Press.

Dalton, Melville 1959. *Men Who Manage: Fusions of Feeling and Theory in Administration.* New York: John Wiley and Sons.

Darroch, G.A. 1979. "Another Look at Ethnicity, Stratification and Social Mobility in Canada." *Canadian Journal of Sociology* 4: 1–25.

Darwin, C. 1871. *The Descent of Man.* New York: Appleton.

Dashefsky, Arnold, and Howard M. Shapiro 1976. "Ethnicity and Identity." In *Ethnic Identity in Society*, edited by Arnold Dashefsky. Chicago: Rand McNally, 5–10.

Davis, Kingsley 1939. "Illegitimacy and Social Structure." *American Journal of Sociology* 43: 213–33.

———. 1949. *Human Society.* New York: Macmillan.

———. 1984. "Wives and Work: The Sex Role Revolution and Its Consequences." *Population and Development Review* 8(3): 495–511.

———. 1987. "Low Fertility in Evolutionary Perspective." In *Below Replacement Fertility in Industrial Societies,* edited by K. Davis, M.S. Bernstam, and R. Ricardo-

Campbell. Supplement to *Population and Development Review* 12: 48–65.

Davis, Kingsley, and Judith Blake 1955–56. "Social Structure and Fertility: An Analytic Framework." *Economic Development and Cultural Change* 4: 211–35.

Davis, Kingsley, and Wilbert E. Moore 1945. "Some Principles of Stratification." *American Sociological Review* 10: 242–49.

Davis, N.J., and C. Stasz 1990. *Social Control of Deviance: A Critical Perspective.* New York: McGraw-Hill.

de Beauvoir, Simone 1952. *The Second Sex,* translated by H.M. Parshley. New York: Alfred A. Knopf.

Defleur, Melvin, William V. D'Antonio, and Lois B. Defleur 1971. *Sociology.* Glenview, Ill.: Scott, Foreman and Company.

de Koninck, Maria 1991. "Double Work and Women's Health." In *Continuity and Change in Marriage and Family,* edited by Jean Veevers. Toronto: Holt, Rinehart and Winston of Canada.

de Vries, John 1988. "Canada's Population: Selected Aspects of Structure and Change." In *Social Issues: Sociological Views of Canada,* 2nd ed., edited by D. Forcese and S. Richer. Scarborough, Ont.: Prentice-Hall, 23–39.

Decker, S.H. 1983. "Comparing Victimization and Official Estimates of Crime: A Re-examination of the Validity of Police Statistics." *American Journal of Police* 2(2): 193–201.

Decore, A.M., and K.O. Ugbor 1991. "The Blocked Mobility Thesis Revisited." *Research Notes.* Edmonton: Department of Educational Foundations, University of Alberta.

Denis, Claude 1993. "Quebec-as-Distinct-Society as Conventional Wisdom: The Constitutional Silence of Anglo-Canadian Sociologists." *Canadian Journal of Sociology* 18(3): 251–69.

Denton, Frank T., Christine H. Feaver, and Byron G. Spencer 1986. "Prospective Aging of the Population and Its Implications for the Labour Force and Government Expenditures." *Canadian Journal on Aging* 5: 75–98.

Derksen, Linda, and John Gartrell 1993. "The Social Context of Recycling in Alberta." *American Sociological Review* 58(3): 434–42.

1992. "Scientific Explanation." In *Encyclopedia of Sociology,* edited by Edgar F. Borgatta and Marie L. Borgatta. New York: Macmillan.

Despelder, L., and A. Strickland 1992. *The Last Dance,* 3rd ed. Mountain View, Calif.: Mayfield Press.

Devereux, Edward C. 1970. "Socialization in Cross-Cultural Perspective: A Comparative Study of England, Germany, and the United States." In *Families in East and West: Socialization Process and Kinship Ties,* edited by Reuben Hill and René König. The Hague: Mouton.

Diamond, Milton 1982. "Sexual Identity: Monozygotic Twins Reared in Discordant Sex Roles and a BBC Follow-Up." *Archives of Sexual Behaviour* 11: 181–86.

Dominion Bureau of Statistics 1901–1911. *Census of Canada: The Marital Condition.* Ottawa: King's Printers.

1969. *Census of Canada, 1966.* Vol. 2, *Population: Households and Families.* Catalogue no. 93-612. Ottawa: Queen's Printers.

Donelson, A.C., P.J. Walsh, and G.C. Haas 1986. *Alcohol Use by Persons Fatally Injured in Motor Vehicle Accidents.* Ottawa, Ontario: Traffic Injury Research Foundation.

Donnerstein, E. 1980. "Aggressive Erotica and Violence against Women." *Journal of Personality and Social Psychology* 39: 269–77.

Doyle, James A. 1982. *The Male Experience,* 2nd ed. Dubuque, Iowa: Wm. C. Brown.

Drache, Daniel, and Meric S. Gertler 1991. *The New Era of Global Competition: State Policy and Market Power.* Montreal and Kingston: McGill-Queen's University Press.

Driedger, Leo 1989. *The Ethnic Factor: Identity in Diversity.* Toronto: McGraw-Hill Ryerson.

Driedger, Leo, and Neena L. Chappell 1987. *Aging and Ethnicity: Toward an Interface.* Toronto: Butterworths.

Dubos, R. 1968. *Determinants of Health and Disease in Man, Medicine and Environment.* New York: Frederick A. Praeger.

Dufour, Christian 1989. *Le défi québécois.* Montreal: L'Hexagone.

1992. *La rupture tranquille.* Montreal: Boréal.

Duke, Vic, and Stephen Edgell 1987. "The Operationalization of Class in British Sociology: Theoretical and Empirical Considerations." *The British Journal of Sociology* 38: 445–63.

Dumas, Jean 1987. *Report on the Demographic Situation in Canada 1986.* Ottawa: Minister of Supply and Services.

1990. *Report on the Demographic Situation in Canada 1990.* Ottawa: Minister of Supply and Services.

Durkheim, Emile 1965 [1912]. *Elementary Forms of the Religious Life,* translated by Joseph Ward Swain. New York: Free Press.

1947 [1933]. *The Division of Labor in Society,* translated by George Simpson. New York: Free Press.

1951 [1897]. *Suicide: A Study in Sociology,* translated by George Simpson. New York: Free Press.

1966 [1897]. *Suicide,* translated by John A. Spaulding and George Simpson, edited by George Simpson. New York: Free Press.

1966 [1938]. *The Rules of Sociological Method,* translated by Sarah A. Solovay and John H. Mueller, edited by George E.G. Catlin. New York: Free Press.

1983 [1964]. *The Division of Labor in Society.* New York: Free Press.

Dworkin, Andrea 1989. "Gynocide: Chinese Footbinding." In *Feminist Frontiers II,* edited by Laurel Richardson and Verta Taylor. New York: Random House, 15–24.

Dyer, E.D. 1963. "Parenthood as Crisis: A Re-study." *Marriage and Family Living* 25: 196–201.

Easterlin, Richard A. 1969. "Towards a Socioeconomic Theory of Fertility: A Survey of Recent Research on Economic Factors in American Fertility." In *Fertility and Family Planning: A World View,* edited by S.J. Berhman, L. Corsa, and R. Friedman. Ann Arbor: The

University of Michigan Press, 127–56.

1980. *Birth and Fortune: The Impact of Numbers on Personal Welfare*. New York: Basic Books.

Eck, J.E., and L.J. Riccio 1979. "Relationship between Reported Crime Rates and Victimization Survey Results: An Empirical and Analytic Study." *Journal of Criminal Justice* 7(4): 293–308.

Economic Council of Canada 1984. *Toward Equity: Proceedings of a Colloquium on the Economic Status of Women in the Labour Market,* November. Ottawa: Economic Council of Canada.

1987. *Innovation and Jobs in Canada*. Ottawa: Economic Council of Canada.

1990. *Good Jobs, Bad Jobs: Employment in the Service Economy: A Statement by the Economic Council of Canada* (Highlights). Ottawa: Economic Council of Canada.

1992. *A Lot to Learn: Education and Training in Canada*. Ottawa: Supply and Services Canada.

Edginton, B. 1989. *Health, Disease and Medicine in Canada: A Sociological Perspective*. Toronto: Butterworths.

The Edmonton Sun 1990. "More RCMP Changes." March 18: 16.

Ehrensaft, Philip, and Warwick Armstrong 1981. "The Formation of Dominion Capitalism: Economic Truncation and Class Structure." In *Inequality: Essays on the Political Economy of Social Welfare,* edited by A. Moscovitch and G. Drover. Toronto: University of Toronto Press.

Ehrich, C. 1971. "The Male Sociologist's Burden: The Place of Women in Marriage and Family Texts." *Journal of Marriage and the Family* 33(3): 421–30.

Eichler, Margrit 1988a. *Families in Canada Today: Recent Changes in Their Policy Consequences*, 2nd ed. Toronto: Gage.

1988b. *Nonsexist Research Methods: A Practical Guide*. Boston: Allen & Unwin.

Eldridge, John 1983. *C. Wright Mills*. London and New York: Ellis Horwood/Tavistock.

Eliade, Mircea 1958. *Rites and Symbols of Initiation*. New York: Harper and Row.

Elliott, David 1988. "Aberhart, William." In *The Canadian Encyclopedia*. 2nd ed. Edmonton: Hurtig Publishers.

Elliott, David R., and Iris Miller 1987. *Bible Bill: A Biography of William Aberhart*. Edmonton: Reidmore Books.

Elliott, D.S., and S. Ageton 1980. "Reconciling Differences in Estimates of Delinquency." *American Sociological Review* 45: 95–110.

Emerson, R.M. 1974a. "Exchange Theory Part I: A Psychological Basis for Social Exchange." In *Sociological Theories in Progress,* Vol. 2, edited by J. Berger, M. Zelditch, Jr., and B. Anderson. New York: Houghton Mifflin.

1974b. "Exchange Theory Part II: Exchange Relations and Network Structures." In *Sociological Theories in Progress,* Vol. 2, edited by J. Berger, M. Zelditch, Jr., and B. Anderson. New York: Houghton Mifflin.

1981. "Social Exchange Theory." In *Social Psychology: Sociological Perspectives*, edited by M. Rosenberg, and R.H. Turner. New York: Basic Books.

1983. *Contemporary Field Research: A Collection of Readings*. Boston: Little, Brown.

Empey, L. 1982. *American Delinquency*. Homewood, Ill.: Dorsey Press.

Employment and Immigration Canada 1989. "Immigration to Canada: A Statistical Overview." Ottawa: Public Affairs and the Immigration Policy Branch, 10–11.

1990. *1990 Annual Report, Employment Equity Act*. Ottawa: Supply and Services Canada.

Enstrom, J. 1989. "Health Practices and Cancer Mortality among Active California Mormons." *Journal of the National Cancer Institute* 81(23): 807–14.

Erasmus, Georges, and Jo Sanders 1992. "Canadian History: An Aboriginal Perspective." In *Nation to Nation: Aboriginal Sovereignty and the Future of Canada*, edited by Diane Engelstad and John Bird. Concord, Ont.: Anansi Press.

Ericson, Richard V. 1981. *Making Crime: A Study of Detective Work*. Toronto: Butterworth and Co. Canada.

Eshleman, J. Ross 1991. *The Family*. Boston: Allyn and Bacon.

Esping-Andersen, Gøsta 1985. *Politics against Markets*. Princeton: Princeton University Press.

1990. *The Three Worlds of Welfare Capitalism*. Cambridge, England: Polity Press.

Farley, John E. 1988. *Majority Minority Relations,* 2nd. ed. Englewood Cliffs, N.J.: Prentice-Hall.

Farrington, Keith, and Ely Chertok 1993. "Social Conflict Theories of the Family." In *Sourcebook of Family Theories and Methods: A Contextual Approach,* edited by Pauline G. Boss, William G. Doherty, Ralph LaRossa, Walter R. Schumm, and Suzanne K. Steinmetz. New York: Plenum Press.

Fasteau, M. 1974. *The Male Machine*. New York: McGraw-Hill.

Fengler, A.P., and N. Goodrich 1979. "Wives of Elderly Disabled Men: The Hidden Patients." *The Gerontologist* 19: 175–83.

Festinger, L. 1957. *A Theory of Cognitive Dissonance*. Evanston, Ill.: Row, Peterson.

Fiebert, M. 1987. "Some Perspectives on the Men's Movement." *Men's Studies Review* 4(4): 8–10.

Figgis, John Neville 1965 [1914]. *The Divine Right of Kings*, 2nd ed. Reprint, New York: Harper Torchbooks.

The Financial Post 1991. "The Top 500." Summer: 94–117.

Finkel, Alvin 1989. *The Social Credit Phenomenon in Alberta*. Toronto: University of Toronto Press.

Finlayson, Ann 1987. "A New Emphasis on the Family." *Maclean's* January 5: 71–2.

1988. *Whose Money Is It Anyway? The Showdown on Pensions*. Markham, Ont.: Viking/Penguin.

Finlayson, Judith 1989. "The Trouble with Superwoman." *Homemaker Magazine* (October): 42–52.

Finley, M.I. 1983. *Politics in the Ancient World*. Cambridge: Cambridge University Press.

Fischer, C.S. 1976. *The Urban Experience*. New York:

Harcourt Brace Jovanovich.

Flugel, J.C. 1930. *The Psychology of Clothes*. London: Leonard and Virginia Woolf.

Flynn, Clifton P. 1987. "Relationship Violence: A Model for Family Professionals." *Family Relations* 36: 295–99.

Forcese, Dennis 1986. *The Canadian Class Structure*. Toronto: McGraw-Hill Ryerson.

Foucault, Michel 1978. *The History of Sexuality*. Vol. 1, *An Introduction*. New York: Random House.

Fournier, Marcel 1986. *L'Entrée dans la modernité. Science, culture et société au Québec*. Montreal: Editions Saint-Martin.

Fox, Bonnie J. 1988. "Conceptualizing Patriarchy." *Canadian Review of Sociology and Anthropology* 25(2): 163–82.

Fox, J., and T.F. Hartnagel 1979. "Changing Social Roles and Female Crime in Canada." *Canadian Review of Sociology and Anthropology* 16: 96–104.

Francis, Daniel 1992. *The Imaginary Indian: The Image of the Indian in Canadian Culture*. Vancouver: Arsenal Pulp Press.

Frank, Andre Gunder 1967. *Capitalism and Underdevelopment in Latin America*. New York: Monthly Review Press.

——— 1969. *Latin America: Underdevelopment or Revolution*. Harmondsworth, England: Penguin.

Franklin, Clyde W., II 1982. *Theoretical Perspectives in Social Psychology*. Boston: Little, Brown and Co.

Freeman, R.B., and J.L. Medoff 1984. *What Do Unions Do?* New York: Basic Books.

Freidson, E. 1984. "The Changing Nature of Professional Control." *Annual Review of Sociology* 10: 1–20.

Freud, Sigmund 1922. *Group Psychology and the Analysis of the Ego*, translated by J. Strachey. London: The Hogarth Press.

Frideres, James S. 1988. *Native Peoples in Canada: Contemporary Conflicts*, 3rd ed. Scarborough, Ont.: Prentice-Hall Canada.

Friedman, A.L. 1977. *Industry and Labour: Class Struggle at Work and Monopoly Capitalism*. London: Macmillan.

Friedman, M., and R.H. Rosenman 1974. *Type A Behavior and Your Heart*. New York: Alfred A. Knopf.

Friedman, Robert I. 1990. "Making Way for the Messiah." *New York Review of Books* October 11: 41–47.

Fries, James F. 1980. "Aging, Natural Death and the Compression of Morbidity." *New England Journal of Medicine* 30: 130–35.

Frisby, David, and Derek Sayer 1986. *Society*. Chichester, London, and New York: Ellis Horwood/Tavistock.

Fromm, Erich 1951. *The Forgotten Language*. New York: Rinehart.

Fry, Christine L. 1985. "Culture, Behavior and Aging in Comparative Perspective." In *Handbook of Psychology of Aging*, 2nd ed., edited by J. Birren. New York: Van Nostrand-Reinhold, 216–44.

Fudge, Judy, and Harry Glasbeek 1992. "Alberta Nurses v. a Contemptuous Supreme Court of Canada." *Constitutional Forum* 4(1): 1–5.

Fullton, E. Kaye 1993. "Babies Having Babies." *Maclean's* February 22: 32–33.

Fulton, R. 1976. *Death, Grief and Bereavement: A Bibliography. 1845–1975*. New York: Arno Press.

Furstenberg, Frank F., and Andrew J. Cherlin 1991. *Divided Families: What Happens to Children when Parents Part?* Cambridge, Mass.: Harvard University Press.

Gagnon, Alain G., ed. 1984. *Quebec: State and Society*. Toronto: Methuen Publications.

Gagnon, Alain G., and A. Brian Tanguay, eds. 1989. *Canadian Parties in Transition: Discourse, Organization, Representation*. Scarborough, Ont.: Nelson Canada.

Garbarino, J.E. Guttman, and J. Seeley 1986. *The Psychologically Battered Child: Strategies for Identification, Assessment, and Intervention*. San Francisco: Jossey-Bass.

Gartrell, John W. 1977. "Status, Inequality and Innovation: The Green Revolution in Andhra Pradesh, India." *American Sociological Review* 42(2): 318–37.

——— 1986. Sarcee Health Needs Assessment, Final Report. Unpublished paper. The University of Alberta, Edmonton, Canada.

Gartrell, John W., and David C. Gartrell 1981. "Inequality within Rural Communities of India." *American Sociological Review* 46(6): 768–82.

Gavigan, S.A.M. 1983. "Women's Crime and Feminist Critiques." *Canadian Criminology Forum* 6(1): 75–90.

Gecas, Viktor, and Monica A. Seff 1990. "Families and Adolescents: A Review of the 1980's." *Journal of Marriage and the Family* 52: 941–58.

Gee, Ellen M., and Susan A. McDaniel 1992. "Social Policy for an Aging Canada." *Journal of Canadian Studies* 27(3).

Gelber, S.M. 1972. "The Underemployed, Underpaid Third of the Labour Force." In *Women's Bureau, 1971*, S.M. Gelber. Ottawa: Information Canada.

Gelles, Richard J., and Claire P. Cornell 1987. "Adolescent-to-Parent Violence." In *Family Violence*, 2nd ed., Richard J. Gelles. Newbury Park: Sage.

Gelles, Richard J., and Murray A. Straus 1987. "Is Violence toward Children Increasing? A Comparison of 1975 and 1985 National Survey Rates." In *Family Violence*, 2nd ed., edited by Richard J. Gelles. Newbury Park: Sage.

Gerbner, George et al. 1986. "Living with Television: The Dynamics of the Cultivation Process." In *Perspectives on Media Effects*, edited by Jennings Bryant and Dolf Zillman. Hillsdale, N.J.: Lawrence Erlbaum, 17–40.

Gerth, Hans, and C.W. Mills 1953. *Character and Social Structure*. New York: Harcourt, Brace and Co.

Gibbs, Jack 1985. "The Methodology of Theory Construction in Criminology." In *Theoretical Methods in Criminology*, edited by R. Meier. Beverly Hills: Sage.

——— 1989. *Control: Sociology's Central Notion*. Urbana, Ill.: University of Illinois Press.

Giddens, Anthony 1971. *Capitalism and Modern Social Theory*. Cambridge: Cambridge University Press.

1984. *The Constitution of Society.* Cambridge, England: Polity Press.

Giffen, P.J. 1965. "Rates of Crime and Delinquency." In *Crime and Its Treatment in Canada,* edited by W.T. McGrath. Toronto: Macmillan.

1976. "Official Rates of Crime and Delinquency." In *Crime and Its Treatment in Canada*, 2nd ed., edited by W.T. McGrath. Toronto: Macmillan.

Gillespie, Marcia Ann 1993. "What Good for the Race?" *Ms.* January/February: 80–81.

Glaser, B.G., and A.L. Strauss 1965. *Awareness of Dying.* Chicago: Aldine Press.

Glenn, Norval D. 1991. "The Recent Trend in Marital Success in the United States." *Journal of Marriage and the Family* 53: 261–70.

Glenny, Misha 1992. *The Fall of Yugoslavia: The Third Balkan War.* London: Penguin.

1993. "What Is to Be Done?" *New York Review of Books* May 27: 14–16.

The Globe and Mail 1990. "Turbans in the RCMP, Kirpans in the Schools." Editorial. July 27: A16.

Glock, Charles Y. 1962. "On the Study of Religious Commitment." Research Supplement to *Religious Education* 57(4). Excerpt reprinted in "The Dimensions of Religious Commitment." In *Religion in Sociological Perspective: Essays in the Empirical Study of Religion*, edited by Charles Y. Glock. Belmont, Calif.: Wadsworth Publishing Company, 1973, 9–11.

1964. "The Role of Deprivation in the Origin and Evolution of Religious Groups." In *Religion and Social Conflict*, edited by Robert Lee and Martin E. Marty. New York: Oxford University Press, 24–36. Reprinted as "On the Origin and Evolution of Religious Groups." In *Religion in Sociological Perspective: Essays in the Empirical Study of Religion*, edited by Charles Y. Glock. Belmont, Calif.: Wadsworth Publishing Company, 1973, 207–20.

Godwin, Deborah D., and John Scanzoni 1989. "Couple Consensus during Marital Joint Decision-Making: A Context, Process, Outcome Model." *Journal of Marriage and the Family* 51: 943–56.

Goldscheider, Calvin 1971. *Population, Modernization, and Social Structure.* Boston: Little, Brown and Company.

Goldschmidt, Walter 1959. *Man's Way: A Preface to the Understanding of Human Society.* New York: Holt.

Goldstein, Walter 1992/93. "Europe after Maastricht." *Foreign Affairs* Winter: 117–32.

Gomme, I.M., M.E. Morton, and W.G. West 1984. "Rates, Types, and Patterns of Male and Female Delinquency in an Ontario Community." *Canadian Journal of Criminology* 26: 313–23.

Goode, Erich 1992. *Collective Behaviour.* Toronto: Harcourt Brace Jovanovich.

Goode, W.J. 1957. "Community within a Community." *American Sociological Review* 11: 194–200.

1960. "Encroachment, Charlatanism, and the Emerging Profession: Psychology, Sociology, and Medicine." *American Sociological Review* 25: 902–14.

Gordon, Milton M. 1964. *Assimilation in American Life.* New York: Oxford University Press.

Gorer, Geoffrey 1965. *Grief and Mourning in Contemporary Britain.* London: Cresset Press.

Gottfredson, Michael R., and Travis Hirschi 1990. *A General Theory of Crime.* Stanford: Stanford University Press.

Gottlieb, Robert, and Peter Wiley 1984. *America's Saints. The Rise of Mormon Power.* New York: G.P. Putnam's Sons.

Gough, E. Kathleen 1960. "Is the Family Universal: The Nayar Case." In *A Modern Introduction to the Family,* edited by Norman Bell and Ezra Vogel. New York: Free Press, 76–92.

Gove, Walter 1973. "Sex, Marital Status and Mortality." *American Journal of Sociology* 79: 45–67.

Grabb, Edward G. 1990. *Theories of Social Inequality.* Toronto: Holt, Rinehart and Winston.

Grabb, Edward G., and Ronald D. Lambert 1982. "The Subjective Meanings of Social Class among Canadians." *Canadian Journal of Sociology* 7(3): 297–307.

Gramsci, Antonio 1971. *Selections from the Prison Notebooks,* edited and translated by Quinton Hoare and Geoffrey Nowell Smith. New York: International Publishers.

Granatstein, Joel 1975. *Canada's War: The Politics of the Mackenzie King Government, 1939-1945.* Toronto: Oxford University Press.

Gray, Ann 1986. "Behind Closed Doors: Video Recorders in the Home." In *Boxed In: Women and Television,* edited by H. Baehr and G. Dyer. London: Pandora. As reported in *Television and Women's Culture: The Politics of the Population,* edited by Mary Ellen Brown. London: Sage, 1990.

Greeley, Andrew 1974. *Ecstasy: A Way of Knowing.* Englewood Cliffs, N.J.: Prentice-Hall.

Green, Melvyn 1979. "A History of Canadian Narcotics Control: The Formative Years." *University of Toronto Faculty of Law Review* 37: 42–79.

Greenaway, W.K. 1980. "Crime and Class: Unequal before the Law." In *Structured Inequality in Canada,* edited by J. Harp and J.R. Hofley. Scarborough, Ont.: Prentice-Hall, 247–65.

Greenberg, David 1977. "Delinquency and the Age Structure of Society." *Contemporary Crises* 1: 189–223.

1979. "Delinquency and the Age Structure of Society." In *Criminology Review Yearbook,* edited by S.L. Messinger and E. Bittner. Beverly Hills: Sage, 586–620.

1981. *Crime and Capitalism.* Palo Alto, Calif.: Mayfield.

Griffith, Janet D., and Helen P. Koo 1984. "Childlessness and Marital Stability in Remarriages." *Journal of Marriage and the Family* 46: 577–85.

Grindstaff, Carl F. 1975. "The Baby Bust: Changes in Fertility Patterns in Canada." *Canadian Studies in Population* 2:15–22.

1981. *Population and Society: A Sociological Perspective.* West Hanover, Mass.: The Christopher Publishing House.

1985. "The Baby Bust Revisited: Canada's Continuing

Pattern of Low Fertility." *Canadian Studies in Population* 12(1): 103–10.

Grindstaff, Carl F., T.R. Balakrishnan, and Paul S. Maxim 1989. "Life Course Alternatives: Factors Associated with Differential Timing Patterns in Fertility among Women Recently Completing Childbearing, Canada, 1981." *Canadian Journal of Sociology* 14: 443–59.

Grossberg, Lawrence, Cary Nelson, and Paula Treichler 1992. *Cultural Studies*. New York: Routledge.

Gruneau, Richard, ed. 1988. *Popular Cultures and Political Practices*. Toronto: Garamond Press.

Habermas, Jürgen 1975. *Legitimation Crisis*. Boston: Beacon.

Hackler, J.C., and K. Don 1990. "Estimating System Biases." *Canadian Journal of Criminology* 32: 243–64.

Hagan, John 1984. *The Disreputable Pleasures: Crime and Deviance in Canada*. Toronto: McGraw-Hill.

1985a. *Crime, Criminal Behavior, and Its Control*. New York: McGraw-Hill.

1985b. "Toward a Structural Theory of Crime, Race and Gender." *Crime and Delinquency* 31: 129–46.

Hagan, John, A.R. Gillis, and John Simpson 1985. "The Class Structure of Gender and Delinquency: Toward a Power-Control Theory of Common Delinquent Behavior." *American Journal of Sociology* 90: 1, 151, 178.

1987. "Class in the Household: A Power-Control Theory of Gender and Delinquency." *American Journal of Sociology* 92: 788–816.

Hagan, J., J. Simpson, and A.R. Gillis 1979. "The Sexual Stratification of Social Control." *British Journal of Sociology* 30: 25–38.

Halli, Shiva S., Frank Trovato, and Leo Driedger, eds. 1990. *Ethnic Demography: Canadian Immigrant, Racial and Cultural Variations*. Ottawa: Carleton University Press.

Halsey, A.H. 1980. "Social Mobility and Education." In *Education and Equality*, edited by David Rubinstein. London: Harper and Row, 44–55.

Hamilton, A.C., and C.M. Sinclair 1991. *The Justice System and Aboriginal People: Report of the Aboriginal Justice Inquiry of Manitoba*. Winnipeg: Queen's Printer.

Hamilton, Peter 1983. *Talcott Parsons*. Chichester, London, and New York: Ellis Horwood/Tavistock.

Hammer, Heather-Jo 1984. Mature Dependency: The Effects of American Direct Investment on Canadian Economic Growth. Ph.D. Dissertation. University of Alberta, Edmonton, Department of Sociology.

Hammer, Heather-Jo, and John W. Gartrell 1986. "American Penetration and Canadian Development: A Case Study of Mature Development." *American Sociological Review* 51(2): 201–13.

Hammersley, Martyn, and Paul Atkinson 1983. *Ethnography: Principles in Practice*. London: Tavistock.

Hampson, J.L., and J.G. Hampson 1961. "The Ontogenesis of Sexual Behavior in Man." In *Sex and Internal Secretions*. Vol. 2, edited by W.C. Yong. Baltimore: Williams and Wilkins, 1401–32.

Hanson, Eric O. 1987. *The Catholic Church in World Politics*. Princeton: Princeton University Press.

Happold, F.C. 1955. *Adventure in Search of a Creed*. London: Faber and Faber.

Haralambos, Michael 1980. *Sociology: Themes and Perspectives*. Slough, United Kingdom: University Tutorial Press.

Harrell, W. Andrew 1985. "Husband's Involvement in Housework: The Effects of Relative Earning Power and Masculine Orientation." *Edmonton Area Series Report No. 39*. Edmonton: Population Research Laboratory.

1990. "Husband's Masculinity, Wife's Power, and Marital Conflict." *Social Behavior and Personality* 18: 207–16.

Harries, K.D. 1974. *The Geography of Crime and Justice*. New York: McGraw-Hill.

Harris, Michael 1990. *Unholy Orders. Tragedy at Mount Cashel*. New York: Viking.

Harrison, Trevor 1993. Right-Wing Populism and the Reform Party of Canada. Ph.D. Dissertation. Department of Sociology, University of Alberta.

Hartnagel, T.F. 1978. "The Effect of Age and Sex Compositions of Provincial Populations on Provincial Crime Rates." *Canadian Journal of Criminology* 20: 28–33.

1987. "Correlates of Criminal Behaviour." In *Criminology: A Canadian Perspective*, edited by R. Linden. Toronto: Holt, Rinehart and Winston.

1989. Social Integration and Canadian Provincial Crime Rates. Discussion Paper, Centre for Criminological Research, Department of Sociology, University of Alberta, Edmonton.

Hartnagel, T.F., and G.W. Lee 1990. "Urban Crime in Canada." *Canadian Journal of Criminology* 32: 591–606.

Hatt, Ken 1985. "Ethnic Discourse in Alberta: Land and the Métis in the Ewing Commission." *Canadian Ethnic Studies* 17(2): 64–79.

Havemann, P., K. Couse, L. Foster, and R. Matonovich 1985. *Law and Order for Canada's Indigenous People*. Regina, Sask.: Prairie Justice Research, School of Human Justice, University of Regina.

Havighurst, Robert J., Bernice L. Neugarten, and Sheldon S. Tobin 1968. "Disengagement and Patterns of Aging." In *Middle Age and Aging*, edited by Bernice L. Neugarten. Chicago: University of Chicago Press, 161–72.

Hawkins, Freda 1988. *Canada and Immigration*, 2nd ed. Kingston: McGill-Queen's University Press.

Health and Welfare Canada 1987. *The Active Health Report: Perspectives on Canada's Health Promotion Survey 1985*. Ottawa: Minister of Supply and Services.

1988. *Canada's Health Promotion Survey: Technical Report*. Ottawa: Minister of Supply and Services.

1989a. *Alcohol in Canada*. Ottawa: Minister of Supply and Services.

1989b. *National Survey on Drinking and Driving: 1988*. Ottawa: Minister of Supply and Services.

1990. *National Health Expenditures in Canada, 1975–1987*. Ottawa: Minister of Supply and Services.

1991. *Canadians and Smoking: An Update*. Ottawa:

Minister of Supply and Services.

Hearn, J., and W. Parkin 1987. *'Sex' and 'Work': The Power and Paradox of Organisation Sexuality.* Britain: Wheatsheaf Books.

Heath, Anthony 1990. "The Sociology of Social Class." In *Biosocial Aspects of Social Class,* edited by C.G. Nicholas Mascie-Taylor. Oxford: Oxford University Press, 1–23.

Heaton, Tim B. 1991. "Religious Group Characteristics, Endogamy, and Interfaith Marriages." *Social Analysis* 51: 363–76.

Heidensohn, F. 1985. *Women and Crime.* Basingstoke, United Kingdom: Macmillan.

Heider, F. 1958. *The Psychology of Interpersonal Relations.* New York: Wiley.

Heilbroner, Robert L. 1963. *The Great Ascent: The Struggle for Economic Development in Our Time.* New York: Harper and Row.

Herberg, Edward N. 1989. *Ethnic Groups in Canada: Adaptations and Transitions.* Scarborough, Ont.: Nelson Canada.

Herold, Edward S. 1984. *Sexual Behaviour of Canadian Young People.* Markham, Ont.: Fitzhenry and Whiteside.

Herzberg, Frederick 1968. "One More Time: How Do You Motivate Employees?" *Harvard Business Review* 46: 53–62.

Hetherington, E. Mavis, and Kathleen A. Camera 1985. "Families in Transition: The Processes of Dissolution and Reconstitution." *Review of Child Development Research* 7: 398–439.

Hewitt, W.E. 1993. "The Quest for the Just Society: Canadian Catholicism in Transition." In *The Sociology of Religion: A Canadian Focus.* Toronto: Butterworths, 253–71.

Hiller, Harry H. 1982. *S.D. Clark and the Development of Canadian Sociology.* Toronto: University of Toronto Press.

Hinch, R. 1992. "Conflict and Marxist Theories." In *Criminology: A Canadian Perspective,* 2nd ed., edited by Rick Linden. Toronto: Harcourt Brace Jovanovich, 267–91.

Hindelang, M.J., T. Hirschi, and J.G. Weis 1979. "Correlates of Delinquency." *American Sociological Review* 44: 995–1014.

Hirschi, Travis 1969. *Causes of Delinquency.* Berkeley: University of California Press.

Hirschi, T., and M. Gottfredson 1983. "Age and the Explanation of Crime." *American Journal of Sociology* 89: 552–84.

Hirschi, Travis, and Rodney Stark 1969. "Hellfire and Delinquency." *Social Problems* 17.

Hobart, Charles 1989. "Experiences of Remarried Families." *Journal of Divorce* 13: 121–44.

1990. Premarital Sexual Standards among Canadian Students at the End of the Eighties. Unpublished manuscript, University of Alberta, Edmonton.

Hobart, Charles, and Frank Grigel 1990. Premarital Sex among Canadian Students at the End of the Eighties. Unpublished manuscript, University of Alberta, Edmonton.

1992. "Cohabitation among Canadian Students at the End of the Eighties." *Journal of Comparative Family Studies* 23: 311–37.

Hobsbawm, Eric J. 1959. *Social Bandits and Primitive Rebels.* New York: Free Press.

1990. *Nations and Nationalism since 1780: Programme, Myth, Reality.* Cambridge: Cambridge University Press.

Hochschild, Arlie 1976. "Disengagement Theory: A Critique and Proposal." *American Sociological Review* 40(5): 553–69.

1989. *The Second Shift: Working Parents and the Revolution at Home.* New York: Avon Books.

Hodson, Randy 1984. "Corporate Structure and Job Satisfaction: A Focus on Employer Characteristics." *Sociology and Social Research* 69: 22–49.

Hoffer, Eric 1951. *The True Believer.* New York: Harper and Brothers.

Hollister, Anne 1984. "From One Life to Two." *Life* October.

Holmes, T.H., and R.H. Rahe 1967. "The Social Readjustment Rating Scale." *Journal of Psychosomatic Research* 11: 213–25.

Homans, G.C. 1974. *Social Behavior: Its Elementary Forms,* 2nd ed. New York: Harcourt, Brace, and Jovanovich.

Horan, P.M. 1978. "Is Status Attainment Research Atheoretical?" *American Sociological Review* 43: 534–41.

Horowitz, Irving 1973. "The Hemispheric Connection: A Critique and Corrective to the Entrepeneurial Thesis of Development with Special Emphasis on the Canadian Case." *Queen's Quarterly* 80: 327–59.

Hostetler, John A. 1974. *Hutterite Society.* Baltimore: The Johns Hopkins University Press.

Hourani, Albert 1991. *A History of the Arab Peoples.* Cambridge, Mass.: Harvard University Press, Belknap Press.

Hubbard, Ruth 1983. "Have Only Men Evolved?" In *Discovering Reality: Feminist Perspectives on Epistemology, Metaphysics, Methodology, and the Philosophy of Science,* edited by S. Harding and M.B. Hintikka. Dordrecht, Holland: D. Reidel.

1990. *The Politics of Women's Biology.* New Brunswick, N.J.: Rutgers University Press.

Hughes, Karen D. 1989. "Office Automation: A Review of the Literature." *Relations industrielles/Industrial Relations* 44: 654–77.

1990. "Trading Places: Men and Women in Non-Traditional Occupations, 1971–86." *Perspectives on Labour and Income* Summer.

Humphreys, Laud 1975 [1970]. *Tearoom Trade: Impersonal Sex in Public Places.* Enlarged edition with a retrospect on ethical issues. New York: Free Press.

Hunsberger, Bruce 1980. "Problems and Promise in the Psychology of Religion: An Emerging Social Psychology of Religion?" *Canadian Journal of Behavioral Science* 12(1).

Hunter, Alfred A. 1986. *Class Tells: On Social Inequality in Canada,* 2nd ed. Toronto: Butterworths.

Hunter, Ross 1992. "Polygamy Law Is Unconstitutional."

Creston Valley Advocate [British Columbia]. June 15: 1, 8.

Ignatieff, Michael 1993. "The Balkan Tragedy." *New York Review of Books* May 13: 4–6.

Irving, Howard H. 1972. *The Family Myth*. Toronto: Copp Clark.

Irving, John A. 1959. *The Social Credit Movement in Alberta*. Toronto: University of Toronto Press.

Isajiw, Wsevolod W. 1974. "Definitions of Ethnicity." *Ethnicity* 1: 111–24.

Ismael, Jacqueline S., ed. 1985. *Canadian Social Welfare Policy: Federal and Provincial Dimensions*. Montreal: McGill-Queen's University Press.

James, J.T.L. 1979. "Toward a Cultural Understanding of the Native Offender." *Canadian Journal of Criminology* 21: 453–62.

James, William 1902. *The Varieties of Religious Experience*. Reprinted with revisions, 1910. London: Longmans, Green, and Co.

Jarvis, G.K. 1987a. *An Overview of Registered Indian Conditions in Alberta*. Ottawa: Indian and Northern Affairs Canada.

——— 1987b. *An Overview of Registered Indian Conditions in Saskatchewan*. Ottawa: Indian and Northern Affairs Canada.

——— 1988a. Alexander Health Survey: Final Report. Unpublished paper. The University of Alberta, Edmonton.

——— 1988b. Final Report: Kehewin Health Survey. Unpublished paper. The University of Alberta, Edmonton.

Jarvis, G.K., and M. Boldt 1982. "Death Styles among Canada's Indians." *Social Science and Medicine* 16: 1345–52.

Jary, David, and Julia Jary 1991. *Collins Dictionary of Sociology*. Glasgow: Harper Collins.

Jencks, Christopher, Susan Bartlett, Mary Corcoran, James Crouse, David Eaglesfield, Gregory Jackson, Kent McClelland, Peter Mueser, Michael Olneck, Joseph Schwartz, Sherry Ward, and Jill Williams 1979. *Who Gets Ahead?* New York: Basic Books.

Jenson, Jane 1989. "'Different' but Not 'Exceptional': Canada's Permeable Fordism." *Canadian Review of Sociology and Anthropology* 26(1): 69–94.

Johnson, H. 1986. *Women and Crime in Canada*. Ottawa: Solicitor General Canada.

——— 1987. "Getting the Facts Straight." In *Too Few To Count,* edited by E. Adelberg and C. Currie. Vancouver: Press Gang Publishers, 23–46.

——— 1988. "Violent Crime." *Canadian Social Trends* Summer: 25–29.

Johnston, W., and M. Ornstein 1985. "Social Class and Political Ideology in Canada." *Canadian Review of Sociology and Anthropology* 22(3): 369–93.

Jones, Frank E. 1985. "Educational and Occupational Attainment: Individual Achievement." In *Ascription and Achievement,* edited by M. Boyd, J. Goyder, F. Jones, H. McRoberts, P. Pineo, and J. Porter. Ottawa: Carleton University Press, 101–61.

Kaden, Joan, and Susan A. McDaniel 1990. "Caregiving and Carereceiving: A Double-Bind for Women in Canada's Aging Society." *Journal of Women and Aging* 2(3): 15–18.

Kaelble, H. 1981. *Historical Research in Social Mobility,* translated by Ingrid Noakes. London: Croom Helm.

Kahle, L.R. 1986. "The Nine Nations of North America and the Value Basis of Geographic Segmentation." *Journal of Marketing* 50: 37–47.

Kaihla, Paul, Ross Laver, Ann McLaughlin, and Barry Came 1993. "The Ant Hill Kids." *Maclean's* February 8: 18–24.

Kalleberg, Arne, and Ivar Berg 1987. *Work and Industry: Structures, Markets, and Processes*. New York: Plenum.

Kalleberg, Arne L., and Rachel A. Rosenfeld 1990. "Work in the Family and in the Labor Market: A Cross-National, Reciprocal Analysis." *Journal of Marriage and the Family* 52: 331–46.

Kammayer, Kenneth C., and Helen Ginn 1986. *An Introduction to Population*. Chicago: The Dorsey Press.

Kanter, Rosabeth Moss 1977. *Men and Women of the Corporation*. New York: Basic Books.

Kantrowitz, B., A. Cohen, and M. Dissly 1990. "Whose Baby Will It Be?" *Newsweek* August 27: 66.

Kaplan, Abraham 1964. *The Conduct of Inquiry: Methodology for Behavioral Science*. Scranton: Chandler.

Kaplan, G., V. Barell, and A. Lusky 1988. "Subjective State of Health and Survival in Elderly Adults." *Journal of Gerontology* 43: S114–S120.

Karasek, Robert, and Tores Theorell 1990. *Health Work: Stress, Productivity and the Reconstruction of Working Life*. New York: Basic Books.

Kashuba, S., P. Hessell, C. Hazlett, G. Jarvis, and L. Laing 1992. Acute Care Hospital Morbidity in the Blood Indian Tribe, 1984–87. Unpublished manuscript. Department of Health Services Administration, The University of Alberta.

Kazdin, A.E. 1989. *Behavior Modification in Applied Settings*. Pacific Groves, Calif.: Brooks/Cole.

Kelley, H.H. 1967. "Attribution Theory in Social Psychology." *Nebraska Symposium on Motivation* 15: 192–238.

——— 1973. "Attribution in Social Interaction." In *Attribution: Perceiving the Causes of Behavior*, edited by E.E. Jones et al. Morristown, N.J.: General Learning Press.

Kelley, H.H., and J.W. Thibaut 1978. *Interpersonal Relations: A Theory of Interdependence*. New York: Wiley.

Kelly, John R., Marjorie W. Steinkamp, and Janice R. Kelley 1987. "Later Life Satisfaction: Does Leisure Contribute?" *Leisure Sciences* 9: 189–200.

Kelman, S. 1975. "The Social Nature of the Definition Problem in Health." *International Journal of Health Services* 5(4).

Kelsall, K., H. Kelsall, and L. Chisholm 1984. *Stratification*. London and New York: Longman.

Kendrick, Martyn 1988. *Anatomy of a Nightmare*. Toronto: Macmillan Canada.

Kennedy, L.W., R.A. Silverman, and D.R. Forde 1988. Homicide from East to West. Discussion Paper 17. Centre for Criminological Research, Department of Sociology, University of Alberta.

Kennedy, Leslie W., and Donald G. Dutton 1989. "The Incidence of Wife Assault in Alberta." *Canadian Journal of Behavioural Science* 21: 40–54.

Kennedy, L.W., and David Forde 1990. "Routine Activities and Crime: An Analysis of Victimization in Canada." *Criminology* 28(1): 101–15.

Kent, Stephen A. 1983. "Weber, Goethe, and the Nietzschean Allusion: Capturing the Source of the 'Iron Cage' Metaphor." *Sociological Analysis* 44(4): 297–319.

1987a. "Psychological and Mystical Interpretations of Early Quakerism: William James and Rufus Jones." *Religion* 17: 251–74.

1987b. "Psychology and Quaker Mysticism: The Legacy of William James and Rufus Jones." *Quaker History* 76(1): 1–17.

1989a. "Mysticism, Quakerism, and Relative Deprivation: A Sociological Reply to R.A. Naulty." *Religion* 19: 157–78.

1989b [1983]. "The Quaker Ethic and the Fixed Price Policy: Max Weber and Beyond." *Sociological Inquiry* 53(1): 16–32. Revised reprint in *Time, Place, and Circumstance: Neo-Weberian Essays in Religion, Culture, and Society,* edited by William Swatos. Albany: State University of New York Press, 139–50, 198–201.

1990. "Deviance Labelling and Normative Strategies in the Canadian 'New Religions/Countercult' Debate." *Canadian Journal of Sociology* 15(4): 393–416.

1993a. "New Religious Movements." In *The Sociology of Religion: A Canadian Focus,* edited by Ted Hewitt. Toronto: Butterworths, 83–105.

1993b. "Deviant Scripturalism and Ritual Satanic Abuse Part One: Possible Judeo-Christian Influences." *Religion* 23(3): 229–41.

1993c. "Deviant Scripturalism and Ritual Satanic Abuse Part Two: Possible Mormon, Magick, and Pagan Influences." *Religion* 23(4).

Kent, Stephen A., and Karyn Mytrash 1990. Social Control in the Children of God: Rewards, Punishments, and Deviant Attributions. Paper presented at the Canadian Sociology and Anthropology Association.

Kettler, David, Volker Meja, and Nico Stehr 1984. *Karl Mannheim.* Chichester, London, and New York: Ellis Horwood/Tavistock.

Keyfitz, Nathan 1987. "The Family That Does Not Reproduce Itself." In *Below Replacement Fertility in Industrial Societies,* edited by K. Davis, M.S. Bernstam, and R. Ricardo-Campbell. Supplement to *Population and Development Review* 12: 139–54.

Kimmel, Michael S., and Michael S. Messner 1989. *Men's Lives.* New York: Macmillan.

Kingsbury, Nancy, and John Scanzoni 1993. "Structural Functionalism." In *Sourcebook of Family Theories and Methods: A Contextual Approach,* edited by Pauline G. Boss, William G. Doherty, Ralph LaRossa, Walter R. Schumm, and Susanne K. Steinmetz. New York: Plenum Press.

Kinsey, Alfred C., Wardell B. Pomery, and Clyde E. Martin 1948. *Sexual Behavior in the Human Male.* Philadelphia: W.B. Saunders.

Kinsey, Alfred C., Wardell B. Pomery, Clyde E. Martin, and Paul H. Gebhard 1953. *Sexual Behavior in the Human Female.* Philadelphia: W.B. Saunders.

Klockars, Carl B. 1974. *The Professional Fence.* New York: Free Press.

Knottnerus, J.D. 1987. "Status Attainment Research and Its Image of Society." *American Sociological Review* 52: 113–21.

Kohn, Melvin L., and Carmi Schooler 1983. *Work and Personality: An Inquiry into the Impact of Social Stratification.* Norwood, N.J.: Ablex.

Koos, E. 1954. *The Health of Regionville.* New York: Columbia University Press.

Krahn, Harvey 1991. "Non-standard Work Arrangements." *Perspectives on Labour and Income* (Winter): 35–45.

1992. *Quality of Work in the Service Sector.* Ottawa: Statistics Canada, General Social Survey Analysis Series 6 (Catalogue no. 11–612E, no. 6).

Krahn, Harvey, and Graham S. Lowe 1991. "Transitions to Work: Findings from a Longitudinal Study of High-School and University Graduates in Three Canadian Cities." In *Making Their Way: Education, Training and the Labour Market in Canada and Britain,* edited by D. Ashton and G. Lowe. Toronto: University of Toronto Press.

1993 [1988]. *Work, Industry, and Canadian Society.* Revised edition, Scarborough, Ont.: Nelson.

Kroker, Arthur 1984. *Technology and the Canadian Mind: Innis/McLuhan/Grant.* Montreal: New World Perspectives.

Kubler-Ross, E. 1969. *On Death and Dying.* New York: Macmillan.

Kumar, Krishan 1986. *Prophecy and Progress: The Sociology of Industrial and Post-Industrial Society.* London: Penguin.

Laclau, Ernest 1977. *Politics and Ideology in Marxist Theory: Capitalism — Fascism — Populism.* London: NLB.

Langford, Thomas 1992. "Social Experiences and Variations in Economic Beliefs among Canadian Workers." *Canadian Review of Sociology and Anthropology* 29(4): 453–87.

LaPrairie, C.P. 1983. "Native Juveniles in Court." In *Deviant Designations,* edited by T. Fleming and L.A. Visano. Toronto: Butterworths, 337–50.

1990. "Native Women and Crime: A Theoretical Model." *The Canadian Journal of Native Studies* 7(1): 121–37.

Larson, Lyle E. 1985. "Marital Breakdown in Canada: A Sociological Analysis." In *Christian Marriage Today — Growth or Breakdown: Interdisciplinary Essays,* edited by Joseph A. Buijs. Toronto: Edwin Mellen Press, 35–70.

1987. "Interpersonal Perception in Marriages: A Research Note." *CATSF Newsletter* 4: 3–7.

Lawrence, Bruce B. 1989. *Defenders of God. The Fundamentalist Revolt against the Modern Age.* Toronto: Harper and Row.

Laxer, Gordon 1989. *Open for Business: The Roots of Foreign Ownership in Canada.* Toronto: Oxford University Press.

Laxer, Robert, ed. 1973. *Canada Ltd.: The Political Economy of Dependency.* Toronto: McClelland and Stewart.

LeBon, Gustave 1960. *The Crowd.* New York: Viking Press.

Lee, Everit, S. 1966. "A Theory of Migration." *Demography* 3: 47–57.

Lee, Robert Mason 1993. "Worldwide Campaign against Logging Hits Forest Firm." *The Vancouver Sun* November 12: A1, A2.

Leenaars, Antoon A., and David Lester 1990. "Suicide in Adolescents: A Comparison of Canada and the United States." *Psychological Reports* 67: 867–73.

LeMasters, E. 1957. "Parenthood as Crisis." *Marriage and Family Living* 19: 352–55.

Lemert, Edwin 1951. *Social Pathology.* New York: McGraw-Hill.

Lenski, Gerhard 1966. *Power and Privilege: A Theory of Social Stratification.* New York: McGraw-Hill.

Lenski, G., and J. Lenski 1974. *Human Societies.* New York: McGraw-Hill.

Lestaeghe, Ron, and Johan Surkyn 1988. "Cultural Dynamics and Economic Theories of Fertility Change." *Population and Development Review* 14(1): 1–45.

Levine, J.P. 1976. "The Potential for Crime Overreporting in Criminal Victimization Surveys." *Criminology* 14(3): 307–30.

Levitt, Kari 1970. *Silent Surrender: The Multinational Corporation in Canada.* Toronto: Macmillan of Canada.

Lewis, Bernard, ed. 1976. *Islam and the Arab World.* New York: Alfred A. Knopf.

Li, Peter S. 1988. *Ethnic Inequality in a Class Society.* Toronto: Wall and Thompson.

Lieberson, Stanley 1961. "A Societal Theory of Race Relations." *American Sociological Review* 26(6): 902–10.

Lincoln, C. Eric 1983. "The American Muslim Mission in the Context of American Social History." In *The Muslim Community in North America,* edited by Earle H. Waugh, Baha Abu-Laban, and Regula Qureshi. Edmonton: University of Alberta Press, 215–33.

Linden, Eric, and James C. Hackler 1973. "Affective Ties and Delinquency." *Pacific Sociological Review* 16: 27–46.

Lindsay, C. 1986. "Trends in the Crime Rate in Canada, 1970–1985." *Canadian Social Trends* Autumn: 33–38.

Linton, Ralph 1936. *The Study of Man.* New York: D. Appleton-Century.

Linz, D., E. Donnerstein, and S. Penrod 1988. "Effects of Long Term Exposure to Violent and Sexually Degrading Depictions of Women." *Journal of Personality and Social Psychology* 55: 758–68.

Lippert, Randy 1990. "The Construction of Satanism as a Social Problem in Canada." *Canadian Journal of Sociology* 15(4): 417–39.

Lipset, Seymour M. 1963. "The Value Patterns of Democracy: A Case Study in Comparative Analysis." *American Sociological Review* 28: 515–31.

———— 1985. "Canada and the United States: The Cultural Dimension." In *Canada and the United States,* edited by C.F. Doran and J.H. Sigler. Englewood Cliffs, N.J.: Prentice-Hall.

———— 1990. *Continental Divide.* New York: Routledge.

Liska, Allen E. 1987. *Perspectives on Deviance,* 2nd ed. Englewood Cliffs, N.J.: Prentice-Hall.

Lithwick, H., M. Schiff, and E. Vernon 1986. *An Overview of Registered Indian Conditions in Canada.* Ottawa: Indian and Northern Affairs Canada.

Littlejohn, J. 1972. *Social Stratification.* London: Allen and Unwin.

Lofland, John, and L.N. Skonovd 1981. "Conversion Motifs." *Journal for the Scientific Study of Religion* 20(4): 373–85.

Lofland, John, and Rodney Stark 1965. "Becoming a World-Saver: A Theory of Conversion to a Deviant Perspective." *American Sociological Review* 30: 862–74.

Long, Richard J. 1989. "Patterns of Workplace Innovation in Canada." *Relations Industrielles/Industrial Relations* 44: 805–24.

Lopez, Alan D., and Lado T. Ruzicka 1983. *Sex Differentials in Mortality: Trends, Determinants and Consequences.* Canberra, Australia: The Australian National University Press.

Lovick, L.D. 1988. "Douglas, Thomas Clement." In *The Canadian Encyclopedia,* 2nd ed. Edmonton: Hurtig.

Lowe, Graham S. 1987. *Women in the Administrative Revolution: The Feminization of Clerical Work.* Toronto: University of Toronto Press.

———— 1989. *Women, Paid/Unpaid Work, and Stress.* Ottawa: Canadian Advisory Council on the Status of Women.

———— 1991. "Computers in the Workplace." *Perspectives on Labour and Income* Summer: 38–50.

Lowe, Graham S., and Harvey Krahn, eds. 1993. *Work in Canada: Readings in the Sociology of Work and Industry.* Scarborough: Nelson Canada.

Lox, E. n.d. *On Being Funny: Woody Allen and Comedy.* New York: McKay Publishing.

Lulat, Y.G. 1988. "Education and National Development: The Continuing Problem of Misdiagnosis and Irrelevant Prescriptions." *International Journal of Educational Development* 8: 315–28.

Lupri, Eugen 1989. "Male Violence in the Home." *Canadian Social Trends* Autumn: 19–21.

Lupri, Eugen, and Donald L. Mills 1987. "The Household Division of Labour in Young Dual-Earner Couples — the Case of Canada." *International Review of Sociology* 2: 33–56.

Lynch, M.J., and B.W. Groves 1989. *A Primer in Radical Criminology.* New York: Harrow and Heston.

Lynd, R.S., and H.M. Lynd 1929. *Middletown: A Study in Contemporary American Culture.* New York: Harcourt, Brace & Co.

Lyon, David 1988. *The Information Society: Issues and Illusions.* London: Polity Press.

Lyons, A.S., and R.J. Petrucelli, II 1987. *Medicine: An Illustrated History.* New York: Harry N. Abrams.

McDaniel, Susan A. 1986. *Canada's Aging Population.* Toronto: Butterworths.

———— 1988a. "Medical Culture and Health Politics: The Ontario Debate." *Environments* 19(3): 52–60.

———— 1988b. "An Aging Canada: Sandwich and Caregiver Dilemmas." *Perspectives: Journal of the Gerontological Nursing Association* 12(2): 15–18.

———— 1988c. "Women's Roles, Reproduction and the New Reproductive Technologies: A New Stork Rising." In

Reconstructing the Canadian Family: Feminist Per-spectives, edited by Nancy Mandell and Ann Duffy. Toronto: Butterworths, 49–81.

1988d. "The Changing Canadian Family: Women's Roles and the Impact of Feminism." In *Changing Patterns: Women in Canada,* edited by Sandra Burt, Lorraine Code, and Lindsay Dorney. Toronto: McClelland and Stewart, 103–28.

1990. *Feminist Perspectives: Towards Family Policy in Canada with Women in Mind.* Ottawa: Canadian Reseach Council for the Advancement of Women.

1991. Interim Report on Family and Friends, 1990: An Analysis of the General Social Survey, Cycle 5. Un-published. Ottawa: Statistics Canada.

McDonald, P. Lynn, and Richard A. Wanner 1990. *Retire-ment in Canada.* Toronto: Butterworths.

McDougall, W. 1908. *Introduction to Social Psychology.* London: Methuen.

McGuire, Meredith B. 1992 *Religion: The Social Context,* 3rd ed. Belmont, Calif.: Wadsworth.

McIntyre, Jennie 1981. "The Structure-Functional Approach to Family Study." In *Emerging Conceptual Frame-works in Family Analysis,* edited by F. Ivan Nye and Felix Berardo. New York: Praeger.

MacIver, R.M., and C.H. Page 1957. *Society: An Introduc-tory Analysis.* London: Macmillan.

MacKenzie, Donald, and Judy Wajcman 1985. *The Social Shaping of Technology: How the Refrigerator Got Its Hum.* Milton Keynes: Open University Press.

McKeown, Thomas 1972. *The Modern Rise of Population.* New York: Academic Press.

1978. "Fertility, Mortality and Causes of Death: An Ex-amination of Issues Related to the Modern Rise of Population." *Population Studies 32*(3): 535–42.

Maclean's 1988. "Death Sentence by Gender." August 22.

1992. "Campus Confidential." November 9: 42–46.

MacLeod, Linda 1987. *Battered but Not Beaten.* Ottawa: Canadian Advisory Council on the Status of Women.

McLuhan, Marshall 1962. *The Gutenberg Galaxy.* Toronto: University of Toronto Press.

Macpherson, C.B. 1953. *Democracy in Alberta: Social Credit and the Party System.* Toronto: University of Toronto Press.

McRoberts, Hugh A. 1985a. "Mobility and Attainment in Canada: The Effects of Origin." In *Ascription and Achievement,* edited by M. Boyd, J. Goyder, F. Jones, H. McRoberts, P. Pineo, and J. Porter. Ottawa: Carleton University Press, 67–100.

1985b. "Language and Mobility: A Comparison of Three Groups." In *Ascription and Achievement,* ed-ited by M. Boyd, J. Goyder, F. Jones, H. McRoberts, P. Pineo, and J. Porter. Ottawa: Carleton University Press, 335–56.

1988. "Patterns of Occupational Mobility." In *Social Inequality in Canada,* edited by J.E. Curtis, E. Grabb, N. Guppy, and S. Gilbert. Scarborough, Ont.: Prentice-Hall, 126–37.

McVey, Wayne W., and Barrie W. Robinson 1981. "Separa-tion in Canada: New Insights Concerning Marital Dissolution." *Canadian Journal of Sociology* 6(3): 353–66.

1985. "The Relative Contributions of Death and Divorce to Marital Dissolution in Canada and the United States." *Journal of Comparative Family Studies* 16: 93–109.

McVey, Wayne W., and Warren E. Kalbach 1994. *Cana-dian Population.* Scarborough, Ont.: Nelson Canada.

Maddox, George 1987. "Aging and Well-Being." Bryn Mawr, Pa.: Boettner Research Institute.

Madigan, Francis C., and S.J. Madigan 1957. "Are Sex Mortality Differentials Biologically Caused?" *Milbank Memorial Fund Quarterly* 35: 202–23.

Magnusson, Warren 1992. "Decentring the State, or Look-ing for Politics." In *Organizing Dissent: Contempo-rary Social Movements in Theory and Practice,* ed-ited by William K. Carroll. Toronto: Garamond Press.

Magnusson, Warren, and Rob Walker 1988. "De-Centring the State: Political Theory and Canadian Political Economy." *Studies in Political Economy* 26, Summer: 37–71.

Maier, Charles S., ed. 1987. *Changing Boundaries of the Political: Essays on the Evolving Balance between the State and Society, Public and Private in Europe.* Cambridge: Cambridge University Press.

Malamuth, Neil M. 1981. "Rape Proclivity among Males." *Journal of Social Issues* 37: 138–57.

1984. "Violence against Women: Cultural and Individual Cases." In *Pornography and Sexual Aggression,* ed-ited by N.M. Malamuth and E. Donnerstein. New York: Academic Press.

Mamiya, Lawrence H. 1983. "Minister Louis Farrakhan and the Final Call: Schism in the Muslim Move-ment." In *The Muslim Community in North America,* edited by Earle H. Waugh, Baha Abu-Laban, and Regula Qureshi. Edmonton: University of Alberta Press, 234–55.

Manitoba 1991. Public Inquiry into the Administration of Justice and Aboriginal People. *Report of the Aborigi-nal Justice Inquiry of Manitoba,* Vol. 2. *The Deaths of Helen Betty Osborne and John Joseph Harper.* A.C. Hamilton and C.M. Sinclair, Commissioners. Winni-peg: Queen's Printer.

Mann, W. E. 1955. *Church, Sect, and Cult in Alberta.* To-ronto: University of Toronto Press.

Manton, Kenneth G. 1982. "Changing Concepts of Mor-bidity and Mortality in Elderly Populations." *Milbank Memorial Quarterly/Health and Society* 60: 183–244.

Mao Tse-Tung 1966. *Problems of War and Strategy.* Pe-king: Foreign Languages Press.

Marchak, Patricia 1985. "Canadian Political Economy." *Canadian Review of Sociology and Anthropology* 22(5): 673–709.

1991. *The Integrated Circus: The New Right and the Restructuring of Global Markets.* Montreal and King-ston: McGill-Queen's University Press.

Markus, H., and R.B. Zajonc 1985. "The Cognitive Per-spective in Social Psychology." In *Handbook of So-cial Psychology,* edited by G. Lindzey and E. Aronson. New York: Random House.

Maroney, Heather J., and Meg Luxton 1987. "From Femi-nism and Political Economy to Feminist Political Economy." In *Feminism and Political Economy:*

Women's Work, Women's Struggles, edited by Heather J. Maroney and Meg Luxton. Toronto: Methuen.

Marron, Kevin 1988. *Ritual Abuse*. Toronto: Seal Books.

——— 1989. *Witches, Pagans and Magic in the New Age*. Toronto: Seal Books.

Marshall, Katherine 1987. "Women in Male-Dominated Professions." *Canadian Social Trends* Winter: 7–11.

——— 1989. "Women in Professional Occupations: Progress in the 1980s." *Canadian Social Trends* Spring: 13–16.

Martin, Emily 1989. *The Woman in the Body: A Cultural Analysis of Reproduction*. Boston: Beacon Press.

Martin, Kay M., and Barbara Voorhies 1975. *Female of the Species*. Toronto: Methuen.

Martin, Lawrence 1993. *Pledge of Allegiance: The Americanization of Canada in the Mulroney Years*. Toronto: McClelland and Stewart.

Martinio, Mario, with Harriet Martinio 1977. *Emergence, A Transsexual Autobiography*. New York: Crown Publishing and New American Library.

Marty, Martin E., and R. Scott Appleby, eds. 1991. *Fundamentalisms Observed*. Chicago: University of Chicago Press.

Marx, Gary 1967. "Religion: Opiate or Inspiration of Civil Rights Militancy among Negroes?" *American Sociological Review* 32: 64–72.

Marx, Karl 1964 [1844]. "Introduction to *Contribution to the Critique of Hegel's Philosophy of Right*." In *Karl Marx and Friedrich Engels on Religion*. 1957. Reprint, New York: Schocken Books, 41–58.

Marx, Karl, and F. Engels 1967. *The Communist Manifesto*. Harmondsworth, England: Penguin.

Mascie-Taylor, C.G. Nicholas 1990. "The Biology of Social Class." In *Biosocial Aspects of Social Class,* edited by C.G.N. Mascie-Taylor. Oxford: Oxford University Press, 117–42.

Matthews, Ralph 1983. *The Creation of Regional Dependency*. Toronto: University of Toronto Press.

——— 1988. "Understanding Regionalism as Effect and Cause." In *Social Issues: Sociological Views of Canada,* 2nd ed., edited by D. Forcese and S. Richer. Scarborough, Ont.: Prentice-Hall Canada.

Matthews, Sarah 1979. *The Social World of Old Women: Management of Self-Identity*. Beverly Hills: Sage.

Mayer, Kurt B., and Walter Buckley 1970. *Class and Society*. New York: Random House.

Mead, G.H. 1932. *The Philosophy of the Present*. Chicago: Open Court.

——— 1934. *Mind, Self, and Society*. Chicago: University of Chicago Press.

——— 1938. *The Philosophy of the Act*. Chicago: University of Chicago Press.

——— 1954. *Mind, Self, and Society*, edited by Charles W. Morris. Chicago: University of Chicago Press.

Mead, Margaret 1963 [1935]. *Sex and Temperament in Three Primitive Societies*. Reprint, New York: William Morrow.

Meissner, Martin 1971. "The Long Arm of the Job: A Study of Work and Leisure." *Industrial Relations* 10: 239–60.

——— 1975. "No Exit for Wives: Sexual Division of Labour and the Cumulation of Household Demands." *Canadian Review of Sociology and Anthropology* 12(4) Part I: 424–31.

——— 1976. "Women and Inequality." *Our Generation*. 11(2).

Meloff, William, and Robert A. Silverman 1992. "Canadian Kids Who Kill." *Canadian Journal of Criminology* January: 15–34.

Mercer, Shirley Litch 1987. *Not a Pretty Picture: An Exploratory Study of Violence against Women in High School Dating Relationships*. Toronto: Education Wife Assault.

Mertl, Steve, and John Ward 1985. *Keegstra: The Trial, The Issues, the Consequences*. Saskatoon, Sask.: Western Producer Prairie Books.

Merton, Robert 1938. "Social Structure and Anomie." *American Sociological Review* 3 (October): 672–82.

——— 1949. "Discrimination and the American Creed." In *Discrimination and National Welfare*, edited by Robert M. MacIver. New York: Harper and Brothers, 99–126.

——— 1957. *Social Theory and Social Structure*. Glencoe, Ill.: Free Press.

Metz, Donald L. 1981. *Running Hot: Structure and Stress in Ambulance Work*. Cambridge, Mass.: Abt Bks.

Michener, H.A., J.D. DeLamater, and S.H. Schwartz 1986. *Social Psychology*. Orlando, Flo.: Harcourt Brace Jovanovich.

Miles, Mathew B., and A. Michael Huberman 1984. *Qualitative Data Analysis: A Sourcebook of New Methods*. Beverly Hills: Sage.

Milgram, Stanley 1963. "Behavioral Study of Obedience." *Journal of Abnormal and Social Psychology* 67: 371–78.

——— 1974. *Obedience to Authority*. New York: Harper and Row.

Milgram, Stanley, and Hans Toch 1969. "Collective Behavior and Social Movements." In *Handbook of Social Psychology*, 2nd ed., edited by Gardner Lindzey and Elliot Aronson, 2nd ed., Vol. 4. Reading, Mass.: Addison-Wesley, 507–79.

Miliband, Ralph 1969. *The State in Capitalist Society*. New York: Basic Books.

——— 1987. "Class Analysis." In *Social Theory Today*, edited by Anthony Giddens and J.H. Turner. Cambridge, England: Polity Press, 323–46.

Miller, David L. 1989. *Introduction to Collective Behavior*. Prospect Heights: Waveland Press.

Miller, Perry 1961 [1939]. *The New England Mind: The Seventeenth Century*. Reprint, Boston: Beacon Press.

Mills, C. Wright 1956. *The Power Elite*. New York: Oxford University Press.

——— 1958. "A Pagan Sermon to the Christian Clergy." *The Nation* March 8: 199–202.

——— 1967 [1959]. *The Sociological Imagination*. London, Oxford, and New York: Oxford University Press.

Mills, Theodore 1967. *The Sociology of Small Groups*. Englewood Cliffs, N.J.: Prentice-Hall.

Milner, Henry 1990. *Sweden: Social Democracy in Practice*. Oxford: Oxford University Press.

Momen, Moojan 1985. *An Introduction to Shi'i Islam: The History and Doctrines of Twelver Shi'ism*. New Haven: Yale University Press.

Money, John 1975. "Ablatio Penis: Normal Male Infant Sex Reassigned as a Girl." *Archives of Sexual Behaviour* 4(1): 65–71.

Montagu, M.F. Ashley 1960. *Introduction to Physical Anthropology*. Springfield, Ill.: Thomas.

Moodley, Kogila 1981. "Canadian Ethnicity in Comparative Perspective: Issues in the Literature." In *Ethnicity, Power and Politics*, edited by Jorgen Dahlie and Tissa Fernando. Toronto: Methuen Publications, 6–21.

Moore, Maureen 1989. "Dual-Earner Families: The New Norm." *Canadian Social Trends* Spring: 24–26.

Moore, S., and D. Wells 1975. *Imperialism and the National Question in Canada*. Toronto: privately published.

Moreland, R.L., and R.B. Zajonc 1982. "Exposure Effects in Person Perception: Familiarity, Similarity, and Attraction." *Journal of Experimental Social Psychology* 8: 395–415.

Morgan, Gareth 1986. *Images of Organization*. Beverly Hills: Sage.

Mori, George A. 1987. "Religious Affiliation in Canada." *Canadian Social Trends* Autumn: 12–16.

Morley, J.T. 1988. "Social Credit." In *The Canadian Encyclopedia*, 2nd ed. Edmonton: Hurtig.

Morris, A. 1987. *Women, Crime and Criminal Justice*. Oxford: Basil Blackwell.

Morris, Jan 1974. *Conundrum*. New York: Harcourt Brace Jovanovich and New American Library.

Morrish, Ivor 1978. *The Sociology of Education*. London: Allen & Unwin.

Morrow, Raymond A. 1985. "Critical Theory and Critical Sociology." *Canadian Review of Sociology and Anthropology* 22: 710–47.

——— 1986. "Marcel Rioux: Critiquing Quebec's Discourse on Science and Technology." *Canadian Journal of Political and Social Theory* 10: 151–73.

——— 1991. "Introduction: The Challenge of Cultural Studies to Canadian Sociology and Anthropology." *Canadian Review of Sociology and Anthropology* 28: 153–72.

——— 1992. "Marxist Sociology." In *Encyclopedia of Sociology*, edited by Edgar Borgatta and Marie Borgatta. New York: Macmillan.

Mossey, J.M., and E. Shapiro 1982. "Self-Rated Health: A Predictor of Mortality among the Elderly." *American Journal of Public Health* 8: 800–8.

Ms. 1988. "I Never Called It Rape: The Ms. Report on Recognizing, Fighting and Surviving Date and Acquaintance Rape."

Mulgrew, Ian 1988. *Unholy Terror. The Sikhs and International Terrorism*. Toronto: Key Porter.

Mullins, Mark 1989. *Religious Minorities in Canada. A Sociological Study of the Japanese Experience*. Queenston, Ont.: The Edwin Mellen Press.

Murdock, George 1949. *Social Structure*. New York: Free Press.

——— 1965. *Culture and Society*. Pittsburgh: Pittsburgh University Press.

Murphy, Emily F. 1920. "The Grave Drug Menace." *Maclean's* 33(3): 1.

——— 1922. *The Black Candle*. Toronto: Thomas Allen.

Murstein, Bernard I. 1980. "Mate Selection in the 1970s." *Journal of Marriage and the Family* 42: 777–92.

Musgrove, Frank 1964. *Youth and the Social Order*. Bloomington: Indiana University Press.

Myles, John F. 1988a. "The Expanding Middle: Some Canadian Evidence on the Deskilling Debate." *Canadian Review of Sociology and Anthropology* 25(3): 335–64.

——— 1988b. "Social Policy in Canada." In *North American Elders: United States and Canadian Perspectives*, edited by E. Rathbone-McCuan and B. Havens. Westport, Conn.: Greenwood.

——— 1989. *Old Age in the Welfare State: The Political Economy of Public Pensions*. Revised edition, Toronto: Little, Brown.

Nagnur, Dhruva 1986. *Longevity and Historical Life Tables 1921-1981 (Abridged): Canada and the Provinces*. Ottawa: Minister of Supply and Services.

Nagnur, Dhruva, and Michael Nagrodski 1991. "Epidemiologic Transition in the Context of Demographic Change: The Evolution of Canadian Mortality Patterns." *Canadian Studies in Population* 17(1): 1–24.

Nathanson, Constance 1984. "Sex Differences in Mortality." *Annual Review of Sociology* 10: 191–213.

National Council of Welfare 1979. *Women and Poverty*. Ottawa: National Council of Welfare.

——— 1989. *A Pension Primer*. Ottawa: National Council of Welfare.

——— 1990a. *Pension Reform*. Ottawa: National Council of Welfare.

——— 1990b. *Progress against Poverty*. Ottawa: National Council of Welfare.

National Organization for Changing Men 1989. "Statement of Principles." In *Men's Lives*, edited by Michael S. Kimmel and Michael A. Messner. New York: Macmillan.

Naylor, C. David 1986. *Private Practice, Public Payments: Canadian Medicine and the Politics of Health Insurance, 1911–1966*. Montreal: McGill-Queen's University Press.

Naylor, R. Tom 1972. "The Rise and Fall of the Third Commercial Empire of the St. Lawrence." In *Capitalism and the National Question in Canada*, edited by G. Teeple. Toronto: University of Toronto Press.

——— 1975. *The History of Canadian Business, 1867-1914*. Toronto: Lorimer.

Nettler, G. 1978. *Explaining Crime*. New York: McGraw Hill.

——— 1984. *Explaining Crime*, 3rd ed. New York: McGraw-Hill.

——— 1991. Letter sent to the editor of *The Economist*.

Neugarten, B.L., ed. 1968. *Middle Age and Aging*. Chicago: University of Chicago Press.

Neugarten, B.L., J.W. Moore, and J.C. Lowe 1965. "Age Norms, Age Constraints, and Adult Socialization." *American Journal of Sociology* 70: 710–17.

Neuman, W. Lawrence 1991. *Social Research Methods: Qualitative and Quantitative Approaches*. Boston: Allyn and Bacon.

Nevitte, Neil 1992. Canada-U.S. Value Change, Free Trade and Integration: The World Values Evidence. Paper presented to the Annual Meeting of the Canadian Sociology and Anthropology Association in Charlottetown, P.E.I.

Newman, Peter C. 1979. *The Canadian Establishment.* Toronto: McClelland and Stewart-Bantam.

Newsweek 1990. "The Reluctant Father." January 2: 52–54.

Ng, Roxana 1988. "Immigrant Women and Institutionalized Racism." In *Changing Patterns: Women in Canada,* edited by Sandra Burt, Lorraine Code, and Lindsay Dorney. Toronto: McClelland and Stewart, 184–203.

Nicholson, Linda J., ed. 1990. *Feminism/Postmodernism.* New York and London: Routledge.

Niebuhr, H. Richard 1929. *The Social Sources of Denominationalism.* New York: World Publishing.

Nightingale, Donald 1982. *Workplace Democracy: An Inquiry into Employee Participation in Canadian Work Organizations.* Toronto: University of Toronto Press.

Niosi, Jorge 1983. "The Canadian Bourgeoisie: Towards a Synthetical Approach." *Canadian Journal of Political and Social Theory* 7(3): 128–49.

Nock, Steven L. 1992. "Defining the Family." In *Sociology of the Family,* 2nd ed., edited by Steven L. Nock. Englewood Cliffs, N.J.: Prentice-Hall.

Northcott, Herbert C. 1982. "Extra-Billing and Physician Remuneration: A Paradox." *Canadian Public Policy* 8: 200–6.

——— 1984. "Widowhood and Remarriage Trends in Canada, 1956–1981." *Canadian Journal on Aging* 3: 63–78.

——— 1985. "The Geographical Mobility of Canada's Elderly." *Canadian Studies in Population* 12: 183–201.

Northcott, Herbert, and Graham S. Lowe 1987. "Job and Gender Influences in the Subjective Experience of Work." *Canadian Review of Sociology and Anthropology* 24: 117–31.

Noss, John B. 1969. *Man's Religions,* 4th ed. London: Collier-Macmillan.

Nye, F. Ivan 1979. "Choice, Exchange, and the Family." In *Contemporary Theories about the Family,* Vol. 2, edited by Wesley R. Burr, Reuben Hill, F. Ivan Nye, and Ira L. Reiss. New York: Free Press.

Oakley, Ann 1974. *The Sociology of Housework.* New York: Pantheon Books.

O'Brien, Robert M. 1985. *Crime and Victimization Data.* Vol. 4, Law and Criminal Justice Series. Beverly Hills: Sage.

Offer, Daniel, Eric Ostrov, Kenneth I. Howard, and Robert Atkinson 1988. *The Teenage World: Adolescents' Self-Image in Ten Countries.* New York: Plenum.

O'Flaherty, Wendy Doniger 1975. *Hindu Myths.* Baltimore: Penguin.

Ogmundson, Rick 1975. "Party Class Images and the Class Vote in Canada." *Canadian Review of Sociology and Anthropology* 40: 506–12.

Oja, Gail 1987. *Changes in the Distribution of Wealth in Canada, 1970–1984.* Ottawa: Minister of Supply and Services.

Omran, Abdul R. 1971. "The Epidemiological Transition: A Theory of Epidemiology of Population Change." *Milbank Memorial Fund Quarterly* 49: 507–37.

Orr, James R., and Scott G. McNall 1991. "Fraternal Orders and Working-Class Formation in Nineteenth-Century Kansas." In *Bringing Class Back In,* edited by S.G. McNall, R.F. Levine, and R. Fantasia. Boulder: Westview Press, 101–17.

Orwell, George 1963. "The Lower Classes Smell." In *Sociology through Literature,* edited by Lewis A. Coser. Englewood Cliffs, N.J.: Prentice-Hall.

Ostry, Sylvia 1970. "Labour Force Participation and Childbearing Status." In *Demography and Educational Planning,* edited by Betty Macleod. Toronto: Ontario Institute for Studies in Education, 143–56.

O'Toole, Roger 1982. "Some Good Purpose: Notes on Religion and Political Culture in Canada." In *Annual Review of the Social Sciences of Religion,* Vol. 6, edited by Joachim Matthes, Bryan R. Wilson, Leo Laeyendecker, Jean Séguy, and Bernice Martin. New York: Mouton, 177–217.

Ouchi, William G. 1981. *Theory Z. How American Business Can Meet the Japanese Challenge.* Reading, Mass.: Addison-Wesley.

Ouchi, William G., and Alan L. Wilkins 1985. "Organizational Culture." *Annual Review of Sociology* 11: 457–83.

Overbeek, Johannes 1974. *History of Population Theories.* Rotterdam: Rotterdam University Press.

Pammett, Jon 1987. "Class Voting and Class Consciousness in Canada." *Canadian Review of Sociology and Anthropology* 24: 269–90.

Pan, Lynn 1989. "Playing the Identity Card." *Far Eastern Economic Review* February 9: 30–32.

Panitch, Leo 1981. "Dependency and Class in Canadian Political Economy." *Studies in Political Economy* 6: 7–33.

Park, Libbie, and Frank Park 1973. *Anatomy of Big Business.* Toronto: James Lewis and Samuel.

Parker, Rozsike, and Griselda Pollock 1981. *Old Mistresses: Women, Art and Ideology.* London: Routledge & Kegan Paul.

Parkin, Frank 1979. *Marxism and Class Theory.* London: Tavistock.

——— 1982. *Max Weber.* London and New York: Ellis Horwood/Tavistock.

Parrinder, Geoffrey 1980. *Sex in the World's Religions.* London: Sheldon Press.

Parsons, Talcott, and Robert F. Bales 1955. *Family, Socialization and Interaction Process.* Glencoe, Ill.: Free Press of Glencoe.

Pascale, Richard T., and Anthony G. Athos 1981. *The Art of Japanese Management.* Harmondsworth, England: Penguin.

Pavlov, I.P. 1927. *Conditioned Reflexes.* Oxford: Oxford University Press.

Penton, M. James 1985. *Apocalypse Delayed: The Story of Jehovah's Witnesses.* Toronto: University of Toronto Press.

Peters, John 1980. "High School Dating: Implications for Equality." *International Journal of Comparative So-*

ciology 21: 109–18.

Pine, V.R. 1977. "A Socio-Historical Portrait of Death Education." *Death Education* 1(1): 57–84.

———. 1986. "The Age of Maturity for Death Education: A Socio-Historical Portrait of the Era 1976–1985." *Death Studies* 14: 209–31.

Pineo, Peter C. 1976. "Social Mobility in Canada: The Current Picture." *Sociological Focus* 9: 109–23.

Pineo, P.C., and J. Porter 1967. "Occupational Prestige in Canada." *Canadian Review of Sociology and Anthropology* 4: 24–40.

———. 1985. "Ethnic Origin and Occupational Attainment." In *Ascription and Achievement,* edited by M. Boyd, J. Goyder, F. Jones, H. McRoberts, P. Pineo, and J. Porter. Ottawa: Carleton University Press, 357–92.

Pleck, Joseph 1989. "The Contemporary Man." In *Men's Lives,* edited by Michael S. Kimmel and Michael A. Messner. New York: Macmillan.

Pleck, Joseph H., and J. Sawyer, eds. 1974. *Men and Masculinity.* Englewood Cliffs, N.J.: Prentice-Hall.

Pollock, Otto 1961. *The Criminality of Women.* Philadelphia: University of Pennsylvania Press.

Polyani, Karl 1957. *The Great Transformation.* Boston: Beacon Press.

Popenoe, David 1993. "American Family Decline, 1960–1990: A Review and Appraisal." *Journal of Marriage and the Family* 55: 527–42.

Population Reference Bureau 1990. *World Population Data Sheet.* Washington, D.C.: The Population Reference Bureau.

———. 1992. *The 1992 World Population Data Sheet.* Washington, D.C.: The Population Reference Bureau.

Population Research Laboratory 1989. *All Alberta Survey, 1989.* University of Alberta. Data on computer tape.

Porter, John 1965. *The Vertical Mosaic.* Toronto: University of Toronto Press.

———. 1985. "Canada: The Societal Context of Occupational Allocation." In *Ascription and Achievement,* edited by M. Boyd, J. Goyder, F. Jones, H. McRoberts, P. Pineo, and J. Porter. Ottawa: Carleton University Press, 29–65.

Porter, M.R., J. Porter, and B.R. Blishen 1979. *Does Money Matter? Prospects of Higher Education in Ontario.* Toronto: Macmillan.

Poulantzas, Nicos 1982. "On Social Classes." In *Classes, Power, and Conflict,* edited by Anthony Giddens and David Held. Berkeley: University of California Press.

Pratt, Michael W., David Green, Judith MacVicar, and Marie Bountrogianni 1992. "The Mathematical Parent: Parental Scaffolding, Parenting Style, and Learning Outcomes in Long-Division Mathematics Homework." *Journal of Applied Developmental Psychology* 13: 17–34.

Prentice, Susan 1988. "The 'Mainstreaming' of Day-Care." *Resources for Feminist Research* 17: 59–63.

Presthus, Robert 1978. *The Organizational Society,* 2nd ed. New York: St. Martin's Press.

Preston, Samuel H. 1976. *Mortality Patterns in National Populations.* New York: Academic Press.

———. 1984. "Children and the Elderly: Divergent Paths for

America's Dependents." *Demography* 21(4): 435–57.

———. 1987. "Changing Values and Falling Birth Rates." In *Below Replacement Fertility in Industrial Societies,* edited by K. Davis, M.S. Bernstam, and R. Ricardo-Campbell. Supplement to *Population and Development Review* 12: 176–95.

Pringle, Rosemary 1988. *Secretaries Talk: Sexuality, Power, and Work.* Sydney, Australia: Allen & Unwin.

Proudfoot, Wayne, and Phillip Shaver 1975. "Attribution Theory and the Psychology of Religion." *Journal for the Scientific Study of Religion* 24(1): 1–118.

Pugh D.S., D.J. Hickson, and C.R. Hinings 1985. *Writers on Organizations.* Beverly Hills: Sage.

Purcell, Kate 1984. "Militancy and Acquiescence amongst Women Workers." In *Fit Work for Women,* edited by Sandra Burman. London: Croom Helm.

Pusey, Michael 1987. *Jürgen Habermas.* Chichester, London, and New York: Ellis Horwood/Tavistock.

Qvortrup, Jens 1985. "Placing Children in the Division of Labour." In *Family and Economy in Modern Society,* edited by P. Close and R. Collins. Basingstoke, England: Macmillan.

Radcliffe-Brown, R. 1959. *African Systems of Kinship and Marriage.* Oxford: Oxford University Press.

Rafter, Nicole Hahn 1986. "Left Out by the Left." *Socialist Review* 16: 7–23.

Ram, Bali 1990. "Current Demographic Analysis." *New Trends in the Family: Demographic Facts and Features.* Catalogue no. 91-535. Ottawa: Minister of Supplies and Services.

Ramet, Sabrina 1992. "War in the Balkans." *Foreign Affairs* Fall: 79–98.

Rank, S.G, and C.K. Jacobsen 1977. "Hospital Nurses' Compliance with Medication Overdose Orders: A Failure to Replicate." *Journal of Health and Social Behavior* 18: 188–93.

Ratner, R.S. 1987. "Rethinking the Sociology of Crime and Justice." In *State Control: Criminal Justice Politics in Canada,* edited by R.S. Ratner and J.L. McMullan. Vancouver: University of British Columbia Press, 3–17.

Razack, Sherene 1991. *Canadian Feminism and the Law. The Women's Legal Education and Action Fund and the Pursuit of Equality.* Toronto: Second Story Press.

Razzell, P.E. 1974. "An Interpretation of the Modern Rise of Population in Europe: A Critique." *Population Studies* 28(1): 517.

Reasons, Charles, Lois Ross, and Craig Patterson 1981. *Occupational Health and Safety in Canada.* Toronto: Butterworths.

Rees, W.D., and S.G. Lutkins 1967. "The Mortality of Bereavement." *British Medical Journal* 4: 13–16.

Reinharz, Shulamit, with the assistance of Lynn Davidman 1992. *Feminist Methods in Social Research.* New York: Oxford Press.

Reiss, Ira 1960. *Premarital Sexual Standards in America.* New York: Free Press.

———. 1965. "The Universality of the Family: A Conceptual Analysis." *Journal of Marriage and the Family* 27: 443–53.

Reiter, Ester 1991. *Making Fast Food.* Montreal: McGill-

Queen's University Press.

Resnick, Philip 1982. "The Maturing of Canadian Capitalism." *Our Generation* 15(3): 11–24.

Retherford, Robert D. 1976. *The Changing Sex Differential in Mortality.* Westport, Conn.: Greenwood Press.

Rhys Davids, T. W. 1965 [1921]. *Sacred Books of the Buddhists,* Vol. 4. Reprint, London: Luzac & Company.

Richard, Madeline A. 1991. *Ethnic Groups and Marital Choices.* Vancouver: University of British Columbia Press.

Richards, John, and Larry Pratt 1979. *Prairie Capitalism: Power and Influence in the New West.* Toronto: McClelland and Stewart.

Richardson, R. Jack 1982. "Merchants against Industry: An Empirical Study of the Canadian Debate." *Canadian Journal of Sociology* 7(3): 279–96.

Richmond, Anthony H. 1986. "Ethnogenerational Variation in Educational Achievement." *Canadian Ethnic Studies* 18: 75–89.

Riesman, David 1953. *The Lonely Crowd.* Garden City, N.Y.: Doubleday.

Rinehart, James 1986. "Improving the Quality of Working Life through Job Redesign: Work Humanization or Work Rationalization." *Canadian Review of Sociology and Anthropology* 23: 507–30.

——— 1987. *The Tyranny of Work: Alienation and the Labour Process,* 2nd ed. Toronto: Harcourt Brace Jovanovich.

Rioux, Marcel 1978 [1969]. *Quebec in Question,* translated by James Boake. Toronto: Lorimer.

Risman, Barbara, and Pepper Schwartz 1988. "Sociological Research on Male and Female Homosexuality." *Annual Review of Sociology:* 125–47.

Ritzer, George 1992. *Contemporary Sociological Theory,* 3rd ed. New York: McGraw-Hill.

Roberts, William L. 1989. "Parents' Stressful Life Events and Social Networks: Relations with Parenting and Children's Competence." *Canadian Journal of Behavioural Science* 21: 132–46.

Robertson, David, and Jeff Wareham 1987. *Technological Change in the Auto Industry: The CAW Technology Project.* Willowdale, Ont.: Canadian Auto Workers Union.

Robertson, Ian 1987. *Sociology,* 3rd ed. New York: Worth Publishers.

——— 1989. *Society.* New York: Worth Publishers.

Rokeach, Milton 1960. *The Open and Closed Mind.* New York: Basic Books.

Romaniuc, Anatole 1984. *Fertility in Canada: From Baby-Boom to Baby-Bust.* Ottawa: Minister of Supply and Services.

——— 1989. "Fertility in Canada: A Long View — A Contribution to the Debate on Population." In *The Family in Crisis: A Population Crisis?* edited by Jacques Légaré, T.R. Balakrishnan, and Roderic P. Beaujot. Ottawa: Royal Society of Canada, 251–70.

Rose, Arnold 1965. "The Subcultures of Aging: A Framework for Research in Social Gerontology." In *Older People and Their Social World,* edited by A. Rose and W. Peterson. Philadelphia: E.A. Davis, 3–16.

Ross, L.D. 1977. "The Intuitive Psychologist and His Shortcomings: Distortions in the Attribution Process." In *Advances in Experimental Social Psychology,* Vol. 10, edited by L. Berkowitz. New York: Academic Press.

Ross, M.W. et al. 1981. "Cross-Cultural Approaches to Transsexualism: A Comparison between Sweden and Australia." *Acta psychiatrica scandinaviana* 63: 75–82.

Ross, Rupert 1992. *Dancing with a Ghost: Exploring Indian Reality.* Markham, Ont.: Octopus Publishing Group.

Rothschild, Joyce, and Raymond Russell 1986. "Alternatives to Bureaucracy: Democratic Participation in the Economy." *Annual Review of Sociology* 12: 307–28.

Rowe, A.R., and C.R. Tittle 1977. "Life Cycle Changes and Criminal Propensity." *The Sociological Quarterly* 18: 223–36.

Roy, Donald 1954. "Efficiency and the Fix: Informal Intergroup Relations in a Piecework Machine Shop." *American Journal of Sociology* 60: 255–66.

Rubin, Z. 1973. *Liking and Loving: An Invitation to Social Psychology.* New York: Holt, Rinehart, and Winston.

Ruch, Libby O., Stephanie R. Amadeo, Joseph J. Leon, and John W. Gartrell 1991. "Repeated Sexual Victimization and Trauma Change During the Acute Phase of the Sexual Assault Trauma Syndrome." *Women and Health* 17(1): 1–19.

Rudé, George 1959. *The Crowd in the French Revolution.* Oxford: Clarendon Press.

Rush, Florence 1975. "Women in the Middle." In *Radical Feminism,* edited by Anne Koedt, Ellen Levine, and Anita Rapone. New York: Times Books.

Russell, Susan 1986. "The Hidden Curriculum of School: Reproducing Gender and Class Hierarchies." In *The Politics of Diversity.* London: Verso, 343–61.

Ryerson, Stanley 1960. *The Founding of Canada.* Toronto: Progress Books.

——— 1968. *Unequal Union: Confederation and the Roots of Conflict in the Canadas, 1815–1873.* Toronto: Progress Books.

Sabom, M.B. 1981. *Recollections of Death: A Medical Investigation.* New York: Harper and Row.

Sacco, V., and H. Johnson 1990a. "Household Property Crime." *Canadian Social Trends* Spring: 15–17.

——— 1990b. "Violent Victimization." *Canadian Social Trends* Summer: 10–13.

——— 1990c. *Patterns of Criminal Victimization in Canada.* Ottawa: Statistics Canada.

Salaman, Graeme 1972. "Major Theories of Stratification." In *Stratification and Social Class.* Coursebook. Milton Keynes: The Open University Press, Units 9-11: 10–26.

Salée, Daniel 1983. "L'analyse socio-politique de la société québécoise: bilan et perspective." In *Espace régionale et nation. Pour un nouveau débat sur le Québec,* edited by Gérard Boismenu, Gilles Bourque, Roch Denis, Jules Duchastel, Lizette Jalbert, and Daniel Salée. Montreal: Boréal Express, 15–49.

Sales, Arnaud, and Lucie Dumais 1985. "La construction sociale de l'économie québécoise." *Recherches sociographiques* 26(3): 318–60.

Samatar, Abdi Ismail 1992a. "Social Classes and Economic Restructuring in Pastoral Africa: Somali Notes." *Af-*

rican Studies Review 35(1): 101–27.

1992b. "Destruction of State and Society in Somalia: Beyond the Tribal Convention." *Journal of Modern African Studies* 30(4): 625–41.

Sampson, R., and J. Wooldredge 1987. "Linking the Micro- and Macro-Level Dimensions of Lifestyle-Routine Activity and Opportunity Models of Predatory Victimization." *Journal of Quantitative Criminology* 3: 371–93.

Samuel, John T. 1990. "Third World Immigration and Multiculturalism." In *Ethnic Demography: Canadian Immigrant, Racial and Cultural Variations,* edited by S. Halli, F. Trovato, and L. Driedger. Ottawa: Carleton University Press, 383–415.

Sargent, S. Stansfeld, and Robert C. Williamson 1966. *Social Psychology,* 3rd ed. New York: The Ronald Press Company.

Sayer, Derek 1991. *Capitalism and Modernity: An Excursus on Marx and Weber.* London and New York: Routledge.

Scanzoni, John 1970. *Opportunity and the Family: A Study of the Conjugal Family in Relation to the Economic Opportunity Structure.* New York: Free Press.

1978. *Sex Roles, Women's Work, and Marital Conflict.* Lexington: D.C. Heath.

1987. "Families in the 1900s: Time to Refocus Our Thinking." *Journal of Family Issues* 8: 394–421.

Scanzoni, John, Karen Polonko, Jay Teachman, and Linda Thompson 1989. *The Sexual Bond: Rethinking Families and Close Relationships.* Newbury Park, Calif.: Sage.

Schwartz, A.M. 1979. "Psychological Dependency: An Emphasis on the Later Years." In *Aging Parents,* edited by P.K. Ragan. Los Angeles: Andrus Gerontology Centre, University of Southern California Press.

Scott, J.F. 1971. *Internalization of Norms: A Sociological Theory of Moral Commitment.* New York: Prentice-Hall.

Scott, Jacqueline, and Duane F. Alwin 1989. "Gender Differences in Parental Strain: Parental Role or Gender Role?" *Journal of Family Issues* 10: 482–503.

Seeley, John R., R. Alexander Sim, and Elizabeth W. Loosley 1956. *Crestwood Heights: A Study of the Culture of Suburban Life.* Toronto: University of Toronto Press.

Shaw, R.P. 1975. *Migration: Theory and Fact.* Philadelphia: Regional Science Research Institute.

Shea, Catherine 1990. "Changes in Women's Occupations." *Canadian Social Trends* 18: 21–23.

Sheehan, Edward R.F. 1993. "In the Heart of Somalia." *New York Review of Books* January 14: 38–43.

Shneidman, E.S., ed. 1984. *Death: Current Perspectives,* 3rd ed. Mountain View, Calif.: Mayfield.

Silberman, M. 1976. "Toward a Theory of Criminal Deterrence." *American Sociological Review* 41(3): 442–61.

Silverman, R.A., J. Teevan, and V. Sacco, eds. 1991. *Crime in Canadian Society,* 4th ed. Toronto: Butterworths.

Silverman, R.A., and M.O. Nielsen, eds. 1992. *Aboriginal Peoples and Canadian Criminal Justice.* Toronto: Harcourt Brace Jovanovich.

Silverman, Robert A., and S.K. Mukherjee 1987. "Intimate Violence: An Analysis of Violent Social Relationships." *Behavioral Sciences and the Law* 5: 37–47.

Simmel, Georg 1984. *On Women, Sexuality and Love,* translated and edited by G. Oakes. New Haven, Conn.: Yale University Press.

Simone, Rose 1992. "Religion Has an Impact on Income, Study Finds." *The Edmonton Journal,* February 12: C8.

Sinclair-Faulkner, Tom 1977. "A Puckish Look at Hockey in Canada." In *Religion and Culture in Canada,* edited by Peter Slater. n.p.: Canadian Corporation for Studies in Religion, 383–405.

Skinner, B.F. 1938. *The Behavior of Organisms.* New York: Appleton-Century-Crofts.

1953. *Science and Human Behavior.* New York: Free Press.

Skipper, James K., and Gilbert Nass 1966. "Dating Behaviour: A Framework for Analysis and an Illustration." *Journal of Marriage and the Family* 28: 412–20.

Skocpol, Theda 1979. *States and Social Revolutions: A Comparative Analysis of France, Russia, and China.* Cambridge: Cambridge University Press.

Skocpol, Theda, and Edwin Amenta 1986. "States and Social Policies." *Annual Review of Sociology* 12: 131–57.

Skogan, W.G. 1981. *Issues in the Measurement of Victimization.* Washington: U.S. Government Printing Office.

1984. "Reporting Crimes to the Police: The Status of World Research." *Journal of Research in Crime and Delinquency* 21: 113–37.

Smart, Barry 1985. *Michel Foucault.* Chichester and London: Ellis Horwood/Tavistock.

Smart, C. 1976. *Women, Crime and Criminology: A Feminist Critique.* London: Routledge & Kegan Paul.

1984. *The Ties that Bind.* London: Routledge & Kegan Paul.

Smart, Ninian 1977. *The Long Search.* Toronto: Little, Brown and Company.

Smelser, Neil 1962. *A Theory of Collective Behavior.* New York: Free Press of Glencoe.

Smith, Dorothy 1977. "Women, the Family and Corporate Capitalism." In *Women in Canada,* 2nd ed., edited by Marylee Stephenson. Don Mills, Ont.: General Publishers, 17–48.

1987. *The Everyday World as Problematic: A Feminist Sociology.* Toronto: University of Toronto Press.

1990. *The Conceptual Practices of Power: A Feminist Sociology of Knowledge.* Toronto: University of Toronto Press.

Smith, M.D. 1987. "The Incidence and Prevalence of Woman Abuse in Toronto." *Violence and Victims* 2: 173–87.

Snider, Laureen 1993. *Bad Business.* Toronto: Nelson Canada.

Snider, L., and W.G. West 1985. "A Critical Perspective on Law in the Canadian State: Delinquency and Corporate Crime." In *The New Criminologies in Canada,* edited by T. Fleming. Toronto: Oxford University Press, 138–69.

Solicitor General of Canada 1983. Bulletin 1. *Victims of Crime*. Ottawa: Minister of Supply and Services.

Spencer, Metta 1990. *Foundations of Modern Sociology*. Scarborough, Ont.: Prentice-Hall.

Spilka, Bernard, Phillip Shaver, and Lee A. Kirkpatrick 1985. "A General Attribution Theory for the Psychology of Religion." *Journal for the Scientific Study of Religion* 24(1): 1–18.

Spiro, Melford E. 1967. "Religion: Problems of Definition and Explanation." In *Anthropological Approaches to the Study of Religion*, edited by M. Bainton. New York: Appleton-Century Crofts, 85–126.

Stark, Rodney, and Charles Y. Glock 1969. "Prejudice and the Churches." In *Prejudice, U.S.A.*, edited by Charles Y. Glock and Ellen Siegelman. New York: Praeger.

Stark, Rodney, Bruce D. Foster, Charles Y. Glock, and Harold E. Quinley 1973. "Ministers as Moral Guides: The Sounds of Silence." In *Religion in Sociological Perspective*, edited by Charles Y. Glock. Belmont, Calif.: Wadsworth, 163–86.

Stark, Rodney, and William Sims Bainbridge 1985. *The Future of Religion: Secularization, Revival, and Cult Formation*. Berkeley: University of California Press.

——— 1987. *The Future of Religion*. New York: Peter Lang.

Stasiulis, Daiva 1988. "Capitalism, Democracy, and the Canadian State." In *Social Issues: Sociological Views of Canada*, edited by D. Forcese and S. Richer. Scarborough, Ont.: Prentice-Hall.

Statistics Canada 1921 to 1986. *Census of Canada: Age, Sex, and Marital Status: The Nation*. Catalogue no. 93–101. Ottawa: King's Queen's Printer, Minister of Supply and Services.

——— 1979. *1976 Census of Canada*, Vol. 4. *Families*. Catalogue no. 93–822. Ottawa: Minister of Supply and Services.

——— 1980. *Perspectives Canada III*. Ottawa: Minister of Supply and Services.

——— 1984. *Charting Canadian Incomes, 1951–1981*. Ottawa: Minister of Supply and Services.

——— 1985. *Canada Yearbook*. Ottawa: Minister of Supply and Services.

——— 1986. *The Distribution of Wealth in Canada, 1984*. Ottawa: Minister of Supply and Services.

——— 1987a. *Census of Canada 1986. Families: Part 1. The Nation*. Catalogue no. 93–106. Ottawa: Minister of Supply and Services.

——— 1987b. *Census of Canada 1986. Dwellings and Households: Part 1. The Nation*. Catalogue no. 93–104. Ottawa: Minister of Supply and Services.

——— 1988a. *1986 Census of Canada. The Nation: Dwellings, Households, Families*. Part 1. Catalogue no. 93–106. Ottawa: Minister of Supply and Services.

——— 1988b. *Vital Statistics, Fertility Rates, 1986*. Catalogue no. 84–204. Ottawa: Minister of Supply and Services.

——— 1988c. *Vital Statistics, Therapeutic Abortions, 1986*. Catalogue no. 82–211. Ottawa: Minister of Supply and Services.

——— 1988d. *Census of Canada 1986. Labour Force Activity*. Catalogue no. 93–111. Ottawa: Minister of Supply and Services.

——— 1988e. *Pension Plans in Canada, 1986*. Catalogue no. 74–401. Ottawa: Minister of Supply and Services.

——— 1989a. *Canadian Crime Statistics, 1988*. Ottawa: Minister of Supply and Services.

——— 1989b. *Adult Correctional Services in Canada*. Ottawa: Minister of Supply and Services.

——— 1989c. *Labour Force Annual Averages 1981–1988*. Catalogue no. 71–529. Ottawa: Minister of Supply and Services.

——— 1990a. *Labour Force Annual Averages*. Catalogue no. 71–220. Ottawa: Minister of Supply and Services.

——— 1990b. *Women in Canada: A Statistical Report*, 2nd ed. Catalogue no. 89–503E. Ottawa: Minister of Supply and Services.

——— 1990c. *Canadian Crime Statistics, 1989*. Ottawa: Minister of Supply and Services.

——— 1990d. *Current Demographic Analysis: New Trends in the Family, Demographic Facts and Figures*, Bali Ram. Ottawa: Minister of Industry, Science and Technology.

——— 1990e. *Postcensal Annual Estimates of Population by Marital Status, Age, Sex and Components of Growth for Canada, Provinces and Territories, June 1, 1990*. Catalogue no. 91–210. Ottawa: Minister of Supply and Services.

——— 1990f. *The Changing Profile of Canadian Families with Low Incomes, 1970-1985*. Ottawa: Minister of Supply and Services.

——— 1991a. *Income Distribution by Size in Canada*. Ottawa: Minister of Industry, Science and Technology.

——— 1991b. *Canada: A Portrait*. Ottawa: Minister of Industry, Science and Technology.

——— 1991c. *Household Facilities by Income and Other Characteristics*. Ottawa: Minister of Supply and Services.

——— 1991d. *Census of Canada*, Catalogue no. 93–315

——— 1991e. *Health Reports*, Supplement no. 16. Catalogue no. 82–003516. Ottawa: Minister of Supply and Services.

——— 1991f. *Labour Force, December, 1990*. Catalogue no. 71–001. Ottawa: Minister of Supply and Services.

——— 1992. *Age, Sex, and Marital Status. 1991 Census of Canada*. Catalogue no. 93–310. Ottawa: Minister of Supply and Services.

——— 1993a. *Employment Income by Occupation. The Nation*. Catalogue no. 93–332. Ottawa: Minister of Industry, Science and Technology.

——— 1993b. *Ethnic Origin*. 1991 Census of Canada. Catalogue no. 93–315, 12–27. Ottawa: Industry, Science and Technology.

Stebbins, Robert A. 1988. *Deviance: Tolerable Differences*. Toronto: McGraw-Hill.

Steffensmeier, D. 1980. "Sex Differences in Patterns of Adult Crime, 1965-77." *Social Forces* 58: 1080–108.

Steffensmeier, D., R.H. Steffensmeier, and A.S. Rosenthal 1989. "Age and the Distribution of Crime." *American Journal of Sociology* 94: 803–31.

Stein, L.I. 1967. "The Doctor-Nurse Game." *Archives of General Psychiatry* 16: 699–703.

Steinem, Gloria 1983. *Outrageous Acts and Everyday Rebellions*. New York: Holt, Rinehart and Winston.

Stephens, T., C.L. Craig, and B.F. Ferris 1986. "Adult Physical Fitness and Hypertension in Canada: Findings from the Canada Fitness Survey II." *Canadian Journal of Public Health* 77(4): 291–95.

Stephens, William N. 1963. *The Family in Cross-Cultural Perspective*. New York: Holt, Rinehart and Winston.

Stets, Jan E. 1991. "Cohabiting and Marital Aggression: The Role of Social Isolation." *Journal of Marriage and the Family* 53: 669–80.

Stets, Jan E., and Murray A. Straus 1989. "The Marriage License as a Hitting License: A Comparison of Assaults in Dating, Cohabiting, and Married Couples." In *Violence in Dating Relationships: Emerging Social Issues,* edited by M. Pirog-Good and J. Stets. New York: Praeger, 33–52.

Stoller, E.P. 1984. "Self-Assessments of Health by the Elderly: The Impact of Informal Assistance." *Journal of Health and Social Behavior* 25: 260–70.

Storey, Robert 1991. "Studying Work in Canada." *Canadian Journal of Sociology* 16: 241–64.

Stout, Cam 1991. "Common Law: A Growing Alternative." *Canadian Social Trends* Winter: 18–20.

Strate, Lance 1992. "Beer Commercials: A Manual on Masculinity." In *Men, Masculinity, and the Media,* edited by Steve Craig. Newbury Park, Calif.: Sage.

Straus, M.A., R.J. Gelles, and S.K. Steinmetz 1980. *Behind Closed Doors: Violence in American Families*. New York: Doubleday.

Straus, Murray A., and Richard J. Gelles 1986. "Societal Change and Change in Family Violence from 1975 to 1985 as Revealed by Two National Surveys." *Journal of Marriage and the Family* 48: 465–79.

Strauss, A. 1966. "Structure and Ideology of the Nursing Profession." In *The Nursing Profession,* edited by F. Davis. New York: John Wiley, 60–104.

Strauss, R. 1957. "The Nature and Status of Medical Sociology." *American Sociological Review* 22: 200–4.

Sudnow, D. 1967. *Passing On: The Social Organization of Dying*. Englewood Cliffs, N.J.: Prentice-Hall.

Sugar, Fran, and Lana Fox 1991. *Survey of Federally Sentenced Aboriginal Women in the Community*. Ottawa: Native Women's Association of Canada, 1990, as reported in *Report of the Aboriginal Justice Inquiry of Manitoba, Vol. 1. The Justice System and Aboriginal People,* A.C. Hamilton and C.M. Sinclair. Winnipeg: Queen's Printer.

Sutherland, Edwin H., and Donald R. Cressey 1970. *Principles of Criminology*. New York: Lippincott.

1978. *Criminology*, 10th ed. Philadelphia: Lippincott.

Sutherland, R.W., and M.J. Fulton 1990. *Health Care in Canada*. Ottawa: The Health Group.

Sydie, R.A. 1987. *Natural Women, Cultured Men: A Feminist Perspective on Sociological Theory*. Toronto: Methuen.

Szinovacz, Maximiliane E. 1987. "Family Power." In *Handbook of Marriage and the Family*, edited by Marvin B. Sussman and Suzanne K. Steinmetz. New York: Plenum Press, 651–94.

Tawney, R.H. 1928. *Religion and the Rise of Capitalism*. New York: Harcourt, Brace.

Teitelbaum, Michael S. 1975. "Relevance of Demographic Transition for Developing Countries." *Science* 188: 420–25.

Tepperman, L. 1977. *Crime Control*. Toronto: McGraw-Hill Ryerson.

Thomlinson, R. 1965. *Population Dynamics*. New York: Random House.

Thompson, Kenneth 1982. *Emile Durkheim*. Chichester, London, and New York: Ellis Horwood/Tavistock.

Thompson, Linda, and Alexis J. Walker 1991. "Gender in Families: Women and Men in Marriage, Work and Parenthood." In *Contemporary Families: Looking Forward, Looking Back,* edited by Alan C. Booth. Minneapolis: National Council on Family Relations, 76–102.

Thompson, Paul 1989. *The Nature of Work: An Introduction to Debates on the Labour Process,* 2nd ed. London: Macmillan.

Thornberry, T.P., and M. Farnworth 1982. "Social Correlates of Criminal Involvement." *American Sociological Review* 47: 505–18.

Tilly, Charles 1978. *From Mobilization to Revolution*. Reading, Mass.: Addison-Wesley.

Tilly, Charles, Louise Tilly, and Richard Tilly 1975. *The Rebellious Century, 1830–1930*. Cambridge, Mass.: Harvard University Press.

Tittle, C.R., W.J. Villemez, and D.A. Smith 1978. "The Myth of Social Class and Criminality." *American Sociological Review* 43: 643–56.

Tönnies, Ferdinand 1957 [1887]. *Community and Society (Gemeinschaft und Gesellschaft)*, edited and translated by Charles P. Loomis. New York: Harper and Row.

Trasler, G. 1980. Aspects of Causality, Culture, and Crime. Paper presented at the 4th International Seminar at the International Centre of Sociological, Penal and Penitentiary Research and Studies, Messina, Sicily.

Tribute 1991. "Black Robe: Bruce Beresford Directs a Canadian Tale of Survival." Famous Players, 8(6): 12.

Triplett, N. 1897. "The Dynamogenic Factors in Pacemaking and Competition." *American Journal of Psychology* 9: 507–33.

Troeltsch, Ernst 1931. *The Social Teaching of the Christian Churches,* 2 vols. London: Allen & Unwin.

Trovato, Frank 1988a. "The Interurban Mobility of the Foreign Born in Canada, 1976-81." *International Migration Review* 22(3): 59–86.

1988b. "Change in the Marriage Rate: Canadian Women, 1921–25 to 1981–85." *Journal of Marriage and the Family* 50: 507–21.

Trovato, Frank, and George K. Jarvis 1986. "Immigrant Suicide in Canada: 1971 and 1981." *Social Forces* 65(2): 433–57.

Trudeau, Pierre E. 1968. "A Few Obstacles to Democracy in Quebec." In *Federalism and the French Canadians*. Toronto: Macmillan of Canada.

Tucker, Judith E. 1985. *Women in Nineteenth-Century Egypt*. New York: Cambridge University Press.

Turchnyiak, G. 1979. "Cemeteries Take Toll of Land for the Living." *The Ring* 5(19). The University of Victoria.

Turk, Austin T. 1969. *Criminality and the Legal Order*. Chicago: Rand McNally.

1976. "Law, Conflict and Order: From Theorizing Toward Theories." *Canadian Review of Sociology and Anthropology* 13(3): 282–94.

Turner, Bryan S., ed. 1990. *Theories of Modernity and Postmodernity*. London: Sage.

Turner, Graeme 1990. *British Cultural Studies: An Introduction*. Boston: Unwin Hyman.

Turner, Jonathan, and Alexandra Maryanski 1979. *Functionalism*. Reading, Mass.: Benjamin Cummings.

Tylor, E.B. 1871. *Religion in Primitive Culture*. Reprint, 1958. New York: Harper Torchbooks.

Ugbor, K.O. 1991. Educational Opportunity and Social Redistribution. Ph.D. Dissertation. University of Alberta, Edmonton.

Ujimoto, K. Victor, and Gordon Hirabayashi, eds. 1980. *Visible Minorities and Multiculturalism: Asians in Canada*. Toronto: Butterworths.

United Nations 1956. *The Aging of Populations and Its Economic and Social Implications*. Population Studies no. 26. New York: United Nations.

University of Alberta 1991 [1985]. *University Standards for the Protection of Human Research Participants*. Edmonton: General Faculties Council.

Urquart, M.C., and K.A.H. Buckley, eds. 1983. *Historical Statistics of Canada*, 2nd ed. Ottawa: Supply and Services Canada.

van den Berghe, Pierre 1978 [1967]. *Race and Racism: A Comparative Perspective*, 2nd ed. New York: John Wiley and Sons.

van Kirk, Sylvia 1980. *"Many Tender Ties": Women in Fur Trade Society, 1670–1870*. Winnipeg: Watson and Dwyer.

Vanier Institute of the Family 1981. *A Mosaic of Family Studies*. Ottawa: Vanier Institute of the Family.

Varga, A.C. 1984. *The Main Issues in Bioethics*. Revised edition. New York: Paulist Press.

Veblen, Thorstein 1912. *The Theory of the Leisure Class: An Economic Study of Institutions*. New York: Macmillan.

Veevers, Jean E. 1988. "The 'Real' Marriage Squeeze: Mate Selection, Mortality, and the Mating Gradient." *Sociological Perspectives* 31: 142–67.

——— ed. 1991. *Continuity and Change in Marriage and Family*. Toronto: Holt, Rinehart and Winston of Canada.

Veltmeyer, Henry 1986. *Canadian Class Structure*. Toronto: Garamond Press.

——— 1987. *Canadian Corporate Power*. Toronto: Garamond Press.

Verdun-Jones, S.N., and G.K. Muirhead 1979/80. "Natives in the Canadian Criminal Justice System." *Crime and Justice* 7-8: 3–21.

Vincent, C. 1972. "An Open Letter to the 'Caught' Generation." *Family Coordinator* 21: 143–50.

Volinets, Irene 1989. Towards an Understanding of Courtship Violence. Unpublished M.A. Thesis. University of Waterloo.

Waldron, Ingrid 1976. "Why Do Women Live Longer than Men?" *Social Science and Medicine* 10: 349–62.

——— 1986. "What Do We Know about Causes of Sex Differences in Mortality? A Review of the Literature." *Social Science and Medicine* 10: 349–62.

1987. "Patterns and Causes of Excess Female Mortality among Children in Developing Countries." *World Health Statistics Quarterly* 40: 194–210.

Wallace, Ruth, ed. 1989. *Feminism and Sociological Theory*. Newbury Park and London: Sage.

Wallace, Ruth A., and Alison Wolf 1986. *Contemporary Sociological Theory: Continuing the Classic Tradition*, 2nd ed. Englewood Cliffs, N.J.: Prentice-Hall.

Wallace, Walter 1971. *The Logic of Science in Sociology*. New York: Aldine.

Wallerstein, Judith S., and Sandra Blakeslee 1989. *Second Chances: Men, Women and Children a Decade after Divorce*. New York: Tichnor and Fields.

Ward, Peter W. 1978. *White Canada Forever*. Montreal: McGill-Queen's University Press.

Ward, Sally K., Kathy Chapman, Ellen Gee, Susan White, and Kirk Williams 1991. "Acquaintance Rape and the College Social Scene." *Family Relations* 40(1): 65–71.

Wargon, Sylvia 1979. *Canadian Households and Families: Recent Demographic Trends*. Catalogue no. 99–753E. Ottawa: Minister of Supply and Services.

Warner, William L. 1961. *The Family of God: A Symbolic Study of Christian Life in America*. New Haven: Yale University Press.

Watkins, Melville 1963. "A Staple Theory of Economic Growth." *The Canadian Journal of Economics and Political Science* 29(2): 141–58.

Watson, J. Mark 1982. "Righteousness on Two Wheels: Bikers as a Secular Sect." *Sociological Spectrum* 2: 333–49.

Weatherly, U.G. 1909. "How Does the Access of Women to Industrial Occupations React on the Family?" *American Journal of Sociology* 14(6): 740–52.

Weber, Max 1930 [1920a]. *The Protestant Ethic and the Spirit of Capitalism*, 2nd ed., translated by Talcott Parsons. London: Allen & Unwin.

——— 1946. *From Max Weber: Essays in Sociology*, edited by Hans Gerth and C. Wright Mills. New York: Oxford University Press.

——— 1951 [1920b]. *The Religion of China*, translated and edited by Hans H. Gerth. Toronto: Collier-Macmillan.

——— 1956 [1922]. *The Sociology of Religion*, 4th ed., revised by Johannes Winckelmann, translated by Ephraim Fischoff. Boston: Beacon Press.

——— 1958 [1920c]. *The Religion of India. The Sociology of Hinduism and Buddhism*, translated and edited by Hans H. Gerth and Don Martindale. Toronto: Collier-Macmillan.

——— 1958. *The Protestant Ethic and the Spirit of Capitalism*. New York: Scribner.

——— 1964. *The Theory of Social and Economic Organization*. New York: Free Press.

——— 1968. *Economy and Society: An Outline of Interpretive Sociology*, 3 vols., edited by Guenther Roth and Claus Wittich. New York: Bedminster Press.

——— 1978 [1968]. *Economy and Society*. Reprint, Berkeley: University of California Press.

Webster, M., Jr., and J.E. Driskell, Jr. 1978. "Status Generalization: A Review and Some New Data." *American Sociological Review* 43: 220–36.

Weeks, David 1972. "Comparative Social Stratification." In *Stratification and Social Class.* Coursebook. Milton Keynes: The Open University Press, Units 9-11, 47–71.

Weeks, Wendy 1980. "Part-Time Work: The Business View on Second-Class Jobs for Housewives and Mothers." *Atlantis* 5: 69–86.

Wells, Don 1986. *Soft Sell: 'Quality of Working Life' Programs and the Productivity Race.* Ottawa: Canadian Centre for Policy Alternatives.

Wells, J. Gipson 1984. *Choices in Marriage and Family.* Jackson: Piedmont Press.

Wells, L.E., and J.H. Rankin 1991. "Families and Delinquency: A Meta-Analysis of Impact of Broken Homes." *Social Problems* 38: 71–93.

Westoff, Charles F. 1983. "Fertility Decline in the West: Causes and Prospects." *Population and Development Review* 9(1): 99–104.

White, G.L., and D. Shapiro 1987. "Don't I Know You? Antecedents and Social Consequences of Perceived Similarity." *Journal of Experimental Social Psychology* 23: 75–92.

Whyte, Donald 1992. "Canadian Sociology." In *Encyclopedia of Sociology*, Vol. 1., edited by Edgar F. Borgatta and Marie L. Borgatta. New York: Macmillan, 159–62.

Whyte, William F. 1981 [1943, 1951]. *Street Corner Society: The Social Structure of an Italian Slum,* 3rd ed. Chicago: University of Chicago Press.

Whyte, William F., with the collaboration of Kathleen King Whyte 1984. *Learning from the Field: A Guide from Experience.* Beverly Hills: Sage.

Wilkins, R., and O. Adams 1983. *The Healthfulness of Life.* Ottawa: The Institute for Research on Public Policy.

Williams, Glen 1979. "The National Policy Tariffs: Industrial Development through Import Substitution." *Canadian Journal of Political Science* 312(2): 333–68.

——— 1989. "Canada in the International Political Economy." In *The New Canadian Political Economy,* edited by Wallace Clement and Glen Williams. Montreal: McGill-Queen's University Press.

Williams, Kirk R., and Richard Hawkins, 1986. "Perceptual Research on General Deterrence: A Critical Review." *Law and Society Review* 20(4): 545–72.

Wilson, Bryan R. 1978. "Becoming a Sectarian: Motivation and Commitment." In *Religious Motivation: Biographical and Sociological Problems for the Church Historian.* Studies in Church History 15, edited by Derek Baker. Oxford: Basil Blackwell, 481–506.

Wilson, E.O. 1975. *Sociobiology: The New Synthesis.* Cambridge, Mass.: Harvard University Press.

Wilson, S.J. 1991. *Women, Families, and Work,* 3rd ed. Toronto: McGraw-Hill Ryerson.

Winter, Gordon A. (Chairman) 1990. *Archdiocesan Commission of Enquiry into the Sexual Abuse of Children by Some Members of the Clergy of the Archdiocese,* 2 vols. St. John's, Nfld: Archdiocese of St. John's.

Wirth, Louis 1938. "Urbanism as a Way of Life." *American Journal of Sociology* 44: 3–24.

——— 1945. "The Problem of Minority Groups." In *The Science of Man in the World Crisis*, edited by Ralph Linton. New York: Columbia University Press, 347–72.

Wolf, Naomi 1990. *The Beauty Myth.* Toronto: Random House of Canada.

Wolfe, David 1989. "The Canadian State in Comparative Perspective." *Canadian Review of Sociology and Anthropology* 26 (1): 95–126.

Wolff, Kurt H. 1950. *The Sociology of Georg Simmel.* Glencoe, Ill.: Free Press.

Wood, Stephen 1989. "The Transformation of Work?" In *The Transformation of Work? Skill, Flexibility and the Labour Process,* edited by Stephen Wood. London: Unwin Hyman.

The World Almanac and Book of Facts 1991. New York: Scripps-Howard.

Wright, Erik O. 1984. *Classes.* London: Verso.

——— 1991. "The Conceptual Status of Class Structure in Class Analysis." In *Bringing Class Back In,* edited by S.G. McNall, R.F. Levine, and R. Fantasia. Boulder: Westview Press, 17–37.

Wright, E.O., and Luca Perrone 1977. "Marxist Class Categories and Income Inequality." *American Sociological Review* 42: 32–55.

Wright, E.O., Cynthia Costello, David Hachen, and Joey Sprague 1982. "The American Class Structure." *American Sociological Review* 47: 709–26.

Yaukey, David 1985. *Demography: The Study of Human Population.* New York: St. Martin's Press.

York, Geoffrey 1990. *The Dispossessed: Life and Death in Native Canada.* London: Vintage U.K.

Young, Jock 1986. "The Failure of Criminology: The Need for a Radical Realism." In *Confronting Crime,* edited by Roger Matthews and Jock Young. London: Sage.

Young, M.F.D., ed. 1971. *Knowledge and Control.* London: Collier-Macmillan.

Zajonc, R.B. 1966. *Social Psychology: An Experimental Approach.* Belmont, Calif.: Brooks/Cole.

Zborowski, Mark 1952. "Cultural Components in Responses to Pain." *Journal of Social Issues* 8: 16–30.

Zehme, Bill 1993. "Jerry & George & Kramer & Elaine: Exposing the Secrets of Seinfeld's success." *Rolling Stone* 660/661.

Zeitlin, Irving M. 1987. *Ideology and the Development of Sociological Theory,* 3rd ed. Englewood Cliffs, N.J.: Prentice-Hall.

Zigler, Edward, and Pamela Ennis 1989. "Child Care: Science and Social Policy, the Child Care Crisis in America." *Canadian Psychology* 30: 116–25.

Ziryanov, P.N. 1988. "The Orthodox Church in the Early Twentieth Century." In *The Russian Orthodox Church: 10th to 20th Centuries*, edited by Alexander Preobrazhensky, translated by Sergei Syrovatkin. Moscow: Progress Publishers, 165–264.

Zuboff, Shoshana 1988. *In the Age of the Smart Machine: The Future of Work and Power.* New York: Basic Books.

Index

deer, though warning him against dangerous beasts. In
e the events were compressed into a single summer's day
At dawn the immortal goddess visited an 'earthly son' and
o woo him with all her charms. Adonis, a coy, self-regard-
ent, rejected her through the hours of daylight. Aspiring
kind of manly prowess, he chose that night to hunt the
was killed for his pains. Next morning Venus discovered his
er grief she forsook the world and laid a curse on human
forth to be linked with perverseness, cruelty and suffering.
of how the spirit of Ovidian narrative might be carried over
n verse, *Scilla's Metamorphosis* set a good formal precedent.
-line stanzas had grace and poise; they kept the action mov-
while allowing scope for elaboration. Early in the poem the
onis was alluded to, with the death of 'the sweet Arcadian
enus's agonized laments:

How on his senseless corse she lay a-crying,
As if the boy were then but new a-dying.

were clear hints for the courtship of Adonis in the descrip-
disdainful Glaucus wooed by the enamoured sea-nymph

How oft with blushes would she plead for grace,
How oft with whisp'rings would she tempt his ears:
How oft with crystal did she wet his face:
How oft she wiped them with her amber hairs:
  So oft, methought I oft in heart desired
  To see the end whereto disdain aspired.

are's imagination was engaged on a variety of levels, and
s he reconceived it had a complexity of its own. Ovid's
andscape merged insensibly with the English countryside,
and woodlands, pastures and hedgerows, foxes and hares,
ises of hunting dogs and lark-song up on high. There was
omedy in the situation of the love-sick goddess of love,
by a callow boy who pouted and turned away his face from
etting and situation came together happily in the escapade
s horse, the paragon of its kind, who breaks his rein and
y to answer the call of 'A breeding jennet, lusty, young and
e natural courtship of the animals supplying implicit com-
e waywardness of the young human male. Lovers' follies,
rse follies of those who rejected love, would be matter for
antic comedies teaching the lesson 'Make the most of the
e'. In the Arden of *As You Like It* and the woods of *A Mid-*
ght's Dream a range of perverse attitudes would be ex-

Young boys and girls
Are level now with men. The odds is gone,
And there is nothing left remarkable
Beneath the visiting moon.   (IV, xv, 65–8)

In Act v Cleopatra presents to Dolabella her vision of Antony in imagery
of breath-taking grandeur, looking up and down the Great Chain of
Being and all through the cosmos for terms of comparison:

His face was as the heav'ns, and therein stuck
A sun and moon, which kept their course and lighted
The little O, the earth.
....
His legs bestrid the ocean; his rear'd arm
Crested the world. His voice was propertied
As all the tuned spheres,...
....
.... His delights
Were dolphin-like.   (V, ii, 82–9)

Who but Shakespeare would dare to puncture such a speech thus:

CLEOPATRA   Think you there was or might be such a man
             As this I dreamt of?
DOLABELLA   Gentle madam, no.

And who else would leave us with the feeling that Cleopatra's vision
both is and is not true? The play's vision of the *range* of possibilities
within a single human life cuts across the simply ethical dimension –
which, of course, is amply represented, too, as in 'the triple pillar of
the world transform'd / Into a strumpet's fool'—and no analysis can
exhaust the reasons why we are so moved at 'a lass unparallel'd'.

Antony and Cleopatra shows Shakespeare's awareness that human
experience is often intangible and ultimately, at its highest reaches or
lowest depths, mysterious. It is amorphous and chaotic. 'The web of
our life is of a mingled yarn, good and ill together.' We look to our
poets to illuminate the mysteries and to our dramatists to make order
out of the chaos. It was the achievement of the greatest poet-dramatist
to create such order without destroying the mystery of human personality and human fate. His lines were indeed 'so richly spun, and wouen
so fit', but, as in Desdemona's handkerchief, there was also magic in
the web.

8

SHAKESPEARE'S NARRATIVE POEMS

J. W. LEVER

In all editions of Shakespeare's collected works, his poems appear after the entire body of thirty-seven plays, making up a kind of non-dramatic appendix. Tradition alone explains this position, with its suggestion of second-class matter. Down the centuries editors have respectfully followed the broad lay-out of the First Folio, which included only the dramas; when in 1778 the poems were added, it seemed inevitable that they should be tacked on at the end of the familiar sequence. There they have since remained. Yet as an introduction to Shakespeare's complex genius, the narrative poems at least might have been more suitably placed at the head of his works. In order of composition *Venus and Adonis*, published in 1593, was not likely to have been what Shakespeare in his dedication termed 'the first heir of my invention', but it was certainly his first work to appear in print. *The Rape of Lucrece* followed in the next year, when the only plays yet published were *Titus Andronicus* and the unauthorized quarto of *2 Henry VI*. More important than matters of chronology, these poems give a striking impression of the energy and range of the early Shakespeare; more so, indeed, than his first experiments on the stage. Written at a time when the theatres were closed on account of plague in the capital, they belong to a phase of rapid maturing and awareness of latent powers. Into them was poured a ferment of intuitions, perceptions, speculations and fancies that had not yet found dramatic expression. Many of the sonnets have these qualities and often show close resemblances in attitudes, imagery and turn of phrase; but as a personal medium they stand at a further remove from the plays. The narrative poems were, in the truest sense, the 'first heirs' of Shakespeare's literary creation.

Both *Venus and Adonis* and *Lucrece* were widely read and admired in their time; both, however, can mislead a modern reader who comes to them unprepared. Their unchecked exuberance, ornamentation and profusion of trope and conceit were characteristic of the younger Shakespeare and the age he grew up in: they were not, as they might be in a present-day writer, marks of a superficial talent. Also the poems need to be seen in their respective settings if their tone is to be under-

stood. *Venus and Adonis* has l
too cold, too fleshly and too a
yet too tragic in nuance. *Lucre*
static for the stage, too rhetori
sincere as they may be, arise
standards foreign to the poer
'dramatic', nor are they 'narrat
work through their distinctive
case of *Venus and Adonis*, tragi
the channels of these Elizabeth
variety of effects. Success was
of myth in *Venus and Adonis*
accord. Elements of humour an
ceptions combined. With som
a triumphant example of divers
less even. The morality form v
structurally the poem was unw
of remarkable power, and the
achievement.

Mythological romance gaine
the sixteenth century. Introduc
(1589), it was taken up by Marlo
inspiration was Ovid's *Metamo*
of story material but also a form
the beauty, sensuousness and
sented a virginal world withou
by figures who were creatures c
forces, archetypes rather than
suits, flights, ardours and recoi
the behaviour of social man. Lo
were part of their world, but t
ironic detachment that held the
a distance from full imaginati
other mediums would evoke
followed in smooth sequence
narrative flow. In this realm of
could be descried and mapped
could provide.

Shakespeare borrowed the ou
tale in *Metamorphoses* X, but
stories. Adonis was described b
whom Venus enjoyed the pas
dressing herself as a huntress a

hares and
Shakespea
and night.
proceeded
ing adoles
to another
boar, and
body: in I
love, henc
As a mode
into Engli
Lodge's si
ing easily,
story of A
boy' and

And there
tion of a
Scilla:

Shakesp
the story
Arcadian
its downs
with the n
inherent c
frustrated
her kiss. S
of Adonis
gallops av
proud'; t
ment on t
and the w
future ror
present ti
summer l

plored. The plight of Venus prefigured Titania's love for a mortal; Adonis's self-regard looked ahead to that of Bertram in *All's Well*. As in these plays, intellectual issues are also joined. At times the dialogue becomes a set *débat*, with the goddess condemning 'fruitless chastity' in arguments drawn from Erasmus's *Encomium Matrimonii*, and the boy countering with a moralist's diatribe against lust, broken off as he remembers that 'The text is old, the orator too green'. Shakespeare was raising questions of major concern in his approach to life and love. The conception of Increase as the only answer to 'never-resting time', as well as concern with the workings of lust in action, would recur throughout the plays and were directly linked with the themes of the sonnets.

Permeating the poem, underlying its romance, its comedy, its fresh descriptions of nature, its theoretical discourses, is a sense of elemental tragedy. The keynote is struck in the opening lines of Venus's first address to Adonis:

> Nature that made thee, with herself at strife,
> Saith that the world hath ending with thy life.

In all Shakespeare's writing, 'Nature with herself at strife' was the deepest apprehension, that no received concept of world order, no Platonist or Christian idealism, could altogether dispel. At the quick of experience no individual could escape the co-presence of beauty and destruction, love and death, creation and chaos. Awareness of this gives a special urgency to Venus's wooing, and her presentiment of the death of Adonis mirrors a universal pessimism:

> For he being dead, with him is beauty slain,
> And, beauty dead, black chaos comes again.

The vision of destruction takes in not only the central figures of the poem, but also its natural setting. Terror is the lot of all creatures. The startled hare who 'Cranks and crosses with a thousand doubles' in a desperate attempt to outrun the hounds; the injured snail struck on its 'tender horns' who

> Shrinks backward to his shelly cave in pain,
> And there, all smoth'red up, in shade doth sit,

share a common experience with the goddess on earth and her human love. The snail's fearful retreat images Venus's eyes shrinking from the sight of dead Adonis. In gruesome contrast, the frothy mouth of the boar after its kill, 'Like milk and blood being mingled both together', resembles the white and red complexion of the living boy. Significantly, Venus in the presence of death has no more serenity than any country girl who has lost her lover; she shares the helplessness of all creatures. Such insights foreshadow the great love tragedies, anticipating Othello's premonition 'Chaos is come again', and Cleopatra's 'No more but e'en a woman, and commanded / By such poor passion as the maid that milks'.

Shakespeare's rehandling of Ovid's myth gives it a new breadth and universality, through which the diverse perceptions are integrated. Venus is not just one more tenuous figure of pastoral, indistinguishable from others in her disguise as a huntress. The poem draws attention to her many attributes as the great goddess of love. Her arrival on earth is sudden and mysterious. She has put on a woman's form, yet she is strangely incorporeal, neither naked nor clothed, neither young nor old, with perennial beauty that 'as the spring doth yearly grow'. The sensuality of her courtship is only apparent: her hand if touched would 'dissolve, or seem to melt'; the primroses she lies on support her 'like sturdy trees'; when the time will come for her to leave earth, two 'strengthless doves' will draw her through the skies. As Venus Genetrix, her wooing proceeds on various levels: through direct sensuous appeal; through charming the intellect and the fancy,

> Bid me discourse, I will enchant thine ear,
> Or, like a fairy, trip along the green,
> Or, like a nymph, with long dishevelled hair,
> Dance on the sands, and yet no footing seen...

through yoking erotic sensations to the pleasures of hillock and brake, making her body a source of delight on the vegetable plane of existence – 'I'll be a park, and thou shalt be my deer'; – through evoking the precedent of fierce animal desire set by the runaway horse. As for Adonis, the commonplace adolescent is transformed in the eyes of Venus, as the friend of the sonnets was transformed in the eyes of Shakespeare the poet, becoming 'the very archetypal pattern and substance of which all beautiful things are but shadows'.[1] The essence of all that was lovely and transient in nature,

> his breath and beauty set
> Gloss on the rose, smell to the violet.

Conversely, the boar that slays Adonis is no common beast like the many wild animals against which he had been warned in Ovid's story. Unique in its blind ferocity, it is presented as the antitype of destruction, unmotivated, brutishly unaware of the death it carries. At the end, Shakespeare keeps Ovid's metamorphosis of Adonis into a windflower; but this is subordinate in importance to the universal change in the nature of love itself. As Venus yokes her doves and despairingly flies back to Paphos, she leaves behind her the fallen world of everyday life.

In terms of Ovid's medium, Shakespeare had created a myth to end myths. But seen in a wider frame of reference, *Venus and Adonis* has affinities with the more elemental Greek myths of nature and human passion. In its tragical aspect it recalls the story of Hippolytus and Phaedra, which Shakespeare must have known from Seneca. There, however, both protagonists were fully human, and Aphrodite had become less a divinity than desire personified. In the purer form of a pagan nature myth, Bion's *Lament for Adonis* had the universality of Shakespeare's poem. Adonis was a superhuman figure, the demigod of vegetation whose death was accompanied by the fall of the season, and who was mourned by all living things. But the treatments differed basically as much as the outlook of the Greek world differed from that of the Renaissance. Bion's elegy described the whole of nature grieving in sympathy with the divine lovers:

Woe, woe for Cypris, the mountains all are saying, and the oak trees answer, *woe for Adonis*. And the rivers bewail the sorrows of Aphrodite, and the wells are weeping Adonis on the mountains.[2]

In *Venus and Adonis*, nature does not go into mourning; on the contrary, there is total indifference. The world knows nothing of its loss; the echoes do not, as in Bion's *Lament*, grieve of their own accord, but senselessly repeat Venus's cries. Summer preserves its outward charm; only in the deeper insight of the bereaved is its beauty seen to be empty:

> The flowers are sweet, their colours fresh and trim,
> But true-sweet beauty liv'd and died with him.

Shakespeare's myth draws its validity not from the outer world but from the human imagination only. All through his poem there is a disparity between physical sight and the vision of the inner eye. Venus might be the embodiment of beauty and love, but to the literal-minded Adonis she is no more than an infatuated older woman. The reader for his part is inclined to see Adonis objectively as an uninteresting youth, callow and self-absorbed; only through the eyes of Venus does he appear as 'The field's chief flower...more lovely than a man'. The ambivalence of truth and seeming was the mainspring of both comedy and tragedy in Shakespeare; only in the imagination of lovers and poets is the transcendent worth of the individual affirmed.

The expression of such antinomies through complex human experience belonged to Shakespeare's life-work as a dramatist. The development was from myth to history, from fictional paradigms to

many-sided individuals. Maturity brought an ever more intense awareness of the duality of life, but also a growing belief in the capacity of
love to transcend it. In the love tragedies the characters were exposed
from all quarters to the disparities of truth and seeming, the destructive
action of time, the chaos that underlay order. *Antony and Cleopatra*
was, in this sense, a vast reworking of *Venus and Adonis*. Not Ovid's
pastoral world but an empire torn by civil war formed the setting.
Instead of one day of frustrated courtship between the goddess of love
and a boy with a mind bent only on hunting, the rival claims of love
and ambition were fought out over years in the souls of a great queen
and a military hero. The desires, ardours and caprices of the immortal
Venus were realized in an all too human Cleopatra. Adonis's youthful
dreams of prowess became the exploits of an ageing Antony who would
at last be caught in 'the world's great snare'. Yet in the realm of the
imagination both lovers at death attained to the rank of demigods. In
Shakespeare's later drama myth was not abandoned, but built itself
a new validity through the workings of whatever was godlike in
human nature.

The Rape of Lucrece, Shakespeare's second narrative poem, was
conceived on a different basis. Again the outlines were taken from Ovid,
but from the *Fasti*, not the *Metamorphoses*; a prose account by Livy
was also consulted, as well as Chaucer's rendering in *The Legende of
Good Women*. The story was of crime, suffering and retribution;
legendary indeed, but rooted in the world of history, not myth,
describing the passions of human beings, not projections of fancy. In
the dedication to *Venus and Adonis* 'some graver labour' had been
promised. *Lucrece*, carefully printed and again dedicated to Southampton, lived up to the description. What Ovid had told in 131 lines of
compact hexameters was expanded into a poem of 1855 lines, composed
in 'rhyme royal' that produced a more weighty effect than the six-line
stanza and lent itself to even more elaborate treatment. Every device
of rhetorical amplification, patterned imagery and intricate conceit
was worked into the texture. Action alternated with reflection; inner
conflicts were set over against generalities; minute detail and large
abstractions both found a place. From start to finish, a strong rhythmic
drive carried the narration on through its varying tempos.

To understand these qualities, some recognition of Shakespeare's
artistic problem is called for. Clearly he was undertaking an essay in
the tragic mode, and on lines very different from the treatment he
found in his sources. The primary object in *Lucrece* was not to portray
a virtuous woman, or to relate a great historical event, but to show
the workings of evil on a universal scale. The theme of creative love
in *Venus and Adonis* was here to be replaced by that of 'lust in action',

vicious, destructive, and serving to typify the dark forces in man and nature alike. *Venus and Adonis*, too, had conveyed a profound sense of the tragical side of existence, but the Ovidian style of narration had maintained an overriding elegance and detachment. For *The Rape of Lucrece* a form was required that would allow the destructive and chaotic elements to predominate. At this stage of Shakespeare's development, the inevitable course was to make use of such models as the poetry of his age could offer.

The form chosen was neither drama nor simple narrative, but stemmed from the Elizabethan 'tragical morality', where an exemplary story, based on history, was made to drive home a moral principle. 'Tragedy' here was essentially rhetorical and didactic, unrelated to drama, and typically defined as 'a lofty kind of poetry, shewing the rueful end of royal personages and their fall from felicity'.[3] The most celebrated work of its kind was *A Mirror For Magistrates* (1555–87), presenting stories of the fall of rulers and statesmen. Written for the most part in solemn stanzas of 'rhyme royal', they served as a series of contemporary warnings against the sins of ambition and lust. Daniel's *Complaint of Rosamund* (1592) continued the tradition, with less concern for teaching a political lesson and a centring of interest in the female victim of corruption amongst the great. Shakespeare's poem was structurally a broad amalgam of the two kinds, and might, in sixteenth-century fashion, have been termed 'The Tragedy of Tarquin and the Complaint of Lucrece'. Instead of monologues interspersed with prose comments there was a framework of third-person narrative, though in the second part much of the poem was devoted to Lucrece's laments. The didactic tone was preserved, but directed not so much to rulers as to persons of high social rank. In momentary recoil from his intended crime Tarquin is made to exclaim:

> O shame to knighthood and to shining arms!
> O foul dishonour to my household's grave!

Historically, as was made clear in the sources and indeed the 'Argument' to the poem,[4] Tarquin was the son of a usurper who had murdered his own father-in-law and practised many tyrannies; he had no family honour to lose. But such anxieties would have been fitting enough for a young Elizabethan nobleman of high lineage. As an example to shun, the Tarquin of this poem was a 'mirror' for individuals like the Earl of Southampton, heir to his dead father's estate, who came of age in the year *Lucrece* was published.

Shakespeare's treatment, however, ranges far beyond the rather narrow limits of the conventional forms. He borrows the rhetorical style; indeed, he heightens it; but he also infuses a stream of complex imagery sprung from his own tragic perceptions. Individual crime and suffering are given a universal resonance. Lust becomes an aspect of that predatory nature implied in *Venus and Adonis* but here made fully explicit. Darkness, clouds, beasts and birds of prey take the place of sunshine, starlight, flowers and innocent animals. Reinforcing the violence in nature are images of aggression and conquest in the human sphere, as well as suggestions of the guilt-ridden psyche of the wrong-doer. In the latter part of the poem Lucrece's laments reach out to indict nature, society, and the very structure of creation. The long account of the picture of Troy presents a sustained metaphor of war and its evils, centring on the treacherous Sinon and Hecuba, 'Time's ruin, beauty's wrack, and grim care's reign'. The morality form, less flexible than myth, is strained to breaking point by the vast creative energy it is made to hold. So long as action carries the poem forward, a remarkable sombre power is generated; but after the first part has reached its climax, an increasing imbalance sets in between the traditional mode for expressing tragedy and Shakespeare's wide apprehensions of what the tragic state involves.

In the dedication, *Lucrece* is described as 'this pamphlet without beginning'. The poem makes no attempt to provide a historical background to events. Nor is mention made of Tarquin's first visit to Lucrece in company with her husband, when her beauty and modest bearing had aroused his desire. Political setting and plausibility alike are sacrificed for an intense concentration on the primary moral theme, the assault of irresistible lust upon innocent chastity. Plunging at once *in medias res* with the furious ride of 'lust-breathed Tarquin', the poem makes headlong action the correlative of the wild urge of desire. Outer and inner realities correspond through images of fire and smoke, torches, coals and darkness. Antithetically Lucrece is introduced, not as in Ovid's realistic description of her, spinning with her maids and weeping at Collatine's absence, but abstracted in a heraldic conceit depicting her face as an emblem of beauty and virtue reconciled. In keeping with the didactic medium, the vanity of lust is explicitly stated in Tarquin's tortuous mental debates ' 'Tween frozen conscience and hot-burning will'. The thing he seeks is 'A dream, a breath, a froth of fleeting joy'; it would bring shame and self-hatred; the scandal would blot his escutcheon and disgrace his descendants. Alternating with debate, the chaos in Tarquin, the calm in Lucrece is presented through patterned imagery that sets up a universal opposition between the two states. Night as an enveloping presence accompanies Tarquin in his movements and meditations. With night go its creatures, owls, wolves, vultures, hawks; types of all that is predatory in animal nature. On the human plane, Tarquin's lust, the 'uproar' in his veins, his 'drumming' heart, even his hand that 'marched', become troops of a squalid army of invasion, 'In bloody death and ravishment delighting'. His thief-like progress towards the bedchamber is punctuated by impediments and alarms: the door grating on the threshold, the shriek of weasels, the successive locks to be forced, the glove with the needle that pricks his finger. The vivid details, charged with dreamlike evocativeness, serve as projections of anxiety and guilt in the soul. In contrast the sight of Lucrece peacefully asleep gives rise to images of another order. Her presence suggests a dazzling beam of sunlight, a 'virtuous monument', 'an April daisy on the grass', symbolizing bright chastity, cold virtue and vulnerable innocence. Rhetoric again supervenes as she awakes and calls reason to her aid with measured arguments. Briefly the assault is held back, but soon desire rudely breaks up the flow of words, and the rape is accomplished. As in the sonnets, lust is 'Enjoy'd no sooner but despised straight'. Like 'full-fed hound or gorged hawk' it withdraws, tame at last, leaving Tarquin's soul defiled. Evil has run its course; but not before its work of destruction and self-destruction has been consummated.

The second and longer portion of the poem is dominated by the figure of Lucrece lamenting her woes and making the decision to end her life. In the 'complaint' medium the heroine usually recounted her story and the circumstances that led to her fall. The line of development led on to full-scale characterization in the manner of Defoe and Richardson. But here the one important action left to relate is Lucrece's suicide. The laments lack narrative constraint and expand in a vacuum. As for character, the intense concentration on Tarquin as a moral example has reduced Lucrece in the first part to an emblem of virtue; in the latter portion she becomes little more than a declamatory voice. Here lies the basic weakness, rather than in the rhetorical style itself, though the opportunities for conscious eloquence tempted Shakespeare's facility and led to a piling up of tropes in imitation of the Senecan grand manner. It was even difficult to manipulate sympathy with the act of suicide, an ethically dubious course for Christian readers who accepted the maxim that 'compelled sins were no sins'. Only in brief phases of action, addressing her maid or giving her letter to the groom, does Lucrece engage interest. On the other hand, the extensive monologues allow Shakespeare to enlarge on major themes implicit in the imagery of the Tarquin section. The properties of evil and the workings of chance and mutability are explored on a cosmic scale. Tarquin's crime is presented as an aspect of the nature of things, challenging any optimistic belief in 'world order'. Night, the accomplice of Tarquin, is a 'vast, sin-concealing chaos'. Opportunity or chance is seen as an autonomous force able to corrupt innocence and frustrate virtue both in nature and man. The view of a tainted world comprehends a society that is heartless and cruel, where 'The orphan pines while the oppressor feeds'. Time, in one aspect the universal healer, in another brings decay and oblivion, destroys monuments and spoils antiquities. On all planes of being duality prevails. The enormous indictment amounts to a statement of the major premises of Shakespearean tragedy.

The Rape of Lucrece has been generally seen as a striking anticipation of *Macbeth*. Actually the resemblance lies mainly in the first part. The conflict in the wrongdoer's soul, the demoniacal drive to evil, the setting of darkness, the imagery of war and creatures of prey closely link the 'tragedy of Tarquin' to the mature drama. The morality form here collaborated fruitfully with Shakespeare's own perceptions and pointed a way forward in his development as a tragedian. No simple reworking of Ovid's narrative technique could have brought about such results. Moreover, in its own right this portion of the poem was a fine achievement. Its kinetic qualities, its use of internal dialogue, its sharply focused details of sight and sound, give it distinctive properties, often outside the scope of drama and in some ways analogous to the art of film. If the heightened rhetoric and emotive imagery are alien to our conceptions of poetry, they have found their modern equivalents in other, non-literary mediums. For Shakespeare's age their recognized place was in narrative verse. After the first powerful episode, however, *Lucrece* loses momentum and formal cohesion. The gap opens ever wider between the poem as an artifact and as a repository for Shakespearean concepts and themes. Yet in this respect, at least, the poem remains of absorbing interest. The great addresses to Night, Opportunity and Time may add little to Lucrece's stature, but they prefigure Shakespeare's vision of tragedy more clearly than anywhere else in his early writing. The detailed description of Troy, though awkwardly linked to the subject matter of the poem, was the first presentation of a recurrent theme, to be returned to in *2 Henry IV* and *Hamlet*, and treated at length, as the archetype of 'wars and lechery', in *Troilus and Cressida*. Indeed, the brief sketches of 'sly Ulysses', the senile Nestor, and 'despairing Hecuba' seem like notes for the stage characters of that play. At the end, the strangely inapposite description of Brutus, with his 'folly's show' disguising 'deep policy', looks ahead to the Antony of *Julius Caesar*.

With its poise, clarity and varied appeal, *Venus and Adonis* is a more successful poem than the over-ambitious but ill-balanced *Rape of Lucrece*. Yet both poems have outstanding merit in their different but complementary modes. Together they are unique forerunners of Shakespeare's fulfilled dramatic powers.

9

SHAKESPEARE THE ELIZABETHAN DRAMATIST

DAVID BEVINGTON

The division between Shakespeare's Elizabethan phase and his Jacobean phase is real and significant. Whatever his reasons, Shakespeare did in fact seek a new direction and emphasis during the second decade of his career as a practising dramatist. By and large, one can say that during the decade of the 1590s, Shakespeare wrote English history plays – the *Henry VI* trilogy and *Richard III* (1590–3), *King John* (*c.* 1594–6), and the famous tetralogy from *Richard II* (1594–5) through *Henry IV* in two parts (*c.* 1596–8) to *Henry V* (1599) – and farcical or festive comedies: the experimental and imitative beginning (*c.* 1589–94) in *Love's Labour's Lost, The Comedy of Errors, The Two Gentlemen of Verona,* and *The Taming of the Shrew*; the mid-decade lyric vein in *A Midsummer Night's Dream* and *The Merchant of Venice*; mature romantic statement in *Much Ado about Nothing, As You Like It,* and *Twelfth Night* (1598–1600); and a late farce in *The Merry Wives of Windsor* (1597–1602). During the 1600s, he wrote the darker 'problem' comedies, virtually all the great tragedies, and finally a group of predominantly tragicomic 'romances'. Even the apparent exceptions to this generalization help confirm a pattern. The late history play *Henry VIII* (1613), written in probable collaboration with Fletcher, lacks the triumphant battle oratory, comic exuberance, and thoughtful analysis of the monarchy so characteristic of Shakespeare's earlier patriotic dramas. Conversely, Shakespeare's two early sporadic attempts at tragedy are an unsuccessful apprenticeship in Senecan blood revenge (*Titus Andronicus, c.* 1589–90) and a touching love story (*Romeo and Juliet, c.* 1594–5). This recognizable distinction between the Elizabethan and the Jacobean Shakespeare is a tribute to the extraordinary intellectual and artistic consistency of this dramatist as he sought constantly to develop new forms.

It is easy to oversimplify the possible motives underlying Shakespeare's change of direction, and to speak knowingly of Shakespeare 'on the heights' or entering the valley of despair, as though the plays might represent little more than his own spiritual odyssey. Or one can pluck out the heart of Shakespeare's mystery by seeing a political reflection in his plays, an indication of a shift from the great Elizabethan compromise (however shaky during its last years) to an era under James I of political and religious confrontation, impasse, and eventually drift toward civil war. More broadly, it is tempting to invoke a change of cultural and philosophic outlook from 'Elizabethan optimism' to 'Jacobean pessimism', which, although gradual rather than sudden, did comprise the challenge of many medieval orthodoxies in such fields as astronomy, geography, medicine, logic and rhetoric, Biblical learning, and political theory. John Donne lamented that the 'new philosophy casts all in doubt'; its apostles were Galileo, Bacon, Montaigne, Machiavelli. Some element of truth may well lie in all these generalizations.

When we view Shakespeare as an artist and man of the theatre, at any rate, we can affirm that he did devote himself to the perfection of certain genres before moving on to new areas of endeavour, and that in doing so he both reflected and influenced the trend of dramatic art generally in the London of his day. When he wrote English history plays and bright comedies, these forms were the stock-in-trade of the London popular stage. The 1590s belonged to the adult companies, such as Shakespeare's the Chamberlain's men and their rivals the Lord Admiral's men. Juvenile theatre was in eclipse, forced to close at the start of the decade and not permitted to reopen until 1599. Competing only among themselves, the adult companies enjoyed an extraordinary financial success, and purveyed entertainments to a widely diversified national audience. Under these conditions, the mores and artistic forms of their plays veered towards popular consensus: England's military and cultural supremacy patriotically defended, the monarchy upheld, Catholic plotting disdained, love and marriage wholesomely affirmed as inseparable, and the like. When on the other hand the boys' theatre reopened in 1599 (significantly the very year of *Henry V*), drama began to gravitate towards the more exclusive precinct of the court. Satire became the fashion, if not the rage. Tragicomedy flourished. The adult companies were compelled to follow suit, especially when their Puritan-leaning audiences began to fall away in the deteriorating atmosphere of court versus London populace.

Shakespeare began his dramatic career, then, at an auspicious moment: the adult companies were about to enter the period of their greatest success, and the English history play was in its merest infancy. Scholarship used to maintain that Shakespeare was a great follower of conventions, perfecting what others had begun – in this case, learning the rudiments of the history play from such contemporaries as George Peele, Robert Greene, Thomas Lodge, and Christopher Marlowe.

The Globe Theatre. From Claes Jans Visscher's 'Long View of London'

Now it seems more likely that Shakespeare was a pioneer as well. To guide his earliest efforts, he may have had little more to go on than *Gorboduc* (1562), the anonymous *The Famous Victories of Henry V* (1583–8), and some experimenting with history in late morality plays such as *Cambises* (1561) or Robert Wilson's *The Three Lords and Three Ladies of London* (1588–90). The popularity of Shakespeare's *Henry VI* plays and *Richard III* may well have figured prominently in establishing a new vogue for patriotic drama, and in prescribing its literary form.

The time was also auspicious for the emergence of Shakespeare's historical genius because of England's recent Armada victory over the Spanish (1588). At least in part, the English history play satisfied a current need for celebratory triumphs of England's national greatness, and conversely for warnings of the dangers to be found in international conspiracy abroad and decadent complacency at home. In this hour of challenge, English dramatists (with Shakespeare in the vanguard) ransacked the nation's annals for illustrations from her glorious past – Crécy, Poitiers, Agincourt – as well as more sobering and instructive instances of political disaster. A new edition of Holinshed's *Chronicles* (1587) was appropriately at hand for source material.

Thus it was that Shakespeare turned first to the saga of Lancaster versus York, England's prolonged agony of civil war during much of the fifteenth century. The Lancastrian claim to the throne belonged to Henry IV and to his heroic son Henry V, since Henry IV's father had been Duke of Lancaster and son of Edward III. But Henry IV had won the throne by the deposition and murder of his cousin, Richard II, and the illegality of this act left the Lancastrian regime vulnerable to rival dynastic claims. These claims emerged with a vengeance after the untimely death of Henry V in 1422, and the accession of his underage and weakminded son Henry VI. The Yorkist family of Richard Plantagenet and his sons Edward (later Edward IV), Clarence, and Richard (later Richard III) could argue a prior descent from Edward III, and consequently seized the opportunity of a minority kingship, squabbling at court, and French hostility abroad. The struggle led to England's loss of her French territories and almost total anarchy at home. It strained to the limit England's ability to exist as a nation, and ended only with the accession of the Tudor Henry VII, Elizabeth's grandfather, in 1485. A century later, it was appropriate to give thanks for the continued stability of Tudor rule, and at the same time to foresee the spectre of renewed dynastic instability under an aging virgin queen with no appointed successor and with many Catholic enemies plotting a return to power.

In the first play of the series, *1 Henry VI*, a chief conclusion seems to be that political division at home leads to military defeat abroad.

The scene shifts rapidly back and forth from the English court to the French camp. The English, normally invincible and contemptuous of the cowardly French, are their own worst enemy. At home, the young King Henry is bedevilled by the aspirations of his closest relatives, such as his corrupt ecclesiastical uncle the Bishop of Winchester, and his conspiratorial Yorkist cousin Richard Plantagenet. The king's ineffectual attempt to appease both Yorkist and Lancastrian factions produces divided responsibility for the French campaign, and the victimization of the valiant general Talbot. This general, Shakespeare's first popular stage hero, appears larger than life. He is martyred in the name of personal and family honour, devotion to God, and service to his country. His old-fashioned virtues contrast not only with the machinations of the English courtiers, but with the devil-worshipping and profligate French. He is everything that the French Dauphin Charles is not: courageous, self-controlled, putting reason above passion in his relationship with women, courteously forbearing and yet stern with the enemy. Even more he is opposite to Joan of Arc, unsympathetically portrayed as a wanton and trafficker in evil spirits. Thus the play derives its thematic focus from a metaphoric conflict between good and evil. England is a family divided against itself, disobedient to the will of heaven, paying for the sins of usurpation and fratricide. The manifestations of this moral enervation are to be found at all levels in the triumph of selfish whim over right reason. Not coincidentally, the play ends with the king's own surrender to the imperious will of a Frenchwoman, Margaret of Anjou.

This Margaret, Henry's French bride, becomes an ever more ominous presence in the subsequent *Henry VI* plays. In concert with her paramour, the conniving Duke of Suffolk, she engineers the downfall of the good Humphrey Duke of Gloucester. He is the victimized hero of the second play. The chief virtue for which he must die is his role as intermediary between the commoners' just complaints and the prerogative of the throne. Royal authority cannot be challenged, in his view, but it must be receptive to petitions and willing to amend injustices on its own authority. This humane view affronts those who insist on despotic absolutism, and he is mercilessly cut down. Without his sane guidance, the commons take matters into their own hands. The communistic rebellion of Jack Cade, with its ludicrous antics, is a fearful reminder of what will happen when the people are goaded too far. Yet the responsibility for their disobedience rests primarily with a defaulted aristocracy. Richard Plantagenet, for his part, cynically whets the ambitions of Cade in order to further the breakdown of civil authority, by which Richard hopes to seize power. Popular unrest is only a prelude to outright civil war among feuding nobles.

And in that war it is Margaret, not Henry VI, who serves as Lancastrian commander-in-chief. By expending frightful vengeance on Richard Plantagenet and his family, she invites an escalation of violence on both sides. After most of the carnage is done, after Margaret herself has lost husband and son, we see her in *Richard III*, withered and impotent, a prophetess of the retaliatory plan by which an angry God exacts an eye for an eye, a Yorkist prince for a Lancastrian prince, until England's penalty for insurrection is fully paid.

It is thus in *Richard III* that providential meaning finally emerges from the chaos of England's suffering. So many deaths are necessary because England's rulers have grown insolent and must be purged to satisfy heaven's wrath. Richard III himself, youngest son of his namesake father Plantagenet, is the scourge appointed by heaven to cleanse a moral wilderness. Richard is the epitome of all of England's wrongs: he is ambitious, ruthless, diabolically inspired, hypocritical, and – in a central theatrical metaphor – he is a masterful actor of many roles. In a superb irony that sustains the play, we see Richard reaching for the throne, gloating in his own success that seems to confirm his godless faith in the unlimited power of the individual will – whereas we know that in fact Richard unwittingly fulfils providential destiny. Most of his victims fittingly condemn themselves out of their own mouths for the wrongs they have committed, or ignore plain warnings of impending disaster. Others, like Richard's pitiful nephews, must pay the price of their fathers' sins. Richard clambers to the throne over the fallen bodies of his kinsmen only to lose it to Henry Tudor, God's appointed minister of the renewed state. Shakespeare minimizes the dubiousness of Henry's own claim to the throne, the usurping manner of his accession, and the historical unattractiveness of his character; instead, Henry is an emblem of rightminded devotion to duty and to God.

In literary form these plays do not conform to any classical ideal. They are neither comedies nor tragedies, but segments of chronicle in sequence. Unity is achieved, as we have seen, by thematic means rather than by single focus of the action. Indeed, the plot lines are numerous, the array of characters vast. Episodic incidents frequently introduce personages whom we never see again. The acting company, following a native homiletic tradition going back to the morality plays and religious cycles, does its utmost to produce multiplicity and panorama. In staging, especially, Shakespeare's early history plays revel in gymnastic feats of scaling operations against the façade of the 'tiring house' or dressing room, actual firing of cannon, alarums and excursions in profusion, appearances 'on the walls'. The scene moves epically from country to country and battlefield to battlefield with the easy fluidity of the open Elizabethan stage. Violence is displayed whenever possible. Comedy is raucous, often anti-foreign; conversely, big scenes of political seriousness do not flinch from revealing the secret counsels of kings and emperors.

Shakespeare's later histories, although vastly superior as works of art, are really continuations of the same popular dramatic genre. In the opening of *1 Henry IV*, for example, we experience the same juxtaposition in alternating scenes of high seriousness and practical joking, the court and the Boar's Head Tavern, wakeful counsellors of the king and a gluttonous, mischief-loving counsellor of the prince. Unity of theme provides the common point of reference; and the theme, stated with growing maturity, bears a close relation to that of the earlier plays. Once again, Shakespeare examines the strengths and potential weaknesses of the English monarchy, and searches for a definition of the ideal ruler through positive and negative example. *King John* obviously provides a negative instance. Shakespeare refuses to glorify this king's reign into anti-Catholic defiance, as more rabidly Protestant dramatists had done. Instead, he portrays a whimsical tyrant and murderer of his kinsman, so evil that well-meaning Englishmen must actively consider the prospect of overthrowing him. Yet the desperate recourse to armed rebellion is invoked only to reveal its ultimate fallacy. The choric Bastard Faulconbridge, instinctively loyal to John, must experience fully the appeal of disaffection so that he can conscientiously transcend it. Rebellion is the worst alternative, for it must rely on foreign alliances and so play into the hands of England's cynical enemies. The violent displacement of the worst of kings (apart from Richard III, who, as predecessor of the Tudors, had to be viewed as an exception) merely teaches others to rebel.

This sad lesson plagues the Henry Bolingbroke who forces his way to the throne in *Richard II*. His reasons for opposing Richard are manifold. Richard is a spendthrift and incompetent ruler, despoiling his subjects for his own decadent luxuries. As his watchful uncles Gaunt and York observe in choric exasperation, Richard subverts the very law of primogeniture by which he rules when he illegally seizes Bolingbroke's birthright. Henry returns to England from exile solely to claim his lands and titles so wrongfully misappropriated. Yet the choric moderates of the play are equally insistent that Henry must not resort to force: God's is the quarrel. They see the far-reaching consequences of rebellion that Henry ignores. Once Richard has capitulated to Henry, what alternative has Henry but to assume the throne? And once king, how can he allow his rival to continue alive? The logic of these silent questions leads to regicide and an illegal regime. In the *Henry IV* plays, the new king tastes the bitter fruit of his having taught others to employ revolution.

The paradox of rule is carefully balanced in *Richard II*. Richard himself is unfit to govern and yet is graced by a regal bearing that never deserts him, especially in his brave death; Henry is an expert administrator and politician, and yet can never achieve the style or charisma of a born monarch. Our sympathies are divided, and the dominant metaphors of the play convey a structure of antithesis – such as the image of two buckets in a well, one rising as the other is lowered. Richard's is the poetic temperament, and his plight is rendered in an interrelated set of cosmic and natural metaphors. He is the neglectful father of an unruly family, the ailing physician of a sick body politic, the indolent gardener of a paradise choked with weeds. His cosmos is disordered by comets, drought, a weeping universe, and a sun in decline. In his death he sees himself as a martyr and saint, and his moving depiction of life as a prison or shadow invokes an ideal of contemplative withdrawal by which Henry's worldly achievement appears crass and vain. Who has in fact triumphed, the rejected poet or the successful but tormented worldling? A latter-day poet, Yeats, has tellingly contrasted these two figures as a vessel of porcelain, exquisite but impractical, and a vessel of clay, hardy but graceless. To put the question thus is to wonder if Shakespeare sees an inherent contradiction in political rule, whereby the polarities of vision and pragmatism can never wholly coalesce.

The question remains central to the education of Prince Hal as he prepares to become Henry V. Can he retain the breadth of compassion and *joie de vivre* he has known under Falstaff's tutelage, and still attain dignity and the calculating, efficient use of power incumbent upon any great administrator? The struggle is posed for Hal by a series of foils, or contrasting yet parallel characters, whom he must both emulate and surpass by avoiding their fatal weaknesses. Falstaff embodies the camaraderie of youth and mirthful escape from responsibility, but is for that reason dangerously akin to licence, rebellion, and anarchy. Hal's own true father, unlike Falstaff, would have Hal grow up preternaturally wary and discreet; but Henry IV's counsel is marred by the insincere expediency of his political cunning. Still another foil character, Hotspur, so close to Hal in age and energy, holds out to the prince the ideal of bright honour. Yet Hotspur is a rebel, humourless, fanatic, so obsessed with honour that it tarnishes into egomania and leads him into a trap created by the Machiavellian intrigues of his own allies. Falstaff can easily puncture the hollowness of this honour, yet is himself deficient in the opposite extreme. Hal must find the middle course between Falstaff and Hotspur, Falstaff and Henry IV.

In *2 Henry IV* the foil to Falstaff is the Lord Chief Justice, and the issues are justice and reputation. Here, however, the structural equation is altered, for the Chief Justice is a man of complete probity whereas Falstaff's genius is on the wane. No longer the constant companion of the prince, Falstaff spends his time with prostitutes, rowdies, or corrupt Justices of the Peace. He fears death, and his hopes of attaining great dignities under Henry V are outlandish and pathetic. Hal's ultimate rejection of his companion seems both inevitable and somewhat heartless; it is incumbent upon him, and he finally accepts the consequences of maturity and kingship. The free play of his winsome personality must dwindle as he embraces the public and ceremonial role of leader; his choice of friends, as of wife, can no longer be simply his own. Still, the choice is made compassionately, on behalf of England's public weal, and is a sacrifice for which the prince too must feel some regret. We cannot seriously charge him with having used Falstaff merely to cultivate the myth of the prodigal son. The love between them, though brief, was too real for that. At least Hal is no replica of his cold-blooded brother, Prince John.

The concluding portrait in *Henry V* is not without its ironies. The war against France, furthered by all the slogans of patriotic fervour, has its seamier underside. The church hopes for war in order to avoid a heavy tax, and Hal chooses war as an instrument of uniting a discordant populace. Under martial law he eliminates political rivals with dispatch. We see him manipulating emotions with his great public speeches and his sportive visits in disguise to his soldiers' firesides. Notwithstanding, he is courageous, generous, and charismatic. He is amusedly condescending yet fond toward Fluellen, the cantankerous and old-fashioned Welshman who upholds the finest traditions of a unified British army. Although Hal's marriage with Katharine of France is a political alliance, he courts her with genuine relish and affection. Perhaps even an ideal English king is the prisoner of 'idol ceremony', since his chief contribution to society is a kind of play-acting, but Hal at least carries it off with style.

In his early comedies, as in his histories, Shakespeare experimented with genres that had only recently made their appearance on the Elizabethan popular stage, and, by the late 1590s, synthesized them into his own successful formula. Even at the very outset, he revealed a genius for transforming his models or sources, often classical or continental in origin, into an unmistakably English humour. *The Comedy of Errors*, for example, is a farce of mistaken identity, derived chiefly from Plautus's *Menaechmi*, or *The Twins*. Shakespeare has preserved from the original what suited him most: the swiftly-paced action and dialogue, the hilarity and improbability of the plot, the compression of events into one place and brief span of time, the farcical consistency of tone, and above all the ingenious structuring of the action whereby the initial error of mistaken identity is elaborated into every conceivable misconception, reaches a climax of confrontation, and then is neatly resolved with virtually every character brought to a suitable account. Shakespeare is indebted to classical tradition, in other words, for rhetoric, dramatic form, and decorum. The form is much unlike that of English popular romance of the period, with its sequential action, episodic multiplicity of event, and loose handling of time and place. Yet the English spirit is also dominant in the moral decency of Shakespeare's characters, the emphasis on the marital bond and on the need for public order.

In *Love's Labour's Lost*, Shakespeare gives us unmistakably English portraits of a hedge-priest, pedantic schoolmaster, small-town constable, clown, and country wench, complete with a rustic dramatic rendition of 'The Nine Worthies'. The main action, contrastingly, is a highly embroidered and courtly debate on love versus contemplative study, in the style of John Lyly. Similarly in *The Two Gentlemen of Verona*, the disputations on love versus friendship are periodically offset by the vaudeville-like clowning of the servants, Speed, and Launce with his dog. *The Taming of the Shrew*, in its double plot, juxtaposes the exquisite neoclassical structure of Ariosto's original, *I Suppositi* (*Supposes*), with the thoroughly English hilarity, slapstick violence, and facetious antifeminism of the wife-taming episode. Even in the neoclassical plot, the love relationships and satiric sketches are modestly expurgated to suit English popular mores.

A Midsummer Night's Dream, for which no extensive source has been found, skilfully interweaves not two but four distinct groups of characters, each with its own plot line and distinctive tone: the royal party of Theseus, the four lovers who flee into the woods, the fairies, and the rude mechanicals of Athens. Furthermore, Shakespeare introduces a structural motif of profound consequence to many of his later romantic comedies: the contrasting of two dramatic worlds, one earthbound, rational, legalistic, and competitive; the other distant, improbable, sylvan, and regenerative. It is 'the sharp Athenian law' urged by the prudent father, Egeus, that compels the lovers to flee from repressive civilization to the mystery and freedom of the forest. There they experience a transforming vision under the whimsical tutelage of the fairies, whose mad love quarrels are not so very different from those of mortal men. The fatuous tradesman, Bottom, also undergoes an enchanted pilgrimage, ludicrous in fashion because of his asininity but nonetheless wondrous. Who among us, after all, can boast that we have been the lover of the Faery Queen? This childlike faith in dream bears fruit in the mechanicals' play of 'Pyramus and Thisbe', so fearfully real to them that they must apologize for the power of artistic creation and so lay bare their contrivances. Theseus and his queen, who laugh at this simplicity, have alone been untouched by the magic of the forest; and Theseus' sardonic rationalism at the expense of all poetic vision, or madness, suggests that he is the poorer for being so worldly-wise. The pattern of this delicate play, and of the imaginative experience in its essence, is one (as in Keats's 'Nightingale') of brief and fantastic journey into the realm of the unseen, borne on the wings of frenzy and intoxication, from which one must awake as though haunted, uncertain what is real and what is not. As the fairies explain in the epilogue, the play itself has been but a shadow. Still, as Theseus knows, 'The best in this kind are but shadows' – the best of art is like a dream.

In *The Merchant of Venice*, the two contrasting worlds are those of Venice and Belmont. The city, dominated by the evil genius of Shylock, is commercial and cut-throat, a place of harsh law and sudden disasters, a man's world. Portia's Belmont is, like its mistress, enchantingly feminine and mysterious, in rarified and pure mountain air, reached only by a journey across water, a place of caskets, rings, fairy-tale riddles, harmonious melodies, nocturnal quietude. Bassanio's quest for Portia is like Jason's quest for the golden fleece, an adventure in which those who risk all deserve to win all. Shylock, contrastingly, holds to the letter of the law, the old dispensation lacking in grace and charity; it is his paradoxical fate to lose all because he has clung to those things dearest to him (even his daughter Jessica) as though they were merchandise. From Belmont, Portia must descend into the sultry and feverish arena of Venice to untangle those problems for which human institutions appear to offer no solutions. Antonio, who has risked all for friendship, is carried off to the regenerative company of Belmont, where he joins Jessica, Lorenzo, and all those who have practised *caritas*. Shylock, however sympathetically portrayed as a persecuted man, is cast by the comic structure of the play into the role of villain.

Much Ado about Nothing does not offer two diverse worlds that can be spatially located. There is, however, an important thematic contrast between appearance and reality, between the masks we show to others and our inner state of mind. The action of the play abounds in masking and overhearing scenes, in which the characters abuse one another with false surmise. Shakespeare characteristically employs a double plot, comparing two sets of lovers who must learn to understand one another as best they can. Claudio and Hero, the more conventional pair, fall easily in love but are only superficially acquainted; accordingly, they are prone to misconceptions based upon stereotyped attitudes. When rumour has it that Don Pedro, Claudio's superior officer and close friend, is wooing Hero for himself, Claudio jumps *a priori* to the predictable but wrong conclusion: all's fair in love and war, and so the rumour must be true. Claudio lacks faith, in other words, in Hero's unseen qualities. He cannot perceive simply that she couldn't do such a thing. The rumour is 'much ado about nothing', for it was based on mere fantasy. Yet it is potentially destructive. The second such delusion, cynically plotted by the villain Don John, is equally baffling to the young lover who has failed to learn his lesson. This time the charge of adultery is grave indeed, and would produce tragic results except for a providential intervention ludicrously appearing in the disguise of an inept police force. Justice stumbles on truth, and offers Claudio a third chance that he scarcely deserves. His Hero, whom he has apparently killed with his accusation, is brought back to life as though by miracle. The other lovers, Benedick and Beatrice, follow a different and more hopeful course to genuine rapport. Although they sardonically abuse one another with insults and swear never to marry, they are in fact idealists about love who need only to be convinced of the other's constancy and true worth. This time the deceptions practised on them take a benign turn, for they are fooled into believing what in fact has always been true. The exposure of one's deepest feeling is painful, because it leaves one vulnerable to callousness or indifference. Benedick and Beatrice struggle to retain what they consider to be the integrity of their personalities, but eventually discover that the most precious things involve risk and demand faith.

In *As You Like It* we again find contrasting worlds, of Duke Frederick's court and the Forest of Arden. The court is above all a place of envy, resenting the fair Orlando, Rosalind, and the banished elder duke for the goodness by which they outshine the practitioners of tyranny. When these fugitives from social oppression band together in the communal fraternity of the forest, they find a restorative natural order that will not reward hypocrisy or grasping ambition. They find also, as Jaques and Touchstone observe, that the forest has its defects: it is indifferent to suffering, and it lacks the graces of civilization. The forest is a means to regeneration, not a final resting place. It has a strange ability to move the hearts even of Frederick and of Orlando's churlish brother Oliver, who, by envying the virtuous, have shown their secret longing to be better than they know how to be. The forest, by stripping away the pretensions of social intercourse, enables man to free himself from the prison of his own insincerity. Still, when Orlando and his old servant Adam are threatened by starvation in the pitiless wilderness, it is the compassion of their fellow-creatures that saves them; and this sudden appearance of Orlando at the rustic banquet prompts the banished duke to think, not of man's ingratitude to man, but of the church-bells and other institutional conventions they have all known in better days, and to which they will return.

Twelfth Night is, like its near contemporary *Henry V*, the triumphant culmination of a popular form Shakespeare had shaped to his own particular genius, and which he was about to lay aside. In its types of comic appeal this play characteristically blends farce (the familiar Plautine business of mistaken identity) with coarse buffoonery (Sir Toby and company), and most of all with Shakespeare's 'philosophic' comedy of love and marriage raised to a Platonic perspective of eternal joyousness. The subplot of Sir Toby and Malvolio also uses the comic device of satirical exposure, so much in vogue on the boy actors' newly-reopened private stage. Yet the genial Shakespeare cannot let satire have the last word: the outraged Malvolio is entreated to a peace, and his compassionate mistress Olivia thinks he has been 'most notoriously abused'. Like its unattractive apologist Jaques, in *As You Like It*, satire is too destructive and potentially sadistic a form of expression to dominate the festive character of *Twelfth Night*. Rather, in a Saturnalian mood of post-Christmas celebration, Malvolio's churlish gospel of denial must be answered by the positive ideal of release. 'Youth's a stuff will not endure', sings the Fool, and Viola echoes this innocently hedonistic spirit when she urges Olivia to give up sterile mourning and embrace the proper uses of beauty. Sin or madness in this play is equated with Malvolio's wish to spoil others' happiness, a madness graphically portrayed through a pervasive metaphor of inversion. We see Malvolio, the apostle of sobriety, imprisoned as a madman for his erratic behaviour in yellow stockings, while the Fool roams freely abroad and is mistaken by Malvolio for a learned clergyman. Illyria thus becomes a joyously improbable world where appearance and reality are wholly reversed. The lovers undergo experiences as though in a dream, and are transformed.

To comment briefly on the tragedies of the Elizabethan period is to underscore the relative lateness of any central artistic preoccupation with this genre. *Titus Andronicus* is hardly an auspicious start. *Romeo and Juliet* is exquisite, but in ways that more resemble the lyric comedies than the late tragedies. Its lovers come from ordinary rather than exalted backgrounds, and are almost totally innocent of the catastrophes engulfing them. In a tragedy of circumstance and family feuding, they are the sacrificial victims. The lessons of their ill-fated passion – the poignant brevity of love, the obstinacy of parents, the misunderstanding of society at large – are those of such comedies as *A Midsummer Night's Dream*; and indeed the deaths of Romeo and Juliet bear a striking resemblance to those of Pyramus and Thisbe.

139

In poetic texture as well, *Romeo and Juliet* is permeated with hilarious bawdry and elaborate Petrarchan metaphors.

Julius Caesar (1598–1600), although approaching tragic maturity, has important affinities with Shakespeare's history plays of the same period. As in *Richard II*, we find a lack of focus on a single protagonist, and witness instead the carefully balanced confrontation between political rivals. Whose actions are more justified, Caesar's or Brutus'? Because the scene is Rome, English standards of monarchical heredity do not apply; nonetheless, in Brutus' eyes Caesar is a usurper, unfit to govern because he has violated senatorial tradition. Yet what can Brutus hope to accomplish by Caesar's death, other than another illegitimacy of rule and an invitation to civil strife? Shakespeare ironically characterizes Brutus as not unlike the very man he would supplant: deaf to counsel, fatally prone to flattery, and proud. Even though Brutus is truly noble, he cannot command a noble revolution; for revolution itself plays into the hands of less scrupulous politicians such as Antony and Octavius.

With *Hamlet* (1599–*c.* 1601), Shakespearean tragedy comes triumphantly into its own right, and in a way that hauntingly depicts the sombre cosmic preoccupations of the 1600s. The recurrent imagery of *Hamlet* is of unweeded gardens, ulcerated sores filmed over, inward poisons, garments of hypocritical seeming. Claudius impresses Denmark with his watchful diplomacy; Polonius is all sagacity; Rosencrantz and Guildenstern are loyal, earnest subjects. Only Hamlet knows the truth, and it is his dreadful secret that alienates him from all the rest. The courtiers think Hamlet mad, and analyse his infirmity in ways that tellingly reveal their own: to Rosencrantz and Guildenstern Hamlet is politically ambitious, and so on. This alienation provokes Hamlet to mistrust exceedingly his erstwhile friends, and to generalize about human nature and the universe in profoundly pessimistic terms. His behaviour is indeed antisocial and his response to Claudius' villainy ineffectual, as he himself observes; but on balance we blame not Hamlet but his corrupted world. Even the Ghost's command is riddling, for it involves cold-blooded murder, and to a man of Hamlet's poetic sensibility such crass action is indefensible. Hamlet is confronted above all with the inherent absurdity of action in an imperfect world. Only when he subscribes to a providential view of destiny is an answer unexpectedly provided him. Truly, as John Donne said, the 'new philosophy' of the 1600s has cast all in doubt.

10

SHAKESPEARE THE JACOBEAN
DRAMATIST

M. C. BRADBROOK

His Jacobean decade (1603–13) includes Shakespeare's major tragedies beyond *Hamlet*, the Roman plays, the last romances, *Timon of Athens*, *King Henry VIII*. In 1609 his sonnets were first printed. By 1613, both Shakespeare and Beaumont left the stage, and the decade had seen also the chief masterpieces of Jonson, Tourneur, Webster and Chapman.

A period of relative social stability permitted the indulgence of creative instability in the arts. In the drama, whilst new Italian influences were brought to bear at court yet London players, and especially Shakespeare's company, were at the height of their prosperity. Practised and confident, the craftsmen had evolved their own native standards to challenge both ecclesiastical opponents and academic legislators. Alleyn and Henslowe, Burbage and Shakespeare, were gentlemen, each with his coat of arms; a truce had prevailed in the war against the sinfulness of the stage which had been waged earlier and was to be resumed later.

Playwrights felt confident enough to turn to self-questioning, which sharpened into satiric comedy or darkened into the tragic mode. In the new intimacy of a closed theatre, the subtlety of the actors brought them and the audience together to study personal conflicts, so that 'to the new age, so often sceptical, tentative and self conscious in its exploration of hidden motives, a new style was necessary, a style that could express the mind as it was in action, could record thought at the moment it arose in the mind'.[1] A theatre rooted in traditional social rituals was being replaced by an art at once more critical and more individual, more sharply divided from popular entertainment. This was the age both of Shakespeare and of Jonson; the deeper probings came from the more traditional craftsman. While Jonson's interests were social and 'politic', and led him towards analysis of a 'Machiavellian' kind, Shakespeare with Montaigne turned from social issues to the proper study of Mankind, a being 'ondoyant et divers'.

In a theatre, the form of the building itself expresses and conditions social response. This period saw a revolution in stage technique, the transition from what was essentially still the medieval open stage, to the ancestor of the closed modern house. It saw also a great development in spectacular staging, in which court productions led the way. But the popular theatres also developed new and better 'machines'.

The general temper of the first Jacobean decade was satiric and critical. With Italian sets, Italianate tragedies also became fashionable; the second wave of Revenge plays – that of Marston, Tourneur and Webster – showed the great influence of *Hamlet*, while Shakespeare himself moved on from the Revenge tradition. Satiric city comedy, and political tragedy were Jonsonian forms designed for the more sophisticated part of the audience; but as the cheats and rogues of the comedy were caricatures, drawn within a set convention, so the evil world of Italy was seen as an aspect of England. As G. K. Hunter has pointed out, it bore little resemblance to the Italy of the Counter Reformation, of Spanish hegemony and Baroque art.

The dark negations of Webster are perhaps finally less disquieting than the new melodramatic art of Fletcher.

a more relaxed drama, which in its character-types mirrored a stable world and yet in its language maintained and indeed further developed the informality of the earliest Jacobean years. The essential property of the new Beaumont and Fletcher drama consists in its dislocation... There is no firm ground for reverence, or for a cosmic scheme, in the great majority of the plays which deeply bear John Fletcher's impress. Neither Fletcher nor Beaumont was ever a declared revolutionary, yet few dramatists can have written plays so fully destructive in implication.[2]

Shakespeare, fifteen years older than Fletcher, evolved no single form. In the space of four years, 1604–8, he appears to have composed *Othello, King Lear, Macbeth, Antony and Cleopatra, Coriolanus* and perhaps some lesser works. The form of each is distinct from the rest, to a much greater degree than had been the case with his Elizabethan comedies and histories. The English history play, to which Shakespeare had given such predominance, passed into rapid decline.[3] Even when it depicted tragic disorder, the history had rested on assumptions of social order reaching back to the great providential history of creation which the craft guilds had presented from Chaucer's time until the Reformation. Of course, the pieties and assurances that sustained civic pageantry had not gone unquestioned in the theatre that saw Marlowe's *Edward II*; and Shakespeare's own sequence reveals a deepening scepticism. The emblematic framework was never quite as stable as critics like Tillyard tend to suggest, and Ulysses' famous speech on degree is a lament for its passing.

Although the presence of the aged Queen Elizabeth had sustained the providential legend of the coming of the Tudors, yet even before her death it had faded. James I was not the stuff of which public images are made, so that the British Solomon was soon replaced in popular idolatry by the youthful Prince Henry. Loss of the royal image symbolized much deeper loss, which on the stage can be registered in scenic terms:

For centuries kings had been presented to the public, whether real kings in public ceremonies, or actor kings in plays and pageants, in a throne backed by a symbol of the realm. That symbol combined elements from the pageant-castles, from the city gates, from triumphal arches, from the choir screen of the church. The throne was framed by columns supporting a canopy, a 'heavens' – exactly the same kind of pavilion-canopy used to frame an altar or a tomb...Its background structure resembled a castle, a throne, a city gate, a tomb, or an altar. It was a symbol of social order and of divine order – of the real ties between man and king, between heaven and earth.[4]

The tomb of Shakespeare's master, Baron Hunsdon, in Westminster Abbey, its black altar shape flanked by gilded obelisks and wreathed trophies is one of the more splendid examples of this kind. Hunsdon died in 1597. After 1603, Shakespeare can show only the vacated throne of Lear, Macbeth's haunted chair. Perhaps the ghost of King Hamlet represents more than the demise of a single royalty.

As a historian, Professor Christopher Hill accepts this as evidence of a change:

All old conventions are being challenged. We could tell simply by reading the literature of the time that two sets of standards were in conflict. In *King Lear*, the traditional feudal patriarchal loyalties are challenged by the blind individualism of Goneril, Regan and Edmund...in later Jacobean and Caroline drama the tension is lost.[5]

The shift from English history to the Roman tragedy of *Julius Caesar* and the Trojan tragedy of *Troilus and Cressida* freed Shakespeare of certain presuppositions. 'Roman society lacked a divine sanction, or at least it seemed to the Christian tradition to have done so; it was therefore a fit ground in which to explore the political behaviour of men empirically, freed from the assumption of a providence shaping their ends.'[6] Ralegh's *History of the World* was to show the conflict still unresolved; and by the time he wrote *Antony and Cleopatra* Shakespeare had enlarged humanity to almost godlike state – though the descendant of Hercules and the incarnation of Isis fall among the defeated.

Meanwhile, however, politics considered as an autonomous activity subjected the greatest heroes to a scrutiny which patriotism had withheld from the hero of Agincourt – Caesar is godlike and ailing, Hector gallant but without a princely sense of responsibility. Hamlet behaves outrageously to Ophelia, yet we believe her when she cries 'O, what a noble mind is here o'erthrown!'

Maynard Mack has distinguished the two voices of Jacobean tragedy as those of the hero and his foil – Hamlet and the gravedigger, Emilia and Desdemona, Cleopatra and the countryman each speak in languages which do not commune; their dialogue can never be finally adjudicated, but the opposites must somehow be reconciled. We believe in Othello's nobility – and we believe Emilia when she calls him 'ignorant as dirt'; Goneril terms Lear an 'idle old man' and Cordelia kneels to the mad-man as 'my royal lord'. Both command assent, but as a saint has said, we must first believe in order that we may understand.

The complexity of character as it is shown directly, and the com-plexity of its conflict-relations with others presupposes a much finer meshed form of acting established between members of the company. After 1608, Shakespeare worked for the closed theatre at Blackfriars as well as for the open stage of the Globe, which marked a decisive break with the old 'playing place' or 'game place' of medieval times. Yet, far from supporting Glynne Wickham's view that this was a move towards the modern stage of naturalism and prose, Shakespeare turned in his final plays towards the old romances and 'drama of the gaps', adapting the purely theatrical trends that were now in ascendancy.

Growing sophistication in the audience altered their relation with the actors and playwright; by 1611, Fletcher was offering a virtuoso display of passion to the judgement of connoisseurs, while at the end of his life, victim of habits he had inculcated, Jonson bitterly carica-tured the critic Damplay.

As social confrontation hardened, leading up to the Civil War, the theatre was to shrink to a vehicle for courtly views, dependent on courtly favour. Social cross currents were still swirling and eddying through the early Jacobean theatre; the turbulence assured its great-ness. Shakespeare's power of synthesis established some community of theme between a popular romance like *Pericles* and the delicate courtly masquing of *The Tempest*, so that modern writers tend to forget that they belong to totally different kinds of theatre.

As in the golden decade, Shakespeare's company dominated without overwhelming the others (in Caroline times it stood far ahead), so it has recently been argued that Shakespeare dominated the play-wrights.[7] By the second decade of James's reign, both Fletcher and Massinger, writing for his company, were capable of stagey writing, that is, of utilizing a theatrical success by borrowing situations, to use as a series of properties. Such a labour-saving device, not unwelcome in a repertory company, perhaps, offered short cuts to the actors, and was quite different from the rhetorical borrowings of Elizabethan times, which were more literary. The plot situation and some key lines of *Othello* were used by Massinger in *The Emperor of the East*, but for the court were given an incongruous happy ending.

Shakespeare's Jacobean tragedies are full of scenes which imprint the character in action upon the minds of the audience. Such great stage moments as Lear on the heath, Othello at Desdemona's bedside, Macbeth and the witches radiate symbolic potency – they have often given themes for painting – yet they do not belong to a ritual tradition like the earlier tourneys, coronations, challenges; they are not loaded with memories of other like events, but are at once representative of the human condition yet stamped with the specific mark of a particular plot and a master craftsman. Free from old emblematic forms, and as yet without a trading stock of melodramatic images, Shakespearian tragedies result from a balance of interest between playwright, actors and audience.

At a much humbler level such a balance can be seen in the collaborative work on city pageants, which Shakespeare's contemporaries were engaged in;[8] and the final proof of it is the collaboration which he engaged in during the composition of his latest plays, *Pericles*, *Two Noble Kinsmen*, the lost *Cardenio* and possibly *King Henry VIII*. In these latest plays, a new kind of emblematic scene is established; it is the language of the poet that validates the stage image, not the image which carries the words as accompaniment. Enobarbus' description of Cleopatra in her barge justifies the abruptness of Antony's 'I will to Egypt' though he himself has not heard the words; to him the soothsayer only appears as an emissary of Egyptian magic power. The statue scene of *The Winter's Tale*, the masques of *The Tempest* provide the climax of action; yet, as I have indicated elsewhere,[9] they evoke the scenic emblems of Shakespeare's youth – the Living Statue, the Ship, the Cave, and other 'devices'. Some of the ancient rôles, the May Queen, Monster and Magician are used to explore an interior world where fine and delicate sensibilities alternate with 'imagination foul as Vulcan's stithy'.

Any attempt to discuss Shakespeare's Jacobean achievement which is not swamped in generalities must be highly selective. Its specific qualities will be more clearly brought out by a consideration of the first Jacobean tragedy, *Othello*, and the first romance, *Pericles*.

Othello was performed at court on 1 November 1604; it captivated the popular stage, where ever since it has been central to the Shakespearian repertory. In Jacobean times, the characters are more often referred to than any others save Hamlet and Falstaff. The story was new to the stage; its bold and splendid roles inverted traditional ones.

All stage Moors were wicked demi-devils; Aaron of *Titus Andronicus*, 'a Moor that has damnation dyed upon his flesh' shares the diabolic gaiety of Marlowe's Ithamore, who like many a later Moor or Turk, is associated in complots with a Machiavellian. Crude atrocity plays depicting such a pair, atheist or infidel, treacherous and parricidal, mechanical bogeymen of the most automatic gesticulations, lasted till Caroline times.[10]

Even in Webster the disguise of a Moor often covers a diabolic 'second self'; but in Shakespeare all the characteristics expected for these familiar figures are transferred to Iago. The tempter is marked, by his malicious wit and Mephistophelian contempt for virtue, as the hero's foil. Iago 'is *homo emancipatus a Deo*, seeing the world and human life as self-sufficient on their own terms...[man] is the king of beasts, crowned by his superior faculties. And society, by the same token, is the arena of endless competition...To the kind of love existing between hero and heroine,...the ancient is the dark counter-type, the adversary...nothing engrosses him so much as the subject of love or receives from him so mordant a negation.'[11] Yet the betrayed Othello sees no cloven hoof – 'I look down towards his feet; but that's a fable' – and turns back with animal cries to the body of his 'girl', all ceremony lost. The spiritually human and the animal blend; behaviour, dominant over doctrine, shapes belief. Othello, a baptised Moor, uses the votive candle as symbol of his earthly saint – 'Put out the light, and then put out the light'. Heaven and Hell gleam through the play, as when Othello and Iago kneel to make their deadly compact:

> Arise, black vengeance, from the hollow hell.
> Yield up, O love, thy crown and hearted throne
> To tyrannous hate!   (III, iii, 451–3)

Yet the play turns on the magic of the lost love token; if the one lover is the descendant of kings, the other daughter of a Venetian senator, a domestic love story challenged the traditional view that high tragedy involved 'the growth, state, and declination of Princes, change of Government and lawes, vicissitudes of sedition, faction, succession, confederacies, plantations, with all other errors, or alterations in publique affaires.'[12]

There is a marked indifference to what every Elizabethan would feel the chief interest of Cyprus – the history of the Turkish attack, their defeat at the Battle of Lepanto, their subsequent conquest.

> When I love thee not
> Chaos is come again.   (III, iii, 92–3)

makes love and not society the regulative principle of Othello's life.
He tells Emilia

> had she been true,
> If heaven would make me such another world
> Of one entire and perfect chrysolite,
> I'd not have sold her for it.   (v, ii, 146–9)

The flawless talismanic stone that no force could crack or break is
symbolized in the fragile web of her soul and body; there was magic
in *this* web. To Desdemona Othello also is a world: 'My heart's sub-
dued / Even to the very quality of my lord' (I, iii, 250–1). When
she hears that Cassio has been killed, Desdemona's cry 'Alas,
he is betrayed and I undone!' implies that she herself cannot be
betrayed for she takes Othello's mistakes and guilt on herself. Though
she knows herself to be falsely murdered and to die guiltless, when
Emilia cries 'O, who hath done this deed?' she can reply 'Nobody;
I myself', for it is herself, her other self, who is guilty. Othello at once
intuitively recognizes and cannot endure the truth of the words, which
assert their unity as one flesh, if not entirely of one mind and heart;
so he repudiates it in a great burst of self-directed rage:

> She's like a liar gone to burning hell;
> 'Twas I that killed her.   (v, ii, 132–3)

To that same hell Emilia at once consigns him:

> O, the more angel she,
> And you the blacker devil!   (v, ii, 134–5)

The angel and the devil are yet one flesh and this is what each is
asserting behind the frantic words.

When a middle-aged alien, honoured yet but a denizen of the state,
wins a love that is hazardous and vulnerable because only imperfectly
in accord with social habit, the Doge endorses the act of free election,
in spite of social disapproval. A warrior among merchants, Othello
had chosen his Venetian masters and served freely; like Desdemona,
he belonged to a new society of chosen and contractual individualism.

Desdemona thereby assumes a servant's obedience ('I will not stay
to offend you'). A wife owed fealty to her husband; if she murdered
him, she was guilty not only of murder but of treason also. To one
bred in the habit of command, wedded to the daughter of his 'very
noble and approved good masters' the revolt from obedience destroyed
the foundations of his being:

> They have the power to hurt us whom we love,
> We lay our sleeping lives within their arms.

A year earlier than this play, in 1603, Thomas Heywood had shown a betrayed husband who could yet allow tenderness full play, banishing his guilty wife – 'It was thy hand cut two hearts out of one'. Her penitent death restored the marriage tie:

> My wife, the mother to my pretty babes!
> Both these lost names I do restore thee back,
> And with this kiss I wed thee once again.[13]

The new principle of character introduced is one of growth and change, felt as a change in relationships. Compared with Heywood's scene of conversion and reconversion, the temptation of Othello in Acts III and IV constitutes a new way of making plays. Organic psychological growth or degeneration, central to Shakespeare's four great tragedies, distinguishes them from his own later plays as from his earlier ones.

The shame of a noble nature is itself a kind of expiation in Cassio and Othello. The hero has become one to be cursed by Emilia, ordered about by Ludovico, disarmed by Montano:

> Soft you; a word or two before you go:
> I have done the state some service and they know it.
>
> (V, ii, 341–2)

This might be a defence plea; the Venetians halt to hear their prisoner. But that he 'forsake the room and go with them' is impossible. Recalling his act of almost suicidal loyalty against the malignant Turk in Aleppo, he looks on his stricken life and his own 'Turkish' self – the theatrical image which Shakespeare has so firmly repudiated – and divides it cleanly from him. Executing the judgement of the court, he fulfils another role of the black-visaged man (as in Peacham's scene from *Titus Andronicus*, he is familiar). For Othello is a soldier, absolute and decisive, used to letting his muscles take over from his mind in crisis. The tears he sheds are like the fruit of the myrrh tree, emblem of death; but they are healing. In death he ventures to kiss his wife, nor does he feel any longer divided from her:

> No way but this:
> Killing myself to die upon a kiss.

The nineteenth century's view of Othello as entirely noble ('there is none we love like Othello', said Swinburne) produced its reaction; few would go so far as the critic who thought Desdemona so guilty in deceiving her father, as to call down a deserved fate. But it has been suggested more than once that Othello is damned for committing suicide, or that his lack of insight alienates. T. S. Eliot's influential words on the final speech set the tone for a whole generation of critics:

I...have never read a more terrible exposure of human weakness...What Othello seems to me to be doing is *cheering himself up*. He is endeavouring to escape reality...dramatizing himself...He takes in the spectator, but the human motive is primarily to take in himself.[14]

Enlarging on this, Leavis thinks Othello's 'habit of self approving dramatization' is often 'a disguise' for 'obtuse and brutal egoism'.

It is significant that Eliot talks of 'reading' the speech. Such an interpretation could never be used in the theatre. It simply is not actable.

Moreover this view, it has been remarked, is quite close to Iago's view of Othello; it is also quite close to that of Shakespeare's source. It is what then might have been expected in such a story, particularly by theatregoers; but the power of Shakespeare's drama is generated by departure from the stock action for an Eleazer, a Muly Mahomet. The conflict and sympathy of this play depends in the first place on the character of the hero contradicting a stereotype, and secondly in the slow poisoning and quick final recovery, the change of speed in his development. Jacobean spectators were used to hearing speeches from the scaffold, in which a dying man put off his guilt.

J. I. M. Stewart sees both Iago and Othello as 'abstractions from a single and, as it were, invisible protagonist...It is less a matter of Othello projecting concealed facets of himself upon Iago...than of the dramatist's abstracting these facets, and embodying them in a figure substantially symbolic.'[15] For W. H. Auden, on the other hand, Iago is far more significant and interesting than Othello; there are as many Iagos as there are characters for him to deceive, and he must display every trick for which great actors are praised. Everything he sets out to do he accomplishes, including his own self-destruction. He exists to play with the lives of others, producing a ruinous change, like that of a cancer cell, in the organic body of relationships; for he could say, with the Serpent of Valéry, 'Je suis Celui qui modifie'.[16]

These divergent views show with what variety it is possible for individuals to identify with each of the characters, and to project the conflict *in toto* rather than single aspects. When A. C. Bradley found in *Othello* 'a certain limitation, a partial suppression of that element in Shakespeare which unites him with the mystical poets and with the greatest musicians and philosophers' he did not recognize that this lack of the symbolic, or of a cosmic dimension was itself a great act of emancipation, a shedding of the taboos and irrational supports which some critics are eager to put back. Shakespeare had gone off the gold standard of conventional judgements, and had gained a floating position where the audience must follow with its own judgement the natural pulses of sympathy. Crowds thronged to see 'kind Lear' and 'the grieved Moor'.[17] It was less than thirty years since feeling had been blocked out by the stage direction for Tamburlaine when he sees Zenocrate with his rival; 'he goes to her and takes her away lovingly by the hand, looking wrathfully on Agydas, and saying nothing'. Othello never holds anything back; his words are always ready to command. In his madness he gains no deepened insight such as comes to Hamlet or Lear. But the sharp orders and animal cries, the hero's fit of delirious rage belong with a new sympathetic acting technique; the feminine part of the audience would have been as responsive to the appeal of the exotic as was Desdemona herself. The sensuous warmth and opulence of the language, the firm rhythm, the sustained simplicity of action join together the leading parts in their interaction on each other and on the audience. In the eavesdropping scene, for instance, Bianca acts the part of a whore, while Cassio responds and Othello interprets the whole thing in terms of his wife (IV, i, 120–44).

Othello's fury at being offered his own love-token to soothe the pain of his brow's 'injury' not only causes Desdemona to drop the handkerchief but to forget where she lost it. The 'faith, half asleep' with which she excuses her half-fainting condition after the brothel scene, her fearful noting in the death-scene of Othello's rolling eyes and the gnawing of his lip demand interpretation and participation from the audience. After the brawl, honest Iago 'looks dead with grieving' (II, iii, 173). The pleasures of variety are joined with firm 'conceit' – or 'conception' – of each part. This 'Method' style must have emanated from Burbage who was famous as a 'Protean' actor, living entirely inside his role, and never putting it off, even in the tiring house. Younger actors, trained by him, would conform – as in modern times, they conformed to Stanislavsky. The chameleon poet, as Keats observed, has as much delight in conceiving an Iago as an Imogen; the poet, like the actor, has no identity. Yet, fundamentally, we talk always out of our own experience; and as this play inverts some conventional stage roles, it reflects – but also inverted – the bitter story of betrayal that is told in the sonnets. The clever servant who so thoroughly dominates his master, who by his talent for acting the blunt man acceptably gets his own way, might have been a role with which Shakespeare in his darkest moments could identify, no less than with the unconditional generosity of forgiveness in Cassio and Desdemona. Physical facts are acknowledged in the sonnets with the very pun that maddens Othello:

> When my love swears that she is made of truth,
> I do believe her, though I know she lies...
> Therefore I lie with her, and she with me,
> And in our faults by lies we flatter'd be.
>
> (Sonnet 138)

'Lie with her! lie on her! they say lie on her, when they belie her!' cries Othello at news of the 'confession' (IV, i, 36–7). If part of the sonnet situation appears in the grief of Othello, the nausea of the sonnets on the Dark Lady, and the straight sexual abuse of others, sounds like Iago's voice; the invisible protagonist in whom Iago and Othello are united wrote the sonnets. Othello's social insecurity, his hesitation about his age, his peculiarly flat use of an emblematic heaven and hell conceived as stage locations could be paralleled, with agonized sense of a metamorphosis in the beloved image:

> Her name, that was as fresh
> As Dian's image, is now begrim'd and black
> As my own face: (III, iii, 390–2)
> But I have sworn thee fair and thought thee bright
> Who art as black as hell, as dark as night.   (Sonnet 147)

Buried at a deep level, with the relation of friendship and love inverted, the older experience, already once shaped in the alembic of the imagination, may have assisted in *Othello*'s deep catharsis, unaccompanied as it is by strain or complexity or the reverberation of further unresolved conflicts. The eloquence and unity of this play, the close relation of all characters in one great household might suggest that behind it lies the old emblem of the Tree of Life, with its many branches:

No man is an island, entire of itself; every man is a piece of the continent, a part of the main; if a clod be washed away by the sea, Europe is the less, as well as if a promontory were, as well as if a manor of thy friends or of thine own were; any man's death diminishes me, because I am involved in mankind. And therefore never send to know for whom the bell tolls; it tolls for thee.[18]

Unity behind the rending divisions, which derives perhaps from the underlying unity in a conflict projected from a personal experience is endorsed by the ease and power of rhythm and movement in the play, its shapeliness and order. Based on natural relations, as expressed by the actors in their sense of an ensemble, this kind of unity is far less direct and obvious than one based on hierarchy and degree, or on social analysis and 'humourous observation' of Jonson's kind.

As social ritual, the Jacobean court masque replaced the Elizabethan history play. Celebrating unity and concord, but designed for the few rather than the many, it depended on those assumptions of order and degree which, whatever their philosophic validity, were no longer socially at the centre. The Platonic assumptions of a great festive poem like Spenser's *Epithalamium* were challenged by a scepticism and pessimism which found its most powerful expression on the public stage, above all perhaps in the world of *King Lear*.

Shakespeare's final plays are related to the masque and also to the older emblematic stages of his youth. Their relation to the masque is attested by their effect on Milton, whose own masques are his most Shakespearian writings. The structure is poetic, but goes well beyond the poetry to spectacle and presentation, and draws on a great range of social and theatrical habit. With a striking unity of theme they offer a range of audience appeal and of staging as wide as the tragedies that precede them. *Coriolanus* and *Antony and Cleopatra* can be contrasted as a play of strict and severe control, and one of great opulence and variety. When Antony sums up his story in the speech to Eros 'Sometimes we see a cloud that's dragonish' he anticipates Prospero's speech on the ending of the revels; the underlying principle has been a succession of pompous and baroque pageants melting into each other. The pageant of Cleopatra as Venus, described by Enobarbus, is directly presented by her in her death scene. A river pageant and a royal performance by a Queen, African and richly robed in pearl and blue and silver, had been seen as early as 1605 on the Whitehall stage. In Ben Jonson's *Masque of Blackness*, Anne of Denmark had appeared in person, seated in a great shell with her maids of honour, and surrounded by sporting Tritons. This masque, in which for the first time the Queen of England appeared as a player, could not have failed to move the imagination of the King's servants who would – including Shakespeare – have been in attendance. It joined perhaps with memories of Elizabethan pageantry on the Thames.

The Winter's Tale and *The Tempest* appear connected in some way with the marriage of Princess Elizabeth, later Queen of Bohemia. The tale of *Cymbeline* reshapes British history, giving a romantic and distanced view of Roman and British elements. But *The Winter's Tale* also refashioned a romance of Shakespeare's old stage enemy, Robert Greene, dead some twenty years; *Cymbeline* recalls other early plays of those far-off times such as *Clyamon and Clamydes*. In *Pericles* and *The Two Noble Kinsmen* Chaucer and Gower, poets of an older time, are invoked as supporters; the second may reshape that famous early lost play, Edwards' *Palamon and Arcite*, and it certainly contains echoes of Shakespeare's own *A Midsummer Night's Dream*.

A popular and perennially attractive romance, *Pericles* incurred the scorn of Ben Jonson, who dismissed it as a 'mouldy tale' a relic of a feast of language, left for alms like 'the shrieve's crusts'. However, in 1619 it was given at a court performance in honour of the departing French ambassador. The performance was divided into two halves – after Act II – the point at which Shakespeare took over the writing.

During this interval especially sumptuous refreshments were served in china dishes, and the late-night show ended at two in the morning. On such an occasion a 'mouldy tale' would seem no fit offering.

Dryden who adapted and improved on *The Tempest* in his *Enchanted Island*, thought *Pericles* 'a ridiculous incoherent story'. Dr Johnson found *The Winter's Tale* 'with all its absurdities, very entertaining' but coming to *Cymbeline*, refused to 'waste criticism upon unresisting imbecility, upon faults too evident for detection and too gross for aggravation'. The popularity of *Pericles* puzzled contemporaries, as it still puzzles critics, for poetry of the gaps is always bewildering. Many references suggest that it had no right to be as popular as it was; though included in the projected edition of Shakespeare's works for 1619, it did not appear in the First Folio of 1623, where *Timon of Athens*, another puzzling play, was inserted only to fill a printer's need. *The Two Noble Kinsmen* was never formally acknowledged; these may represent only a portion of Shakespeare's minor uncompleted work, in which he reverted to the older habit of working with a collaborator.

These 'tales, tempests and such drolleries' as Jonson scornfully termed them, combined shows (or drolleries) of great splendour with violent action, and passages of concentrated writing, sometimes delicate, sometimes ferocious. The disturbed imagination that confers insight on a Hamlet, a Lear, a Macbeth is here presenting the play. The intuitive linking of character with character – so that, for example, in *King Lear* the Fool 'serves as a screen on which Shakespeare flashes readings from the psychic life of the protagonist' – now extends itself so that the total drama is seen from outside the normal range of view by one, like Gower, 'assuming man's infirmities' but not really subject to them. Imogen waking beside the headless trunk of Cloten dressed in her husband's garments 'produces an effect like that of the modern Theatre of the Absurd in its violence and incongruity. The devouring of Paulina's husband by the bear is reinforced in its comic horror by the clownish jocularity of the shepherd: 'I have not winked since I saw these sights; the men are not yet cold under water, nor the bear half din'd on the gentleman; he's at it now' (*The Winter's Tale* III, iii, 101–4).

The Two Noble Kinsmen is sprinkled with images of horror to parallel the tableau of slain knights at the opening of *Pericles*; an unburied king that

> I' the blood cizd field lay swoln,
> Shewing the Sun his teeth, grinning at the moon　(I, i, 103–4)

and women that have

> sod their Infants in (and after eat them)
> The brine they wept at killing 'em.　(I, ii, 24–5)

The colloquial violence of the brothel scenes in *Pericles* stands out from the homespun texture of the rest no less than does the poetry of the final recognition scene, for which perhaps the whole play was devised. In the beautiful trance-like calm of this 'Ship' scene, silence is broken only by deliberately inadequate words till Pericles finally hears the music of the spheres, inaudible to mortals:

> Such harmony is in immortal souls,
> But while this muddy vesture of decay
> Doth grossly close it in, we cannot hear it.
> (*Merchant of Venice* v, i, 63–5)

The presenter, Gower, from whose *Confessio Amantis* the story comes, stands 'i' the gaps to teach you / The stages of our story' and promises the audience

> What's done in action, more if might,
> Shall be discover'd; please you sit and hark.

His final trite moral summary, like the even more trite summary concluding *The Two Noble Kinsmen*, underlines how little can be discovered. Sudden transforming of humanity into puppets, or *vice versa*, as if charmed by Prospero's rod, constitutes the shock treatment of these plays; the jagged join of old and new styles, the turbulence of subtle feelings and preposterous violence is made explicit by the presenter.

The framework of a medieval Romance or tale of adventure had been provided by those fixed and regular habits from which it gave a momentary escape. The struggle to retain and transform the old form is part of the history of Elizabethan literature. In the theatre, romance had been decried from the time of Philip Sidney, with his mocking account of adventurous stage journeys. Shakespeare returned to these old forms (being himself already mocked in *The Knight of the Burning Pestle* for the inflated rhetoric of his Hotspur). He could only attempt to invoke something beyond the ordinary framework.

The 'play within a play' was by this time familiar enough; what is presented in these plays is something like 'the play beyond the play' – those larger and unheard harmonies of which it is an echo.

Cervantes had found another way to this humane achievement of reconciliation; but it is to Cervantes that anyone in search of a comparable imagination must turn. As *Othello* gains its effect by concentrating upon the natural and shutting out cosmic reverberations, the romances are designed to reverberate and vibrate in accordance with what is brought to them. In a doctrinal and critical age, they appeal, they charm or sometimes repel, but 'the poet never affirmeth and therefor never lieth'. And yet, as one of Shakespeare's jesters knew, 'the truest poetry is the most feigning'.

The unity of time and place in *The Tempest* is masterly, a direct evidence of control; but it does not, compared with the other romances, give the sense of relief of a dislocated joint falling into place; for the logic of Time as chorus in *The Winter's Tale* works in a different way. The speedy fall and slow recovery of faith may be contrasted with the movement of Othello's mind; and in that play, the 'double time' skilfully controls the tension and response. Nowadays, being used to working with two-clock systems, even analytic pedants may accept what was perhaps, originally, the craftsman's intuitive cunning.

A Caroline defender of the poet, feigning disapproval of both Jonson 'the Dagon-poet' and Shakespeare, declares:

> Shakespeare, the Plebeian Driller, was
> Founder'd in's *Pericles* and must not pass.[19]

To drill could mean to *whirl, twirl*, or *churn*, i.e Shakespeare devised this popular whirligig of a plot and 'founder'd' in the turbulence he created. At the time, a number of plays had appeared with such titles as *Cupid's Whirligig*, or *A Woman is a Weathercock*, but Shakespeare worked and reworked this same theme many times; and to the end in *The Tempest*, it images forth a conflict only partly resolved.

In positive terms, this suggests that the audience was meant to reach a state which cannot be defined, a state of being overwhelmed. It had sometimes been described as 'rapture' or 'delight' and perhaps it is what the fastidious but susceptible young Milton was trying to describe when he wrote for the Second Folio:

> Thou in our wonder and astonishment
> Hast built thyself a live-long Monument...
> Those Delphick lines with deep impression took,
> Then thou our fancy of itself bereaving,
> Dost make us Marble with too much conceiving.

To judge by *Comus*, Milton must have received the deepest impression from *The Tempest*, which in spite of its classic design, has received such diversity of interpretation that it remains 'deliberately enigmatic'. The most notable thing about the hero is 'the impossibility of charting the movements of his mind', and 'it is rarely possible to be sure what is going on inside these people, or that there is one right way of acting the parts'.[20] The play is susceptible of almost any interpretation that the audience chooses to put on it; it is a *new* myth, with all the openness, the invitation to personal variety that is characteristic of the older rituals. Its simplicity is deceptive, and won perhaps at great cost.

Even its shows, the plays within the play, are profoundly unclear; the audience seem to move through such a country as Othello described to Desdemona. Caliban is as strange as the anthropophagi. It is also a dream country; the slanders and plots of Antonio and Sebastian, who speak with the accents of Iago – the sneering and derisive confederacy of 'the joker in the pack' – are silenced. Yet, like Iago, they do not repent. The play is truly 'Delphic'.

The enigmatic and puzzling nature of the latest products of Shakespeare's Jacobean workshop would seem to indicate that he was experimenting to integrate old and new conventions of the stage, conscious of the widening gap between the forms of his youth and that of his age. He could use the old framework – but always to some new purpose. A coronation earthly and heavenly are built into a plot that replaces the old Wheel of Fortune by the personal fiat of Henry VIII, determining the rise and fall of Buckingham, Katherine, Anne, Wolsey and Cranmer.[21] In the whirligig that shifts the characters of *The Two Noble Kinsmen* and *Pericles* some symmetry is kept; the comic madness of the jailer's daughter, like that of the madmen in Middleton's *Changeling*, is based on an immediate sense of the 'difference of men' whereas the heroine cannot distinguish Palamon from Arcite, and prefers school-girl friendships to either. Pericles' love for Marina and Antiochus' incestuous relation with his daughter are contrasted by Gower, whose motto, if not wholly acceptable, is not wholly irrelevant either:

Et bonum quo antiquius, eo melius.   (Prologue 1, 10)

Accepting, as Chaucer had done before him, the role of an unlearned writer, combining all the arts of the theatre with a full sense of their range, Shakespeare in these latest plays yet implies that actors, audience and poet share an event brought only into being by full action. Words can only bear witness to silence, as shadows bear witness to light. He did not seek to print his plays, perhaps from assurance as much as from humility.

In the first phase of his Jacobean writings, Shakespeare set against the analytic and critical drama led by Jonson the 'esemplastic power' of a tragedy built on principles of growth and change in human relations. Against the purely spectacular and theatrical display of Fletcher's baroque theatre, and the court masque, he worked for continuity. Of Wisdom, it is said, that remaining in herself, she makes all things new.

11

SHAKESPEARE AND MUSIC

F. W. STERNFELD

In order to assess the employment of music in Shakespeare's plays we must remember that a wealth of dramatic music was available to him both in England and abroad as model and analogue. The tragedies and comedies of native dramatists were not lacking in sung lyrics or instrumental pieces, and there were moreover the influences, whether direct or indirect, of the Italian *intermedio* and the French *ballet*. It will be seen that no mention has been made of Italian opera which existed contemporary with Shakespeare. In this respect one must remember that Shakespeare's characters speak naturally and predominantly in verbal cadences, whereas in Italian opera song is the natural and exclusive mode of utterance.

From time immemorial, however, men of the theatre have found it useful to intersperse spoken plays with music since audiences subjected to an exclusive diet of speech, much of it in verse, tend to get restless. Music (in addition to stage machinery and other spectacular effects) seems one of the means to alleviate that condition. Apart from this practical consideration, many theatrical artists have felt that music adds another dimension to the play, conveys ideas which cannot be as well set forth in verbal discourse. Certainly, many of Shakespeare's predecessors and contemporaries shared these practical and aesthetic doctrines.

The obvious place to insert music in a spoken play is between the acts. For one thing, competence to declaim and competence to sing are not too frequently combined, and this comparatively simple device gives one group of performers, namely, the actors, a chance to rest, while another group, namely the musicians, keep the audience amused. Italian spoken comedies were sometimes punctuated by musical *intermedi* between the acts, notably in performances at court, given in the second half of the sixteenth century. And similarly, in Sackville's and Norton's *Gorboduc*, a tragedy in blank verse acted before Queen Elizabeth in 1562, each act is preceded by a dumbshow to the accompaniment of instrumental music. But with the rapid development of dramatic art in the later sixteenth century and its growing independence of Senecan and other humanist models, no such neat division was attempted, and music crept into the very body of spoken plays to an increasing degree. In later Elizabethan and Jacobean drama the dumb-show became an integral device of the play, as witnessed by Kyd's *Spanish Tragedy*, Shakespeare's *Titus Andronicus* and *Hamlet*, and Webster's *Duchess of Malfi*. Altogether, strains of instrumental music were frequently employed to endow a particular sequence with especial, if not magic significance. It is music's sound to which the ghost of Helen of Troy is conjured up in Marlowe's *Doctor Faustus*. On the other hand, the *intermedio* tradition, where music framed the play, survives somewhat in the musical finale which sometimes concludes a play, notably a comedy. Here Feste's epilogue to *Twelfth Night* offers a distinguished example. No doubt there were many precedents: the spring and winter song at the end of *Love's Labour's Lost*, the tradition of the Elizabethan jig which often concluded plays, and the related Italian tradition of the joyous choral dancing finale at the conclusion of *intermedi*.

Before proceeding to a more detailed examination of vocal and instrumental music in Shakespeare's plays, it may be well to enumerate the major categories into which these various cues can usefully be divided. (One would hesitate to call these musical cues 'insertions', for to term them thus in the mature and late plays would be to deny them their chief value: to be an integrated part of the drama itself.)

There is, first of all, what may be called stage music: an action on the stage which functionally demands music, for example, a banquet, serenade, or call to battle.

The second category may, for the sake of brevity, be termed magic music, employed, for instance, to make someone fall in love, or fall asleep, or be miraculously healed. Naturally, these classifications may overlap; a call to battle may be functional stage music, but it may also steel the nerves of the faltering. It is, perhaps, fair to say that scholars in the first half of this century have paid a good deal of attention to the magic function of music in Elizabethan plays, and well they might in view of the numerous examples extending from the way in which Glendower's daughter sings Mortimer to sleep in *Henry IV* to the manner in which Ariel entices Ferdinand 'to these yellow sands' in *The Tempest*. Of course, some magic effects on the stage are brought about by human cunning and suggestion, but frequently these events are supernatural, and both Lady Mortimer and Ariel are aided by the supernatural powers commanded by Glendower and Prospero respectively. Glendower's musicians who

> Hang in the air a thousand leagues from hence,
> And straight they shall be here:

are clearly concealed, perhaps behind a curtain, as are the spirits who accompany Ariel, as well as the Masque of Shapes in Act III of *The Tempest*. At other points this concealment of supernatural, magic music seems to be brought about by placing music under a trap-door, as when the strange sound of oboes which presages the fall of the hero in *Antony and Cleopatra* is accompanied by the stage direction

[Music of the hautboys is under the stage].

In this instance nobody would wish to draw a neat line between the magic, the superstitious and the prophetic; but it is a fair generalization to say that magic music, when supernatural, is as a rule concealed and invisible. Frequently it is also inaudible to the rest of the cast and heard only by those to whom it is addressed, as in the Music of the Spheres in *Pericles*.

A third category could be described as character music, that is to say, as music which portrays or reveals the character of one of the protagonists. In *Troilus and Cressida* the nature of Pandarus, the provider of soft luxuries, the pander, is characterized by the sophisticated lecherous song which he sings

Love, love, nothing but love, still love, still more!

Beyond that it also portrays Paris and Helen for whom he sings, as well as the Elizabethan gentry whom Shakespeare satirizes. Sometimes the character expressed through music is assumed rather than real. In *Othello* honest Iago pretends to conviviality and kindliness when he sings:

And let me the canakin clink, clink.

Fondness for music is usually a criterion of kindliness in Shakespeare; in Pandarus this trait may degenerate into excessive sweetness and softness; in Iago it is merely the disguise behind which he hides. Lack of fondness for music (and plays), as in the case of Cassius who 'has a lean and hungry look', is taken as a symptom of lack of charity, and so this attitude toward music may become a negative characterization. There is nothing lean and hungry about clowns, and when Feste in *Twelfth Night* sings

O Mistress mine, where are you roaming?

this easy-going gospel of *joie de vivre* marks both him and his audience, Toby and Andrew. When he asks them whether they want 'a love song, or a song of good life' for their sixpence, they clearly demand the former, because they 'care not for good life', that is, Puritan restrictions. Often it is desirable and dramatically economical that a character be portrayed in song, but there are times when Shakespeare's characters are good at verse but not at singing; at other times their social station requires that they don't sing themselves but bid a servant to do so. Duke Orsino's excessive melancholy and love-sickness is marvellously portrayed by Feste's recital of

> Come away, come away, death;

a lyric the Duke expressly commands to be performed for his gratification. A similar case of self-indulgence occurs in *Measure for Measure* when the unhappy and deserted Mariana asks a boy singer to recite the melancholy

> Take, O take those lips away,

to 'please her woe'. But probably the supreme example of characterization, of revealing a protagonist's true mind beneath the surface, occurs in Ophelia's famous mad scene. When the heroine sings numerous songs (and snatches of songs) before the King, the Queen and Horatio; when she breaks into song spontaneously without being urged to perform by the others and without polite protestations on her own part, she betrays to the audience several crucial facts. First, that her mind is deranged, for the object of the devotions of the Prince of Denmark should not break into song in a manner quite unbecoming to her social station. (On that point the etiquette books, whether Italian or English, are quite clear. Note that Shakespeare is careful to insert polite disclaimers in the surrounding dialogue when a member of the nobility does sing, as Balthasar does in *Much Ado About Nothing* and Pandarus in *Troilus and Cressida*.) Secondly, Ophelia's lyrics are a clear indication of the profound grief over her father's death:

> White his shroud as the mountain snow,
> Larded with sweet flowers;
> Which bewept to the grave did not go
> With true-love showers.

Here the insertion of the monosyllable 'not' in the third line illustrates a method much employed in Shakespeare's use of song. In a popular lyric he departs from the text, presumably well-known to the audience, to convey the state of mind of the singer. The syllable 'not' is metrically superfluous and its omission would agree with the over-all sense of the stanza (for which reason older editors often emended 'to the grave did go'). But by singing 'to the grave did not go' Ophelia indicates her sense of shock at the absence of pomp and circumstance on the occasion of her father's burial. If one of the strands of Ophelia's consciousness, or subconsciousness, is concerned with her filial grief, the other is her love for Hamlet, and in that connection concern for her chastity 'not too delicately avowed by her father and her brother', as Coleridge puts it. Whether she sings a mere snatch, such as

> For Bonny sweet Robin is all my joy

or four entire stanzas of a St Valentine's Day song, her concern with love, moreover extramarital love, is quite clear. Both the fact of her singing and the subject matter of her songs characterize her state of mind and her preoccupations.

A fourth category of music is distinctly present. It foretells a change of tone within the drama; from suspicion to trust, from vengeance to forgiveness, from hate (or coldness) to love. The employment of music to indicate to the audience a general change of tone is a most economical way of indicating the different style of the proceedings ahead. It obviates tiresome verbal explanations and asides and has been used in this capacity both in ritual and in drama from time immemorial. The most felicitous examples in Shakespeare occur in his last comedies where the miraculous element functions not so much in its own right than as a token of expiation and happiness. In *The Tempest*, the wedding masque in Act IV and Ariel's song in Act V

> Where the bee sucks, there suck I;

certainly prefigure

> ...calm seas, auspicious gales.
> And sail so expeditious that shall catch
> Your royal fleet far off.

To be sure, the functions of the music overlap, the wedding masque is also stage music, and Ariel's lyric serves also, in a manner of speaking, as a character song. The airy spirit sings to himself about his future life, revealing his bent of mind. Yet the larger aesthetic meaning is unmistakable. The intervention of music in *The Winter's Tale* to prepare for the denouement is similarly timed. There is a masque in Act IV and the sheep-shearing in Bohemia is followed by a striking musical interlude in Act V. When Paulina commands

> Music, awake her: strike

and the statue comes to life, we know that the complete reconciliation within the older generation will soon follow that between Florizel and his father. This instrumental music, to the sound of which Hermione descends from the pedestal, is some mere fifty lines from the end of the play. It may be that Shakespeare, who concluded both *The Tempest* and *The Winter's Tale* with spoken verse and thereby deprived himself of a musical finale effect, wished to place near the conclusion of the drama pieces of incidental music, fairly prominent within the play's frame. From what we may infer about the playwright's methods from the extant plays, such a combination of mundane and lofty considerations would not be alien to his customary procedure.

So far this discussion of Shakespeare's employment of music has dealt with the manner in which songs or instrumental passages are woven into the spoken text, without reference to the notes themselves or to their instrumentation.

In regard to the actual music, our knowledge is fairly scant though it must be granted that, in particular since the Second World War, modern bibliographical methods, extensive concordances of incipits and their variants have filled several gaps in our knowledge. By reference to the monographs cited at the end of this book the interested reader will find numerous musical settings for the songs in Shakespeare's plays. In a few instances it is more than likely that these represent the actual notes employed by the King's men, if not in a first performance, at least in an early revival. But more often than not we cannot be certain that a particular tune was used on the stage, as when a melody with the appropriate title, or incipit, or rubric occurs in a commonplace book or other source of the period, and the setting represents a likely hypothesis. In still other cases no certainty of any kind exists, but an Elizabethan or Jacobean tune has been found which fits the text metrically and whose melodic contours suggest an atmosphere not at odds with the dramatic situation. Here we deal with a working hypothesis which, at least on historical and stylistic grounds, seems acceptable *faute de mieux*. If we count all the songs in Shakespeare, including quotations of mere snatches, and if we include lyrics that were, perhaps, only declaimed but might have been sung, the total is fairly near to a hundred. In about forty instances we have music, extending from near certainty to a hypothesis that is historically not unacceptable.

Once more, the music which provided the setting for these lyrics covered a wide range. At one end we have simple, ballad-like ditties, presumably well known to contemporary audiences. These tunes easily fitted a variety of lyrics composed of lines of three stresses or four stresses or an alternation of the two. We must assume that these melodies, accommodating various texts, were well enough known so as not to require musical notation, for in the broadsides of the period one usually meets merely such verbal rubrics as 'To the tune of Greensleeves' or 'To the tune of Walsingham'. In the few instances where melodies are given in musical notation it is a one-staff notation, that is to say, a melody without accompaniment. Indeed, most of these melodies, although capable of being harmonized, do not require harmonization. A person calling them to mind could sing them spontaneously or hum them without carrying an instrument, such as a lute or a cittern, which is rarely carried about unless one plans a musical performance. Of such a nature are most of the ballad-like ditties sung by the Fool in *King Lear*, by Silence in *Henry IV*, and by Ophelia in *Hamlet*. True, the first quarto of *Hamlet* has the stage direction

Enter Ophelia playing on a lute, and her hair down, singing.

But this stage direction does not occur in the second quarto or the Folio, and there is no reference to a musical instrument in the surrounding dialogue. Certainly, Ophelia's songs do not require accompaniment, though a few strummed chords would do them no harm. In *Othello*, on the other hand, it would be extremely awkward for Desdemona to accompany herself on a lute when she sings the Willow Song and while Emilia undresses her. The lyric which she recalls is an old song, which survives in two commonplace lute books of the sixteenth century (one in Dublin, one in Washington, D.C.). As she remembers, she sings, and to search at this point for a musical instrument would break dramatic continuity and spoil the impression of spontaneity.

In modern literature these ditties are sometimes referred to as ballads, sometimes as folksongs. The term folksong is unobjectionable provided it does not imply anonymity but conveys the fact of popularity with 'folk', regardless of whether or not we know the name of the composer. A case in point is the song of Peter (enacted by Will Kemp, who preceded Robert Armin as the company's clown) in *Romeo and Juliet*. The verbal text of Peter's lyric was first printed in an anthology in 1576 and attributed to Richard Edwards. The music survives in two manuscripts, unattributed, but is probably also by Edwards. To all intents and purposes, then, Shakespeare has the clown quote a lyric by Edwards, a playright and poet of an older generation. But functionally the song sounds like a ballad, not like a humanist poem in praise of music (as which it is revealed when one contemplates the entire lyric and not merely the lines quoted by Peter). Its four-stress lines, its simple, fairly syllabic melody which is easily sung or hummed without accompaniment, the puns and jokes to which its content is subjected in the surrounding dialogue, all of these aspects combine to make the clown's song the equivalent of a ballad or an anonymous folksong, if there be such a thing except in the minds of nineteenth century scholars.

These simple ditties, then, provide music for many of Shakespeare's lyrics. In contrast there are also songs that might be described as art music rather than quasi folk music. These are characterized either by the prosodic complexity of the verbal text or simply by the dramatic context. A protagonist sings a song, not spontaneously as it springs to his mind, but as a studied and considered performance, either after entreaties by his friends or at the express command of his master. As a rule the singing requires an instrumental accompaniment, and this accompaniment is often referred to in the dialogue surrounding the lyric. In *Julius Caesar* Brutus refers three times to the 'instrument' with which Lucius accompanies himself, and in *Henry VIII* Queen Katherine commands, 'Take thy lute, wench'. Pandarus's song in *Troilus and Cressida* is another example. Before beginning he says at one point, 'Come, give me an instrument' and at another 'I'll sing you a song now'. And when Helen commands, 'Let thy song be love', Pandarus obliges with a lyric which in finesse and sophistication is far removed from the metrical simplicity of the songs and ditties sung by Autolycus in *The Winter's Tale*. Ariel in *The Tempest* is another artful singer of whom professional skill is demanded, notably in 'Full fathom five' and 'Where the bee sucks'. Of these songs we fortunately possess settings from the early seventeenth century, attributed to the lutenist Robert Johnson (*c.* 1582–1633) and printed by John Wilson (1595–1674) in the latter's *Cheerful Ayres*, MDCLX (*recte* 1659). It is impossible to establish whether these settings were composed for the first performance in 1611 or for the revival in 1612–13 or later, but there seem to be no good historical or stylistic grounds for doubting that Johnson's music was expressly composed for Shakespeare's play and that the date of composition falls within Shakespeare's lifetime. It is also possible that Thomas Morley, next to William Byrd Shakespeare's most famous musical contemporary, was connected with two other lyrics which were performed on the stage by professional musicians, each consisting of several stanzas. In *As You Like It* two singing boys sing four stanzas of 'It was a lover and his lass'. When one of them asks

Shall we clap into't roundly, without hawking, or spitting, or saying we are hoarse, which are the only prologues to a bad voice?

he is poking fun at the polite disclaimers of aristocratic amateurs. A musical setting for single voice and lute appears in the printed edition of Morley's *First Book of Ayres*, 1600, and can easily be adapted for two voices. In *Twelfth Night* Feste sings two stanzas of 'O Mistress mine, where are you roaming?' Feste is clearly a professional musician who gives a professional performance for pay. An instrumental piece entitled 'O Mistress mine' was printed in Morley's *Consort Lessons*, 1599, and its melody fits Shakespeare's words very well. In both cases, though, Morley's music requires adaptation, which Johnson's does not, and for a variety of reasons collaboration between Morley and Shakespeare is less likely, though by no means impossible.

A word must be said about the 'scoring' of Shakespeare's vocal and instrumental resources. A modern audience listening to a Bach cantata or mass performed by a choral society of men and women experiences a sonority greatly at variance with that envisaged by the composer who wrote for boys and countertenors (as did Byrd and Palestrina), rather than female sopranos and altos. Similarly, the modern theatre-goer must remember that the only performers for Shakespeare's songs were men and boys, a fact which makes a crucial difference to the sonority and overtones of the lyrics of Ophelia and Desdemona. A thin, sexless sound in contrast to a reverberant and chesty tone will stress the aspects of pathos and helplessness of a deserted or cruelly disappointed heroine. It will also help to accentuate interest on the turns and twists of the plot rather than on the sensuous aspects of the action. In this regard a comparison between Shakespeare's *Othello* and Verdi's opera *Otello* is illuminating. But boys by no means sang only the lyrics of the heroines, they also performed the songs of the fairies in *A Midsummer Night's Dream*, the children disguised as fairies in *The Merry Wives of Windsor*, and the music of Ariel and his troupe in *The Tempest*. Clearly, in these and other instances their size and the tone colour of their voices added to the illusion of the supernatural. In this regard the Chamberlain's/King's men had little advantage over the St Paul's and Blackfriar's boys. On the contrary, the group of 'little eyasses' would contain a greater number of musically trained boys. But Shakespeare's troupe of adult players had one cardinal advantage: it could offer, within the same drama, in addition to boys, an adult singer who in size, maturity and sonority was a welcome contrast. To watch the playwright developing this resource over the years within his 'orchestra' is a fascinating spectacle. Naturally, it was the clown who was most easily available as a trained musician among the adult personnel and in the chronological progression from Balthasar to Amiens, to the gravedigger (in *Hamlet*) to Feste to Pandarus to Lear's fool to Autolycus, some of the best parts belong to clowns. Notwithstanding, the part of Pandarus is not to be despised and Pandarus's song has been called by Richmond Noble 'one of the very greatest dramatic masterpieces in our language'. In any event, it is obvious that after Armin succeeded Kemp Shakespeare steadily increased both the importance of the speaking part and the singing part of the adult singer until, in the role of Autolycus, he created a figure which is both essential to the theme and at the same time adds another dimension to the play through its music. This dimension has a great deal to do with the turn from farce to 'romance' as Shakespeare's last plays are usually designated. By the time the function of the boy-singer had reached a somewhat similar apotheosis, as in the part of Ariel, the perfection of the vocal resources in Shakespeare's orchestra is complete.

As to the instrumental forces, these greatly contributed to the atmosphere the playwright wished to evoke by virtue of the symbolism attached to various families of instruments. Whether a scene was military or courtly or domestic, whether the influences at work were divine or diabolical, whether the outlook was one for peace or for bloodshed, all these and many other matters could be suggested to an audience by the sound of certain instruments and instrumental combinations. It did not matter so much what was played as rather how it was played: harsh versus still, fast versus slow, loud versus soft, wind instruments versus stringed instruments, and so forth. In themselves the instrumental pieces did not command a great deal of intrinsic musical interest, it was the overtones of their sonorities that mattered. In that regard Shakespeare and Milton were perhaps the last poets who could still count on a fairly wide knowledge of certain traditions stretching back to the Middle Ages and even Antiquity. Not that Dryden and Johnson and Keats and Yeats were less knowledgeable, but with the exception of a few cognoscenti familiarity with these concepts could no longer be counted upon on the part of their listeners and readers. Very little instrumental music for the stage has survived, and such little that has suggests dances, marches and other pieces of great brevity and simplicity, homophonic in nature, posing no problem of comprehension. (It would be naïve to expect in the theatre music of the length and complexity of a Dowland Fantasia, a Bach Fugue, a Beethoven Quartet.) At the most obvious level trumpets (and sometimes drums) connoted a military or courtly scene, whereas plucked instruments such as the lute and cittern suggested domesticity. The contrast between the silver strings of Apollo and the Muses and the pipes (wind instruments) of Pan and Marsyas was steadily employed in medieval and Elizabethan drama, but it is probably less immediately apparent to a modern audience. Shakespeare's groundlings, even if they could not read and write, were familiar with the 'lute' of the Biblical David and the classical Orpheus, the 'silver-tuned strings' of the Muses from many an Elizabethan play. Again, the music of the spheres and its 'invisible fiddlers' occurs in many a stage play, and the popular picture books of the sixteenth century contain instances of teaching the beholder the contrast between the aristocratic lute and the plebeian pipes. No classical education was required, therefore, to grasp the symbolism of musical instruments to which Shakespeare frequently resorts at crucial stages of his plot.

The belief that heavenly music rewards the good, punishes the bad, heals the sick, and foretells divine plans to anguished mortals operates in the masque-like episodes in *Pericles*, *Cymbeline*, *The Winter's Tale*, and *The Tempest*. On the stage this heavenly music is usually represented by the soft music of strings, gentleness being a commendable quality not only in the speaking voice of women (witness Cordelia) but also in the tone colour of instruments. By contrast, the harsh squealing of oboes and the brazen din of trumpets usually connotes excessive egotism, unnecessary bloodshed, and civil strife. This contrast between instruments 'haut' and 'bas', to use the medieval terms, is noticeable in those scenes where music plays a therapeutic role to assist an ailing patient. In *2 Henry IV* the dying king appeals for quiet

> KING   Let there be no noise made, my gentle friends;
> Unless some dull and favourable hand
> Will whisper music to my weary spirit.
> WARWICK   Call for the music in the other room.

Clearly, strings are called for on this occasion, as in *King Lear* when soft music restores 'the untuned and jarring senses' of the King. When Cordelia agrees to have her father awakened, the doctor commands

> Louder the music there![1]

And when in *Pericles* Cerimon employs music to revive Thaisa he again has recourse to the tradition:

> The still[2] and woeful music that we have,
> Cause it to sound, beseech you.
> The viol[3] once more. How thou stirr'st, thou block!

Opposed to these healing strains was the sound of oboes. (The oboes of the sixteenth and seventeenth centuries were much harsher and louder than those encountered in a modern symphony orchestra.) The banqueting scenes in *Titus Andronicus* and *Macbeth*, and the ominous music, under the stage, in *Antony and Cleopatra* are instances. Between these two extremes is a wealth of passages from short alarums and dead marches to morris dances and masques, illustrating the playwright's discriminating utilization of instrumental passages; always, to be sure, in the greater service of his central objective: poetic drama.

12

THE HISTORICAL AND
SOCIAL BACKGROUND

JOEL HURSTFIELD

A historian who is not himself a literary critic is perhaps too ready to see Shakespeare's plays as historical sources rather than in terms of their form, plot, language and imagery. He may indeed be guilty of putting Shakespeare too much in his time and too little in the context of the historical development of English drama. Yet so handicapped, and perhaps also helped, the historian does see in Shakespeare's work reflections of the two societies in England or, to anticipate the phrase of Disraeli, the two nations. If this conclusion is correct, and not merely a subjective discovery in literature of what the historian finds in Elizabethan and Jacobean society, then the plays – whether histories or not – show over and over again the insecure grasp of crown and government upon the authority they have inherited and claim. The crown which sits so uneasily on the head of Henry IV is a burden to all Shakespeare's rulers. 'To be a King and wear a crown', said Elizabeth I to her parliamentarians in 1601, 'is a thing more glorious to them that see it, than it is pleasant to them that bear it.'[1] The force which destroys Julius Caesar, Coriolanus, Richard II, Richard III is a force which threatened the Tudor and Stuart monarchy. 'I am Richard II,' said Elizabeth on another occasion to the historian Lambarde, when referring to Shakespeare's play, 'know ye not that?'[2]

For here was a monarchy which rested on two claims: that it was of divine origin and that it governed by consent of the whole people. These claims were not inherently contradictory since, in sixteenth century political thought, representation did not imply election. The overwhelming majority of Englishmen in the time of Shakespeare did not possess the right to vote; and of those who had it, few ever had the opportunity to use it. Direct patronage, or agreement between factions, usually determined who should sit in Parliament. The basic assumption was that the leading men of the shire, however they were elected, spoke for their whole community; and this was not questioned until the middle of the seventeenth century when, in the tumult of revolution, a small minority called for a wider suffrage. But what was becoming a significant issue was whether the monarch made policy in the light only of divine guidance, or modified it where necessary on the advice of some four hundred men gathered in the House of Commons and some sixty in the House of Lords. Was James I answerable for his policy in the next world only, as he believed, or could he be called to a reckoning in this?

It is often assumed that in Ulysses's plea for order and degree in *Troilus and Cressida* is an account of the Elizabethan form of social hierarchy as it existed. Yet what Ulysses is saying is that the Greek camp is sick because order and degree no longer prevail. In Shakespeare's England order and degree, where they existed at all, existed much more in form than substance; and so it had been throughout the sixteenth century. Indeed the real malaise was not because order and degree were in dissolution but because they were being imposed upon a society which had in many respects broken free from their rigidities. The tragedy of the Stuarts was that Charles I took degree, with monarchy at its apex, more seriously than had any of his predecessors, and far more seriously than would any of his parliamentarians.

For Tudor society was fluid and pressing against the narrow channels into which church and state would confine it. To grasp this is fundamental to any understanding of Elizabethan or Jacobean society. It is not that the old order was dissolving. It was that a new more rigid order and degree were being imposed. It is not that the Tudor monarchy was fighting to retain its inherited powers, but it had enlarged these powers in a measure never enjoyed by its predecessors.

The central event which was to dominate the history of a whole century occurred a generation before Shakespeare's birth. In the 1530s Henry assumed on behalf of the monarchy powers which no other king of England had ever possessed. We call this event the English Reformation and the term is valid provided it is taken to describe a profound change in the constitution and society, perhaps more important than the religious change with which the term is associated. (I am not referring to the administrative 'revolution' associated with the name of Thomas Cromwell, which turns out to be less significant than was at one time thought.)

Henry assumed the headship of the English church; and one uses the word assumed deliberately because the king did not derive his authority from parliament – which did not possess the power to give it – but as he stated, from God alone. Parliament was there simply to confirm, not grant this title, and to impose the penalties for disobedience. 'The King's Majesty,' says the Act of Supremacy of 1534,

'justly and rightfully is and oweth [ought] to be the supreme head.'
The truth or otherwise of this statement could only be known when
its author got to heaven; but in practice it became increasingly difficult
for Henry VIII's successors to treat the whole religious settlement as
if it were a private treaty between himself and the Almighty. The changes,
first to Anglicanism under Henry VIII, then to radical Protestantism
in the course of Edward VI's short reign, then sharply back to Catholicism during Mary's equally short reign, then back again to a moderate
Protestant Anglicanism under Elizabeth I, had been too fundamental
and too swift to permit a monarch to carry through by himself.
Parliament came to see its own role, not simply as that of confirming
the king's claims and executing his policy, but also as advising and
commenting upon, criticizing and modifying the shape and content of
the English church. It is the fashion to speak of a 'partnership' between
crown and Parliament in the Tudor period. By the end of Shakespeare's
lifetime this 'partnership' resembled much more the unsettled relationship between one firm, the crown, which had overvalued its assets, and
another, a more aggressive consortium, the parliamentarians, which
was thinking in terms of a take-over bid, so that it could run the
business of government more efficiently and according to modern
managerial techniques, in a new partnership.

When Shakespeare came to London much of this struggle lay in the
future, but it was not very far away at the time that he left. What,
however, we are seeing from Henry VIII's day onward is the emergence
of the unitary, sovereign, state, the state seeking supremacy in secular
and spiritual things alike, and which was trying to reach into every
crevice of men's thoughts and actions. Recognizing this process, More
resigned his office of Lord Chancellor and then renounced life itself.
We who can see the full-length Holbein portrait of Henry VIII with
his legs astride his gorgeous costume, his arrogant, beady eyes staring
out on the world, see the visual image of the Leviathan state, sparing
no man in its inexorable advance to power. Order and degree formed
part of the new concept of the state, pressed on the nation by the crown
and its servants.

But below the flamboyant language of Henry VIII, the supreme
head, the more modest language of Elizabeth I, and the renewed
extravagance of James I, there was, in fact, an unstable and shifting
balance of power. For though parliament was, in the design of
Henry VIII, no more than a ratifying and enforcing instrument for
carrying through his revolution, the parliamentarians were beginning
to think otherwise. To understand the basis and framework of these
advancing claims we must look beyond the court to the few million
people who were Shakespeare's fellow countrymen.

It so happens that we have the work of two of Shakespeare's contemporaries to guide us in this. The first is Sir Thomas Smith, scholar, politician and diplomat, who wrote his *De Republica Anglorum* – only the title is in Latin – in 1565, the year after Shakespeare's birth. The second is Thomas Wilson, a minor figure in government circles, who wrote a survey of English society in about the year 1600, roughly halfway between the time of Shakespeare's arrival in London and his return to Stratford.

Smith wrote his book, which is enormously interesting as the only contemporary account of English government and society, while he was ambassador at the Court of the Valois. He distrusted the French government and loathed the conditions of political and religious disorder which he saw all around him. By contrast, as he looked homeward, he saw indeed an ordered society secure in its internal peace, with each man acknowledging his appointed place in this happy commonwealth. (Even the criminals sentenced to death did not complain because they realized that the sentence had been lawfully given).[3] Monarchy, aristocracy, gentry, burgesses, yeomen, all of them lived in settled, stable conditions, and performed duties appropriate to their rank. Smith even found a 'fourth sort of men which do not rule';[4] and these, by the way, though he does not say so, were the overwhelming majority of the queen's subjects. It is indeed, he argues, possible to identify each class by its very appearance: 'a gentleman (if he will be so accounted) must go like a gentleman, a yeoman like a yeoman, and a rascal like a rascal.'[5] But what is a gentleman? It is here that Smith lets reality break through the smooth surface of his two-dimensional survey. Gentlemen, he says, are being made 'good cheap' in England;[6] and the College of Heralds was always available to discover or invent an ancient lineage. Unkind critics, he acknowledges, scornfully call these *arrivistes* 'gentlemen of the first head'. Anyone, he says, who can afford to behave like a gentleman – 'who will bear the port, charge and countenance of a gentleman' – can soon be acknowledged as one.[7] Smith accepts that the *nouveaux riches* can make good their claim to gentility.

Thomas Wilson, writing about 35 years later, is less sure than is Smith about the ordered stability of England. Smith, of course, knows perfectly well that Tudor society is far more complex and indeterminate than his ordered hierarchy would imply. He gently tilts at the new families but assumes that they will rapidly adopt the postures of their class. Wilson's comments are not gently ironic but bitter. He was himself a younger son whose lot he laments, one of those, as he says, who inherit no more than 'that which the cat left on the malt heap'.[8] He is without land and without prospects. But he sees all around him the discouraging signs of an aggressive expansionist class from among whom he selects the upstart yeomen and lawyers for his most caustic comments.

The yeoman, he complains, 'must skip into his velvet breeches and silken doublet and, getting to be admitted into some Inn of Court or Chancery, must ever after think scorn to be called any other than gentleman.'[9] (It is good to be reminded of the somewhat different kind of yeomen from those to whom Shakespeare's Henry V and Richard III addressed their memorable words.) 'Prithee, nuncle,' asks the Fool of King Lear, 'tell me whether a madman be a gentleman or a yeoman' (III, vi, 9–13). To Lear's reply that the answer must be a king, the Fool retorts: No, a madman is 'a yeoman that has a gentleman to his son; for he's a mad yeoman that sees his son a gentleman before him'. Often these ambitions of the yeoman class are snuffed out in extravagance, but, says Wilson, the lawyers do better.

Many lawyers, says Wilson, are 'grown so great, so rich and so proud, that no other sort dare meddle with them'. The most eminent lawyers were, indeed, getting most of the profitable business, and the rest of the members of this overcrowded profession had to 'live by pettifogging'. So they pry into records and provoke litigation with the result that they 'undo the country people and buy up all the lands that are to be sold'. These parasites are to be found everywhere, except perhaps in the Isle of Anglesey 'which boast they never had lawyers nor foxes'.[10] It was, of course, not only the gentry who suffered.'The first thing we do,' says Dick, the crony of Jack Cade, the rebel, 'let's kill all the lawyers' (2 Henry VI IV, ii, 73–7). 'Nay, that I mean to do,' replies Cade, 'Is not this a lamentable thing, that of the skin of an innocent lamb should be made parchment? That parchment, being scribbl'd o'er, should undo a man?'

Though England, of course, was not populated solely by lawyers, gentlemen and yeomen, we hear much of them in contemporary literature and politics because England was still essentially a rural country, and land the measure of a man's wealth and standing. Cloth, the only English industry of major importance, was still mainly a rural industry. But most men did not possess land, for example, the agricultural labourer, the textile worker in town and country, the retailer, the seaman, the schoolmaster and many others. It is true that the enclosure movement, much of it for converting corn-land to sheep rearing, accompanied often by depopulation, had passed its peak by the time that Shakespeare was born; but its effects were still felt and remembered. Wealthy merchants and civil servants did own land for, as ever, the wealthy townsman sought to take root in the country. But, wherever they lived, they were alike acutely subject to the violent fluctuations of climate and harvest, of famine and plague, of commercial boom and slump, of war and peace.

During the whole of Shakespeare's lifetime there was not a single year when Europe was not engaged in war. England was not itself involved the whole time. From his birth until 1585 – roughly the time when he came to London – England was at peace, apart from isolated skirmishes. But for the rest of Elizabeth's reign, that is, for more than half the time that he spent in London, she was at war, deeply committed, and at a prodigious cost, to a stubborn struggle in the Netherlands, in Ireland and on the high seas. The new reign brought peace; but there could have been no period during Shakespeare's adult life when he would not see broken men returning from battle to which they had gone as volunteers or conscripts in defence of their own country, or as soldiers of fortune in foreign wars. 'What! a young knave and begging!' exclaims Falstaff. 'Is there not wars?' (2 *Henry IV* 1, ii, 68–9). One should not be surprised that there are few plays of Shakespeare, whether history, comedy or tragedy, in which the sounds of war are not heard either on the stage or from the wings.

But far more widespread in their effects and implications were the threats of hunger and disease. The primitive state of English agriculture, and the inaccessibility of alternative supplies, meant that a wet summer and a ruined harvest brought high prices and hunger. Three wet summers in succession spelled out a major disaster as happened in the period 1594–6 and is best described in Titania's speech in *A Midsummer Night's Dream*. The price of corn, as compared with wages, has never been as high, before or since. London could sometimes import urgently needed corn via Danzig; other places using waterborne supplies might gain some relief. But inland transport, whether by water or land, was subject to all sorts of climatic hazards and was expensive for bulky commodities. Corn could double its price over relatively short distances.

Severe as these physical handicaps were, they were worsened by the sharp rise in population which extended for about a century after the 1530s. Probably, the population doubled during this period, rising from about two and a half to five million, though the pace was uneven; and the population of London may have quadrupled, reaching a quarter of a million by the end of Shakespeare's life. Historians have not yet taken the measure or discovered the cause of this upward trend; but about its existence there is no doubt. Men like Hakluyt saw it clearly enough and used this evidence to urge emigration and colonial settlement. Again, the effects of this growth were intensified by the backward state of the economy. Industry had neither the capital, nor the markets, nor the raw materials, nor the technical resources to absorb this increased labour; nor had farmers the knowledge to force up production to meet the pressure of demand. Hence England faced the situation, familiar enough to us today in the West Indies and India, of a population outgrowing its industry and its subsistence, and forced therefore to leave. It gives us some insight into both Shakespeare's age and our own to reflect that England today, with some fifty million people is, in certain respects, underpopulated while his England, with some five million, was threatened with overpopulation.

The other consequences of this are also familiar: unemployment, underemployment and inflation. Underemployment, as we can see today in Spain, southern Italy and some of the emergent nations, was more widespread than unemployment. It is a condition in which men are not wholly without work, but work only part of the week or part of the day. In the earlier centuries this was in some respects masked by two characteristics of medieval life: a part of the population was taken out of the labour market into monasteries and nunneries; and secondly, the large number of saints' days in any case reduced the length of the working week. When Protestant England abolished monasteries and drastically reduced the saints' days, the implicit conditions of underemployment became explicit.

But even more widespread were the effects of inflation. This, as always, affected the whole population. But it did not affect the whole population in the same way. It is a common enough phenomenon, in any time of inflation, that some of the rich grow richer and some of the poor grow poorer. So it was in Tudor England. Fortune, says Henry IV

> ...either gives a stomach and no food –
> Such are the poor, in health – or else a feast,
> And takes away the stomach – such are the rich...
>
> (2 *Henry IV* IV, iv, 105–7)

Many lost, for example, tenants (including copyholders) whose legal insecurity of tenure, or sheer weakness, made it possible to evict them; those landlords who found no means of raising rents to meet a changed situation, or had to bankrupt themselves to meet the heavy cost of litigation, or even dowries for a string of daughters; artisans whose labour was more plentiful than the food they ate; and the crown whose income simply could not be enlarged to meet the increased cost of living, administration, diplomacy and war. Who gained? Many merchants who sold on a rising market; those landlords who could force rents up and generally modernize their estates; many lawyers whose services are always needed in time of rapid change. All the evidence points to the increasing importance of these classes in society. We ask, therefore, what was their role in government?

The provincial gentry supplied the justices of the peace and the sheriffs. They served as amateurs but many of them had spent a year or more at either Oxford or Cambridge, or at the Inns of Court in London, the third university of England. They had both judicial and administrative duties, including the maintenance of order, the supervision of roads and bridges, the apprenticing of poor children, the fixing of wages and the organization of poor relief. A proportion of them worked hard and conscientiously but others were slack and easily responded to favour or gifts. They were not as bad as Shallow and Silence but some were probably not much better. The provincial administration for military affairs was no better. Under a leading nobleman as lord lieutenant it was factious, sometimes corrupt and thoroughly amateur.

Any study of Tudor provincial administration displays the great gap between the claims and the powers of the crown. Its writ ran only as far as the gentry cared to obey it. Behind the writ lay the threat; and a summons to appear before the Star Chamber in London was not lightheartedly received by justices who corrupted administration or juries who falsified verdicts. Many a great person in his shire was cut down to size by the government in London. But there were limits to the amount that it could do against the pressures of vested interests or just simply idleness or stupidity in the shire. Hence it is nowadays said by many historians that this was not an autocracy and that 'Tudor despotism' is a nineteenth century myth.

Yet this ignores one important element in government power: its control over communication. If the printing press in one sense weakens central authority because it makes possible the dissemination of minority opinions, in another it comes to its aid. Certainly, the government used pamphlets and homilies, addresses by high court judges at the assizes, sermons, proclamations, preambles to statutes to expound and popularize its aims to all who could read, write or listen. And the royal progress provided a dazzling, theatrical cavalcade through the towns and villages of southern England – these costly, elaborate processions never got to the north – and helped to implant in the popular imagination the divine attributes of the sovereign. Meanwhile, on the negative side, the strong censorship exercised over all forms of literature, secular no less than divine, did much to uphold the sacred virtues of the established order. The penalties for dissent were heavy and they grew heavier in the generation after Shakespeare's death as the fundamental dispute within the nation intensified and the country drifted into civil war. The dispute centred upon the nature of authority, and it dominates many of his plays.

The Tudor crown under Henry VIII had absorbed too much power over church and state, over thought and action. Divinity might hedge a king – if there were also arms to defend him; but it could not shield him from the doubts of his critics, or provide him with the necessary funds to govern. By the end of the sixteenth century, even the relatively austere Elizabeth was being forced to sell land to meet the exhausting costs of war. The more she lived on capital, the more she and her successors would have to call on parliamentary support. But it was the same kind of men who were influential in the shires who were also influential in Parliament, and Parliament was unwilling to grant money without a direct influence on government policy. Yet this control no monarch of the day was willing to accept, least of all the goddess Elizabeth or the kingly Solomon, James I. Hence the conditions of deadlock which were developing during Shakespeare's last decade in London. The anointed king held the spiritual and constitutional titles and the authority to determine policy, without the economic power to carry it through. The Commons possessed the economic power without the constitutional right to make policy.

'The state of monarchy', James I once told his faithful parliamentarians, 'is the supremest thing upon earth. For kings are not only God's lieutenants upon earth and sit upon God's throne, but even by God himself they are called gods.'[11] These parliamentarians were many of them astute, experienced men of the world who were hearing one thing and seeing another. They looked upon this man, ungainly, undignified, impoverished. They saw a patronage system which under Elizabeth, in spite of her mistakes, was usually used skilfully to distribute power and to bring the ablest men to the top. They had seen the whole system shudder at the end of the reign when the Earl of Essex had declined to submit to the controls essential to monarchical rule. The Essex rebellion, in which the Earl of Southampton, Shakespeare's patron, was involved, had it succeeded, would have put the clock back to the Wars of the Roses. Elizabeth regained control; and royal patronage remained the only viable system of government between the decline of medieval feudalism and the rise of modern party government. But James never grasped its full purpose. To him the criteria for the elevation of his public servants were not their wisdom and statecraft but their physical charms and his personal affection. The monarch who declared that kings were called gods by God himself could thus write to his favourite, the Earl of Somerset: 'Do not all courtesies and places come through your office as Chamberlain, and rewards through your father-in-law as Treasurer. Do not you two as it were hedge in all the court with a manner of necessity to depend upon you?'[12] Patronage was debased into favouritism; and it was there for all men to see. Was divinity enough to hedge a king?

Decay and division spread out from the court to the upper ranks of society and on through the shires. So, too, contempt and resistance began to find voice among those who had always measured monarchy against the divine criteria of the Bible. For Puritanism was now a force to be reckoned with.

When it first emerged under that name, early in Elizabeth's reign, the term was applied to a minority of churchmen, Members of Parliament and others who felt that the Anglican Reformation had stopped short of its goal. It had not established anything resembling a biblical commonwealth, now developing in Geneva, nor had it purged the English church of Romish rituals and organization. Some of the leaders of Puritanism were to be found in the upper ranks of church and state, and among the *jeunesse dorée* of the age, of which the best example was the Earl of Essex. Some of these political leaders had a deep and fervent interest in religion, as had the Earl of Huntingdon, others saw it much more as part of a political alignment. Many M.P.s saw it also as a great force for resisting the alien power of Spain, and the alien influence represented by Mary, Queen of Scots.

From our point of view, however, a new and important element became apparent, late in the reign, in the shape of moral puritanism and, more especially, sabbatarianism. Since Puritans used the Bible as a guide to conduct, not simply to faith, but to political and social life, and since they could read it in their own language, it took on for them a greater importance than it had ever held. They made a serious attempt to recreate some of the conditions and standards of behaviour which had been adopted by the biblical Children of Israel. Part of this was the Mosaic injunction to remember the Sabbath day and keep it holy. In 1595 the publication of Nicholas Bound's *Doctrine of the Sabbath* gave formal exposition to this developing theme; but this was only part, albeit an important part, of the increasingly rigid moral stance assumed by the Puritans. The long struggle between the Puritans and the theatre had begun. To be virtuous was to renounce cakes and ale. The controversy over sabbatarianism was bitterly fought for decades with the result, said Thomas Fuller, that 'the sabbath itself had no rest'.[13] Puritan dissent challenged the fundamentals of church, state and society.

Catholic dissent was less dangerous though the government was bound to take it seriously in the light of the whole European situation of national and civil war. Catholicism in England, it is true, collected its own extremists who played dangerous political games with foreign powers, but they were a tiny minority. The crown for its part tried to stamp out Catholicism by increasingly severe penalties. Yet in spite of this, the overwhelming majority of the Catholics remained loyal subjects of the crown in the time of its danger, as during the threat of the Spanish Armada in 1588, and Gunpowder Plot in 1605. Only in Ireland, where Catholicism formed part of a domestic desire for self-expression and independence, did it become a truly hostile movement. But in England Puritanism was more of a threat than Catholicism, partly because the Puritans functioned *within* the governing class, and partly because their whole philosophy found its source and authority, not in monarchy and hierarchy, but in a quasi-egalitarian biblical commonwealth.

Here then was evidence that the elaborate, gilded superstructure of a divine royal order rested insecurely on its religious foundations. And when the House of Commons became the sounding board for religious criticism and political discontent, as it did during the last years of Shakespeare's life, the whole system was under severe strain. Yet it would be wrong to paint these later years of Shakespeare's life in sombre colours. For the growing intensity of the debate was itself a sign of the intellectual vigour, independence and adventurousness distributed widely within the nation.

It was a time, too, of the growth of a social conscience. In the early sixteenth century Hythlodaye in More's *Utopia* could write bitterly: 'When I consider and weigh in my mind all these commonwealths which nowadays anywhere do flourish, so God help me, I can perceive nothing but a certain conspiracy of rich men procuring their own commodities under the name and title of the commonwealth.'[14] There was still the division between the two nations; and Smith's 'Fourth sort of men which do not rule' lived often in dire poverty at the edge of starvation. Yet Elizabeth's reign had seen the emergence of imaginative policies for social welfare, and the formulation of good machinery for carrying them through. There was at last the open recognition that innocent and hardworking men could be caught up in the harsh consequences of an economic slump. It was now acknowledged that somehow work must be found or relief given. The state too, in the shape of the county or town, was assuming some degree of responsibility for the orphan, the sick and the aged. Unevenly, pragmatically, the governing classes saw that their own strength and the survival of their society were bound up with the recognition of social responsibility for their fellow Englishmen. One unforeseen result of this was that the civil war of the seventeenth century was not a social revolution as well.

London had been a pioneer in welfare matters, as in so much else. And here in the capital, in the years when Shakespeare was turning his thoughts towards London, was gathered the greatest talent in politics, law and administration. Here were the palace, its law courts, Parliament, the city gilds and companies; here was diversity, a teeming thrusting population, a questing interest in novelty. Here were poets, church-men, politicians, lawyers, pamphleteers. Here was money seeking an outlet in commerce, piracy and the gentler arts of peace. Never before in English history had there been such a concentration of wealth, talent and opportunity. Here, then, was a 'wide and universal theatre' embracing the whole capital, with an audience in their places waiting for the play to start.

13

SHAKESPEARE AND THE THOUGHT
OF HIS AGE

W. R. ELTON

Shakespeare's works, formed in the changing thought of his age, require a recognition of Renaissance intellectual conventions. These conventions, also, affected the attitude of Shakespeare's audience. This outline will identify some Renaissance conceptual modes which may usefully be recalled to the twentieth-century reader.

Despite an influential portrayal of '*the* Elizabethan world picture' as unaltered from the medieval, its notable features were complexity and variety, inconsistency and fluidity. Similarly, the recently reiterated 'frame of order' may be regarded, for our purposes, as, to a large extent, a background of Elizabethan commonplaces against which Shakespeare played complex and ironical variations. While his dramas assert the 'great chain of being', for instance, and the hierarchy of order, they also as frequently act out the opposite, the reality of disorder. Considering the rapidity of Renaissance change, moreover, generalizations about Shakespeare's age, or about such complex patterns as Renaissance Christianity, should ordinarily specify, with as much precision as possible, the time and place in question.

Transitional beyond many eras, mingling divided and distinguished worlds, the Shakespearian age witnessed numerous revaluations and reversals. Not unexpectedly, a favourite metaphor was the 'world upside down'; while a repeated mode of a central Renaissance work such as *Hamlet* is the interrogative. In view of Elizabethan complexities, the present condensed notes are thus subject to their own appropriate qualifications.

I ANALOGY

Most generally, for Shakespeare and his audience, a prevailing intellectual mode differing from our own was the analogical. Though an analogical world-view relating God and man, inherited from the Middle Ages, was in process of dissolution, the analogical habit of mind, with its correspondences, hierarchies, and microcosmic–macrocosmic relationships survived. Levels of existence, including human and cosmic, were habitually correlated, and correspondences and resemblances were perceived everywhere. Man as microcosmic model was thus a mediator between himself and the universe; and knowledge of one element in the microcosm-macrocosm analogy was knowledge of the other. Blending faith with knowledge, actuality with metaphysics, analogy also joined symbol with concept, the internal with the external world. Analogy, indeed, provided the perceiver with the impression of aesthetically and philosophically comprehending experience.

While medieval analogical thought, including 'analogy of being' which likened man and God, had been largely regulated within the Church, Reformation and Renaissance |currents tended to transform it. The Reformers' re-emphasis on man's fallen nature and darkened reason denied such human-divine likeness (at best, an analogy of faith). In the Renaissance revival of antiquity, including Stoic, Pythagorean, neo-Platonic, and hermetic influences, analogy became increasingly a syncretic and secularized instrument for unlocking what Paracelsus called the 'great secret wisdom'. Through this unified theory of the human imagination, poets sought with scientists to interpret the Book of Nature and to discover the harmonious, ordered, and inter-related universe.

In the Shakespearian theatre, analogy, in this sense a momentary leap between levels, correlated the disparate planes of earth (the stage), hell (the cellerage), and heaven (the 'heavens' projecting above part of the stage). Upon that stage, moreover, were spoken lines which might, through analogy, simultaneously allude to the universe, to the state or body politic, to the family, and to the microcosmic individual. Without awareness of analogical (rather than, e.g., allegorical) Christ-allusions, Shakespeare's auditors might have condemned as blasphemous Richard II's comments upon himself:

> Did they not sometime cry 'All hail!' to me?
> So Judas did to Christ; but he, in twelve,
> Found truth in all but one; I, in twelve thousand, none.
>
> (IV, i, 169–71)

Or, among other instances, in *King Lear* they might have missed the relevant overtones of Cordelia's reference to her father's 'business' (IV, iv, 24).

Shakespearian analogy connected a scale of creation which ordered the world's diversity. From Aquinas to Richard Hooker (d. 1600) that pattern, it has been held, comprised such principles as plenitude, or the view that the universe, created by God out of nothing, was, by the Creator's desire, to be populated through all possible kinds.

A second principle was hierarchy or unilinear gradation; upon this scale, each of God's diverse creatures, in accordance with his distance from divine perfection, had an allotted position, observing 'degree, priority, and place' (*Troilus and Cressida* I, iii, 86). The final principle, continuity, implied regular, rather than uneven or saltatory, progression in this universal chain of being. Thus, from God and the angels, man, woman, the lower animals, vegetation, to the most inferior 'stones' or 'senseless things' (*Julius Caesar* I, i, 36), creation was unifiedly and uninterruptedly graded.

Because he possessed both soul and body, man occupied a pivotal place in the great chain of being. Externally, his individual actions found their implications echoed in macrocosmic nature. Macbeth's murder of Duncan reverberates through hell and heaven; Lear's madness embraces an inner and outer storm; and even contemplation of a crime, or the prospect of moral choice, might affect the outward world. Brutus observes, meditating on the cosmic correlatives preceding 'the acting of a dreadful thing', that

> The Genius and the mortal instruments
> Are then in council; and the state of man,
> Like to a little kingdom, suffers then
> The nature of an insurrection.
>
> (*Julius Caesar* II, i, 66–9)

As moral choice brought into focus the cosmos, it simultaneously brought into question the identity of the chooser. Internally, man's mingled nature was expressed in a conflict between his divine soul or reason, and his baser appetites or passion. Precluded by the Fall from ascending in perfection to the angelic level, he might easily be tempted to descend to the bestial plane. In contrast to the more modern idea of human goodness, consciousness of Original Sin was uppermost. Shakespearian drama ponders the extremes of human possibilities, as in *The Tempest*'s magically learned Prospero and bestially ignorant Caliban. Recalling Pico della Mirandola's admiration, Hamlet's wonder at man's workmanship (II, ii, 304–5) is, however, contrasted by the murderous Captain's conception in *King Lear* of 'man's work' (v, iii, 40).

Inwardly, sinful predisposition, marked by pride, predominance of passion over reason, and neglect of degree, was outwardly analogous to political disorder, as well as to the decay of nature. The primitive Edenic 'golden age' was irrecoverable; and the predicted end of the world – 'The poor world,' notes Rosalind, 'is almost six thousand years old' (*As You Like It* IV, i, 83–4) – was imminent. Natural degeneration, in contrast to our optimistic idea of progress, was everywhere evident: physically, man was a pygmy compared to his longer-lived progenitors; artistically, the ancients had been superior; and even in suffering, as the closing lines of *King Lear* declare, the young 'Shall never see so much nor live so long' (v, iii, 325–6). While above the moon all had been considered permanent, below the moon ordinary matter, such as the body – 'this muddy vesture of decay' (*The Merchant of Venice* v, i, 64) – was subject to mutability. Mutability itself was ruled with fearful, eroding effect by Time: life, the dying Hotspur observed, was 'time's fool' (*1 Henry IV* v, iv, 81) – man was also, like Romeo, the unpredictable 'fortune's fool' (*Romeo and Juliet* III, i, 133). For many Elizabethans, despite their religious beliefs, 'injurious time' (*Troilus and Cressida* IV, iv, 41) was obsessively a murderer. Except for such figures as Giordano Bruno (1548?–1600), on the other hand, it was left to the later seventeenth century, to John Milton and Blaise Pascal, to emphasize the fearful immensities of Space.

In addition to cosmic correspondences, analogical thinking implied hierarchy and order in the political realm. Proceeding from the idea of God as ruler of the macrocosm to the idea of monarch as ruler of the political world, argument by correspondence had evident royalist implications. That mode of argument led inevitably to the widespread Renaissance employment, derived largely from Aristotle's *Politics*, of the analogy of the body politic. The latter corresponded to the human body, whose heart or head corresponded to the king, and whose lower members resembled the lower members of the social organism. As the body obeyed the soul, and the world the Creator, so subjects were to obey the king. In *Coriolanus* a variation of the body analogy occurs in which the belly, compared by Menenius to the senators, is said to sustain the ungrateful and 'mutinous parts', including the 'great toe of this assembly' (I, i, 94–153). That the body-politic correspondence was natural could be verified, in turn, by analogy with the family and its patriarchal head, as well as with the animal kingdom. Throughout the divine creation were primacies of various orders: like God in the macrocosm and the sun in the heavens were, for instance, the eagle among creatures of the air, and the lion among beasts of earth. Within all mankind, moreover, innately implanted by God, was an absolute 'law of nature', by which his rational creatures everywhere recognized right and wrong. In the scholastic tradition, the habitual knowledge of natural law, or the willingness to recognize right reason – synderesis – is the faculty of Macbeth's conscience implicitly dwelt upon in the tragedy after his murder of Duncan.

Hierarchically, the human soul, of which Malvolio professed to 'think nobly' (*Twelfth Night* IV, ii, 53), was threefold: the highest, or rational soul, which man on earth possessed uniquely; the sensible,

sensitive, or appetitive soul, which man shared with lower animals –
its concupiscible impulse drove him towards, and its irascible away
from objects; and the lowest, or vegetative (vegetable; nutritive) soul,
distributed still more widely and concerned mainly with reproduction
and growth. Further, the rational soul was itself divided into two kinds:
the intuitive or angelic, whose knowledge was immediately infused,
without any intervening process; and the discursive, involving rational
effort and sense data. The soul was facilitated in its work by the body's
three main organs, liver, heart, and brain: the liver served the soul's
vegetal, the heart its vital, and the brain its animal faculties – the last
contained motive, sensitive, and principal virtues (i.e. involving commonsense, fantasy, and imagination, as well as reason, judgement, and
memory).

Central to earth, lowest and heaviest planet in creation, man himself
was formed by the natural combination within him of the four elements:
in ascending hierarchical order, 'the dull elements of earth and water'
(*Henry V* III, vii, 22–3), both tending to fall to the centre of the universe,
and air and fire, both tending to rise. At point of death, Cleopatra
exclaims,

> I am fire and air; my other elements
> I give to baser life.　　(v, ii, 287–8)

While, if unmixed, the elements would separate into their proper
spheres, in a mixed state they both abetted terrestrial instability and
shaped man's temperament. Antony's eulogy of Brutus's qualities
observes the exemplary mingling in him of the elements (*Julius Caesar*
v, v, 73–5). Each element possessed two of the four primary qualities
which combined into a 'humour' or human temperament: earth (cold
and dry: melancholy); water (cold and moist: phlegmatic); air (hot
and moist: sanguine); fire (hot and dry: choleric).

Like his soul and his humours, man's body possessed cosmic
affinities: e.g. the brain with the Moon; the liver with the planet
Jupiter; the spleen with the planet Saturn. Assigned to each of the
planets and the sphere of the fixed stars, and guiding them, was a hierarchy of incorporeal spirits, angels or daemons – intelligences which
may be alluded to in Lear's proposal to Cordelia that they 'take upon'
them 'the mystery of things' as if they were 'God's spies' (v, iii, 16–17).
In parallel fashion, on earth, the fallen angels and Satan, along with
such occult forces as witches, continued to tempt man and lead him
on to sin. For a time, Martin Luther (1483–1546), for example, was
afflicted by doubts whether his calling to reform the Church was, in
inspiration, divine or diabolic. Hamlet expresses such fears of the Ghost,
since 'the devil hath power/T'assume a pleasing shape' (II, ii, 595–6).

Macbeth finds himself all too susceptible to the weird sisters. And the disillusioned Othello suspects Satan's presence in Iago:

> I look down towards his feet – but that's a fable.
> (v, ii, 289)

Although controversial, belief in the influence of the stars upon man's life was held by a majority of Shakespeare's audience. Indeed, distinguished astronomers, such as Tycho Brahe (1546–1601) and Johannes Kepler (1571–1630), were practising astrologers, and the eminent physicist, William Gilbert (c. 1540–1603), physician to Queen Elizabeth, maintained astrological views. Natural astrology (useful, e.g. for meteorological predictions governing such matters as the influence of planets on crops) was widely credited, but differentiated from judicial astrology (more suspect, as involving details of personal lives and political prognostications). While astrologers agreed that man's fate was determined by his planetary conjunctions, they continued to dispute whether the determining moment was that of conception or that of birth. Rejecting his father's supernatural determinism and astrological notions, the illegitimate and naturalistic-deterministic Edmund voices the attitudes of sceptical Renaissance spectators (*King Lear* I, ii, 98–127). Opposed to primogeniture and exclusion by accident of birth, Edmund's anti-legal and anti-social view holds that the heat of the conceptual moment itself determines the natural superiority of bastards (I, ii, 11–12).

Renaissance astrological views operated within a finite universe of spherical shape – the circle was regarded as perfection in form and motion – and the very small planet earth was at its centre and lowest point. Motionless itself, earth was at the centre of a series of moving concentric crystalline spheres, those of the Moon, Mercury, Venus, the Sun, Mars, Jupiter, and Saturn. Beyond Saturn were the fixed stars; beyond these was the *Primum Mobile* or First Mover; and beyond that was the void, containing neither time nor space. As the planets revolved, they produced, inaudible to mortal sense, the Pythagorean 'music of the spheres':

> There's not the smallest orb which thou behold'st
> But in his motion like an angel sings,
> Still quiring to the young-ey'd cherubins.
> (*The Merchant of Venice* v, i, 60–2)

Recognizing Renaissance uses of analogy, the modern student should also note the radical differences between the philosophical preconceptions of our scientific age and those of the Shakespearian era. In addition to such influences as those of Francis Bacon (1561–1626) and

Thomas Hobbes (1588–1679), as well as those of Kepler and Galileo
Galilei (1564–1642), a major cleavage between the Shakespearian world-
view and our own was effected by René Descartes (1596–1650).
Towards the mid-seventeenth century, Cartesian dualism separated
off mind from matter, and soul from body. While influential, this body-
soul dichotomy was hardly new, and Descartes, as Professor Ryle
reminds us, 'was reformulating already prevalent theological doctrines
of the soul in the new syntax of Galileo. The theologian's privacy of
conscience became the philosopher's privacy of consciousness, and
what had been the bogy of Predestination reappeared as the bogy of
Determinism'. For Descartes, all nature was to be explained as either
thought or extension; hence, the mind became a purely thinking substance, the body a soulless mechanical system. Exalting philosophical
rationalism and evicting mystery, casting doubt on the objective reality
of the outside world, Cartesianism held that we can know only our own
clear and distinct ideas. Putting aside, like Bacon, as unknowable or
uncertain, final causes – the 'why' or purposefulness of things –
Descartes considered objects as intelligible only as we bring our
judgements to bear upon them. If only such knowledge alone were
possible, it would follow that the analogical method of knowing the
universe was thenceforth outmoded. Further, from the Cartesian
preference for clarity and its suspicion of our illusory and sensory
judgements resulted in turn the misprising of feeling and the affective
life as no more than a confused idea. Such Cartesian scepticism and
subjectivism led to the rejection as meaningless or obscure of the
previous centuries' Aristotelian perspectives.

For, in contrast to the Cartesian disjunction and its dissolution of
the world of correspondences, the Elizabethan universe still held to
the Aristotelian premises of teleology, or purposefulness, and causal
action. According to Aristotle, to know the cause of things was to
know their nature. Familiar to Shakespeare's contemporaries were the
Aristotelian four causes: the final cause, or purpose or end for which
a change is made; the efficient cause, or that by which some change is
made; the material cause, or that in which a change is made; and the
formal cause, or that into which something is changed. Renaissance
concern with causation may be seen in Polonius' labouring of the
efficient 'cause' of Hamlet's madness, 'For this effect defective comes
by cause' (II, ii, 101–3). Reflecting the controversy over final versus
natural causes, Lear's pagan interrogation of the 'philosopher' concerns the 'cause of thunder?' (III, iv, 150–1), traditionally a divine
manifestation, like the 'cause in nature that make these hard hearts'
(III, vi, 77–8). Ironically, Othello's 'causeless' murder of Desdemona
is prologued by a reiteration of 'cause':

It is the cause, it is the cause, my soul –
...It is the cause.   (v, ii, 1–3)

Further, in Shakespearian use of the language of formal logic may be found remains of the Aristotelian and scholastic modes: e.g. 'syllogism' (*Twelfth Night* I, v, 45); 'discourse of reason' (*Hamlet* I, ii, 150; *Troilus and Cressida* II, ii, 116); 'dilemma' (*The Merry Wives of Windsor* IV, v, 78; *All's Well that Ends Well* III, vi, 67); 'major', i.e. premise (*1 Henry IV* II, iv, 478); 'premises' themselves (*All's Well that Ends Well* II, i, 200; *Henry VIII* II, i, 63); 'fallacy' (*The Comedy of Errors* II, ii, 185); 'accident' (*Troilus and Cressida* III, iii, 83); etc. In Hamlet's 'Sense, sure, you have, / Else could you not have motion' (III, iv, 71–2) and in his 'forms, moods, shapes...denote' (I, ii, 82–3), among other of his expressions, may be found further echoes of the Aristotelian tradition.

In the Aristotelian view, change involves a unity between potential matter and actualized form. Although matter in one of its potentialities is transformed by change, it endures through the altering process, as the wood endures in one of its actualizations, e.g. a table. Change is thus a process of becoming, affected by a cause which acts determinately towards a goal to produce a result. Implicit in the Elizabethan world-view was the Aristotelian idea of causation as encompassing both potentiality and act, matter and mind. Rejecting as self-contradictory the Aristotelian notion of 'changeful potency' (*Troilus and Cressida* IV, iv, 96), Descartes, in contrast, considers process as a simple quality which things either have or do not have. Since it is merely extension, or passive geometrical space, he argues, the physical world cannot possess intrinsic possibilities for action. Implicit in a post-Cartesian world-view is thus the heritage presupposing a disjunction between mind and matter; a static and disparate, rather than interrelated idea of change; and a conception of motion as machine-like and activated by no final cause. In contrast, Elizabethan intellectual modes sustained the traditional notion of causation within a continuous and purposeful universe. Within that context, motion and action were engaged in a causal relationship extending throughout creation.

Shakespeare's pre-Cartesian universe, indeed, tended to retain a sense of the purposefulness of natural objects and their place in the divine scheme. While objects in the Aristotelian view of nature were distinguished by their own kind of movement – e.g. of fire, naturally upward; of earth, naturally downward – modern mechanics holds that laws of motion are the same for all material objects. For the Middle Ages and the Renaissance, objects, not as dead artifacts, influenced each other through mutual affinities and antipathies. Regarding nature ethically, for instance, Elizabethans could accept, medically, the correspondences of sympathies and antipathies in nature, including a homeopathic notion that 'like cures like'. Insufficiently evident to a post-Enlightenment spectator, moreover, the Elizabethan world was animistic and vitalistic, indeed, panpsychistic, magically-oriented, and, from our viewpoint, credulous. Well into the seventeenth century, alchemical, hermetical, astrological, and other pre-scientific beliefs continued to exert, even on the minds of distinguished scientists, a discernible influence.

In contrast to our belief through experimental verification, Elizabethans tended to a greater degree to believe by authority, by imaginative appeal, as in myth, and by disposition to entertain the marvellous, as in Othello's

> ...Anthropophagi, and men whose heads
> Do grow beneath their shoulders.   (I, iii, 144–5)

Concerned with the need to believe, in an age of incipient doubt, Shakespeare's audiences witnessed in his central tragedies such struggles to sustain belief: Hamlet's need, in contrast to Horatio's, who at first 'will not let belief take hold of him' (I, i, 24), to trust the Ghost; Lear's wracked concern regarding the heavenly powers; and Othello's desperate necessity to preserve his belief in Desdemona – 'and when I love thee not / Chaos is come again' (III, iii, 92–3). For Othello and Lear, belief is sanity: their agon involves the striving to retain both. Although within Elizabethan belief of various kinds might be found numerous shades between total credence and heretical doubt, over all there lingered a credulity, or a need for belief, that permeated their cosmos and penetrated the nascent sciences themselves.

II TRANSITIONS

While such inherited modes of thought provided some premises of Shakespeare's age, elements of his world as well as of his work often enough point towards the incipient disordering or breakdown of the analogical and pre-Cartesian tradition. In numerous spheres of Elizabethan thought occurred transitions and revaluations, if not actual crises and reversals.

Theologically, in the later sixteenth century, divine providence seemed increasingly to be questioned, or at least to be regarded as more bafflingly inscrutable. New orientations between man and the heavenly power, disintegrating the relative medieval sense of security, were in process of formation. Those changes coincided with such circumstances

as the Renaissance revival of Epicureanism, which stressed the indifference of the powers above to man's concerns; the renewal of the
ancient atomist and materialist traditions, along with other sceptical
currents; and the reflection of the Reformation, especially of Calvinism, which argued, in effect, an incomprehensible and unappealable
God, whose judgements of election and reprobation had already,
beyond human intervention, been determined. In place of a special
providence, capricious Fortune, with its counterpoise of *virtù*, or
personal power, was re-emphasized in Machiavelli (1469–1527), and
other Renaissance writers. Further, the Reformers, on the one hand,
and such sceptics as Montaigne (1533–92), on the other, substituted
for the earlier Deity a divine power who, beyond man's darkened
reason, inscrutably hid himself. Like Calvin (1509–64), depreciating
human reason and pride, Montaigne helped demolish man's own self-
image which placed him above the animals, specially created and
favoured by an analogical, anthropomorphic Deity. In sum, this new
distancing of man from the now 'totally other' God had the effect of
a Copernican revolution in man's pride in his privileged status. Despite
his self-flattering conception, he might have discovered, like Lear,
that he was not 'ague-proof' (IV, vi, 105). In claiming special providence, as a speaker in one of Galileo's dialogues observes, 'We arrogate
too much to ourselves.'

Such changes in the relations of man and his Deity inevitably provided an altered climate for tragedy, within which both divine justice
(as in *King Lear*) and meaningful action (as in *Hamlet*) seemed equally
unattainable. In a decreasingly anthropocentric as well as geocentric
universe, *King Lear* appears to question the forces above man's life,
and *Hamlet* the powers beyond his death. For that northern European
student, Hamlet, the quest for meaningful action, moreover, seems
complicated by the irrelevance, from a Reformation viewpoint, of
works towards salvation. The path to salvation – the major concern of
most Elizabethans – depended, according to that view, not on personal
merit or action, but upon impenetrable divine election. For Hamlet,
in relation to the Ghost, the Reformation rejection of Purgatory
appears further to complicate his task. Contrasting the Reformation
and the Middle Ages, moreover, R. H. Tawney observes, 'Grace no
longer completed nature: it was the antithesis of it.' The Reformers'
radical split between the realm of grace and that of nature required, in
a disorderly, brutal, and amoral world, a leap of faith. Alienated from
the objective structure of the traditional Church, as well as from the
release of the confessional, post-Reformation man, with burdened and
isolated conscience, turned his guilt inward.

In contrast to *Hamlet* and *King Lear*, where evil appears more universally diffused, *Othello* and *Macbeth* evoke even more sharply a radical universe of evil, ever ready, seemingly, to work mankind harm. In Shakespearian tragedy generally, the extreme intensities of 'punishment' appear disproportionately incommensurate with 'guilt', or the instigating frailties of the human condition. Poetic justice and its twin, the 'tragic flaw', seem quantitatively as well as qualitatively less than adequate to account for the intense torments of Shakespeare's tragic explorations. Rather than the complacent satisfactions of poetic justice, many in Shakespearian tragic audiences may be said to have participated in a solemn celebration of the irreducible mystery of human suffering.

To turn from theological to philosophical contexts, the Renaissance epistemological crisis emphasized the notion of the relativity of perception, recalling the appearance-versus-reality motif recurrent through Renaissance drama. Present throughout dramatic history, it was a manifestation as well of theatrical illusion and the new theatre of the baroque. The confusion between appearance and reality and the exploration of their validity is a feature of such contemporary writing as Cervantes' *Don Quixote* (Pt. I, published in 1605). The separation of reality from illusion, truth from mere hallucination, is, in part, the task set Hamlet by the Ghost. Recognizing the contradictoriness of all truth, as well as the conflicts in his intellectual heritage, the influential Montaigne, doubting whether mankind would ever attain certainty, turned inward to explore his ambiguous and changing self. Perhaps, as Merleau-Ponty suggests, Montaigne ends with the awareness, related to the dialectic of drama, that contradiction is truth. As in Shakespearian drama, without dogmatic or reductive exclusions, he experiments, 'essays', and questions, in an open-ended and inconclusive manner, the world of experience. Of Shakespearian pertinence are numerous observations in Montaigne's essays: e.g. 'I engage myself with difficulty' (III, x); and 'In fine, we must live with the quick' (III, viii). In the plays of his English successor, Montaigne might have found that ideal work he had imagined, which not only expressed ideas, but also the very life in which they appear that qualifies their significance.

Although, for some Renaissance philosophers, words retained the magic power or essence of the thing named, late medieval and Renaissance nominalism, such as Montaigne's, questioned the relation of language and reality. As do the speeches of some Shakespearian villains, Hamlet's 'Words, words, words' (II, ii, 191) may, in the light of his other remarks, reflect a nominalistic tendency. Concerning 'honour', for instance, Falstaff's celebrated casuistry (*1 Henry IV* v, i, 131–40) suggests the tenuous state in that term's usage by 1598.

Analogously, upper-class social mobility had led, in the Elizabethan scramble for 'honour', to a confusion in social hierarchy. Such lack of discrimination is indicated, more generally, in Hamlet's observation that 'the toe of the peasant comes so near the heel of the courtier, he galls his kibe' (v, i, 136–8).

If the limits of language may be said to mark the limits of social life or civil existence, the abdication, for example, of Lear and his severance of the bonds of social duty help to isolate him from the orderly intercourse of dialogue. Reduced to communication outside the social order, he must resort to the discordant babble of madman, beggar, and Fool, sharing especially the Fool's disordered obliquity. Further, in *Coriolanus*, a profound exploration of the relation of language to civil life, of the word to the city itself, Coriolanus refuses the name, bestowed on him as an honour by the citizens, when he rejects the city that has rejected him. For Macbeth, like Lear, language crumbles when he loses his sense of purpose in life: time is creepingly measured out 'to the last syllable' (v, v, 21); and life itself becomes an idiot's disordered and furious account (v, v, 26–8), reduced, that is, to verbal nonsense.

Such questioning of language emerges in the relativism of Montaigne, to which, among other elements, the Renaissance problem of the noble savage contributed. A man playing with a cat, the essayist had suggested, might, depending on perspective, be regarded as a cat playing with a man. Depending on perspective, too, how was man to evaluate his place in the chain of being in relation to the New World's recently discovered natives? Without European civilization, yet lacking the conflicts and corruption of their cultivated discoverers, such creatures as the Brazilian Indian, for instance, might well be superior in manner of life. Thus, Montaigne's cultural relativism sounded a note which was, partly owing to new geographical discoveries that literally reshaped man's world, and partly to influences set in motion by the Renaissance and Reformation, more widely echoed by the sixteenth century's close. Furthermore, the new cosmography and the cultural relativism of explorers and missionaries stimulated self-consciously critical questions regarding European institutions and values. When, at times, the Renaissance attempted to substitute Arcadia for Eden, displacing Adam by the noble savage, it set an earthly paradise in the New Isles of America. Like *The Tempest*'s, Montaigne's idyllic account of the primitive isles employs a negative form to catalogue utopian aspects. His description thus helps provide an intellectual context for Shakespeare's play, rather than a demonstrable source, since there were a number of such Renaissance accounts. In that New World romance, the old counsellor Gonzalo, in an inset speech reflecting the play's political-utopian preoccupations, unfolds a soft-primitivistic Golden Age revery.

Relativism inhered, too, in the Renaissance's mingling of contradictory and disparate Christian and non-Christian currents. In its revival of Greek and Hebrew, and the introduction of radically different ways of regarding the cosmos, relativism as well as scepticism flourished. Moreover, a multiple and shifting hermeneutic, including the revival of ancient emblematic, metaphorical, and symbolic traditions, furthered the questioning of absolute and authoritative readings. In such fundamental doctrines as the Creation, for example, a counter-orthodoxy existed in the Renaissance, involving the cosmogony of chaos. In addition to creation out of nothing by divine design, Renaissance thought, through Near Eastern and hermetic influences, also affirmed creation from pre-existing chaos. Such views and their attendant amphibious-monster imagery appear not only in Spenser and other Renaissance writers, but in Shakespeare as well. In *Antony and Cleopatra*, for instance, contrasted with such orthodox order figures as Octavia and Octavius, is Cleopatra, 'serpent of old Nile' (I, v, 25).

Philosophic value attitudes were also in process of relativistic transition. Shakespearian drama reflects the conflict between traditional views, found in Aquinas, for whom value is present and bound up in the object, and the newer views of such figures as Bruno, with his aesthetic relativism, and Hobbes (b. 1588), with his notion of value as relative to a market-situation. Such later positions are implicit especially in the politic Ulysses' exchanges in *Troilus and Cressida*, where the wily counsellor is a manipulator both of men and of the market in honour. In Renaissance value theory, a turning point may also be reflected in Troilus' individualistic and wilful demand, 'What's aught but as 'tis valued?' (II, ii, 52). To this anarchic and subjective relativism, Hector's comprises a traditional restraining reply:

> But value dwells not in particular will:
> It holds his estimate and dignity
> As well wherein 'tis precious of itself
> As in the prizer.   (II, ii, 53–6)

In Edmund's libertine naturalism, similarly, is heard the dissolution of ethical absolutes and natural law, regarded as mere 'plague of custom' (*King Lear* I, ii, 1–4). Reaffirming the Sophists' distinction between 'natural right' and man-made law, and between nature (or *physis*) and convention (or *nomos*), Edmund's challenge shatters traditional absolutistic confidence in the universality of God's law. For Montaigne, as for Agrippa von Nettesheim a half century before him, what is in one place a virtue is elsewhere a vice; what was once a vice is regarded as a virtue. In the Shakespearian era, custom, previously linked with natural law, was regarded by some as a merely relative, or local rather than universal, hindrance to natural desire. Shakespeare's work, therefore, marks a transition between absolute natural *law* bestowed by God, and relativistic *natural* law, recognized by man. In this transformation, the new explorations of previously unfamiliar lands and customs led to a more tolerant perspective.

Apropos of such explorations, if it is true, as Lord Keynes has suggested, that England was 'just in a financial position to afford Shakespeare at the moment when he presented himself', the following may also be true: Shakespeare reflected in his works the financial condition which could afford him. To the typical acquisitive enterprise, for example, of such English explorers as Richard Hakluyt (1552?–1616), England was indebted in large part for her possession of the American colonies. Significantly, Shakespeare's age participated in the transition between the older 'use value', by which price was conceived according to a form of intrinsic utility, and 'market value', the price rising or falling according to scarcity or plenty of the commodity. Against the traditions of Aristotle and Aquinas, his age took part also in the conflict over forbidden usury, which, reflected in *The Merchant of Venice*, was being practically resolved in favour of the new Puritan class of lenders and investors. Often, though not always, handled negatively, mercantile imagery occurs in other Shakespearian plays, such as *Troilus and Cressida*, which, like Jonsonian comedy, is replete with buying and selling references. In *King Lear* notably, the Renaissance clash between love and quantity – *how much* love? – is most powerfully observed. Like *King Lear*, *Timon of Athens* condemningly explores, with more specific monetary allusion, the new acquisitive impulse.

If analogical relationships had, in the theological sphere, been questioned, the hierarchical correspondences supporting political order had also been challenged. While Shakespeare maintains the medieval image of the state as the body (e.g. in *Coriolanus*), the sense of unity sustaining the metaphor was, even in that play itself, in process of dissolution. Despite, moreover, a received notion of Shakespeare's subscription to the 'Tudor myth', the complexities both of his age and the plays should qualify that view. According to the 'Tudor myth', Shakespeare's histories were devoted to the glorification of Elizabeth's line, to propagandizing on behalf of the sanctity of the legitimate ruler, and to preaching against the sinfulness of rebellion. In short, Shakespeare's histories are held to be didactic dramatizations espousing the doctrines of the Establishment homilies (e.g. 'Against disobedience and wilfull Rebellion'), directed to be read in the obli-gatorily-attended Elizabethan church.

Against those who consider the plays orthodox 'mirrors of policy', it should be recalled that Elizabethan political views were themselves in process of change. For instance, the deposition scene of *Richard II*, which could be staged at one time, was omitted in the published quarto of 1597. Since the argument for divine right was bound up with Christian cosmology, alterations in the latter had begun to undermine the hierarchical argument by correspondence. If man and his specially-created earth were no longer at the centre of the great scheme, human frailty at the Fall would seem to have had less occasion to corrupt the enormous or limitless universe. In addition, the monarchic analogy with God, or the First Cause, was also weakened by the tendency of Renaissance empiricists to distance the First Cause as unknowable, in favour of the study of God's visible second cause, nature. Further, such analogical principles as plenitude and the even scale of creation suggested, without evidence, a kind of rigid determinism and pre-arranged perfection. Reformation thought, moreover, had tended to uphold a God of will, rather than one of visible reason, and a world whose supposed rational order was imperceptible to man's darkened faculties. Such human depravity argued against mankind's exemplary and unique state, a little lower than the angels. From the point of view of practical politics, on the other hand, the accelerated rise of the 'gentry' suggested less a fixed and immutable order than one that could be shaped by the human will.

Furthermore, the premises themselves of Elizabethan political thought were paradoxical, being based, as derived from Henry VIII, at once on the divinity and mortality of the king's two bodies. Divinely enthroned, he is also 'elected', his power being drawn from Parliament or people, and his tenure dependent on his beneficent behaviour. In the con-tradictory Henrician propaganda to which Elizabeth was heir, the monarch could not be usurped. But if he were, the usurper himself should not be replaced, for the orderliness of the commonwealth had priority. These contradictions led, on the one hand, to Samuel Daniel's urging of total submission to authority, to prevent the disorders of war; and, on the other, to Michael Drayton's insistence on the ill effects of unfit rulers. Such paradoxical attitudes were part of the intellectual heritage of Shakespeare, and helped provide the foundations of his ironical, dialectical art. Those positions support the dramatic am-bivalences, for instance, of *Richard II* and *Henry IV*. In the former, an inadequate ruler is usurped; in the latter, the son of a usurper plays out his ambivalent role as man and king-to-be, a contradiction under-lying his duality of relationships. In *Richard II*, the pathos of Richard as suffering monarch is evoked at the same time that his unsuitability for kingship is affirmed; while Bolingbroke's usurpation is shown as simultaneously dubious and inevitable. In addition, a related reductive view affirms that the deposition and killing of Richard II recurs in *Henry VI* and *Richard III* as a central theme of England's guilt, the whole tetralogy being structured on sin and atonement for Boling-broke's crime. Yet Richard II seems curiously absent from the plays his ghost is supposed to haunt, while the moralizing implications of God's vengeance upon England for usurpation and regicide appear textually unsustained. While he affirms the primacy of the common welfare, further, Shakespeare complexly transcends the accepted view's simple didacticism and poetically-just formula of right and wrong and of the orderly sequence of sinfulness and atonement.

For Machiavelli and Machiavellianism, moreover, whose influence on Shakespeare's England has been demonstrated, worldly politics were shaped not by the City of God but by the will, desire, cunning, *virtù*, and energy of man. Machiavelli's anti-Aristotelian separation of politics from ethics proposes a behavioural study of 'policy', power, and reason of state. Among Elizabethan playwrights, it is Shakespeare who apparently provides the most numerous instances of 'policy' in the Machiavellian sense, e.g. in *Timon of Athens* where 'policy' is said to sit 'above conscience' (III, ii, 86). Machiavellian 'reason of state', the relativistic view that the interests of the state supersede principles of morality, was a recognized political notion of the later sixteenth century. In Ulysses' behaviour as well as in his celebration of the 'mystery of state' are discernible apologies for 'reason of state' and 'The providence that's in a watchful state' (*Troilus and Cressida* III, iii, 196–204).

Among the strongest testimonies to the new Renaissance relativism is the transformation of the traditional geocentric and well-enclosed Ptolemaic universe. While the Copernican revolution was only gradually accepted in England, its implications regarding man's conception of his status could not have been ignored in the Shakespearian climate. Indeed, Lear's shocked discovery of a universe apparently no longer specially concerned for his welfare, and ruled by apparently un-benevolent powers, suggests an analogue to the Renaissance questioning of scripturally-based anthropocentricity and geocentricity. In addition, implications of infinity and a plurality of worlds, proposed by the Copernican-influenced Bruno, were recognized, for instance, in Robert Burton's compendium of Renaissance thought, *The Anatomy of Melancholy* (1621). Suggesting discrepancies with religious orthodoxy, and Christ's unique incarnation in time, Burton asked, regarding a plurality of worlds and their possible inhabitants, '. . . are we or they lords of the world, and how are all things made for man?' Having broken the world's circle, how was man to reconstitute his own centuries-secured identity in the new vast and unfamiliar cosmos? To add to Copernicus' innovations, and modifications in them by Tycho Brahe, other disturbing developments included the recognition that corruption and mutability affected not only the sublunar, but also the supralunar, universe. In 1572, a bright new star, or *nova* – followed by others in 1600 and 1604 – suddenly appeared, and gradually disappeared, an event interpreted as demonstrating the impermanence even of the translunary cosmos. For the Renaissance, the terrifying effect of such phenomena was traceable not merely to their novelty. They reinforced, in addition, a contemporary pessimism which tended to anticipate signs of decay as apocalyptic portents of the approaching universal dissolution. 'O ruin'd piece of nature!' exclaims Gloucester at sight of his king. 'This great world / Shall so wear out to nought' (*King Lear* IV, vi, 134–5).

Between an innovating Renaissance empiricism and an obsolescent scholasticism, Shakespeare's plays move critically. From one point of view, it may be possible to approach *Othello* as a testing of that new empiricism. For, concerning Cassio and Desdemona, Iago has provided Othello with virtually all the evidence that a dehumanized and efficient empirical mind, devoid of the testimony of faith, love, and intuitive reason, might circumstantially collect. Indeed, the limitations of empiricism, albeit perversely distorted in the case of Iago, may suggest a critique of empirical data unmixed with human value. Yet, in its apparent scrutiny of empiricism, science, and what may be related to the inductive method, *Othello* seems to involve less an argument, as has been urged, on behalf of intuitive or angelic reason, than a negatively realistic, even Calvinist, commentary on the powers of human reason at all.

For Shakespeare's spectator, finally, this world no longer, as in the medieval metaphor, mirrored the reality of the next. As doubts and 'dread of something after death' increased concerning 'The undiscover'd country' (*Hamlet* III, i, 78), the beyond seemed more tantalizingly inaccessible. Instead of world-mirror, Shakespeare's era topically and repeatedly figured the world as stage, and man as actor in temporary and borrowed costume, strutting and fretting his meaningless hour. Continually, his theatrical self-reflexivity allows Shakespeare to resort to the temporary and illusory materials of the stage to depict man's worldly estate. Rather than acting out a meaningful role pointing towards the Last Judgement, Renaissance man might at times resemble a trivial plaything for the amusement of questionably benevolent higher powers. On such a stage he moved dialectically between the hopes and fears implicit in 'a special providence in the fall of a sparrow' (*Hamlet* v, ii, 212–13) and 'As flies to wanton boys are we to th' gods' (*King Lear* iv, i, 37).

III   DIALECTIC

For the intellectual tensions of his analogical yet transitional age, Shakespeare's drama provided an appropriate conflict structure: a dialectic of ironies and ambivalences, avoiding in its complex movement and dialogue the simplifications of direct statement and reductive resolution. Further, the theatrical form itself permitted such internalizing of conflicts. For example, the questioning of identity inherent in drama, especially Renaissance drama, might be self-reflexively mirrored in the actor's assumed role as actor, and in his shifting of costumes; Renaissance ethical problems could be reflected in the necessity, within the dramatic action, of the actor's decision to take one direction rather than another, a movement tending to involve moral choice; and the Renaissance epistemological crisis might be evoked through the emphasis on illusion and appearance-versus-reality of the theatrical setting itself, as well as through the ambiguous juxtaposition of scenes, particularly in multiple plot structure. Embracing and juxtaposing the contradictions of his age, Shakespeare contrived an artistic virtue out of a contemporary necessity. Within his heterogeneous audience, playing off one antithetical preconception against another, he structured his works partly on numerous current issues of controversy. Manipulating such diverse attitudes, while engaging the attention of all, he achieved a unified, yet complex and multifaceted dramatic form.

Nothing if not critical, Shakespeare utilized such 'built-in' conceptual possibilities for his dramatic exploration of values. That exploring movement might be symbolized in a two-edged sword which, as it advances through the play, cuts with ironic sharpness in both directions. Recalling, for example, Augustine's view that, without justice, a kingdom is merely a band of robbers, Shakespeare shows us, in *1 Henry IV*, a kingdom as a band of robbers. In that piece, the thieves of the tavern are measured ironically against the greater thieves of the court, the prize being literally in both cases, the 'King's exchequer' (ii, ii, 53). Contrapuntally, the dialectic of 'robber robbing the robber' (travellers – Falstaff – Hal at Gadshill; Henry IV – the rebels – Hal) is played out on several social levels. As usual in Shakespeare, while judgements of value are orchestrated, commentary, depending on the spectator's theatrical perceptions, is tacit.

When T. S. Eliot, finally, in reply to Coleridge, questions Shakespeare's philosophical mind, denying that 'Shakespeare did any think-ing on his own', it is apparent that the issues have been confused. Since drama operates dialectically, the main care must be not to decon-textualize lines and interpret them apart from their fluid and dynamic ironies. The great thing is to grasp Shakespeare's unparalleled pro-fundities within, as Dryden called it, 'the living labour of a play'.

14

SHAKESPEARE'S PLAYS ON THE ENGLISH STAGE

A. C. SPRAGUE

I FROM THE RESTORATION TO GARRICK

Not much is known about Shakespearian performances between 1616 and 1642. Such evidence as is afforded by literary allusions or the appearance of quarto editions is largely ambiguous. Even our scanty play-lists are of very limited use. The fact that *The Winter's Tale* was acted several times at court does not necessarily imply that the play was appreciated at the Globe. It is reassuring to come upon the clean-cut assertions of Leonard Digges. In commendatory verses to the 1640 collection of Shakespeare's *Poems*, Digges contrasts the lively appeal of *Julius Caesar* and *Othello* with the tedium of Ben Jonson's tragedies. Even *Volpone* and *The Alchemist*, great comedies admittedly, have sometimes had poor houses,

> When let but Falstaff come,
> Hal, Poins, the rest, you scarce shall have a room,
> All is so pester'd; let but Beatrice
> And Benedick be seen, loe in a trice
> The cockpit, galleries, boxes, all are full
> To hear Malvolio, that cross-garter'd gull.

In September 1642 the playhouses were closed by a Puritan-dominated Parliament. The excuse given, a good one so far as it went, was the outbreak of civil war. But Puritan hostility toward the theatre was deep seated, and it is significant that there was no move to re-open the playhouses when the fighting ceased. The actors got on as best they could. A number served with distinction in the King's army. Others had recourse to publishing their manuscript plays – it was a great play-reading time. There was a certain amount of surreptitious acting, but this was stamped out by new stringent measures, enforced by disastrous raids, in 1648. Inheritances from this desolate time are what were known as 'drolls' – excerpts, usually farcical in character, from earlier plays. Three are from Shakespeare: 'The Bouncing Knight' (Falstaff, of course), from *1 Henry IV*; 'The Grave Makers', from

199

Hamlet, and 'The Merry Conceited Humours of Bottom the Weaver', from *A Midsummer Night's Dream.*

With the re-opening of the theatres at the Restoration came changes of an enduring consequence. Women presently replaced boys as actresses, the earliest instance being, we are assured, in *Othello*, though where and just when this performance took place, and who the actress was, remain matters of conjecture and dispute. It is remarkable how early these actresses were taken seriously as artists (that no one of these was peculiarly associated with Shakespearian roles I find somewhat curious).

Another change had been anticipated in some productions before the wars. Although the action of the play usually took place well forward, in front of rather than within the proscenium arch, it was now regularly illustrated by painted scenes, which were supplemented for spectacular effects by descents, through traps, and devices for flying, exploited to the full by the Witches in *Macbeth*. Finally, in the patents granted to two courtier-dramatists, Davenant and Killigrew, in August 1660, we have the beginnings of a theatre monopoly which was to endure well into the nineteenth century. This last development, the limiting of authorized companies to two, encouraged tradition, so far as tradition existed after the suspension of playing for eighteen years.

Shakespeare's popularity in the new age was of slow growth. Even by 1710, when his plays were no longer outnumbered on the stage by those of Beaumont and Fletcher, some were still unrevived while others had been so modernized and 'improved' as to be scarcely themselves. Among the long neglected plays were several which were to be the favourites of a later time. Thomas Doggett played Shylock as a comic character in 1701, but the fact is of no great significance since *The Merchant of Venice* had been out of the acting repertory for years and its interpretation cannot have been traditional. *Hamlet*, on the other hand, and *Othello* were performed steadily and without serious mutilation. Indeed, when *Hamlet* was revived in 1663, we have the word of John Downes, the prompter, that Davenant coached Betterton, who was to play the Prince, and Davenant had seen 'Mr Taylor of the Blackfriars Company' act it, and this Mr Taylor (which is a little less likely) had been instructed in the part by Shakespeare himself. Any hint of how Betterton played Hamlet, as that he used miniatures in the Closet Scene with Gertrude, is thus of peculiar importance.

The identification of Betterton with his Shakespearian parts was remarked upon in his time. He was for those who saw him their only Brutus, Othello, Macbeth, and Hamlet; their Hotspur, till he grew old, and near the close of his career the best of Falstaffs. He was a student of the plays (we have Nicholas Rowe's word for this) and no one better understood Shakespeare's 'manner of expression'. The restraint of his acting was often praised. He neither ranted nor chanted. And if his voice left something to be desired, he could yet so tune it as to win the attention of the least responsive members of his audience, the very fops and orange-girls.

Some of the Restoration versions of Shakespeare's plays were mere modernizations, of critical interest only occasionally in their substitution of words or correction of images. Others are expressions of neo-classical thought, the practical applications of dramatic theory. The pseudo-Aristotelian unities of time and place were imposed, where possible, on works which continually violated them. Ideas of decorum led to the removal of such comic intrusions in tragedy as Macbeth's Porter and Lear's Fool. Poetic justice was served by ending *King Lear* happily, 'in a success to the innocent distressed persons'. On the other hand, the reducing of Shakespeare's long casts, effected in most of these versions, was desirable on theatrical grounds (it made for neatness too), and the frequent exploiting of the new scenic resources of the stage was only to be expected.

Into the merits of these strange plays it is unnecessary to enter. Enough, perhaps, to note a growth of tolerance towards them in recent years. What does concern us is the fact that several of the altered versions long supplanted the originals on the stage. Thus Dryden and Davenant in revising *The Tempest* gave Miranda a sister, Dorinda, and Ferdinand a rival, Hippolito, and these two added characters (Hippolito personated by an actress) figure in casts of the play well into the nineteenth century. Davenant's singing witches and the famous *Macbeth* music were other lasting inheritances. Nahum Tate's *King Lear* was the only form in which Lamb could have seen the play acted when he set forth his preference for merely reading Shakespeare's tragedies. It was with trepidation that Macready at last restored the Fool in 1838. Colley Cibber's *Richard III* (1700) flourished even longer. Both Phelps and Edwin Booth, after attempting Shakespeare's history, returned to what was felt to be the safer version, and this was acted in America by Fritz Leiber as recently as 1930. Sacrificing the larger reaches of the earlier play, Cibber concentrated upon Richard, his rise to power, his reign and death, treating these matters with much liveliness and an uncanny ability to imitate Richard's manner of speech. The famous claptraps,

Off with his head. – So much for Buckingham,

and 'Richard's himself again' are by no means isolated examples of this. Both have passed, on occasion, as Shakespeare's own.

The death of Betterton in 1710 marks the end of a theatrical era almost as convincingly as the advent of Garrick in 1741 marks the beginning of one. Between, lies a generation which saw a decline in the quality of tragic acting, not unfairly represented by the monotonous declamation of James Quin. Cibber (for whom this age has sometimes been named) must have been quite impossible in tragedy. Yet Shakespeare's popularity was advancing strongly all the while. The appearance of such readily accessible editions as Nicholas Rowe's in 1709, and those published subsequently by Tonson for a shilling or less a play, contributed to this. In the theatre it shows in the gradual enlargement of the Shakespearian repertory. Up to now this had included, among the tragedies: *Hamlet*, *Othello*, *Julius Caesar*, Tate's *King Lear*, and Davenant's *Macbeth*. *Timon of Athens* was given in Shadwell's adaptation, *Troilus and Cressida* in Dryden's, and *Romeo and Juliet* only in the distantly related *Caius Marius* of Otway. The tragedies came first with audiences, as indeed they had done since the re-opening of the theatres, but both the histories and the comedies were gaining in number. To the firmly established *1 Henry IV*, *Henry VIII*, and, as altered by Cibber, *Richard III*, were added *2 Henry IV* and, somewhat later, *King John* and *Henry V*. It was a flourishing period for the histories. As for the comedies, *The Merry Wives of Windsor*, not unknown earlier, began now to be much performed, thanks to Quin's Falstaff. In 1741 a revival of *The Merchant of Venice* (as Shakespeare wrote it) was made memorable by the passionate, evil Shylock of Charles Macklin. *Measure for Measure*, the original once more, was also played; and near the close of this transitional time, *Much Ado about Nothing*, *As You Like It* and *Twelfth Night*, favourite plays of the last years of the century.

II THE ACTOR'S THEATRE

The general esteem in which Betterton was held, remarkable as it was, fell short of the fame which was to attend Garrick. Reasons for this are not far to seek. Unlike Betterton, or any earlier English actor, Garrick was a public figure, one whose death in Dr Johnson's well-known phrase 'eclipsed the gaiety of nations'. He wrote and talked well; moved in literary and polite circles; was painted by Gainsborough and Sir Joshua Reynolds. His social gifts, his vivacity, amiability and *savoir faire*, were extraordinary. Acting, he made clear by demonstration, was an art to be taken as seriously, it might be, as painting. An age which delighted in connoisseurship welcomed the thought.

The range of parts in which Garrick excelled was extraordinary. It was questionable whether he was to be preferred as Archer, in *The Beaux' Stratagem*, Abel Drugger, in *The Alchemist*, or King Lear. In strong contrast to the pompous recitation of his predecessors, his characteristic effects were visual and arresting. He delighted in sudden starts: as in Richard III (pictured by Hogarth) starting from his couch in the Tent Scene; or Hamlet, upon sight of the Ghost. A famous passage in Cibber's *Apology* describes Betterton in the *Hamlet* scene and the comparison with Garrick is illuminating. The earlier actor is praised for rightness of conception; for restraint and propriety of speech. Garrick's start, the horror shown in his face, and a prolonged and elaborated exit, as he followed the Ghost out, are what impressed those who saw him.

But can it be said that this brilliant performer, who made fulsome protestations of loyalty to Shakespeare, really did much to serve his interests? It used to be questioned whether he did, and the fact that he altered a number of his plays, including *Hamlet*, was advanced as evidence. The work of an American scholar, George Winchester Stone, has largely succeeded in silencing the sceptics. Even the altered *Hamlet* proved upon examination somewhat less offensive than descriptions of it had suggested. Like Garrick's other adaptations, which include the long popular *Katharine and Petruchio*, it suffered mainly from cutting. The fashion of adding to the text, and improving Shakespeare's poetry, had passed.

There is no questioning Garrick's genius or, for that matter, the healthy state of the theatre in his time. That it was a theatre dominated by stars, an actor's theatre, is equally clear. The balanced strength of Garrick's company still permitted the adequate casting of as exacting a work as Ben Jonson's *Alchemist* but, with the emphasis where it now lay, deterioration was certain. Already one's chief purpose in attending the playhouse might be to see a particular actor as Romeo or Lear and then compare him with some rival – Garrick, say, with Spranger Barry. This habit of comparing one interpretation with another is closely related to a new and lively interest in the art of acting, which is reflected in the appearance of poems like Churchill's once famous *Rosciad*. Significantly, the provincial theatres, now flourishing at York, Norwich, and elsewhere, sent to London as their discoveries, not new plays but promising young players, like John Henderson, 'The Bath Roscius'. Texts were wanted, finally, for the numerous actors, amateur as well as professional, who were now appearing in the plays, and we have Bell's Shakespeare (in the 1770s), and a succession of acting editions, right down to that published by Samuel French in our time.

In judging a performance much importance came to be attached to

certain awaited moments and to what were known as 'new readings':
Hamlet's 'Did *you* not speak to it?' as he distinguished Horatio from
the other watchers, or Lady Macbeth's supremely confident 'Give *me*
the daggers'. Both these were points made by the Kembles. For the
style of acting introduced to London audiences in 1783 by John Philip
Kemble, and carried to heights beyond his reach by Sarah Siddons, was
at once heroic and meticulous. In him attention to detail might seem
pedantic. In his sister it was subordinate to passion and a strong sense
of character. Constance, Volumnia, Katharine (in *Henry VIII*), and
of course Lady Macbeth, were among her greatest performances – and
they were unsurpassed, in the memory of those who saw her. It is
absurd to dwell on her deficiencies in comedy or to judge her acting by
the performances of her later years.

Kemble's Shakespearian productions, his *Coriolanus*, for instance,
and *Henry VIII*, were heavy with pomp. Not much attention was
paid to historical verisimilitude (that was to come a little later) but
enthusiasm for detail appears in other ways. Kemble looked after the
proprieties and the observance of ceremonial form. He found names for
many of the little anonymous people in the plays and raised Servants
to the dignity of being 'Officers'. Typically the Messenger who brings
news of the Turkish fleet to the Duke and Senators in *Othello* gave
his letters to 'Marco', who in turn presented them to the Duke.

Garrick's last season came to an end in the spring of 1776. Edmund
Kean's first appearance as Shylock at Drury Lane was on 26 January
1814. There were persons who had seen both actors and declared that
Kean reminded them of Garrick. He was profoundly unlike Kemble.
The effects for which the new actor was lauded, his moments of illumination, 'flashes of lightning', depended on vivid pantomimic action or
some sudden, unexpected transition in speech. At times he seems
deliberately to have 'thrown away' lines. He achieved sustained beauty
in Othello's farewell (III, iii, 347), in which he was profoundly moving,
and Othello was certainly his greatest part. His desperate fighting and
death, in *Richard III*, are described unforgettably by Hazlitt, to whom
Kean owes much, as Hazlitt something, no doubt, to Kean. His spiritual
kinship with the romantic poets was early recognized and he was
their favourite actor.

During Kean's later years (he died in 1833) the condition of the two
patent theatres was going from bad to worse. Many causes contributed
to this, and when at last Macready took over the management of
Covent Garden (1837–9) and Drury Lane (1841–3) he was fighting
a losing battle. What he accomplished is the more remarkable. In
Shakespeare's case there were most obviously the restorations. That
of *King Lear* for Tate's *King Lear* took courage. Macready was worried

about the introduction of the Fool (would this not 'either weary and annoy or distract the spectator'). The choice of a young actress, Priscilla Horton, for the part relieved his mind, and the same Priscilla Horton as Ariel (an Ariel who flew as well as sang) delighted audiences in Macready's highly spectacular revival of *The Tempest*. His inclusion of the choruses in *Henry V* was unusual, and as if distrustful of their appeal to the imagination he 'illustrated' them by means of a diorama. In *As You Like It*, with greater subtlety, he used off-stage sounds, the tinkling of sheep bells especially, to create atmosphere.

In his own performances Macready concentrated upon the interpretation of characters as wholes rather than on the making of points. The definiteness of his conceptions was as unusual in his time as the seriousness with which he rehearsed. His name is associated with no single role, as Kean's was with Othello, but he was at his best in Macbeth and in another thoughtful study of moral deterioration, King John.

With the ending of the theatre monopoly, in 1843, the Shakespearian repertory, once the property of Covent Garden and Drury Lane, became available for production elsewhere, and good use was made of it at Sadler's Wells, first, and in the 1850s at the Princess's. Between 1844 and 1862 the strong company assembled by Samuel Phelps at Sadler's Wells gave all but six of Shakespeare's plays, omitting only the three parts of *Henry VI*, *Titus Andronicus*, *Troilus and Cressida*, and less predictably *Richard II*. They gave them well, too, and before popular audiences who, like those of the Old Vic at a later time, became genuinely appreciative of them. Phelps himself was an actor of fine ability. Indeed, the variety of parts which he assumed has rarely been matched. He passed with ease from the tragic heroes to Bully Bottom, and as a feat of virtuosity doubled Henry IV and Justice Shallow. His Shakespearian texts, though they were bowdlerized for Islington ears, contained a number of restorations. He even attempted a *Richard III* without recourse to Cibber.

It was said that Shakespeare's plays were always 'poems' at Sadler's Wells. At the Princess's under Charles Kean, they were more like educational pageants – but very magnificent. Archaeological enthusiasm had been finding expression in the theatre for some time, as in the remarkable production of *King John* at Covent Garden, on 24 November 1823, for which J. R. Planché, the antiquary, was engaged to devise the costumes and armour. But Kean went farther, even to distributing 'flyleaves', in which he indicated the learned authorities for what one was seeing on the stage. His carefully rehearsed crowds, as in an interpolated episode of the return of Henry V to London, and the effect of spaciousness which he sometimes gained on a comparatively small stage, are to be remembered to his credit. *Punch* ridiculed him destructively as the 'upholsterer' of Shakespeare.

Henry Irving's great productions of *Romeo and Juliet* and *Much Ado about Nothing* at the Lyceum in 1882 were different from those of Kean, but the difference lay chiefly in the artistic refinement of the later master. Kean would have accepted Irving's statement of purpose: that of showing his audience a hovel, if the scene was a hovel, and if it was the palace of Cleopatra, then as gorgeous a palace as 'the possibilities of art would allow'. If, however, at one point his accomplishment is perceptibly within a tradition, at another it was amazingly original. To Charles Fechter, a continental player who brought to performances of *Hamlet* and *Othello* at the Princess's the methods, comparatively realistic, of melodrama, Irving may have owed something. As an actor he had few other debts. His apprenticeship in the provinces was in a repertory which no longer contained much Shakespeare. His first successes in London were in modern plays. Then, too, his mannerisms of speech and movement were limiting and set him apart. Was he not always himself?

Yet even very critical playgoers yielded to their enthusiasm. For them there was no other actor, as there was no theatre except Irving's Lyceum. He had intellect and an almost hypnotic power of attraction. He used for his purposes as an actor the resources of a stage which he controlled. Romeo's macabre descent into the tomb, Hamlet's seizing of the throne at the close of the Play Scene, above all, Shylock's lonely homecoming, these were wonderful moments most skilfully stage-managed, or as we would say today directed, by the actor himself.

III   THE RISE OF THE DIRECTOR

That there was an alternative to Irving's manner of presenting Shakespeare would have seemed incredible to most playgoers. Yet as early as the spring of 1881 when an obscure actor named William Poel directed his now celebrated matinée of the First Quarto *Hamlet*, there were persons who advocated a return to the stage for which the plays were designed. Poel had no theatre of his own and only amateur actors. The demonstration of his ideas remained incomplete. What his productions did make clear was that Shakespeare played before plain curtains was still perfectly intelligible, and that the time saved in shifting heavy scenery could be spent to great advantage in restoring some of the many lines omitted in contemporary performances. That Shakespeare was a craftsman of amazing skill, who in any given instance pretty certainly 'knew what he was about', was not a truism to Poel's generation.

Even the generally hostile William Archer gave Poel credit for the care which he bestowed on rehearsing plays and the 'perfect smoothness' with which as a rule they went in performance. His responsibility for a production was complete. His interest extended even to such matters as the speaking of the verse. Yet he did not always appear in the cast himself and was not a star actor. This fact instantly differentiates his connection with a performance from that of Irving or Macready, who whatever concern they might show for the play as a whole could not be expected to forget the central importance of one character in it.

Poel's ideas gained wide currency through the productions of Ben Greet, given sometimes on the 'draped stage', more frequently out-of-doors, and those of Nugent Monck at the excellent Maddermarket Theatre, Norwich. How far the same ideas influenced Harley Granville-Barker is difficult to determine, because of the latter's eclecticism. Granville-Barker had appeared under Poel's direction as Richard II. Both men departed wholly from the heavily cut, constantly interrupted texts then current in the theatre. But it is only with effort that one thinks of Granville-Barker's productions at the Savoy as belonging to an Elizabethan revival. There *The Winter's Tale* and *Twelfth Night*, in 1912, and *A Midsummer Night's Dream*, in 1914, were given in startling, fantastic dresses. Those for *The Winter's Tale*, designed by Albert Rothenstein, were sophisticated in colour and quite forsook any single period. In *A Midsummer Night's Dream* the fairies had gilded faces, an idea much ridiculed by the conservative. There were important innovations in lighting, as well, and the sets were rather decorative than realistic and could be shifted in a moment. Granville-Barker planned also to give *Antony and Cleopatra* and *Macbeth*, but hope of these was destroyed by the outbreak of the First World War.

Before its close there were other losses as well, though none quite so serious. The famous Benson Company paid its final visit to Stratford-upon-Avon. Sir Herbert Beerbohm Tree gave the last of his many Shakespearian revivals at His Majesty's Theatre. The success of these last, grandiose productions is a little hard to account for, as we read of them today, since they were enough like Irving's to make comparison inevitable. And Tree, for all his flamboyance and inventiveness, was very far from being Irving's equal, whether as actor or producer. Frank Benson had brought his company to Stratford-upon-Avon for the first time in 1886. By 1914 they had performed almost, but not quite all of Shakespeare's works, with an unusual bent for the histories. Benson himself is associated particularly with Richard II (memorably reviewed by C. E. Montague) and Henry V. Many actors of subsequent fame served their apprenticeship with this happy, healthy company who gave the people of a great many provincial towns their only chance to see Shakespeare's plays.

Two new men came into prominence in the years immediately after the war. At Stratford, W. Bridges-Adams as director of a recently established company there used simple sets of great beauty and texts of notable completeness. What he accomplished, with the means at his disposal, was extraordinary. At the Old Vic, where Shakespeare (under Greet and others) had begun to be played during the war years, Robert Atkins, a follower of Poel's, became manager in 1920. Of Mr Atkins it has been well remarked that he might have 'entered and taken charge of an Elizabethan playhouse'. In the five years of his stay at the Vic he produced all of the Folio plays (except *Cymbeline*), and *Pericles* as well. The Old Vic was to be identified with Shakespeare's plays for a full generation to come.

I shall not attempt to describe the events of this busy time (1920–51). Characteristic of it was the great increase in the number of Shakespearian productions: some three hundred in London alone, not counting those at the Old Vic. Long neglected works now became familiar. In *The Theatrical World of 1895* William Archer lists those he had not yet seen after years of industrious playgoing. They included: *Richard II, The Tempest, Coriolanus*, and *2 Henry IV*. *1 Henry IV, Love's Labour's Lost*, and *Measure for Measure*, he had seen only in performances by amateurs; *Julius Caesar* had been acted in London, 'within the memory of man', but only by a German company. Archer's ambition (he confessed) stopped short of *Troilus and Cressida*, 'which was not intended for the stage'. He would be able to see many of the others before long. What is remarkable is that he had not yet seen them. *Richard II* was to be particularly successful in the new time of Gielgud and Maurice Evans, when there would be audiences to whom the idea that *Troilus and Cressida* was not an acting play, and a very effective one, would be strange indeed.

Not only were there more productions, a much larger number of Shakespeare's lines were now spoken. Bowdlerization, where it existed, had become an amusing anachronism and cuts were not made for reasons of propriety. The speech of actors, those of Bridges-Adams, for instance (as earlier those of Granville-Barker), was far more rapid than it had once been. Such scenery as was still used no longer demanded frequent and lengthy pauses for its manipulation. Tree's intervals between acts and scenes might take up something like a third of one's evening; the new way was to have only one or two breaks in all.

With the restoration of Shakespeare's text, and the greater swiftness and continuity of many performances, it became possible to appreciate aspects of his technique which had long been obscured. Episodes once thought irrelevant assumed meaning. The opposing of consecutive scenes – as Marc Antony's oration and the murder of the harmless poet Cinna – seemed deliberately ironic. Any sweeping restoration of Elizabeth stage conditions was impossible in the theatres available. But the actor, as if on intimate terms with his audience, now tended to address them in soliloquy, abandoning any attempt at abstraction. Only low comedians had done this, earlier in the century, when the practice was considered destructive of illusion.

As for the directors, with their newly gained, despotic power, they used it with varying degrees of wisdom but on the whole benevolently. The idea that so far as Shakespeare was concerned the director's function was to bring out qualities in the work itself, rather than impose novel interpretations upon it, was pretty generally accepted as an idea, though it was sometimes forgotten in practice. From the early 1920s there were lively experiments with modern dress. This did well for certain scenes, for the Gravediggers and Christopher Sly, the banquet in *Macbeth* and three whole acts of *Julius Caesar*, and very badly for others. There were experiments also with costumes belonging to some serviceable period, more recent than that of the play, but not quite our own, and ingenuity was displayed in substituting characters of this period for their Elizabethan counterparts. With romance as such, that delight in strangeness and wonder which Shakespeare shared with many of his contemporaries, there was little sympathy; but most directors stopped short of deliberate travesty.

The year 1951 does well as a terminal date. In that Festival of Britain year the characteristics which I have been describing showed to particular advantage. At Stratford the production of *Richard II*, the two parts of *Henry IV*, and *Henry V* brought out the closeness of their relationships, the larger unity which they possessed as a group. It was a purpose of immediate appeal to scholars. In London the two great actors of our time were both to be seen in Shakespearian roles; and if Laurence Olivier was disappointing as Antony, in *Antony and Cleopatra*, John Gielgud was near his best as Leontes in a finely sensitive production of *The Winter's Tale* by Peter Brook. More exciting still, for some playgoers, was 2 *Henry VI*, directed by Douglas Seale at the Birmingham Repertory Theatre. This was to be followed, next year, by the Third Part, and all three histories were finally given in sequence with a degree of success which few readers would have prophesied for them.

Since 1951 there have been signs of reaction against the popularity of Shakespearian drama on the stage. When the plays were given, and there was no want of productions during these years, it was with less obvious liking and respect on the part of the director. For him what mattered most was to be creative, to have ideas of his own. Critics, too, grown tired of a familiar work, were ready to welcome almost any sort of originality in its production. Fault has been found with the plays on ideological grounds. They were not what their author should have written, not what is wanted here and now. The temptation to alter and improve them became irresistible. At Stratford itself, where simple persons might have expected to see Shakespeare's plays acted as Shakespeare wrote them, Mr John Barton added some hundreds of lines to the three parts of *Henry VI*, given as two plays in 1963. His adaptations were repeated in 1964 as items in a long succession of histories. That the original versions had been successfully revived only a few years before, when they proved to be quite intelligible as they stood, and exciting 'theatre', mattered not at all.

The danger of over-emphasizing what may have been no more than a passing mood is obvious. The English stage between 1951 and 1970 has not been without Shakespearian productions comparable to the best of the generation before. It is enough to recall Peter Brook's *Titus Andronicus*, and, as given in Edinburgh in 1962, Peter Hall's *Troilus and Cressida*. In both these there was an unusual and strangely effective mingling of symbol and savage realism. In the tragedy, ritual was frequently introduced as well. In *Troilus and Cressida*, a play of impermanence, dominated by the presence of Time, the stage itself was deeply covered with sand.

15

SHAKESPEARE AND THE
DRAMA OF HIS TIME

PETER URE

I INTRODUCTORY

Shakespeare sometimes drew upon plays (or other works) by fellow-dramatists for his own plays and poems. He often remembered bits of what they had written. Occasionally, he chose a play as his main source: an old two-part play by George Whetstone (1578) was the basis of *Measure for Measure*. This chapter is not about sources in that sense, although they cannot be completely excluded; it is about Shakespeare's contacts with the work of other Elizabethan playwrights, with special reference to those who might have shaped his own art in important ways. He borrowed a whole play from Whetstone, a thing which he never did to Marlowe; but it is Marlowe who is discussed here, and not Whetstone. We are concerned with those playwrights who may have induced Shakespeare to attend to them enough to accept (or reject) them as artists, in the fullest sense. Absolute proofs of the 'contacts' themselves are often missing; when discussing this topic, modern literary criticism has sometimes built bricks without straw. It is easy to imagine the distorted face of a contemporary in Shakespeare's vast mirror – one can dream up a Marlovian Shakespeare even more easily than a Brechtian one. Ingenuities of this sort have had to be overlooked here, together with much other work and detail of greater value.

II MARLOWE

Shakespeare alludes to or echoes Marlowe's writings every now and then, but it is likely that there was also a complex artistic encounter between the two dramatists; the matter works itself out in elaborate topics such as the Machiavel in *The Jew of Malta* and *Richard III*, king and kingdom in *Edward II* and *Richard II*, or even more speculatively: humanism and orthodoxy are examined, or a contrast is proposed between Marlowe's 'restless scepticism' and Shakespeare's 'optimistic view of life'. Shakespeare was the same age as Marlowe (about thirty when Marlowe was murdered in 1593) but there is no good evidence that they ever collaborated or that they thought of themselves as rivals, friendly or unfriendly.

Shakespeare may or may not have invented the popular English history play, but there can be little doubt that in his three plays on Henry VI (?December 1589–June 1592), he and he alone gave life to the form and made it thematically and poetically coherent. In *Henry VI* the supposed influence of *Tamburlaine* on the blank verse, the rhetoric and the construction proves fairly hard to pin down; and certainly Shakespeare does not seem to endorse and involve himself, in Marlowe's way, with the over-reaching tone and imperative rhythms which he derives from Marlowe's huf-cap hero (heard, for example, in the speeches of the aspiring Duke of York and of his son Richard). With this son, the future Richard III, Shakespeare's response to Marlowe crystallizes. Richard, in *3 Henry VI* and its sequel *Richard III*, is his first full-scale study of the Marlovian superman in his Machiavel role. During the years it was being fashioned (?1591–3), Shakespeare had not only Tamburlaine but probably also the Guise (in *The Massacre at Paris*) and Barabas (in *The Jew of Malta*) to think about. In these characters Marlowe had established the murderous Machiavel of the playhouse, ruthless and magnetic, self-delighting and self-destructive. Their author is himself implicated in the disturbing union of intensity and (apparently) cynical indifference found in these plays. Shakespeare, on the other hand, is able to embody all the energies of Machiavellism in his Richard and yet to interrelate them with the positives that elsewhere in the play spring from conscience, providence or pity (as, for example, pity for Clarence, one of Richard's victims, a figure outside Marlowe's range). It is not – or not wholly – a case of Shakespeare's being more orthodox and complacent, but of his being willing to take a more penetrating look at Machiavellism itself than Marlowe did. Shakespeare may have arrived at this by way of *Titus Andronicus* (?1589–90): Aaron, in that play, is a creation of Marlovian exuberance, almost a 'villain as hero', like Richard and Barabas.

An even more famous case of interaction concerns Marlowe's *Edward II* (*c.* 1590–2), which was influenced by at least the last two parts of the *Henry VI* trilogy. The general resemblances between *Henry VI* and Marlowe's play include a weak king murdered after a rebellion, varying fortunes in a civil war, and characters towards whom our sympathies fluctuate accordingly. Though Marlowe was learning from Shakespeare, his attitude to history is so different that he has been accused of writing it 'without morality', detached from ordinary human sympathies and in rejection of life. Others have found the verse arid: Edward's inlaid, ranting apostrophes seem too often to proceed only from the author's pen, while Richard III has already internalized his speech.

In his turn Shakespeare must have had *Edward II* well in mind when he wrote *Richard II* about 1594–5. His close knowledge of the piece, though it left its marks, sometimes decisive ones such as the deposition scene (IV, i), would have been perfectly compatible with what C. H. Herford termed a 'decisive reaction' *against* Marlowe. For me, the shared ingredient is the helpless king, the personal tragedy of the 'king who must', ruled by those who have wrested from his own power to rule. Marlowe's handling of Edward brought the tragic impropriety into focus for Shakespeare, but it is already hinted at in much that befalls Henry VI. The characteristically Shakespearian device of gradually re-ordering our feelings about individuals (from detachment or reproof to sympathy, or *vice versa*) is found in Marlowe, too; but Shakespeare (in *Henry VI*) seems to have been first to try it. This makes it less likely that he needed an impulsion from Marlowe to build it into the great thing that it is in *Julius Caesar* and *The Merchant of Venice*.

These are the other two Shakespeare plays for which a major Marlovian influence has been invoked. Although it must be easier for those who can see Caesar as a 'Roman Tamburlaine' (in Dover Wilson's phrase), it is much more difficult to detect Marlowe in *Julius Caesar* than in *The Merchant of Venice*. They were the only dramatists of their era to make a Jew a central figure in a play; there are verbal parallels which include the deliberate assignment of Tamburlaine–and Guise - like rhodomontade to the solemn princes of Morocco and Arragon. As for Shylock and Jessica, editors mostly agree that *The Jew of Malta* must be regarded as a major source – though, again, as is the case with *Richard II*, Shakespeare's use of Marlowe is by no means incompatible with a 'decisive reaction' against his limited, if incandescent, vision. A recent editor says sensibly that Marlowe's Jewish father and daughter are the 'complements rather than the parallels' to Shakespeare's.

Marlowe's work seems, in Yeats's phrase, to finish in a flare. The mind that made it so blaze up must have been very unlike Shakespeare's; but there are signs that it invited his admiring compassion, and that he had to come to terms with it before he could go on.

III   LYLY AND OTHER WITS

The idea that Lyly's *Euphues* (1578) was an aberration has given place to the view that euphuism – or the movement of which it was the climax – was a big step in the development of sixteenth-century prose away from invertebrate muddle towards dealing with complex material in an adequately ordered and logical way (productive, in drama, of poised elegance, bite and sparkle). If this is true, Shakespeare, like many of his contemporaries, stayed Lyly's beneficiary to the end; it has been said that *all* Shakespeare's prose has some resemblances to euphuism. A debt of a more particular kind has been observed in the influence of Lyly's court-comedies (mostly performed in the 1580s) on Shakespeare's five earlier comedies, *The Comedy of Errors, The Taming of the Shrew, The Two Gentlemen of Verona, Love's Labour's Lost* and *A Midsummer Night's Dream.*

One of the obscurities of this topic is that specific source-type links are disputable, because the two dramatists may have been drawing independently on the traditions of Roman or Italian comedy; and, when the debt seems necessarily more generalized (as in the treatment of love and lovers), Shakespeare's reliable gift for seeing further and more finely has persuaded commentators to study his improvements upon Lyly, rather than his resemblances to him. Lyly, however, was the first writer to produce a substantial collection of English prose comedies; they display wit-combats between courtiers and ladies; and offer us engaging servants and their encounters with their lords, malapert little boys and shining nymphs, girls disguised as boys, songs, fairies, and a fine-grained and deferential cultivation of the audience's 'delight', its 'soft smiling'. Lyly makes a little world of harmonies, which is linked with Ovidian poetry through its mythology and metamorphoses, and with dance, tapestry, masque and pastoral. English comedy before Lyly had been vigorous enough; now it was elegant. The great symbolic activity of this comedy is courtship, and a search, half-humorous and half-serious, for a definition of love; and its maiden-meditations extend to nature and society as well.

The *general* resemblances between that kind of comedy and Shakespeare's up to *Twelfth Night* are obvious. Indeed, it is broadly true that Lyly and Shakespeare are the *only* Elizabethan playwrights whose comedies enact a manifest concern with the definition of love, its meaning, value and order in the life of the individual and society. 'Being in love' is often the central experience of their comedy; it is not, as in most comedy, a mere datum from which interest is displaced onto the bustle of intrigue against the detested rival or tyrannical parent. Like Lyly, Shakespeare constructed his comic societies by placing different groups in apposition to one another (courtiers, ladies; masters, servants; fairies, humans; schoolboys, pedants; and so on); but he not only deepened the reality of individuals (Lyly has no 'stock types' so rammed with life as Launce, Armado or Bottom), he also bound the groups to one another in an elaborate, critical and relativistic way, often under-cutting Lyly's courtly values with subtle analogies and parody. As G. K. Hunter puts it, Shakespeare *interlaces* his episodes (as he does his servants and masters), but Lyly's are kept separate.

Love's Labour's Lost and *A Midsummer Night's Dream*, especially the former, are the plays that (as wholes) approach nearest to Lylian court-entertainment. Shakespeare has adopted many Lylian conventions, and the parallels are generally (though not universally) admitted. The stylish wit, the love-debates, the complementarily arranged groups are all like Lyly's. But Shakespeare is much more concerned with the emotional history of his lovers and with their struggle to understand their own experience. (Valentine and Proteus in *The Two Gentleman of Verona*, Hermia and Lysander in *A Midsummer Night's Dream*, Berowne and his company in *Love's Labour's Lost* are all alike in this). The result is that we become involved with that experience, too, especially when we are helped by the exquisitely penetrating verisimilitude of Shakespeare's verse and prose. But Lyly's less individuated courtiers are shielded from us inside the crystal cabinet of their courtly professionalism: by it alone, by nothing more universal, can they submit to be judged.

Participation in the heart-mysteries of comedy Shakespeare brought about for the first time in English. Lyly's example seems to have marked an important phase in a movement from intrigue-comedy of a chiefly Plautine sort (*The Comedy of Errors*) to the mature love-comedies which are so uniquely Shakespearian. It is a fair guess that the poise and radiance and other unnameable qualities of even Shakespeare's most triumphant heroines – Beatrice or Rosalind or Viola – owe something to him. Shakespeare just intensified the 'delight' – almost, but not entirely, beyond recognition.

A conceivable exception to the rule that only Lyly and Shakespeare are profoundly concerned with 'being in love' might be sought in the work of another university wit, Robert Greene. From time to time good cases have been made out for his kinship with Shakespeare. This appears in their common interest in romantic love and romantic heroines (sometimes dressed up as boys), in their multiple plots, in their use of play-framing devices (like Christopher Sly in *The Taming of the Shrew* and Bohan in Greene's *James IV*) and playlets-within-the-play (compare the eavesdropping scenes in *Much Ado about Nothing* with the 'prospective glass' scenes in Greene's *Friar Bacon and Friar Bungay*). Kinship is a hard thing to be sure about, and both playwrights were using their inheritance of improbable old fictions, the Hellenistic romances and Italian *novelle*; but the hypothesis, accepted or rejected, does help to define features not only of Shakespeare's earlier comedies but of his late romances as well. In Greene's best plays there is a spirit – it has been called magnanimity and loving insight – which resembles Shakespeare's.[1]

Thomas Kyd did not go to a university, but he learnt his wit and his Latin at a famous school in company with Spenser, so perhaps he may be considered here. He was apparently the first man to write plays about revenge for murder, thereby founding a tradition which includes *Titus Andronicus* and *Hamlet*. He may have written the old Hamlet play (the model for Shakespeare's *Hamlet*) which had – for we know what its sources must have been, though we have lost the play itself – a ghost, a son's (delayed) revenge for a father, a hero who goes crazy, and a play within a play. His *The Spanish Tragedy* (?1587), the first extant full-blown revenge-play, has a number of similar episodes.

Kyd was, in the strictest sense, a very great dramatist – greater, as T. S. Eliot declared, than Marlowe. He used his theatre brilliantly, and knew of many different ways in which to show it off. His savage ironies have a more personal thrust than Marlowe's. He used soliloquy, dialogue and gesture for actualizing inner confusion, grief, solitary brooding, tragic foolery. All this can be underrated if we do not recognize how subtly he animates the modes which he derived largely from medieval metrical tragedies (there is very little 'Senecanism' in him). When all is said, a scene such as Hieronimo's discovery of the dead body of his son hanging in the garden (*The Spanish Tragedy* II, v) is one of the most tremendous in English drama. He was amongst the first to contrive that intensification of tragic by comic modes that everybody knows about in *Hamlet* and *King Lear* and *Macbeth*. He created personages of unusual awareness and located the motives for the action in them and not in the gods or their innumerable surrogates. It is easy to believe that Shakespeare was deeply impressed; and that he may have owed much more to Kyd than just the *schema* of revenge-tragedy.

All the major Wits fell on evil days; nearly all died before their time. It is Shakespeare himself and his work as actor and playwright, which most obviously bridges the gap between their plays and the new writers whom we begin to hear about in the late 1590s. Embodying that continuity must have been a salient part of his life-experience.

IV JONSON AND THE SATIRISTS

Shakespeare acted in Jonson's *Every Man in his Humour* (1598). This play, or its immediate forerunner Chapman's *An Humorous Day's Mirth* (1597), started the vogue for humour-comedy, shifting into its cognate modes, comical (and tragical) satires, black comedy, malcontent plays. Culminating in Jonson's *Sejanus* (1603) or Marston's

The Malcontent (1604), the movement left its mark on much subsequent writing, on Webster's tragedies and Chapman's comedies, on Middleton, on Tourneur, and on Jonson's own comic masterpieces from *Volpone* (1606) onwards. Satire (increasingly agile and provocative in the late 1590s) had got a lodgement in the drama and proved its kinship by sprouting out into all kinds of daring devices. The 'comical satires' of Jonson and Marston offer combinations which are new to the theatre, though much indebted to both Roman and medieval satirical ideas: first, affected (= 'humorous') or vicious or criminal persons, commonly subjugated by *one* affectation, vice, or crime, in the same way that a diseased humour was believed to surcharge the human body and discompose its elements. Secondly, there takes his place inside the play the necessary counterpoise to these satirized persons – the satirist himself: he may be the virtuous, temperate, four-square Poet (like Horace in Jonson's *Poetaster*), or (more frequently) he is the flailing commentator, the scourge who is not immune from the 'strange surquedries' that he castigates; a darker version of the same figure is the malcontent-revenger, like Malevole in *The Malcontent* or Vindice in *The Revenger's Tragedy*, who, in inhibiting vices, especially sexual ones, enjoys a prurient complicity with a world which to him appears a graveyard, muck-heap, and pestilential congregation of vapours. Thirdly, comical satires are built up from the development of these characters through their own internal logic, especially during their submission to some ramifying court or city intrigue. The humour-character needs, because of his obsessions, continually to exhibit his viciousness or folly. This is where satire approaches close to allegory. It is the business of the penal agent in satire whether revenger, homilist, righteous victim, or cynic dog, to induce the humour-character to act out his humour fully, to wind up the clock of his mania until it strikes; it is also the business of the play as a whole to move steadily towards the place and moment when the affectations and vices are finally stripped bare, punished, and ejected with contempt from the society of the play. The process is mythic enough – the scapegoat purifies his community of burdens otherwise pernicious to it. But the commonest metaphors in the plays are of scourging and purging; these were mirrored in the penal code, and literally enacted on the stage in Dekker's *Satiromastix* and Jonson's *Poetaster*.

Shakespeare's mature art of the middle period, from *Henry V* (1599) onwards, was undoubtedly affected by all this. His artistic acknowledgement of it is perhaps the clearest demonstration we have, once the formative years are over, of his being always wide awake to what other playwrights were doing. This seems clear enough even though Shakespeare, like them, was also responding to something in the 'spirit of the age', a new restlessness and sardonic intellectuality, which would have affected his art anyway. But he never went in whole-heartedly for these paradigms of punishment. The satirical elements are scattered here and there, but they do not take control. Even his early humour-characters, Pistol and Nym in *Henry V*, have got an extra un-Jonsonian dimension. His unequalled genius for seeing the man beneath the mask unfitted him for the wall-eyed stare of the humour-satirist.

The wariness of Shakespeare's response is clearly seen in *Troilus and Cressida*. Thersites in that play is an uncompromising version of the immoderate, contemptible railer. *Troilus and Cressida* is unique, and hard to construe, but the claim that it is an example of comical (or tragical) satire, with everybody in it held up to ridicule (as though Thersites had *written* the play) must, I believe, be denied. Jacques and *As You Like It* make up, *mutatis mutandis*, a parallel case. Malvolio in *Twelfth Night* has many affinities with satirical and humour-comedy and is temperately subjected to its purgative and dismissive routines; but no one has claimed *Twelfth Night* as a whole for the Jonsonian mode (though Sir Toby is a more squalid figure than is usually recognized). *Measure for Measure* can only be allocated a 'basic satiric anatomy' on the hypothesis that Isabella and her cause upset an original design; the play that we have, though things in it may have been derived from Marston or Middleton, achieves a final effect unlike either's work. Hamlet takes malcontentism in his stride, and is not encompassed by it. He has some affinity (as indeed has Lear) with Timon, but the view that *Timon of Athens* is a 'tragical satire' (like *Sejanus*) depends upon a reading which ignores too much in the play to be plausible. In short, we can justifiably talk of Shakespeare's satire, and all the plays and characters I have just mentioned, and others beside, can be illuminated by some knowledge of what was going on in the theatre from 1598 to 1604 or later; but we cannot talk of Shakespeare's satires.[2]

V FLETCHER AND THE LAST PLAYS

The four last plays or romances, beginning with *Pericles* (?1607–8), make up a constellation rather different from any other in Shakespeare. Each of the four has its own character, nor ought we to exaggerate the apartness of their group: in earlier plays, such as *All's Well that Ends Well* and *Troilus and Cressida*, there are the same qualities – discontinuous characterization, 'baroque' or 'old comedy' forms, satire mixed with far-fetched story, an analytic approach to ideas – that are to be more richly and magniloquently deployed in *The Tempest* and its immediate predecessors.

It is, therefore, extraordinarily difficult to say how much of the new strain grows out of earlier achievements and how much may be due to new dramatists and a changing theatrical climate. Early in 1609 the King's men started playing in the Blackfriars theatre and were launched on their great experiment of being the first adult company to run two London theatres simultaneously. Although a recent habit of referring to it as a 'coterie' theatre is perfectly misleading, the Blackfriars was smaller, dearer and more exclusive than the Globe; this must have made the company think a bit more about fashion and refinement, as well as about music and masques. John Fletcher started working for them in 1609 – Shakespeare's junior by fifteen years, he had been writing (for other companies) for about two. His career overlapped with Shakespeare's for four or five years (1609–13), and it was he who, in the theatrical and professional sense, was to be Shakespeare's successor as chief poet. In the artistic sense Fletcher (and his partner during the vital period, Beaumont) were so far below Shakespeare as to be virtually invisible; but the fact that their work was to be highly esteemed during the rest of the era indicates the sort of changes in taste, just then beginning, to which Shakespeare may have wished to respond.

Did Fletcher influence the last plays? Behind this puzzle stands the common belief that Shakespeare actually collaborated with Fletcher in *Henry VIII* and *The Two Noble Kinsmen* (current theories that Shakespeare wrote them unaided are exceptionally improbable). But both these collaborative exercises, as well as that involving the lost *Cardenio*, are very late (1612–13), probably done during the semi-retirement at Stratford; they cast only a retrospective light on the main problem. This problem cannot be solved in terms of contact between play and play in the *Edward II/Richard II* manner. Efforts to prove the specific indebtedness of *Cymbeline* to *Philaster* (or *vice versa*), or of *The Tempest* to *The Faithful Shepherdess*, have not succeeded. We are driven to compare the art of the two playwrights at a higher level of generalization, to talk about patterns. A pattern may be defined simply as an aggregate of various characteristic features, or, more obscurely, as a critically abstracted principle of design or development. Either way, there is a certain liberty of interpreting.

It is wrong to feel that Shakespeare would have refused to learn – about, for example, the modish Italian-style pastoral – from younger men, especially in the new Blackfriars situation (perhaps it was Shakespeare himself who spotted Fletcher's timeliness). But, before Fletcher's advent, he had written or rewritten the last three acts of *Pericles*, the prototype of the romances – and for the Globe, too. The taste for romance was old as well as new, as is shown by the King's men revival of *Mucedorus*, an old tragical-comical-pastoral thriller, which left its traces in *The Winter's Tale* and *The Tempest*; similarly another old (1582) play of the same kind, *The Rare Triumphs of Love and Fortune*, may have affected *Cymbeline*. When we *can* specify, what come first to mind are 'old plays', Spenser, *Arcadia*, *Pandosto*, the archaic fictions that we hear about in *The Winter's Tale* and the Hellenistic romances which had long supplied material for popular writers such as Greene or Peele.

And yet these borrowings underline the kinship between the old romantic thrillers and the new sumptuous tragicomedy that, like *Philaster* and *Cymbeline*, 'wants deaths...yet brings some near it'. The basic patterns of Fletcherian tragicomedy resemble the patterns of generations lost-and-found explored in the last plays, though tragicomedy itself is not new to Shakespeare and has a long history on the English stage before Fletcher: one thinks of Richard Edwardes's *Damon and Pithias* (1565) or of the romance elements in *The Comedy of Errors* or of the 'deaths' of Claudio or Hero; likewise, the conjunction of *satyr* and *pastor*, complicated in Fletcher, had been clearly established by Jaques and Touchstone. Even the conscious theatrical artifice, the play's exposure of its own machinery, the virtuoso daring of much of the plotting in the romances, the declamatory and passionate arias – these are things Shakespeare has in common with Fletcher; yet there is no phase of his earlier work that does not forecast their magnification in the final plays. The Fletcherian stigma – a peculiar, mawkish intensity of tone and language – did not afflict Shakespeare: even *Cymbeline*, the most Fletcher-like of the plays, keeps a toughly obscure late-Shakespearian style; and all of them contain writing that, for solemnity and splendour of imagination, outpaces Fletcher beyond any reckoning. What we are dealing with is a confluence rather than an influence; Fletcher's art was one of a number of tributaries running in the same direction, its waters now drowned in the great river. Indeed, the really incalculable gulf between the insight of genius, more penetrating than ever in the last plays, and Fletcher's rather vapid talent, makes any comparison between them, however much it is stated in terms of *underlying* patterns, seem inescapably of the surface.

VI CONCLUSION

With the possible exception of two or three of the great tragedies – more distinctly *sui generis* than any other group – a less summary treatment of the subject of this chapter would need to give some consideration to every one of Shakespeare's plays: for none is without some kind of contextual relationship to other plays of the time. 'Shakespeare,' G. E. Bentley says, 'was more completely and continuously involved with theatres and acting companies than any other Elizabethan dramatist whose life we know.' The inescapable corollary of this is Hazlitt's '. . . distinguished from his immediate contemporaries, not in kind, but in degree and greater variety of excellence. . . He did not form a class or species by himself, but belonged to a class or species.' On the other hand, classification, though it may help or hinder them, has no necessary overlap with literary criticism or theatre-performance. This may explain why we have had tolerable productions and suggestive criticism neither of which has appeared to be much damaged by a stupendous indifference to the rest of the species.

16

SHAKESPEARE'S TEXT: APPROACHES AND PROBLEMS

G. BLAKEMORE EVANS

Interest, even a passionate interest, in the challenging problems raised by the text of Shakespeare's plays and poems is scarcely a modern phenomenon. From the beginning of the eighteenth century many scholars and amateurs have devoted themselves, in the light of current textual approaches, to establishing what they firmly believed represented the 'best' or 'true' text. The seventeenth century, on the other hand, had adopted a much less idolatrous view of the sanctity of Shakespeare's every word, and a progressive and unauthorized tendency to modernize grammar, syntax, and language may be traced from the early quartos to the First Folio (1623) and then on through the Second (1632), Third (1664) and Fourth (1685) Folios.

This accumulation of compounded error and thoughtless if well-intentioned meddling was the inheritance of Shakespeare's early editors, and nearly a hundred years passed before these surface blemishes were finally sloughed off and the primacy of the earliest printed editions vindicated. This done, the basic problems were, as we shall see, only partially understood and it was not until the present century that their full implications were squarely faced. Even today, after two hundred and fifty years devoted to the study of Shakespeare's text, there is much that remains to be learned, much that is only hypothetically explained, much that we can probably never know with any certainty. What we do know, what we guess, and, by implication, what we would still like to know is the subject of the present essay.

The extant materials for an examination of Shakespeare's text may be quickly listed. Thirty-nine plays, in whole or in part by Shakespeare, the poems *Venus and Adonis* and *Lucrece*, the sonnets, and a few other short poems form the body of the Shakespeare canon. Thirty-six of these plays were gathered together in the earliest collected edition of Shakespeare's works (1623), now generally known as the First Folio (F1).[1] Eighteen plays appeared there for the first time in any printed form and for these F1 furnishes the sole authority for the text, any changes that were made in the later folios being entirely without

Addition (D) to Sir Thomas More, *lines 126–140*

what Country by the nature of yor error
fhoold gyve you harber go yo^u to ffraunc or flanders
to any Jarman pvince, ~~to~~ fpane or portigall
nay any where ~~why yo^u~~ that not adheres to Ingland
why yo^u muft neede be ftraingers, woold yo^u be pleafd
to find a nation of fuch barbarous temper
that breaking out in hiddious violence
woold not afoord yo^u, an abode on earth
whett their detefted knyves againft yor throtes
fpurne yo^u lyke dogge, and lyke as yf that god
owed not nor made not yo^u, nor that the elamente
                              yor
wer not all appropriat to ~~their~~ Comforte.
but Charterd vnto them, what woold yo^u thinck
to be thus vfd, this is the ftraingers cafe
and this your momtanifh inhumanyty

Our deereſt *Regan*, wife to *Cornwell*, ſpeake?

Reg. Sir I am made of the ſelfe ſame mettall that my ſiſter is,
And prize me at her worth in my true heart,
I find ſhe names my very deed of loue, onely ſhe came ſhort,
That I profeſſe my ſelfe an enemie to all other ioyes,
Which the moſt precious ſquare of ſence poſſeſſes,
And find I am alone felicitate, in your deere highnes loue.

Cord. Then poore *Cord.* & yet not ſo, ſince I am ſure
My loues more richer then my tongue.

Lear. To thee and thine hereditarie euer
Remaine this ample third of our faire kingdome,
No leſſe in ſpace, validity, and pleaſure,
Then that confirm'd on *Gonorill*, but now our ioy,
Although the laſt, not leaſt in our deere loue,
What can you ſay to win a third, more opulent
Then your ſiſters.

Cord. Nothing my Lord.   (againe.
Lear. How, nothing can come of nothing, ſpeake
Cord. Vnhappie that I am, I cannot heaue my heart into my
mouth, I loue your Maieſtie according to my bond, nor more nor
leſſe.

Lear. Goe to, goe to, mend your ſpeech a little,
Leaſt it may mar your fortunes.

Cord. Good my Lord,
You haue begot me, bred me, loued me,
I returne thoſe duties backe as are right fit,
Obey you, loue you, and moſt honour you,
Why haue my ſiſters huſbands if they ſay they loue you all,
Happely when I ſhall wed, that Lord whoſe hand
Muſt take my plight, ſhall cary halfe my loue with him,
Halfe my care and duty, ſure I ſhall neuer
Mary like my ſiſters, to loue my father all,

Lear. But goes this with thy heart?
Cord. I good my Lord.
Lear. So yong and ſo vntender.
Cord. So yong my Lord and true.
Lear. Well let it be ſo, thy truth then be thy dower,
For by the ſacred radience of the Sunne,

B 2   The

Our deereſt *Regan*, wife of *Cornwall* ?

Reg. I am made of that ſelfe-mettle as my Siſter,
And prize me at her worth. In my true heart,
I finde ſhe names my very deede of loue :
Onely ſhe comes too ſhort, that I profeſſe
My ſelfe an enemy to all other ioyes,
Which the moſt precious ſquare of ſenſe profeſſes,
And finde I am alone felicitate
In your deere Highneſſe loue.

Cor. Then poore *Cordelia*,
And yet not ſo, ſince I am ſure my loue's
More ponderous then my tongue.

Lear. To thee, and thine hereditarie euer,
Remaine this ample third of our faire Kingdome,
No leſſe in ſpace, validitie, and pleaſure
Then that conferr'd on *Gonerill*. Now our Ioy,
Although our laſt and leaſt ; to whoſe yong loue,
The Vines of France, and Milke of Burgundie,
Striue to be intereſt. What can you ſay, to draw
A third, more opilent then your Siſters? ſpeake.

Cor. Nothing my Lord.

Lear. Nothing ?

Cor. Nothing.

Lear. Nothing will come of nothing, ſpeake againe.

Cor. Vnhappie that I am, I cannot heaue
My heart into my mouth: I loue your Maieſty
According to my bond, no more nor leſſe.

Lear. How, how *Cordelia*? mend your ſpeec ah little,
Leaſt you may marre your Fortunes.

Cor. Good my Lord,
You haue begot me, bred me, lou'd me.
I returne thoſe duties backe as are right fit,
Obey you, Loue you, and moſt Honour you.
Why haue my Siſters Husbands, if they ſay
They loue you all ? Happily when I ſhall wed,
That Lord, whoſe hand muſt take my plight, ſhall carry
Halfe my loue with him, halfe my Care, and Dutie,
Sure I ſhall neuer marry like my Siſters.

Lear. But goes thy heart with this ?

Cor. I my good Lord.

Lear. So young, and ſo vntender ?

Cor. So young my Lord, and true.

Lear. Let it be ſo, thy truth then be thy dowre:
For by the ſacred radience of the Sunne,

From the Folio of 1623.

independent manuscript authority. The remaining eighteen plays in F1 had been published earlier in separate quarto editions[2] and for all but seven these quartos furnish the most authoritative texts. Three other plays, now generally admitted as at least in part by Shakespeare, were not included in F1: *Pericles*, published in quarto in 1608, was added to the F1 collection in the Third Folio (1664);[3] *The Two Noble Kinsmen*, probably by Fletcher and Shakespeare, appeared in quarto in 1634; and *Sir Thomas More*, a play in which Shakespeare is usually accorded a single scene of 147 lines and (in the opinion of some) one other speech, was printed from a manuscript, now in the British Museum, for the first time in 1844. This so-called *More* fragment, since the single scene is believed to be in Shakespeare's autograph, is of special interest and will be referred to in later discussions. These, then, simply listed, are the primary materials with which the student of Shakespeare has to work, but the many-faceted problems raised by this body of materials are far from simple.

Two basic questions at once present themselves, questions which, curiously enough, were never seriously or systematically considered until about sixty years ago. First, what kind or kinds of manuscripts can be postulated as lying behind the earliest printed texts? Second, what sort of treatment, both editorial and mechanical, did these manuscripts undergo in the Elizabethan–Jacobean printing house? Or, to reduce the two questions to one: how close do the printed texts bring us to what Shakespeare actually wrote? The answers to these questions, fundamental as they are, are extremely complex and not infrequently still hypothetical.

Let us consider, first, the matter of the manuscripts from which the earliest printed texts were necessarily derived. The modern reader will naturally tend to assume that Shakespeare's plays were printed from carefully prepared author's final copy, 'absolute in their numbers, as he conceived them'. Such, indeed, was the claim Heminges and Condell, Shakespeare's fellow actors and the 'editors' of F1, made in their preface, 'To the Great Variety of Readers', for the texts in that volume. But recent investigations, begun under the leadership of R. B. McKerrow, A. W. Pollard, W. W. Greg, and J. Dover Wilson, have painted a sadly different picture. Except, possibly, in the case of *2 Henry VI* and *3 Henry VI*, *Troilus and Cressida*, *Antony and Cleopatra*, and *Coriolanus*, it has been demonstrated that, even when it is possible to postulate Shakespearian autograph as the source of a printed text, the manuscript involved must be recognized as Shakespeare's 'foul papers' (i.e. the original, or an early draft of the play) and not his final (or 'fair') copy. The reasons for this state of affairs are not difficult to guess. Once an author had sold his play to a company of actors (in

Shakespeare's case the Chamberlain's men, later known as the King's men), he ceased, except in special circumstances, to have any personal rights in the play, and, when a company decided to make a little extra money by selling the printing rights to a publisher, the manuscript they turned over, since they probably possessed only one official copy (the prompt-book), was most likely to be some state of the author's original draft ('foul papers'), something presumably of no further value to them. Such a manuscript would inevitably tend to be untidy and carelessly written, containing unclearly marked deletions, additions, revisions, interlineations, inconsistent speech-prefixes, incomplete and sporadic stage directions. Enough examples of this kind of manuscript have survived (including parts of the *Sir Thomas More* manuscript) to support such a generalization. It is scarcely surprising, therefore, that compositors when faced with 'foul papers' for printer's copy frequently produced a confused and inaccurate text. Certainly, the hypothetically difficult and potentially confusing condition of Shakespeare's 'foul papers' will go far to explain the compositorial misreadings and mis-understandings found in such basic texts as the second quartos of *Romeo and Juliet* and *Hamlet*. In addition to these two plays, *The Comedy of Errors, Titus Andronicus, The Taming of the Shrew, Love's Labour's Lost, Richard II, A Midsummer Night's Dream, King John, The Merchant of Venice, 1 Henry IV* and *2 Henry IV, Much Ado about Nothing, Henry V, All's Well that Ends Well*, and *Timon of Athens* have been widely thought to have been printed more or less directly from some stage of Shakespeare's 'foul papers'. Such, at least, is W. W. Greg's final judgement (1955). But there is disagreement, and some recent opinion prefers to postulate an intermediate scribal transcript from the 'foul papers' as the manuscript copy for certain of these plays.

But, even if we accept Greg's view, author's copy, fair or foul, will account for only about half of the plays. At least four other kinds of what may be termed secondary copy have to be allowed for: scribal copy (either from author's foul or fair copy or from another scribal copy); theatre prompt copy (a manuscript possibly authorial, but more often scribal, which has served as the prompt-book for stage produc-tion); memorially reconstructed copy (the hypothetical source of the so-called 'bad' quartos); and what may be called combination-copy, partly printed (the quartos), partly manuscript (the manuscript in question again being of several possible kinds).

The first two categories, scribal and theatre copy, clearly overlap, since theatre copy seems usually to have been a scribal transcript, not infrequently, one suspects, made from a late stage of an author's 'foul papers'. There is, however, a class of scribal copy prepared for such a non-theatrical occasion as a manuscript gift (perhaps such a Shake-spearian fair copy lies behind the quarto edition of *Troilus and Cressida*) or publication. This kind of scribal copy is believed to be the basis of the F I texts of *The Tempest, The Two Gentlemen of Verona, The Merry Wives of Windsor, Measure for Measure,* and *The Winter's Tale,* the manuscript copy for which is now generally accepted as the work of Ralph Crane, who is sometimes loosely described as scrivener to the King's men. These transcripts are thought to have been specially pre-pared for publication in F I, and Crane's characteristics as a scribe, strongly marked and well documented from other non-Shakespearian Crane transcripts, are still recognizable even after being filtered through the F I compositors. The texts of these plays in F I are comparatively clean and present few serious textual problems, but two nagging and essentially unanswerable questions must always remain. How much editorial tinkering and tidying up did Crane (or any other scribe) undertake in the process of transcription? And, from what kinds of manuscripts, authorial, scribal, or theatrical, were the transcripts made?

Theatre copy is thought to lie behind such plays as *Julius Caesar, As You Like It, Twelfth Night, Macbeth, Cymbeline,* and to some extent the F I texts of *Hamlet, Othello* and *King Lear.* Again these folio texts are relatively clean and tidy, but the problems noticed in con-nection with scribal copy are in most cases again present, aggravated by the additional interference of theatrical provenience. *Macbeth,* an extreme case, satisfactory as it may appear in some respects, almost certainly represents a shortened and somewhat telescoped stage version, which, short as it is compared with any of the other tragedies except *Timon of Athens* (probably never completed by Shakespeare), ironically preserves some fifty additional lines (the Hecate appearances) com-monly attributed to Thomas Middleton. *The Taming of the Shrew,* although probably printed from Shakespeare's 'foul papers', illustrates the danger of theatre influence even on manuscripts which did not serve as the official prompt-book. The F I text lacks the conclusion to the inimitable Christopher Sly framework and all but one of the interscene commentaries by Sly, a sad state of affairs that can best be explained by supposing that the 'foul papers' had been marked for cutting (fortunately not always very clearly) preparatory to the tran-scription of a prompt-book that would limit the play to the central taming plots. In this instance, however, we are fortunate enough to possess an earlier play (considered indeed by some critics to be a 'bad' quarto version of Shakespeare's play) called *The Taming of a Shrew* from which Shakespeare's treatment of the missing Sly material can in part be reconstructed.

The third kind of secondary manuscript copy, one based on some form of memorial reporting, introduces the question of the so-called 'bad' quartos. In the early years of this century, A. W. Pollard suggested the distinction, now regularly accepted, between what he termed 'good' and 'bad' quartos. Heminges and Condell in their preface to F1 talked disparagingly about certain earlier editions of the plays as 'stolen, and surreptitious copies'. Before Pollard's important distinction, although certain quartos were recognized as offering good texts, Heminges and Condell's remark was interpreted as a blanket attack on all the pre-Folio quartos, inspired by their desire to puff the authenticity of the texts in F1. Pollard, however, proposed that they were referring only to a special group of quartos, which he thereupon dubbed 'bad' quartos, the texts of which had been in some way piratically obtained, hence 'stolen, and surreptitious'. In this category are now included the first quartos of *Romeo and Juliet* (1597) and *Hamlet* (1603) and the quartos of *The Merry Wives of Windsor* (1602), *Henry V* (1600), *The Contention* (1594) and *True Tragedy of Richard Duke of York* (1595) (i.e. *2 Henry VI* and *3 Henry VI*), *Richard III* (1597), *King Lear* (1608), and *Pericles* (1609).[4] The quartos of *Richard III* and *King Lear* present special problems that make their inclusion here open to some question. The textual difficulties in *Richard III* will be discussed in some detail later. The 1608 quarto of *King Lear*, although it suffers seriously from some kind of memorial contamination, also gives evidence in parts of being printed from a transcription (perhaps through dictation) from Shakespeare's 'foul papers'.

At about this same time, an older theory, first suggested in the eighteenth century, was revived to account for the kinds of texts that, in varying degrees of 'badness', comprise this group of nine quartos. In his introduction to an edition (1910) of the quarto of *The Merry Wives of Windsor*, W. W. Greg offered the first detailed exploration of what is now called the memorial theory. Prior to this, these texts had been usually viewed either as early drafts by Shakespeare or others of plays which he later revised, or as shorthand reports of the plays taken down during performance. The memorial reconstruction theory is now commonly accepted, though with various qualifications and emphases, depending upon the particular play under consideration. In a later classic monograph, Greg extended the memorial theory in his discussion of Greene's *Orlando Furioso* and illustrated another kind of maimed text in an examination of Peele's *Battle of Alcazar*, an officially cut and simplified version prepared for provincial touring. Although none of the Shakespearian 'bad' quartos seems exactly to fit into this second category, a provincial tour probably explains the genesis of some of the unofficially perpetrated 'bad' quarto texts.

Briefly put, a memorially reconstructed text is one based primarily on what an actor (or actors) could recall from having played one or more roles, usually of a comparatively minor sort, in an authorized production of a play. The resulting version would thus produce, more or less accurately, the basic action of the original play, although not always in correct sequence, but its verbal text would, in greater or lesser degree, evidence the various tricks which memory can play: anticipation (placing phrases, lines, even scenes too early in the play), recollection (the reverse of anticipation), unconscious borrowing (using lines and phrases from other plays which are suggested by the immediate context), and, above all, simple forgetfulness, which forced the 'author' to ad-lib in an effort to give some semblance of logic and connection to his half-remembered bits and pieces. It has been observed that these texts tend to be more reliable when certain characters are present in a scene and this phenomenon, not without disagreement, has been used to suggest the actor (or actors) most likely to be responsible for the report (e.g. the Host in the quarto of *The Merry Wives of Windsor* or Marcellus and Lucianus, probably played by one actor, in Q1 of *Hamlet*). One other characteristic of many 'bad' quarto texts should be noticed – their employment of the visual memory. Again and again these texts give us visually recollected reports on stage business or costume of a sort not commonly found in texts printed from authorial or even theatrical copy. It is from the 'bad' quarto of *Hamlet*, for example, that we learn that the Ghost enters in his nightgown in the famous bedroom scene and that Hamlet leaps into Ophelia's grave after Laertes. The 'bad' quartos of *Romeo and Juliet*, *2 Henry VI* and *3 Henry VI*, and *The Merry Wives of Windsor* are also rewarding in affording this sort of sudden insight into a contemporary production.

The fourth kind of secondary printer's copy, combination-copy – part manuscript, part printed – appears largely in connection with F1 texts. Several (*Richard III*, *2 Henry VI* and *3 Henry VI*, *Henry V*, *King Lear*, *Troilus and Cressida*, and probably *Hamlet* and *Othello*) can be shown to have been printed from an earlier quarto edition (or editions) that had been collated and corrected against an independent manuscript, in most cases probably the official prompt-book. Words, phrases and lines from the manuscript were added to the printed copy, or substituted for readings already there, and longer passages, copied on slips, attached for insertion. Ideally, this method should produce something like a substantive facsimile of the manuscript, but given human carelessness, abetted by probable haste, the resulting printer's copy was in fact far from ideal.

For the eighteen plays which were printed for the first time in any form in F1 no problem can arise for an editor in his choice of basic copy-text, since, whatever kind of manuscript we may decide underlies these F1 texts, no other choice is possible. But the problem is potentially more complicated for the remaining eighteen plays in F1 where there are earlier quarto editions and a question may be posed as to the relative authority of quarto versus folio. For thirteen of these plays, however, no serious conflict exists. For four of them (*2 Henry VI* and *3 Henry VI*, *Henry V*, *The Merry Wives of Windsor*), the F1 texts are unchallenged because the only earlier quarto editions fall into the category of 'bad' quartos. For another nine (*Titus Andronicus*, *Romeo and Juliet*, *Love's Labour's Lost*, *A Midsummer Night's Dream*, *The Merchant of Venice*, *Richard II*, *1 Henry IV* and *2 Henry IV*, *Much Ado about Nothing*), a quarto edition is now generally accepted as the basic copy-text because the F1 texts, though they may contain additional lines from an independent source, are essentially only slightly sophisticated and edited reprints of the earlier quartos. But with such plays as *Richard III*, *Hamlet*, *Troilus and Cressida*, *Othello*, and *King Lear* various difficulties arise that tend to confuse the choice of copy-text and present an editor with many problems, some of them beyond any entirely satisfactory solution. Two case-histories (*Richard III* and *Hamlet*) may serve to clarify some of these difficulties and uncertainties and, at the same time, illustrate more concretely certain of the generalities treated in earlier parts of the discussion.

There are two important early texts of *Richard III*: Q1 printed in 1597 and the F1 text. Between Q1 and F1 five more quarto editions were published. Recent scholarship is now generally agreed that F1 should be taken as the basis for any modern edition and that Q1 is some kind of memorially reported version and must be classified as a 'bad' quarto, though what may be called a good 'bad' quarto, similar in this respect to the quarto of *King Lear*. Although F1 is thus accorded a primary place, the resulting textual situation is far from satisfactory. The greater part of the F1 text was set from a copy of Q6 (or possibly Q3), corrected and amplified (by some 190 lines) from an authoritative manuscript, probably Shakespeare's 'foul papers'. For some reason, however, at which we can do no more than guess, about five hundred lines of the play (a short stretch, III, i, 1–158, and all of the play after v, iii, 48) were printed from an uncorrected copy of Q3 (1602). For these five hundred lines, then, we are thrown back to the authority – or lack of it – of Q1. Since, moreover, the F1 text was, in great part, set up from a corrected late quarto, one that had amassed in a mounting spiral of error all the mistakes added along the way as each new quarto edition was printed from the one immediately preceding it, we are able to check the accuracy of the person making the collation between Q6 and the manuscript. Where, for example, F1 retains a reading first introduced in Q 2–6 (readings which were without any authority, mere printing-house guesses or errors), we can be relatively certain that the collator has failed to make the necessary correction in his copy of Q 6. Forty-one such readings were overlooked by the collator out of a possible 340, that is, he failed to correct one out of every eight readings. In these instances we are able to check his accuracy, but in the thousands of readings common to Q 1 and F 1 (remembering that Q 1 is a memorially reported text and its readings consequently of doubtful authority), we have no means of checking the collator's accuracy. Alice Walker, for example, calculates that at least 110 corrections from the manuscript were missed and others would put the figure even higher. Baldly stated, the only substantial parts of *Richard III* that we can be relatively sure represent what Shakespeare wrote are the 190 lines that appear for the first time in F 1 and that must have been derived directly from the manuscript.

The some thirty-seven hundred lines which we read today as *Hamlet* were never read by an Elizabethan and almost certainly at no single reading even by Shakespeare himself. Our modern *Hamlet* is in fact an eclectic text combining materials from three sources: Q 2 (1604), F 1 (1623), and Q 1 (1603), a 'bad' quarto. Of these, however, only Q 2 and F 1 figure in the choice of a copy-text. Q 2 is now, since the important work of Dover Wilson in 1934, recognized as the more authoritative, being for the most part demonstrably set from Shakespeare's 'foul papers', and it contains roughly 200 lines found neither in F 1 nor Q 1. F 1, which contains some 85 lines not in Q 1 or Q 2, shows obvious connections with an official theatre prompt-book, though whether it was printed directly from that prompt-book manuscript or from a copy of Q 2 collated against and augmented from such a manuscript remains a debatable question that affects the relative independent authority of the F 1 text. Recent research has shown, moreover, that the F 1 text evidences considerable indications of contamination by long use in the theatre (an important factor in the gradual corruption of a text), and its readings are becoming increasingly suspect – except, of course, for the more substantial additional passages, which we must suppose to be genuine Shakespearian additions made at some point between the writing of the play around 1600 and Shakespeare's death in 1616.

Q 1 is a typical example of a 'bad' quarto. It is about half as long as Q 2 and offers a text that suffers markedly from all the characteristic weaknesses of a memorial reconstruction – misplaced scenes and groups of lines, garbled and farced-out speeches, sophomoric and unmetrical verse, commonplace word substitutions and flat prosaic paraphrases, bits and pieces from other plays – even, perhaps, a scene (between

SHAKESPEARE'S TEXT: APPROACHES AND PROBLEMS

Gertrude and Horatio, which will be found in no modern critical text) from the original *Hamlet* play on which Shakespeare based his own version. But even this miserable excuse for *Hamlet* makes its comparatively small contribution to a modern edition: first, through its stage directions that reflect visually reported Elizabethan stage business (see the examples noted earlier, p. 230); and second, through the number of single readings (usually corroborated by F 1) through which it corrects the authoritative Q 2 text. This second debt to a 'bad' quarto (the textual situation in *Romeo and Juliet* offers an exactly parallel case) is one of the ironies that confront an editor. Given an edition like *Hamlet* Q 2, printed from Shakespeare's own manuscript, one might suppose that the text would be relatively free from error. But it is apparent in this case (and in *Romeo and Juliet*) that Shakespeare's 'foul papers' were just exactly that – foul, and that the two compositors who set Q 2 had a difficult time deciphering Shakespeare's handwriting, frequently botching the job badly. Finally, to confound confusion another step, it is highly probable that the whole of the first act of Q 2 was printed, where possible, from a copy of Q 1 corrected by collation with Shakespeare's manuscript. The uncertainty of this sort of copy was illustrated in the discussion of *Richard III* and throws doubt on all readings for Act I shared by Q 2 and Q 1, while it increases the potential authority of F 1 variants for this act.

What then are the implications of the complicated textual picture just sketched? Perhaps the simplest answer is to record the distressing fact that a modern critical edition of *Hamlet* contains roughly 190 emended substantive readings, that is, readings which do not follow the basic Q 2 copy-text but have been adopted either from F 1 and Q 1 or from a long line of later editorial conjectures.

We must turn now from the manuscript sources of Shakespeare's text and the various influences that shaped those sources to some consideration of what happened to the manuscript of a play in the printing house and how printing-house practices may have influenced the reliability of the printed text. Concentrated interest in this matter is comparatively recent and was given its first significant statement in E. E. Willoughby's *The Printing of the First Folio of Shakespeare* (1932). Later studies, particularly Charlton Hinman's magisterial two volumes, *The Printing and Proof-Reading of the First Folio of Shakespeare* (1963), and Alice Walker's *Textual Problems of the First Folio* (1953), have greatly extended and corrected Willoughby's pioneer work.

The various and intricate techniques of printing-house practice in the sixteenth and seventeenth centuries cannot be dealt with here. For this sort of information the student should consult R. B. McKerrow's

Introduction to Bibliography for Literary Students (1927) and the new edition (edited by Herbert Davis and Harry Carter, 1958) of Moxon's *Mechanick Exercises* (1683). Nevertheless, certain aspects of the printing process that may have affected the accuracy and completeness of the text may be briefly discussed.

(1) *The compositor.* Being human, compositors were liable to error, some more liable than others. Such seems to have been the case, for example, with Compositors A (less) and B (more), the two principal compositors for F 1. Moreover, a compositor might be an inexperienced apprentice and hence tend to multiply mistakes (as Compositor E in F 1). Since dramatic manuscripts were generally very sporadically and lightly punctuated (the 147 lines of the *More* scene attributed to Shakespeare contain only two or three examples of line-end punctuation and some 35 of internal punctuation), the task of 'pointing' the text seems in great part to have been the responsibility of the compositor. This was a large responsibility and, again varying with the expertness and literary sense of the compositor, often led to misunderstandings of an author's meaning. Despite the dangers, however, it should always be remembered that the pointing in the early printed editions was done by men who had a contemporary feeling for the spoken relation of words and the rhythm and emphasis of Elizabethan English, and editors who, like those of the eighteenth and nineteenth centuries, tamper with it unnecessarily do so at their peril and with unfortunate strait-jacketing of the idiomatic turn and run of the dialogue.

Spelling was also in the hands of the compositor. Unlike modern prescriptive spelling, Elizabethan spelling was a highly idiosyncratic affair and Shakespeare's was no exception. The *More* scene evidences a handful of unusual spellings, a number of which appear in other plays believed to have been set from Shakespeare's autograph. It also shows how inconsistent a writer could be: *sheriff* (in the form *shrieve*) is spelled five different ways within five lines and *More* three within a single line. Generally, compositors (and scribes) tended to 'normalize' an author's spelling by imposing on it their own spelling habits or the general forms favoured by the establishment for which they worked, but, even so, many authorial spellings escaped into print and can be a helpful guide in determining what kind of manuscript underlies a printed text.

In recent years, work has been done on what is called compositor determination with a view to establishing, so far as possible, the special characteristics and relative reliability of certain compositors, notably those concerned with the printing of F 1. A compositor's characteristic spelling preferences have formed the basis for much of this investigation, an approach first suggested by Thomas Satchell in 1929, when he distinguished what he called the work of Compositors A and B in the F1 text of *Macbeth*. Since that time, the investigation has been greatly extended by Alice Walker and Charlton Hinman, the latter refining the technique by proving for F1 that, through the identification of 'distinctive types' (i.e. pieces of type characteristically enough damaged to be individually identified), a particular case of type could regularly be associated with a particular compositor. Further, where a control exists, an earlier printed text, for example, from which it can be shown a compositor is working – as in those plays in F1 printed from quarto copy – it is possible to gain a general impression of the probable accuracy, faithfulness to copy, and dependability of the compositor. Theoretically, the knowledge gained from this kind of study places an editor in the position of being able to say that certain portions of a text were set by a compositor liable to eyeskip, carelessness, etc., and that therefore one may expect to find such weaknesses in his work and feel freer to emend what appear to be unsatisfactory passages. In practice, however, the whole approach is fraught with evident dangers and even in expert hands tends to produce editions which seriously threaten whatever stability Shakespeare's text may lay claim to.

(2) *Press correction.* It is often said, with probable truth, that no two extant copies of F1 are textually exactly alike. Behind this statement lies the fact of what is called press correction. In printing off either side of a sheet (outer or inner forme), it was the general practice to send the first sheet printed off to the press-corrector (or an equivalent functionary), who marked whatever errors in the typesetting caught his eye. While he was thus engaged, printing continued and a number of sides of the sheet (inner or outer) were printed off in what is called the uncorrected state. When the corrected proof was returned to the press worker, the type was removed from the press, corrected, returned to the press, and printing resumed. Sometimes such an interruption might happen two, or even more, times in the printing off of either side of the sheet, further errors being spotted in the course of the run. The sheets printed from the uncorrected type were not discarded. In this way, an Elizabethan book is usually made up of a mixture of corrected and uncorrected sheets, and until as many copies as is reasonably possible have been minutely compared – a process now made quicker and more accurate by the Hinman collator – an editor cannot be sure that he has not missed significant corrected states of the text. It is equally important to be able to examine the uncorrected states, since, first, the press corrector seems usually to have 'corrected'

without consulting the printer's copy and his 'corrections' are often little better than guesses, which can themselves be corrected by an examination of the uncorrected state, and second, the compositor making the indicated changes was liable to fresh error in the process of supposed correction.

(3) *Cancels.* A cancel leaf (or leaves) is called for when textual changes are necessary in a part of a book already printed off. Since the type will in most cases have been redistributed, both sides of the leaf (recto and verso) will have to be completely reset, the resulting leaf (or leaves) being substituted for the original setting when the sheets are assembled to form the book. Occasionally copies of the volume can be discovered that preserve either the original setting or both the original and the reset leaves. The detection of a cancel (the *cancellans*) and where possible the retrieval of the original setting of the leaf (the *cancellandum*) are obviously matters of importance for the establishment of a text, particularly where the textual changes involved may have been authorial or dictated by political or religious censorship.

(4) *Casting-off copy.* The potential importance to the completeness and accuracy of a text of what is called the process of casting- (counting-) off copy has only recently begun to be realized. Simply put, to cast-off copy means to estimate how much of a manuscript text may be fitted into a page of the chosen printed format and then to divide up the copy into clearly marked sections. Charlton Hinman has shown, for example, that casting-off was used extensively throughout F 1, and it is becoming clear that the process was employed also in the setting of some of the quartos. A saving in time (i.e. the possibility of simultaneous composition by two, or more, compositors and the concurrent use of more than one press) and in type (i.e. the freeing of type for earlier redistribution and re-use, particularly in the printing of folios) is the rationale behind the use of this technique, but it had its special dangers. If the casting-off process had been carelessly performed, a compositor might well find himself with either too much or too little copy and nowhere to go, since the following (or preceding) page had already been printed off. He may thus have to stretch his material by heavier 'leading' – and here no great harm results except aesthetically – or he may have to compress by crowding or printing verse as prose. Worse, he may be forced to omit words or lines. In instances where the use of cast-off copy can be supported by bibliographical evidence, an editor can now at least sometimes explain why there seems to be some dislocation in the text, even though he can rarely do anything to remedy the fault.

Our discussion so far has mainly concerned itself with approaches to Shakespeare's text developed during the last sixty years. But much work by generations of textual scholars lies behind these approaches and, in fact, made them possible. The eighteenth century brought the beginning of a significant split between what may be termed 'the theatre' and 'the study'. Shakespeare became increasingly a 'classic' and was accorded all the learned attention formerly lavished only on Greek and Latin authors. Editor after editor, beginning with Nicholas Rowe, in 1709, on through Alexander Pope (1723–4), Lewis Theobald (1733), Thomas Hanmer (1744), William Warburton (1747), Samuel Johnson (1765), Edward Capell (1768), George Steevens (1778) and Edmond Malone (1790), expended endless hours and untold pains in seeking to establish what they believed was the 'true text'. Each in his way made his contribution, particularly Theobald, Capell, and Malone, but they were relatively hampered by the lack of any clear conception of the kinds of problems outlined earlier in this study and depended largely on ingenuity in emendation and the exercise of contemporary 'taste' in grammar and language to solve what seemed to them the problems of the text. Among them Capell stands apart, and has, with good cause, been called the first 'modern'. In his crabbed way (his contemporaries insisted, not without reason, that he could not write English), he sorted out the relative authority of the early texts, particularly the quartos, and laid the foundation of the principle of copy-text. He also published the first extensive textual apparatus, recording the readings of all the early editions and his editorial predecessors. By such fundamental work he struck a blow against the widely eclectic approach of earlier editors and pointed the way towards the textual approaches of the twentieth century. Unfortunately, his edition was derided by his two principal successors, Steevens and Malone, who silently pillaged his text and notes, and largely ignored the significant implications of his textual approach.

The nineteenth century, though it produced a large number of new editions by men of distinguished reputations as Shakespearian scholars (Charles Knight, J. Payne Collier, Grant White, Halliwell-Phillipps, Alexander Dyce), did little to advance any understanding of basic textual problems and continued the tradition of eclecticism little changed from pre-Capell times. The culmination of the tradition was the impressive and vastly influential Cambridge *Shakespeare*, edited by W. G. Clark and W. A. Wright (1863–6) and revised by Wright in 1892–3, a text on which the famous 'Globe' (1864) one-volume edition was based. Here, for the first time since Capell, the student was afforded a full textual apparatus. It was a remarkable work and crystallized the editorial labours of a hundred and fifty years. Out of it grew the monumental American *New Variorum*, begun under the tireless hand of H. H. Furness in 1871 (with *Romeo and Juliet*) and still, with ten plays to go, in the process of completion.

The present century has seen the advent of what is called the 'new bibliography'. Under the aegis of pioneers like R. B. McKerrow, W. W. Greg, A. W. Pollard, and J. Dover Wilson the approaches outlined in the first part of this essay were laid down and their work has been carried on and refined by many later textual critics, notably Peter Alexander, Fredson Bowers, Charlton Hinman, Charles Sisson, and Alice Walker. Out of this ferment has come the most challenging edition of Shakespeare yet published – the New Cambridge Shakespeare (1921–66) under the editorship primarily of Dover Wilson. Full of energy and new ideas (many later jettisoned by Wilson himself) it aroused a new and lively interest in Shakespeare, even when the interest was generated by healthy and productive disagreement, and has inspired other important new attacks on the problems of the text: the editions by G. L. Kittredge (1936), Peter Alexander (1952), C. J. Sisson (1954), and John Munro (1958), as well as the individually edited volumes of the New Arden (1951–), and the collected Pelican *Shakespeare* (1969, general editor, Alfred Harbage). Each of these editions not only has contributed to a better critical understanding of Shakespeare but has served to bring us one step nearer to what we wistfully dream of as his 'true text'.

17

SHAKESPEARE CRITICISM: DRYDEN TO BRADLEY

M. A. SHAABER

The first critic of Shakespeare is Dryden. Earlier comment on the plays and their author, abundant enough, is as a rule simply admiring or anecdotal. It is true that Jonson, in differentiating Shakespeare's natural gifts from his art, and Milton, in making by implication the same distinction, defined an issue over which critical battle was to be joined by future generations. In the poem he wrote for the First Folio Jonson praised both the natural gifts and the art; in his gossip with Drummond and in his note-book, however, he found that Shakespeare 'wanted art'. 'But he redeemed his vices, with his virtues. There was ever more in him to be praised than to be pardoned.' The latter opinion is also Dryden's and that of many of his successors.

The vices that Dryden found in Shakespeare were chiefly faults of expression. 'He is many times flat, insipid; his Comick Wit degenerating into Clenches, his serious Swelling into Bombast' (*Of Dramatic Poesy*). Dryden's aversion to Shakespeare's comic wit remained insuperable: the wit of the Elizabethan age 'was not that of Gentlemen, there was ever somewhat that was ill-bred and Clownish in it' (*An Essay on the Dramatic Poetry of the Last Age*), distasteful to the more refined times in which he lived. His attitude towards Shakespeare's bombast is somewhat ambivalent. 'I will not say of so great a Poet, that he distinguish'd not the blown puffy stile, from true sublimity; but I may venture to maintain that the fury of his fancy often transported him, beyond the bounds of Judgment, either in coyning of new words and phrases, or racking words which were in use, into the violence of a Catachresis:...to say nothing without a Metaphor, a Simile, an Image, or description, is I doubt to smell a little too strongly of the Buskin' (preface to *Troilus and Cressida*). Yet in *The Author's Apology* to *The State of Innocence* (1677), without specific reference to Shakespeare, he denies that 'the flights of Heroick Poetry ...[are] bombast, unnatural, and meer madness', and affirms that 'the boldest strokes of Poetry, when they are manag'd Artfully, are those which most delight the Reader'. Two other shortcomings upon which Dryden insists much less frequently also became parts of the usual eighteenth-century view of Shakespeare. One of them is 'lameness' of plot, a fault which he imputes to all the Elizabethan playwrights, and by which he perhaps means chiefly plots violating the unities, for he stigmatizes such a plot as 'some ridiculous, incoherent story, which, in one Play many times took up the business of an Age' (*An Essay on the Dramatic Poetry of the Last Age*). The other is violations of 'the decorum of the stage'. It is possible partly to discount these strictures since they all occur in essays and prefaces whose overriding purpose was to justify Dryden's own plays and those of his contemporaries to (among others) *laudatores temporis acti*. Moreover Dryden himself discounted them by putting some of the blame for Shakespeare's defects on the barbarity of the age in which he lived. On balance, however, he always comes down on the side of Shakespeare, as in *Of Dramatic Poesy*:

he was the Man who of all Modern, and perhaps Ancient Poets, had the largest and most comprehensive soul. All the Images of Nature were still present to him, and he drew them not laboriously, but luckily: when he describes any thing, you more than see it, you feel it too. Those who accuse him to have wanted learning, give him the greater commendation: he was naturally learn'd; he needed not the Spectacles of Books to read Nature; he look'd inwards, and found her there...But he is always great, when some great occasion is presented to him; no Man can say he ever had a fit subject for his wit, and did not then raise himself as high above the rest of Poets,

Quantum lenta solent inter Viburna Cupressi.

The eighteenth century adopted and cherished this picture of Shakespeare as an untutored genius who lived in a rude society and wrote for mean and undiscriminating audiences, who, though he committed many faults through ignorance of what Pope called 'the rules of writing', by his extraordinary natural gifts excelled all other poets or equalled the best of them. 'The Poetry of *Shakespear* was Inspiration indeed,' said Pope: 'he is not so much an Imitator, as an Instrument, of Nature; and 'tis not so just to say that he speaks from her, as that she speaks thro' him.' Pope enumerates Shakespeare's excellences as follows:

His *Characters* are so much Nature her self, that 'tis a sort of injury to call them by so distant a name as Copies of her...

The *Power* over our *Passions* was never possess'd in a more eminent degree, or display'd in so different instances...

Nor does he only excell in the Passions: In the coolness of Reflection and Reasoning he is full as admirable.

The palinode duly follows:

It must be own'd that with all these great excellencies, he has almost as great defects; and that as he has certainly written better, so he has perhaps written worse than any other.

But the disparity between the pleasure which the plays gave readers and theatregoers and the displeasure expressed by critics of the rigid sect sometimes led admirers of Shakespeare to question the fundamental assumptions of the latter. Dryden, Addison, Pope, and Johnson all depreciated the importance of observing the unities. The strict notions of decorum applied to the plays by Rymer and Voltaire were often shrugged off. Rymer (*A Short View of Tragedy*, 1693) objected to the character given Iago because it does not conform to the type of soldier fixed by Horace; to Voltaire 'Not a mouse stirring' was too mean for tragedy. Few English critics felt that Shakespeare must be held to such strict standards. Even Shakespeare's learning was upgraded as close readers discovered evidence or presumed evidence of some acquaintance with the classics. Sometimes the critics' bark is worse than their bite. In *The Adventurer* of 25 September 1753 Joseph Warton begins the first of two essays on *The Tempest* with an echo of Pope: 'he exhibits more numerous examples of excellencies and faults, of every kind, than are, perhaps, to be discovered in any other author'; then he summarizes briefly both the faults and the excellencies. But in his discussion of the play it is only the excellencies that he expatiates on. In a subsequent series on *King Lear* (4, 15 December 1753, 5 January 1754) the faults appear only in the final paragraph.

If Shakespeare's plays were blemished by faults of expression, the faulty passages might be expunged and what was left read with greater pleasure. In his edition Pope excised lines and passages so displeasing to him that he thought Shakespeare could never have written them and he also put inverted commas at the beginning of lines and series of lines that he found specially admirable. The plays came to be admired for their beauties rather than as wholes. Charles Gildon's *Remarks on the Plays of Shakespeare* (added to the seventh volume of Rowe's 1709 edition) consist largely of lists of the most praiseworthy episodes and passages. Regarding the plays as puddings from which plums may be pulled colours much subsequent criticism, even as late as that of Hazlitt. A little later, in *The Complete Art of Poetry* (1718), Gildon published the first anthology of 'Shakespeare's Beauties'. Many more followed. The most durable, William Dodd's *Beauties of Shakespear* (1752), was still in print one hundred and fifty years later.

The prevailing attitude is summed up most memorably – and very nearly for the last time – in Dr Johnson's preface to his edition of the plays (1765). Its comprehensive scope, its magisterial style, and its judicial temper make it not only the most considerable criticism so far written but also the best. Johnson praises Shakespeare as 'the poet of nature',

the poet that holds up to his readers a faithful mirror of manners and of life. His characters are not modified by the customs of particular places, unpractised by the rest of the world; by the peculiarities of studies or professions, which can operate but upon small numbers; or by the accidents of transient fashions or temporary opinions; they are the genuine progeny of common humanity, such as the world will always supply, and observation will always find...In the writings of other poets a character is too often an individual; in those of Shakespeare it is commonly a species.

He also praises Shakespeare as the founder of English drama and commends his differentiation of his characters, his power of expressing the passions, his mastery of a style 'above grossness and below refinement' which is 'more agreeable to the ears of the present age than any other author equally remote'. He defends Shakespeare against some of the charges usually lodged against him. He finds that 'the unities of time and place are not essential to a just drama'. He justifies the mixture of the serious and the comic: '*Shakespeare*'s plays are not in the rigorous and critical sense either tragedies or comedies, but compositions of a distinct kind; exhibiting the real state of sublunary nature, which partakes of good and evil, joy and sorrow, mingled with endless variety of proportion and innumerable modes of combination.' The indecorum imputed to Shakespeare's characters he brushes aside. He even relents so far as to admit that 'The mind, which has feasted on the luxurious wonders of fiction, has no taste of the insipidity of truth' and thus to ascribe the extravagance he finds in the plays to the immaturity of Shakespeare's audiences.

At the same time he specifies a number of faults. Shakespeare's plots are often 'loosely formed' and his fifth acts carelessly huddled up. Anachronisms abound. He is deplorably prone to quibbling and playing on words. His comic wit is too often gross and licentious, his tragic speeches strained, his narrative passages inflated. He is too often content with something less than his best: when his plays 'would satisfy the audience, they satisfied the writer'. Johnson is uncomfortable about Shakespeare's failures to satisfy poetic justice: the destruction of Claudius, a usurper and a murderer, affords him 'gratification', but the death of innocents like Ophelia and Cordelia pains him. His chief charge against Shakespeare is his lack of moral purpose: 'He sacrifices virtue to convenience, and is so much more careful to please than to instruct, that he seems to write without any moral purpose.'

Johnson's judicial posture may seem at times to give the preface a too-lofty tone, but his praise is always splendid.

This therefore is the praise of *Shakespeare*, that his drama is the mirror of life; that he who has mazed his imagination, in following the phantoms which other writers raise up before him, may here be cured of his delirious extasies, by reading human sentiments in human language; by scenes from which a hermit may estimate the transactions of the world, and a confessor predict the progress of the passions.

But when Johnson wrote his preface the winds of romanticism had already begun to stir. It was only a few years later that Lessing rejected French classical tragedy and exalted Shakespeare above Corneille and Voltaire (*Hamburgische Dramaturgie*, 1769). The continental revolters against neo-classical rigidity often held up Shakespeare as its antithesis. In 1796 Goethe, in *Wilhelm Meister*, gave the world the delicate and impotent Hamlet. In a letter of 14 April 1818 Stendhal wrote: 'I am a mad romantic, that is to say I am for Shakespeare against Racine.'

In England, while the full-blown romantic idea of Shakespeare hardly appears before Coleridge, there are signs of altered emphases in the latter part of the eighteenth century. It has even been argued that Dr Johnson's 'sense of the inseparability of a man and his work makes him the first of our Romantic critics' (H. V. D. Dyson and John Butt, *Augustans and Romantics*, 1940, p. 67). In 1774 William Richardson published *A Philosophical Analysis of some of Shakespeare's Remarkable Characters*, an early example of the growing interest in Shakespeare's characters as the aspect of his plays in which his excellence is most evident. Richardson was a moral philosopher rather than a literary critic and he deduces from the characters 'the principles of human conduct'. In his *Essay on the Dramatic Character of Sir John Falstaff* (1777) Maurice Morgann anticipates the romantic attitude towards Shakespeare at several points. His ostensible purpose is to vindicate Falstaff's courage. He enjoyed Falstaff, and therefore admired him, and therefore disliked hearing him derided as a coward. To prove that Falstaff is not a constitutional coward he transcends the evidence of the text of the play and appeals to 'secret Impressions' which Shakespeare contrives to make upon us and which endow Falstaff with a real character different from his apparent one – the courageous, dignified, honoured character of Morgann's imagination. His reasoning is of course specious and the impressions upon which he builds up a more respectable character for Falstaff sometimes naive (e.g. because he invites Master Gower to dinner and to supper, Falstaff must have kept a regular table). But Morgann also describes Shakespeare's art as 'exquisite', not irregular or defective; he thinks that 'True Poesy is *magic*, not *nature*; an effect from causes hidden or unknown', and that all dramatic truth consists in the impressions made on the feelings of readers rather than in what the understanding derives from the external action. Shakespeare, he finds, infuses 'his own spirit' into his characters and must 'have spoken thro' the organ he had formed'. Clearly Morgann is breaking away from the attitude of his predecessors. When he says, 'If the characters of *Shakespeare* are thus *whole*, and as it were original,...it may be fit to consider them rather as Historic than Dramatic beings; and, when occasion requires, to account for their conduct from the *whole* of character, from general principles, from latent motives, and from policies not avowed', he opens a Pandora's box. In 1794 Walter Whiter published a pioneering study of Shakespeare's imagery (*A Specimen of a Commentary on Shakspeare*), an aspect of the plays to which criticism had paid little attention and, in spite of Whiter's example, was to continue paying little attention until the twentieth century.

Whether August Wilhelm Schlegel in Vienna or Samuel Taylor Coleridge in London created the Shakespeare of the romantics is matter for dispute, of unimportant dispute despite the fact that Coleridge resented the charge that he derived his ideas from Schlegel. Schlegel's celebrated course of lectures *Über dramatische Kunst und Literatur* and Coleridge's first course of lectures were delivered in the same year, 1808. Schlegel, however, had anticipated some of his ideas about Shakespeare in essays published twelve years earlier; of Coleridge's first series there is little record, though it is unlikely that he then expressed ideas different from those expounded in later series. For the most part Schlegel and Coleridge agree. Schlegel's lectures on Shakespeare form part of a much broader discussion of dramatic art in which he tosses the debate over neo-classical and romantic standards out of the window by assuming essential differences between ancient and modern poetry which make comparisons idle. Shakespeare is 'a profound artist, and not a blind and wildly luxuriant genius'. Shakespeare's plays are romantic works of art: 'In all Art and Poetry, but most especially in the romantic, the Fancy lays claim to be considered as an independent mental power governed according to its own laws'; from the great plays 'nothing could be taken away, nothing added, nothing otherwise arranged, without mutilating and disfiguring the perfect work'. 'Never perhaps was there so comprehensive a talent for characterization as Shakespeare.' He has 'the capability of transporting himself so completely into every situation...that he is enabled ...to act and speak in the name of every individual'. Shakespeare 'gives us the history of minds'. 'In strength a demigod, in profundity of view a prophet, in all-seeing wisdom a guardian spirit of a higher order, he lowers himself to mortals as if unconscious of his superiority, and is as open and unassuming as a child.'

Coleridge's writings on Shakespeare are mostly desultory and unsystematic: a chapter of the *Biographia Literaria* (1817), scraps of lecture notes, reports, of various degrees of completeness and accuracy, of eight courses of lectures (as a rule not wholly devoted to Shakespeare), marginalia, and *obiter dicta* written down by friends. They are nevertheless seminal and most subsequent criticism derives from them. Coleridge demands reverence for Shakespeare: criticism 'will be genial in proportion as the criticism is reverential' (ed. Raysor, 1960, i, 113). He scorns the idea of the untutored genius: 'does God choose idiots to convey divine truths by?' (i, 202). 'The judgement of Shakespeare is commensurate with his genius' (i, 114); his was 'a most profound, energetic, and philosophical mind' (i, 189). The form of his plays is not determined by mechanical rules; each one has organic form determined by its own nature. Shakespeare's greatest excellence is his portrayal of character; 'The plot interests us on account of the characters, not *vice versa*' (i, 199). 'Shakespeare's characters are like those in life, to be *inferred* by the reader, not *told to him*' (i, 201). Shakespeare projects himself into his characters: 'he had only to imitate certain parts of his own character, or to exaggerate such as existed in possibility, and they were at once true to nature, and fragments of the divine mind that drew them' (ii, 85); he 'darts himself forth, and passes into all the forms of human character and passion' (*Biographia Literaria* xv). As the products of Shakespeare's meditation, the characters are ideal (ii, 123), as is poetry itself, which results from 'the effort of perfecting ourselves' (ii, 53). At the same time Shakespeare keeps 'at all times the high road of life' (ii, 216). Since Coleridge believed in 'the close and reciprocal connections of just taste with pure morality' (i, 226), he vindicates Shakespeare's moral purity along with his taste. Coleridge's discussions of particular plays are, with a few notable exceptions, too fragmentary to carry much weight; his achievement was to define new canons of criticism, a new perspective which his successors enthusiastically adopted. He deployed and passed on a new critical vocabulary with key words such as 'divine', 'sublime', 'philosophical', 'intellectual'.

Many of the contemporaries of Coleridge engaged themselves with Shakespeare. Hazlitt's *Characters of Shakespear's Plays* (1817) is, as Francis Jeffrey said of it, an encomium rather than a critique. Hazlitt preferred Schlegel's version of Shakespeare to Dr Johnson's, which he found wanting in sensibility and ardour of response. But, except when he disputes some of Johnson's pronouncements, he is little given to generalization; he deals with particulars – plays, scenes, characters, speeches – without much attempt to erect his responses into critical principles. The responses are as a rule warmly sympathetic. That inveterate theatregoer Charles Lamb wrote a few descriptions of favourite actors in Shakespearian roles which interpret the roles. De Quincey wrote a fine criticism *On the Knocking at the Gate in Macbeth*. Shakespeare is the topic in a number of the *Imaginary Conversations* of Landor, who thought that 'a rib of Shakspeare would have made a Milton: the same portion of Milton, all poets born ever since' ('Southey and Landor'). Keats records a few shrewd insights in his letters, including his imputation to Shakespeare of 'negative capability' – 'when man is capable of being in uncertainties, Mysteries, doubts, without any irritable reaching after fact and reason...with a great poet the sense of Beauty overcomes every other consideration, or rather obliterates all consideration' (21 December 1817) – a phrase which has become a shibboleth of recent criticism.

The romantic critics usually divorce Shakespeare from the theatre or ignore the fact that he wrote plays. Charles Lamb (*On the Tragedies of Shakespeare*, 1811) pronounced the tragedies impossible to realize at their full potential on the stage; to be sure, the performances he saw and was dissatisfied with were not of Shakespeare's plays but of Tate's, Cibber's, and Garrick's denatured versions. Goethe thought that 'Shakespeare's whole method finds in the stage itself something unwieldy and hostile' (*Schäkspear und kein Ende*, 1815). Carlyle laments: 'Alas, Shakspeare had to write for the Globe Playhouse: his great soul had to crush itself, as it could, into that and no other mould' (*On Heroes, Hero-worship, and the Heroic in History*, 1841).

On one point the romantic critics divided – the presence of Shakespeare himself in his works. To Coleridge 'Shakespeare's poetry is characterless; that is, it does not reflect the individual Shakespeare' (*Table Talk*, 12 May 1830). To Schlegel it does. On the whole, Schlegel's opinion has prevailed over Coleridge's; at any rate, the subsequent attempts to infer Shakespeare's interests and opinions, to align him with this or that cause or philosophy, are countless. Edward Dowden, whose *Shakspere: a Critical Study of his Mind and Art* (1875) exerted a pervasive influence for a quarter century or more, saw the plays as explorations of moral problems that oppressed Shakespeare in his private life. To 'have built up his own moral nature, and have fortified himself for the conduct of life, was...to Shakspere the chief outcome of his toil'. Shakespeare was subject to two temptations to excess – 'the Romeo form and the Hamlet form – abandonment to passion, abandonment to brooding thought' – and his plays record his gradual attainment of equilibrium. In a 'primer' published in 1877 Dowden divided Shakespeare's career into four periods which he labelled, a little apologetically, 'In the workshop', 'In the world', 'Out of the depths', 'On the heights'.

Thus the nineteenth century invented the oracular Shakespeare, a demiurge who created characters embodying the deepest insights into human nature and speaking lines impregnated with sublime wisdom. For the most part, his artistry is taken for granted or examined only when it can be used to support the picture of him as a seer; whatever does not easily fit this view, like his bawdry, is ignored. Shakespeare is the Poet (the capital letter is almost invariable) rather than the playwright, and the Poet includes the Philosopher. The weakness of nineteenth-century criticism, if it is agreed that Shakespeare *is* a supreme oracle, is its tendency to turn its back on the text in order to write philosophical and moralistic speculation in the margins.

The writings of A. C. Bradley are among the last and the best of the romantic school of critics. They are of limited scope: a book on *Shakespearean Tragedy* (1904), which discusses *Hamlet*, *Othello*, *Macbeth*, and *King Lear*, essays on 'The Rejection of Falstaff' (1902) and *Antony and Cleopatra* (1906), and a lecture on *Coriolanus* (1912). Bradley's prestige nevertheless has been very great and is deserved. The book is highly intelligent, conscientious, and suavely written. After an opening chapter on Shakespearian tragedy in which Bradley pursues that will o' the wisp, a concept of tragedy that will fit all of Shakespeare's tragedies, and a chapter on the structure of the plays, he proceeds to an examination of his four tragedies, or rather of their leading characters. He assumes that everything in a play is explicable, that Shakespeare knew all the answers, and that we can discover them too if we apply our minds with sufficient discernment and sympathy. He assumes that Shakespeare would allow no part to inconsistency or chance or unreason in the scheme of a play and labours to eliminate them wherever he finds them. When Shakespeare offers insufficient explanation Bradley supplies what is wanting. The result is a psychological analysis of each character which fully accounts for his behaviour and vindicates the consistency and completeness of the presentation. In doing so, Bradley often comes perilously close to treating the characters as real people. In doing so, he sometimes, like Morgann, trusts his own impressions rather than the statements of the text (e.g. though Kent says he is forty-eight years old, 'we get the impression' that he is over sixty). In doing so, he often ignores aspects of the plays that other schools of critics make great play with. Of its kind there is nothing better than Bradley's criticism, but like all his predecessors and all his successors, he is prone to picturing Shakespeare in his own image.

The triumph of nineteenth-century criticism was the canonization of Shakespeare. Earlier objections to his violation of the rules of writing were nullified by explaining away the violations or cancelling the rules. The improbability and looseness of some of his plays and scenes were reconciled with romantic taste. Even the most stubborn objection of all, the exuberance of his style, his propensity for torturing the language out of 'an irritability of fancy', as Matthew Arnold, a firm objector, put it, was submerged in the concentration on Shakespeare's philosophy and morality. The nineteenth century passed on to the twentieth a Shakespeare securely placed on his towering pinnacle.

18

SHAKESPEARE CRITICISM
SINCE BRADLEY

STANLEY WELLS

A. C. Bradley's *Shakespearean Tragedy*, published in 1904, serves as a convenient landmark by virtue of its date as well as its stature. It comes almost at the beginning of a century that has seen an astonishing growth of professionalism in Shakespeare studies. Bradley is characteristic of an earlier period in that his training was not primarily in English literature. But he anticipates the shape of things to come in that his great book was published when he was a Professor of English, and is a development of lectures he gave in that capacity. In some ways he was himself anticipated by Edward Dowden, whose *Shakspere: His Mind and Art* appeared in 1875 and is still in print. But before Dowden the great names in Shakespeare criticism are not those of professional teachers of literature. Dryden, Pope, Johnson, Morgann, Hazlitt, Coleridge: most of them are primarily men of letters, only secondarily teachers and lecturers. They are in the highest sense amateurs, writing on Shakespeare because his plays are at the forefront of their minds and there is something they feel impelled to say about him. Such an attitude is not extinct, nor can it be wholly isolated from that of the professional academic. Robert Bridges, John Masefield, T. S. Eliot, P. Wyndham Lewis, Harley Granville-Barker, and W. H. Auden are among the creative writers of this century who have written stimulatingly about Shakespeare; and of some academics (G. Wilson Knight is only one example) we feel that this is what they would have been doing even had it not been part of their professional duty.

Nevertheless, by far the larger part of the mass of Shakespeare criticism produced since Bradley's time has been academic, some of it obviously originating in the lecture room, and some of it still more restricted in appeal, being published in learned journals that are read only by a limited number of specialists. This situation is partly the result of a great swing in the bias of literary education which occurred during Bradley's lifetime, and of which his own career is a result. The literature on which he was educated was classical literature. When he went to Liverpool, where he was the first Professor of English, he thought seriously of applying for the Chair of Philosophy and Political Economy. G. K. Hunter has written of the image of *Shakespearean Tragedy* 'as an Establishment synthesis, making possible the absorption of Shakespeare into the higher educational system, long dominated by the Greats syllabus of Classics and Philosophy'. The absorption has been complete; Shakespeare's plays are now regarded as the foundation of a literary education.

When Bradley's book appeared, only one periodical devoted itself to Shakespeare. It was, significantly, the *Shakespeare-Jahrbuch*, published by the Deutsche Shakespeare Gesellschaft. The systematic study of Shakespeare appeared earlier in Germany than anywhere else, and there it was closely linked with the structure of the higher-educational system. Now the *Jahrbuch* has doubled itself (partly, it is true, for political rather than academic reasons), *Shakespeare Survey* has appeared annually since 1948, the American *Shakespeare Quarterly* has flourished for almost as long, and *Shakespeare Studies* made the first of its annual appearances in 1965. Many other periodicals concern themselves at least partly with Shakespeare. Some of the criticism that appears in the periodicals represents work in progress and later appears as part of more substantial studies in book-form. Other essays receive a wider circulation in the critical anthologies that help non-specialist readers with their problem of choice. If the remainder of this chapter shows little concern with articles in the journals, it is not from any feeling that important work appears only in book-form. More respect may be felt for the man who writes economically to a given point than for one who inflates a comparatively minor insight into excessive proportions. A critic may have something to say on *As You Like It* without wanting to write a book on all Shakespeare's comedies. Thus, to give only one example, Harold Jenkins's essay on that play, which first appeared in *Shakespeare Survey 8*, is acknowledged as one of the best to have been written; and there are other outstanding essays by critics who have not attempted longer studies.

Bradley has been important both as a critic to be agreed with and as one to be reacted against. It is because of influence provoked by disagreement that he may be held responsible for part of the emphasis given in scholarly journals and elsewhere to writing that attempts to interpret a Shakespeare play by reference to historical factors. Two critics who were early to express disagreement with Bradley's method were E. E. Stoll and L. L. Schücking, both of whom insisted on the need to see Shakespeare in the context of the life and literature of his age, and opposed themselves against what they regarded as the subjectivism of their colleagues. Schücking's *Character Problems in Shake-*

speare's Plays was first published in German in 1917, and was translated into English in 1922. He does not hesitate to find fault with Shakespeare's art, and in this respect he was reacting against a bardolatrous attitude not uncommon in Romantic and Victorian times. Two famous authors, one English and one Russian, had already given notable vent to adverse criticism. Robert Bridges, in his brief but trenchant essay 'On the Influence of the Audience', published in the tenth volume (1907) of the Shakespeare Head Press edition, had been concerned almost entirely to define in Shakespeare's works 'the matters that most offended my simple feelings', and he alighted especially on what he regarded as bad jokes and obscenities, as brutalities, and as the too easy forgiveness of 'offences of the first rank' such as Angelo's in *Measure for Measure*. He anticipates Stoll and Schücking especially in his accusation that Shakespeare produced his effects by deliberately pandering to the supposed stupidity and 'moral bluntness' of Elizabethan audiences, in the process deliberately blurring motives and sacrificing logic and consistency in order merely to surprise. Tolstoy's extraordinary diatribe, *Shakespeare and the Drama*, which appeared in 1906, is so extreme in expression, and so indicative of a failure to comprehend the nature of any kind of poetic drama, that it is more likely to have had an emotional appeal to those who shared his prejudices (it first appeared along with an article called 'Shakespeare and the Working Classes', to which it had been intended as a Preface, and was published by the Free Age Press) than a rational one to those who were seeking the truth. But salvoes such as these, coming from creative writers, must have done something to breach a gap for more academic studies that also took a somewhat sceptical view.

Schücking, in the book referred to, develops the thesis that Shakespeare's 'art-form is in fact a mixture of the most highly developed with quite primitive elements'. Like Bridges, he finds that Shakespeare neglects consistency and logic, and seeks the immediate effect at the expense of the overall design. Also like Bridges, he regards such characteristics as flaws in Shakespeare's art, and does not, as some later critics have done, attempt to justify them in terms of a higher appropriateness. He agrees in fact with Ben Jonson, that Shakespeare 'wanted art'. Adopting commonsense explanations where they are available, he tends to reduce everything to its lowest terms; but his book is a good corrective to over-subjective attitudes.

Schücking has much in common with E. E. Stoll, who began before him and went on to publish a much larger body of writing on Shakespeare over a period of many years. '*Othello*': *An Historical and Comparative Study* appeared in 1915, '*Hamlet*': *An Historical and Comparative Study* in 1919, *Shakespeare Studies* in 1927, *Art and Artifice in*

Shakespeare in 1933, *Shakespeare's Young Lovers* in 1935, and *Shakespeare and Other Masters* in 1940. Like Schücking's, Stoll's is a hardheaded, down-to-earth approach. He asserts the primacy of plot over characterization, and the importance of poetry: 'one's ear, not one's reason, is the best judge of Shakespeare's characters' he wrote in *Art and Artifice in Shakespeare*, reminding us of George Bernard Shaw's similar remarks in connection with *Othello*. In spite of this, he does not offer detailed examination of the verse. Also like Shaw, Stoll makes frequent analogies with music, discussing the ways in which the playwright, like the composer, plays upon and manipulates his audience's responses. He is much concerned with dramatic convention, and fails sometimes to consider that a convention may also express truth. Like Schücking he reacts against that kind of criticism that lays great emphasis on the dramatist's 'creation of character', as if the principal value of a play lay in the sense it gives us of individual character. Such a view has often been attributed to Bradley, and much subsequent criticism takes as its starting point the debate about character in which Bradley stands as spokesman for one side, Stoll and Schücking for the other. For a while, indeed, Bradley was in danger of becoming a whipping boy, just as Dowden's unfortunate simplification in his *Shakespeare Primer* of Shakespeare's development into periods to which he gave such labels as 'Out of the Depths' and 'On the Heights' has been too easily taken as representative of his critical achievement. Lytton Strachey, in his well-known essay, 'Shakespeare's Final Period' (1906), uttered a counterblast to Dowden, suggesting that boredom rather than a hard-earned serenity was responsible for the special characteristics of the late plays. Inevitably the 'realists' have themselves been reacted against, and later critics have even drawn on the evidence and techniques of Freudian and post-Freudian psychological research in their Shakespearian investigations, and in the process have rendered themselves as liable to the charge of importing private preoccupations into their reading of the plays as did earlier critics who employed less sophisticated methods. Freud himself wrote several papers on Shakespeare, but more influential has been *Hamlet and Oedipus* by Ernest Jones (the book of 1949 is the final development of ideas first published in 1910), who is more convincing on *Hamlet* itself than in his attempts to investigate Shakespeare's personality on the basis of the play.

Attention to Shakespeare's portrayal of character became unfashionable with the increasing emphasis in the 1930s on verbal criticism, so that in 1938 H. B. Charlton, taking a reactionary stand-point, wrote in *Shakespearian Comedy*: 'the present trend of fashionable criticism appears to have little use even for drama. To our most modern coteries, drama is poetry or it is nothing; and by poetry they mean some sort of allegorical arabesque in which the images of Shakespeare's plays are far more important than their men and women.' In his attitude to character Charlton proclaimed himself a disciple of Bradley, and J. I. M. Stewart, in *Character and Motive in Shakespeare* (1949), attempted to reassert the view that 'Shakespeare understood the passions and described, or conveyed, their several and conjoined operations with certainty, subtlety and power'. Bridges, Schücking, and Stoll are the principal critics whose views he examines. He is more aware than they are of Shakespeare's complexity – partly perhaps because of some of the criticism that intervenes between the date of his book and the time when their views were first formulated – but goes too far the other way in some of his own interpretative comments. Later writers, too, have been willing to discuss certain characters, at least, in language resembling that used by Bradley. Actors, especially, need to think in terms of individual character, so it is understandable that Granville-Barker's *Prefaces* include sections on the principal characters in the play under discussion. John Palmer's writings on the comic and political characters have been popular, and John Bayley's chapter on *Othello* in *The Characters of Love* (1960) is a sophisticated example of the kind.

The tendency to study Shakespeare's plays in the context of the literature and thought of their time has had a considerable influence both on critics whose main concern is with Shakespeare, and on others who have concentrated rather on the background. The direct sources of the plays have been fruitfully studied in the introductory chapters of Geoffrey Bullough's *Narrative and Dramatic Sources of Shakespeare* (from 1957) and in Kenneth Muir's *Shakespeare's Sources* (vol. 1, 1957), and many critics have brought investigations of analogous material to bear on their explorations of Shakespeare's creative processes. W. W. Lawrence in *Shakespeare's Problem Comedies* (1931) approaches a particular group of plays by way of a study of the conventions of narrative writing, and to a lesser extent of social behaviour, that lie behind them. Even so valuable a specimen of this kind of study occasionally reveals some of the dangers of the method, perhaps the most serious being the assumption that Shakespeare can properly be judged by the supposed standards of his age.

Some writers have studied dramatic conventions, often making comparisons with Shakespeare's forebears and contemporaries. This has been one of the approaches employed by M. C. Bradbrook in a series of books more or less directly concerned with Shakespeare, of which two of the most influential have been *Themes and Conventions of Elizabethan Tragedy* (1935) and *Shakespeare and Elizabethan Poetry* (1951). Her work is valuable especially for the way in which it places

Shakespeare in the full intellectual, dramatic, and theatrical context of his time, showing an unusual awareness of the possible significance of such matters as the social environment, the physical conditions of the theatres, and the overall literary milieu. S. L. Bethell in *Shakespeare and the Popular Dramatic Tradition* (1949) suggestively examines Shakespeare's capacity to manipulate responses, showing how features of the plays that 'realist' critics regard as primitivist can just as well be seen as a sophisticated exploitation of various levels of the spectator's awareness. Alfred Harbage, in books such as *Shakespeare's Audience* (1941), *As They Liked It* (1947), and *Shakespeare and the Rival Traditions* (1952), has been specially concerned with Shakespeare's relationship with his audience and the artistry with which he responded to their demands. In *Theatre for Shakespeare* (1955) he stimulatingly examines the problems of presenting the plays in modern conditions. His books are among the most attractively written of modern contributions. Bernard Spivack's *Shakespeare and the Allegory of Evil* (1958) is an impressive study of Shakespeare's portrayal of certain types of character (particularly Iago and his antecedents) in relation to earlier English drama.

Many studies of theatrical conventions are inextricably bound up with researches into the structure of Elizabethan theatres and the social composition of the audiences, and so fit more easily into the history of scholarship than that of criticism. The dividing line is exceedingly difficult to draw, since much work that reveals detailed scholarly investigation has a critical aim, and few even of the most subjective among critics rely entirely on their own unaided response to a work of art. Some studies of Elizabethan life and literature which are not centred on Shakespeare, and even some which hardly refer to him, probably would not have been written except in the hope of casting light, directly or indirectly, on his plays. Enid Welsford's *The Fool: His Social and Literary History* (1935) ranges from classical literature to Charlie Chaplin, but begins with a quotation from *Twelfth Night* and includes a valuable section on *King Lear*. Books wholly or partly concerned with Elizabethan thought, such as A. O. Lovejoy's *The Great Chain of Being* (1936), Hardin Craig's *The Enchanted Glass* (1936), and E. M. W. Tillyard's *The Elizabethan World Picture* (1943), have done much to activate response both to large patterns and to poetic details of Shakespeare's plays, and even the most determined advocate of the examination of verbal techniques could not deny the relevance of such studies, as also of far starker tools of scholarship, such as above all the *New English Dictionary*. Editors too have contributed to the critical as well as the more evidently 'scholarly' scene. In many respects the editor's task may be regarded as mainly 'scholarly'.

He is establishing his text, glossing and annotating it, providing information rather than interpretation. Yet even in the choice of information to provide he is exercising critical judgement, and in most editions he is given the opportunity to expound his own views. The editorial discipline at its fullest demands close familiarity with all aspects of the text, and some of the soundest critical writing on Shakespeare comes in introductions written no doubt at the end of the editorial agony, such as some of those in the New Cambridge, new Arden, and New Penguin series. Some editors, too, have found their thoughts on the plays overflowing into independent critical writings such as John Dover Wilson's *What Happens in Hamlet* (1935) and *The Fortunes of Falstaff* (1943).

Although, contrary to common belief, there is evidence even in the pages of *Shakespearean Tragedy* that Bradley sometimes attended the theatre, he is not noted for having considered the plays in close relation to their theatrical effect. Schücking and especially Stoll are more aware of the need to give this its due, but undoubtedly the most theatrically concerned of the major Shakespeare critics since Bradley has been Harley Granville-Barker, himself an actor, playwright, and producer. His *Prefaces*, which began to appear in full-dress form in 1927, are valuable above all because they appeal on two important fronts. Academics with little interest in the practical theatre can read Granville-Barker, and theatre people to whom academic criticism is a closed library can find practical help in him too. His awareness of the theatrical potential of Shakespeare's plays when thought of in relation to the conditions for which they were written has been immensely influential and valuable, encouraging the performance of previously neglected plays, such as *Love's Labour's Lost*, the reinstatement of passages that had been generally omitted in the theatre from others, and the rethinking of the staging of Shakespeare in modern conditions.

This influence on the practical theatre has indirectly affected literary criticism too. Some critics have written directly on Shakespeare in relation to the stage of both his own and later times. G. C. D. Odell's *Shakespeare – from Betterton to Irving* (1920) is critically naive, and valuable rather for the information it conveys than the attitudes lying behind it, but Arthur Colby Sprague's writings on stage history such as *Shakespeare and the Actors* (1944) are informed by a wise critical judgement and, in a book such as his *Shakespeare's Histories: Plays for the Stage* (1964), are applied to critical ends. Shakespeare critics have become increasingly aware of the theatre, and this trend seems likely to continue. The critical terminology associated with plays in performance is limited, and even those professionally concerned with the theatre are apt to talk and write in surprisingly academic language, but some critics seem to be making an attempt to write about the plays with their effect in performance at the forefront of their minds. Marvin Rosenberg in *The Masks of Othello* (1961) draws together the history of the play on the stage and in the study in the effort to investigate our response to it, John Russell Brown in *Shakespeare's Plays in Performance* (1965) interestingly explores the unwritten theatrical dimension in the texts of plays, and Maynard Mack makes good critical use of stage-history in *'King Lear' in Our Time* (1965). This kind of study reflects awareness that our response to Shakespeare is inevitably coloured by what has happened to the plays between his time and ours. We have inherited prejudices and attitudes of which we may be hardly aware. As T. J. B. Spencer has written, 'The great task of criticism is, no doubt, to see the object as it really is. But in order to do this we need to disentangle ourselves from the past as well as, to some extent, the present.' This is true in relation to areas other than stage history, but its truth is a justification of the use in critical work of scholarly investigations into the history of Shakespeare's plays on the stage.

Shakespeare criticism inevitably reflects changes in general critical method and fashion. It would scarcely be unfair to say that the most powerful literary critics of the century so far have not been the major Shakespeare critics. Many of them have nevertheless exerted considerable influence, direct and indirect. T. S. Eliot's essay on *Hamlet*, especially his pronouncement that it is 'an artistic failure', has teased later writers on the play more perhaps than he would ever have thought likely; and his view of *Othello*, especially that in his final speech the hero is 'cheering himself up', has influenced actors as well as critics. Eliot's essays on Elizabethan dramatists other than Shakespeare have cast light on Shakespeare's technique, and his writings on poetic drama in general have stimulated those concerned mainly with Shakespeare. F. R. Leavis's influence has been even less direct, working largely through the dissemination of attitudes and critical techniques, and not infrequently through a reaction against them. Many of the pieces on Shakespeare first published in *Scrutiny* were written under his powerful influence. Northrop Frye's essay 'The Argument of Comedy' (1948, incorporated in *Anatomy of Criticism*, 1957) has had a seminal influence, but his more extended Shakespeare studies, in *A Natural Perspective: The Development of Shakespearean Comedy and Romance* (1965) and *Fools of Time: Studies in Shakespearean Tragedy* (1967), are remarkable rather for the sparks that are thrown off than for the illumination of a sustained argument.

The emergence round about 1930 of a school of criticism much concerned with close verbal analysis had a major effect on Shakespeare criticism. The work of I. A. Richards looms behind the movement, though he has contributed little to the Shakespearian side of it. In

1933 appeared L. C. Knights's clever 'How Many Children had Lady Macbeth?'. The title parodies those of Bradley's less happy appendices (it is said to have been suggested by Leavis), and in attacking the study of the plays as if they were novels, and especially the Bradleian approach through character, Knights propounds the view that 'a Shakespeare play is a dramatic poem'. The emphasis is on the poem, not the drama, and in this respect Knights's trenchant essay seems now to belong to its time as much as Bradley's book does to his. Bradley has some interesting remarks on style, but Stoll and Schücking had been little concerned with details of language. Now within a few years there appeared Caroline Spurgeon's essays on imagery (1930, 1931) and her book *Shakespeare's Imagery and What it Tells Us* (1935), G. Wilson Knight's *Myth and Miracle* (1929), *The Wheel of Fire* (1930), *The Imperial Theme* (1931), and *The Shakespearian Tempest* (1932), William Empson's *Seven Types of Ambiguity* (1930) and *Some Versions of Pastoral* (1935), the essay by L. C. Knights already referred to, and, in German, W. H. Clemen's book (1936) later translated as *The Development of Shakespeare's Imagery* (1951). These were all by critics with a highly developed interest in language. Critically, Caroline Spurgeon's book is the least sophisticated. Often referred to as a 'pioneering' study, it suffers from a limited definition of imagery, an excessively statistical approach, and too strong an emphasis on imagery as biographical evidence. But it remains a book that has to be consulted, and its influence has been widespread. Clemen's study is more rigorous in approach and more consistently rewarding in its results. L. C. Knights's later writings on Shakespeare, while preserving a perceptive concern with the texture of language, have increasingly adopted the moralistic tone associated with *Scrutiny*. Similar preoccupations characterize the work of D. A. Traversi, another contributor to *Scrutiny* who has gone on to write extensively about Shakespeare. His is a judicial approach, much concerned to relate details of poetic language to overall moral attitudes. He displays little interest in historical considerations, in this resembling Wilson Knight, who followed up his early spate of books with many others, including *The Crown of Life* (1947), *The Mutual Flame* (1955), and *The Sovereign Flower* (1958). Together they form a complex, highly interrelated body of work. *Shakespearian Production* (1964), a revision of *Principles of Shakespearian Production* (1936 and 1949), most obviously reflects his concern with the practical theatre – he has performed some of the great tragic roles. Knight ought, one feels, to be the major Shakespeare critic after Bradley. He is a verbal critic of great subtlety. Stressing 'interpretation' as distinguished from 'criticism' he tends to work from an assumption of 'organic unity', of the play as an 'expanded metaphor', and to proceed to expound underlying themes and symbols. The critic's attempt to submit himself totally to the work can be immensely valuable. Knight has been partly responsible for a broadening of our view of the possibilities of Shakespeare's art of which only a minor result is the rehabilitation into the Shakespeare canon of parts of the plays, such as the vision in *Cymbeline* and Antigonus's dream speech in *The Winter's Tale*, that previously had often seemed unrelatable to the overall design. He is especially interesting too on the relationships between the plays, on for instance the symbolical significance of storms and music. He has been justly described as 'one of the great seminal critics'. Yet his potential seems not to have been fully realized, and some readers are understandably deterred by his obscurities of style, a feeling that he tends to lose hold on reality, and an excessively personal approach that causes us sometimes to suspect that he is concerned to interpret himself through Shakespeare rather than the reverse.

Later critics, too, have pursued studies in which an interest in the devices of linguistic style is paramount. E. A. Armstrong's *Shakespeare's Imagination* (1946) is a fascinating exploration of Shakespeare's creative processes as revealed by a study of a number of 'image clusters'. In *Shakespeare and the Arts of Language* (1947), Sister Miriam Joseph is concerned especially with rhetorical devices. R. B. Heilman writes thorough and perceptive studies of individual plays in *This Great Stage: Image and Structure in 'King Lear'* (1948), and *Magic in the Web: Action and Language in 'Othello'* (1956). M. M. Mahood's *Shakespeare's Wordplay* (1957), which concentrates on five plays and the Sonnets, is a clever assault on some of Shakespeare's verbal complexities. Those who have written usefully on the poems include Edward Hubler in *The Sense of Shakespeare's Sonnets* (1952), Patrick Cruttwell in *The Shakespearean Moment* (1956), and J. B. Leishman in *Themes and Variations in Shakespeare's Sonnets* (1961). On the whole, writers on Shakespeare's verbal techniques have shown more interest in the verse than the prose, but Brian Vickers's *The Artistry of Shakespeare's Prose* (1968) does something to redress the balance. Still, no one has yet written with sufficient passion on the fact that Shakespeare is our greatest prose-writer as well as our greatest poet.

Bradley is known above all for *Shakespearean Tragedy*, and many critics have followed him in writing on particular groups of plays, sometimes in the effort to arrive at a definition of Shakespeare's concept of the genre in which he was working, sometimes (perhaps more usefully) trying to define the characteristic effects of the genre. Lily B. Campbell, in *Shakespeare's Tragic Heroes: Slaves of Passion* (1930), follows Bradley in concentrating on the four 'great' tragedies. Studying them against the background of contemporary medicine and philosophy, with which she believes Shakespeare to have been familiar, she sees the hero of each play as a study in the influence of one dominating passion. She is not a disciple of Bradley, and has two appendices criticizing his criticism. H. B. Charlton, on the other hand, proclaimed himself 'a devout Bradleyite', and, in *Shakespearian Tragedy* (1948), attempts to reaffirm Bradley's approach to character. In *The Story of the Night* (1961) John Holloway attempts an anthropologically based study of the tragedies with results that are sometimes brilliant, though uneven.

M. W. MacCallum's *Shakespeare's Roman Plays and their Background* (1910) remains the standard, most comprehensive study of this group of plays. It makes extensive use of source study, and also attempts lengthy character studies of the main figures. Maurice Charney's *Shakespeare's Roman Plays: the Function of Imagery in the Drama* (1961) is more specialized. The two principal studies of the plays that take English history as their subject matter both consider the political implications of the plays as well as their historical background. E. M. W. Tillyard in *Shakespeare's History Plays* (1944) is the more historiographical in his approach, whereas Lily B. Campbell, in *Shakespeare's 'Histories': Mirrors of Elizabethan Policy* (1947), offers more thorough consideration of the contemporary political background, which she finds specially relevant. M. M. Reese's *The Cease of Majesty* (1961) is a useful corrective to some of the more extreme features of Tillyard's approach.

Although the comedies form the largest single group of Shakespeare's plays, criticism of them lagged behind that of the tragedies and histories except in relation to a few dominating characters, such as Shylock. As a character of potentially tragic status Shylock received attention from Stoll, yet the same critic wrote that 'the essential thing for comedy, the critical spirit...is not abundant in Shakespeare'. Stoll thus associates himself with the satirical tradition of comedy which, as Nevill Coghill shows in his essay 'The Basis of Shakespearian Comedy' (1950), flourished in Renaissance England, and which has perhaps been more amenable to analysis than the romantic tradition which Shakespeare found more congenial. The twentieth century is to be credited with a realization on the part of at least some commentators that the greatness of Shakespearian comedy is not necessarily in proportion to its critical intent, and various writers have tried to define its characteristic modes and effects. The concept of Shakespearian comedy has proved even more difficult to pin down than that of Shakespearian tragedy, and the plays have yielded more to individual analysis than to the application of single-minded theories or rigorously defined critical techniques. H. B. Charlton's *Shakespearian Comedy* (1938) employs a scholarly approach through literary analogues, related to that used by Lawrence in *Shakespeare's Problem Comedies*. Charlton's is a substantial study, dated by a ponderous style. C. L. Barber in *Shakespeare's Festive Comedy* (1959) succeeds more than most critics in finding a rewarding framework of discussion. His approach is anthropological. His subtitle is *A Study of Dramatic Form and its Relation to Social Custom*, and he finds in the comedies up to *Twelfth Night* a 'saturnalian pattern' derived from both social and artistic traditions. Bertrand Evans in *Shakespeare's Comedies* (1960) closely examines the artistry by which Shakespeare manipulates the reactions of his audience, creating 'exploitable gaps or discrepancies among the awarenesses of participants and between the awarenesses of participants and audience'. The method is not equally illuminating for all plays.

Shakespeare's works remain (more or less) constant, but those who read and see them are always changing. In this lies the justification for the continuous stream of writing about them. As T. S. Eliot wrote in the previous *Companion*, 'Shakespeare criticism will always change as the world changes.' As the plays become more remote in time they stand more in need of explanation and interpretation. Not all who write about them are, or should be, trying hard to say something new. Moreover, even the most original critics often need their mediators, whether in print or in the lecture hall. For this reason, much good writing on Shakespeare is not specially exciting. The truest, most balanced criticism is that which takes account of many different points of view, which synthesizes a variety of approaches. Inevitably it is likely to seem judicious rather than brilliant, sound rather than revelatory. Conversely, extremist approaches are liable to be one-sided. John Holloway, in the Introduction to *The Story of the Night*, which is an independent and stimulating discussion of fundamental critical issues, speaks of the need 'to restore traditional clarity by removing modernistic over-ingenuity'. But even over-ingenious critics can perform useful functions. Theirs are likely to be more readable, because more surprising, than middle-of-the-road interpretations. This is sad, because the obvious is often true, and a generally accepted view of a play is liable to be just. But the older the truth, the better it needs to be put. It takes a writer of real skill to present forcefully an established point of view. The critic who writes with the excitement that comes from a knowledge that he is being shocking, that he is challenging received opinion, may attract attention; and even if he does not convince he may usefully disturb. This is a valid function of criticism. Readers, especially those for whom familiarity is in danger of dulling their responses, need to be shaken up. Even so extreme a piece as Jan Kott's chapter on *A Midsummer Night's Dream* in *Shakespeare Our Contemporary* (1965, revised 1967), may vivify our response to aspects of the play, however violently we reject his total argument. But the best criticism, and that which stands the best chance of survival, is that which combines a balanced approach with the ability to engage and sustain the attention of the reader without excessive concern with local and temporal matters. It is too early yet to sort out with any confidence the post-Bradleian sheep from the goats. Certain names would be likely to figure in any account, however brief, but many which might have been included have been omitted here, and to others a different degree of prominence might easily have been accorded. And those who are working now may well develop in different and surprising ways. Criticism based on a strong sense of the play as something that is incomplete until it is performed seems likely to grow in importance, but it is a difficult area of discussion. The study of linguistics is likely to be applied to Shakespeare, but will not have much immediate effect unless its practitioners can devise a more readily comprehensible terminology than that in which they communicate with one another. But it is useless to speculate, for what happens in the future is not conditioned by what we may feel to be desirable, but by the future itself: the needs of readers, and the capacities of the individuals who write for them.

NOTES AND READING LISTS

1. THE LIFE OF SHAKESPEARE

Note

1 Much confusion has arisen from the entry of licence, made the previous day in the Bishop of Worcester's *Register*, which names Anne Whateley of Temple Grafton as the bride. Presumably the entry clerk made a careless mistake. That Shakespeare's wife was a Hathaway is confirmed by the independent tradition reported in Rowe's *Account* (1709).

Reading List

Baldwin, T. W., *William Shakspere's Small Latine & Lesse Greeke*, 2 vols. (Urbana, Ill., 1944)

Bentley, G. E., *Shakespeare: A Biographical Handbook* (New Haven, 1961)

Chambers, E. K., *William Shakespeare: A Study of Facts and Problems*, 2 vols. (Oxford, 1930)

Eccles, Mark, *Shakespeare in Warwickshire* (Madison, Wis., 1961)

Fripp, Edgar I., *Shakespeare, Man and Artist*, 2 vols. (1938)

Hotson, Leslie, *I, William Shakespeare, Do Appoint Thomas Russell, Esq.* (1937)

Shakespeare versus Shallow (1931)

Reese, M. M., *Shakespeare: His World and His Work* (1953)

Rowse, A. L., *William Shakespeare: A Biography* (1963)

Schoenbaum, S., *Shakespeare's Lives* (1970)

Smart, J. S., *Shakespeare: Truth and Tradition* (1928)

2. THE PLAYHOUSES AND THE STAGE

Notes

1 Herbert Berry, 'The Playhouse in the Boar's Head Inn, Whitechapel', in *The Elizabethan Theatre*, ed. David Galloway (Toronto, 1969).

2 Alfred Harbage, *Shakespeare and the Rival Traditions* (New York, 1952).

3 William A. Armstrong, *The Elizabethan Private Theatres* (1958).

4 'Reconstitution du théâtre du Swan', in *Le Lieu théâtral à la Renaissance*, ed. Jean Jacquot (Paris, 1964), pp. 295–316.

5 Texts of the two contracts and reproductions of most of the pictorial sources cited in this chapter may be found in *The Globe Restored* (1953) by C. Walter Hodges.

6 Irwin Smith, 'Theatre into Globe', *Shakespeare Quarterly*, III (1952), pp. 113–200.

7 'A Reconstruction of the Second Blackfriars', in *The Elizabethan Theatre*, ed. David Galloway.

8 See the article by D. F. Rowan in *The New Theatre Magazine* (1969).

9 See 'The Staging of the Monument Scenes in *Antony and Cleopatra*', *The Library Chronicle*, XXX (University of Pennsylvania), (1964), pp. 62–71.
10 'The Discovery-space in Shakespeare's Globe', *Shakespeare Survey 12* (Cambridge, 1959), pp. 35–46.
11 'The Staging of Desdemona's Bed', *Shakespeare Quarterly*, XIV (1963), pp. 57–65.
12 'The Gallery over the Stage in the Public Playhouse of Shakespeare's Time', *Shakespeare Quarterly*, VIII (1957), pp. 15–31; 'Shakespeare's Use of a Gallery over the Stage', *Shakespeare Survey 10* (Cambridge, 1957), pp. 77–89.
13 'Was There a Music-room in Shakespeare's Globe?', *Shakespeare Survey 13* (Cambridge, 1960), pp. 113–23.
14 See 'The Origins of the So-called Elizabethan Multiple Stage', *The Drama Review*, XII, 2 (1967–8), pp. 28–50.
15 It is a pleasure to record my indebtedness to Dr Richard Southern for making the drawings that illustrate this chapter.

Reading List

Adams, Joseph Quincy, *Shakespearean Playhouses* (Boston, 1917)
Armstrong, William A., *The Elizabethan Private Theatres: Facts and Problems* (1958)
Beckerman, Bernard, *Shakespeare at the Globe* (New York, 1962)
Bentley, Gerald Eades, *The Jacobean and Caroline Stage*, 7 vols. (Oxford, 1941–68), vol. 6: *Theatres*, 1968.
Chambers, E. K., *The Elizabethan Stage*, 4 vols. (Oxford, 1923), vols. 2 and 3
Harbage, Alfred, *Shakespeare's Audience* (New York, 1941)
    Theatre for Shakespeare (Toronto, 1955)
Hodges, C. Walter, *The Globe Restored* (1953; rev. ed., 1968)
    Shakespeare's Theatre (1964)
Nicoll, Allardyce, *Stuart Masques and the Renaissance Stage* (1937)
Reynolds, George F., *The Staging of Elizabethan Plays at the Red Bull Theater, 1605–1625* (New York, 1940)
Southern, Richard, *Changeable Scenery* (1952)
    The Medieval Theatre in the Round (1957)
    The Open Stage (1953)
Wickham, Glynne H., *Early English Stages, 1300 to 1660*, vol. 1 (1959); vol. 2, pt. 1 (1963)

3. THE ACTORS AND STAGING

Notes

1 E. H. Gombrich, *Art and Illusion* (1960), p. 394.
2 See Reading List.
3 *Cf.* Bernard Beckerman, *Shakespeare at the Globe, 1599–1609* (New York, 1962), pp. 183–6.
4 Although such computation as this is naturally limited by a factor of

individual interpretation, I have tried to include for consideration only those lines in which evidence is definite; i.e. for which there is an explicit stage direction of theatrical provenance, for which another character is explicit in descriptive terms of business being acted, or for which certain business would have to be conducted simultaneously to make sense of the lines. Two relevant facts should be noted about this evidence: first, that so far as can be determined from the texts considered for this study, the figures pertain as much to performance in private theatres as in public ones; and, second, that commonsense leads one to assume that any category of action for which documentation exists would also take place less apparently in other parts of a text. For what it is worth, categories of stage business such as those being investigated here cover, ordinarily, at least half of the words of most modern plays; and even if one acknowledges that our theatre may be more physically and psychologically 'busy' than the Elizabethan, we may assume with some confidence that the percentage figures noted above must be minimal, and that much more stage business of all kinds took place than we will ever be able to detect and document.

5 Prologue, *Summer's Last Will and Testament.*
6 Cited by Alfred Harbage, *Theatre for Shakespeare* (Toronto, 1955), Appendix B, p. 109.
7 In computing these averages, I have omitted consideration of 'massed' scenes, such as those taking place in a monarch's court, before a battle, trials, etc.
8 Beckerman, *op. cit.*, p. 184.
9 John Russell Brown, 'On the Acting of Shakespeare's Plays', *Quarterly Journal of Speech*, XXXIX (1953), 479.

Reading List

Beckerman, Bernard, see 2, above
Bradbrook, M. C., *Themes and Conventions of Elizabethan Tragedy* (Cambridge, 1935), ch. I and III.
Brown, John Russell, *Shakespeare's Plays in Performance* (1966)
Chambers, E. K., see 2, above
Coghill, Nevill, *Shakespeare's Professional Skills* (Cambridge, 1964)
Foakes, R. A., 'The Player's Passion', *Essays and Studies* (1954)
Harbage, Alfred. see 2, above
Joseph, Bertram, *Acting Shakespeare* (1960)
  Elizabethan Acting (1951; rev. 1964)
  The Tragic Actor (1959)
Rosenberg, Marvin, 'Elizabethan Actors: Men or Marionettes?', *PMLA*, LXIX (1954), 915–27
Seltzer, Daniel, 'Elizabethan Acting in *Othello*', *Shakespeare Quarterly*, X (1959), 201–10
  'The Staging of the Last Plays', *Stratford-upon-Avon Studies*, vol. 8 (1966)
Styan, J. L., *Shakespeare's Stagecraft* (Cambridge, 1967)

4. SHAKESPEARE'S READING

Reading List

The books in this list are arranged in the order in which the topics they cover are dealt with in this chapter.

Anders, H. R. D., *Shakespeare's Books* (Berlin, 1904)

Muir, Kenneth, *Shakespeare's Sources I* (1957)

Wilson, F. P., 'Shakespeare's Reading', *Shakespeare Survey 3* (1950)

Bullough, Geoffrey, *Narrative and Dramatic Sources of Shakespeare*, 7 vols. (1957–72)

Whiter, Walter, *A Specimen of a Commentary on Shakespeare* (1794), ed. Over and Bell (1967)

Armstrong, Edward A., *Shakespeare's Imagination* (1946)

Isaacs, J., 'Shakespeare's earliest years in the theatre', *Proc. Brit. Acad.* XXXIX (1953), 119–38

Weiss, Roberto, *Humanism in England in the Fifteenth Century* (1941)

Walker, Alice, 'The reading of an Elizabethan', *R.E.S.*, VIII (1932), 264–81

Thomson, J. A. K., *Shakespeare and the Classics* (1952)

Farmer, Richard, 'An Essay on the Learning of Shakespeare' (1767) in *Eighteenth Century Essays on Shakespeare*, ed. D. Nichol Smith (Oxford, 1903)

Baldwin, T. W., see 1, above

Baldwin, T. W., *William Shakespeare's Five Act Structure* (Urbana, 1947)

Salingar, L. G., 'The design of *Twelfth Night*', *Shakespeare Quarterly*, IX (1958), 117–39

Jenkins, Harold, 'Shakespeare's *Twelfth Night*', *Rice Institute Pamphlets*, XLV (1959), 19–42

Prouty, C. T., *The Sources of 'Much Ado About Nothing'* (New Haven, 1950)

Noble, Richmond, *Shakespeare's Biblical Knowledge* (1935)

Hart, Alfred, *Shakespeare and the Homilies* (Melbourne, 1934)

Wilson, F. P., *Marlowe and the Early Shakespeare* (Oxford, 1953)

Honigmann, E. A. J., 'Shakespeare's lost source-plays', *Modern Language Review*, XLIX (1954), 293–307

Lascelles, Mary, *Shakespeare's 'Measure for Measure'* (1953)

Spencer, Theodore, *Shakespeare and the Nature of Man* (Cambridge, Mass., 1942)

Whitaker, Virgil K., *Shakespeare's Use of Learning* (San Marino, 1953)

Taylor, G. Coffin, *Shakespeare's Debt to Montaigne* (Cambridge, Mass., 1925)

Hogden, Margaret, 'Montaigne and Shakespeare', *Huntington Library Quarterly*, XVI (1952), 23–42

Wilson, J. Dover, *What Happens in 'Hamlet'* (Cambridge, 1935)

Bald, R. C., 'Edmund and Renaissance Free thought', *Joseph Quincy Adams Memorial Studies*, ed. J. G. McManaway *et al.* (Washington, D.C., 1948), pp. 337–49.

5. SHAKESPEARE AND THE ENGLISH LANGUAGE

Reading List

Abbott, E. A., *A Shakespearian Grammar* (3rd ed., 1872)

Byrne, M. St. Clare, 'The Foundations of Elizabethan Language', *Shakespeare Survey 17* (1964), pp. 223–39

Clemen, W. H., *The Development of Shakespeare's Imagery* (1951)

Dobson, E. J., *English pronunciation 1500–1700* (Oxford, 2nd ed., 1968)

Evans, B. Ifor, *The Language of Shakespeare's Plays* (2nd ed., 1959)

Franz, W., *Die Sprache Shakespeares in Vers und Prosa* (Halle, 4th ed., 1939)

Hulme, Hilda M., *Explorations in Shakespeare's Language* (1962)

Kökeritz, H., *Shakespeare's Pronunciation* (New Haven, 1953)

McIntosh, A., '*As You Like It*: A Grammatical Clue to Character', *R.E.L.*, IV (1963)

Mahood, M. M., *Shakespeare's Wordplay* (1957)

Millward, C., 'Pronominal Case in Shakespearian Imperatives', *Lg*, XLII (1966)

Mulholland, J., ' "Thou" and "You" in Shakespeare', *E.S.*, XLVIII (1967)

Onions, C. T., *A Shakespeare Glossary* (Oxford, 2nd ed., 1919)

Salmon, V., 'Elizabethan Colloquial English in the Falstaff Plays', *Leeds Studies in English*, n.s. 1 (1967)

'Sentence Structures in Colloquial Shakespearian English', *TPS* (1965)

Schmidt, A., *Shakespeare-Lexicon*, rev. G. Sarrazin (Berlin and Leipzig, 4th ed., 1923)

Willcock, G. D., 'Shakespeare and Elizabethan English', *Shakespeare Survey 7* (1954)

'Language and Poetry in Shakespeare's Early Plays', *Proc. Brit. Acad.*, XL (1954)

6. SHAKESPEARE'S USE OF RHETORIC

Reading List

Abrams, M. H., *The Mirror and the Lamp: Romantic Theory and the Critical Tradition* (New York, 1953)

Baldwin, C. S., *Medieval Rhetoric and Poetic* (New York, 1928)

Baldwin, T. W., see 1, above

Bolgar, R. R., *The Classical Heritage and its Beneficiaries* (Cambridge, 1954)

Barish, J. A., 'The Antitheatrical Prejudice', *Critical Quarterly*, VIII (1966), 329–48

Curtius, E. R., *European Literature and the Latin Middle Ages*, tr. W. R. Trask (New York, 1953)

Faral, E., *Les Arts Poétiques du XIIe et du XIIIe Siècle* (Paris, 1924)

Hoskins, J., *Directions for Speech and Style*, ed. H. Hudson (Princeton, 1935)

Howell, W. S., *Logic and Rhetoric in England 1500–1700* (Princeton, 1956)
Joseph, Sister Miriam, *Shakespeare's Use of the Arts of Language* (New York, 1947)
Kennedy, G. A., *The Art of Persuasion in Greece* (London 1963)
Marrou, H. I., *A History of Education in Antiquity*, trans. G. Lamb (London, 1956)
Peacham, H., *The Garden of Eloquence*, ed. W. G. Crane (Florida, 1954)
Puttenham, G., *The Arte of Englishe Poesie*, ed. G. Willcock and A. Walker (Cambridge, 1936, 1970)
Sonnino, L. A., *A Handbook to Sixteenth-Century Rhetoric* (1968)
Stone, P. W. K., *The Art of Poetry 1750–1820*. (London, 1967)
Tuve, Rosemond, *Elizabethan and Metaphysical Imagery* (Chicago, 1947)
Vickers, Brian, *The Artistry of Shakespeare's Prose* (1968)
    Classical Rhetoric in English Poetry (1970)

7. SHAKESPEARE'S POETRY

Reading List

Clemen, W. H., *The Development of Shakespeare's Imagery* (1951)
Hubler, Edward, *The Sense of Shakespeare's Sonnets* (Princeton, 1952)
Knight, G. Wilson, *The Wheel of Fire* (1930)
    The Imperial Theme (1931)
    The Crown of Life (1947)
Lever, J. W., *The Elizabethan Love Sonnet* (1956)
Nicoll, Allardyce (ed.), *Shakespeare Survey 15* (1962)
Nowottny, Winifred, *The Language Poets Use* (1962)
Spurgeon, Caroline F. E., *Shakespeare's Imagery and What It Tells Us* (Cambridge, 1935)

8. SHAKESPEARE'S NARRATIVE POEMS

Notes

1 George Wyndham, *The Poems of Shakespeare* (1898), Introduction, p. cxxii.
2 Bion, *Idyl* I, trans. Andrew Lang.
3 Adrian Junius, *Nomenclator*, trans. John Higgins, 1585. Cited in Madeleine Doran, *Endeavors of Art* (1954), p. 382.
4 The 'Argument' differs in many respects from the version of events in the poem. Shakespeare's authorship has been questioned; alternatively it has been thought of as an early outline for the later work.

Reading List

Allen, D. C., *Image and Meaning*, 2nd ed. (Maryland, 1968)
Baldwin, T. W., *On the Literary Genetics of Shakespeare's Poems and Sonnets* (Urbana, 1950)

Bradbrook, M. C., *Shakespeare and Elizabethan Poetry* (1951)
Coleridge, S. T., *Biographia Literaria* (1817), ch. xv
Hamilton, A. C., 'Venus and Adonis', *Studies in English Literature, 1500–1900*, I (1961)
The Early Shakespeare (San Marino, 1967)
Maxwell, J. C. (ed.), *The Poems* (Cambridge, 1966)
Muir, Kenneth, '*A Lover's Complaint*: A Reconsideration' in *Shakespeare 1564–1964*, ed. E. A. Bloom (Providence, R. I., 1964)
Nicoll, Allardyce, *Shakespeare Survey 15* (1962)
Price, Hereward T., 'The Function of Imagery in *Venus and Adonis*' (*Papers of the Michigan Academy*, 1945), pp. 275–97
Prince, F. T. (ed.), The Arden Shakespeare: *The Poems* (1960)
Rollins, H. E. (ed.), New Variorum Shakespeare: *The Poems* (Philadelphia, 1938)
Smith, Hallett, *Elizabethan Poetry* (Cambridge, Mass., 1952)
Wyndham, George, *The Poems of Shakespeare* (1898)

9. SHAKESPEARE THE ELIZABETHAN DRAMATIST

Reading List

Barber, C. L., *Shakespeare's Festive Comedy* (Princeton, 1959)
Frye, Northrop, 'The Argument of Comedy', *English Institute Essays* (New York, 1949)
'Characterization in Shakespearean Comedy', *Shakespeare Quarterly*, IV (1953), 271–7
Granville-Barker, H., *Prefaces to Shakespeare* (1927, 1930)
Hunter, G. K., 'Shakespeare's Politics and the Rejection of Falstaff', *Critical Quarterly*, I (1959), 229–36
Hunter, R. G., *Shakespeare and the Comedy of Forgiveness* (New York, 1965)
Reese, M. M., *The Cease of Majesty* (1961)
Rossiter, A. P., 'Much Ado about Nothing', *Angel with Horns* (1961), pp. 67–81
Tillyard, E. M. W., *Shakespeare's History Plays* (1944)
Wilson, J. Dover, *The Fortunes of Falstaff* (Cambridge, 1944)
Young, David, *Something of Great Constancy; The Art of 'A Midsummer Night's Dream'* (New Haven, 1966)

10. SHAKESPEARE THE JACOBEAN DRAMATIST

Notes

1 F. P. Wilson, *Elizabethan and Jacobean* (1945), p. 26.
2 Clifford Leech, *The John Fletcher Plays* (1962), p. 32.
3 See Irving Ribner, *The English History Play in the Age of Shakespeare* (New York, 1965), ch. 9.
4 George Kernodle, 'Open stage; Elizabethan or Existentialist?', *Shakespeare Survey 12* (1959), 2–3.

5 *A Century of Revolution* (1961), p. 96.
6 Nicholas Brooke, *Shakespeare's Early Tragedies* (1968), p. 143.
7 By David Frost, *The School of Shakespeare* (1968).
8 See Glynne Wickham, *Early English Stages*, vol. II (1963), 242.
9 In 'Shakespeare's Primitive Art', *British Academy Annual Shakespeare Lecture* (1965)
10 With such titles as *The Raging Turk*. See the introduction to *Mulleasses the Turk* in Bang's *Materialien*.
11 Bernard Spivack, *Shakespeare and the Allegory of Evil* (New York and London, 1958), pp. 424, 426.
12 Fulke Greville, *Life of Sir Philip Sidney* (ed. Nowell Smith, 1907), p. 15.
13 Thomas Heywood, *A Woman Killed with Kindness*, V, vi.
14 T. S. Eliot, 'Shakespeare and the Stoicism of Seneca', *Selected Essays* (1951), pp. 130–1.
15 J. I. M. Stewart, *Character and Motive in Shakespeare* (1949), pp. 108–9.
16 W. H. Auden, 'The Joker in the Pack', *The Dyer's Hand* (1963), pp. 246–72.
17 See M. C. Bradbrook, *Shakespeare the Craftsman* (1969), ch. 3.
18 John Donne, *Devotions upon Emergent Occasions* (1624), No. XVII.
19 *The Shakespeare Allusion Book*, II, p. 23.
20 Anne Righter, Introduction to *The Tempest*, New Penguin Shakespeare (1968), p. 17.
21 See *Shakespeare the Craftsman*, ch. I, pp. 22–6.

Reading List

Elton, W. R., *King Lear and the Gods* (San Marino, 1966)
Empson, William, *The Structure of Complex Words* (1951)
Farnham, Willard, *Shakespeare's Tragic Frontier* (Berkeley, 1950)
Jacquot, Jean (ed.), *Les Fêtes de la Renaissance*, 2 vols. (Paris, 1956–60)
  Le Lieu Théâtral à la Renaissance (Paris, 1964)
Leech, Clifford, *Shakespeare's Tragedies and other studies in Seventeenth Century Drama* (1950)
Mack, Maynard, 'The Jacobean Shakespeare' in *Jacobean Theatre*, ed. J. R. Brown and B. Harris (1960)
Muir, Kenneth (ed.), *Shakespeare Survey 21* (1968) (on *Othello*)
Nicoll, Allardyce (ed.), *Shakespeare Survey 10* (1957) (on Roman Plays)
  Shakespeare Survey 11 (1958) (on Last Plays)
Raab, Felix, *The English Face of Machiavelli* (1964)

11. SHAKESPEARE AND MUSIC

Notes

1 This half-line is supplied from Q1, as in K. Muir's Arden edn., 1952.
2 Q1 has 'rough'. The emendation 'still' is based on Wilkins's *Pericles*: 'that they should command some still music to sound'; cf. E. Schanzer's Signet edn., 1965.
3 Q1 reads 'viole', Q4 has 'viall'; cf. Schanzer's edn.

Reading List

Bowden, W. R., *English Dramatic Lyric, 1603–1642* (New Haven, 1951)

Cutts, John P., *Musique de la troupe de Shakespeare* (Paris, 1959)

Fellowes, E. H. (ed.), *English Madrigal Verse* (3rd ed. rev. F. W. Sternfeld and D. Greer, Oxford, 1967)

English School of Lutenist Song Writers, 32 vols., (1920–32)

Hartnoll, P. (ed.) *Shakespeare in Music* (1964)

Long, John H. (ed.), *Music in English Renaissance Drama* (Lexington, 1968)

Shakespeare's Use of Music – Comedies, 2 vols. (Gainesville, 1955, 1961)

Naylor, Edward W. (ed.), *Shakespeare Music*, 2nd ed. (1928)

Shakespeare and Music, 2nd ed. (1931)

Noble, Richmond, *Shakespeare's Use of Song* (1923)

Seng, Peter J., *Vocal Songs in the Plays of Shakespeare* (Cambridge, Mass., 1967)

Sternfeld, F. W., *Music in Shakespearean Tragedy*, 2nd impr. (1967)

(ed.) *Songs from Shakespeare's Tragedies* (1964)

12. THE HISTORICAL AND SOCIAL BACKGROUND

Notes

1 J. E. Neale, *Elizabeth I and her Parliaments* (1957), II, 391.

2 J. E. Neale, *Elizabeth I* (1934), p. 381.

3 Thomas Smith, *De Republica Anglorum*, ed. L. Alston (Cambridge, 1906), p. 106.

4 *Ibid.*, p. 46.

5 *Ibid.*, p. 41.

6 *Ibid.*, p. 39.

7 *Ibid.*, p. 40. Cf. W. Harrison, *Description of England* (1577), upon which Smith almost certainly drew.

8 Thomas Wilson, *The State of England Anno Domini 1600*, ed. F. J. Fisher, *Camden Miscellany*, 1936, XVI, 24.

9 *Ibid.*, p. 19.

10 *Ibid.*, p. 24–5.

11 D. H. Willson, *King James VI and I* (1956), p. 243.

12 *Ibid.*, p. 350.

13 Cited in P. Collinson, 'The Beginnings of English Sabbatarianism', *Studies in Church History*, I, 221.

14 Thomas More, *Utopia*, ed. J. R. Lumby (Cambridge, 1885), p. 162. I am using the Tudor translation not the modern one.

Reading List

Bindoff, S. T., *Tudor England* (Harmondsworth, 1950)

Morris, C., *Political Thought from Tyndale to Hooker* (London, 1953)

Neale, J. E., *Elizabeth I* (1934)

Ramsey, P., *Tudor Economic Problems* (1963)
Rowse, A. L., *The England of Elizabeth* (1951)
Smith, A. G. R., *The Government of Elizabethan England* (1967)
Smith, Sir Thomas, *De Republica Anglorum*, ed. L. Alston (Cambridge, 1906)
Willson, D. H., *King James VI and I* (1956)
Wilson, Thomas, 'The State of England Anno Domini 1600', ed. F. J. Fisher, *Camden Miscellany*, XVI (1936)

13. SHAKESPEARE AND THE THOUGHT OF HIS AGE

Reading List

Anderson, Ruth L., *Elizabethan Psychology and Shakespeare's Plays* (New York, 2nd ed., 1966)
Baker, Herschel, *The Image of Man* (New York, 1961)
   The Wars of Truth (Cambridge, Mass., 1952)
Bamborough, J. B., *The Little World of Man* (1952)
Cassirer, Ernst, *The Individual and the Cosmos in Renaissance Philosophy* (New York, 1964)
Craig, Hardin, *The Enchanted Glass: The Elizabethan Mind in Literature* (New York, 1936)
Curry, Walter C., *Shakespeare's Philosophical Patterns* (Baton Rouge, La., 2nd ed. 1959)
Greenleaf, W. H., *Order, Empiricism, and Politics: Two Traditions of English Political Thought, 1500–1700* (1964)
Haydn, Hiram, *The Counter-Renaissance* (New York, 1950)
Johnson, Francis R., *Astronomical Thought in Renaissance England: A Study of the English Scientific Writings from 1500 to 1645* (Baltimore, 1937)
Kantorowicz, Ernst H., *The King's Two Bodies: A Study in Mediaeval Political Theology* (Princeton, 1957)
Kocher, Paul H., *Science and Religion in Elizabethan England* (San Marino, Calif., 1953)
Kristeller, P. O., *Renaissance Thought: the Classic, Scholastic, and Humanist Strains* (New York, 1961)
Lewis, C. S., *The Discarded Image* (1967)
Lovejoy, A. O., *The Great Chain of Being: A Study of the History of an Idea* (Cambridge, Mass., 1936)
Nicoll, Allardyce (ed.), 'Shakespeare in his own Age', *Shakespeare Survey 17* (1964)
Popkin, Richard H., *The History of Scepticism: from Erasmus to Descartes* (New York, 1968)
Tillyard, E. M. W., *The Elizabethan World Picture* (1943)
Walker, D. P., *Spiritual and Demonic Magic from Ficino to Campanella* (1958)

Winny, James, ed., *The Frame of Order: An Outline of Elizabethan Belief...* (1957)

Yates, Frances A., *Giordano Bruno and the Hermetic Tradition* (1964)

14. SHAKESPEARE'S PLAYS ON THE ENGLISH STAGE

Reading List

Crosse, Gordon, *Shakespearean Playgoing 1890–1952* (1953)

Dickins, Richard, *Forty Years of Shakespeare on the English Stage: August, 1867 to August, 1907* (1907)

Hogan, C. B., *Shakespeare in the Theatre*, 2 vols. (Oxford, 1952–7)

Odell, G. C. D., *Shakespeare from Betterton to Irving*, 2 vols. (New York, 1920)

Spencer, Christopher (ed.), *Five Restoration Adaptations of Shakespeare* (Urbana, 1965)

Spencer, Hazelton, *Shakespeare Improved* (Cambridge, Mass., 1927)

Sprague, A. C., *Shakespeare and the Actors: The Stage Business in his Plays* (New York, 1963) [First published in 1944]

Shakespearian Players and Performances (1954)

Shakespeare's Histories: Plays for the Stage (1964)

Sprague, A. C. and Trewin, J. C., *Shakespeare's Plays Today: Some Customs and Conventions of the Stage* (1970)

Trewin, J. C., *Shakespeare on the English Stage 1900–1964* (1964)

Trewin, J. C. and Kemp, T. C., *The Stratford Festival* (Birmingham, 1953)

Winter, William, *Shakespeare on the Stage*, 3 vols. (New York, 1911–16)

There are good brief stage histories of the separate plays by Harold Child, continued by C. B. Young, in the New Cambridge Shakespeare. Marvin Rosenberg, *The Masks of Othello* (Berkeley, 1961), and Joseph Price, *The Unfortunate Comedy* [*All's Well That Ends Well*] (Liverpool, 1968), are excellent recent books.

15. SHAKESPEARE AND THE DRAMA OF HIS TIME

Notes

1 Apart from his debt to Greene's romance *Pandosto* (the source for *The Winter's Tale*), there is plenty of evidence that Shakespeare had read some of Greene's other novels and pamphlets, as also that he knew work by other playwriting Wits of the 1580s and 1590s – Nashe, Lodge, Mundy, Peele, Chettle. The question of his kinship with any or all of them is an open one. As an established actor and playwright by or before 1592, he should have had by that date unusually good opportunities for getting to know their work for the stage.

2 What was going on included the 'War of the Theatres' (1599–1602), an intensification of the satirical spirit and a quarrel of personality and principle which involved Jonson, Marston, Dekker, Heywood and perhaps Shakespeare himself. Its development is obscure. If it is true

(as has been argued) that the War was simply a phase during which a conscious and enduring opposition of literary ideals between the 'popular' and 'coterie' theatres temporarily broke surface, it is plain from his work that Shakespeare ordinarily inclined to the former. One may agree that there were differences between two sorts of theatre, public and private, without adopting an attitude of moralistic-sentimental approval for Shakespeare's side and of reproof for the other. Shakespeare does not on the whole go in for urbanities about homosexuality, faithless wives and longing heirs, but it is overzealous to regard them as, in Alfred Harbage's phrase, conducting us straight towards a 'perversion and defeat of the human spirit'. It was zeal of that kind that so ingloriously shut down the theatres in 1642.

Reading List

A *Marlowe*

Bakeless, John, *The Tragicall Historie of Christopher Marlowe* (Cambridge, Mass., 1942)

Brooke, Nicholas, 'Marlowe as a Provocative Agent in Shakespeare's Early Plays', *Shakespeare Survey 14* (1961)

Wilson, F. P., *Marlowe and the Early Shakespeare* (Oxford, 1953)

B *Lyly and other Wits*

Bradbrook, M. C., *The Growth and Structure of Elizabethan Comedy* (1955)

Freeman, Arthur, *Thomas Kyd: Facts and Problems* (Oxford, 1965)

Hunter, G. K., *John Lyly: The Humanist as Courtier* (1962)

Mincoff, Marco, 'Shakespeare and Lyly', *Shakespeare Survey 14* (1961)

Sanders, Norman, 'The Comedy of Greene and Shakespeare', *Early Shakespeare*, ed. J. R. Brown and B. Harris (1961)

C *Jonson and the Satirists*

Campbell, Oscar J., *Shakespeare's Satire* (New York, 1943)

Harbage, Alfred, *Shakespeare and the Rival Traditions* (New York, 1952)

D *Fletcher and the Last Plays*

Bentley, G. E., 'Shakespeare and the Blackfriars Theatre', *Shakespeare Survey 1* (1948)

Edwards, Philip, 'Shakespeare's Romances, 1900–1957', *Shakespeare Survey 11* (1958)

Leech, Clifford, *The John Fletcher Plays* (1962)

Pettet, E. C., *Shakespeare and the Romance Tradition* (1949)

16. SHAKESPEARE'S TEXT

Notes

1 *Folio* is a printer's term describing a book in which the sheet, the basic unit of any book, has been folded once to produce two leaves (four pages). In the Shakespeare First Folio three sheets were placed together

and then folded once to form a single gathering of six leaves (twelve pages). Abbreviated as F.

2 *Quarto*, also a printer's term, is used to describe a book, roughly half the size of a folio, in which the sheet has been folded twice to produce four leaves (eight pages) to a gathering. Abbreviated as Q.

3 In addition to *Pericles*, six other plays, attributed to Shakespeare, were included in F3 (and F4): *The London Prodigal*, *The Life and Death of Thomas Lord Cromwell*, *The History of Sir John Oldcastle*, *The Puritan*, *A Yorkshire Tragedy*, and *The Tragedy of Locrine*. None of these plays is now accepted as even in part by Shakespeare. *The Reign of King Edward the Third* (1596) was claimed for Shakespeare by Edward Capell in the eighteenth century and is still considered by a few critics to be partly his work. Finally, two 'lost' plays (*Love's Labour's Won* and *Cardenio*) have been associated with Shakespeare. *Love's Labour's Won* was included by Francis Meres in a list of twelve of Shakespeare's plays in his *Palladis Tamia* in 1598. It is now known that a play so titled was actually published, since the volume formed part of a bookseller's stock in 1603 (see T. W. Baldwin, *Shakspere's 'Love's Labor's Won'*, 1957), but no copy of the quarto has survived. It is possible, though less likely since Baldwin's discovery, that the play was included in F1 under another title. *The History of Cardenio* was first assigned to John Fletcher and Shakespeare by the publisher Humphrey Moseley in an entry on the Stationers' Register in 1653, but never published. In 1728 Lewis Theobald published his *Double Falsehood*, claiming that he had adapted it from three manuscript copies (since lost) of the hitherto missing *Cardenio* and attributing the original play wholly to Shakespeare. Recent scholarship now generally admits that some vestiges of Shakespeare's and Fletcher's hands, both rather dolefully disguised, may indeed be detected in Theobald's play.

4 There is growing support for the view that *The Taming of a Shrew* (1594) is a 'bad' quarto of *The Taming of the Shrew*; some scholars would also include *The Troublesome Reign of John, King of England* (1591 two parts) as a 'bad' quarto version of *King John*.

Reading List

Bowers, Fredson, *Bibliography and Textual Criticism* (Oxford, 1964)
  On Editing Shakespeare (Charlottesville, Virginia, 1966)
Chambers, E. K., *William Shakespeare: A Study of Facts and Problems*, 2 vols. (Oxford, 1930)
Greg, W. W., *The Variants in the First Quarto of 'King Lear'*, Bibliographical Society (1940)
  The Editorial Problem in Shakespeare: A Survey of the Foundations of the Text, 3rd. ed. (Oxford, 1954)
  The Shakespeare First Folio: Its Bibliographical and Textual History (Oxford, 1955)
Hinman, Charlton, *The Printing and Proof-Reading of the First Folio of Shakespeare*, 2 vols. (Oxford, 1963)

Honigmann, E. A. J., *The Stability of Shakespeare's Text* (1965)

McKerrow, R. B., *An Introduction to Bibliography for Literary Students*, rev. ed. (Oxford, 1928)

Prolegomena for the Oxford Shakespeare (Oxford, 1939)

Pollard, A. W., *Shakespeare Folios and Quartos, 1594–1685* (1909)

Shakespeare's Hand in the Play of Sir Thomas More (Cambridge, 1923) [A collection of essays by Pollard, W. W. Greg, E. M. Thompson, J. D. Wilson, R. W. Chambers; Wilson's essay on Shakespeare's spellings is important for general study of the text.]

Walker, Alice, *Textual Problems of the First Folio* (Cambridge, 1953)

Walton, J. K., *The Quarto Copy for the First Folio of Shakespeare* (Dublin, 1971)

Wilson, John Dover, *The Manuscript of Shakespeare's 'Hamlet'*, 2 vols. (Cambridge, 1934)

Important textual studies of individual plays: *2 Henry VI* and *3 Henry VI* (Madeleine Doran, Peter Alexander); *Richard III* (Peter Alexander, D. L. Patrick, Kristian Smidt); *Romeo and Juliet* (H. R. Hoppe, G. W. Williams); *Hamlet* (G. I. Duthie); *King Lear* (G. I. Duthie). See also the textual discussions in the more recent volumes of the *New Variorum Shakespeare* (*1 Henry IV* and *2 Henry IV*, *Richard II*, *Troilus and Cressida*, the Poems, and the Sonnets) and in the separate introductions to the New Cambridge and New Arden editions. Articles dealing with various aspects of Shakespeare's text may be found in *The Library*, *Studies in Bibliography*, *Shakespeare Survey*, and *Shakespeare Quarterly*.

17. SHAKESPEARE CRITICISM: DRYDEN TO BRADLEY

Reading List

Anthologies of criticism

Halliday, F. E., *Shakespeare and his Critics* (1949; 2nd ed., 1958)

Kermode, Frank, *Four Centuries of Shakespearian Criticism* (New York, 1965)

Siegel, Paul N., *His Infinite Variety: Major Shakespeare Criticism since Johnson* (Philadelphia, 1964)

Smith, D. Nichol, *Eighteenth Century Essays on Shakespeare*, 2nd ed. (Oxford, 1963)

Shakespeare Criticism, a Selection (1916)

The writings of particular critics

Samuel Johnson. Ed. Walter Raleigh (1908); ed. W. K. Wimsatt, Jr. (New York, 1960); ed. Arthur Sherbo (New Haven, 1968)

Walter Whiter. See 4, above

S. T. Coleridge. Ed. Thomas M. Raysor (Cambridge, Mass., 1930; 2nd ed. 1960); ed. Terence Hawkes (New York, 1959)

William Hazlitt, *Characters of Shakespeare's Plays* (numerous editions)

Histories of the criticism of Shakespeare

Babcock, R. W., *The Genesis of Shakespeare Idolatry 1766–1799* (Chapel Hill, 1931)

Eastman, A. M., *A Short History of Shakespearean Criticism* (New York, 1968)

Lounsbury, Thomas R., *Shakespeare as a Dramatic Artist, with an Account of his Reputation at Various Periods* (New York, 1901)

Ralli, Augustus, *A History of Shakespeare Criticism*, 2 vols. (Oxford, 1932)

Smith, D. Nichol, *Shakespeare in the Eighteenth Century* (Oxford, 1928)

Westfall, A. V. R., *American Shakespearian Criticism, 1607–1865* (New York, 1939)

18. SHAKESPEARE CRITICISM SINCE BRADLEY

Reading List

Eastman, A. M., See 17, above

Holloway, John, 'Criticism – 20th Century' in *The Reader's Encyclopedia of Shakespeare*, ed. Oscar J. Campbell (New York, 1966)

Muir, Kenneth, 'Fifty Years of Shakespearian Criticism: 1900–1950', *Shakespeare Survey 4* (1951), pp. 1–25

Murray, Patrick, *The Shakespearian Scene* (1969)

Ralli, Augustus. See 17, above

CHRONOLOGICAL TABLE

The following chronological table covering Shakespeare's working years shows (*a*) some important national and theatrical events; (*b*) the date of publication of some important books; (*c*) approximate date of the first production of the most important plays during Shakespeare's career; (*d*) the dates of their first publication. The evidence for (*c*) and (*d*) will be found principally in Sir E. K. Chambers's *Elizabethan Stage* and *William Shakespeare: a study of facts and problems*. It is seldom possible to date the first appearance of a play exactly: before 1595 and after 1605 the margin of error may be as much as five years. Nor is there general agreement on the dates of Shakespeare's earliest and latest plays: some scholars would date the first as early as 1587. Plays which may be dated with some precision are marked ‡.

EVENTS	BOOKS PUBLISHED
1587 Execution of Mary Queen of Scots Funeral of Sir Philip Sidney	
1588 Defeat of the Spanish Armada Robert, Earl of Leicester, died	Greene's *Perimedes* and *Pandosto* Marprelate controversy
1589 A Parliament held The Portugal Voyage Duke of Guise and Henri III murdered Civil war in France	Hakluyt's *Voyages* Greene's *Menaphon*
1590 Sir Francis Walsingham died	Lodge's *Rosalynde* Spenser's *Faerie Queene*, Bks 1–3
1591 Hacket's treason The loss of the 'Revenge' Proclamation against Jesuits and seminaries	Harington's *Orlando Furioso* Sidney's *Astrophel and Stella* Spenser's *Complaints*

1592 Scottish Witchcraft trials
Greene died
The Great Carrack captured
Edward Alleyn marries
  Henslowe's step-daughter
	Greene's *The Conny-catching*
	  pamphlets. Groatsworth of Wit
	Nashe's *Piers Penniless*
	Constable's *Diana*
	Daniel's *Delia*
	Chettle's *Kind Heart's Dream*

1593 Parliament held Marlowe killed Plague stops playing	VENUS AND ADONIS *The Phœnix Nest* Hooker's *Laws of Ecclesiastical* *Polity*

1594 Plague till summer
Playing reorganized: the
  Admiral's men at Rose;
  Chamberlain's at Theatre
Kyd died
	LUCRECE
	Willobie his Avisa
	Nashe's *Jack Wilton*
	Drayton's *Idea's Mirror*
	Chapman's *Shadow of Night*

PLAYS FIRST PRODUCED	PLAYS PUBLISHED
I Tamburlaine	
Alphonsus, King of Aragon	
Dido, Queen of Carthage	
Endimion	
II Tamburlaine	
Two Angry Women of Abingdon	
Spanish Tragedy	*Rare Triumphs of Love and Fortune*
Jew of Malta	
Friar Bacon and Friar Bungay	
Midas	
John a Kent and John a Cumber	
Mother Bombie	
Looking Glass for London and England	*Three Lords and three Ladies of London*
Love's Metamorphosis	*I and II Tamburlaine*
I HENRY VI	
TITUS ANDRONICUS	
Orlando Furioso	*Endimion*
James IV	*I and II Troublesome Reign of King John*
The Woman in the Moon	
II, III HENRY VI	
Dr Faustus	*Arden of Feversham*
Edward II	*Spanish Tragedy*
RICHARD III	*Galathea*
	Midas
Massacre at Paris	*Edward II*
COMEDY OF ERRORS	*Edward I*
TWO GENTLEMEN OF VERONA	*Fair Em*
LOVE'S LABOUR'S LOST	*Orlando Furioso**
TAMING OF THE SHREW	*Knack to Know a Knave*
	TITUS ANDRONICUS
	Looking Glass for London and England

* The probable explanation of the sudden increase in printed plays in 1594 is that the companies were so disorganized by the plague that they raised money by selling their MSS.

279

EVENTS	BOOKS PUBLISHED

1594
(cont.)

	EVENTS	BOOKS PUBLISHED
1595	Riots in London Ralegh's Guiana Voyage Last expedition of Drake and Hawkins (both died)	Spenser's *Amoretti* Sidney's *Defence of Poesy* Southwell's *St Peter's Complaint*
1596	Calais captured by Spaniards The Cadiz expedition	Harington's *Metamorphosis of Ajax* Lodge's *Wit's Misery* Spenser's *Faerie Queene*, Bks 4–6; *Four Hymns* Drayton's *Mortimeriados* Davies's *Orchestra*

1597	The Islands Voyage
	A Spanish armada wrecked
	A Parliament held
		Bacon's *Essays* (1st version)
		Hall's *Virgidemiarum*
		Deloney's *Jack of Newbury* and
		  Gentle Craft (entered in
		  Stationers' Register)

1598	Rebellion and disaster in Ireland The Queen boxes Essex's ears Lord Burghley died Philip II of Spain died The 'Theatre' demolished	Marlowe's *Hero and Leander* Chapman's Trans. of *Iliad* (7 books) Meres's *Palladis Tamia* Marston's *Scourge of Villainy*

1599	Spenser died
	Essex in Ireland
	Satires burnt
	Chamberlain's men occupy new
	  'Globe'
	Invasion scare
	Essex fails in Ireland and returns
	  in disgrace
	Children of Paul's begin playing
		Hayward's *Henry IV*
		THE PASSIONATE PILGRIM
		Davies's *Nosce teipsum*

PLAYS FIRST PRODUCED	PLAYS PUBLISHED
	II Henry VI
	Taming of a Shrew
	Friar Bacon and Friar Bungay
	Wounds of Civil War
	Cobbler's Prophecy
	True Tragedy of Richard III
	Battle of Alcazar
	Selimus
	Dido, Queen of Carthage
MIDSUMMER NIGHT'S DREAM	*Old Wives' Tale*
RICHARD II	*Pedlar's Prophecy*
ROMEO AND JULIET	*Locrine*
	III Henry VI
Blind Beggar of Alexandria‡	*Knack to Know an Honest Man*
KING JOHN	*Edward III*
MERCHANT OF VENICE	
Humorous Day's Mirth‡	RICHARD II
Isle of Dogs (lost)‡	RICHARD III
The Case is Altered	ROMEO AND JULIET
I HENRY IV	*Woman in the Moon*
I and II Robert, Earl of Huntingdon	I HENRY IV
Englishmen for my Money	*Blind Beggar of Alexandria*
Every Man in his Humour‡	LOVE'S LABOUR'S LOST
Pilgrimage to Parnassus‡	*Mucedorus*
II HENRY IV	*Famous Victories of Henry V*
MUCH ADO ABOUT NOTHING	*James IV*
Shoemakers' Holiday‡	*I and II Edward IV*
Every Man out of his Humour	*Warning for Fair Women*
I Sir John Oldcastle‡	*Humorous Day's Mirth*
Histriomastix	*Two Angry Women of Abingdon*
Antonio and Mellida	*Alphonsus of Aragon*
Antonio's Revenge	*David and Bethsabe*
Old Fortunatus‡	*George a Greene*
I Return from Parnassus‡	
HENRY V‡	
AS YOU LIKE IT	
JULIUS CAESAR‡	

EVENTS	BOOKS PUBLISHED
1600 Mountjoy in Ireland	*England's Helicon*
Kempe's dance to Norwich	Exorcism controversy
Alleyn builds 'Fortune' theatre	
The Gowry conspiracy	
Children of Chapel begin playing	
at Blackfriars	
East India Company formed	
1601 Essex's rebellion and execution	Catholic controversy
The 'War of the Theatres'	Holland's Translation of Pliny
Siege of Ostend begun	
Spanish expedition lands in	
Ireland	
A Parliament held: the agitation	
concerning monopolies	
1602 Tyrone defeated in Ireland	Campion's *Observations in the Art*
Spaniards surrender	*of English Poesy*
Biron's conspiracy	Deloney's *Thomas of Reading*
	(entered in Stationers' Register)
1603 Tyrone submits	Davies's *Microcosmos*
QUEEN ELIZABETH DIED	Dekker's *Wonderful Year*
ACCESSION OF JAMES I	Daniel's *Defence of Rhyme*
Chamberlain's men become	Florio Translation of Montaigne's
King's men	*Essays*
Plague stops playing	James I's *Dæmonology* (London
Ralegh and others tried and	ed.)
condemned	
Renewed vogue of Court	
masques	
1604 Hampton Court Conference	
End of Siege of Ostend	
James's first Parliament	
Peace with Spain	

PLAYS FIRST PRODUCED	PLAYS PUBLISHED
Blind Beggar of Bethnal Green‡	*Old Fortunatus*
Patient Grissell‡	*Every Man out of his Humour*
MERRY WIVES OF WINDSOR	*Maid's Metamorphosis*
TWELFTH NIGHT‡	HENRY V
	MUCH ADO ABOUT NOTHING
	I Sir John Oldcastle
	II HENRY IV
	MIDSUMMER NIGHT'S DREAM
	MERCHANT OF VENICE
	Shoemakers' Holiday
Cynthia's Revels	*Love's Metamorphosis*
Poetaster	*I and II Robert, Earl of Huntingdon*
Satiromastix	*Cynthia's Revels*
Blurt Master Constable	*Every Man in his Humour*
What You Will	(1st version)
II Return from Parnassus	*Jack Drum's Entertainment*
HAMLET	
Gentleman Usher	*Antonio and Mellida*
Family of Love	*Antonio's Revenge*
Sir Thomas Wyatt‡	*Satiromastix*
TROILUS AND CRESSIDA	*Poetaster*
Hoffman	MERRY WIVES OF WINDSOR
	Blurt Master Constable
	Thomas Lord Cromwell
	A Larum for London
Woman Killed with Kindness‡	HAMLET (Q 1)
Sejanus	*Patient Grissell*
The Phœnix	
OTHELLO	
Dutch Courtesan	*The Malcontent*
All Fools	*I Honest Whore*
The Malcontent	HAMLET (Q 2)
Wise Woman of Hogsdon	*Dr Faustus*
Monsieur D'Olive	
Law Tricks	
Bussy D'Ambois	

283

EVENTS	BOOKS PUBLISHED

1604 (cont.)

1605   Act to expel Jesuits and   Bacon's *Advancement of Learning*
        seminary priests
        Gunpowder plot

1606   Gunpowder plotters executed   Dekker's *Seven Deadly Sins of*
        State visit of King of Denmark   *London*

1607   Renewed troubles in Ireland
        Virginia colonized
        Riots over enclosures
        A great frost

PLAYS FIRST PRODUCED	PLAYS PUBLISHED
I and II Honest Whore	
Westward Hoe	
ALL'S WELL THAT ENDS WELL	
MEASURE FOR MEASURE	
The Fawn	*Sejanus*
Eastward Hoe‡	*King Leir*
Northward Hoe	*Fair Maid of Bristow*
I and II If you Know Not me	*When you See me, you Know Me*
Trick to Catch the Old One	*Dutch Courtesan*
KING LEAR	*I If you Know Not me*
	Eastward Hoe
	All Fools
	London Prodigal
	I Jeronimo
Whore of Babylon	*II If you Know me Not*
Sophonisba	*II Return from Parnassus*
Woman Hater	*Gentleman Usher*
Volpone	*Sir Giles Goosecap*
Isle of Gulls‡	*The Fawn*
Rape of Lucrece	*Sophonisba*
MACBETH	*Wily Beguiled*
	Monsieur D'Olive
	Isle of Gulls
Knight of the Burning Pestle	*Westward Hoe*
Travels of the Three English	*Whore of Babylon*
Brothers	*Fair Maid of the Exchange*
Humour out of Breath	*The Phœnix*
ANTONY AND CLEOPATRA	*Michaelmas Term*
CORIOLANUS	*Woman Hater*
TIMON OF ATHENS	*Bussy D'Ambois*
	Cupid's Whirligig
	Travels of the Three English
	Brothers
	Miseries of Enforced Marriage
	The Puritan
	Northward Hoe
	What You Will
	Revenger's Tragedy
	Devil's Charter
	Volpone
	Woman Killed with Kindness
	Sir Thomas Wyatt

EVENTS	BOOKS PUBLISHED
1608 Children at Blackfriars disbanded King's men take over the private playhouse Notorious pirates executed	Dekker's *Belman of London*
1609 Jonson's *Masque of Queens* at Court Truce in the Netherlands The Oath of Allegiance administered	Dekker's *Gull's Hornbook* Shakespeare's SONNETS
1610 The plantation of Ulster Henri IV murdered A great drought	
1611 Carr made Viscount Rochester James quarrels with Parliament	A.V. Translation of Bible Chapman's Translation of *Iliad* completed Donne's *Anatomy of the World*
1612 Sir Thomas Overbury poisoned in the Tower Robert Cecil, Earl of Salisbury, died Prince Henry died	Shelton's Translation of *Don Quixote* Drayton's *Polyolbion*

PLAYS FIRST PRODUCED	PLAYS PUBLISHED
Faithful Shepherdess	*Trick to Catch the Old One*
Philaster	*Family of Love*
Maid's Tragedy	*Merry Devil of Edmonton*
Charles, Duke of Biron‡	KING LEAR
PERICLES	*Law Tricks*
	Humour out of Breath
	Yorkshire Tragedy
	Rape of Lucrece
	Tragedy of Biron
	Mad World, my Masters
	Dumb Knight
Epicœne	PERICLES
Woman is a Weathercock	*The Case is Altered*
Atheist's Tragedy	*Every Woman in her Humour*
	Two Maids of Moreclack
	Faithful Shepherdess
The Alchemist	*Histriomastix*
Revenge of Bussy D'Ambois	
Roaring Girl	
CYMBELINE	
King and no King	*Ram Alley*
Catiline	*Atheist's Tragedy*
Amends for Ladies	*Golden Age*
Golden Age	*Catiline*
Silver Age	*May Day*
If it be not Good, the Devil is in It	*Roaring Girl*
THE WINTER'S TALE	
THE TEMPEST	
Brazen Age	*The Alchemist*
White Devil	*Woman is a Weathercock*
	Christian Turned Turk
	Widow's Tears
	White Devil
	If it be not Good the Devil is in It

EVENTS	BOOKS PUBLISHED
1613 Marriage of Princess Elizabeth	Browne's *Britannia's Pastorals*
The Essex divorce suit	
The Globe Theatre burnt	
1616 Death of William Shakespeare	
1623 The first Folio published	

PLAYS FIRST PRODUCED	PLAYS PUBLISHED
Bonduca	*Revenge of Bussy D'Ambois*
Chaste maid in Cheapside	*Silver Age*
Duchess of Malfi	*Brazen Age*
Honest Man's Fortune	*Insatiate Countess*
Iron Age	*Knight of the Burning Pestle*
TWO NOBLE KINSMEN	
HENRY VIII	

INDEX

Abusez, Les, 62

Act of Common Council of the City of London, 17, 19

acting companies: Benson Company, the, 207, 208; Blackfriars' boys company, 165, 200; Chamberlain's men, the, 128, 165, 227; King's men, 21, 33, 162, 165, 219, 227, 228; Leicester's touring company, 5; Lord Admiral's men, the, 128; Queen's touring company, the, 5; St Paul's boys, 165; Warwick's touring company, 5

acting methods, 35–53; change of styles, 45–7; development of skills, 35–9; projection of psychology, 41–5; use of soliloquy, 47–52

actors, 202–6

different styles of, 203–4; increasing importance of, 203

Barry, Spranger, 203; Betterton, Thomas, 200, 201, 202, 203; Garrick, David, 202–4; Henderson, John, 203; Kemble, John P., 204; Kean, Edmund, 204

actresses, introduction of, 200

Horton, Priscilla, 205; Siddons, Sarah, 204

Ad Herennium, 85, 86

Aethiopica, The, 62

Alchemist, The, 199, 203

Alexander, Peter, 238

All's Well That Ends Well, 50, 119, 187, 218, 227

Altick, Richard D., 104, 112

Amadis de Gaule, 62

analogy, 180–8

Anatomy of Melancholy, The, 42, 195

animal-baiting ring as playhouse, 16, 18, 19, 22, 24

Annesley, Brian, 64

Antony and Cleopatra, 72, 111, 122, 142, 143, 144, 184, 192, 226, 247; elements of masque in, 152; poetic imagery in, 79, 111, 113, 114–15, 120, 145; sources of, 61; staging of, 30, 39–40, 159, 167; use of soliloquy in, 50, 52

Appius and Virginia, 48

Aquinas, Thomas, 181, 192, 193

Arcadia, 62, 64, 220

Archer, William, 207, 208

Arden of Feversham, 45

Arden Shakespeare, The, 238, 255

Ariodanto and Jenevra, 59

Ariosto, L., 59, 62, 136

Aristotle, 61, 83, 183, 186, 187, 193, 195, 201

Armin, Robert, 163, 165

Armstrong, E. A., 55, 258

Arnold, Matthew, 248

Ars Poetica, 61

Arte of English Poesie, The, 77, 91

Arte of Rhetorique, The, 78

Astrology, 184–5

As You Like It, 7, 118, 127, 164, 182, 218, 228, 250; dramatic structure of, 138–9; staging of, 205; use of language in, 69, 76, 81

Auden, W. H., 149, 249

Bacon, Francis, 128, 185, 186

Baker, George, 76

Baldwin, T. W., 61

Bandello, M., 59, 62

Barber, C. L., 260

Battle of Alcazar, 229

Bayley, John, 253

Beaumont, Francis, 141, 142, 200, 219

Beaux' Stratagem, The, 203

Belleforest, F. de, 59, 62

Bellot, Jacques, 73

Bell's Shakespeare, 203

Bentley, Eric, 113

Bentley, G. E., 5, 221

Berners, Lord, 63

Bethell, S. L., 254

Beverley, Peter, 59

Bion, 121

Boccaccio, G., 62

Bodin, Jean, 66

Booth, Edwin, 201

booth stage, 15, 17, 18, 19, 22

Bound, Nicholas, 177

Bowers, Fredson, 238

Boys' companies, 20, 128; boys as singers, 165; plays written for, 53; see also under acting companies